D0081060
1011 Holtz Lane
Chaska, MN 55318
Office: (651) 648-8879

The Journey of Adulthood

Photo © Joel Gordon. Reprinted with permission.

SECOND EDITION

The Journey of Adulthood

HELEN L. BEE

MACMILLAN PUBLISHING COMPANY
New York
MAXWELL MACMILLAN CANADA, INC.
Toronto
MAXWELL MACMILLAN INTERNATIONAL
New York Oxford Singapore Sydney

Editor: Christine Cardone
Production Supervisor: Publication Services, Inc.
Text Designer: Mary Sarah Quinn
Cover Designer: Blake Logan
Photo Researcher: Chris Migdol

This book was set in Garamond by Publication Services, Inc., and was printed and bound by Arcata Graphics. The cover was printed by Lehigh Press.

Chapter opening art credits appear on pp. 569 and 570, which constitute a continuation of the copyright page.

Printed in the United States of America

Macmillan Publishing Company
866 Third Avenue, New York, New York 10022

Maxwell Macmillan Canada, Inc.
1200 Eglinton Avenue East
Suite 200
Don Mills, Ontario M3C 3N1

Library of Congress Cataloging-in-Publication Data
Bee, Helen L., 1939-
The journey of adulthood / Helen L. Bee. – 2nd ed.
p. cm.
Includes bibliographical references and indexes.
ISBN 0-02-308101-5
1. Adulthood–Psychological aspects. 2. Aging-Psychological aspects 3. Adulthood. 4. Aging. I. Title.
BF724.5.B44 1992
155.6–dc20 90-22732
CIP

PRINTING 23456789 YEAR 23456789

To Carl,
who journeys with me

PREFACE

As was true of the first edition, this is a book about adult *development.* It is not just a catalogue of facts about adults or a text about the characteristics of adults compared to children or a discussion of old age. Instead, this book is about adults over the full range of adult years, from 18 to 100 or more. Most importantly, it is about the ways in which adults change or develop in both shared and individual ways over those years. My interest continues to be in the *process* of development—in those biological, psychological, or social forces or laws that may govern the changes and the continuities that we see among adults. At the same time, I am fascinated by the ways in which individual adults differ from one another and by the effects those differences have on the processes or patterns of adult development. These twin interests lead me to ask the same questions again and again about each facet of adult development: What changes (or continuities) do we observe with age? Do those changes (or continuities) differ among subgroups, such as women versus men, or from one ethnic group or one culture to another? How can we explain both the changes and the continuities? How can we explain the individual or group differences? What rules or theories best describe the process?

As in the first edition, I have approached the answering of such questions by dividing the book into three main sections. In the first three chapters I have laid the groundwork, describing some of the key dimensions on which adults differ at the start of their journey through adulthood and introducing some of the major concepts and theories of adult development. In the second section, Chapters 4 through 11, I have described the major empirical information we now have about changes and continuities in functioning over the years of adulthood. In the final group of chapters, I have attempted to pull some of the threads together.

New Features in This Edition

Although the central emphasis and the basic structure of the book remain the same, I have made a few key changes. Most noticeably, I have *added two chapters.* The first of these, Chapter 5, describes what we know about changes in health in adulthood. Some of this material was contained in the first edition in the chapter on physical changes, but I have greatly expanded the coverage and placed it in a separate chapter. The second new chapter, Chapter 13, provides a new form of synthesis—"putting the adult back together" by combining the information from all the prior descriptive chapters to give a picture of the simultaneous changes and features of each age period in adult life: young adulthood, middle age, the "young old," and the "old old."

Several other *chapters have been extensively reorganized,* most notably the chapter on personality development (now Chapter 10), and of course all chapters have been *completely updated,* with current research examples used throughout.

Some Other Key Features

This text, like the field of adult development, continues to be highly interdisciplinary. I have drawn not only from the work of psychologists, but also from that of sociologists, demographers, physicians, epidemiologists, industrial psychologists, vocational specialists, and gerontologists. I continue to find it a challenge both to delve into the literature of all these fields and to combine the research results from such varied disciplines into some kind of meaningful and comprehensible whole.

Equally challenging is my continued effort to strike a balance among research rigor, theoretical clarity, and practical relevance. I don't want this book to be so full of descriptions of individual research studies that you lose sight of the forest for the trees. Nor do I want it to be so general that you never have a sense of the existing research findings on some issue. I have tried always to tell you clearly when we don't know something, or when conclusions must be tentative because of a thin or poor research base. But I have tried not to flood you with detail.

You will also see that I continue to speak to you directly in this book, as if you and I were having a conversation. To make the encounter even more personal as well as to heighten the sense of personal relevance of many of the key points, I have often used my own experiences as illustrations. I find being an adult an immensely fascinating, maddening, and enjoyable learning process. I hope you will find the material in this book to be food for thought for your own journey.

Your learning may also be made easier by a series of pedagogical features built into the book: boldfaced key words, which are defined in a glossary at the end of the book; chapter-ending summaries; an annotated list of suggested readings for each chapter; and a summary table in each of the basic empirical chapters (Chapters 4–11) that shows the main changes or continuities with age in that particular domain.

Some Bouquets

No textbook author can function without excellent reviewers. I am grateful not only to those who reviewed the first edition and offered helpful suggestions about needed revisions but also to those who read the first draft of the revision and suggested further changes. It is, of course, very nice when reviewers have positive things to say, but I am equally grateful for their criticisms, their pickiness, and their suggestions for sources I had not discovered on my own. Thanks go to Freda Rebelsky Camp, Boston University; Kathleen Fox, Salisbury State University; Anne P. Glass, Virginia Polytechnic Institute & State University; Harriet Gordon, Bloomfield College; Ruth G. Lyell, San Jose State University; Jonathan Rich, California State University-Fullerton; and James Thomas, Northern Kentucky University.

As always, thanks go to my own personal "convoy" as well. My partner (now husband) Carl is always immensely supportive, even when he does not understand my dilemmas in detail; my family and friends provide sanity when I can no longer bear to look at a computer screen or think about another journal article. By helping me to develop, all these important people in my life also help to change the perspective from which I examine all the theories and evidence I have talked about in this book. Without them I would wither and blow away.

Finally, thanks to Chris Cardone, Psychology Editor, Aliza Greenblatt, Freelance Manager, and the other Macmillan staff . . .

BRIEF CONTENTS

CONTENTS

3 Theories of Adult Change or Development 63

4 Physical Changes in Adulthood 97

5 Changes in Health and Health Habits in Adulthood 135

6 Intellectual Changes in Adulthood 163

CHAPTER 1

Defining the Journey: Some Assumptions, Definitions, and Methods

Some of you reading this are just beginning the journey of your own adult life; some of you are part way along the road, having traveled through your 20s, 30s, or perhaps 40s or 50s. Whatever your age, you *are* traveling, moving through the years and through the changes and transformations that come with the years. We do not all follow the same itinerary on this journey; you may spend a long time in one country that I do not visit at all; I may make an unusual side trip. Or we may visit the same places but experience them very differently. If you and I both visited Paris for five days, we would not see precisely the same sights, or eat the same food, or—more importantly—come away with precisely the same impressions or understandings. You might be most impressed by the beauty of the city, the broad boulevards, the parks, the incredible buildings. I might be more struck by the unfriendliness of many of the shopkeepers and waiters or by their impatience with my limited French.

Every journey is unique. No two adult lives are exactly alike. Still, there have to be some common themes or there would be no reason for a book on adult development. Amidst the variability, there are some typical itineraries, some commonly shared experiences, some shared lessons or tasks. My task is obviously to explore both—both the uniqueness and the common ground of adult lives.

One person's journey can perhaps help illustrate both:

> It seems in retrospect that I have uprooted myself every five to seven years and gone off in a different direction. Sometimes these changes have been physical, moving from place to place; sometimes they have been inner changes, when there has been a turning inward or a turning away from.
>
> After college, I completed a Ph.D. in four years and started off on a traditional academic career with a first job at Clark University in Worcester, Massachusetts and then a shift to the University of Washington, in Seattle, changing jobs mostly because I was dying to get back to the Pacific Northwest, where I had been raised and where my friends and family all were. I spent a total of eight years being a young professor, doing all the customary things: teaching huge classes as well as seminars, doing research, sitting on endless committees, and having anxiety attacks about whether I'd get tenure or not (I did). I loved the teaching, eventually enjoyed the research, loathed the committee meetings and the anxiety, and in the end disliked the life of a professor as a whole. After a year's sabbatical, during which I went around the world looking at child care arrangements in other countries (Russia, Israel, Scandinavia, France, and spots in between), I resigned my tenured job. For me, the "average day" of a professor contained too many things I did not like and too few that brought pleasure or satisfaction. And it was too much the life of the mind, too narrow a preoccupation. So at the age of 32, to the astonishment and consternation of a great many people, I quit, having no clear idea of how I would make a living but knowing that it would not be with a traditional academic job.
>
> Shortly afterward I married and we moved with my husband's two children (ages 3 and 11 at the time) to a small island north of Seattle, where we lived for six years. I adopted the children and settled into full time motherhood as well as into marriage. In retrospect, I also think of this as my "back to the land" phase, though it was much more than that. I began to write books as a way to earn a living, which turned out to be both enjoyable and successful. I spent three years at the thankless but fascinating community job of school board director, grew a

> huge garden, and learned how to make bread and butter and to can produce. It is difficult to exaggerate the pleasure I felt each fall at the sight of the shelves all stacked with canning jars filled with colorful produce: green beans, tomatoes, peaches, blackberry and raspberry jam, and applesauce. In those same years I also grew up in some quite different ways and discovered some parts of myself that logic didn't touch.
>
> Unfortunately, the marriage did not hold together. Eventually I moved back to Seattle, where I began work on some research with colleagues, began teaching again part time, and generally stuck my toe back into the traditional academic waters. (For a while there I was in at least up to my waist, but I have resisted any further immersion.) At the same time I became much more interested in what I now think of as the "inner journey," the search for understanding of what each of us is all about. Over the next few years I began to read the literature of mysticism; meditation became part of my daily routine; and I struggled with the problem of applying fundamental ethical principles to my everyday living. My friendships deepened, my capacity to care for others seemed to grow, and my willingness to make commitments to others expanded.
>
> And just when I was sure that there would be no more romance in my life, sure that I would be able to find much contentment in solitude, I fell in love again and moved to the Midwest to live with this new love—a man who is, ironically, a university professor. This shift has not only taken me away from my beloved Northwest and my family; it has brought a whole new set of lessons about intimacy, about friendships, about independence and dependence.
>
> Something else has begun to happen, too, now that I am in my early 50s. I feel a whole lot freer from the constraints of all those expectations that seemed to dominate my earlier life. Of course it helps that my youngest child is nearly through with college, so some of the responsibilities of being a parent are almost completed. But it is more than that. It is a sense that I *know* better who I am, and can *be* that person with greater freedom and ease. I don't any longer need to bend myself into some other sort of shape to fit into the expected molds—whether it is the mold of "young professor" or the mold of "wife" or "mother." When I turned 50, I decided I was old enough to start being seriously eccentric—and then had to laugh when my friends all told me that I had been eccentric for quite some time! I am sure there is more—vastly more—growing to do, but I am finally feeling like a grown-up person and looking forward with relish to the many good years still ahead of me.

As you may well have guessed, this is my own life I am describing. Most of this is taken from the description I wrote for my college's twenty-fifth reunion yearbook, with some updating for the years since. Since the women in my family live to be *very* old (typically into their late 90s), I am, at 51, just past the middle of my expected span of years.

Chances are good that my journey and yours have many differences. I chose a fairly high-powered career at a time when it was not so common for women to do that, and then I changed gears professionally in an unusually radical way. I married late and have no natural-born children. These deviations from the norm are obvious. Describing them may be useful for introducing myself to you so that you can have at least a brief acquaintance with the person who will be talking to you in these pages, but they are not important in themselves. What is much more interesting, to me at least, are the possible common themes and key issues about adult development that may be hidden behind the obvious variability of our experiences. Let me point to a few of those issues.

First of all, when I think about myself, and read what I wrote, I experience both a sense of continuity and a sense of change. I'm still very much an intellectual, so that is constant. Yet I feel that my relationships with others have changed greatly. Is this typical? How much do people really change in adulthood? Most of us like to *think* that we are maturing, growing, getting "better." But are we really? How much do we just take ourselves with us through the years, bringing the same patterns, the same styles to each new situation? This issue of continuity versus change will form one of the major themes of this book.

A second issue that may have struck you as you read my brief life history is the occurrence of episodes, phases, or even stages. I established stable life patterns, then reassessed them and changed, only to establish a new life pattern for a number of years. And each of these periods or stages seemed to be focused on a different set of tasks, goals, or issues: getting a career started and achieving success; rearing a family and exploring the tenderer side of myself; searching for the reasons, the meaning; accepting myself as I am. Is this kind of life pattern

Figure 1–1 There could be hundreds of reasons for this man's obvious distress. He might have just heard of his father's death; he might have lost his job; he might be facing up to his own alcoholism. Or perhaps he is in the midst of some major life transition—often called a "midlife crisis"—and is searching for a new pattern. Does everyone go through such a change at midlife? If we do, is it always painful and distressing? What causes such transformations when they do occur? (Photo © Joel Gordon, 1978. Reprinted with permission.)

typical? Is adult life made up of phases or stages? If it is, are these stages shared by all adults? Are the tasks and issues the same for all 20-year-olds, or all 40-year-olds, or all 70-year-olds? Is there, in other words, a predictable or expectable rhythm to adult life? This theme, too, will recur frequently in the pages ahead.

Still a third theme has to do with inner versus outer changes. My life has gone through a variety of "outer" changes—shifts in the jobs I held, in the people I lived with, in the roles I tried to fill with those people. I went from student to professor to wife and parent to researcher to "significant other," for example. At the same time I changed physically: my hair turned prematurely white, I gained and then lost weight, I lost fitness and then regained it. All of these changes can be seen by someone observing from the outside, and represent, in a sense, an "outer journey" through the adult years.

But we can talk about an inner journey as well—a set of changes that are experienced by the individual but that may not be so obvious to someone on the outside. My own sense of "growing up" is one such inner change, as is the shift I described from a preoccupation with success and family to the more recent preoccupation with inner growth and spiritual development.

I do not at all mean to imply that these inner and outer changes are independent of one another. They are not, as we will see again and again through the book. The shifts we all experience in the roles we fill (e.g., student, spouse, parent, young worker, older worker, mentor, friend) affect the way we feel about ourselves and the issues that concern us. I am freer now to "be myself" in part precisely because my youngest child is nearly grown and flown, not because I turned 50. Yet physical aging, too, can influence our inner processing. The moment (at age 38) when I realized that walking up a flight of stairs made me puff was not just a recognition of a physical change; it was a shock to my image of myself. I felt middle-aged for the first time, and that realization changed my inner perspective. The influences go the other way, too; the inner shifts influence our outward behavior in important ways. Thinking of myself as middle-aged resulted in a new exercise program, weight loss, and a significant change in my appearance. Another adult may change jobs at age 30 or at 40 because of a major shift in the issues that preoccupy him. One of my tasks in this book is to try to sort out the causal links between the inner and the outer threads of change.

The Basic Questions

These fundamental themes can be described a bit differently. My questions about adult development are of two basic kinds: descriptive and explanatory.

Descriptive Questions

The first task with any scientific endeavor is description. What happens? What kinds of changes occur over the adult years? What kinds of continuities exist? Are these changes or continuities widely shared or universal, or, alternatively, are there subgroups that seem to share distinctive patterns of change and continuity? To understand development, we must be able to answer such questions about each facet or aspect of human functioning: the way the body works, the way the mind works, the kinds of roles and relationships adults have, the inner patterns such as personality or temperament, and the issues of concern to the individual.

Merely describing such change and continuity is no small task. And as you will discover very quickly, we lack the data to provide good, basic description in a great many areas. Still, we can begin.

Explanatory Questions

Equally important are questions that ask "how" or "why." We will be searching for causes, both for shared patterns of change and for individual variations. For example, we will see in Chapter 6 that beginning in perhaps their 40s, adults experience some decline in the speed with which they can do mental tasks. By age 60 or 70, this difference in speed is quite noticeable. How can we account for this? Such a loss of speed could certainly be the result of one or more physical changes, such as the slower rate by which the nervous system conducts signals. But slower performance on mental tasks could also result from a change in the amount of time older adults, compared to younger adults, spend doing complex mental tasks. Maybe they are just out of practice. Still a third possibility is that older adults may be much less motivated to compete or to strive to succeed at such tasks. Working quickly may simply not be a high value.

Virtually every pattern of change over adulthood that we can identify or describe has such multiple possible explanations. In most instances, we are a very long way from understanding the causes of the patterns we observe. But psychologists and sociologists who study adult development have at least reached some preliminary agreement on three major categories of influences that help to explain both the ways in which we tend to be alike in our adult journeys and the ways in which we differ from one another: (1) shared, "age-graded" change, (2) cohort effects, and (3) unique experiences (Baltes, Reese, & Lipsitt, 1980; Riley, 1976).

The major emphasis here is on explaining *change.* Since the subject we are studying is adult *development,* it surely makes sense to focus most of our attention on the ways in which adults change as they age. But be assured that I have not forgotten about the issue of individual continuity—that sense that we each stay much the same throughout our adult lives. Ultimately, if we are going to describe or explain adult journeys adequately, we will have to account not only for the changes but for the things that do *not* change. Still, for now, let me focus on the potential changes.

Change in Adults: The Basic Explanations

Shared, Age-Graded Changes

This type of change is probably what you assume is meant when you hear the phrase "adult development." These are changes linked to age in some way and shared by most or all adults in every generation. I find it useful to divide this further into three sub-types.

Figure 1–2 If you asked these older people about the kinds of physical changes they have found most disturbing about aging, no doubt quite a few would list loss of taste as a major annoyance. Among the many shared biological changes we experience as we get older is a gradual loss of taste buds in the tongue, which makes it harder to enjoy food. (Photo © Anita Bartsch, c/o Design Conceptions, 1990. Reprinted with permission.)

BIOLOGICALLY INFLUENCED CHANGES Some of the changes we see in adults are shared by all of us because we are all biological organisms undergoing natural aging processes. Many such changes are easy to see, such as hair gradually turning gray, or skin becoming more wrinkly as it loses elasticity and becomes dryer. Others are not directly visible from the outside but are experienced inwardly quite clearly, such as the loss of taste buds that occurs gradually over the adult years. Babies typically prefer bland food in part because they have many more taste buds than adults do, so to them it may not be "bland" at all. But as we move through adulthood, we lose taste buds, so many of us begin to experiment with more highly spiced food. My grandmother, in her late 80s and early 90s, complained bitterly that food had no taste anymore. It is ironic, of course, that one of the actions we might take to counteract this is to add more salt to our food—an action that has detrimental effects elsewhere in the body.

Biological changes are also significantly involved in the speed with which we can process information. Fifty- and sixty-year-olds don't learn quite as quickly as they did at 20, and they find it takes a bit longer to remember names or other items of information. This loss of speed seems to be caused at least partly by a loss of efficiency in the synapses in the brain. The *rate* at which these (and equivalent) changes occur varies quite a lot from one adult to another, but the *sequence* seems to be highly similar.

Such biological explanations of adult change have not been terribly popular (perhaps because most of us, including the researchers and the theorists, don't like to think about our own physical aging), but we need to keep steadily in mind that each of us has an aging body, that there are common chemical and biological changes that occur with aging, and that those common changes affect the rest of our experience of adulthood.

For example, my sense of being "middle-aged" when I was 38 was based on the physical reality that I had lost fitness. To be sure, it was possible to improve my fitness; but the very fact that I could stay fit with little effort at 20, yet had to take up an exercise program to maintain my aerobic capacity when I was 38, emphasizes the fact that some underlying change may have occurred. It seems likely that at least some of the reported "crises" of midlife might be due either to the indirect effects of such realizations of physical aging, or conceivably to another, more direct, biological effect, namely the hormonal changes of the menopause in women and the equivalent changes in men. In a similar way, perhaps we will find that changes in work attitudes are linked in some ways to natural declines in physical or mental efficiency. Thus, in each area we need at least to look for potential direct or indirect biological explanations.

Changes Produced by Shared Experiences Another highly significant cause of the changes we have in common in adult life is simply shared experience. There are obvious individual variations, but most of us move through adulthood encountering similar tasks, similar options, similar experiences. Furthermore, these shared experiences are organized at least roughly by age. Sociologist Matilda White Riley and her colleagues (Riley, 1976, 1986; Riley, Johnson, & Foner, 1972) point out that virtually all societies are organized into **age strata**—periods in the life span which have shared demands, expectations, privileges. In our culture, for example, we have quite different expectations of, and attitudes toward, 18-year-olds, 35-year-olds, and 60-year-olds. We expect them to do different things, to form different kinds of relationships, to have different pleasures. We also afford these three age groups different amounts of recognition, responsibility, or power. Such collections of expectations and responsibilities for each age constitute the **age norms** for that culture or sub-culture. Over the course of adulthood, each individual passes through the sequence of age strata with their accompanying norms, and this shared age-graded experience exerts a powerful influence on the pattern of change we see in individuals over their lifetimes.

One of the most significant elements in age stratification and age norms in virtually all cultures is the pattern of experiences associated with marriage and family life—what sociologists call the **family life cycle**. In the United States, for example, about 90 percent of adults marry (and that number has been stable through this century). Furthermore, the vast majority (80–90 percent) of married couples have children (Glick, 1979). Once the first child is born, the parents are locked into a powerful sequence of experiences linked to the child's developmental stage: infancy, toddlerhood, school age, adolescence, and finally, departure from home.

Figure 1–3 Every society is organized into **age strata,** *with different rules and expectations for the members of each age group. What different age strata are represented here? What are the different expectations? (Photo © Joel Gordon, 1990. Reprinted with permission.)*

Each of these periods in the child's life makes a different set of demands on the parents, and this sequence of demands shapes 20 or 30 years of most adults' lives.

The impact of such a shared pattern may extend well beyond the family relationships themselves. For example, one of the findings I'll talk about in Chapter 8 is an intriguing decline in friendship formation from approximately age 30 to 45. This seems to be a widely shared pattern, but how can we explain it? I can think of no obvious biological explanation, but it might well be one of the offshoots of the family life cycle. When your children are small, your energy is focused on the relationships in the immediate family. There is less time, and perhaps less opportunity, for forming and maintaining new friendships.

There are a great many widely shared, age-related, cultural patterns other than the family life cycle. To take just one more example: For the past several generations at least, most adults have become more physically (and mentally) sedentary with age. Our jobs are becoming more automated; we read less, move less. So the common experience of lowered fitness in one's 30s or 40s may be caused not by some inevitable body changes but may be instead a side effect of the age norm of a more sedentary life in middle-age. More generally, we will need to explore the intriguing possibility that many aspects of the apparent deterioration of our bodies as we age, which might seem to be biologically inevitable, are really the indirect result of the increasing disuse that is part of our age norms.

INTERNAL CHANGE PROCESSES A third kind of shared, age-graded change is more difficult to describe because it involves inner processes. The basic idea is that each of us must face and cope with a set of tasks or dilemmas in our adult life. In the process of coping, we undergo a series of inner adjustments. We may become more "integrated," we may learn to express a wider range of emotions, we may become more "mature." Movement through the family life cycle or other shared experiences may be part of what triggers this set of inner changes, but the internal transformations may go beyond this. For some adults at least, values change, ways of thinking change.

For example, one of the current notions is that in early adulthood, particularly after the birth of children, there is a kind of exaggeration of masculine or feminine qualities for many adults. Then at midlife, men and women both seek to "balance" their feminine and masculine qualities more completely (e.g., Giele, 1982a). For most of us, this means expanding the expression of the less practiced aspect. If this is true, we might find that men at midlife become more emotionally expressive and warm, whereas women become more assertive and independent. In fact, there is some evidence that such a sex role "crossover" does occur in many cultures, as I'll describe more fully later. For now, my point is simply that this is an example of the kind of internal change, linked to age but neither caused by biological change nor entirely defined by age norms, that many theorists have both searched for and found most intriguing.

If we are to understand adult development, we must eventually be able to sort out the effects of and the interactions among these several types of age-graded change. If we observe the same pattern of change between age 20 and age 60 in many cultures, and in many generations in the same culture, we still will not know whether that particular change is biologically based, culturally defined, or determined by some natural or inevitable internal psychological change, or some combination of the three.

Cohort Effects

When I try to explain some pattern of change with age in terms of shared experiences or shared age-graded changes, I'm searching for *universal* patterns in adult lives. What is the common ground that makes us *all* alike? But there are also narrower bands of influence—experiences that shape the adult lives of some subgroups but not others.

The culture in which we grow up and in which we spend our adult lives is obviously one such influence. Cultures vary enormously in the ways they structure the expected life pattern: the typical age of marriage or child bearing, the typical number of children, the roles of men and women, caste or class structures, and the like. I am well aware of the fact that virtually all of the research and theorizing we have about adult development is based on studies of only a few cultures, most particularly Western cultures. It may well be that some of the patterns of change or development that we have come to think of as universal are really much more culture-specific than that—a possibility I will remind you of fairly regularly.

But even *within* a culture there are significant variations in adult life experience from one generation to the next, and this variability we can and do study. The key concept is that of a **cohort**.

The term *cohort* may be new to you, but the basic idea is not. It is roughly synonymous with the word generation. Thus, it is a group of people who were born at approximately the same time and share certain cultural influences and historical experiences. The difference is that a generation is normally defined as a 20-year span, whereas a cohort, as the term is used by psychologists, sociologists, and demographers, can refer to a much smaller band of years, perhaps as few as two or three.

For our purposes, the concept of a cohort is important for two reasons: (1) it helps to explain how and why adults of any given era will be like one another in their values, life experiences, or attitudes, and (2) it can help explain *differences* in attitudes, values, skills, or life experiences that we may see between groups of adults of different ages. I can make both these points clearer with some examples.

One relatively easy way to see the effect of variations in the experiences of adjacent cohorts is to look at major social upheavals, such as (in our culture) the Great Depression of the 1930s, World War II, or the Vietnam war. To be sure, everyone who was alive during one of these eras was affected in *some* way by the upheaval, but because these events hit each cohort at a different age, the effects are remarkably cohort-specific.

Glen Elder's research on the depression is a wonderful example (Elder, 1974, 1978; Elder, Liker, & Cross, 1984). He has found that those who were teenagers in the depths of the depression showed fewer long-term effects than did those who had been in early elementary school when the depression struck full force. The younger cohorts spent a greater portion of their childhood under conditions of economic hardship. The hardship altered family interaction patterns, educational opportunities, and even the personalities of the children, so that the negative effects could still be detected in adulthood. Those who were teenagers during the depression did not show negative effects in adult life; on the contrary, some of them seemed to have grown from the experience of hardship and, as a result, showed more independence and initiative as adults. Thus two cohorts, rather close in actual age, experienced the same historical event differently because they were different ages at the time.

The same point emerges from a study by Abigail Stewart and Joseph Healy, Jr. (1989) of a group of women who had all been in graduate school between 1945 and 1951 but who actually represented three different cohorts—those who were fully grown before World War II (born between 1906 and 1914), those who reached adulthood *during* the war (born 1918–1922), and those who reached adulthood *after* the war (born 1925–1929). Those in the oldest group had grown up during the depression, when self reliance and financial security were strongly valued but traditional family values were also very strong. The value structure of that era was such that they believed that a woman must choose between a career and a home; she could not do both and do justice to the important family values. In contrast, the women from the last of the three cohorts had been adolescents during the war, at a time when it was very common for women to work; they

Figure 1–4 *The Great Depression was so widespread, and its impact so significant for most families, that every cohort that passed through it was influenced by the experience. But the specific influence was different for adjacent cohorts, depending on how old they had been during the worst of the economic hardship. (Photo © The Bettmann Archive. Reprinted with permission.)*

then spent their young adulthood in the postwar period, when women were expected to devote themselves gladly to family life. Stewart and Healy argue that these women, conditioned by both experiences, fully expected to marry and have children but also valued work and thought it "natural" for women. They believed that one could have both career and family. When the life histories of these women were then examined, the contrast was clear: Only a quarter of those in the earliest cohort ever had children, while 88 percent of those in the latest cohort gave birth to at least one child.

A particular cohort, then, has not only lived through specific historical or cultural events but has lived through them *at the same time in their lives.* The timing of the events interacts with the tasks, issues, or age norms for that age, producing unique patterns of influence for each cohort and helping to create common adult life trajectories for those born into the same cohort. Thus, the concept gives us a powerful tool in understanding the similarities in adult lives.

At the same time, the concept of a cohort has been enormously helpful in explaining differences as well—not only differences between adjacent cohorts such as those Elder or Stewart and Healy studied, but differences among widely spaced cohorts. Most importantly, it helps us to differentiate between "real" developmental change—universal or nearly universal changes with age that are grounded in basic biology or in common psychological processes—and *apparent* change that is, in fact, not individual change at all but merely cohort differences.

Suppose I interview a group of 50- and 60-year-old men and women and a group of 20 to 25-year-olds and ask each person to tell me her or his views about the appropriate male and female sex roles: "Should a woman work if she has small children?" "Who should be responsible for running the household?" "What jobs should husbands or wives do in a home?" "If your wife made more money than you did (or if you made more money than your husband), how would you feel about it?" When I compare the answers of the different age groups, I find that the adults in their 50s and 60s hold much more "traditional" ideas about sex roles than do the 20-year-olds. The older subjects are much more likely to tell me that women should not work if they have young children, that it would make them uncomfortable if a woman made more money than her husband, and so forth.

How do I explain this finding? Is there some underlying shift here from liberal to conservative that might be a common thread in adult lives? That's possible, but not likely. It seems much more plausible to argue that what we have here is a **cohort effect:** The current 20-year-olds have been influenced by the women's movement and the change in values about adult sex roles. The older group grew up at a different time, when values were different. The difference between the 20-year-olds and the 60-year-olds in this case probably does not really reflect a *change* in the individuals over time. The current 60-year-olds probably held much the same values when they were 20, and it seems unlikely that the current 20-year-olds will get more traditional as they get older (though that is an empirical question). Thus, what looks like an age *change* is most likely cohort *difference.*

Another example comes from studies of IQ in adulthood. Does IQ change (go up or down) as we age? Or is it stable? Early researchers studying IQ in adulthood (e.g., Wechsler, 1955; Matarazzo, 1972) compared average IQ scores of adults of different ages. They found that the older the group, the lower the average score. Alas, it looked as if we all declined in mental power as we got older. But there is a cohort effect lurking in the data: Older cohorts in our culture have had significantly less education than have younger cohorts. So it could be education, and not age, that is related to IQ. As you'll see in Chapter 5, that is roughly what researchers have found when they have explored the question from a different angle.

A "cohort effect," in general, describes differences between groups of adults of different ages that are due not to age or aging or to any other developmental process but simply to the fact that the different age groups have grown up in different historical or cultural circumstances.

As we look at descriptions of age-related differences in adulthood in the rest of this book, we need to be steadily alert for possible cohort effects. Cohort differences make it harder to develop broad, general statements or universal principles about adult development. But such differences are not just "noise" in the system. They are interesting in and of themselves. They tell us something about how major social forces shift the developmental patterns for adults.

Unique, Nonshared Events

For any one individual, changes over the adult years are also shaped by a wide range of experiences that are not shared with all adults, or even with all members of a cohort. Having your parents die when you are in your 20s or 30s, a significant illness early in life, the early death of a spouse or a child, losing a job, whether you marry early or late (or not at all), whether you have a special teacher in highschool who inspires you to go on for a specific kind of training—all of these and hundreds more experiences like them can alter the pathway a particular individual will follow through adulthood. Even experiences like marital separation or divorce, which are widely shared, belong in this category of "unique or nonshared events," since divorce is neither universal nor age-graded.

You'll see as we go along that the *timing* of particular unique events seems to be a highly significant factor influencing the degree or direction of impact. Bernice Neugarten (1979), in particular, has emphasized that events that are "on time," that follow a "normal expectable life cycle" are less disruptive or difficult than those that are "off time." So having your parents die when you are in your 20s (which is "off time") is more difficult to deal with, more likely to lead to significant life-disruption, than is the death of your parents when you are in your

Figure 1–5 This woman's husband died while she was still young. Widowhood is hard enough at any time, but it is still harder when it is "off time" like this. In fact, any major life change that is "off time" for your cohort creates more stress, and is more likely to change the basic trajectory of your life than is true for life changes shared with your cohort. (Photo © Art Stein, Photo Researchers, Inc., 1981. Reprinted with permission.)

40s or 50s. Similarly, losing your job in your 30s is harder to handle than is retirement at 65. In some sense, this is another way of saying that those adults who deviate from the age norms in significant ways are likely to show more distinctive or unusual patterns of development than do those whose lives more closely follow the culturally defined age norms.

Obviously, in a book like this I cannot begin to explore the effects of every possible combination of unique and shared experiences in the lives of adults. But I can and will try to search for any underlying patterns that may exist that will help us understand types of unique events, their timing, and their combined effects.

Some Definitions

Before I go further, I think it is important to pause and define some terms. Perhaps you have already been confused by having so many different words used apparently interchangeably—words like development, change, aging, and maturing. So far I have used these words rather loosely, but if I am going to create any order at all out of the evidence and the theories, I need to be more precise and more strict in the way I label various concepts. At the very least, we need terms for the following processes or concepts: (1) basic physiological change that is an inevitable accompaniment of the passage of years; (2) "improvements" that occur with age, such as greater personality flexibility, or successful completion of a series of tasks or dilemmas; (3) "declines" that may occur with age (that may or may not be physiologically based); and (4) all other patterns of variation in behavior or attitudes that are associated or linked with age but that don't fit the other categories.

My choices for terms to describe these different patterns may not altogether fit your preconceived notions, but I will use these terms consistently throughout the book.

Adulthood. I will define adulthood as that period from age 18 to death. Eighteen is an arbitrary age, but it represents (in our culture at least) the time when young people graduate from high school, and many then immediately take on the duties and responsibilities of adulthood. To be sure, many other young people continue in a semidependent status for some years after 18, but it is still a convenient demarcation.

Aging. To be consistent, I will use this term to describe simply the passage of years, although the everyday meaning also includes the notion of decline or "getting worse," as in "She's certainly aged since we saw her last, hasn't she?" I will make every effort to avoid that sort of implication for the word aging.

Maturation. This is a term used commonly in the study of children's development to refer to those processes of change with age that are governed by underlying physiological processes, largely determined by the genetic code. We can speak, for example, of the maturational changes that underlie the infant's progression from sitting to crawling to walking, or the maturational changes of puberty. I will use the term in the same way in this book to describe any sequence of physical changes that appears to be governed by systematic, shared genetic, or other biological processes. For example, the complex sequence of changes in sexual and reproductive functioning between age 40 and 60 (referred to most generally as the climacteric in both men and women, also called menopause in women) is a maturational change parallel to the changes of puberty. Note that maturation, in this sense, is quite different from the common parlance word "maturing," which often connotes "becoming wiser" or "becoming psychologically better balanced." Any increase in wisdom or balance *might* be the result of fundamental maturational (physiological) processes but could also reflect any one of a host of other growth or development processes as well. Note also that a maturational change might involve either the addition or the loss of skills or physical functions. With increasing age, adults lose taste buds but gain ear size; we lose speed in nerve synapses but gain plaque in our blood vessels.

Development. In my use of the term "development" I am following, at least roughly, the definitions given by Heinz Werner and Bernard Kaplan (Werner & Kaplan, 1956; Kaplan, 1983), who define development in terms of increasingly higher, more integrated levels of functioning. Whether development in this sense of the word actually exists in adulthood is one of the key questions I will be asking in this book. Do some adults, or all adults, become "more mature," "wiser," more altruistic, and compassionate? Obviously the decision of what constitutes "better" or "more mature" is a question as much of values and philosophy as of fact. But I am not content merely to describe strings of changes with age without at least addressing the question of value, or "growth."

This use of the word development, I realize, does not fit well with common parlance. The word is used in normal conversation, and even among psychologists, to mean roughly "change with age," or "change over time." So you will have to make an effort to remember that when I use the term I do not mean it in this looser way but much more narrowly to refer to only a subset of changes with age—those changes that arguably reflect the emergence of some more complex or more integrated system or structure.

Gain and Decline. These two terms I will use, as nonpejoratively as possible, to describe changes that involve increases or decreases in some function or skill over age. It is important to be clear about the fact that *development,* as I have defined it here, may result from either gains or declines. It is possible, for example, to gain in wisdom as a result of loss of health: Illness causes some people to examine themselves and their lives in constructive and beneficial ways.

Change. Where it is not clear whether some pattern of variation with age is a gain, or a loss, or reflects some development, I will simply talk about change. Descriptions of change or stability will nearly always be the beginning point in our explorations of adulthood. What is the pattern of frequency and depth of friendship over the adult years? What is the pattern of hearing loss in older adults? What happens to scores on IQ tests over time in adulthood? All of these are questions at the descriptive level that call for data on change or stability over age. It is when we turn to the task of explanation that terms like maturation or development are likely to enter the discussion. Is some observed change the result of biological maturation? Does it reflect some basic inner restructuring, some development? Or, might the difference between old and young that we observe be some kind of cohort effect?

Collecting the Information to Answer the Questions

To answer questions like these is no simple task. More importantly, the specific research methods an investigator chooses have a powerful effect on the range of questions that can be answered with that particular study. Examining research methodology is always an important part of understanding the findings in any field but never more so than in studying adult change or development.

Let me take as an example the issue I pointed to just a few paragraphs back: What is the pattern of change or stability in frequency, duration, or quality of friendships over the adult years? What decisions would I have to make in trying to answer such a question? Here are some of the key issues:

Should I study groups of people of different ages, or should I study the same group of people over time, or some combination of the two? This is a question dealing with basic *research design*.

How shall I find out about friendships in the subjects I decide to study? Shall I simply ask people to tell me how many friends they have? How shall I define "friend" for this purpose? Shall I ask about specific relationships, and how close they are? Should I do this with a questionnaire or an interview? What else would I want to know about each subject aside from numbers of friendships and age? These are questions of *research methodology*.

How shall I analyze and interpret the responses that people give me? Is it enough merely to determine the average number of friends described by subjects of each age group? What else would I want to do in order to tease out some of the possible explanations? These are questions of *research analysis*.

You need to have at least a basic working knowledge of the options involved in such research decisions if you are going to be able to interpret the findings from the research I'll be describing in this book.

Research Design

Choosing a research design is perhaps the most crucial decision the researcher makes. This is true in any area of psychology or sociology, but there are special considerations when the subject of study is change or development with age. There are essentially three choices: (1) You can pick different groups of subjects at each of a series of ages and compare their responses. This is called a **cross-sectional** design. (2) You can study the *same* subjects over a period of time, observing whether their responses remain the same or change in systematic ways. This is called a **longitudinal** design. (3) You can combine the two in any of several ways, collectively called **sequential designs** (Achenbach, 1978; Schaie, 1983a).

Cross-sectional Designs

The essential characteristic of cross-sectional studies is that they include *different* groups of subjects at *different* ages. Each subject is tested only once. Such comparisons tell us about age *differences,* but—as you may have figured out from my discussion of cohort differences—they do not tell us directly about age *change.*

As an example, suppose once again that I am interested in friendship changes over the adult years. I could select a group of adults in their 20s, another group of adults in their 30s, and so forth. I could then compare the average number of friends reported by subjects in each age group. The results from one study like this are in Figure 1–6 (Lowenthal, Thurnher, & Chiriboga, 1975).

These results tell us that numbers of friendships are different in the various age groups (at least in these cohorts in this culture), with a low point in the 40s. Some researchers might also try to read these findings as saying that friendships *decline* in one's middle years and then rise again later. But there are several problems with drawing conclusions about age *changes* from results like these. First and foremost, there is very probably a cohort effect here. The 60-year-olds are from a distinctly different generation than are the 25-year-olds. With only these findings, there is no way for us to tell whether the different levels of friendships represent genuine, life-cycle changes that would occur with successive generations, or whether these are simply cohort differences. That is, we cannot assume that today's 25-year-

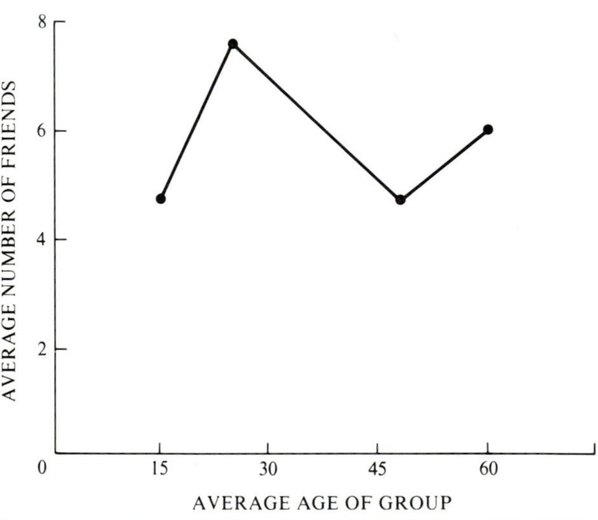

Figure 1–6 Lowenthal and her colleagues studied four separate groups of adults, of differing ages, asking each one how many friends he or she had. These cross-sectional results tell us about an age difference in number of friends, but they do not *tell us that friendship patterns* change *with age. (Source: Lowenthal, Thurnher, & Chiriboga, 1975, data from Table 4, p. 50.)*

olds, when they are 60, will show the same pattern of friendships that current 60-year-olds show. The technical term for such built-in coexistence of effects is **confounding.** Thus *in any cross-sectional study, age and cohort are totally confounded.* They vary simultaneously, so that we cannot ascribe an observed pattern of age differences unequivocally to either age or cohort.

A second difficulty in this particular study is that the subjects at each age were actually selected not for their age per se, but because they occupied particular statuses or roles. The youngest group is made up of highschool students; the next-oldest group included only newlyweds (in their first marriages) who ranged in age from 20 to 38; the middle-aged group (average age 50) were all married and had children nearly grown and ready to leave home; the oldest group consisted of married adults whose children had left home and who were about ready to retire. Thus, these results, if they tell us anything, may tell us more about the relationship between family life status and friendships than they do about age and friendships. We would need to look at other adults in their 20s who were not newlyweds, or who had been married for some years, to see if the pattern was actually linked to age.

This variant of cross-sectional research in which subjects are chosen on the basis of their stage in the family life cycle rather than by age is very common in research by family sociologists. For example, a great deal of what we know about marriages over the adult years is based on research following such a design.

Sociologists also commonly use another variant of a cross-sectional design. Instead of selecting subjects initially in specific age groups, they simply sample randomly across a wide age range. The group of subjects—often quite a large group, perhaps several thousand—may be chosen to represent the characteristics of the total population, or it may include only women who work, or only families that have telephones, or the like. If all ages are included in the group, then the researcher can later either combine the subjects into groups on the basis of age or can look at age as a continuous dimension. Research of this kind, rich as it can be, does not solve the cohort problem. Age and cohort are still confounded.

Longitudinal Designs

One obvious solution to the cohort problem is to follow the same subjects over time. There are several variants of such a design. Among psychologists, the most common procedure is to select a relatively small group of children or adults who are all roughly the same age at the beginning of the study, and then study them intensively and repeatedly as they move through some interesting period of years. Perhaps the most famous such study, at least in the field of adult development, is the Berkeley Intergenerational Study, in which several hundred children born between 1918 and 1928 were followed until they were in their 50s (Eichorn, Clausen, Haan, Honzik, & Mussen, 1981). They were observed, tested, and interviewed as children, their families were observed and interviewed, and then they were reinterviewed and tested at roughly 10-year intervals in adulthood. The result is a remarkably rich body of information, albeit on a small (and not necessarily representative) group of individuals.

Among sociologists, the more common procedure, called a **panel study,** aims for greater representativeness by starting with a much larger sample of individuals, usually chosen so as to be statistically representative of the national population or some sub-group of the population, such as heads of households, or single mothers, or whatever. Usually the initial sample differs quite widely in age. All of these subjects are then reinterviewed on a regular schedule over the succeeding years. In long-term panel studies, as subjects drop out or die they are replaced, so that in any given year the entire sample is still representative of the population from which it was drawn, even though the sample does not now include precisely the same individuals from year to year. Still, the lives or experiences of those individuals who do remain in the study can be traced over time.

One of the richest and most influential of the panel studies of adult development is the Michigan Panel Study of Income Dynamics (e.g., Duncan and Morgan, 1985), which began with a nationally-representative sample of 5,000 *families* in 1968. The study has followed not only the individuals in those original families, but also the families formed by the grown children, and the families formed by remarriages of the original spouses. At the moment, about 6,500 families (over 16,000 individuals) are included. Each year, one member of each family is interviewed in detail, and that individual gives information not only about him/herself but about other members of the family.

Either of these types of longitudinal study can tell us about changes or continuities over age that are common in a particular group of people. Do most people become more conservative as they get older? Does awareness of physical aging commonly become a central concern of adults in their 40s or 50s? Longitudinal studies can also tell us, as cross-sectional studies never can, how consistent or inconsistent each *individual* is over time. Are moody and irritable 20-year-olds also likely to be moody and irritable as 50-year-olds? Is a young adult with a high IQ likely still to have a relatively high IQ at 80? Finally, longitudinal studies can allow us to look at both group and individual effects at the same time and to ask whether certain sub-groups of individuals—such as, perhaps, very shy adults compared to the more gregarious, or working class versus middle class adults—follow different pathways.

Both cross-sectional and longitudinal studies can be useful. However, it is confusing when the two sorts of studies seem to point to very different conclusions about the course of adult life. When that happens, it tells us that some kind of cohort effect is at work. For example, as I pointed out earlier (and as I'll detail more fully in Chapter 5), cross-sectional studies of IQ consistently showed that IQ was lower among older adults than younger, a difference usually interpreted as showing a *decline* in IQ, beginning in middle-age or even earlier. But longitudinal studies do not show declines until quite late in old age (for example, Schaie, 1983b). The obvious explanation is that the older subjects in the cross-sectional studies had less education and less exposure to standardized tests. When cross-sectional groups were compared, the older groups were both older and less educated. The longitudinal studies showed that *individuals* showed relatively little change in IQ over their own lifetimes.

It may seem from this discussion that a longitudinal study solves all our problems. As Paul Mussen puts it:

> . . . for understanding real people, living, growing, and changing in the real world, interacting with others and coping with real problems and transitions, there is no satisfactory alternative to the longitudinal method. (1987, p. 375)

But while this is true, longitudinal studies are *not* trouble free. They have their own built-in difficulties, of which three are particularly troublesome.

THE DROP OUT OR SELECTIVE ATTRITION PROBLEM Whenever you study the same people over a period of time, it is impossible to keep in touch with all of them. Some move, and you can't find them again. Some decline to participate at later testing points. Some die or become too ill to participate. In general, the healthiest and best educated subjects are more likely to continue to participate in longitudinal research, so that over time your sample becomes more and more biased toward those with the best functioning. This is a problem with all longitudinal research but a particularly troublesome one in studies of the final decades of life. Since the least healthy older adults die, we may underestimate the degree of actual decline in some function (such as memory speed, or IQ, or whatever) because each succeeding test includes only those healthy enough to have survived.

An excellent example of this effect comes from an analysis by Ilene Siegler and her colleagues (Siegler, McCarty, & Logue, 1982) of some findings from the first Duke Longitudinal Study of Aging, which you can see in Figure 1–7. The subjects, who initially ranged in age from 63 to 87, were tested repeatedly over 16 years on a wide range of measures. This particular figure shows scores on a test of verbal memory for the oldest subjects, those who were 71 or older at the beginning of the study. As you can see, those who remained in this study the longest had initially had the highest verbal memory scores.

Similar analyses from Warner Schaie's Seattle Longitudinal Study—a study with which you will become very familiar in Chapter 5—show that not all types of drop outs are equally problematical. Schaie found that those subjects who dropped out because they were no longer interested had about the same initial qualities as did those who remained in the study all along. It was those who dropped out because they died, or who were too ill to continue, who led to biased results since they had differed from the continuing subjects at the beginning (Cooney, Schaie, and Willis, 1988).

Because of such difficulties, we must be cautious about drawing overly optimistic conclusions from longitudinal studies that appear to show that skills are retained or even improved in old age.

TIME OF MEASUREMENT, OR HISTORICAL EFFECTS A second problem is that in many longitudinal studies, particularly those done by psychologists, the sample is drawn from a single cohort—so we haven't really gotten rid of the cohort problem entirely. We cannot be sure that any pattern of age change

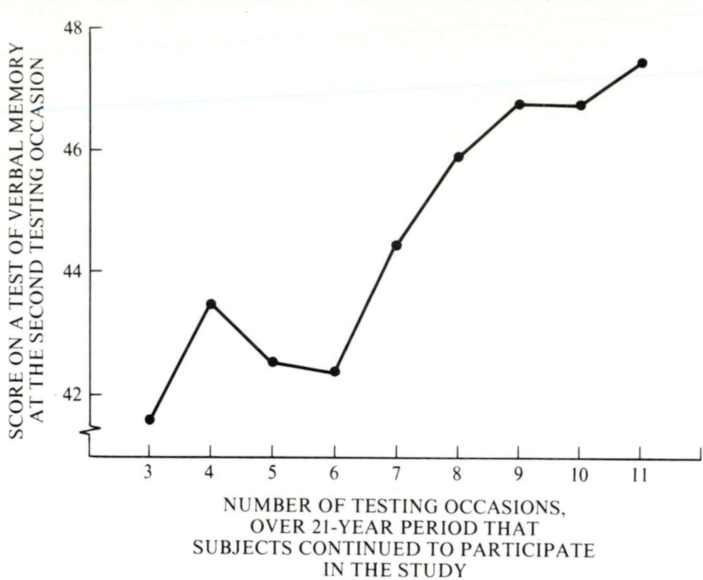

Figure 1–7 Selective attrition—the steady loss of the least healthy, the least educated, or least cooperative subjects over repeated testings—can be a serious problem in longitudinal research. These results from the first Duke Longitudinal Study show that for adults who were 71 years or older when the study began, those who lasted the longest in the study had started out with higher scores on the verbal memory test. Since these initially brighter subjects are the only ones left in the study at later ages, we may end up underestimating the effects of aging on memory loss or maintenance. (Source: Siegler, McCarty, & Logue, 1982, Figure 1, page 179. Reprinted by permission of the Journal of Gerontology, *1982, 37, 176–181.)*

we observe in our longitudinal study would *also* describe another cohort studied longitudinally. The example I gave earlier, of changes in attitudes about sex roles, may help make this clear.

If I had studied sex role attitudes longitudinally in a group of adults born in 1925 (those now about 65), I might well find that the subjects' attitudes had become more egalitarian in their late 40s or 50s. But would such a change really reflect some age-linked or *developmental* process that normally occurs at midlife, or does it merely reflect the fact that for this cohort, the women's movement coincided with their 40s and 50s? The only way to know would be to study *other* cohorts longitudinally, such as perhaps those who were born in 1935 and 1945.

Panel studies in which individuals from several different cohorts are followed over time do not share this problem. But among the more psychologically-oriented longitudinal studies this cohort-specificity is particularly problematic. Many of the most thorough of these studies—those that have examined the widest range of adult functioning and followed the subjects for the greatest number of years—

involve essentially the same cohort: those born between about 1920 and 1930 (e.g. Eichorn, Clausen, Haan, Honzik, & Mussen, 1981; Vaillant, 1977a, 1977b). And this is, in some respects, a highly atypical group. They grew up during the depression, lived through World War II, formed their families during that unusual time immediately following the war when women returned to full-time homemaking and birth rates soared. Both preceding and succeeding cohorts had very different life experiences. Longitudinal data on this cohort *may* point to basic developmental processes in adult life; or they may tell us only something about adult life patterns in this cohort. Thus when we look at longitudinal data we must be sensitive to the potential impact of experiences unique to the cohort being studied.

CHANGING THEORIES AND MEASURES A third frustration for longitudinal researchers is that they usually find, 5 or 10 or 20 years into the study, that they are now interested in somewhat different aspects of development than they were at the beginning; and they find that they did not measure initially the qualities or aspects they now find intriguing. Theories change, new data emerge that alter the way issues are framed, new tests and measurement strategies are devised. With a longitudinal study, one is locked into a set of measurement decisions that had to be made in a different era. (Having been involved myself in one 10-year study, I know how frustrating this can be!).

Sequential Designs

A third type of research design can give us the best of both worlds—potentially achieving the relative speed and flexibility of cross-sectional designs while at the same time retaining the study of sequence and consistency that is the hallmark of longitudinal research (Baltes, Reese, & Nesselroade, 1977; Schaie, 1986). Collectively, these are called sequential designs, and each involves studying more than one cohort.

The easiest way for me to lay out the alternatives for you is to have you look very carefully at Figure 1–8. (I guarantee that this will take some thought; I have to rethink the alternatives myself every so often to be sure I still have them straight in my mind. But it is worth the effort, since you will understand the research I'll be describing throughout the book a lot better if you take the time to understand these alternatives now.)

Figure 1–8 shows all the logical possibilities in schematic form. On the top of the table are the years in which the researcher might actually study the subjects. On the left are the years of *birth* of the subjects (cohorts). The numbers entered into the body of the table are the *ages* of the subjects of that cohort studied in that particular year.

Let me start with the already-familiar possibilities: A cross sectional study involves a comparison of the cells of any *one column.* A longitudinal study involves a comparison of the cells of any *one row.* A third relatively simple possibility, which I have not yet mentioned, involves comparisons along any *one northwest/southeast diagonal.* This is called a **time-lag design.**

YEAR OF BIRTH OF COHORT	TIME OF MEASUREMENT 1945	1950	1955	1960	1965	1970	1975	1980	1985	1990	1995	2000
1905					60							
1910					55	60						
1915					50	55	60					
1920					45	50	55	60				
1925	20	25	30	35	40	45	50	55	60			
1930		20	25	30	35	40	45	50	55	60		
1935			20	25	30	35	40	45	50	55	60	
1940				20	25	30	35	40	45	50	55	60
1945					20	25	30	35	40			
1950						20	25	30	35			
1955							20	25	30			
1960								20	25			
1965									20			

Figure 1–8 *All the research designs used for studying age differences or age change can be shown here. The numbers entered in the table are the ages of the subjects in that cohort at each time of testing. A* cross-sectional *design involves comparisons of several entries in any one column; a* longitudinal *design involves comparisons across any one row or portion of a row; a* time-lag *design involves comparisons on any one northwest/southeast diagonal; a* time-sequential *design involves essentially two or more cross-sectional studies done at different times, thus including two or more columns; a* cohort-sequential *design is essentially a repeated longitudinal design, thus involving comparison of more than one row; a* cross-sequential *design includes both multiple rows and columns, such as all the cells in the marked rectangle.*

Suppose I had studied the sex role attitudes of a group of college students in 1970. In 1980 I got interested in whether sex role attitudes had changed at all in the last 10 years, so I studied *another* group of college students in 1980. Then I did the same thing again in 1990. I now have three samples, each from a different cohort, but all the subjects were the same age when they were tested. This allows me to look directly at cohort effects without any confounding of age and is the simplest of the so-called sequential designs.

But suppose, instead, that in 1970 I had done a cross-sectional study, including not just college students but also 30-year-olds, 40-year-olds, and 50-year-olds. And then in 1980 I again studied 20-, 30-, 40-, and 50-year-olds. That is, I did one cross-sectional study in 1970 and *another* in 1980. Now I have what is called a **time-sequential design.** In Figure 1–8, this would involve studying at least *two columns.* You can see immediately that this type of design gives you a lot more information. If I had observed some differences among the responses of the adults of different ages in my first longitudinal study and had been tempted to interpret these differences as reflecting some inner or developmental change, I could now check and see if the same pattern of change occurred in the next cross-sectional comparison. If it did, I would be more confident (although not yet sure) of my interpretation. I could also look at the *same* cohort as it moved through time by comparing the scores of those groups who had all been born in 1950 (those who were 20 in 1970, 30 in 1980, and 40 in 1990), or I could look at those born in 1940, who were 30 in 1970, and 40 in 1980. It's not the same *people* each time, but it is the same *cohort.* Thus by doing two (or more) relatively simple cross-sectional studies several years apart, I gain enormously in explanatory power.

A real-life example comes from the work of Joseph Veroff, Elizabeth Douvan, and Richard Kulka (1981), who completed a major survey of the life experiences of a large representative sample of Americans in 1957 and then repeated essentially the same design, with different subjects, in 1976. Since both surveys included more than 2,000 subjects, it was possible for Veroff and his colleagues to subdivide the total sample into age groups and to compare the responses of different age groups in two different series of cohorts.

In one comparison, for example, they found that in their 1957 sample the percentage of adults who described themselves as highly anxious went up steadily with age. Those over 65 were almost three times as likely to describe such high anxiety as were those in their 20s. But in the 1976 sample, *every* age group reported much higher anxiety than had been true among the 1957 sample, and there were no clear age trends. In 1976, 65-year-olds reported about the same amount of anxiety as did 20-year-olds. But another aspect of mental health, which they called "immobilization," (difficulty getting up in the morning, drinking, hands sweating, can't get going) showed exactly the same age pattern in 1957 and 1976: Adults in their 20s reported the most immobilization, and it declined steadily with age. The anxiety differences thus look like cohort effects, while the differences with age in immobilization *might* reflect some more basic developmental process.

Time-sequential designs, like the Veroff study, call for two or more consecutive cross-sectional studies. The next logical possibility, called a **cohort sequential design,** is obviously to do two or more consecutive longitudinal studies. Think back again to the original time-lag design I described: I studied a group of 20-year-olds in 1970, and another group of 20-year-olds in 1980. I could turn this design into a cohort sequential design by now studying *each* of those groups longitudinally. So I might re-interview each group of 20-year-olds when they turn 30 and again when they turn 40. This now gives me three parallel *longitudinal studies,* one begun in 1970, one begun in 1980, and one begun in 1990. In Figure 1–8, such a design involves any comparison of two or more *rows.*

This design is also powerful, since it now allows me both to look at change within each individual and also to discover whether the same kind of change within individuals occurs for more than one cohort.

The obvious remaining logical possibility, called a **cross-sequential design,** involves studying both rows and columns at the same time, such as studying all the cells within the outlined box. A good example of such a design is the second of the Duke Longitudinal Studies of Aging (Palmore, 1981; Siegler, 1983), which I've shown in Figure 1–9. The researchers began with five cohorts, ages 45, 50, 55, 60, and 65 at the start of the study. Each group was then seen three more times, at two year intervals. Thus they have five separate longitudinal studies,

	COHORTS		AGE AT EACH MEASUREMENT DATE			
	AGE AT START OF STUDY	YEAR BORN	1968	1970	1972	1974
A	45	1919	45	47	49	51
B	50	1914	50	52	54	56
C	55	1909	55	57	59	61
D	60	1904	60	62	64	66
E	65	1899	65	67	69	71

Figure 1–9 The design of the second Duke Longitudinal Study illustrates a cross-sequential *design. Five different cohorts were identified at the start of the study, and each was followed for six years. If we compare the scores for the five cohorts in 1968, or in 1972, or 1974, we would have a cross-sectional study; if we look at each cohort over time, we have a longitudinal study. (Source: Palmore, 1981.)*

each lasting 6 years. They also have potentially a series of cross-sectional studies: at each testing year, they can compare the responses of subjects of differing ages. But because the ages of the cohorts began to overlap as the longitudinal study progressed, the researchers also have a third option: They can compare the responses of *different* cohorts at roughly the *same* ages. For example, they could see whether Cohort A at age 50 responded similarly on their tests as had Cohort B when they had been 50, six years earlier. This allows the same test of cohort effects as one can have in the simpler time-lag designs.

If you think back to the description I gave of panel designs a few pages ago you'll realize that many panel studies are variations of cross-sequential designs. They start with adults of many different ages and follow all of them over time.

When several of these types of sequential designs are combined, as Schaie has done in the Seattle Longitudinal Study (Schaie, 1983b, Schaie & Hertzog, 1983), remarkably rich and powerful data may emerge. Schaie first selected and gave IQ tests to a series of cohorts 7 years apart in age, ranging from 25 to 67 at the start of the study. This first study was thus cross-sectional. Then some of the subjects *of each age* were followed longitudinally, with retesting at 7-year intervals for 21 years. This now gives him a cross-sequential analysis, essentially like the Duke studies only over a longer period of time.

Not content with that, however, every 7 years Schaie also selected *another* set of cross-sectional samples with new 25-year-olds, new 32-year-olds, and so on, and followed some of them longitudinally as well, which gives him a cohort-sequential design. In the end, he had one set of parallel longitudinal subjects he had followed for 21 years, another set he had followed for 14 years, and others he had followed for 7 years. He also had four full cross-sectional studies, 7 years apart. It is a remarkable study. Few researchers have had either the patience or the resources to complete designs of this complexity. But all the sequential designs allow us to shift from talking merely about age differences to talking about age *changes* and their variations. They also allow us to separate out the impact of unique cohort experiences (time of measurement effects) from that of more enduring developmental patterns.

Research Methods

Choosing the Subjects: Sample Selection

In addition to questions of when and how often one will observe or assess subjects, and at what ages, a critical element in research design is the selection of the actual individuals to be included as subjects. Ideally, the sample should accurately represent the population the researcher is hoping to describe. If we are really searching for age changes or developmental patterns valid for all adults, we should select random samples of adults from all cultures of the world. Since that—or anything even close to it—is clearly impractical, researchers make a variety of compromises in selecting subjects, each of which may affect the generalizability of the findings. As you can see from the descriptions of some key studies in Table 1.1, the most representative samples are typically found in the large sociological panel or survey studies, in which subjects are selected randomly within one or more cities, or from across the country. In contrast, most of the longest-term, in-depth longitudinal studies include relatively small samples (100–300), more middle class than working class, and usually predominantly white subjects. Many frequently quoted studies include only men. As a consequence, we know more about the adult development of white middle-class American men born between 1920 and 1930 than we do about any other group.

Given the enormous investment of time and effort required to do research of this kind, it is remarkable that there are as many decent studies as there are. But we do need to keep limitations in both design and sampling in mind as we move through the various chapters of the book.

Collecting Information About Subjects

Once the research design is determined, the next major set of decisions has to do with the ways in which information will be collected from subjects. Each of the basic strategies has distinct advantages. Since you have encountered descriptions of these techniques in earlier courses, I will assume that each of you has at least some knowledge of the pros and cons of the alternatives. Therefore, I will describe them only very briefly.

OBSERVATION The most open-ended way to explore adult behavior is to observe adults in natural surroundings. This is a common technique in studies of children but is rarely done with adults. Even structured observations, or observations of adults in specially created or artificial situations, are relatively rare. Most of what we know about adulthood comes from asking people about themselves in one way or another.

TABLE 1.1. Design and Sampling Characteristics of Some Major Longitudinal and Sequential Studies.

Name of Study	Recent Source	Years of Study	Average of Range of Ages of Ss at Start (and end) of Study	Birth Year of Oldest Cohort	Number of Ss at start (and end) of Study	Sample Characteristics	Design and Measures
Long-Term Longtitudinal Studies							
Grant Study	Vaillant, 1977	1937–1970	19(49)	1918	268 (95)	Harvard under-graduates, all male	Longitudinal; psychological adjustment, health.
Berkeley Intergenerational Studies	Eichorn, Clausen, Haan, Honzik, & Mussen, 1981	(a)1928–1970	birth (40)	1928	248(144)	Sample from Berkeley, CA, male & female, mostly middle class, mostly white	Longitudinal; personality, IQ, health.
		(b) 1932–1970	10–12(48)	1920	212(107)	Sample from Oakland, CA, all white, middle & working class	Same measures as in (a)
AT&T longitudinal Studies	Bray & Howard 1982	1946–1967	24–30 (44–50)	1926	422(226)	All male, begin-ning managers at AT&T, college & noncollege; white	Longitudinal; work success, personality
Terman Study of Gifted	Sears, 1977	1922–1972	11(62)	1911	1,528(916)	Children with IQs of 135 or above, from California	Work success; personality

			Sequential Studies				
Duke Studies of Aging	Palmore, 1981	(a) 1955–1976	59–94 (76–102)	1870	270(44)	Southeastern city, reasonably representative, white & black	Cross-sequential; health, personality, IQ, work history
		(b) 1968–1976	46–70 (51–77)	1899	502(375)	Southeastern city, all white, more middle class, both male and female	Cross-sequential; health, personality, work, IQ
Seattle Longitudinal Study	Schaie, 1983a	1956–1977	25–67 (46–88)	1889	21-year sample: 120 14-year sample: 300	Seattle, WA: all participants in a health maintenance organization, male & female, mixed social class	Cross-sequential & time-sequential; heavy focus on intellectual measures
Baltimore Longitudinal Studies of Aging	Costa, McCrae, & Arenberg, 1983	1958–1978	17–77 (37–97)	1881	769(171)	All male volunteers; quite well educated	Cross-sequential; personality and health
Michigan Survey Research Center Study of Mental Illness & Health	Veroff, Douvan, Kulka, 1981	1957 & 1976	21 and older in each sample	approx 1877	2,460 in 1956; 2,267 in 1977	National probability sample; all social classes and races, men & women	Time-sequential; two cross-sectional studies 20 years apart; values, family, work, health
National Longitudinal Surveys	Parnes, 1981	1966–1976	45–59 (55–69)	1907	5,020 (3,185)	All male, with blacks intentionally overrepresented; national sample	Cross-sequential; work history, family economics
Panel Study of Income Dynamics	Duncan & Morgan, 1985	1968–1983	full adult age range	1900	5000 families (6500 families)	Nationally representative sample	Panel design, with all ages selected initially and then reassessed repeatedly. Can be used as cross-sequential design; work history, family dynamics, income.

INTERVIEWS Interviews are extremely common in research on adulthood. The longitudinal studies described in Table 1.1 all included extensive interviews in their test procedures; many sociological studies of aspects of adult life also involve structured interviews. Sometimes the transcripts of subjects' responses to interview questions are later rated on broad dimensions by other psychologists or researchers; sometimes the data from the interviews are coded in a more direct fashion.

QUESTIONNAIRES Still more structured is a questionnaire in which the alternative answers are provided. The questions may request factual information about the subject (age, occupation, number of friends of various types, marital status, income, etc.). Standardized instruments designed to assess attitudes or aspects of personality, such as sex role attitudes, or rigidity/flexibility, are also widely used.

OTHER STANDARDIZED TESTS IQ tests and tests of other specific abilities are also used widely, sometimes administered individually, sometimes given in groups.

Most of the longitudinal studies have included all or most of these techniques in their testing procedures, yielding a very rich body of data. Most of the shorter-term longitudinal studies or the cross-sectional studies involve a more focused set of questions and a narrower range of assessment techniques.

Understanding the Answers: Analysis of Research Findings

Once the data have been collected, researchers must make another set of decisions about how to analyze the findings. Some of the statistical methods now being used are extremely sophisticated and complex. I'll be describing a few of these in later chapters, as I discuss specific studies that include them. At this early point, all I want to do is talk about the two most common ways of looking at the results of studies of adult change and continuity.

The most common way to describe age differences is simply to calculate average (mean) scores on some measure for each of several different age groups. Then the means are compared in some fashion. When longitudinal data are available, a comparison of mean scores at different ages is also involved. In each case, we are usually looking for a trend, a pattern of scores linked to age.

If the sample studied is large enough, it is often possible to subdivide it and look for age differences or equivalences separately in various subgroups, such as women vs. men, working class vs. middle class, those with young children vs. those without young children, and the like. If every group shows essentially the same pattern over age, and if the same pattern occurred in longitudinal studies as well, we'd be much more likely to conclude that this is a significant age-linked or developmental pattern. If the changes and continuities are very different for different subgroups, however, (as is often the case) then we are led to ask other kinds of follow-up questions: Why might the groups differ? What do the differences tell us about the possible pathways through adulthood?

Let me give you a quick example. One of the consistent findings in sociological research on families is that marital satisfaction is related to the presence and age of children. Figure 1–10 shows the results from one of the early studies (Rollins & Feldman, 1970). You can see that the percentage of couples who say they are happy "all the time" goes down with the birth of the first child and stays relatively low until retirement age. I'll be talking much more about this intriguing pattern in Chapter 7. For now I merely want to have you think about the way in which these findings are analyzed and interpreted. These are cross-sectional comparisons, so we don't know if *individual* families actually go through this sequence. All we know from this study is that when we compute separate means for each age/family stage group, we find a robust pattern of age or stage differences. Since other researchers reported the same results when they studied somewhat different cohorts, (Rollins & Galligan, 1978), confidence in the consistency of this pattern is increased.

But other research shows that this curvilinear pattern is much more typical of some types of families than of others. Stephen Anderson and his

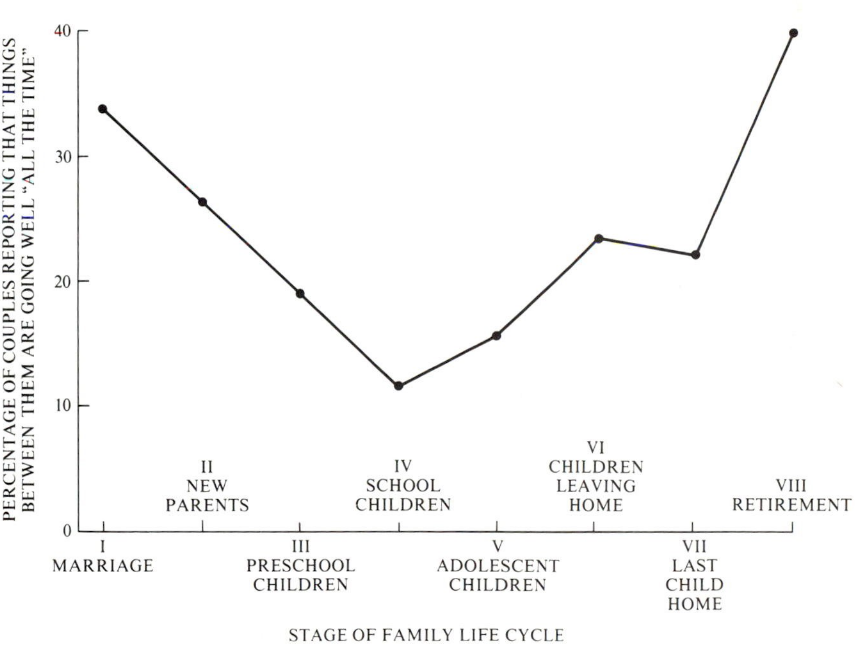

Figure 1–10 These cross-sectional findings, replicated by other researchers studying other cohorts, show a consistent pattern of age differences related to stage of family life cycle: Couples with young children are less satisfied with their marriages than are couples with no children or with children gone from home. (Source: Rollins & Feldman, 1970, data from Tables 2 and 3, page 24. Copyrighted 1970 by the National Council on Family Relations, 1910 West County Road B, Suite 147, St. Paul, MN 55113. Reprinted by permission.)

colleagues (Anderson, Russell, & Schumm, 1983) looked at this same pattern for three different kinds of spouses: those who were high, medium, or low in "marital conventionalization." Subjects high in conventionalization were those who agreed with statements like "My marriage is a perfect success" or "every new thing I have learned about my husband has pleased me," and disagreed with statements like "I have some needs that are not being met by my marriage." Subjects low in marital conventionalization showed the reverse pattern and thus reported a few warts and wrinkles in their marriages. When the researchers looked at the relationship between marital satisfaction and age/family stage in each of these three groups, the results in Figure 1–11 emerged.

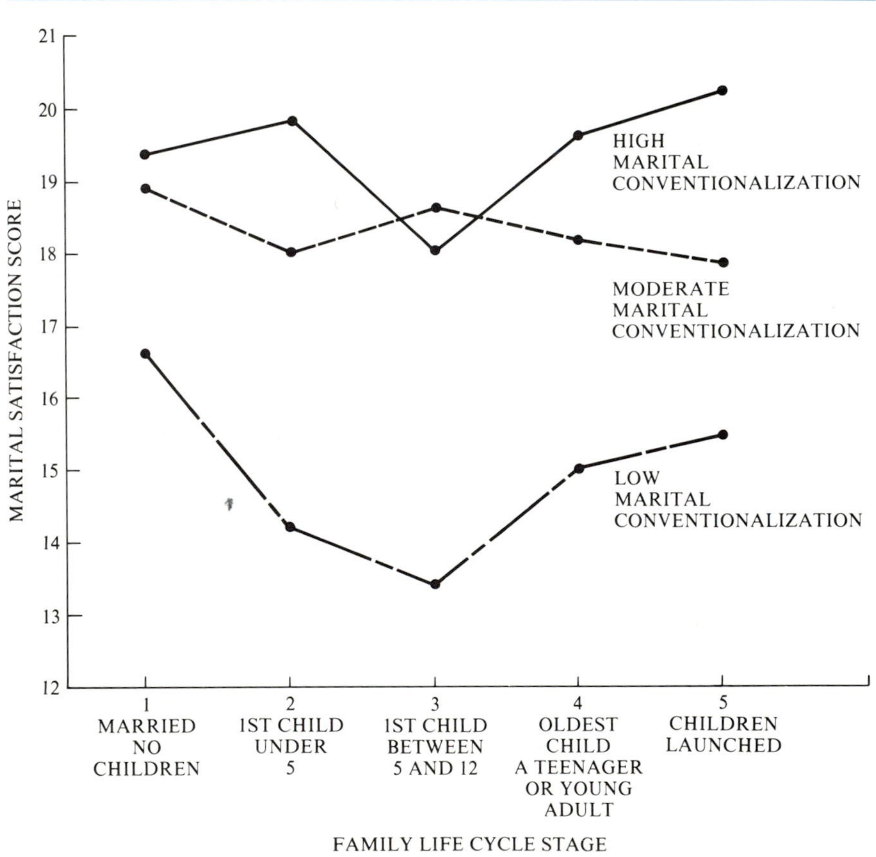

Figure 1–11 *Compare the curves in this figure with those in Figure 1–10. Here we see that the apparent "drop" in marital satisfaction after the birth of a child or when children are young occurred clearly only in one subgroup, those with low "marital conventionalization." By using analyses like these, even simple comparisons of mean scores in cross-sectional studies can be very informative. (Source: Anderson et al., 1983, Figure 2, page 135. Copyrighted 1983 by the National Council on Family Relations, 1910 West Country Road B, Suite 147, St. Paul, MN 55113. Reprinted by permission.)*

As you can see, the clearest curvilinear pattern occurred for those couples low in conventionalization. Intriguing, isn't it? This could mean that children have a negative effect on marital satisfaction only for those couples who are already lower in satisfaction, or it could mean that those couples who are more *honest* in their description of their marriage are also more willing to acknowledge negative reactions to the birth of a child. The point for now, though, is that all of this information emerges from quite simple analytic techniques: the comparison of mean (average) scores for different age or life stage subgroups.

Such comparisons of means for different age groups, either cross-sectionally or longitudinally, can give us some insights about possible age changes or developmental patterns. But they cannot tell us whether there has been continuity or change *within individuals.* For this, a different type of analysis is required, namely correlational techniques. A **correlation** is simply a statistic that tells us the extent to which two sets of scores on the same people tend to vary together. Correlations (symbolized **r**) can range from +1.00 to −1.00, with a positive correlation showing that high scores on the two dimensions occur together. A negative correlation tells us that high scores on one dimension go with low scores on the other. The closer the number to 1.00, the stronger the relationship. A correlation of .00 indicates no relationship.

For example, height and weight are positively correlated: Taller people generally weigh more, shorter people less. But the correlation is not perfect (*not* 1.00) because there are some short, heavy people, and some tall, light people. If you are on a diet, the number of pounds you lose is *negatively* correlated with the number of calories you eat: High calories go with low weight loss. But this correlation, too, is not perfect (as any of you who has dieted knows full well!).

When we go searching for continuities or discontinuities in individual patterns over adulthood, the correlation is the main tool we use. A researcher will measure some skill or quality in each member of a sample at several time points and then use the correlation statistic to describe the degree to which the scores at any two time points are similar to one another. For example, do adults who have high IQs at 20 still have high IQs at 40? Yes. In one study, Dorothy Eichorn and her colleagues (Eichorn, Hunt, & Honzik, 1981) found a correlation between IQ at 18 and at 40 of about .80, which is very high indeed.

Correlations are also used to search for explanations for patterns of change or continuity that we may have already observed. If we were interested in knowing why some adults remain satisfied with their lives into old age, while others do not, (as Palmore, 1981, has been) we could look at the correlations between life-satisfaction and a wide range of other measures, such as education, or income, or presence of family members, or availability of friends, or health.

Ultimately, however, correlations can tell us only about relationship; they cannot tell us about causality, even though it is very often tempting to make the conceptual leap from a correlation to a cause. Some cases are easy. If I told you that there was a negative correlation between the per capita incidence of refrigerators in the countries of the world and the infant mortality rates in those countries, you would not be tempted to conclude that the presence of more refrigerators causes lower infant mortality. You'd look for other kinds of societal changes that might explain the link between the two events. But if I tell you that there is a positive correlation between the amount of time adults spend with friends and family and the overall life happiness those adults report, you would be much more tempted to jump to the conclusion that greater happiness is caused by contact with friends and family. And it may be. But the correlation all by itself doesn't tell us that. It only tells us that there is a relationship. It remains for further research and theorizing to uncover the causal links, if any.

There are many variations on these analytical themes, but nearly all the research on adult development involves one or the other (or both) of these basic techniques.

Experimental Designs

The type of research design I have not mentioned thus far—an omission you may have noted, particularly if you are familiar with research in other areas of psychology—is the **experiment.** In an experiment, the researcher systematically controls or manipulates one or more variables, assigning subjects randomly to various treatment or non treatment groups. Because the questions we are interested in when we study development have to do with changes or continuities with age, and since we cannot assign subjects randomly to age groups nor manipulate or speed up the process of aging, there is not a great deal of experimental research in the study of adult development. But there are important ways in which experiments can help to explore alternative explanations of age-related patterns that may be observed in cross-sectional or longitudinal studies.

For example, take the observation that older adults perform many intellectual tasks at a slower speed than do younger adults. There are several possible explanations of this pattern, some of which I sketched earlier: It could reflect fundamental maturational changes in the brain or nervous system; it could reflect differences in practice at such tasks; it could reflect differences in motivation to compete or achieve; or it could reflect the differences in years of education between young and old cohorts being compared.

Controlled experiments might help us choose among these alternatives. We could, for example, select groups of young, middle-aged, and older subjects, and randomly assign half of each age group to a special training group in which extra practice was given on some particular intellectual task. The other half of the subjects at each age might be given no training, or might be given training at some other kind of task altogether. If we then tested all the subjects before and after training, we could determine whether the older group benefited more, equally, or less from training than did the younger groups. If they benefited more, it would provide support for the "lack of practice" explanation for speed differences. If they benefited less it would provide some support (though not conclusive) for a biological/maturational explanation of the basic observed difference.

Perhaps there are so few experiments of this kind in the study of adult development because we are still, in this field, primarily concerned with problems of description rather than explanation. In those areas in which the basic descriptive research is more complete—such as the study of changes in intellectual performance over adulthood—experiments like this are done, and we will encounter a few as we go along. But at the moment, systematic, controlled experimentation is not one of the major modes of research in this field.

A Final Word

Since I began this chapter on a personal note, let me end it the same way. I approach the topic of this book both as a psychologist and as an adult. My interest is both scientific and personal. I want to understand how it all works and why, both because that is inherently interesting to me, and because it may help me to understand and deepen my own development. Your own journey through adulthood will be like my own in many ways and very unlike it in others. What I am searching for in this book are the basic rules or processes that account for both those similarities and differences. I hope you can share with me the sense of adventure in the scientific search, as well as in the personal journey.

Summary

1. Several central themes run through the study of adult development: Is there continuity, or is there change within the individual? Are there stages or phases? Is there both inner and outer change? In each instance it is important to look both at descriptive and explanatory evidence.
2. Three major kinds of influences help to shape adult experiences. The first are shared, age-graded experiences, which can be further subdivided into three types: shared, inevitable biological changes that are part of aging; shared cultural experiences, such as those associated with the family life cycle; and internal changes that may be common to all adults.
3. A second source of influence is the impact of experiences unique to individual cohorts. Such influences, such as the impact of the Great Depression, or the Vietnam war, or the women's movement, make the adult experiences of any given cohort more alike and distinct from the experiences of other cohorts.
4. Unique experiences encountered by each adult, shared neither within cohort nor across cohorts, form a third source of influence. Examples: the unexpectedly early death of your parent; losing your job in middle age; serious illness or disability at an early age; divorce; winning the lottery.
5. The term *maturation* will be used to describe those age-graded changes due to fundamental, universally shared biological changes. The term *development* will be used to describe changes with age that involve improvement or growth.
6. Researchers exploring questions of adult continuity and change must choose one of several basic research designs. Cross-sectional designs involve studying separate groups at each of several ages or stages; longitudinal designs involve repeated study of the same group of individuals over time; sequential designs involve some combination of the two, such as repeated cross-sectional studies (time-sequential design), replications of longitudinal studies (cohort-sequential design), or both (cross-sequential design).

7. Cross-sectional designs inevitably confound age and cohort, while longitudinal studies involving assessment of a single cohort over time confound age change and time of testing. Longitudinal designs also suffer from problems of selective attrition. Sequential designs can help sort out some of the differing effects.
8. A second series of decisions for the researcher concerns the way in which information will be collected from subjects. The most common strategies in adult research are individual interviews (in person or over the phone), questionnaires, and standardized tests, such as measures of depression or life satisfaction.
9. Analysis of findings typically involve one of two techniques: comparison of means for groups of different ages (or for the same people across age); or calculation of correlations between scores for the same people at different ages (to check for individual consistency) or for the same people at the same time on different measures.
10. True experiments, in which the experimenter systematically manipulates one or more variables and assigns subjects at random to experimental and control groups, are not common in the study of adult development, although they can help us to choose among competing explanations for patterns of change or continuity over age.

Suggested Readings

ACHENBACH, T. M. (1978). *Research in developmental psychology.* New York: Free Press. If you are interested in some of the intricacies of research design and analysis, this is a good source. I especially recommend pages 89–104.

NEUGARTEN, B. L., & NEUGARTEN, D. A. (May, 1987). The changing meanings of age. *Psychology Today, 21* (5), 29–33. In this brief paper, Neugarten argues that age strata in our culture are shifting rather rapidly, with new strata created (such as "middle aged," which was not a recognizable stratum until a few decades ago) and redefinitions of others.

SCHAIE, K. W. (1983A). What can we learn from the longitudinal study of adult psychological development? In K. W. Schaie (Ed.), *Longitudinal studies of adult psychological development.* New York: Guilford Press. Schaie has been one of the foremost advocates of many of the more complex and elegant sequential designs for studying adult development. Many of his writings on the subject are quite dense and difficult, but this particular chapter is reasonably readable.

VAILLANT, G. E. (1977). *Adaptation to life.* Boston, MA: Little, Brown. If you are dying to get started reading about some real people actually moving through adulthood, try this book. I have found it to be one of the most intriguing of the descriptions of longitudinal evidence, full of fascinating case studies as well as provocative theory.

CHAPTER 2

The Journey Takes Shape: Starting Points

Let me introduce some people to you—each at the starting point of the journey of adulthood but with many of their qualities already established and significant choices made.

Tom Kleck is a big, raw-boned, friendly young man of 22 with a thick, blond mustache and neatly cut hair. His ready smile and his outgoing manner make him easy to talk to and helped to make him one of the most popular kids in his high school class. He is usually pretty optimistic about himself and his future and is hard to rile.

Tom grew up in a working class neighborhood with his parents, two brothers, and a sister. His father is a truck driver; his mother mostly stayed home to care for the children, taking odd jobs only when the family needed the money badly. Neither of his parents went to college, but his father has had higher hopes for Tom. After Tom did well in high school, his folks encouraged him to go to the local community college where he finished a two-year business degree. He's now working as a low-level manager in the same trucking firm for which his father drives, which pleases them both. Although he has his own apartment, he sees his folks often, usually having supper with them on Sundays.

Tom likes the routine his life has fallen into—time with his girlfriend, Marianne, and for his folks; time for some sports with his highschool buddies, a few beers at the tavern. But there is a bit of a daredevil in Tom, too. If he could afford it, he'd like to try sky diving, or river rafting, or driving a racing car on a track. Those choices seem beyond his reach at the moment, but he's still on the lookout for new experiences, new chances. He's planning to take some more college courses, likes to try new sports and new foods; for a lark last year he taught himself to bake bread. When he looks down the road a few years, he sees himself married and with a family but maybe with a different job, one with more challenge and variety.

Cathy Stevens, also 22, might fit your image of the "All American Girl." When you first meet her, it is her smile that strikes you; and her face is open, guileless. She laughs often, and her face is already developing a few smile wrinkles.

She went through many of the usual stages and phases in childhood—a tomboy stretch when you could hardly get her out of the nearest tree (with a broken arm from a fall as a reminder of those days), braces on her teeth, Girl Scouts. But since her family was always well off—her father's a banker, and both her parents went to college—she also had some special advantages like horseback riding lessons and ballet classes. These days she stays in shape with aerobic dancing classes, and she rides whenever she can find the time.

Her parents say that practically from the moment she was born Cathy had a remarkably sunny disposition. Unlike her brother and sister, she was usually obedient and rarely made trouble. When all three kids were in high school, her parents worried about her brother and sister, but they always trusted Cathy. Her grades were only average, but they were good enough to get her into the local state university. She has never thought of herself as a great brain, but she enjoyed school and graduated last year with a degree in psychology. She counted herself lucky to have found a job right away as a secretary and girl Friday for a mental health clinic in her home town. Within a few months she plans to marry Pete, whom she met in college. He's just finishing his master's degree in business administration and hopes to get a good job with a local brokerage firm. After they marry, Cathy is planning to work until their first child is born and then to stay home with the kids while they are little. She thinks that later she may want to go back to school and get a degree in something like social work, but that is all a long way off.

Laura Rogers' life has been sharply different from either Cathy's or Tom's, something you might guess when you meet her, since she already has a permanent frown line between her eyebrows. Otherwise she is an attractive woman with intense, brown eyes.

Her folks were working class people. Her dad worked in a steel mill, and her mom worked a lot of the time as a clerk in a nearby drugstore. It seemed to Laura that her parents were so busy with work and keeping the household going that they didn't have much time for her. On the other hand, Laura wasn't such an easy child to raise, either. She was a bit cranky, didn't sleep regularly as a baby, got upset easily, and became a somewhat willful teenager. But she was also outgoing and usually friendly, so although she was not the most popular girl in school, she had a group of friends she enjoyed. Life changed abruptly at 15 when she got pregnant. Her family and her boyfriend's family pressured them to marry, so by 16 Laura was married and the mother of an infant. She dropped out of high school and quickly got pregnant for the second time. She is now 22 and divorced, with two children to rear on her own. Her ex-husband is not very good about making child-support payments, and things are very tight financially. Right now she has a pretty good job as a waitress, but mostly she's been on welfare since the divorce. Both sets of grandparents help out when they can, but she often feels quite hopeless about her future. She takes pains with her appearance, but you can see the fatigue in her face, in her posture. One of her hopes is that she will eventually marry again—someone steady and more mature than her first husband.

Like Laura, Walter Washington has had a rockier start than either Tom or Cathy. His father left when he was about 3, and Walter has seen his dad only occasionally since then. Walter was the youngest of the four kids; his mother was left to bring them up on her own, trying to make ends meet on her pay as an aide in a nursing home. They lived in a crowded apartment in a black neighborhood in Chicago, and all the kids spent a lot of their time on the streets. Walter was part of a street gang for a while when he was in his early teens, and several times he was picked up by the police. But in high school things turned around a bit for him.

Walter was tall enough and just good enough to make the varsity basketball team at his high school, and the coach happened to be a man who pushed the kids hard to study and to get good grades as well as to play ball. Walter just scraped by in English, and always hated history, but somewhat to his surprise he found that he liked math and science. There was something about the orderliness of both subjects that appealed to him, and he was good at them both. When he got out of high school, his coach and his science teacher helped to get Walter into a TV repair training program, which at least used a little of his technical interests. For three years now Walter has had a pretty good job as a repairman.

But Walter is not satisfied. He wants more—a better job, more money, more education. He is fascinated with computers and is taking night school classes in computer programming and engineering. It is this ambition, this drive, that most distinguishes Walter at 22. His long, lean, black face has a firmness around the mouth, an unsmiling quality that is quite striking. It is not an angry expression, although he can get quite angry about the discrimination against blacks in the computer field; rather, it is a quality of determination.

Socially, Walter is a loner. He has had a few girlfriends, but he would rather spend his time tinkering with computers or machines than with people. He plays a little pick-up basketball, sees his family once in a while; but mostly he lives a pretty solitary life—and that suits him fine.

The fifth member of this quintet of young people is Christopher Linton, who at 22 is just starting his last year of law school. He's a couple of years ahead of most of his peers in school since he skipped a grade in elementary school. He learned to read when he was four, and his parents had a hard time keeping his nose out of a book from then on. Needless to say, Chris did extremely well in school, but he didn't have many friends. An only child of highly educated and financially successful parents, he seemed quite content with the company of his books, his parents, and their friends.

Chris doesn't look much like the stereotypical "egg head." He's quite broad shouldered and well-muscled. But he dresses the part, wearing mostly tweeds and crewneck sweaters. Women find him attractive, but they sometimes have a hard time getting past his shyness. At the moment he does not have a steady girlfriend, though he is dating more now than he did in high school. Aside from being shy, Chris's major problem is that he tends to take things very hard—things like setbacks in his school work, or rejection by a girlfriend. He tends to brood about such things, to be pessimistic and grumpy. If you ask him if he's happy, he guesses he is "o.k." but not much better than that.

When he looks ahead, he sees himself as a partner in a top law firm, probably involved in corporate or tax law. Marriage seems far off, although he says he'd like to have children "eventually." He also assumes that whomever he marries will probably have a career, just as his Mom did. But his Mom also did all the cooking and most of the housework, and Chris figures his wife will probably do most of that, too.

These five young people illustrate an absolutely critical point about development in adulthood: Each of us *begins* adulthood already strongly shaped by such built-in characteristics as gender or race, by internal qualities such as intelligence or personality, by such external conditions as our family background, and by the amount of education we complete. At 22, these five young adults differ along all these dimensions. As a result, they have already embarked on different pathways

Figure 2–1 *Your high school year book no doubt includes all sorts of predictions about the future of each of your classmates. How accurate have those predictions been? Can you really make good guesses about how people will turn out based on what they're like at 18 or 22? Amazingly enough, you can. At least some key features of the lives of these older adults enjoying their 50th reunion could have been predicted. Of course, one of the attractions of reunions is that it gives you a chance to see the instances in which the predictions were* not *accurate—when some of your classmates did a lot better or a lot worse than you had expected. (Photo © Polly Brown, Actuality Inc. Reprinted with permission.)*

through adulthood. These pathways, or *trajectories,* are not permanently fixed; no one's adulthood is completely determined by these starting points. People can and do shift from one pathway to another. But for most of us, there is a "line of least resistance," a pathway that opens in front of us in early adulthood, shaped by our family background, our school experiences, our abilities, and our personalities.

In most of the chapters of this book I will be searching for or talking about the ways in which all our adult trajectories are the same. In such a search, it is easy to overlook the individual variations in both the starting points and the roads that those different starting points may lead to. So I want to begin by talking about differences rather than about similarities. How is an adult's pathway or trajectory shaped by differences in gender, or family wealth, or personality? Do extraverted adults (like both Tom Kleck and Cathy Stevens) experience adulthood differently from those who are more introverted (like Chris Linton or Walter Washington)? What *patterns* can we see in these variations? Knowing something about a young adult's background and qualities, can I make some reasonable predictions about the trajectory he or she is most likely to follow over the succeeding decades?

Specifically, let me look at the impact of six qualities or conditions: gender, race, family status, education, intelligence, and personality.

Gender Differences in Adult Lives

Children discover at about age five that they are stuck with whatever gender they are, and by adulthood each of us is well socialized into the roles for our gender. Since gender roles vary somewhat from one culture to the next, what I can say about the impact of gender on adult lives is necessarily culture-specific. But the basic point is not culture-specific: Gender affects adult lives profoundly, determining choices (or whether you will have certain choices at all), relationships, and sequences of experiences.

Since I will be talking about sex differences in adult lives in virtually every chapter of this book, I will not give you a detailed analysis here, but let me list a few of the most significant differences that exist in our culture:

Women's work patterns are much more likely to be interrupted by periods of nonwork than are men's (Moen, 1985; Spenner, 1988). This is less true today than it was ten or 15 years ago; more women now work continuously through

Figure 2–2 Knowing nothing about these young people except their gender, I can still make some reasonable bets about their future life courses. (Photo © Susan Lapides, 1986, c/o Design Conceptions. Reprinted with permission.)

their adult lives. But interruptions are still far more likely for women than they are for men, both because of childbearing and childrearing, and because women are less often the primary wage earner in a family. An interrupted work pattern, in turn, reduces a woman's chances at job advancement, success, and higher income.

- Women's family roles include much more childcare, housework, and nurturing of both children and spouse than do men's family roles even when both spouses are employed full time (e.g. Spitze, 1988; Coverman & Sheley, 1986). The most recent data we have on this question, by the way, were collected in the early 1980s, so it is possible that there has been a dramatic change in this pattern since then. But I doubt it; there was only slight change in the distribution of household work between men and women between 1965 and 1980—a period in which there was a rapid and major change in women's work patterns. Women's continued responsibility for childcare and household work has implications not only for the relationship between the spouses, but also for the sequence in which women and men take up the various emotional and developmental "tasks" of adulthood. For men, for example, nurturance and emotional expressiveness appear to flower in middle age, while for women they are expressed strongly in the 20s and 30s.
- Men and women have different patterns of relationships with friends. Compared to men's, women's friendships are more intimate, with more personal disclosure, more emotion expressed. Men's friendships are more based on shared activities or interests (Ginsberg & Gottman, 1986). Women also typically have more friends than do men and are more likely to have a close confidant (Perlman & Fehr, 1987). These differences have an impact throughout life but perhaps most strongly when an individual adult is facing high levels of stress or personal crisis. Many men, lacking a close personal confidant, find dealing with such crises as the death of a spouse, or unexpected unemployment, far more traumatic than do women.
- In developed countries today, women live longer than men do. At the moment in the United States, the sex difference in life expectancy at birth is about 7 years, although the gap seems now to be narrowing. The existing difference not only means that most women will be widowed and living alone in old age. Combined with the U.S. pension system, it also means that women are much more likely to be poor in old age (e.g. Verbrugge, 1984).

If we look at the lives of the five young people I described at the beginning of the chapter, we can make some educated guesses about their life paths, knowing only their gender. To be sure, there is a great deal of variation in life patterns within each gender. There are many women (of whom I have been one) who follow a more typical "male" occupational and family pathway, working continuously throughout adulthood, sharing family duties, or having no children. There are certainly many man with deep and intimate friendships, and many who share fully in the rearing of children. But it is no accident that the first thing we ask about any newborn baby is "is it a boy or a girl?" We expect boys and girls to be different and to lead different lives. Those expectations are grounded in the facts of gender roles in our culture.

Racial and Ethnic Differences in Adult Life

Like gender, race is an unchangeable characteristic of the individual, and like gender, a person's race has a profound effect on the patterns of adulthood.

Most of what I can say about racial differences in the experiences of adults in the United States relates to black/white comparisons. There has been relatively little research on Spanish-surname adults, still less on Asians, and least of all on Native Americans. So if, in the following summary statements, I seem to be saying mostly "blacks" and "whites," take that as a reflection of the state of our knowledge, rather than a statement about the importance of other racial groups.

Here is a sampling of the findings:

Life expectancy in the United States is five to six years longer among whites than among nonwhites for both men and women (U.S. Bureau of the Census, 1989a). A white girl born in the United States in 1987 could expect to live to be 78.8 years old; a black girl could expect to live until age 73.8. (The equivalent figures for males are 72.1 and 65.4 years respectively). What is more, this life expectancy gap has been increasing in the United States in the past few years, from an average difference of 5.6 years in 1984 to 6.2 years in 1987 (the last year for which national figures are available). Life expectancies are still shorter for Mexican Americans, and shortest of all for Native Americans. The racial difference is very clear in Figure 2–3, which shows the number of black and white adults, out of each 1,000 born, who could expect to live to various ages. As you can see, the largest difference is in the likelihood that a black male will reach the age of 65. Interestingly, however, this racial difference in life expectancy is much smaller for those adults who actually reach the age of 65. For example, a white woman who had reached the age of 65 in 1986 could expect to live an additional 18.7 years, while a black woman of the same age could expect to live an additional 17 years (U.S. Bureau of the Census, 1989a). Among the very old the pattern actually reverses, with nonwhite 85-year-olds having longer life expectancies than whites—a crossover usually explained in terms of the unusual hardiness required of any minority adult who has reached such an advanced age.

Blacks have lower social status, less well paying jobs, and lower incomes than do whites. In 1986, for example, the average household income of blacks was $18,100 whereas that of whites was $32,270. For Spanish-surname households, the average was $20,310 (U.S. Bureau of the Census, 1989b). In 1987 (the most recent year for which we have complete information), one-third of all black households were below the poverty line, compared to 10.5 percent of white households and 28 percent of Hispanics (U.S. Bureau of the Census, 1989b). These differences exist at all ages (Palmore, Burchett, Fillenbaum,

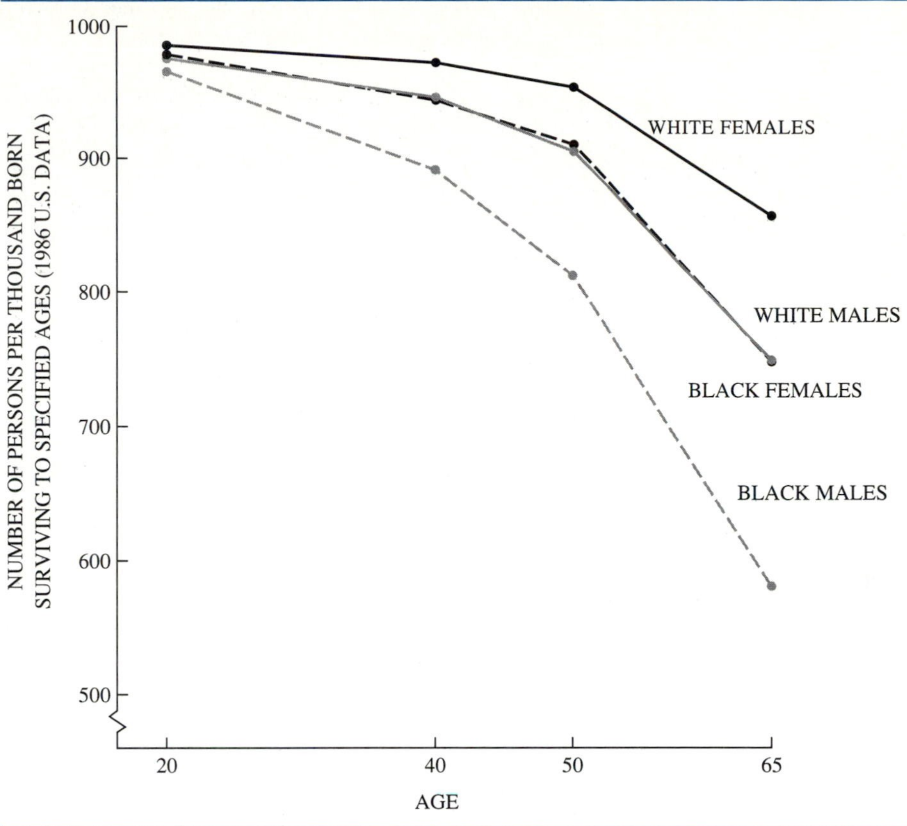

Figure 2–3 The difference in life expectancy between blacks and whites is really striking in these numbers, which show the number of adults out of each 1,000 born who will live to be each of several ages. As you can see, women have higher survival rates than do men, but blacks are consistently lower than whites of the same gender. In particular, black males show a marked drop in survival between age 50 and age 65. (Source: U.S. Bureau of the Census, 1989a, Table 107, p. 72.)

George, & Wallman, 1985). Among the elderly, over half of the blacks are living below the poverty line, compared to approximately 15 to 20 percent for whites (Dressel, 1988).

- Family experiences are, on average, quite different in black than in white families. Henry Walker, in his review of this set of information puts it this way:

> Compared to whites, blacks are less likely to marry, less likely to remain married, more likely to bear children while unmarried, and more likely to reside in households headed by women. (Walker, 1988, p. 87)

All these differences are plain in the data in Table 2.1, which also shows that Hispanic adults, on these indices at least, are much more like white than like

TABLE 2.1. Differences between Blacks, Whites, and Hispanics in Marriage, Divorce, and Family Composition, Based on 1988 National Data.

		Blacks		Whites		Hispanics	
		Men	*Women*	*Men*	*Women*	*Men*	*Women*
Percent	age 25–29	55.0	49.6	41.3	26.3	39.3	26.9
Never	age 30–34	42.0	36.9	22.6	13.0	27.9	16.7
Married	age 35–39	24.5	19.8	12.8	7.5	12.1	9.9
Percent of families with children headed by women		55.6		18.1		29.4	
Percent of children born to never-married mothers		54.2		18.0		32.8	

SOURCE: Rawlings, 1989.

black adults. Collectively, these differences mean not only that (in the United States) at least three quarters of black children—like Walter Washington—spend at least a part of their childhood in a single parent household (compared to somewhat less than half of white children in current cohorts), but that the sequence of roles assumed by black and white adults over their lifetimes may be somewhat different. Thus, black youth arrive at the start of adulthood with different family histories and follow different family pathways in adulthood.

- Blacks have traditionally received fewer years of education than have whites. In 1960, for example, the median years of school completed was 10.9 for whites and 8.0 for blacks. By 1987 this difference had shrunk to almost nothing (12.7 vs. 12.4 years), with Hispanic Americans lagging slightly further at a median of 12.0 years (U.S. Bureau of the Census, 1989a). However, we should not let this narrowing of the difference in median years of education mask the real difference that still exists. If one compares the percentage from different races who have completed at least 4 years of high school (77.7 for whites vs. 63.3 for blacks), or the percentage who have completed four years of college (20.9 for whites vs. 11.3 for blacks) there are still sharp discrepancies. The gap is getting smaller, but it has not been eliminated (U.S. Bureau of the Census, 1989b).
- On average, blacks report lower overall life satisfaction than do whites (Harris, 1981; Schaie, Orchowsky, & Parham, 1982), no doubt in part because of lower income, fewer job opportunities, and outright prejudice encountered throughout life. Interestingly, however, suicide rates are higher for whites than for blacks (McIntosh, 1985), particularly among those 30 and older, and particularly for men.

The overall picture is one of an extra set of hurdles for blacks and for those of other minority races. Since all the summary statements represent averages, not individuals, we can be quite sure that a great many minority race adults surmount those extra hurdles and achieve not only satisfaction in their lives, but genuine development or growth. Still, in this culture, at this moment, the pathways of adulthood are strewn with more obstacles for blacks and other minority group adults than they are for the average white. Given his determination and the good fortune of having had encouragement from teachers, Walter Washington may well pull himself up by his economic bootstraps and achieve considerable occupational and financial success. But because of persisting prejudice in the workplace (and elsewhere), that task will be harder for him than it would be for a white young man with similar education, skills, and family background.

Social Class and Family Background Differences in Adult Life

Both gender and race are built-in at birth. Important as they are, they are at least equaled by the importance of the specific family and cultural circumstances in which a young person grows up. Both the general economic or social conditions in a family and the attitudes, aspirations, and personal skills acquired in a family can have a powerful influence on the course any given adult will follow through adulthood.

Social Class Variations

Every society is divided into strata of some kind. I talked about age strata in Chapter 1, but perhaps the more familiar division is in terms of **social status.** There are bosses and workers, rich and poor, or even explicit castes. In western societies, an individual's social status (often called **social class**) is typically defined or measured in terms of three dimensions: education, income, and occupation. Thus, a person with higher status is one with more education, higher income, and a more prestigious occupation. In other societies, the dimensions of status might be different, but some status differences exist in every society. Distinctions between "blue-collar" and "white-collar" or "middle class" and "working class" are fundamentally status distinctions.

Each of us was reared to young adulthood in a family occupying some position in such a status hierarchy. Walter Washington grew up in a poverty level or lower class family. Both Tom Kleck and Laura Rogers grew up in working class families. Cathy Stevens and Chris Linton grew up in middle class families. If we look at a group of young adults, we can see the effects of these differences in family background in a host of ways—in varying education levels, in differing life expectations, in attitudes. If we then follow those young adults through the next decades, we would see that—like gender and race—the social class of the family you grow up in influences the pathway you are likely to follow through adult life.

- In the United States, over the past several generations at least, the majority of both men and women end up in occupations at the same broad level of social status as their parents'. A young man's occupational level seems to be more strongly affected by his father's occupation, and a young woman's by her mother's (particularly if her mother is in a professional-level job), but both parents' occupations have some effect (Stevens, 1986). You can see the male half of this effect in Figure 2–4, from nationally representative samples studied in 1972 (Featherman & Hauser, 1975; Featherman, 1980). About 60 percent of the men from blue-collar families were themselves in blue-collar jobs, whereas two thirds of those from white-collar families had similar jobs themselves. There is a good deal more movement within levels than Figure 2–4 suggests; many individuals shift between higher- and lower-status white collar jobs, or higher- and lower-status blue-collar jobs. But if we look just

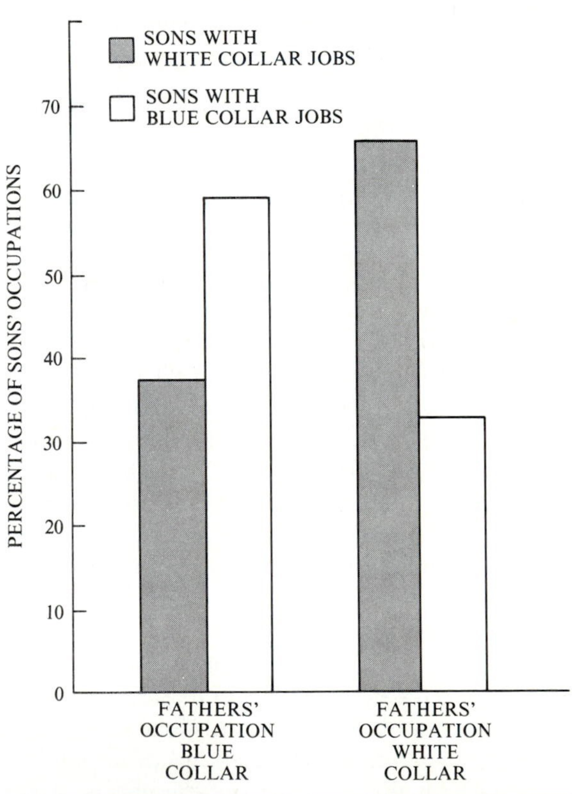

Figure 2–4 The majority of young men from both blue-collar and white-collar families will end up spending their adult lives in the same broad social class as their fathers. But significant minorities will show shifts, either upward or downward in social class. (Source: Featherman, 1980, p. 704, and Featherman and Hauser, 1975.)

at the two broad social strata in our culture, there is quite a strong degree of persistence from one generation to the next.

- For women, a related social process increases the likelihood that a woman will remain in the same social class as her family of origin: The principle of **marital homogamy** says that people tend to marry those like themselves—in religious background, in race, in social status. So women from working class backgrounds tend to marry men from the same background, and the couple is then likely to remain in that broad social status group throughout adulthood.
- Middle class adults as a group marry later and have fewer children than do working class adults. Both of these differences affect the timing of various subsequent life experiences, such as the departure of the last child.
- The life course of middle class adults is more likely to be advantaged in a variety of ways: They are less likely to experience periods of unemployment (Pearlin & Lieberman, 1979); they are healthier and live longer (Longino, Warheit, & Green, 1989); they are more likely to be sexually active in late adulthood (especially true for women) (Palmore & Stone, 1973); they have more stable and satisfying marriages (Locksley, 1982), retain a higher level of intellectual functioning longer into old age (Palmore, 1981), and are, in general, more satisfied with their lives (Campbell, 1981) and more likely to show "development" over adulthood in the sense in which I am using that word. For example, Farrell and Rosenberg (1981), in a study of young and middle-aged working class and middle class men, found that the working class men showed not growth but a kind of alienation and disintegration of personality at midlife.

Some of these effects are more or less direct effects of a person's occupational status. Working class jobs are more likely to be physically strenuous or dangerous, so it is not surprising that working class adults have shorter life expectancies. Differences in income can also have a fairly direct impact on life satisfaction if the culturally defined ingredients of satisfaction are dependent on money.

But some of the effects of social class on adult life patterns are indirect, operating through differences in aspirations, expectations, attitudes. There is some research evidence, for example, that suggests that young people who grew up in middle class families are more likely to have learned basic social skills: they know better how to get along with bosses, how to solve personal problems. Furthermore, such young people are likely to have been encouraged to think of themselves as capable of succeeding at a difficult career. And such belief in yourself, the conviction that you *can* do something, which Albert Bandura (1989) calls **self efficacy**, has been shown repeatedly to be strongly related to later success.

On average, middle class families are more likely to instill such confidence and high expectations in their children than are working class families. But *within* each strata there are wide variations. What the research shows is that any young adult whose family fostered such qualities, regardless of the social class of the family, is more likely to follow a middle class pathway through adult life.

As one example, Lawrence Schiamberg and Chong-Hee Chin (1987), in a 14-year longitudinal study of a group of teenagers from low income rural areas, found that *regardless of the specific economic circumstances of a teenager's family,* those teenagers with the greatest confidence and the highest career aspirations had achieved the highest level jobs in their early 20s.

Findings from two of the longitudinal studies I listed in the last chapter in Table 1.1 show much the same thing. Upwardly mobile men in the Berkeley Longitudinal Studies had, as teenagers, placed a stronger value on intellectual matters and appeared brighter to the adults who interviewed them than did those who turned out to be less mobile. They were also rated as more socially perceptive, more dependable, and more highly motivated to achieve (Clausen, 1981). Similarly, men from working class backgrounds in the AT&T Study of Managers who had moved up to and been successful at management level jobs, had had somewhat higher IQ scores, a wide range of interests, and strong internal motivations to achieve at the beginning of their careers (Bray & Howard, 1983). Both Tom Kleck and Walter Washington, whom you met at the beginning of this chapter, have a number of these qualities, and both are already at higher occupational levels than their parents. We might predict from these studies that Tom and Walter will continue to move upward in the occupational and social ladder.

On the whole, then, although there is a strong tendency for young people to spend their adult lives in the same broad social status group as their parents, **social mobility** (upward or downward) is common. Particularly in recent decades, as the number of blue collar jobs has declined and the number of white collar jobs has increased, there has been an overall increase in status throughout our society. At the same time, mobility is not (primarily) a matter of luck. The family in which one grows up not only creates an economic and social class climate, it also teaches attitudes toward work and toward the self, fosters or inhibits confidence, encourages or discourages achievement. These attitudes, in turn, can have profound effects on the pathway the young adult may follow in the decades that follow.

More Specific Family Characteristics

I do not want to leave you with the impression that the only thing that is significant about the family you grow up in is how much money your father makes, or whether your family fosters confidence and high achievement aspirations. There are obviously uncountable other aspects of family life in a person's first 20 years that help to form us into the people we are at that age. I'll be talking a bit more about some of those factors later in this chapter when I talk about the impact of personality differences on adult trajectories. But let me say at least a word about one more *structural* property of families—other than social class—that seems to have a potent impact on the adult lives of offspring, namely whether the family is intact or not.

The research findings are not unanimous, but the current evidence points to some long-term effects of having grown up in a divorced or single parent family. Adults with such backgrounds are more likely to go through a divorce themselves and are likely to have lower levels of education and lower level jobs, possibly because there was less financial support available to assist in educational costs when they reached young adulthood (McLanahan & Booth, 1989; Mueller & Cooper, 1986). These differences are greatest for those raised primarily in single parent families (as opposed to those raised with a natural parent and a step-parent), and for those whose families are *also* working class or poor. Parental divorce has less impact on the adult lives among those whose mothers are well educated (Keith & Finlay, 1988).

Education Differences and Adult Lives

You may have noticed in what I have already said, that one of the ingredients that pops up often in the various predictive statements is the amount of education a young person has had. Years of education are the *result,* in part, of family social class, attitudes, and confidence engendered by the family, available finances, role models, and the like. But in our society the number of years of education itself has a major independent effect on adult life trajectories (Farmer, Reis, Nickinovich, Kamo, & Borgatta, 1990; Featherman, 1980).

The effects can be striking. Laura Rogers' life course is likely to be strongly shaped by the fact that she dropped out of high school when she got pregnant. Given her lack of education, she is not eligible for any but the lowest levels of jobs. In general, education influences a person's *first job,* and that first job in turn affects later jobs as well (a pattern I will describe in detail in Chapter 9). Put another way, how far you can travel on the "job ladder" over your lifetime is strongly influenced by the rung at which you enter it. And the rung-of-entry is itself strongly influenced by the years of education you have completed (Featherman, 1980).

For example, in an extremely complete study of workers for a large corporation over a 13-year period, James Rosenbaum (1984) found that the level of entry was one of the biggest factors in determining a worker's job level or income 13 years later. Level of entry, in turn, was strongly influenced by whether the worker had a BA degree or not (which is one more reason why the persisting difference between whites and blacks—and other racial groups—in the percentage receiving BA degrees is so significant). This finding is echoed in Bray and Howard's longitudinal studies of AT&T workers (Bray and Howard, 1983). They found that even when basic ability (IQ or acquired job skill) was roughly equated, promotions more often went to workers with college degrees.

For women, education is also strongly related to work success. Featherman (1980) points out that because many women move in and out of the work force rather than having continuous job patterns, their level of education continues to influence the sorts of jobs they are able to get well past the point of first job entry. For someone who has been continuously employed, a strong work history may override low education in a subsequent hiring or promotion decision. But in evaluating a job candidate who has been out of the job market for a time, an employer may place greater emphasis on the credential of a BA degree or other educational achievement.

Of course, it is also true that more intellectually able young people are more likely to go to school longer. So perhaps these correlational findings simply tell us that capable people both go to school longer and have more successful work histories. To some extent, that is true. But the amount of education a young person receives is only partially predicted by school grades or achievement test scores. At the level of job entry, it appears to be the credential (or lack of it) conferred by a BA degree or some other educational achievement that has the major effect. And when ability is held constant, as in the AT&T studies, number of years of education is still a strong predictor of later job success.

The best current guess is that the causal chain runs roughly this way: Young people from middle class homes are more likely to acquire a sense of self confidence or self efficacy as well as high achievement aspirations. Their families also value education highly and can afford to provide it. As a result of all these things, middle class young adults go to school longer. But it is the *schooling* and not the middle-classness itself that seems to be the crucial variable in promoting greater

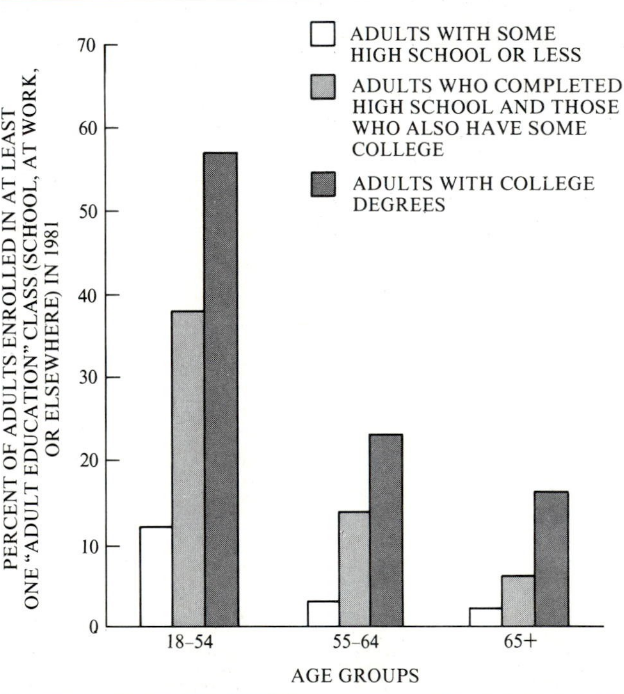

Figure 2–5 We have become a nation of class takers. Based on a national survey taken in 1981, Harris estimates that 20 percent of all adults over 18 are taking at least one "adult education" class at any one time. As you can see in the figure, though, better educated adults are more likely to continue their education in this way, thus increasing the differences in education over the years of adulthood. (Source: Harris, 1981, data from Table 1–16, p. 34.)

work success later on, since we know that middle class adults with less schooling do not follow the same path.

On the other end of the continuum, young people growing up in working class or poverty level homes are far less likely to have extended education, and that lack shapes their options for decades to come.

In our culture, then, variation in the years of education is the mechanism that tends to perpetuate existing class differences. But education is also the vehicle for change in status: As a general rule, more education leads you up the status ladder; less education leads you down, regardless of the social class level of the family in which you grew up.

In talking here about the impact of education on work lives, I do not want to imply that education has no effect on other aspects of adult life. Better educated adults also share the other advantages of higher status adults that I listed earlier: They have better health, remain mentally alert longer into old age, are more satisfied with their marriages and with their lives. Doubtless the financial security that typically accompanies higher education is part of the reason for those differences. But education may also create, or reinforce, habits that will affect later life experiences as well: A habit of reading and discussing ideas; a tendency to be active socially and politically; analytic skills that assist in real-life problem solving. Among other things, those adults who had more education at the beginning of their adult years are much more likely to continue to educate themselves over succeeding decades (Harris, 1981), as you can see in Figure 2–5. Thus, the effect of early education tends to be cumulative as the educationally rich become richer still in later years.

Intelligence and Personality Differences in Adult Life

So far I have talked about four important qualities or characteristics young people bring with them to the adult journey: gender, race, social class, and education. The first two are built-in genetically and are not altered by experience; the second two are largely environmental (although one can certainly make a good argument for some genetic influence on both social class and education). The final two qualities I want to talk about, intelligence and personality differences, are clearly a product of both heredity and environment.

Intelligence Differences

I am not going to delve into the literature that demonstrates that intelligence, as measured by an IQ test, is a product of both environment and heredity (Scarr, 1981). What I want to emphasize is that differences in intellectual "power," in ability to remember things, to analyze ideas, or to recognize relationships, are well established and quite stable from about age five or six (Bloom, 1964) and remain highly stable through adulthood—findings I'll talk more about in Chapter 6. In children, IQ differences are correlated not only with school performance but also with popularity and ability to deal with such inevitable crises as adolescence (Sattler, 1974; Asher, Renshaw, & Hymel, 1982; Rowe & Marcia, 1980). It seems reasonable to assume that differences in intelligence would have equal impact on adults. The evidence is not hard to find.

- Teenagers with higher IQ complete more years of school than do those with lower IQ (Brody & Brody, 1976), and the number of years of education, as I have just pointed out, is a key to many later differences in adult lives.
- Higher IQ young adults are more likely to end up in higher-prestige occupations (Brody & Brody, 1976), and earn higher incomes (Hauser & Dickinson, 1974).
- Higher IQ adults show less decline in intellectual ability in old age than do lower IQ adults (e.g. Jarvik & Bank, 1983).

The relationship between IQ and occupational success, however, is more complex than this list may imply. Many occupations have "entrance requirements," including IQ-like measures. To get into law school or medical school, for example, a student must do well on special examinations, which means that those in such occupations all have relatively high IQs. In these occupations, among those who pass the entrance requirement, IQ does *not* predict ultimate job success well. (See Brody & Brody, 1976, for a review of this research.) Lawyers with IQs of 150 do not earn more money or make better advocates than those with IQs of 120.

However, among jobs that have fewer intellectual entrance requirements but that nonetheless demand skill—jobs like secretary or bookkeeper or even mid-level managers in businesses—IQ scores are positively correlated with adequacy of job performance and with both income and promotions (Brody & Brody, 1976; Hunter, 1986). In reviewing hundreds of studies performed by the military services, John Hunter finds that the more complex the job, the stronger the correlation between measures of general cognitive ability and job performance, but even in very undemanding jobs, those with better intellectual skills perform somewhat better. So IQ serves as a credential for higher status jobs and as a predictor of significant job-related skills in most other jobs, particularly those with some complexity.

If you look at the list I have just given, you may well suspect that in many instances the impact of IQ is indirect rather than direct. It is not that high IQ *causes* higher income or retention of greater intellectual skill in old age. Instead, IQ influences such things as the years of education or interest in intellectual pursuits (reading, doing crossword puzzles, playing intellectual games), and these in turn affect the life patterns. Still, differences in intelligence among young adults may suggest a good deal about the direction of their future lives.

Temperament and Personality Differences

Far more intriguing is the rapidly accumulating evidence telling us that the temperament and personality a young person brings to adult life can profoundly influence not only the specific experiences he or she may have as an adult but the happiness or unhappiness he or she may feel.

Let me pause for a few definitions of what psychologists mean by **personality** or **temperament.** Personality is the broader term referring to "the individual's distinctive, consistent, patterned methods of relating to the environment" (Houston, Bee & Rimm, 1983). The term *temperament* is normally used more narrowly to describe individual variation on a small number of constitutionally-based, relatively stable aspects of personal style or emotional response to stimulation (Buss & Plomin, 1986; Rothbart & Derryberry, 1981; Thomas & Chess, 1977, 1986). Such aspects as basic sociability or emotionality are now typically described as temperament, whereas such characteristics as levels of aggressiveness or dependency or altruism would be described as personality. Personality differences appear to be the result of an interaction between in-born temperamental qualities and environmental influences such as the family's response to the child's temperament.

We now have two fascinating bodies of research that seem to be telling us that at least some personality differences are potent forces in shaping adult experience.

The first approach, typified by the research of Paul Costa and Robert McCrae (1980a, 1984, 1986), begins by trying to identify stable personality traits in adults, and then asks whether adults whose personalities differ on those traits have different life experiences. Costa and McCrae propose three such personality dimensions, which I've summarized in Table 2.2.

To get some sense of what differences in these dimensions might look like in an actual person, think back to the descriptions of the five young people with which I began this chapter. Both Tom Kleck and Cathy Stevens are high in extraversion; Walter Washington and Chris Linton are both much more introverted. Of the five, the two highest on neuroticism are probably Chris and Laura Rogers; the most open to experience would seem to be Tom, whereas the least open is probably Chris Linton.

Costa and McCrae's own work, as well as the work of others, points to a number of implications of such variations for adult lives. Let me give you a few examples.

- Job choice is related to personality, particularly to the dimension of extraversion vs. introversion. Extraverts are more likely to prefer occupations like social

TABLE 2.2. Three Stable Aspects of Personality.

Neuroticism	Included in this dimension of personality are such tendencies as: hostility, impulsiveness, vulnerability, self-consciousness, a tendency toward depression, and high levels of anxiety. A person low on this dimension would be low on all of these qualities.
Extraversion	An individual high in extraversion (vs. introversion) shows high levels of activity, positive emotions, excitement seeking, gregariousness, assertiveness, and attachment to others.
Openness	An individual high in openness shows willingness to explore new values, new actions, new aesthetics or fantasy, new feelings and ideas.

SOURCE: from Costa & McCrae, 1980a.

work or business administration, advertising, or law. Introverts prefer such occupations as architecture, physics, or carpentry (Costa, Fozard, & McCrae, 1977).

- Once in a job, personality may have some effect on success. Within the business world, at least in the United States, certain aspects of openness, lack of rigidity, or lack of authoritarianism seem to be related to success, as are high levels of achievement motivation. In the AT&T studies of success in management over a twenty-year period (Bray & Howard, 1983; Rychlak, 1982), men who advanced further in the corporate hierarchy started out not only brighter (higher IQ), but also with wider interests, greater dominance, and greater achievement motivation. Rychlak describes these men as "enlargers." Their goals included change, innovation, and growth, much of which sounds a great deal like the dimension of openness listed by Costa & McCrae. This is not to say that success in all jobs requires these same qualities. There are doubtless many jobs that require stability, thoroughness, even repetition (bookkeeping or accountancy comes to mind.) For an adult life course, what may be particularly significant is whether a given adult finds herself in a job with demands and payoffs that *match* her own temperament or style. When this occurs, the individual is likely to be more successful at that job.
- The most general impact of personality on adult life is on overall life satisfaction. Costa and McCrae have found, for example, that adults high on aspects of neuroticism are consistently less satisfied with their lives, while those high in extraversion are consistently more satisfied. Openness appears to have little link to satisfaction. (Costa & McCrae, 1984.) The correlations are only of moderate magnitude (on the order of .35 to .50), but they have been found repeatedly. More impressive is the fact that Costa and McCrae can demonstrate longitudinal effects: Measures of neuroticism or extraversion at one point in adult life can predict happiness or satisfaction 10 or even 20 years later.

> To the extent that wellbeing depends on personality, it follows that an individual's wellbeing can be predicted years in advance by assessment of personality. Psychologists are not prophets, and we cannot predict whether life will hold wealth or poverty, health or illness, love or loss. But if our model is correct, we can predict how individuals will evaluate whatever life circumstances they encounter, whether they will be happy or unhappy with their lot. (Costa & McCrae, 1984, p. 150–151)

Thus, it appears not to be maturity, or wisdom, or even wealth or success that are the primary determinants of happiness or life satisfaction. Rather, it is the adult's tendency to respond to life with optimism and cheerfulness, or with depression and complaint, that is the most significant factor. Personality thus affects not only specific occupations, or life success; it helps to shape the emotional fabric of adult life.

A similar conclusion emerges from the work of Avashalom Caspi and Glen Elder, Jr. (Caspi, Elder, & Bem, 1987, 1988; Caspi & Elder, 1988; Elder, Caspi, & Downey, 1986). They begin by identifying children with patterns of maladaptive behavior—such as extreme shyness, or aggressive, or ill-tempered behavior—and then ask what kind of adult lives such children are likely to have compared to the adult lives of less deviant children.

Obviously, this type of approach requires a very special kind of longitudinal data. We have to have information on the same individuals over a very broad range of time, from at least middle childhood through adulthood. And we have to know a lot about those individuals' behavior and personality at each age. There are not many sets of data that meet those criteria, but Caspi and Elder have been able to use the results of the Berkeley Intergenerational Studies to very good effect. Recall from Table 1.1 that these studies involve two adjacent cohorts, one born in 1920 and the other in 1928. Each group has since been studied for 40 to 50 years.

Caspi and Elder have focused their attention particularly on two subgroups: those who were unusually shy as children and those who were unusually ill-tempered as children, with many temper tantrums and high irritability. What they have found is that children in each of these groups went on to have distinctly different adult life patterns than did children with less extreme temperament or behavior.

Shy boys, as adults, married later and had their families later, as you can see in Figure 2–6. They also established stable careers later and had not achieved the same level of occupational success by age 40 as had less shy men. Many of these men were quite consistently "off time" in their life course, a pattern that seems generally to have high personal and emotional costs. For example, while shy boys as a group did not have less stable marriages in adulthood, those shy men who were particularly late in establishing a stable career *were* more likely to divorce.

Shy girls, in contrast, did not marry later (presumably since, for these cohorts certainly, the cultural pattern required the male to do the asking, not the woman), but the shy girls had very different work histories in adulthood than did nonshy girls. They were far more likely to have had no job at all; if they worked at all it was likely to be before marriage, after which they withdrew from the labor force. Interestingly, shy girls were also more likely to marry men *higher* in occupational status than were nonshy girls. So shyness had quite different effects on social mobility for women than for men.

Ill-tempered children from this same sample have had equally distinct pathways in adulthood. Men who had shown high levels of tantrums and other ill-tempered behavior as children, compared to more even-tempered individuals, completed fewer years of education, had more erratic work lives with more job changes and more periods of unemployment, lower status jobs both at the start of their adult lives and at age 40, and were more likely to divorce. Table 2.3 shows the differences in the status of the first jobs the men obtained in early adulthood. The negative impact of ill temper is stronger among young men from middle class backgrounds than for those from working class backgrounds, but the effect is notable in both groups.

Among women, those who had a childhood history of ill temper tended to marry lower-status men, were more likely to divorce, and more likely to become ill-tempered mothers. Indeed Caspi and Elder have been able to show transmis-

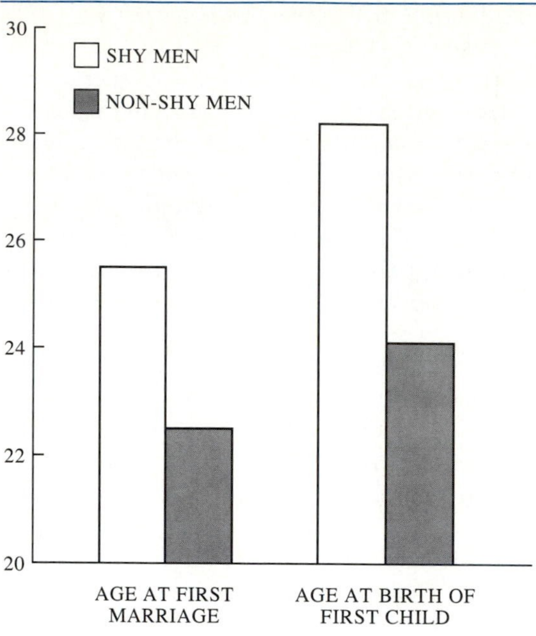

Figure 2–6 Caspi and Elder have found that among men in the Berkeley longitudinal sample, those who were unusually shy as children married later and had their first child later than men who were less shy. Being "off-time" in such major life events typically carries an emotional price. At the very least, we know that it alters a man's life pattern not only in his 20s, but also in later decades, since his children are still at home still needing support when he is in his 50s. (Source: Caspi, Elder, & Bem, 1988, from Figure 1, page 827.)

sion of this pattern across several generations, since the Berkeley archives contain information not only on the parents of the subjects but on their own children as well. Children reared by these ill-tempered women not only describe their mothers as irritable and erratic, they are also more likely to display problem behavior themselves. So the pattern is passed on (Elder, Caspi, & Downey, 1986).

My confidence that results like these are not restricted to this specific study or these specific cohorts is bolstered by the results of a similarly designed study by Leonard Eron and his colleagues (Eron, 1987; Eron, Huesmann, Dubow, Romanoff, & Yarmel, 1987). Eron began in 1960 with a group of 600 eight-year-olds, 400 of whom he has now followed up to age 30. He did not measure tantrums or ill temper, but he did measure aggressiveness in the eight-year-olds, particularly aggressiveness with peers. He found that those adults who had been high in aggressiveness as children are more likely to have a criminal record, to have more moving traffic violations, more convictions for driving while intoxicated, and show more aggressive behavior toward both their spouses and their children. You can see one of these results in Figure 2–7.

TABLE 2.3. Status of Men's First Jobs After Completing Schooling as a Function of their Parents' Social Class and the Men's Temper Tantrum Pattern in Childhood.

		Family Social Class	
		Middle Class	*Working Class*
Temper Tantrum Rating	Low	5.48	3.95
	High	3.95	3.00

Note: The numbers entered in this table are the mean scores on an occupational status scale that runs from 1 (= unskilled employee) to 7 (= higher executive).

SOURCE: Caspi, Elder, & Bem, 1987, Table 2, p. 310.

Even with this general corroboration from Eron's study, we need to be careful about generalizing the *specific* findings of these two pieces of research too broadly. Only a few hundred adults are included, and although both samples contained working class and middle class families, neither sample was designed to be representative of the whole population. There may also be significant cohort effects

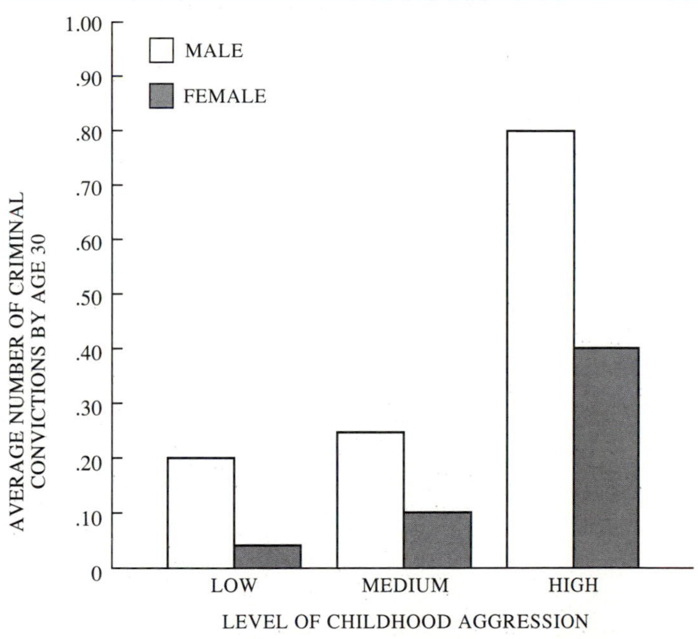

Figure 2–7 Leonard Eron's study of young adults whose childhood pattern of aggression had been observed 20 years earlier shows long-term links between childhood behaviors and adult life experiences. Both men and women who had been more aggressive as children were more likely to be convicted of crimes in adulthood than were men and women who had been less aggressive as children. (Source: Eron, 1987, Figure 2, p. 440.)

at work. We cannot be sure, for example, that shy girls growing up today, in cultural circumstances that may make more demand for assertiveness from women than was true in the 1930s and 1940s, would have the same apparent advantages that shy girls seemed to have had in the Berkeley sample.

Still, I think the central point from these studies is extremely important: The specific temperament or behavioral patterns we bring with us to adult life, particularly if those patterns are extreme, interact with the demands of adult life—in whatever era—to produce distinctive trajectories. Caspi and Elder, in summarizing the effects, quote a much earlier observation by Smith (1968) that makes the point especially clearly—not only about differences in temperament or personality but also for differences in education or even social class:

> Launched on the right trajectory, the person is likely to accumulate successes that strengthen the effectiveness of his orientation toward the world while at the same time he acquires the knowledge and skills to make his further success more probable. His environmental involvements generally lead to gratification and to increased competence and favorable development. Off to a bad start, on the other hand, he soon encounters failures that make him hesitant to try. What to others are challenges appear to him as threats; he becomes preoccupied with defense of his small claims on life at the expense of energies to invest in constructive coping. And he falls increasingly behind his fellows in acquiring the knowledge and skill that are needed for success on those occasions when he does try. (p. 277)

In a psychological sense as well as in an economic one, the rich tend to get richer and the poor tend to get poorer.

The six elements I have talked about—gender, race, intelligence, personality, social class, and education—do not exhaust the list of characteristics of young people that will affect their later life courses. We could make a much longer list, including such physical qualities as stature, body type, physical attractiveness, coordination, or athletic skill. (Michael Jordan's most significant quality at age 22 was not the family he came from, how bright he was, or what his personality was, but the fact that he was a phenomenally good basketball player.) We could also include many other qualities of family life, such as whether a young adult grew up with brothers or sisters, or whether she is first born or later born in the family. Each of these elements, too, has an impact on adult lives. But the six I have mentioned help to set the agenda for adulthood for each of us. We do not begin the adult years with equal characteristics, equal choices, or equal opportunities. And to the extent that the initial qualities and choices remain stable or consistent over the adult years, adults will tend to remain on the same trajectory on which they first began the journey.

In the rest of the book, I will be searching for ways in which adult lives move in the *same* ways, for developmental shifts, for shared changes. But let us not forget these powerful forces creating differences in developmental patterns. If we are to understand adulthood, we have to understand the ways in which these two sets of forces interact.

Summary

1. Adults do not begin the journey of adulthood with clean slates. They already differ in ways that will have a major impact on the pathways they will follow. Particularly significant are differences in gender, race, social class, level of education, intelligence, and personality.
2. Gender differences are pervasive, affecting family roles, work patterns, and the sequencing of the tasks of adult life.
3. Race differences, too, are predictive of different family patterns, work opportunities, health and longevity, and life satisfaction.
4. The majority of adults spend their adult life in the same broad social class strata as did their parents. However, 40 percent or more show shifts in social class. Upward mobility is predicted by higher levels of education, and by higher IQ, as well as by some personal qualities.
5. The social class in which an adult spends his or her adult years has a major effect on a wide range of adult experiences, including job security, marital satisfaction, life satisfaction, and health.
6. Families also affect the young person's expectations of success and desire to achieve, both of which influence later education and occupational success.
7. Whether a young person grew up in an intact family or in a family that divorced also appears to have a long-term effect, with children of divorced (or single parent) families having a higher likelihood of divorce in their own adult life, as well as lower levels of occupational achievement.
8. Differences in years of education achieved, at least in this culture, have a powerful impact on work history and thus on social class, tending to perpetuate social class differences. But education also offers the most significant route to upward occupational mobility; the number of years of education is a better predictor of eventual occupational success than is the social class level of one's parents.
9. Variations in intelligence are also significant. Adults with higher IQs achieve more occupational success and greater intellectual vigor in old age.
10. Studies of personality traits, such as extraversion, neuroticism, and openness to experience, show that such personality differences affect not only job choices but also overall emotional tone or life satisfaction.
11. Studies of adults who as children had shown extreme forms of temperament or behavior show long-term consequences of such variations. For example, men who as boys had been ill-tempered or aggressive have lower occupational success and poorer marriages than do men who had less extreme temperament or behavior.
12. The consistences and shared developments of adult lives must be played out against the background of these individual variations.

Suggested Readings

Birren, J. E., & Schaie, K. W. (Eds.). (1990). *Handbook of the psychology of aging* (3rd ed.). San Diego: Academic Press. This very up-to-date series of reviews of the literature includes two papers that may be helpful for a next-step exploration of some of these issues: one by Jackson et al. on racial and ethnic differences in patterns of aging and one by Huyck on gender differences.

COSTA, P. T., Jr., & MCCRAE, R. R. (1984). Personality as a lifelong determinant of wellbeing. In C. Z. Malatesta & C. E. Izard (Eds.), *Emotion in adult development.* Beverly Hills, CA: Sage Publications. I find this collection of work extremely interesting. These authors describe complex findings with both clarity and verve.

ERON, L. D. (1987). The development of aggressive behavior from the perspective of a developing behaviorism. *American Psychologist, 42,* 435-442. Most of this paper talks about the theoretical underpinnings of Eron's work, but he also describes here the 22-year longitudinal study of aggressive boys and girls that I have talked about in this chapter.

FEATHERMAN, D. L. (1980). Schooling and occupational careers: constancy and change in worldly success. In O. G. Brim, Jr., & J. Kagan (Eds.), *Constancy and change in human development.* Cambridge, MA: Harvard University Press. This dense but excellent chapter will introduce you to some of the complexities of studying the effects of education, intelligence, and social class on adult lives.

CHAPTER 3

Theories of Adult Change or Development

Having just spent an entire chapter persuading you that adult life is powerfully shaped by persistent, durable characteristics of individuals, it may seem contradictory to turn now to an examination of the ways in which adult lives move in the same directions or share similar patterns. But the fact that both of these ways of looking at adulthood are simultaneously true is one of the basic points I want to make in this book. Each of us may enter and move through adulthood on a somewhat different trajectory, but all adult trajectories may still have important elements in common. We are both all alike and all different.

The empirical search for the common elements is the subject of the eight chapters in the next section. Before looking at the data, though, I want to lay the groundwork by talking about theories of adult continuity and change. I find these theories fascinating in themselves. But they also serve to point us at some of the critical questions that research might answer and to illustrate the variety of ways of thinking about adulthood.

Varieties of Theories

Twenty-five years ago, any discussion of theories of adult development would have been almost totally dominated by one theory: Erik Erikson's model of psychosocial development. Erikson's view is still highly influential, but today there has been a real flowering of ideas, some of them distinctly different from Erikson's views.

This wide variety of existing theories will form a better framework for later discussions if I organize the approaches along several dimensions, as I have done in Figure 3–1. Any categorization scheme, including this one, is inevitably an oversimplification. Each theory contains its own unique combination of ideas. But I can still use the two dimensions shown in Figure 3–1 as one helpful basis for organizing the options.

The first dimension on which theories may be organized is their relative emphasis on development versus change. The fundamental difference—as I am using the terms "development" and "change" in this book—is that a development theory assumes there is some goal or end point toward which the adult moves, and that this end point is potentially "better" or more mature than what is seen at earlier ages. A theory of adult change, in contrast, assumes no such end point or goal nor any "improvement" or growth. Among developmental theorists, for example, Erikson talks about "ego integrity" as being the final state, accompanied by wisdom. Vaillant describes a developmental continuum from immature to more mature forms of defense mechanisms. Other theorists, such as Levinson, or Pearlin, while agreeing that there are significant changes taking place over the adult years, do not see those changes as leading anywhere that is more mature, or more integrated, or more wise. Your great aunt Elsie is different from you in specific, predictable ways; but she is not necessarily better (or worse), wiser or more mature.

Note that among the theorists I have listed in Figure 3–1 are several who fall at in-between points on the development/change dimension. It is not necessary to

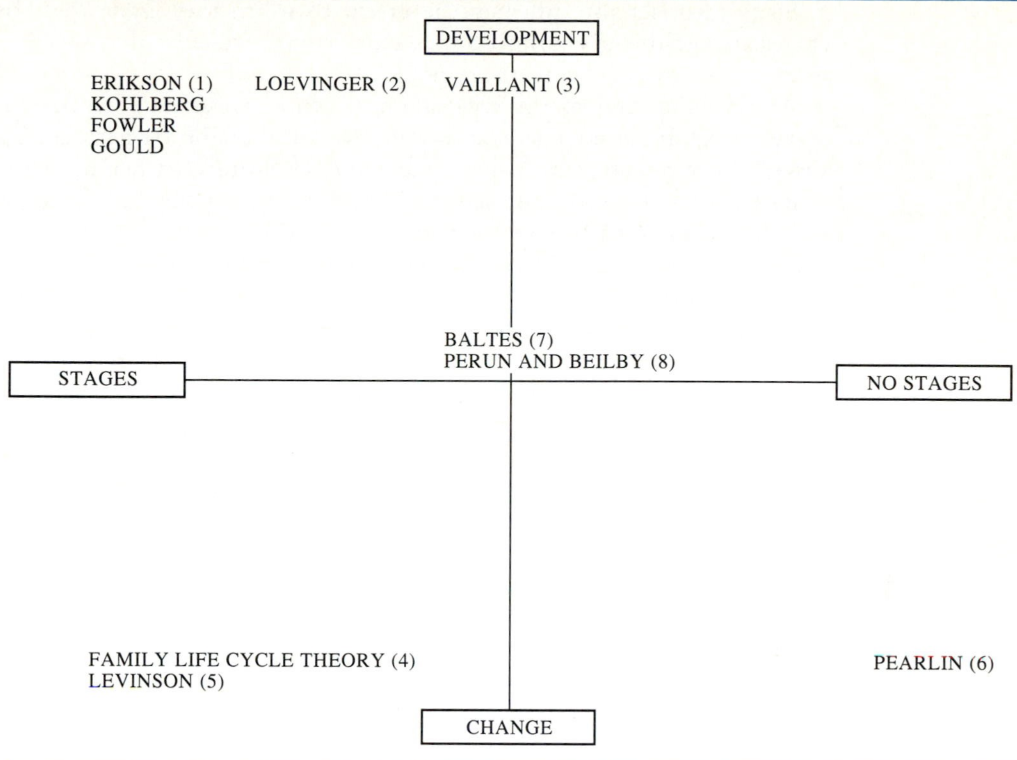

Figure 3–1 This two-dimensional grid, with development versus change as one dimension and stage versus nonstage theories as the other, allows us to contrast several of the major theories of development. (The numbers in parentheses indicate the sequence in which these theories are discussed in the chapter.)

assert one position or the other; one might argue, for example, that both occur under some conditions.

The second dimension I have used to categorize theories of adulthood is that of the presence or absence of stages in each theory. This is a somewhat risky organizational rubric, since the term "stage" is used to describe several different concepts. Most broadly, stages refer to fixed sequences of experiences or events over time, such as the family life-cycle stages I mentioned briefly in Chapter 1. More narrowly (and more commonly in psychological theories), stages imply systematic, sequential, *qualitative* changes in some skill or underlying psychological structure. When Jean Piaget talks about stages in children's cognitive development, for example, he does not mean merely that children learn to add and subtract before they learn to multiply and divide, but rather that the ability to multiply and divide requires fundamentally different understandings, logic, or mental structures. Each stage is thought of as being a structural whole, as having its own logic. Most (but not all) stage theories of adult development make similar assumptions about the nature of changes in adulthood.

Stage theorists also differ on the extent to which they argue that the various stages are age-linked. Levinson's stages are strongly connected to specific ages, for example, whereas Loevinger's are not.

At the other end of the continuum are those theorists who do not see any stages in adult development at all, in any sense of the term stage. Sociologist Orville Brim represents this anti-stage point of view nicely when he says that stage theories "are a little like horoscopes. They are vague enough so that everyone can see something of themselves in them. That's why they're so popular" (quoted in Rosenfeld & Stark, 1987, p. 68). The opposing view is that there are no stages at all—no shared "midlife crises," no "integrity" in old age but only constant change or flux. In between these two extremes lie a number of theorists who argue that there are *sequences* but not stages. That is, there may be orderly, predictable sequences of experiences or changes in adulthood, but these changes may not be integrated into inclusive, shared internal or external structures.

When we put these two dimensions together, as in Figure 3–1, some combinations are obviously more common than others. (In fact, I cannot think of a theory that clearly belongs in the upper right hand corner—a nonstage theory of development—although such a theory is logically possible, even plausible. One could argue that individuals become more wise or more integrated but that the paths they follow toward this end are highly individual, without shared stages or sequences.) At the moment, stage theories of development are probably the most common and the most influential. But many of the current attempts at theoretical integration, such as both Baltes' and Perun & Bielby's theories, lie in the middle.

Because of the current dominance of the stage/developmental theories, let me start the detailed discussion of these theories in the upper left, and then work my way slowly toward the theories that lie in the middle. (The sequence I will use is indicated in Figure 3–1 by the numbers in parentheses after each theorist's name.)

Developmental Stage Theories of Adulthood

Erik Erikson's Theory of Identity Development

Erikson's theory (1950, 1959; 1980; Erikson, Erikson, & Kivnick, 1986; Evans, 1969) has clearly been the most influential view of adult development proposed thus far. There are traces of this theory in every other stage theory of adulthood, and his terminology has been widely adopted.

He proposes that psychosocial development continues over the entire lifespan, resulting from the interaction between inner instincts and drives and outer cultural and social demands. For Erikson, a key concept is the gradual, step-wise emergence of a sense of **identity**. Erikson explicitly stated that development follows a basic, built-in "ground plan" (1959, p. 53) which shapes a sequence of "potentialities for significant interaction" with those around the child or the adult. To develop a complete, stable identity, the individual must move through and successfully resolve eight "crises" or "dilemmas" over the course of the lifetime (see Table 3.1). Each dilemma emerges as the child or adult is challenged by new relationships, new tasks, or demands. The fourth stage of "industry versus inferiority," for example, begins when the child starts school and is challenged by the demand to learn to read and write and absorb great chunks of new information.

Each dilemma or stage is defined by a pair of opposing possibilities, one of which describes the optimum outcome of that dilemma, the other the potential negative or less healthy outcome, such as trust versus mistrust, or integrity versus despair. In his later writings (e.g., Erikson et al., 1986) Erikson also talked about

TABLE 3.1. Erik Erikson's Stages of Psychosocial Development.

Approx. Age	Stage	Potential Strength to be gained	Description
0–1 years	I. Basic trust versus mistrust	Hope	The infant must form a first, loving, trusting, relationship with the caregiver or risk a persisting sense of mistrust.
2–3 years	II. Autonomy versus shame and doubt	Will	The child's energies are directed toward the development of key physical skills, including walking and grasping and sphincter control. The child learns control but may develop shame if not handled properly.
4–5 years	III. Initiative versus guilt	Purpose	The child continues to become more assertive, to take more initiative but may be too forceful and may injure others or objects, which leads to guilt.
6–12 years	IV. Industry versus inferiority	Competence	The school-age child must deal with the demands to learn new, complex skills or risk a sense of inferiority.
13–18 years	V. Identity versus role confusion	Fidelity	The teenager (or young adult) must achieve a sense of identity—both who she is and what she will be—in several areas, including occupation, sex role, politics, and religion.
19–25 years	VI. Intimacy versus isolation	Love	The young adult must risk the immersion of self in a sense of "we," creating one or more truly intimate relationships or suffer feelings of isolation.
25–50 years	VII. Generativity versus stagnation	Care	In early and middle adulthood, each adult must find some way to satisfy the need to be generative, to support the next generation, or turn outward from the self toward others.
50+ years	VIII. Ego integrity versus despair	Wisdom	The culmination, if all previous stages have been reasonably well dealt with, is an acceptance of oneself as one is.

SOURCES: Erikson, 1950, 1959, 1980; Erikson, et al., 1986.

the potential *strength* to be gained from a healthy resolution of each dilemma, as you can see in Table 3.1.

A "healthy resolution," however, does not mean moving totally to the apparently positive end of any one of the continua Erikson describes. An infant can have too much trust; too much industriousness can lead to narrow virtuosity; too much identity cohesion in adolescence can result in fanaticism. The best resolution, in this view, is some balance in between.

Another key point about Erikson's theory that bears emphasis is his contention that these dilemmas/crises are forced on each of us as we move through the life cycle. Unlike some other stage theorists, such as Loevinger, Erikson does not think that you simply stay at a given stage until you have completed it before going on to the next. He argues instead that each person is pushed through this sequence of dilemmas by biological maturation, by social pressures, by the demands of the roles she takes on. You can't stay a 20-year-old until you get it right! On that next birthday you are 21, and then 22, whether you are ready or not. And with increasing age there are new demands, new dilemmas. When you arrive at 60 or 70, the tasks you didn't fully deal with will remain as unresolved issues, interfering with your ability to find true integrity. Erikson's theory thus belongs in the upper corner of this quadrant of the diagram because he not only thinks that the ultimate result of coping with these dilemmas *can* be maturity and wisdom, but because he thinks that the stages come along at roughly the same ages for all of us and must be dealt with in sequence, regardless of how well or poorly we may have resolved the previous stages.

THE DILEMMAS OF ADULT LIFE As you can see in Table 3.1, there are four dilemmas that describe adulthood, beginning with Stage 5, **identity versus role confusion,** which is the central task of adolescence and the early 20s. The young person must develop some specific ideology, some set of personal values and goals. In part, this is a shift from the here-and-now orientation of the child to a future orientation; the teenager must not only consider what or who she *is* but who or what she *will be.* Erikson (and others who have explored this stage following Erikson's lead, such as James Marcia, 1980, or Alan Waterman [Waterman & Archer, 1990]), suggests that the teenager or young adult must develop several linked identities: an occupational identity (what work will I do?), a sexual or sex role identity (how do I go about being a man or a woman?), and political and religious identities (what do I believe in?). If these identities are not worked out, then the young person suffers from a sense of confusion, a sense of not knowing what or who he is.

Stage 6, **intimacy versus isolation,** builds upon the newly forged identity of adolescence. Erikson says:

> . . . it is only after a reasonable sense of identity has been established that real *intimacy* with the other sex (or, for that matter, with any other person or even with oneself) is possible. Sexual intimacy is only part of what I have in mind . . . . The youth who is not sure of his identity shies away from interpersonal intimacy; but the surer he becomes of himself, the more he seeks it in the form of friendship, combat, leadership, love, and inspiration. (Erikson, 1959, p. 101)

Intimacy is "the ability to fuse your identity with somebody else's without fear that you're going to lose something yourself" (Erikson, in Evans, 1969). Many young people, Erikson thought, make the mistake of thinking they will find their identity in a relationship, but in his view, it is only those who have already formed (or are well on the way to forming) a clear identity who can successfully enter this fusion of identities that he calls intimacy. For those whose identities are weak or unformed, relationships will remain shallow, and the young person will experience a sense of isolation or loneliness.

Although in his earliest descriptions of the stages, Erikson had assumed that everyone passes through these stages in the same order, in later writings (Erikson, 1968) he suggested that this sequence of identity formation followed by intimacy may not be true for many women for whom the identity may be *created* in a network of relationships. Other authors (e.g., Sangiuliano, 1978), argue that many women simply reverse the sequence of the tasks of identity and intimacy, while Carol Gilligan (1982), in her influential book *In a Different Voice*, argues that women's identity development is, from the beginning, *inter*dependent rather than *in*dependent. Women define themselves and think about their choices and dilemmas in terms of relationships, whereas men appear to define themselves more by what they do or what they are, separate from their relationships. For women, then, there may simply not be a separate stage of intimacy; rather, intimacy may form the backdrop for all women's stages.

Whatever the resolution of the controversy concerning the stage of intimacy, there is reasonably good agreement that for both men and women there is a subsequent stage, Stage 7 in Erikson's model, **generativity versus stagnation.** An adult in this stage takes her place in society and helps in the development of the next generation or adds to the society in some fashion. Erikson says:

> We understand middle adulthood's generative responsibility for the 'maintenance of the world' in terms of the interrelated realms of people, products, and ideals. It is therefore the responsibility of each generation of adults to bear, nurture, and guide those people who will succeed them as adults, as well as to develop and maintain those societal institutions and natural resources without which successive generations will not be able to survive. (Erikson, Erikson, & Kivnick, 1986, p. 73–74)

The bearing and rearing of children is clearly a key element in Erikson's view of generativity, but it is not the only element. Serving as mentor for younger colleagues, doing charitable work in society—these, too, are part of generativity. Those adults who cannot achieve a satisfying sense of generativity may experience a sense of stagnation. Erikson also uses the term "self-absorption" to describe the flip side of generativity.

Erikson's final stage is **ego integrity versus despair.** I can best describe it using Erikson's own eloquent words:

> Only he who in some way has taken care of things and people and has adapted himself to the triumphs and disappointments of being, by necessity, the originator of others and the generator of things and ideas—only he may gradually grow

> the fruit of the seven stages. I know no better word for it than *integrity.* (1959, p. 104)
>
> Burdened by physical limitations and confronting a personal future that may seem more inescapably finite than ever before, those nearing the end of the life cycle find themselves struggling to accept the inalterability of the past and the unknowability of the future, to acknowledge possible mistakes and omissions, and to balance consequent despair with the sense of overall integrity that is essential to carrying on. (Erikson et al., 1986, p. 56)

I read recently a nice example of a person obviously moving toward such a position of integrity. Actress Audrey Hepburn, now in her 60s (and not yet "burdened by physical limitations"!), reflecting on her life, was quoted as saying:

> But the greatest victory has been to be able to live with myself, to accept my shortcomings and those of others. I'm a long way from the human being I'd like to be. But I've decided I'm not so bad after all. (Klein, 1989, p. 6)

Erikson argues that this sense of integrity must be built upon the foundation of successful resolution of all the crises and dilemmas that came before. Those adults who cannot achieve a sense of integrity, perhaps because they carry forward a residue of distrust, guilt, diffusion, isolation, or self-absorption from earlier stages, experience a sense of despair. They feel that time is too short, or that their life has been a failure, or that they wish they had it to do over again.

A key point implied here is that, in Erikson's view, these stages build on and affect one another. The unsuccessful resolution of any one stage leaves the individual with "unfinished business," unresolved conflicts, that are carried forward to the next stage, making it then more difficult to resolve the next stage successfully. Thus, Erikson is proposing a set of stages that are not only inevitable and in a fixed sequence but are also cumulative.

Jane Loevinger's Theory of Ego Development

In contrast, the stages Jane Loevinger proposes in her theory of ego development (1976) are sequential and cumulative but *not* inevitable, which is why I have placed her slightly more toward the center of the dimension of stages/no stages in Figure 3–1.

She proposes ten stages from birth through adulthood, each building on the one that precedes. But in Loevinger's view, a shift to the next stage occurs *only* when an individual has completed the development of the current stage. Although the first few stages are typically completed in childhood, the stages have only very loose connections to particular ages. Among a group of adults of any given age, a wide range of stages of ego development would be visible. What Loevinger is describing, in essence, is a pathway (or, perhaps a better image, a flight of stairs) along which she thinks we all must move. But the rate of movement and the final stage (step) achieved differ widely from one person to the next.

The ten stages or levels are listed in Table 3.2. Loevinger suggests that virtually all adults successfully move through the first three stages. Some then get stuck at the **self-protective stage,** while still others move to the **conformist stage** and no

TABLE 3.2. Jane Loevinger's Stages of Ego Development.

Stage	Description
Presocial Stage	The baby must learn to differentiate himself from his surroundings, to develop object constancy.
Symbiotic Stage	Baby retains a symbiotic relationship with the mother (or other major caregiver). Major task is to emerge from that symbiosis, through language in part.
Impulsive Stage	The child asserts his separate identity, partly by giving free rein to impulses. Others are valued in terms of what they can give. Those remaining too long at this stage may be "uncontrollable" or "incorrigible."
Self-protective Stage	The child learns self-control of impulses by anticipating immediate, short-term rewards or punishments. The child understands existence of rules but tries always to maximize his own gain. Some adults function at this stage.
Conformist Stage	Child or adult identifies his own welfare with that of the group and attempts to model his behavior along the lines of group expectations. Individuals in this stage tend to be insensitive to individual differences, to be highly stereotyped in response, particularly about sex roles. Inner life is seen in black and white: happy/sad, good/bad.
Self-aware Level	This is a transition level between conformist and conscientious stages. Self-awareness increases as does acceptance of individual differences and shadings of feelings and opinions. Stereotypic categories such as gender, marital status, education, however, are likely to be the basis of judgments, rather than other people's individual traits or needs.
Conscientious Stage	Individually created rules and ideals have now been formed, and the person attempts to live by them. Adults at this stage have a richer inner life, with many more shadings of feelings; similarly, the view of other people becomes more individualistic, the realtionships more mutual.
Individualistic Level	This is a transition level between the conscientious and autonomous stages. Individuals at this level are focused heavily on the question of independence and dependence. They are also more aware of inner conflict.
Autonomous Stage	Adults at this stage (comparatively rare) are fully independent individuals, with a capacity to acknowledge and deal with inner conflict. Other people are accepted and cherished for what and who they are, with no attempt to make them over.
Integrated Stage	This final stage, which is extremely rare, transcends the conflict of the autonomous stage.

SOURCE: Loevinger, 1976.

further. Most adults, however, reach at least the transition that she calls the **self-aware level,** and many go beyond this to the **conscientious stage** or further.

The final four stages are particularly interesting for a study of adulthood. The conscientious stage is really defined by the emergence of a set of self-chosen and self-evaluated rules. It is thus in some ways like Erikson's stage of "identity versus diffusion," except that Loevinger argues that the transition to the conscientious stage often occurs well past adolescence, if it occurs at all. Another aspect of the conscientious stage is the ability to see other people in complex, three-dimensional terms, in contrast to the greater stereotyping and two-dimensionality of relationships of earlier stages. "With the deepened understanding of other people's viewpoints, mutuality in interpersonal relations becomes possible" (p. 22). An adult at this stage would no longer describe (or think of) some particular friend as "a stockbroker who grew up in New York," but perhaps as "a highly achievement-oriented, determined, but somewhat lonely man."

The key to the **individualistic level,** which represents a transition stage between the conscientious and the autonomous, is the development of greater tolerance for both self and others. Individuals are experienced as unique; their flaws and their virtues are seen clearly. There is also a renewed struggle with the problem of dependence on others. The individualistic adult realizes that independence is not achieved merely by earning your own money or having your own house. There is an inner level of independence as well. The individualistic person has not yet reached the point of full independence but knows that it is possible.

The next full stage in Loevinger's model is the **autonomous stage,** when that inner independence has been reached. Autonomy does not at all imply indifference toward others. On the contrary, the autonomous adult cherishes the individuality of others and finds richness in personal relationships. But he is willing to let his friends and family be themselves. He has let his wife step off her pedestal or realized his father had been a partial failure in his business, but he loves them both the more deeply for his acceptance of their flaws and failings.

Another key to this stage is the acceptance of the fact of conflict and paradox in human lives. The autonomous adult no longer sees the world in terms of opposites (good and bad, right and wrong) as the conscientious person tends to do; rather, he sees gradations, exceptions, complexities.

The highest stage in this model is the **integrated stage.** On the surface, it is somewhat like Erikson's stage of ego integrity, but Loevinger thinks that it is a more developed stage than integrity. The integrated person arrives at a personal reconciliation of the conflicts examined at the autonomous stage and gives up the quest for the unattainable.

Loevinger's theory has become increasingly influential in the past 10 years for several reasons. First of all, the fact that the stages are not linked to specific ages can be a real strength. As our empirical information about adult development has grown, it has become increasingly clear that strict age-linked stages, while appealing, are hard to find in real life. Adults of any one age are widely different from one another. Loevinger's theory can help to describe those differences. Second, Loevinger and her colleagues have developed an instrument, the Washington University Sentence Completion Test, to measure a subject's position in the stage continuum. It includes items like: "A woman feels good when ______" or "My main problem is ______ ." Subjects' answers are then evaluated according to well-defined criteria, to yield a stage score. The existence of such a measure has made it possible for Loevinger's model to be used in research on a range of aspects of adult development, as you will see as you move through this book.

George Vaillant's View of Adaptation in Adult Life

A third theorist in the upper left quadrant of Figure 3–1 is George Vaillant, whose approach (1977a) has been strongly influenced by Erikson. Vaillant begins by accepting Erikson's stages as the basic framework of development, although he inserts an additional stage, which he calls **career consolidation,** between Erikson's stages of intimacy and generativity, at some time around age 30. Adults in this career consolidation stage, as Vaillant sees them, are intent on establishing their own competence, on mastering a craft, on acquiring higher status, or a positive reputation.

Despite his acknowledgement of these stages, however, Vaillant's theory is in many respects more like Loevinger's than like Erikson's. Like Loevinger, Vaillant describes a direction in which growth or development *may* occur but does not assume that everyone moves the same distance in this direction. In particular, Vaillant has been interested in potential progressive change in the ways in which adults adapt psychologically to the trials and tribulations they face. The major form of adaptation he discusses is the **defense mechanism.**

Freud used the phrase "defense mechanisms" to describe a set of unconscious strategies for dealing with anxiety. Everyone has some anxiety, so everyone uses some kinds of defense mechanisms. All involve self-deception or distortion of reality of some kind. We forget things that make us uncomfortable or remember them in a way that is not so unpleasant; we give ourselves reasons for doing something we know we shouldn't do; we project our unacceptable feelings onto others rather than acknowledging them in ourselves. Freud, Vaillant (and most other psychologists) agree that defending yourself against anxiety in this way is perfectly normal. What Vaillant has added to Freud's concept is the notion that some defense mechanisms are more mature than others.

Table 3.3 lists the four "levels" of defense mechanisms in Vaillant's classification. In general, mature defenses involve less distortion of reality. They reflect more graceful, less uncomfortable ways of coping with difficulties. Vaillant's central thesis is that for an adult to be able to cope effectively with the slings and arrows of normal life, his defense mechanisms must mature.

Don't be confused by the "levels" listed in Table 3.3. Vaillant is not saying that an adult, at any one moment, uses only defenses that are at one, and only one, level. On the contrary, most of us use a wide range of defenses covering several levels. And most of us show "regression" to less mature kinds of defenses when we are under stress. Facing a serious operation, most of us go through repression (of fear), or intellectualization (such as studying the details of the operation very abstractly), or projection ("my husband is the one who's afraid, I'm not"), or acting out (getting furious with the nurse for needing to jab you twice to get blood). Despite such regressions, according to Vaillant, in the normal course of adult life most adults add some of the more mature mechanisms or use them

TABLE 3.3. Levels of Defense Mechanisms Proposed by Vaillant.

Level	Description
I. "Psychotic" Mechanisms	*Delusional Projection:* frank delusions, such as delusions of persecution.
	Denial: denial of external reality.
	Distortion: grossly reshaping external reality to suit inner needs, including hallucinations, wish-fulfilling delusions (Prince Charming will find me any day now).
II. Immature Mechanisms	*Projection:* attributing one's own unacknowledged feelings to others ("You're the one who's afraid, not me").
	Schizoid Fantasy: the use of fantasy or inner retreat to resolve conflict.
	Hypochondriasis: Reproach toward others turned into complaints of physical illness. Often used to avoid making dependency demands directly or to avoid complaining directly about being ignored.
	Passive-Aggressive Behavior: Aggression toward others expressed indirectly and effectively through passivity or directed toward the self.
	Acting Out: Direct expression of an unconscious wish but without acknowledging the emotion that goes with it. It includes delinquent behavior, but also "tempers."
III. "Neurotic" Mechanisms	*Intellectualization:* Thinking about wishes or desires in formal, emotionally bland terms and not acting on them.
	Repression: Memory lapses or failure to acknowledge some information. Putting out of conscious memory.
	Displacement: Directing your feelings toward something or someone other than the original object. (e.g., cuddling your cat, when you really want to hold a lover).
	Reaction Formation: Behaving in a fashion directly opposite to what you would really (unconsciously) like to do (such as being exceptionally nice to a co-worker you detest, since you cannot acknowledge your hatred to yourself).
	Dissociation: Temporary, drastic modification of one's sense of character, such as a sudden devil-may-care attitude, periods of irresponsibility.
IV. Mature Mechanisms	*Altruism:* Vicarious but constructive service to others.
	Humor: Overt expression of ideas or feelings but without discomfort and without unpleasant effects on others (does not include sarcasm).
	Suppression: Conscious or semiconscious decision to postpone dealing with some impulse or conflict.
	Anticipation: Realistic expectation of future problem or discomfort, and planning for it.
	Sublimation: Indirect expression of some desire or need but without loss of pleasure or adverse consequences (such as expressing aggression through sports). Instincts are channeled rather than dammed up.

SOURCE: Vaillant, 1977, pp. 383–386.

more frequently, and at the same time use the less mature mechanisms less often. Furthermore, Vaillant argues that individuals vary in the extent to which they show such maturing. It is those who move most toward mature defenses who will be most successful in their personal and professional lives.

Vaillant's theory is thus clearly *developmental* in emphasis, since he is charting the progress each adult makes toward higher levels of maturity. But his theory is less easily categorized on the dimension of stage versus non stage. He accepts Erikson's stages as the background against which adult development occurs. But the primary process of maturing he describes is not stage-like at all. The move from immature to mature defenses is a gradual one, not step-like as Loevinger's stages are. But like Loevinger, Vaillant assumes that the more mature levels are not achieved by all adults.

Other Stage-Developmental Theories

There are many other theories of this same broad type which describe narrower dimensions of development, such as Lawrence Kohlberg's theory of moral development (Kohlberg, 1964, 1981, 1984), or James Fowler's theory of faith development (1981), both of which I will describe in Chapter 11.

Still other theories in this group, although broad in scope, cover a narrower age range than do Erikson, Loevinger, or Vaillant, such as Roger Gould's extremely interesting theory of personal transformation (1978, 1980). Gould's theory effectively covers only the period from about 20 to about 45 and says nothing about the later years. He proposed, in essence, that the process of adult development is one of identifying and then giving up a series of "myths" about the world and your place in it. Some of these myths are individual, but Gould argued that there are also shared, age-linked myths, such as the one common in one's early and middle twenties that says something like "as long as I follow the rules, I will be rewarded and be happy." In midlife, there is the myth of immortality that must be faced and abandoned if full adult psychological potential is to be achieved.

Whether narrow or broad, covering all ages or only a portion of the age span, all of these theories share the basic assumption that adults actually develop—that we can become more mature or can create more complex or higher orders of understanding—and that the development occurs in stages, steps, or sequences.

Stage Theories of Adult Change

When we move to the next group of theories (in the lower left quadrant of Figure 3–1) the concept of stages or sequences remains. What is eliminated is the assumption that movement through these stages involves "development." Let me describe two such approaches, one drawn from sociology, the other representing a strongly psychological view.

Family Life Stages: A Sociological Stage Theory

In order to understand the concept of family life stages, it is necessary to understand the concept of a **role.** Sociologists describe social systems as being made up of linked or interlocking *positions* (also called *statuses*), such as teacher and student, parent and child, or employer and employee. The *content* of a particular position is called a role. A role is thus a kind of job description for a particular position, a set of skills or qualities expected in a person who occupies that position. The person who fills the role of Girl Scout Leader, for example, is expected to know about camping, cooking, and crafts, and about organizing activities that will keep young children interested. Such a person is also expected to be friendly and cheerful.

The concept of role is an important one in any discussion of adulthood. In fact, we can describe (or even define) any one adult's life in terms of the roles he or she performs. I am a mother, a daughter, a sister, a partner (a role I often refer to as "spouse-like person"), a psychologist, an author, a friend, a school board member, and so on and on. Filling these roles takes up a good portion of my time and energy.

We can also examine the frictions that emerge when an individual attempts to fulfill the demands of two or more roles simultaneously (as virtually all of us do). **Role conflict** occurs when two or more roles are partially or wholly incompatible, logistically or psychologically. When you are trying to juggle the competing demands of your school, your job, and your family, you are experiencing role conflict. There are not enough hours in the day to fulfill the expectations of all three roles. **Role strain** occurs when a person's own qualities or skills are a poor match for the demands of any one role. If you have been out of school for a while so that your study skills are rusty, you may experience role strain when you go back to school. If you are promoted to a job for which you are only marginally prepared, you will feel role strain.

There are a number of roles that change somewhat systematically with age. As I pointed out in Chapter 1, there are age strata in any society which have accompanying roles. In our culture, teenagers have one role, young adults another, retired persons still another. Work roles also change with age, as I'll detail in Chapter 9. The sequence of role changes that has been the focus of the greatest research and theoretical interest, however, is that of *family roles.*

A number of sociologists (e.g., Evelyn Duvall, 1962) have proposed that adult life can be understood in terms of systematic changes in family roles. At least for those adults who marry and have children (the vast majority of adults), adult life marches to the rhythm of shifts in family roles. As you can see in Table 3.4, eight stages have been proposed, each reflecting either additions or deletions to the family (new child, or children leaving) or changes in the content of the parent role as the children shift from infancy to toddlerhood to school-age to adolescence.

You may note some interesting omissions in this list. The role of grandparent is not included. For most adults, this role coincides with the postparental and "aging family" stages. Nor is the role of caregiver to one's own aging parents included

TABLE 3.4. Stages in Family Life Cycle Proposed by Duvall and Others.

Stage	Description
1	Newly married with no children. The role of spouse has been added.
2	New parents: first child is an infant, so the new role of parent has been added.
3	Families with preschool children: oldest child is between two and six; other younger children may also be in the family.
4	Families with school-age children: The oldest child is between 6 and 12; there may be younger children as well.
5	Families with adolescent children: Oldest child is now a teenager, which changes the parental role in specific ways.
6	Families with the oldest child gone from the home. There may well be other children still at home, but the "launching center" role of the family has begun.
7	Families in which all children have left home. This is also often called the "post-parental" stage.
8	Aging families: One or both spouses has retired.

SOURCE: Duvall, 1962.

in this list, a role that many adults acquire in their 50s. These important family roles are omitted perhaps because they are less clearly sequential than are those associated with the bearing and rearing of one's own children. Grandparenthood might come at any of a wide variety of times, as could caring for an aging parent. But you should bear in mind that this conception of the family life cycle is an oversimplified description of the roles involved in family life.

Nonetheless, this conception has served as an organizing model for a great deal of sociological research on adulthood. Instead of comparing adults of different ages, researchers compare adults in different life-cycle stages. You have already seen an example of this in Chapter 1 (Figures 1–10 and 1–11), and there will be many more examples throughout the book. The basic idea, obviously, is that an individual's behavior and attitudes are shaped by the roles she occupies. And since these roles change with age in systematic and predictable ways, adults will also change systematically and predictably. There is no notion here that some roles are better than others, or that the family life cycle (or any other age-related change in roles) leads to "growth" or "improvement" in some fashion. But there are definable stages, widely shared in this and other cultures. Knowing that a person has a new infant tells you something about his life. If you knew that another person's youngest child had just gone off to college, you would quite correctly infer very different things about her daily existence.

The obvious difficulty with this theoretical position in today's world is that while the roles themselves do continue to make predictable demands, the *sequence* of roles is much less widely shared today than it was even a few decades ago. In western industrial countries at least, many more adults today do not marry; many more do not have children; many more divorce and move through complex combinations of family roles. To use myself as an example again, I did not marry until I was 32; then I became the instant mother of two stepchildren who now no longer live with me.

Psychologists and sociologists who find the basic concept of family stage theory to be useful have struggled to find ways to update the concept so that it can continue to be applied to current cohorts. One such updating has been offered by Avshalom Caspi and Glen Elder, Jr., whose research on the long-term outcomes of childhood personality patterns I described in Chapter 2.

Caspi and Elder (1988) say:

> An emphasis on the age-related life schedules of individuals in particular societies and cohorts organizes the study of lives in terms of patterned movements into, along, and out of multiple role paths such as education, work, marriage, and parenthood. . . . In this fashion, the life course can be charted as a sequence of social positions or trajectories of social roles that are enacted over time . . . . Successful transitions and adjustments to age-graded roles are the core developmental tasks faced by the individual across the life course. The . . . agenda for . . . psychology is to examine how individuals confront, adapt, and make adjustments to age-graded roles and transitions. (p. 120–121)

What Caspi and Elder are saying, then, is that family life stages need not be precisely the same for all adults for the basic theoretical model to remain useful. The specific sequence of roles or the timing of those roles may change from one cohort to the next, from one culture to the next or even for different subgroups within a given culture, but dealing with *some* normative sequence of roles is the very stuff of adult life.

Daniel Levinson's Theory of Seasons of Adulthood

The concept of roles also figures in Daniel Levinson's theory of adult change (1978, 1980, 1986), but he has incorporated it into a more inclusive theoretical concept, that of the **life structure.** According to this idea, each adult at each of several ages creates a life structure that is made up of some integrated combination of roles (work roles, family roles, relationships), adapted to, or filtered through, that person's specific personality and skills. In other words, each of us *adapts* to our environment, to the demands made upon us. We create a pattern to our lives, a rhythm, a system. It is this adaptive pattern Levinson calls the life structure, which is "the underlying pattern or design of a person's life at a given time" (1986, p. 6).

Each life structure is an individual creation. Two individuals dealing with the same roles and relationships will not create precisely the same life structure. But the demands of particular roles (such as family life-cycle roles) do have a significant impact on the shape the life structure will have.

Because life structures are designed (by the individual) to adapt to a set of inner and outer conditions, they cannot remain stable throughout life. Life conditions change, in no small part because roles change. So life structures must change, too. Levinson proposes, therefore, that adult life is made up of alternating periods of stable life structures and transition periods during which the old life structure is reexamined, adjusted, or altered.

The overall sequence he suggests is fairly complex, as you can see in Figure 3–2. He first divides adult life into a sequence of broad *eras,* each lasting roughly 25 years, and each marked with a distinct "biopsychosocial character" (1986, p. 5). Between eras there are major transitions, such as the early adulthood transition, or the midlife transition. But there are also transition periods *within* each era. Levinson suggests that each era begins with a *novice phase,* during which the individual tries out an initial life structure designed to deal with the new demands of that era. This first try at a suitable life structure is then reassessed in a mid-era transition, after which there is a *culminating phase,* in which an improved or more adaptive life structure is created, bringing the efforts of that era to fruition. This culminating life structure is itself reassessed and modified at the end of the era when the transition to the new era begins.

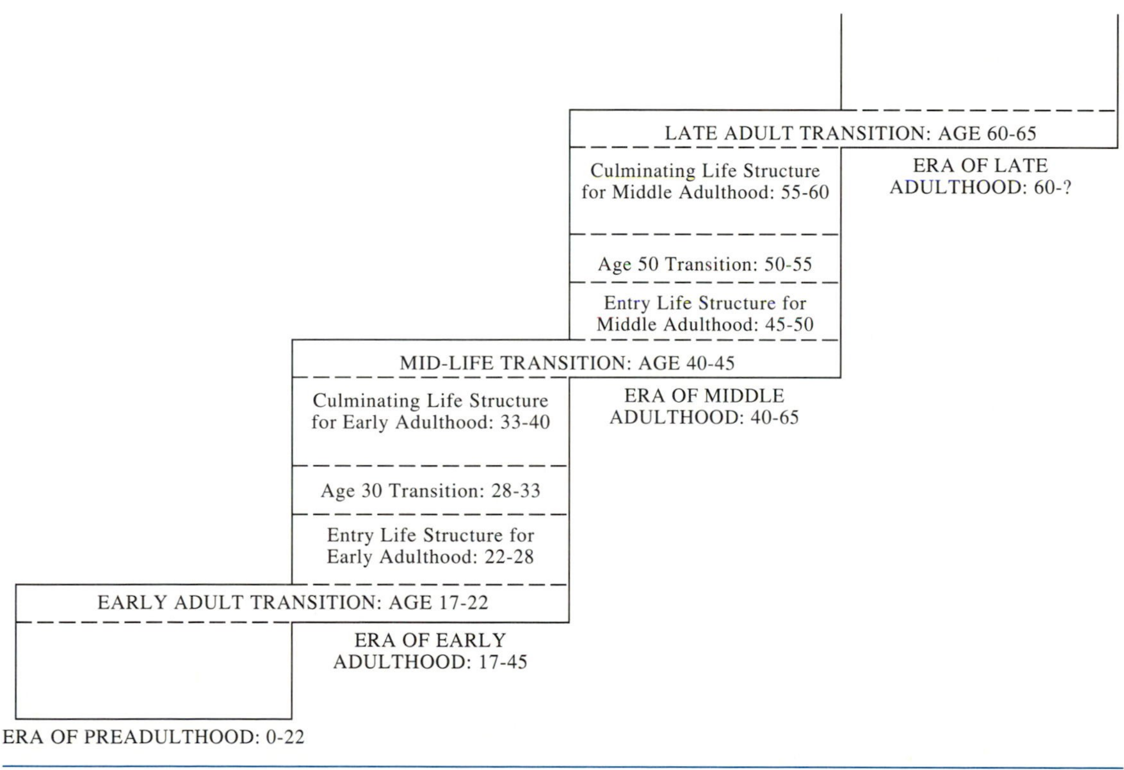

Figure 3–2 Levinson's model of adult development. You can see the alternation of periods of stable life structures (such as "entering the adult world" or "settling down") and periods of transition. Transitions between one era and the next are likely to be more pervasive than are those within any given era. (Source: Levinson, 1986, adapted from Levinson 1978. Copyright 1978 by Daniel J. Levinson. Reprinted by permission of Alfred A. Knopf, Inc.)

Levinson suggests that each era, each stable period within an era, and each transition, has a particular content, some of which I have summarized in Table 3.5. The Early Adult Transition deals with the problem of independence, of establishing an identity and a life separate from one's family (thus, it is similar in some respects to Erikson's stage of identity versus diffusion). Young adults must explore the adult world, find work, create relationships. This first inner and outer exploration leads to the creation of a first life structure in the 20s.

This "novice" life structure of early adulthood is commonly distinguished by two elements that Levinson thinks play a critical part in an adult's life: the creation of a relationship with a **mentor**, and the establishment of the **dream.**

The dream is a sort of fantasy or a set of imagined possibilities showing what one wants to become—a mental picture of oneself winning the Nobel Prize, or playing professional basketball against Abdul-Jabbar, or bringing about racial equality in the country (Martin Luther King's "I have a dream" speech). Many young adults dream of becoming rich, or finding the perfect mate, or living happily ever after in a lovely house in the suburbs with two well-behaved children. As the young person pursues this dream, he may establish a mentor relationship. The mentor is ordinarily 8 to 15 years older (someone, perhaps, in his own stage of generativity) who takes the young person under his wing, who teaches, advises, sponsors, supports, serves as a model for the young person. A mentor is often found in a work setting, but it could also be an older relative or a friend. He (or she) is both a parent figure and a peer and must be both if the relationship is going to work. The function of the mentor is to help the young person make the transition from reliance on the parents and their world to reliance on himself.

The life structure of the 20s, including both the dream and (for some) a mentor, does not last, in part because the goals may not be reached but also because the roles and demands change. At the very least, the novice-phase life structure of the 20s must be reexamined to see if it still fits, if the goals are still the same, if the strategies are working. In Levinson's view, the age-30 transition is focused on just such a reassessment, and it is followed by the culminating phase of this era, which he calls "settling down."

The major between-era transition in the early 40s deals with another set of issues—with awareness of mortality, with the realization that the dream may not have been fulfilled. A further major transition, at around age 60 to 65, is focused on the sense of loss of physical powers or possible illness, on accepting that one has achieved as much as one can.

Levinson is not saying that all adult lives are exactly alike. Indeed, he emphasizes that the specific life structures created in these various stages and eras will be widely different. But he is saying that the underlying sequence of eras, of stable and transitional stages, holds for all adults:

> It is abundantly evident that, at the level of events, roles, or personality, individual lives unfold in myriad ways. I make no claim for order in the concrete individual life course . . . I do propose, however, that there is an *underlying* order in the human life course, an order shaped by the eras and by the periods in life structure development. Personality, social structure, culture, social roles, major life events, biology—these

TABLE 3.5. The Major Tasks of Each Developmental Period Proposed by Levinson.

Development Period	Age	Tasks
Early Adult Transition	17–22	Terminate pre-adulthood and move out of pre-adult world, taking preliminary steps into the adult world. Explore possibilities and make tentative commitments.
Entering the Adult World	22–28	Create a first major life structure, which may include marriage and a separate home, a mentoring relationship, and the Dream. Attempt to pursue the Dream.
Age-30 Transition	28–33	Become aware of the flaws of the first life structure and reassess it. Reconsider earlier choices and make new ones as needed.
Settling Down	33–40	Create a second adult life structure; invest yourself in work, family, friendships, community. Establish a niche in society and strive to "make it," to achieve the Dream.
Midlife Transition	40–45	A bridge from early to middle adulthood: Ask basic questions, such as "What have I done with my life?" or "What do I want for myself and others?" May or may not involve crisis.
Entering Middle Adulthood	45–50	Create a new life structure, often (but not always) with a new job, or a new marriage, or a change in nature of work life.
Age-50 Transition	50–55	Similar in function to the Age-30 Transition; a more minor adjustment to the middle adult life structure. However, if no crisis occurred at Midlife Transition, one is likely to occur now.
Culmination of Middle Adulthood	55–60	Build a second midlife structure, analogous to Settling Down in middle adulthood. May be a particularly satisfying time if the adult has successfully adapted the life structures to changes in roles and self.
Late Adult Transition	60–65	Termination of middle adulthood and bridge to late adulthood. Conclude the efforts of middle adulthood, prepare for retirement and the physical declines of old age. A major turning point in the life cycle.
Late Adulthood	65+	Create a new life structure that will suit the new patterns in retirement and the increasing physical declines. Cope with illness. Deal with the psychological issue of loss of youth.

SOURCE: Levinson, 1978.

> and other influences exert a powerful effect on the actual character of the individual life structure at a given time. . . . It is my hypothesis, however, that the basic nature and timing of life structure development are given in the life cycle at this time in human evolution. (1986, p. 11)

At the same time, Levinson explicitly rejects the idea that these sequences of life structures, these "seasons of a man's life," involve any movement from worse to better or less mature to more mature—which is why I have placed his theory in the lower left quadrant of Figure 3–1 rather than in the upper left quadrant. He assumes change, even systematic change, with age but not development. As he says:

> The tasks of one period are not better or more advanced than those of another, except in the general sense that each period builds upon the work of the earlier ones and represents a later phase in the cycle. There are losses as well as gains in the shift from every period or era to the next. (Levinson, 1978, p. 320)

You may have noticed, in both Levinson's writings and in my descriptions of his theory, a certain male bias. The original theory was based *entirely* on an intensive study of a small group of middle-aged men. Levinson has since studied a parallel group of women (from which the results are not yet published), and several smaller studies of women were undertaken by others (Roberts & Newton, 1987). He now claims that precisely the same sequence of eras and stages occurs in women's lives, although the specific timing of life events is typically quite different for women than for men. I'll be coming back to questions about personality change and possible sex-differences in such changes in Chapter 10. For now, let me merely say that Levinson's view has been at least partially supported by the research on women. The majority of women studied intensively do go through an age-30 transition, for example. On the other side of the ledger, there is little support for Levinson's notions of the universality of the dream or the mentor role. A distinct subset of the women studied have described no dream, and only a fraction of them have had a mentor (Roberts & Newton, 1987). Still, at the deepest level Levinson describes, the level at which there are alternating periods of stable life structures and transitions, there is some support for his view.

Change Without Stages: Non Stage Theories of Adult Change

Stage or sequence theories are attractive in part because they describe the transit of adult life as an orderly process. But there is good reason to think that ordinary people's lives are *not* that orderly. Not all researchers who have looked for evidence of widely shared psychosocial or psychological stages have found them (e.g., Pearlin, 1980; Fiske, 1980). And as I pointed out a few pages ago, there are many men and women whose lives do not follow the clear pattern of the family life cycle, either.

It does appear that some of the issues or tasks that Erikson, Levinson, and others describe are reflected in adult lives. But widely shared, clear stages are harder to find. In the view of some theorists, it is more fruitful to examine the ways adults adapt to the unique constellations of life experiences they may face rather than to search for elusive (or nonexistent) patterns of shared stages.

Many of the theories in this group are really preliminary models rather than complete theories, proposed by researchers who have struggled to apply earlier, stage-like concepts to their observations of adult life, and who have found the stage theories wanting. The term "eclectic" would be a reasonable general description of theories in this group. What they have in common, other than their strong data-based orientation, is skepticism about the usefulness of simple stage models of adult development and similar doubt about conceptualizing changes in adulthood as "development." Leonard Pearlin's approach is a good example of a theory of this type.

Leonard Pearlin's Model of Psychological Distress in Adults

Leonard Pearlin (1980, 1982a; Pearlin & Lieberman, 1979), working from a background in sociology, has offered a useful synthesis of concepts from both psychology and sociology. His major interest has been in sources of distress over the adult years and in people's methods of coping with such distress. But his suggestions about the adult years are not limited to the domain of distress.

Pearlin grants that there may be life tasks or psychological issues that are characteristic of particular age periods. But in his view, such age-related issues form only a minor part of the experience of aging. Pearlin is much more struck by the diversity of pathways:

> Because people are at the same age or life cycle phase, it cannot be assumed that they have either traveled the same route to reach their present locations or that they are headed in the same future directions. (1982a, p. 64)

The elements in individual lives that determine the route a person follows, in Pearlin's view, are several: (1) all the dimensions of individual difference I talked about in Chapter 2, particularly the social or economic class in which the individual finds himself; (2) the range of skills the individual has for coping with stress or life change. The wider the range of such coping skills, the less distress the person will feel; (3) the availability and usefulness of social support networks. Adults with strongly supportive networks experience any form of potential distress less acutely; (4) the nature and timing of the sources of stress or distress the person must face.

Pearlin divides sources of distress into three types. First, there are the chronic or durable strains that are built into any life—the complaining mother-in-law, the boring job, the role conflict inherent in trying to work and care for a family at the same time, the need to stretch the budget to meet inflation. Second, there are *scheduled* or predictable changes or events, such as the birth of a child, the departure of a young adult from home, retirement. These are all anticipated role changes. Finally, there are the unexpected, *unscheduled* changes, such as being laid off work, or an automobile accident, or the unexpected death of a parent or close friend—a concept rather similar to Neugarten's notion of "on time" and "off time" life events.

Pearlin's research findings persuade him that scheduled changes have relatively little effect on feelings of distress or well-being, while unscheduled changes frequently have major effects. But even unexpected or unscheduled events have most of their impact indirectly, by increasing the daily life strains. Being widowed, for example, has a relatively small impact on adults who have adequate financial and emotional resources. Those adults who are forced to change their daily lives sharply, however—go to work, or live at a lower economic level, or cope with rearing children alone—show far more distress, depression, and anxiety. Pearlin appears to be saying that the unplanned disruption of a life structure (to borrow Levinson's concept) is what causes maximum distress.

It should be clear from even this limited description of Pearlin's work that although this is a theory about *changes* in adult lives, it is definitely not a theory about development. Pearlin specifically rejects the idea that there is any inner unfolding, any "growth."

Figure 3–3 Which is likely to be more stressful for an adult's life: retiring at 65, or losing your job when you are in the middle of adulthood, as these adults have apparently done? Pearlin's theory tells us that "scheduled" changes are much less stressful than "unscheduled" changes. (Photo © Ray Ellis, Photo Researchers, Inc., 1976. Reprinted with permission.)

> We hold, first, that adult emotional development does not represent the gradual surfacing of conditions that happen to reside within individuals. Instead, we see it as a continuing process of adjustment to external circumstances. . . . (1980, p. 180)

Since adults of any given age are likely to share certain external circumstances, there *may* be common experiences at different points in the life course, at least for subgroups within any given cohort. But Pearlin is arguing that real understanding of adult lives will be found, not in defining those shared experiences as universal stages, but in searching for those principles that govern the way individual adults cope with the changing demands of adult life.

Additional Theoretical Complexities

The classification of theories I have offered in Figure 3–1 highlights two dimensions on which theories of adulthood differ from one another. But even the brief descriptions I have given of these theories point to other important dimensions on which theories of adult lives might be arrayed. Two such additional dimensions seem to me to be especially critical.

First, there is the question of *universality versus diversity.* Are there ways in which *all* adults change or develop in the same way, in the same sequences, or at the same rates? Some theorists, such as Erikson or Loevinger or Levinson, obviously think so. They are searching for underlying sameness in the face of apparent difference. Other researchers, including Pearlin and even Vaillant, have been much more struck by the diversity of adult pathways, sequences, and coping strategies. For theorists in this second group, understanding adulthood means to understand *why* people develop differently, or in different sequences, or more or less fully. What are the characteristics of the individual, the background characteristics, or the life experiences, that lead one adult to an integrated, satisfied old age, and another to a bitter, maladaptive, or lonely old age?

A second key issue that separates the theorists I have talked about is whether they see change (or development) as primarily resulting from some kind of internal "psychological clock," or from primarily external influences, such as social roles, subcultural norms, or cohort experiences.

To some degree, this particular debate has divided the psychologists and the sociologists who study adulthood. As sociologist Dale Dannefer has pointed out somewhat scathingly (1984a, 1984b, 1988), a psychologist faced with any research results that look even remotely like a common pattern is very likely to assume that she has uncovered a basic, normative process of aging. Dannefer describes the psychologists' typical assumption as the *ontogenetic fallacy:* The assumption that "change in adulthood [is] a natural property of the individual which tends to be uniform across individuals and relatively unaffected by context." (1984, p. 109).

In contrast, many theorists emerging from a sociological tradition have been more interested in understanding the impact on adult lives of such contextual forces as cohort differences and subcultural norms (such as the differences in life expectations for working class and middle class adults in any cohort). To psychologists searching for internal orderliness, cohort differences are "noise" in the system; they want to look beyond or behind such variation for the common pattern they assume is there. To sociologists, cohort and subcultural differences are precisely the data of interest.

Clearly, such a difference in basic assumptions is going to lead theorists of the several persuasions to study very different aspects of individual lives. Psychologists typically focus on measuring internal states, such as personality, coping skills, or mental abilities. Sociologists are much more likely to focus on changes in roles, such as retirement or the birth of the first child. Even when the same event is studied, the two groups ask very different questions. A psychologist looking at the impact of the birth of an adult's first child is likely to study the impact on his or her personality or on sex role attitudes; the sociologist is likely to look at structural changes in family roles resulting from the child's inclusion in the family system.

To be sure, this demarcation line between the two disciplines is often crossed. Nonetheless, this disagreement about which aspects of adulthood should be studied, and about whether we should search for understanding in internal or in external forces, runs through all of the literature on adulthood and makes synthesis of theory and data extremely difficult.

Undaunted, a number of recent authors have attempted such syntheses, some of which I find intriguing. Let me describe two such attempts and then add several suggestions of my own.

Theoretical Syntheses

Paul Baltes' Life-Span Perspective

Paul Baltes, along with colleagues such as Richard Lerner and David Featherman, is quick to point out that the **life-span perspective** is a *perspective* and not a theory (Baltes, 1987; Baltes & Reese, 1984; Featherman, 1983; Dixon & Lerner, 1988; Lerner, 1986). As Dixon and Lerner put it:

> What is the life-span perspective? It should be noted immediately that it does not constitute a theory, a collection of theories, or a metatheory of development; rather, it offers a perspective on psychology based on the proposition that the changes (growth, development, aging) shown by people from the time of their conception, throughout their lives, and until the time of their death are usefully conceptualized as developmental. (1988, p. 34)

In some respects, this perspective is an antidote to the common assumption two decades ago that "development" occurred only in childhood and adolescence. Among other things, we know that development in childhood clearly had at least some biological, maturational base. Children and adolescents are clearly growing and changing physically, and those physical changes affect everything else. When we applied the same model to adulthood, all we saw in the way of change was the decay of the physical organism. Baltes, and those of like mind, see this as a very narrow view. He argues that development continues over the lifetime and is influenced not just by biological change but by a whole set of other factors, age-graded changes dictated by culture, historical (cohort) effects, and unique individual experiences.

The starting point for the life-span perspective, then, was simply the assumption that there is more to study in adult development than physical decline. Over the past two decades, however, this perspective has become richer. As Baltes describes it in his more recent writings, it now includes a set of assumptions, propositions, or "family of beliefs" (to use Baltes' own phrase), listed in Table 3.6, that guide both thinking and programs of research.

TABLE 3.6. Major Theoretical Propositions of Life-Span Perspective (as proposed by Baltes and others).

Concepts	Propositions
Life-span development	Development is a life-long process. No age period holds supremacy in regulating the nature of development. At all stages of the life span, continous (cumulative) and discontinuous processes are at work.
Multidirectionality	There is no single direction of change in development even within the same domain (such as intellectual development). Some functions show increases, some decreases. And at any given age, some systems of behavior show increases whereas others show declines.
Development as gain/loss	The process of development is not a simple move toward higher efficacy, such as incremental gain. Rather, throughout life, development always consists of the joint occurrence of gain (growth) and loss (decline.)
Plasticity	There is considerable capacity for change (either growth or decline) within each individual at any point in the life course. Thus, depending on the conditions and experiences, the developmental course of a given individual can take many forms.
Historical embeddedness	Life-span development can also vary substantially in accordance with historical-cultural conditions, cohort differences, differences within cohorts in the same culture, and differences between cultures.
Contextualism	Any particular course of individual development is understood as the outcome of the interactions of three systems of developmental influences: age-graded, history-graded, and nonnormative.
Multidisciplinary approach	Understanding of human development will be furthered by collaborative work among several disciplines, including anthropology, biology, and sociology as well as psychology.

SOURCE: Adapted from Baltes, 1987, Table 1, p. 613.

When you read through these propositions, you'll see that Baltes and his colleagues are not rejecting totally the notion that there may be shared stages of development. There might even be many different sets of stages or sequences, each connected to or characteristic of one facet of development, such as changes in certain kinds of intellectual skills, or changes in levels of rigidity. But researchers and theorists like Baltes, working within this general perspective, also assume *plasticity.* The human organism is capable of change throughout the life span. Plasticity clearly has some limits, and it may be that those limits get narrower as we get older—an empirical question of great interest to Baltes—but he assumes that there is at least some plasticity at all times. Stage theorists like Loevinger or Erikson also assume the potential for change, but in many stage theories change is unidirectional. Those who follow a life-span development perspective do not make such an assumption; in their view, change can go in many directions.

If after reading the list in Table 3.6 and after reading my brief description of this perspective, you have a sense of fuzziness, you are not alone. In some sense, the life-span developmental perspective offers a theoretical synthesis by simply taking a great many things in under the tent. At first, this may seem like trying to be all things to all people. But there is more to it than that. Baltes and his colleagues are assuming that there is *lawfulness* to the changes we see in adult life and that those laws go beyond processes of physiological decline. Our task as psychologists (or sociologists or anthropologists or biologists) is to uncover and understand the nature of that lawfulness. They do *not* assume that the specific pathways followed by adults will be necessarily all the same; they do not assume that all pathways lead toward either decline or higher efficacy. They do assume that the underlying lawfulness will create many different surface patterns, just as Levinson assumes that myriad specific life patterns can reflect the same underlying sequence of basic eras and periods of transition. Thus, though it is true that the life-span perspective offers a very large tent, the tent is not unlimited.

Within the broad category of the life-span perspective, we can find much more specific theoretical proposals, some of which also offer potential theoretical synthesis. One such is Pamela Perun and Denise Bielby's (1980) *timing* model of development.

Perun and Bielby's Timing Model of Adult Development

Perun and Bielby conceive of adult life as being made up of a large number of *temporal progressions*—sequences of experiences or internal changes each of which follows some timetable. The physical changes in the body over adulthood represent one such temporal progression, as do the changes in the family life cycle, or the ego developments described by Loevinger, or alterations in work roles or sex roles.

Figure 3–4 shows this model graphically, which may help to convey the complexity. Each of these disks, rather like machine gears moving at different rates, represents a single temporal progression, such as the life cycle within the nuclear family (marrying, having children, having those children grow up), or a separate life cycle within the extended family (such as the timing of one's parents' deaths). Each of these progressions moves at a different rate for each individual, thus

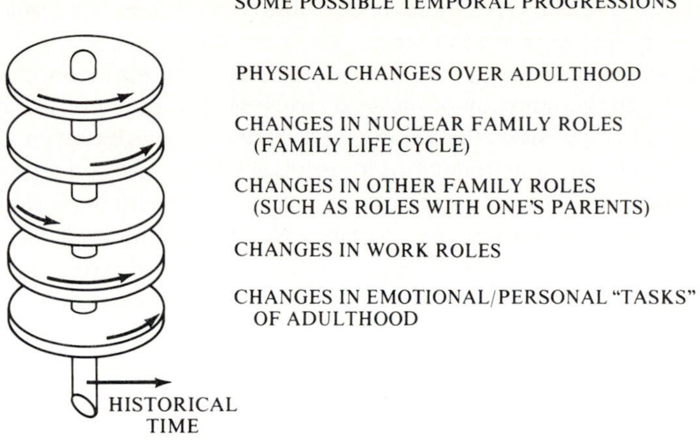

Figure 3–4 Perun and Bielby's timing model of the life course. Each of these disks represents one "temporal progression," a set of sequential changes in one aspect of adult functioning. Each of these progressions moves along its own timetable, at its own speed, with both speed and timetable affected by cohort, culture, gender, race, etc., creating a unique pattern of interlocking changes for each individual. (Source: From Perun & Bielby, 1980, Figure 1, page 102. Reprinted by permission of Westview Press, Boulder, CO.)

creating a unique pattern for each adult. Laura Rogers, who married at 16, has speeded up the family life cycle progression; another adult who exercises three times a week for his whole adult life may slow down the rate of the physical change progression.

Furthermore, this entire process is embedded within a particular period of historical time (a cohort), which will affect the process as well. For each of us, this collection of temporal progressions forms a whole. We do not experience this as a set of independent gears crunching away inside. What we experience are the interrelationships among these progressions.

Perun and Bielby suggest that one of the key interrelationships is the *synchrony* or *asynchrony* of these temporal progressions. Do the several timetables dovetail, support one another, match? If so, then synchrony exists, and the person will experience low levels of stress. In Levinson's terms, when there is synchrony, a stable life structure exists.

> Asynchrony occurs when one or more dimensions is off-time in relation to others. (Perun & Bielby, p. 105)

This creates friction, as if the gears did not quite mesh. We experience such friction as stress or as a crisis and strive to change in one or more dimensions until synchrony is again achieved. To get the gears to mesh again, you may have to move one of the other gears to a new position. The man who, at 45, finds that he puffs when he walks up a flight of stairs or can no longer beat his younger colleagues at tennis, may well experience this as asynchronous with his sense of increased effectiveness and responsibility at work. He could deal with this asynchrony in several ways, each of which involves "moving another gear." He might get into better physical shape (moving back or slowing down the rate of change of the progression of physical changes). Or he might go through some sort of internal reappraisal that would change the way he perceived the importance of physical competition. In coming to terms with his physical aging, he might shift to a higher level of ego development and again experience relative synchrony.

Thus, there are two sources of change within this model: First, the basic temporal progressions themselves describe changes, some of which are either inevitable or widely shared and some of which may be stage-like. Second, asynchrony triggers additional change.

Several intriguing and potentially useful implications or expansions of this model occur to me.

1. The rate of movement along any one temporal dimension may be influenced by those individual differences I talked about in Chapter 2—by gender, race, intelligence, temperament, education, or social class. For example, women from working class families marry earlier and have their children earlier. This changes the timing of at least one of the "gears" in the model, which will in turn alter the points at which asynchrony will be experienced. If we could add to this model some equations describing factors that affect the rate of change in each progression, we could come closer to being able to predict individual life patterns.
2. Following Pearlin's lead, we might also hypothesize that anticipated or scheduled shifts on any one progression will create less disrupting asynchrony than will unanticipated or unscheduled changes. If I plan to retire at 65, I can think about the changes that will be involved and partially adjust to the change ahead of time.
3. Being significantly off time in any one progression should produce relatively high rates of asynchrony throughout the life course. Women who have children in their teens, or those who do not have their first child until they are in their late 30s, would be two examples of such off time patterns. Bernice Neugarten (1979), who was one of the first to talk about the impact of "on time" and "off time" events, has indeed found that there is a price to be paid for off-timeness. But Perun & Bielby's model also suggests that there is a potential reward to be reaped as well, since coping with the asynchrony produced by the off time pattern *may* lead to higher levels of personal adaptation or growth.
4. Despite individual differences in the rate of movement along the several progressions, there are still widely shared (though not universal) points of asynchrony. At midlife, for example, those adults who follow a modal pattern are likely to have their children begin leaving home, their parents begin to fail in health, their own bodies begin to show signs of decline, and their jobs "peak out," all at approximately the same time. Such shared asynchronies may produce the somewhat illusory appearance of broad stages in adult lives.

5. If asynchrony is one of the keys to personal change (and possibly to personal growth), then adults who find themselves in situations that force change are also likely to show the greatest growth. As an example, Melvin Kohn (1980) (whose work I'll describe more fully in Chapter 9) has found that adults in complex jobs show greater growth in intellectual skill than do adults who have more routine jobs. Some of this is self-selection, of course: Adults with less intellectual skill to start with are more likely to end up with less complex jobs. But Kohn has shown that job complexity has an independent effect. High job complexity pushes everyone toward more complex and elaborated ways of thinking.
6. Given asynchrony, growth is not the only possible outcome. Synchrony can be recreated by regression or retreat in some progression. For example, if a new job requires you to learn a whole new set of complex skills, thus creating asynchrony, you could give up the job and go back to something more familiar. A midlife man may respond to the asynchronies of that age not by becoming physically fit or accepting limitations but by increased drinking or by depression. Each of these is a kind of adaptation. In Vaillant's terms, each of these is a defense against the anxiety produced by the asynchrony.

These implications and expansions illustrate, I hope, the potential richness of this model or models like it. An approach like this goes beyond the broadness of the life span perspective and suggests several of the basic laws that may govern adult life change and development. Nonetheless, there is clearly a great deal that is not dealt with in such a model. As an example, when an individual is faced with asynchrony, what determines the coping method that he uses? Given what appears to be the same crisis, why do some people respond constructively, others destructively? And what determines the form that a new life structure will take? If we think of each of these asynchronies as a large freeway cloverleaf intersection, then each represents a set of choices. You can choose to continue along the same road; you can turn off onto a new road, or you can turn around and go back on the road by which you came. What determines such choices? Is there lawfulness here, too? Are these choices affected by personality, by social class, by race, or gender?

Erikson would undoubtedly suggest that each choice affects all that follow it. So unsuccessful resolutions of early dilemmas (perhaps particularly the very first dilemma of trust versus mistrust) will increase the chances that later dilemmas will be unsuccessfully, or even destructively, resolved. To predict the future life course of any one individual, then, we would need to know his life history in detail—a very tall order.

Some Shared Flaws and Weaknesses in the Theories

Before leaving this excursion through the research landscape and beginning our much longer journey through the empirical evidence on specific changes and continuities in adulthood, I would be remiss if I did not point out several major weaknesses shared by most or all of these theories.

First, the data base for these theories is typically extremely small. In Table 3.7 I have described briefly the major studies or clinical data from which these several theories have emerged. As you can see, most of the theories—particularly those offered by psychologists—are based on only very limited observations of actual adults. Vaillant interviewed 100 middle-aged men; Erikson's theory is based primarily on his own clinical observations. Of course this need not mean that the theories are wrong. Many remarkable theoretical insights have been based on only a few clinical observations (Freud's work, and that of Piaget, come immediately

TABLE 3.7. Major Sources of Data on Which the Several Theories of Adult Development Are Based.

Theorist	Data Base
Erikson	Primarily Erikson's own clinical observations as a child analyst and extensive reading of anthropological descriptions of other cultures.
Loevinger	Loevinger's own clinical judgment, supplemented and supported by fairly extensive research with the Sentence Completion Test of Ego Development, including studies of both black and white children, high school and college students studied longitudinally over four to six years, numerous college samples, and many studies relating this measure to other assessments. Less extensive evidence on the higher stages.
Vaillant	Vaillant's own clinical judgment as a psychiatrist but primarily based on interviews with 100 of the all-male Grant Study participants at about age 50, plus all other information on these Harvard men in the Grant Study files.
Family Life Cycle Theory	Proposed by several sociologists as a synthesizing concept, based on hundreds of studies of families in earlier decades, and since used as an organizational rubric and theoretical concept in hundreds more studies. Very extensive data base.
Levinson	Original source was an extensive set of interviews and assessments of 40 men between the ages of 35 and 45, equally divided into four occupations: hourly industrial workers, business executives, university biologists, and novelists. Samples of women have since been studied by both Levinson and several others but few data published.
Pearlin	Major source is a short-term longitudinal study of adults from wide range of socioeconomic levels, both male and female, ages 18 to 65; 2,300 adults were interviewed once, and a subset reinterviewed four years later, covering all aspects of labor and love.
Baltes	A theoretical approach not based on a specific study, although research on changes in adult intellectual functioning has been especially influential.
Perun & Bielby	A theoretical synthesis based on both theory and empirical evidence from others but applied principally to a sample of 41 married women with Ph.D's.

to mind). But it does mean that the wide applicability of any one theory has not been well tested.

Second, there are several marked biases built into many (but not all) of the data sources and the theories themselves. Most theorists have studied primarily middle class, white adults. All have studied only western culture. In addition, several of the major theories are based largely or entirely on interviews with or observations of men only. Whether any theory emerging from such observations will be applicable to women, to working-class adults, or to adults of other cultures, is open to serious doubt. More particularly, any theory based on such limited observations that proposes that all adults develop in the same way or in precisely the same sequence seems to me to be particularly suspect—precisely the point made by sociologist Dale Dannefer in his critique of psychological theories of adulthood. That does not mean that we cannot learn from such theories, but it does mean that we should be suitably skeptical about their wide applicability. Those theories that explicitly attempt to account for variations in individual responses to the tasks of adulthood seem to me the most flexible, and of these, I obviously find the timing model the most useful.

Incomplete as it is and limited though the data base is, the timing model, in my view, comes closer to describing real-life adult patterns than any other single approach. What I need to do now is to look at each of the gears or cogs shown in Figure 3–4 one at a time, so that you can get some sense of the kinds of changes that occur in each dimension over the adult years. I will then come back to the task of putting the pieces together in Chapter 15, when I will attempt another synthesis.

Summary

1. Theories of adulthood differ on a number of important dimensions, among them the distinction between development and change, and between stage-like and non stage-like change. Theorists who assume that there is some common direction in which adults move can be described as *development* theorists; those who assume change without shared direction can be described as *change* theorists. Some in each group further assume that the movement (change or development) occurs in fixed stages of some kind; others assume no such stages.
2. Developmental-stage theorists include Erik Erikson, Jane Loevinger, Roger Gould, and many others.
3. Erikson's theory of identity development describes eight stages or dilemmas spread over the entire life span, each of which is linked to a particular age. The individual moves into a new stage because of changes in cultural or role demands, or physical changes, and must then resolve the dilemma associated with that stage.
4. Incomplete or imperfect resolution of a dilemma leaves unfinished business to be carried forward to the next stage, increasing the likelihood that the next stage, too, will be imperfectly resolved.

5. The four stages Erikson describes that are part of adulthood are identity versus role diffusion, intimacy versus isolation, generativity versus stagnation, and integrity versus despair.
6. The stages in Loevinger's theory are not tied to age. Children and adults move along a progression of 10 steps or levels, each built on the preceding ones, with movement occurring only when the preceding stage has been completed. A group of adults of a given age will thus contain individuals who may be functioning at any one of several different levels.
7. The stages particularly relevant to the study of adulthood are the conformist, the self-aware, the conscientious, the individualistic, the autonomous, and the integrated.
8. George Vaillant assumes the validity of Erikson's stages but adds the concept of maturing defense mechanisms. He describes several levels of maturity of defenses and suggests that a) as a group, adults move toward more and more mature defenses, and b) that adults vary in the degree to which that movement occurs.
9. Another group of theories retains the concept of stage but eliminates the concept of directional development. Included in this group are models of family life cycles and Levinson's theory of seasons of life.
10. Life cycle theories emphasize the formative influence of the predictably changing set of roles associated with marriage, bearing and rearing children, and seeing the children leave home.
11. Levinson proposes a universally shared rhythm of stable life structures alternating with periods of transition. These alternations occur at particular ages, as adults come to terms with particular issues that are relevant for that age.
12. More eclectic models assuming neither development nor stages also exist, such as Leonard Pearlin's model of methods of handling distress in adulthood.
13. These theories also differ on other dimensions, such as whether they assume universality or diversity of patterns and whether they focus on internal or external change. As a general rule, sociologists have emphasized the potency of such external forces as cohort effects and subcultural influences; psychologists have emphasized the importance of some kind of shared "psychological clock" that leads to common inner changes.
14. Several attempts at synthesis involve intermediate positions on the two key theoretical dimensions. Baltes' life span perspective is a broad view that emphasizes the importance of both internal and external forces, both development and change. He assumes that some type of development continues over the whole lifetime, that the process is lawful but that individual pathways may diverge sharply.
15. Perun & Bielby's timing model is a second form of synthesis. They assume that within each adult there is a series of separate temporal progressions, each moving at its own speed. Asynchrony among these several progressions produces stress, which the individual resolves by some kind of change in one or more progressions. This theory appears to provide a better (albeit much more complex) view of adult development than many of the previous theories.

16. All of these theories, to a greater or lesser extent, share two weaknesses: They are based on a paucity of data, and they tend to be biased toward descriptions of the adult lives of white, middle class, American males.

Suggested Readings

BALTES, P. B. (1987). Theoretical propositions of life-span developmental psychology: On the dynamics between growth and decline. *Developmental Psychology, 3,* 611–626. In the past, I have found the life-span perspective hard to grasp. It seemed unbearably broad and fuzzy. But Baltes, in this most recent systematic statement, has made it much clearer.

GILLIGAN, C. (1982). *In a different voice.* Cambridge, MA: Harvard University Press. Gilligan speaks here—eloquently and passionately—to the specific point of male bias in existing theories of adult development. She analyzes many existing theories and presents evidence supporting the view that women's development is qualitatively different in key aspects.

GOULD, R. (1978). *Transformations: Growth and change in adult life.* New York: Simon and Schuster. I am particularly fond of this book, since it is written in an unusually engaging and clear style, with a great deal of clinical case material. It is perhaps the least technical and complex of the series of theoretical books (including also Vaillant's and Levinson's) that came out at about that same time.

LERNER, R. M. (1986). *Concepts and theories of human development* (2nd ed.). New York: Random House. If you are looking for a book that will give you more detail and depth on many of the basic theories of development—both in childhood and adulthood—this is an excellent source.

ROSENFELD, A., & STARK, E. (1987, MAY). The prime of our lives. *Psychology Today, 21,* pp. 62–72. Like all articles in *Psychology Today,* this is semi-technical, intended to be easily accessible to the general public, not just to fellow psychologists. The authors talk briefly and critically about some of the current theories of adult development and cite some of the most current research.

SMELSER, N. J., & ERIKSON, E. H. (1980). *Themes of work and love in adulthood.* Cambridge, MA: Harvard University Press. This is a wonderful collection of papers by many of the major theoretical figures I have talked about in this chapter, including Levinson, Gould, and Pearlin. The chapters are not overly technical but each gives a good overview of that particular approach.

CHAPTER 4

Physical Changes in Adulthood

My maternal grandparents both lived into their 90s and were physically in quite good shape until their final few years. They remained active and vital people through the final decades, keeping house for themselves and each keeping up an extensive correspondence with friends and family. (My grandfather always tried to answer letters the day he got them. No matter how hard I tried, I always seemed to owe him a letter!). My grandmother was working on her third book in her late 80s and early 90s. Despite their continuing vigor, though, they were both acutely aware of the physical changes that had significantly altered their lives. My grandmother complained particularly of the fact that she "couldn't taste anything anymore." Unless food was highly spiced or had a strong natural taste (like strong coffee), it seemed totally bland to her. They also reported loss of energy and vitality; they simply couldn't carry on long at any one activity before they tired. And large groups of people were difficult for them to deal with; it got harder and harder to follow conversations in large groups, and there was too much noise and confusion. We also noticed that they both lost quite a lot of physical coordination in the last years, and both became extremely thin.

How typical are these changes? We all know that adults get grayer, more wrinkled, and a bit slower as they age. But what other changes take place? We can catalogue quite a lot of changes—as I will do in a moment. But such a first level of description, however useful, does not tell the whole story. Equally important, we need to know whether the changes we observe are inevitable or resistant to intervention, and what impact they have on the daily functioning of adults.

Isadore Rossman defines true aging processes as "possessing the characteristics of universality, progressiveness, irreversibility, and being essentially detrimental" (1980, p. 125). In the terminology I am using in this book, these would be *maturational* changes. One of the dilemmas for researchers and physicians has been to discover how many of the observed physical changes that seem to accompany the passage of years are really "aging" (in Rossman's sense) or maturation. Alternatively, some observed changes could be due to increased inactivity, poor diet, or living among environmental hazards. Some of these changes may actually be reversible, and some genuinely universal and irreversible changes, while measurable, may have negligible or small impact on the ability of an older person to function on a day-to-day basis.

In all of this, there is an important distinction to be made between changes that are due to age alone—what we might think of as the underlying physiological maturation or aging—and those that result from the fact that with increasing age, more people suffer from diseases of various kinds that may alter some physiological process. What makes this problem still trickier is the apparent fact that greater *vulnerability* to disease is itself one of the effects of the underlying physiological processes of aging.

Caleb Finch, one of the major researchers and thinkers in this area, distinguishes between two types of changes: *pathogeric* changes, which are disease correlated, and *eugeric* changes, which are related to age but not as a secondary consequence of age-correlated disease (Finch, 1986). The terminology seems a bit artificial, but the distinction is not. To have any hope of sorting out the two kinds of change, we need to look primarily at the results of studies in which *healthy* adults of various ages have been compared or followed over time. A description of the physical changes associated with aging based on such studies may not describe the experience of the *average* person, since the average older adult is affected by disease as well (as I'll describe in the next chapter). But it may come closer to describing the basic processes.

The Facts of Physical Aging

Longevity, Life Expectancy, and Life Span

Let me get the confusing terminology out of the way at the start. **Life span** refers to the upper boundary of years a given species can expect to live. For cats, the life span (the upper boundary) is roughly 20 years; for humans it appears to be roughly 110 years. **Longevity** refers to the *average* expected length of life at any particular time in history, in a particular culture. Finally, the related concept of **life expectancy** refers to the average number of years remaining for a person of a particular age. So we can talk about life expectancy at birth, or life expectancy at age 40, or 65, or 80.

One of the most striking facts about physical aging at this point in history is that longevity has increased very sharply among adults living in developed countries. People are just living longer. This is true partly because fewer people die in infancy, childhood, or early adulthood than was true several generations ago. Among children born in the United States in 1840, 25 percent were dead by the age of 3. Among those born in 1910, in contrast, it wasn't until age 55 that a quarter of the cohort had died (Jacobson, 1964). But life expectancy has also been extended at the upper end, primarily through the virtual elimination of infectious diseases and through reduction of risk of major disorders like heart disease. In 1940 in the United States, a woman of 65 could expect to live an average of another 13.6 years. In 1986, she could expect to live another 18.6 years. (For men, the equivalent figures are 12.1 and 14.7 years) (Verbrugge, 1984; U.S. Bureau of the Census, 1989a). What is more, this pattern of increased life expectancy is expected to continue. By the year 2050, according to at least some estimates, the average life expectancy at birth may be as high as 75 for men and 83 for women, and life expectancy for those who reach the age of 65 may then be as high as 17 years for men and 23 years for women (Crimmins, 1984).

Despite these advances, however, the *life span* probably has not changed at all. A few people have always lived to be 100 or a bit older; now, by *postponing* death from such degenerative diseases as heart disease or diabetes, we have enabled more people to approach the maximum potential span of years. But all the improvements in health care and disease prevention do not appear to have stretched the upper boundary (Hayflick, 1975; Yin & Shine, 1985). As physician Melvin Konner puts it:

> Transcendence of those [life span] limits is not even on the horizon of science. So what we can hope for is not an endlessly lengthening life span, but a prospect that

Figure 4–1 *More and more of us are living to enjoy our 100th birthday parties, and more and more of us will reach that age as healthy as this woman appears to be. But, 100 or a bit more is still the effective upper limit of the life span, and that upper limit has not been increasing, despite medical advances. (Photo © Carolyn Wendt. Reprinted with permission.)*

> has been likened to "the wonderful one-hoss shay" of the poem, that "ran a hundred years to a day." Without wearing down or faltering, it then simply crumbled. . . . individual diseases of the elderly could be cured one by one, leaving the body's aging clocks alone to cause total collapse—but only after a ripe and very vital old age. (1988, p. 100)

One other fact about longevity and life expectancy is worth emphasizing: in our culture at least, women live longer than do men (go back and look again at Figure 2-3 for an illustration). In 1986, the average difference in life expectancy at birth was 7 years—78.3 for women, 71.3 for men (U.S. Bureau of the Census, 1989a).

There are several possible reasons for such a sex difference (Verbrugge, 1984): (1) women may have greater immunity to certain diseases such as heart disease, possibly because of differences in hormone patterns; (2) women's work may expose them less to environmental hazards; (3) women appear to seek medical attention earlier in any illness, improving the chances of cure or amelioration; and (4) women's personal health practices may be better—a factor I'll be talking more about in the next chapter.

Taking all of these facts together, I can quite confidently predict that the vast majority of you now in your 20s or 30s can expect to live to be 65 or older, and a large percentage of you will live well into your 80s or even 90s. Just what will your bodies be like in those later years of adulthood?

Changes in the Way You Look

For many adults, the most obvious changes with age are the ones they see in their mirror every day—those changes in physical shape and contour, in skin and hair that visibly chart the passage of years. The catalogue of such changes includes the following:

LOSS OF HEIGHT Longitudinal research of healthy adults, such as the Baltimore Longitudinal Study of Aging, shows that over the years from about age 40 to age 80 or so, adults lose 1–2 inches in height (Rossman, 1980; Shock, 1985). Most of this loss occurs in the spine where the discs between vertebrae first shrink, and then the vertebrae themselves eventually lose height. The overall effect is that the trunk becomes shorter while the arms and legs remain about the same length.

CHANGES IN WEIGHT Changes in weight follow a different pattern, first rising in the 30s and 40s, and then declining (by about 10 lbs), beginning sometime in the 50s (Shock, 1985). Whether this pattern represents a universal age-related series of changes in weight is less clear since the underlying reasons for the changes in weight are not known. All we can say for now is that in our culture at least, weight changes follow approximately the shape of an inverted U.

BODY SHAPE CHANGES The contour of the body also changes. Up to about age 30 or 40, the head actually grows, following the pattern shown in Figure 4–2 (Guillen, 1984). And both the nose and ears grow fairly steadily until one's 70s (Smith, Bierman, & Robinson, 1978). (Pinocchio is not the only one whose nose grows!) More significantly, the fat deposits in the body shift locations. Past about age 50, fat is lost in the face and in the legs and lower arms, while it is added in the upper arm (particularly among women) and in the belly and buttocks, producing the famous "middle-aged spread" (Shimokata, Tobin, Muller, Elahi, Coon, & Andres, 1989). A graphic personal example of this change came from a woman friend of mine (roughly age 50) who has just lost 60 pounds on a careful diet. She has been disappointed and frustrated to discover that at her "ideal" weight she can no longer get into clothes that fit her ten years ago when she was last at that same weight. The fat is simply in different places now, mostly around the middle. Such redistributions of fat deposits not only affect the way clothes fit; they can also give the impression that the older person is heavier, even after the middle 50s when weight begins to decline.

CHANGES IN SKIN AND HAIR Wrinkled skin, which becomes particularly evident beginning at 40 or 50, results in part from the loss of fat just under the skin—part of the redistribution of fat I've just described. It also occurs because of a loss of elasticity in the skin itself. This loss of elasticity is one of the pervasive

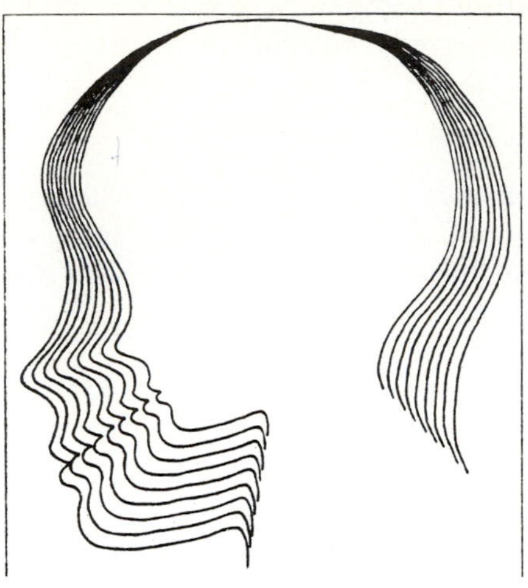

Figure 4–2 A computer simulation of the changes in head contours from infancy to adulthood. It turns out that these changes follow a specific mathematical formula, apparently as a result of the predictable effect of gravitation on the structures of the head. There is a general "sinking" of both bone and tissue toward the lower part of the skull. Because these changes are so regular and predictable, most of us use them unconsciously as part of our basis for judging the age of a child or adult. (Source: Guillen, 1984, p. 77. Reprinted by permission of Dr. Leonard S. Mark, Psychology Department, Miami University, Oxford, OH.)

changes of aging and affects muscles, tendons, blood vessels, and internal organs as well as skin. It is especially noticeable in skin that has been continually exposed to the sun, such as the skin of the face and hands (Selmanowitz, Rizer & Orentriech, 1977). Two other important changes in the skin are the reduction in the efficient functioning of both the sweat glands and the oil secreting glands. Older adults sweat less, which means that they cannot cool their bodies as effectively in high heat. And their skins become drier, subject to cracking.

Hair loss is also a common characteristic of aging in both men and women. Some men, of course, begin to lose hair very early in adulthood, but virtually all adults experience thinning of hair beginning in the 50s or 60s (post-menopausally for women). Graying of hair differs widely, but nearly all adults show some graying.

Changes in the Senses

A second series of body changes noted by many adults as they age affects vision, hearing, tasting, and feeling.

VISUAL CHANGES Two major types of changes in the eye begin sometime in one's 30s, although most of us do not experience the effects of those changes until somewhat later.

First, the lens of the eye thickens, adding layer after layer of slightly pigmented material. This layering process actually starts in childhood but begins to alter visual acuity and clarity only in adulthood as more layers accumulate. Light entering the eye must pass through this accumulating, yellowed material, which reduces the total amount of light reaching the retina and lowers overall sensitivity, particularly to the shorter wave lengths. One result is that with increasing age, adults are less and less able to discriminate between short wave–length colors: blue, blue–green, and violet (Bornstein, 1988).

Second, the eye begins to lose its accommodative power: It becomes less elastic, (just as the skin does), so it adjusts more and more slowly to changes in focal point or distance, a change that affects not only distance vision, but also depth perception. Response to light and darkness is also affected by this loss of elasticity in the lens as well as other changes in the eye. This makes older adults more sensitive to glare (such as headlights from oncoming cars, or glare from a rainy road surface) and less able to see in the dark. Most adults notice the consequences of these changes sometime in their 40s or early 50s when driving at night seems to become more troublesome, and when those who previously got along without glasses rather suddenly find they need glasses to read. (As I write this, I am wearing the glasses I was forced to begin wearing when I was about 45, without which the screen of my word processor is a total blur).

Because of such changes, overall visual acuity declines over the adult years, as you can see in Figure 4–3. Over 95 percent of adults over 65 require glasses at least some of the time (U.S. Bureau of the Census, 1989a) and most older adults require more illumination to see well. Certainly, these visual changes are noticeable (both by the individual experiencing them and by those observing) but because compensations like proper glasses are readily available, most adults are not disabled by the changes. Only three percent of adults over 65 are actually blind in either eye, and only 1.2 percent are blind in both eyes.

CHANGES IN HEARING From about age 50 onward, virtually all adults begin to lose some auditory acuity, especially for the high and very low frequency sounds—a form of hearing loss technically called **presbycusis** (Olsho, Harkins & Lenhardt, 1985). By age 75, roughly three quarters of the U.S. population shows some such loss. The basic cause of this loss appears to be gradual degeneration of the auditory nerves and structures of the inner ear, particularly the hair cells within the cochlea, as a result of basic wear and tear.

As with vision, for the majority of adults the loss of hearing is not so large as to produce serious impairment, particularly since the largest hearing loss is for pitches outside the range of the human voice. There is typically some loss of the ability to discriminate speech sounds, but for most older adults this is fairly readily compensated for by increased loudness (turning up the radio or TV, asking others to speak slightly louder).

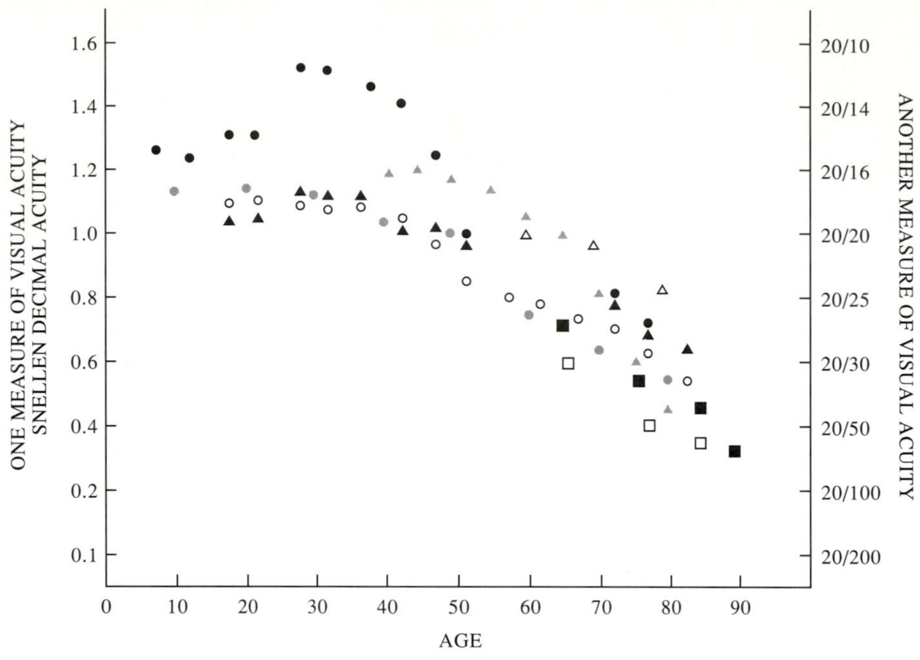

Figure 4–3 *Data from eight different cross-sectional studies are represented here (each with a different symbol), so you can see that the same pattern of loss of visual acuity with age has been found by many researchers. Most investigators have found essentially no loss of acuity until roughly 45 or 50, after which the decline is fairly regular. (Source: Pitts, 1982. Reprinted by permission of Alan R. Liss Inc., © 1982.)*

But the rate of serious impairment is higher for hearing loss than for visual loss. Perhaps 30 percent of adults over 65 have some significant hearing impairment. Roughly 13 percent are deaf in one or both ears and another 8–10 percent wear hearing aids (U.S. Bureau of the Census, 1989a). Helpful as they are, hearing aids do not compensate completely, especially for those with more significant loss. These adults may experience markedly greater difficulty in social situations, particularly in settings in which there are several conversations going on at once.

Smell and Taste My grandmother's complaint about losing her sense of taste is based on a series of real physical changes. For example, the salivary glands (like most glands) secrete less as we age, so that many older people experience a dry or "woolly" mouth. More significantly, the number of taste buds on each bump on the tongue decreases over the years of adulthood with a particularly sharp decline after age 75 (Charness, 1985).

This loss of taste buds seems to have two kinds of effects. First, the threshold for various tastes rises. The threshold is the amount of a particular flavor, such as sweet or sour or salty, that has to be present before you can detect it. So it takes more of a particular flavor before an older person can identify it (Charness, 1985). Second, above the threshold, older adults aren't as able to discriminate between a lot and a little of a particular flavor (Weiffenbach, Cowart, & Baum, 1986).

Thus, as we age we may lose not only some sensitivity to tastes, but some ability to discriminate among them—a sad thought for those of us who like to eat well!

Since the senses of smell and taste are highly related (as you certainly know from your loss of taste sensitivity when your nose is clogged up with a cold), it is not surprising to find that there is also a loss of smell sensitivity during the adult years. Richard Doty and his colleagues (Doty, Shaman, & Dann, 1984) tested this in a cross-sectional study of nearly 2,000 children and adults, using 40 different smells—ranging from pizza to mint to gasoline. He observed that peak olfactory ability (best and most rapid discrimination) is found among young adults between about age 20 and 40. Each succeeding age group has less and less good sense of smell, with a particularly sharp dropoff among those over 70. In this study, about 60 percent of those adults between 65 and 80 had severe losses in the sense of smell, of whom a quarter had lost all sense of smell. (Incidentally, smokers lost their sense of smell more than non-smokers did).

Aside from the aesthetic loss, the practical consequences of the loss of taste and smell can be substantial, since it is hard to work up enthusiasm for eating when you can't taste much. Poor eating habits may result—either eating too little, or skipping important nutrients, or adding too much of another (such as salt).

PAIN AND TOUCH There is scarcer and more conflicting evidence about changes in both touch and pain sensitivity. The evidence, which is virtually all cross-sectional, points to a slight loss of sensitivity to touch and to vibration, but no loss of sensitivity to heat and warmth (e.g. Kenshalo, 1977, 1986) and essentially no change in sensitivity to painful stimuli such as high heat, or electrical stimulation of the teeth (Harkins & Warner, 1980). What does increase is the frequency of pain *reports* by older adults, which may reflect decreased tolerance of chronic pain, or changes in the social acceptability of pain reports as we get older, or other psychological processes. There is a great deal more we need to know about pain experiences—not only in older adults but throughout the age range—if for no other reason than to know better how to treat pain in hospitalized or chronically ill patients.

Internal Physical Changes

Many of these changes in both appearance and sensory acuity are related to a much broader set of changes with age in internal organs or body systems.

CHANGES IN MUSCLES AND BONES There is a significant loss of muscle tissue (actual muscle cells) over the adult years, with the most rapid decline occurring after age 50 (Rossman, 1980). In this instance, we are fortunate to have both longitudinal and cross-sectional data, drawn from the Baltimore Longitudinal Study of Aging (Kallman, Plato, & Tobin, 1990), and both sets of analyses show the same pattern of decline. There is some indication that the greatest loss is in so-called "fast twitch" muscle fibers, which are the ones primarily involved in rapid bursts of speed or strength (such as sprinting), with slower loss in "slow twitch" fibers, which are involved in prolonged activity (such as jogging) (Ostrow, 1984).

The major effect of this loss of fibers is a reduction in physical strength. Figure 4–4 gives both the cross-sectional and the longitudinal data from the Baltimore sample, based on a group of 864 men studied over a period of nine years. You can see that the decline begins at roughly age 45 or 50. Nathan Shock (1984) estimates the loss in muscle strength among the men in the Baltimore studies to be roughly 28 percent by age 80, although this seems to be partly due to the fact that the older men weigh less. When you correct for weight, the loss is estimated to be only about 19 percent. However, when strength is turned into motion, as when subjects are asked to turn cranks or to pedal a bike, the combination of loss of muscle tissue and some loss of coordination results in both an earlier and larger loss of *work* output.

It is important to emphasize that *all* muscles show these changes, including the muscles of the diaphragm and chest, used for breathing, and those of the bladder,

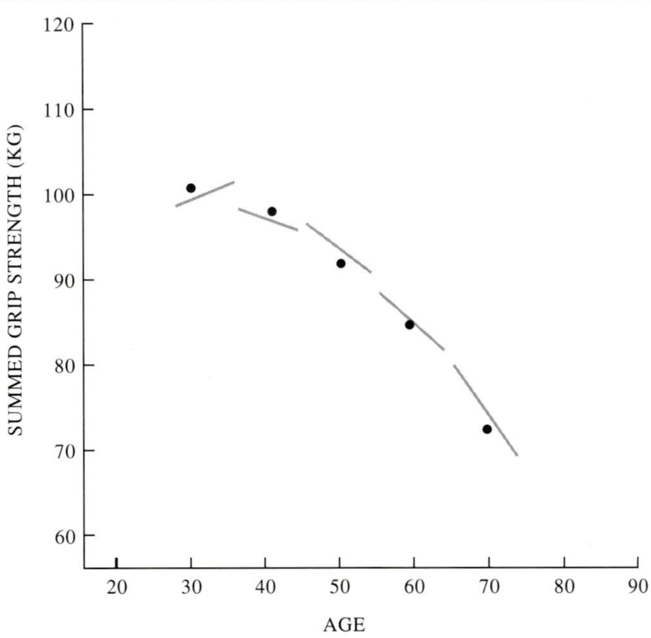

Figure 4–4 One of the consequences of loss of muscle tissue in adulthood is a loss of strength, such as these changes in grip strength in a group of men who participated in the Baltimore Longitudinal Studies of Aging. The dots represent cross-sectional data based on 847 men; 342 of these men were then followed longitudinally for an average of 9 years; their data are shown in the lines. You can see that there is excellent agreement between the two sets of information. Part of the loss of strength could be due to less use of the muscles at older ages, but that does not account for all of it. Some muscle tissue is lost with age even among adults who do hard physical activity or exercise regularly. (Source: Kallman, Plato, & Tobin, 1990, Figure 2, p. M84.)

used for elimination. Muscle loss in these parts of the body, no doubt, has much more impact on daily physical functioning than does loss of arm strength.

In the bones, there are several significant changes associated with age. First, bone marrow (in which blood cells are made) gradually disappears in arms and legs and becomes concentrated in the bones of the trunk. Second, calcium is lost from the bones, making bones more brittle and porous, a process called **osteoporosis.** As a consequence, bone fractures increase markedly in frequency after about age 45 in women and 75 in men (Lindsay, 1985). Osteoporosis is far more likely to be severe in women, particularly post-menopausally. The loss of ovarian hormones that is part of the menopausal process seems to be one of the causal factors, but diet and life style factors also make a difference. The sex difference is also partially attributable to the fact that women have less bone mass to begin with. The major known risk factors are listed in Table 4.1.

Third, changes in the bones of the joints, resulting primarily from the wear and tear of years of body movements, appear to be virtually universal. When such changes become marked, they are called **osteoarthritis** (Rossman, 1980), an extremely common complaint of old age. In 1986 in the United States, 44 percent of those age 65 to 74, and 54 percent of those 75 and older reported some chronic "arthritis" (U.S. Bureau of the Census, 1989a). Like osteoporosis, arthritis is more common among women. In one national health survey (Verbrugge, 1984, 1985), half of women and a third of men over 65 reported having "arthritis" of some form.

Changes in the Cardiovascular and Respiratory Systems

The conventional wisdom for many years has been that there is a systematic decline in the functioning of both cardiovascular and respiratory systems. Recent research, however—particularly research in which only *healthy* adults have been studied—points to a somewhat different conclusion: There are relatively few decrements with age when measurements are taken *at rest.* It is when the system

TABLE 4.1. Risk Factors for Osteoporosis.

Factor	Direction of Effect
Race	Whites have higher risk than other races.
Gender	Females have considerably higher risk than males.
Weight	Those who are light for their height have higher risk.
Timing of Climacteric	Women with early menopause or those who have had their ovaries removed are at higher risk.
Family History	Those with family history of osteoporosis have higher risk.
Diet	Diet low in calcium and high in caffeine and/or alcohol leads to higher risk.
Lifestyle	Sedentary lifestyle associated with higher risk.
Number of Children	Women who have borne any children are at higher risk.

SOURCE: Lindsay, 1985.

is stressed in any way, such as by physical work or exercise (or perhaps even by anxiety or fear) that the age differences show up. For example:

1. The ability to take in and transport oxygen to the various body organs decreases with age, but this shows up primarily in studies of exercise or stress. The measure most often used to assess this is **Maximum oxygen uptake,** or VO_2 max, commonly used as an index of overall aerobic fitness. Both longitudinal and cross-sectional studies show that under exercise conditions, VO_2 max typically declines about one percent per year in adulthood. You can see some typical results in Figure 4–5, which shows both longitudinal and cross-sectional findings (Ostrow, 1984).
2. Cardiac output (oxygen-carrying blood flow from the heart) under *resting* conditions does not decline with age, but it does show decline under exercise or work conditions, on the order of 30 to 40 percent from age 25 to age 65 (Lakatta, 1985; Rossman, 1980).
3. Heart rate shows a parallel change: Under resting conditions, there is very little change with age; with exercise, however, we see an effect of age, with older adults' heart rate rising *less* when exercising than younger adults'.

Edward Lakatta says of these findings: "Thus the notion that an 'aging process' *per se* commands a substantial *obligatory* decline in cardiovascular function at rest is not supported by these results" (1985, p. 393–394).

One exception to this general rule is blood pressure—the force with which the blood is being pushed through the arterial system. Systolic blood pressure (the force when the heart is contracting, and the higher number of the two that are quoted to you when your blood pressure is measured) rises fairly steadily with age until at least age 70 or 80, after which it may decline. This is true under all testing conditions among healthy adults. This change apparently results from loss of elasticity in the aortic wall—yet another indication that pervasive loss of elasticity is one of the major characteristics of physical aging (Lakatta, 1985).

CHANGES IN THE NERVOUS SYSTEM Just as recent research on healthy adults has altered the conventional wisdom about age changes in heart and lung capacity, similar new analyses have led to reassessments of the common assumptions about neurological changes with age. For many years, the common statement in texts and elsewhere has been that, with age, we all lose a great many neurons. The most widely quoted figure has been 100,000 neurons lost per day (Burns, 1958). It now appears that this conclusion was based on cross-sectional comparisons which included many older adults with specific pathologic conditions, such as Alzheimer's disease, which are known to affect brain composition and functioning. Caleb Finch (1986) points out that when only healthy individuals are studied, "abundant evidence now shows that neuronal loss is modest during most of the lifespan in adult mammals . . . whereas striking deficits in neurons and decreases in cerebral metabolism can occur with pathologic conditions, such as Alzheimer's disease" (p. 18). Of course such pathologic conditions do increase

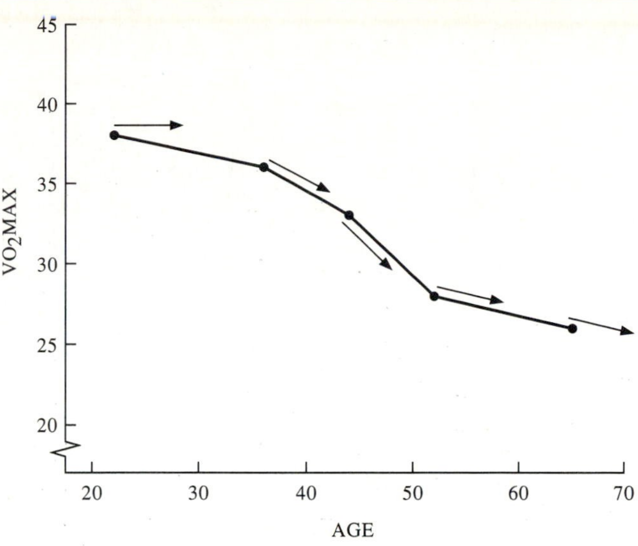

Figure 4–5 The line in this figure represents the mean VO_2 max for groups of women studied cross-sectionally. The arrows reflect scores on this same measure for other groups of women studied longitudinally. As you can see, there is remarkable agreement between the cross-sectional and the longitudinal results which lends further credence to the conclusion that this drop in aerobic efficiency is a normal part of physical aging. (Source: Drinkwater, Horvath, & Wells, 1975; Plowman, Drinkwater, & Horvath, 1979.)

in frequency with age, but it is important to realize that Alzheimer's disease, along with other forms of *dementia*, are not *normal* patterns of aging.

What does seem to be a part of the normal aging of the nervous system is a loss of density of the tree-like branching on each nerve cell, called **dendrites,** which are crucial ingredients in the process of linkage between nerve cells (Duara, London, & Rapoport, 1985). There is also a loss in the receptors for neurotransmitters that are another key part of the neural communication system. You can see the nature of the changes in the dendrites in Figure 4–6, which shows parallel results from studies of rats and humans. In humans, the decrements in these dendrites and in neurotransmitters seem to be perhaps 10 to 20 percent by age 45 and perhaps 40 percent by age 80.

Because we now know that there is relatively little loss of actual neurons, it may sound as if the neuronal changes are rather minor. But the loss of dendritic density is not trivial: ". . . it is the loss of the interconnections, not that of the neurons, that is functionally important" (Bondareff, 1985, p. 104). For example, one of the results of the reductions in neurotransmitters and dendritic connections is a slowing of speed of nerve response. If you measure the response of individual nerves to some stimulus (such as a sound), you find that in older adults the nerves "fire" somewhat more slowly than is true in young adults (Smith, Thompson, & Michalewski, 1980).

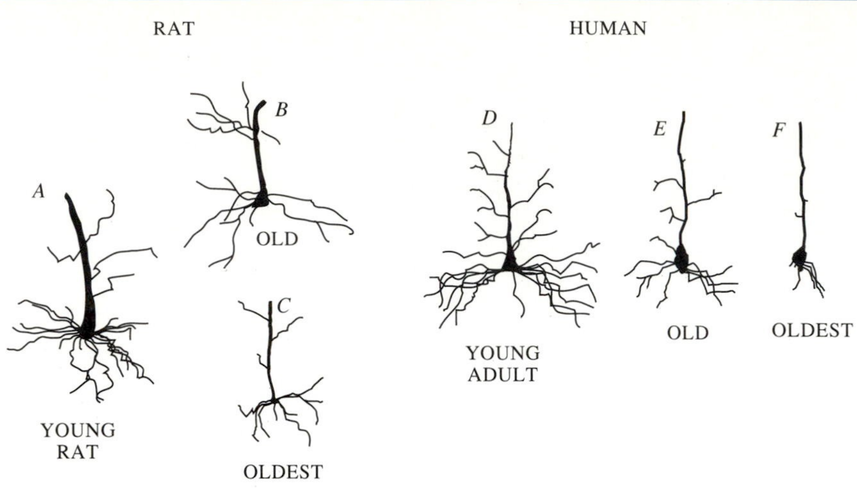

Figure 4–6 Both sets of pictures show changes in neurons with age—one series for humans, the other for rats. You can see that the branch-like elements (dendrites) become much less numerous in older cells. (Source: Cotman & Holets, 1985, fig 1, p. 621, who obtained the original figures from Scheibel, 1978, Fig 5, p. 363, and Vaughn, 1977, Fig 2, p. 505.)

At a behavioral level, you can see the effect of such slowing in measures of *reaction time,* which is the time between the onset of some stimulus and a person's response. For example, in one very large cross-sectional study in England involving over 5,000 subjects ranging in age from children through adults over 70, Robert Wilkinson and Sue Allison (1989) had subjects watch a number display that originally showed 0000. Each subject was told that as soon as she (or he) saw numbers begin to appear in the number window, she was to stop them as quickly as possible by pressing a red button. The subject then repeated this same sequence of watching/red button pushing for one minute. The results are in Figure 4–7. You can see that the average reaction time got slower and slower with increasing age. Interestingly, Wilkinson and Allison found that if they looked at each subject's *fastest* reaction time rather than their average score over one minute of testing, there was much less slowing with age. But the older adults had greater difficulty sustaining the faster speeds.

Such slowing of response—or perhaps also loss of vigilance—has widespread consequences for everyday life, as any older adult can tell you. It affects not only reaction time for such tasks as driving but also may contribute to the greater difficulty older adults experience in learning new things—changes I'll be describing in Chapter 6.

Changes in the Immune System Equally widespread and significant changes occur in the immune system with age. We are all more aware these days of the immense importance of the immune system because we have seen very graphically in AIDS patients what can happen when the immune system

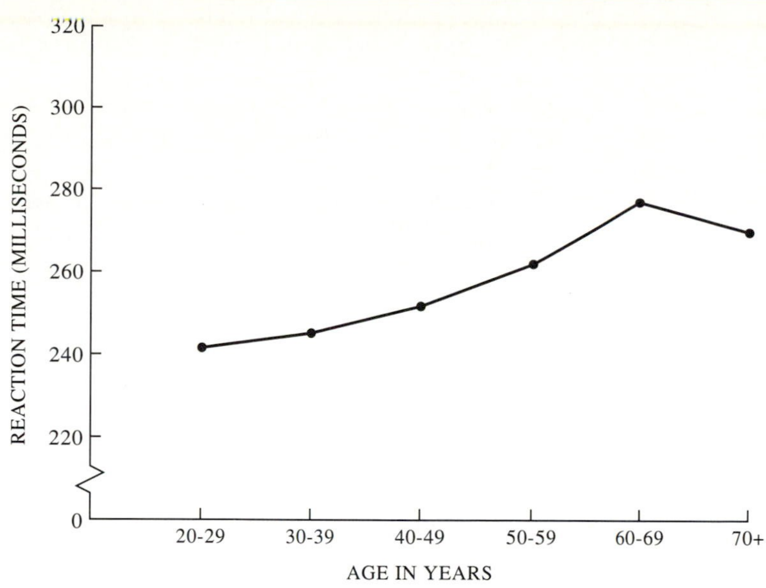

Figure 4–7 When thousands of individual adults were tested on Wilkinson and Allison's reaction time apparatus, clear age differences in speed of response emerged, as you can see here. (Source: Wilkinson & Allison, 1989, Figure 2, p. P31. Copyright 1989 Gerontological Society of America. Reprinted by permission).

no longer functions normally. But age, in addition to disease, brings significant changes in this system.

The key organs of the immune system are the bone marrow (which creates some lymph cells) and the thymus gland. Collectively, the immune system protects the body in two ways: by producing antibodies which react to foreign organisms (such as viruses and other infectious agents) and by producing special cells (T cells) that are programmed to reject and consume harmful or mutant cells, such as cancers or transplanted organs.

With age, the thymus gland decreases dramatically in size and mass. By age 45 or 50, adults retain only about five to ten percent of the cellular mass of thymus gland they had at puberty (Hausman & Weksler, 1985; Braveman, 1987). One result seems to be that the smaller, less functional thymus becomes less able to turn the immature T cells produced by the bone marrow into fully "adult" cells. As a result, both the basic protective mechanisms work less efficiently. Adults produce fewer antibodies than do children or teenagers. In addition, T cells partially lose their ability to "recognize" a foreign cell, so that some disease cells (cancer cells, for example) may not be fought. Thus, one of the key features of *normal* aging may be an increased susceptibility to disease.

More intriguing is the fact that in adulthood the body begins to form antibodies against its *own* cells. This *autoimmune* response seems to lie behind a number of diseases of adulthood, including rheumatoid arthritis, some kinds of diabetes, and perhaps multiple sclerosis (Shock, 1977).

Changes in the Reproductive System Major changes in the reproductive system do not typically begin until after age 40, often not until after age 50. The term **climacteric** is used to describe the gradual or rapid loss of reproductive capacity that occurs then in *both* men and women. It involves changes in hormones, resultant changes in the body and its functioning, and (for some) an overlay of psychological symptoms.

Research on the climacteric in men is undergoing the same kind of transformations as I have described for research on heart and lung function. In the last edition of this text, I stated rather flatly that a key aspect of this change in men is a gradual decline in testosterone (the major male hormone) beginning at roughly age 40 or 50. Some earlier studies suggested that the decline might be as much as 60 percent. However, some (but not all) more recent studies involving only healthy men, with age groups matched for education, social class, and life circumstances, show essentially no decline in testosterone with age (Harman & Talbert, 1985). The question obviously remains open. At the very least, it appears that the hormone changes that are part of the climacteric in men are more complex than first supposed, involving changes in the hormones secreted by the hypothalamus and the pituitary, as well as testosterone created in the testes.

There is better agreement about the physical and behavioral effects of these collective hormone changes. There is diminished production of sperm, some shrinkage of the testes, and a reduction in volume of seminal fluid. It typically takes longer for an older man to achieve erection, and a longer latent period is required before the next erection can be achieved, although once achieved the erection can often be sustained for much longer (Weg, 1983). Some men, particularly after age 60, experience temporary or long-term impotence, an experience that becomes increasingly common after age 80 or so. Estimates of the incidence of impotence vary considerably. For example, among men aged 60–65, the amount of impotence reported in various surveys ranges from 18 percent to 40 percent (Rossman, 1980).

There is also recent (and still very preliminary) evidence that at least some men experience a more significant emotional/physical upheaval during the climacteric, including insomnia or other sleep disturbances, depression, and loss of interest in sex (Weg, 1983). Just how large a segment of middle-aged men may experience such symptoms is not at all clear. Tamir's (1982) analysis of some of the cross-sectional results from the 1976 national sample of the Michigan Survey Research Center Study of Mental Illness and Health (recall Table 1.1) suggests that there are peaks between age 40 and 50 in "psychological immobilization," in drinking problems and drug use, and in ill health *only* among college-educated men. But these same middle-aged college-educated men did not show any higher level of anxiety or depression symptoms—such as sleep disturbances, nervousness, or loss of appetite. My best guess, based on very limited data, is that perhaps 5 to 10 percent of men may experience fairly extreme symptoms coinciding with the climacteric (Weg, 1983), but it is not at all clear whether these symptoms are *caused* by the hormonal or physiological changes of mid-life or are psychological/cultural in origin.

Despite the physiological (and psychological) changes of the climacteric, however, the great majority of men can and do remain sexually vigorous well into old age, (as I'll discuss in detail shortly). Men in their 70s and 80s can and do father children.

For women, there is no dispute about the drop in the key hormone, estrogen, although there are complex changes in other hormones as well. Table 4.2 summarizes the changes in two forms of estrogen and in progesterone (the latter being an important ingredient in the menstrual cycle, triggering the sloughing off of the accumulated material in the uterus) in pre- and post-menopausal women. As these hormones decline, the ovaries begin to respond irregularly to the less-loud signals to release ova, menstruation becomes less regular and finally stops altogether—the **menopause.** In the U.S. today, menopause occurs between age 45 and 55, with an average of roughly 50.

As with men, this series of hormone changes is accompanied by changes in the genitals and other tissues. There is some loss of tissue in the genitals and in the breasts, the ovaries and uterus become smaller, the vagina becomes shorter and smaller in diameter with thinner and less elastic walls, and there is less lubrication produced during intercourse—the latter being a direct result of insufficient estrogen and not an indirect result of the changes in the vaginal walls (Harman & Talbert, 1985).

The other major physical symptom experienced by the majority of women is the "hot flash," a brief, abrupt rise in body temperature which may be accompanied by sudden sweating and skin flushing. (I first experienced this somewhat startling phenomenon at age 46 when I happened to be on a trip to China. The flashes then recurred as often as 30 or 40 times per day, and I was continually flushed and damp with sweat. I came to think of the entire trip as "Hot Flashing Through China.")

These various symptoms of the climacteric in women can be sharply reduced by the oral administration of estrogen and progesterone. Such "hormone replacement therapy" was extremely common in the United States in the 1950s and 1960s, when only estrogen was administered. In one survey in 1973–1974 (Stadel & Weiss, 1975), 51 percent of menopausal women reported having used estrogen, the majority for 10 years or more. Prescription of replacement estrogen then dropped sharply, after evidence accumulated that the risk of endometrial cancer

TABLE 4.2. Levels of Estrogens and Progesterone Before and After Menopause.

	Estrogens		Progesterone
	Estradiol	*Estrone*	
Premenopausal women	50–200	35–500	300–20,000
Postmenopausal women	35–54	12–21	160–220

Note: All values here are pg/ml of plasma.

SOURCE: Harman & Talbert, 1985, p. 466, Table 3.

(cancer of the lining of the uterus) was multiplied 3 to 10 times when estrogen was used in this way (Nathanson & Lorenz, 1982). Subsequently, researchers found that a combination of low dosages of estrogen and progesterone eliminated the increased risk of endometrial cancer. So once again such hormone replacement is common. Not only does such hormone therapy eliminate hot flashes, it also helps to maintain adequate lubrication during intercourse and greatly reduces the risk of osteoporosis. On the other side of the ledger, it is also interfering with "natural" aging processes. It seems to be very much an individual decision.

One other aspect of the female climacteric deserves emphasis: Until quite recently, it was widely assumed that depression and other psychological symptoms were a standard accompaniment of the climacteric in women. There is now a good deal of dispute about this (Eisdorfer & Raskind, 1975; Weg, 1983). Certainly some women do show depression or anxiety in their 40s and 50s, but there is no clear *increase* in such symptoms at midlife, and no indication that such symptoms, when they do occur, are a result of the hormonal changes of the climacteric rather than a response to significant life changes at the same ages. For example, Neugarten (1976), reports that in one intensive study of 100 normal women between 43 and 53, menopausal status (no irregularity of periods, some irregularity, or cessation) did not differentiate among the women on any of the psychological variables they had measured, including anxiety, life satisfaction, or self-concept.

It is clear that most women experience at least some symptoms during menopause, especially hot flashes; for a minority, these symptoms are severe enough to be significantly unpleasant or debilitating. But there is simply little support for the old stereotype of the inevitably disturbed, depressed, anxious, cranky middle-aged, pre-menopausal woman. (The stereotype is not yet gone, though. Seven years ago, when I was 44, I was told by a physician that the cause of dizziness I was experiencing was "pre-menopausal anxiety.")

The Effects of Physical Aging on Behavior

All of these changes form the substrate of physical aging. To understand what we are each likely to experience as we get older it is obviously important to know something about changes in individual organs or in individual cells. Still, for most of us the crucial question is somewhat different: How will these changes affect my daily life? I've alluded to bits of answers to this question already, but let me focus on it more directly.

Slowing Down

The most significant general change in behavior resulting from all the body changes I have described is a quite distinct (and accurate) feeling of being slower as you get older.

You can see (or experience) this effect quite directly in athletic performance. In any sport, the top performers are in their teens or twenties, as you can see in Table 4.3. Even in sports in which endurance rather than speed is a critical variable, such as the marathon or long-distance swimming, record holders or top

TABLE 4.3. Age of Peak Performances in Various Sports.

Age	Men	Women
17		Swimming
18		
19	Swimming	
20		
21		
22		Running short distances
23	Running short distances	Jumping
24	Running medium distances	Running medium distances
	Jumping	
	Tennis	Tennis
25		
26		
27	Running long distances	Running long distances
28	Baseball	
29		
30		
31	Golf	Golf

SOURCE: Schulz & Curnow, 1988, Table 8, page P119. Reprinted with permission from *Journal of Gerontology: Psychological Sciences,* 43, pp. 113–120, 1988.

performers are in their twenties. Only among golfers are the peak performers in their 30s (Schulz and Curnow, 1988). It is true, of course, that sedentary 30-, 40-, 50-, or 60-year-olds can greatly improve their athletic performance by beginning and maintaining some sort of training. But for those who maintain fitness and high levels of competitive skill throughout their adult years, peak performance comes relatively early, after which there is a slowing down.

You can see (and experience) the loss of speed in your reaction time for various everyday activities as well, such as driving. Motor vehicle accidents are *most* common among young adults (presumably because they drive faster), but after a plateau in the years of middle adulthood, there is a rise in accident rate in the later years. The risk for a serious or fatal accident per mile driven is roughly half again greater for a 65-year-old than for a 40-year-old (Evans, 1988). Of course not all of this increased risk results from slower reaction time. Loss of visual acuity and slower visual response to changes in light and dark are also important ingredients. But the collective effect is that you lose some skill at such complex motor activities as driving.

You're likely to experience another kind of slowing down when your body has to adapt to extreme environments, such as heat, cold, or a large intake of sugar. The body's metabolism doesn't work as quickly, and the heating and cooling systems don't work as well either: Once you get cold, it is harder to warm up, and vice versa.

In later years, it also simply takes longer to do everyday tasks like tying your shoes or getting dressed. Not only is there a loss of some sensation in the fingers, there are also the arthritic changes in the joints to deal with. Stamina is also less for various reasons (e.g. the heart is less efficient, the lungs take in less air, the muscles are weaker), so older adults find that they can sustain mild or vigorous activity for shorter periods.

Sleep

Another consequence of the changes in the neurological system seems to be an increased likelihood of problems with sleeping. William Dement, one of the major sleep researchers, reports that with increasing age, especially after perhaps age 50 or 60, older adults wake up more often during the night and have fewer total hours of the type of sleep associated with the slowest brain waves—what in layman's terms we would call *deep sleep*—although there is no change in the number of hours of dreaming sleep (REM sleep). Breathing disturbances during sleep also become more common (Dement, Richardson, Prinz, Carskadon, Kripke, & Czeisler, 1985). Since repeated wakefulness in the night and lessened deep sleep mean that older adults are often getting insufficient night sleep, daytime napping becomes much more frequent. Thus, as we age, we are likely to experience a gradual but highly significant shift of our basic daily rhythms, with the once-a-day sleep/wake pattern broken up into much shorter cycles. Older adults nap more not because they are bored, but because they are not getting sufficient sleep at night. And the need for daytime napping, in turn, can have a major impact on one's daily life.

Sexual Activity

Another area in which many adults experience the consequences of all the changes of physical aging is in their sexual activity. As Kinsey reported years ago (Kinsey, Pomeroy & Martin, 1948, 1953), sexual activity in married couples declines quite steadily over the adult years. Kinsey's own figures showed a drop in the average frequency of intercourse from about 10 times per month in the early 20s to perhaps 2 times a month past 65. Other authors have observed higher rates at every age (e.g. Hunt, 1974), but the same basic pattern of decline. Of course the actual frequencies reported may be inflated, since these researchers are relying on self-reports from subjects who may tend to exaggerate sexual activity, but the overall decline with age is a consistent finding.

This is not just a "cohort problem," either, since longitudinal data show the same pattern, as you can see in Figure 4–8. These findings from the Duke longitudinal studies (Palmore, 1981) show that each group studied reported a decline in frequency of sexual intercourse over the years of the study (Palmore, 1981).

The rates of sexual activity are generally lower for women than for men, in large part because more women are unmarried (especially in the older years) and have difficulty finding a partner. But the shape of the age change pattern is the same for men and women.

What I find remarkable about the findings on sexual activity in adults is not that there is an average decline—a pattern we would expect, given the physical

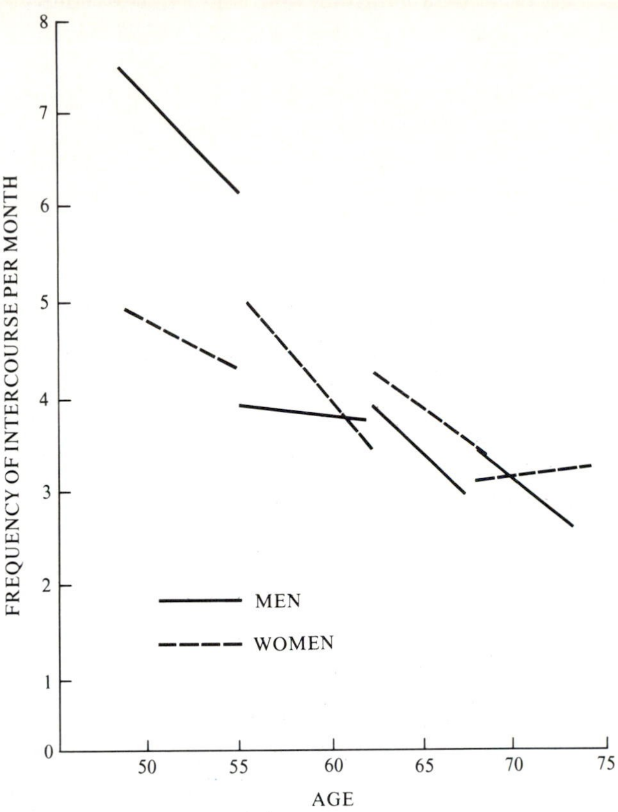

Figure 4–8 These longitudinal data show clearly that the frequency of sexual intercourse declines with age even among married adults, but that regular sexual activity is typical even among adults in their 70s. Each line in this graph reflects the reported sexual activity of one group of men or women over a period of six years. So, for example, the line in the upper left shows that men who were 50 at the beginning of the study reported intercourse an average of 7.5 times per month. Six years later, when they were 56, they reported an average of slightly over 6 times per month. (Source: Palmore, Erdman, Social Patterns in Normal Aging, *p. 88, Figure 6-4. Copyright 1981 Duke University Press.)*

changes occurring—but how many adults remain sexually active well into old age. In one questionnaire study by Consumers Union (Brecher, 1984) including 4,246 respondents over 50, 81 percent of married women and 50 percent of unmarried women over 70 reported at least *some* sexual activity during the past month (including masturbation as well as sex with a partner). The equivalent figures for married and unmarried men over 50 were 81 percent and 75 percent. And of those sexually active in this study, the majority reported that they had sex at least once a week, that they enjoyed sex, and that they experienced orgasm every time or almost every time.

These numbers do not come from a random sample of adults. The respondents in this study were all subscribers (or friends of subscribers) to *Consumers Report*. As a group they are well-educated and middle-class. But similar findings have emerged from the Duke longitudinal studies, which include a more representative sample of older adults. In the Duke study, like the Consumer Union study, over half of adults over 70 were still sexually active. Of those married and sexually active, as you can see in Figure 4–8, frequency of sex was about once a week.

These findings underline yet again an important point about physical changes in adulthood that I have made before: Yes, there is a slowing down of many reactions including sexual responses such as erection or lubrication. And yes, most adults experience an increase in physical ailments as they get older, some of which interfere with their daily functioning. But it is simultaneously true that most adults adapt to these changes with inventiveness and some grace, finding ways to continue activities that they enjoy. The *frequency* or vigor of various activities may decline (as sex does), but *enjoyment* of them need not.

Explanations of Physical Aging

So far, I've been giving descriptions of physical changes with age, some of them well documented, others not. But if accurate descriptions are difficult to come by, explanations of those changes are still harder. Joan Waring's summary of a decade ago is still valid:

> How the physical organism grows older is better understood than why. As yet there is no universally accepted theory as to what mechanism triggers the senescent changes that seem inevitably to increase the risk of death with increasing age. There is, however, an emerging consensus that more than one process is at work: Nature has an arsenal of fail-safe devices to ensure that people do not live forever. If disease or accident do not prove fatal, old age will. (Waring, 1981, p. 471)

Two categories of explanations are currently debated, one of which assumes that aging results from the accumulation of a long series of essentially random environmental insults or injuries to cells or genetic material, the other of which assumes that there is some built-in aging clock.

Random Events Theories of Aging

The basic argument is that, over time, the genetic material in cells is damaged in some fashion. Gerontologists who hold to this view (sometimes called the "hit" theory of aging) do not assume that the organism is actually programmed for specific maturational changes in senescence, but rather that the whole mechanism grinds slowly to a halt as the genetic information in cells throughout the body becomes more and more inaccurate through damage to the DNA within each cell. Such damage could occur from any of a series of random events, including particularly exposure to background levels of radiation. Such theories, once very popular, have gone out of favor as non-corroborating research information has accumulated (Cristofalo, 1988; Tice & Setlow, 1985). For example, when animals have been deliberately exposed to varying levels of radiation, researchers do often find that their lifespans have been shortened, but the shortening seems more often to come from increased disease than from processes that look like speeded-up normal aging.

Developmental-Genetic Theories: Aging Clocks

Currently more popular are theories that focus on aging as a built-in, programmed process. Just as the physical changes of childhood are maturationally controlled, so the sequence and rate of aging may be genetically programmed in some way. The disagreements among theorists in this group center on just what body system is the key to the process.

HAYFLICK LIMITS The most basic genetic argument centers around the observation that each species has a characteristic maximum life span. As I pointed out earlier, 100 or 110 years appears to be the effective maximum life span for humans (Hayflick, 1977, 1987) despite improvements in health care and successful campaigns against infectious diseases. This persuades biologists that there may be a genetic program setting the upper limit of functioning of each organism. Leonard Hayflick (1965, 1975) has provided further support for this idea from his research on the behavior of cells.

Hayflick observes that when human embryo cells are placed in nutrient solutions and observed over a period of time, the cells divide (doubling each time) only about 50 times, after which the cell colony degenerates. Even when the cells are frozen part way through this doubling process, when they are later thawed they "remember" where they were in the sequence, and still double only a total of about 50 times. When cells are taken from human adults, they double fewer times (perhaps 20 times) before the cell colony degenerates. Furthermore, cells from the embryos of longer-lived creatures (such as the Galapagos tortoise) double perhaps 100 times, whereas chicken cells double only about 25 times. Thus, there appears to be a rough correlation between the typical longevity of each species and the number of cell divisions each organism's cells are "programmed" to complete. Thus aging, or at least ultimate death, may result from reaching the "Hayflick Limit," and exhausting the ability of the cells to replicate themselves.

REPAIR OF GENETIC MATERIAL Another theory in this category focuses on changes in the ability of cells to repair breaks in DNA. Some breaks in DNA strands are apparently a common daily event, resulting from some unknown metabolic processes. Such DNA damage could result in aging in either of two ways. First, if the organism is not able to repair all of the damage (as appears to be the case), then over time the accumulation of unrepaired damage would produce gradual decline. As Raymond Tice and Richard Setlow put it:

> The number of DNA damages . . . is not trivial. Presumably, when the frequency of DNA lesions reaches a certain level and/or specific genes become inactive, a loss in cellular function ensues. As the proportion of such cells increases in various tissues, the organism "ages."(1985, p. 209)

Alternatively, or additionally, perhaps the ability to repair DNA breakage itself decreases as the organism gets older. Some research does support this second alternative (e.g. Hartnell, Morley, & Mooradian, 1989) but the findings have been very inconsistent. We simply don't yet know if older organisms are less able to repair cellular or genetic damage than are younger ones. But such a finding is not necessary for the damage theory to account for aging, as long as one assumes that the organism at any given age is unable to repair all of the damage that occurs so that the total amount of damage accumulates.

A related type of theory focuses on another cellular process called **cross-linking,** which *has* been found to occur more often in cell proteins in older than in younger adults. In skin and in connective tissue, for example, two proteins called collagen and elastin form bonds, called cross-linkages, either between molecules, or within a given protein molecule. This decreases the efficiency of the protein. Since collagen and elastin are involved in the elasticity of many tissues, including the skin and the blood vessels, cross-linking helps to explain the increased wrinkling of the skin with age and may also be one cause of some kinds of cardiovascular disease. It seems probable that similar accumulations of cellular malfunctions may lie at the heart of other observed patterns of bodily aging.

ORGAN SYSTEM BREAKDOWNS Still other theorists focus their attention not on individual cells but on entire organ systems. They argue that what we see as aging is the result of progressive failures of key organs or organ systems—failure that is, in turn, assumed to be programmed directly into the system.

We know, for example, that there are certain predictable changes that take place in blood vessels, such as increasing brittleness and loss of elasticity, as well as narrowing resulting from the accumulation of fatty acid deposits (such as cholesterol). Since circulation of the blood is one of the keys to the nourishment of the entire body, any decrease in the efficiency of circulation will affect all other organ systems.

We also know that the immune system becomes gradually less efficient with age as the thymus becomes less and less able to facilitate the full maturation of T cells. And we know that the neurological system undergoes systematic changes with age, as cells lose dendrites and inter-cell communication declines in both speed and efficiency. Any one of these sets of changes may lie at the heart of what we see as aging.

Combining Theories

No one of these views seems to account for all of what we see as physical aging. We might do better by combining elements of several of the theories I have described: Over time there appears to be an accumulation of changes at the cellular level, either because the system is reaching the end point of its genetically programmed reproductive capacity or because small errors accumulate. Eventually these cellular changes are enough to alter the efficient functioning of many organ systems, which in turn makes us each more susceptible to various diseases or major breakdown. At the same time, hormonal changes (such as the changes of the climacteric), and perhaps others of the changes in body systems or cells, appear to be programmed in the genetic code itself. What we see as physical aging is the result of *all* of these factors working together. Another form of synthesis is offered by Vincent Cristofalo:

> One way to envision the organism's aging scenario is that each cell and tissue type has its own aging trajectory. Death occurs when homeostasis in one of the more rapidly aging components of the organism falls beyond the point necessary to maintain the organism. (1988, p. 126)

Pulling the Threads Together: An Overview of Body Changes in Adulthood

From the myriad details of physical aging I have given you in the past few pages, I can extract some summary statements that may help you to organize the information. Vincent Cristofalo (1988) suggests five such generalizations, to which Caleb Finch (1988) adds a sixth: With increasing age in adulthood

1. There is increased mortality (a pretty basic point, but worth restating!).
2. There are many changes in the chemical composition of the body, including quantities and balance of hormones, change in lean body mass and fat, reduction in neurotransmitters in the nervous system, and many others.
3. There is a broad range of progressive deteriorative changes, such as loss of tissue elasticity, reduction of dendrites in the nerve cells, wear and tear in the joints and in the ear, loss of visual acuity, etc.
4. There is a reduced ability to respond adaptively to environmental change, such as exercise, stress, darkness, light, or high or low temperature.
5. There is increased vulnerability to disease as the immune system works less and less efficiently.
6. There is increased instability of biorhythms, not only in such monthly cycles as menstruation in women in their 30s and 40s, but sleep-wake patterns as well.

The same basic information can also be arrayed in a table like Table 4.4, summarizing the physical characteristics of young, middle-aged, and older adults. When you look at the information this way, you can see that adults are clearly at their physical peak in the years from 20 to 35 or 40. They have the greatest strength, the most efficient functioning of body systems, the least likelihood of chronic disease. Reaction times are fast, and everyday tasks are easily accomplished. In the years of midlife, from 40 to 60 or 65, the rate of physical change or ill health varies widely from one individual to the next, with some experiencing a loss of physical function quite early, others much later. Reaction time does begin to decline in this age span, however, as does strength, and there are measurable changes in cellular functioning beginning to accumulate. The risk of death rises, as does the risk of chronic disease.

TABLE 4.4. Summary of Age Changes in the Physical Body.

Age 20–40	Age 40–65	Age 65 and older
The head grows and changes shape.	Height is lost slowly.	Height continues to be lost.
	Skin and other tissues begin to lose elasticity.	Continuation of loss of elasticity of tissues
Peak of sensory acuity	Senses begin to be less acute starting at about age 50, but these changes are still small enough to make little difference in daily life.	More rapid loss of sensory acuity; loss of taste, smell, and hearing are particularly noticeable and may have significant effects on daily living.
Peak of physical strength, stamina, aerobic fitness, athletic skill	Beginning decline in strength, in heart and lung function under work conditions; large individual differences, and little effect on daily life	Continued loss of strength, stamina, aerobic fitness; less change in physically active adults. Loss begins to affect daily life.
Nervous system at maximum efficiency	Beginning changes in nervous system	Further loss of dendrites and nerve conductance speed;
Optimum reproductive period	Climacteric, with accompanying changes in hormones and genitalia	Possibly additional hormone changes
Immune system at peak efficiency	Loss of size of thymus; loss of efficiency of immune system	Significant increase in susceptibility to disease as immune system declines further
Peak of sexual activity	Sexual activity declines in frequency, but virtually all adults are still sexually active.	Frequency of sexual activity declines further, but majority with sexual partners continue some sexual activity.

In the later years of adulthood, from 65 onward, the loss of speed of response continues and is now matched by loss of sensory acuity and by significant increases in chronic diseases. But here, too, there are wide individual differences in the rate of change, and effective compensations that can maintain perfectly adequate (or even excellent) physical functioning for many adults well into their 70s or 80s.

I am sure that summaries like this one are helpful; no doubt this is the section you will come back to when you are reviewing for examinations. But I don't want to end here. Given the state of our knowledge about physical aging, especially in view of rapidly shifting views about the speed or inevitability of certain changes, these summaries are too tidy. They gloss over both our ignorance and the wide individual variation in aging experience that actually exists. So let me end this chapter by commenting on some of the recurrent questions and themes.

Some Recurrent Themes and Remaining Questions

Are the Changes Gradual?

I've described a great many changes in our physical bodies, usually including some phrase such as "the change begins at roughly age 50 and continues thereafter." Such statements imply that the changes are gradual and at a constant rate, but is that really true?

Certainly it is not true for every aspect of physical aging. In some cases, such as the loss of smell sensitivity, there seems to be a very gradual decline until roughly age 65 or 70, after which the decline becomes much more marked. In Chapter 6 you'll see that declines in many mental abilities follow a similar trajectory. In other cases, there may be a more gradual decline that begins in early adulthood and simply continues, like the increasing layers in the lens of the eye. The truth seems to be that different body systems "age" at quite widely different rates. So it is a mistake for us to think of "aging" as some uniform process.

Another facet of the same point is that even for some physical functions in which there *is* gradual change beginning fairly early in adult life, there may be no *functional* change—no required change in behavior, no new compensation—until much later. Changes in the eye are already going on in your 20s but do not reach the critical point at which you will probably need glasses until you are in your 40s; loss of calcium in the bones begins after menopause for women (unless they take hormone replacements) but typically does not reach the point of major risks of fractures until several decades later; changes in the male reproductive system begin in your 40s but, at least for many men, do not require adjustment of sexual practices until much later—if then.

Are These Changes Basic Processes of Aging? Or Are They Results of Disease or Environmental Events?

I've already given you examples of a number of previously widely-accepted conclusions about aging that have recently been called into question as studies of healthy adults have pointed to very different conclusions. Loss of neurons is much less than we'd estimated from studies that included adults with neurological disease; lung and circulatory efficiency at rest is retained better through adult life than we had thought; testosterone levels seem to be maintained in healthy men well into old age.

Clearly we need to know a good deal more about *healthy* aging before we draw too gloomy a picture. But let us not swing too far into rosy optimism, either. Even healthy adults do age. The degree and kind of that aging seems to be a result of some interaction between basic aging processes and specific environmental influences.

A very nice example of this kind of interaction comes from studies of hearing loss. Figure 4–9 shows, in simplified form, both the basic descriptive evidence on the relationship between age and hearing loss and explanatory evidence exploring

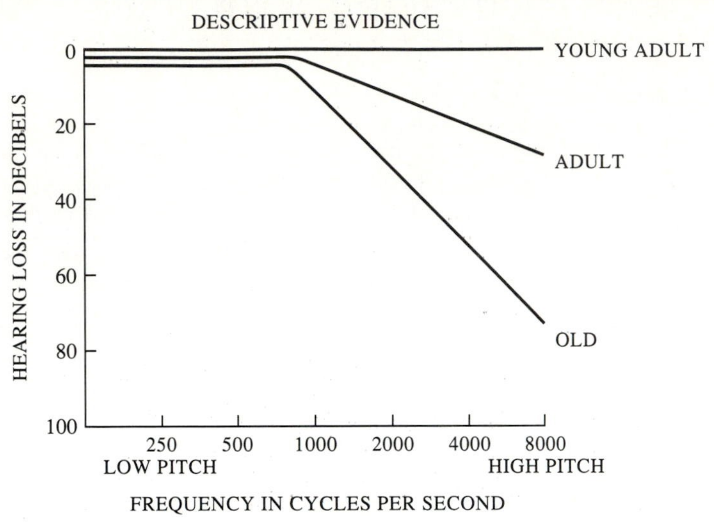

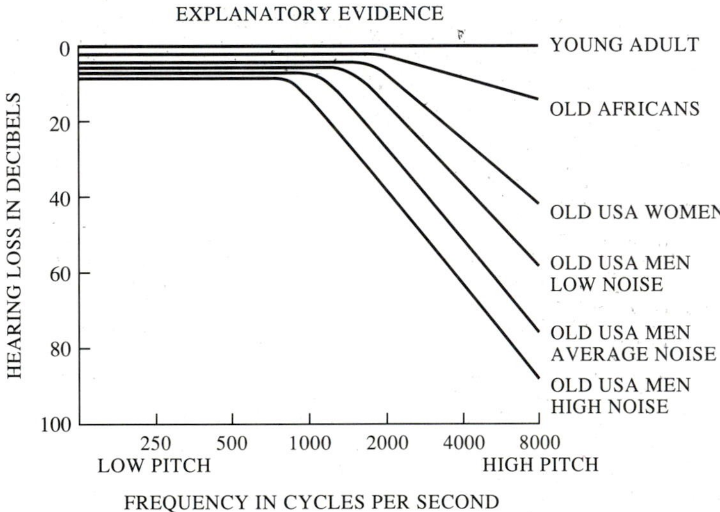

Figure 4–9 The upper figure shows the general pattern of age changes in hearing loss at various pitches (cycles per second). All this gives us is the basic descriptive information. It does not tell us if such declines are a part of normal aging, or whether they are produced by specific environmental events. The lower figure explores one set of explanatory possibilities, namely that the hearing loss is the result of noise exposure. Not only do these results tell us something about hearing loss; they also illustrate the usefulness of comparing aging patterns in different subgroups of adults who have had different life experiences. (Source: Baltes, Reese, & Nesselroade, 1977. Copyright Wadsworth Publishing Company. Reprinted with permission.)

the role of environmental influences. What this suggests is that while *some* hearing loss is a normal aspect of aging—since even adults in very quiet environments have some wear and tear on the auditory system—a great deal of the loss we associate with aging in this country is linked not just to age but to exposure to noise. Within U.S. samples, men with greater noise exposure have far more hearing loss than do those with less exposure. Women, with possibly even less exposure to high decibel noise in their work places, show still less, and adults from other cultures in which there is very low noise level show still less. Pursuing the same line of reasoning, audiologists are concerned that today's younger generations, many of whom have made a practice of listening to extremely loud music, especially over earphones, will have much higher rates of hearing loss in middle and old age.

In a similar vein, loss of elasticity in the skin has been linked to sun exposure: The more exposure to sun, the faster the rate of deterioration of skin tissue is a research conclusion that has led to recent recommendations from dermatologists and others that we should all avoid sunburn or tanning as much as possible.

A similar message comes from recent studies of the impact of stress on the immune system (Braveman, 1987). It begins to look as if the immune system shows declines in efficiency not only as a normal aspect of aging but also in response to stress. Adults who experience some major life stress, such as the death of a spouse or a close friend, show at least temporarily lower levels of T cells than do other adults of the same ages. Thus, specific experience can not only affect body functioning, it also interacts with underlying maturational processes to produce faster "aging."

At the other end of the spectrum, some environments may retard the changes we describe as normal aging or even reverse it. There are hints, for example, that adult animals placed in environments with younger animals, or in visually enriched environments, show actual increases in thickness of their cortexes and in speed of neuronal processes. These hints are supported by findings with humans. Those adults who remain physically active and who choose more stimulating activities and environments appear to "age" more slowly.

These examples, and many more like them, should lead us all to be cautious about drawing too sweeping conclusions about "normal aging." In particular, they point to the wide variability in individual experiences of aging.

Individual Differences in Aging Patterns and Rate

When we look directly at individual differences, it becomes even more clear that almost any generalization about physical aging is going to be inaccurate.

When we study groups, whether cross-sectionally or longitudinally, and then display the results as averages for each age range (as I have done repeatedly in figures in this chapter) we run the risk of conveying the impression that each person's pattern or trajectory is roughly the same as the overall curve. What we are discovering from the ongoing longitudinal studies is that that is simply not the case. There are really huge individual differences in the pattern and rate of physical changes with age. Nathan Shock, who has been involved in one of the major longitudinal studies, the Baltimore Longitudinal Studies of Aging, puts it this way:

> . . . relatively few individuals follow the pattern of age changes predicted from averages based on measurements made on different subjects. Aging is so highly individual that average curves [even from longitudinal data] give only a rough approximation of the pattern of aging followed by individuals. (Shock, 1985, p. 740)

He goes on to point out that because of the wide variability at any one age, age itself is actually quite a poor predictor of performance. That is, if all you know about someone is his or her age, you could *not* make a very good prediction of her blood pressure, weight, hormone levels, immune system response, or whatever. Even for those functions where we are reasonably sure that the *average* changes with age reflect basic, underlying, inevitable processes of physical aging/maturation, there are still very large individual differences at any given age, and wide differences in the patterns of change with age.

Two examples from the Baltimore studies make this clear. Shock reports on a measure of kidney function (creatinine clearance) in three different men, each of whom had been studied over a period of years. Averaged across many subjects, creatinine clearance shows the typical decline with age, even in a sample of healthy adults. But as you can see in Figure 4–10, when we look at individuals we see much less commonality. One of the older men in the figure showed a gradual decline from age 60 to age 80; the other showed much higher levels until roughly age 70, after which his kidney function declined rapidly.

As a second example, in the longitudinal study of changes in muscle mass among the Baltimore subjects that I showed in Figure 4–4, nearly a quarter of subjects between the ages of 40 to 59 and 15 percent of those over 60 showed *no* decline in grip strength over the nine years of this study, even though the averages declined quite markedly during those same years (Kallman, Plato, & Tobin, 1990).

I could give many other examples. Physical aging is simply not nearly as uniform as is the maturation of the early years of life. If we know a child is 2 years old we can make some very good predictions about a whole range of physical functions. To be sure, over *wide* differences in adult age, we could also make some reasonable predictions; 20-year-olds *are* different from 80-year-olds, no matter what environment the 80-year-old has been living in. But certainly between 30 and 65 or 70, there are a great many pathways.

What could account for such differences? A number of obvious possibilities come immediately to mind:

Specific Experience The most obvious possibility is that our specific experiences affect the rate, or even the pattern, of physical aging. (Of course, the very fact that this is true changes the whole meaning of the idea of "normal aging.") I've already given a number of examples of environmental factors that we know make a difference, including noise level, emotional stress, and general

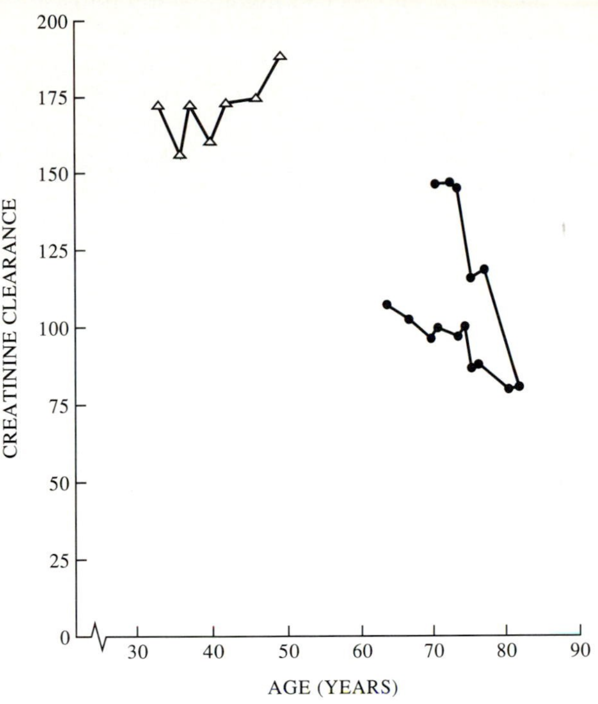

Figure 4–10 *You can get some sense of the degree of individual variation in physical aging from this figure, which shows repeated scores on one measure of kidney function (creatinine clearance) for three different men, each followed longitudinally. The youngest subject in this figure actually improved in kidney function during middle adulthood, and of the two older subjects, one showed a gradual drop, the other a very rapid drop after a period of maintenance. (Source: Shock, 1985, Figure 3, p. 732).*

level of stimulation. One I have not talked about, but that appears to be a highly significant factor, is exercise.

Exercise: Use it or Lose it My interest in this particular aspect of aging stems in part, I am sure, from my own decision at the age of 38 to begin exercising and running or walking regularly. Like most "converts" (such as ex-smokers) I can be a bit of a bore on the subject. But in this case, my point is well-buttressed by research.

For example, I pointed out earlier that maximum oxygen uptake (VO_2 max) under work conditions typically declines about 40 percent in adulthood, which means that older adults, except when at rest, are getting less oxygen to the brain, the muscles, and all other parts of the body. At any age, however, VO_2 max can be significantly increased with exercise (Ostrow, 1984; Blumenthal, Emery, Madden, George, Coleman, Riddle, McKee, Reasoner, & Williams, 1989). And adults who have maintained fitness continuously beginning in their 20s have still higher levels of oxygen uptake.

Regular exercise also seems to slow other specific aspects of "normal aging," including loss of calcium in the bone (Sorock, Bush, Golden, Fried, Breuer, & Hale, 1988) and loss of reaction time speed (Baylor & Spirduso, 1988). It also reduces significantly the risk of some diseases, most particularly coronary heart disease (Paffenbarger & Hyde, 1984; Serfass & Gerberich, 1984), and may even increase longevity (Holloszy, 1988). Current evidence suggests that the minimum amount of exercise required to maintain fitness is about 20-60 minutes, three times a week, at an intensity level that will bring the heart rate to about 70-80 percent of maximum (Serfass & Gerberich, 1984).

The growing body of evidence on the link between physical functioning and exercise points to an intriguing possibility: At least *some* of the patterns of body change that we think of as inevitable facets of aging may instead (or in addition) be the result of disuse. In specific support of this possibility, Walter Bortz (1982) points out that astronauts in weightlessness and patients given prolonged bed rest show many of the body changes we normally think of as aging, including increases in blood pressure, loss of a sense of balance, loss of red blood cells, loss of body weight and increase in body fat, a loss of calcium in the bones, even decreased taste sensitivity. Since most adults (in Western societies) become less active as they grow older, at least some "aging" changes may be "disuse" changes. As the adage goes, "use it or lose it."

Nancy Denney (1982) has proposed a very useful general model (Figure 4–11) to describe the relationship between activity/exercise and functioning. (The model works equally well for describing patterns of aging of intellectual abilities, by the way, so we will meet it again in Chapter 6.) She proposes that over age there is a common pattern of rise and then fall in many skills, abilities, or body functions. The particular shape of the curve may differ for different abilities or functions, but the general pattern is certainly common. This basic curve holds whether the person "uses" or "exercises" that ability or body function or not. But the *level* of the curve is higher for those skills or functions that are well exercised.

Two implications of the model are worth emphasizing. First, at any given age, adults who have exercised some ability (such as those who have increased their maximum oxygen uptake by aerobic exercise, or those who have used their taste buds more by sampling a wide variety of flavors, or who have lifted weights or have kept up typing skills, or whatever) will show a level of that skill or body function which is like that of a younger, unexercised person. So in this sense, the process of aging can be slowed.

A second implication of Denney's model is that it should be possible at any age to improve the level of any unexercised skill or body function by beginning to exercise it. *The maximum level you will be able to reach will decline as you get older,* but some improvement should be possible. Research on the effect of aerobic exercise on maximum oxygen uptake confirms this: Regardless of age, adults who begin physical exercise show some increase in aerobic capacity (Ostrow, 1984; Shock, 1977; Blumenthal et al., 1989).

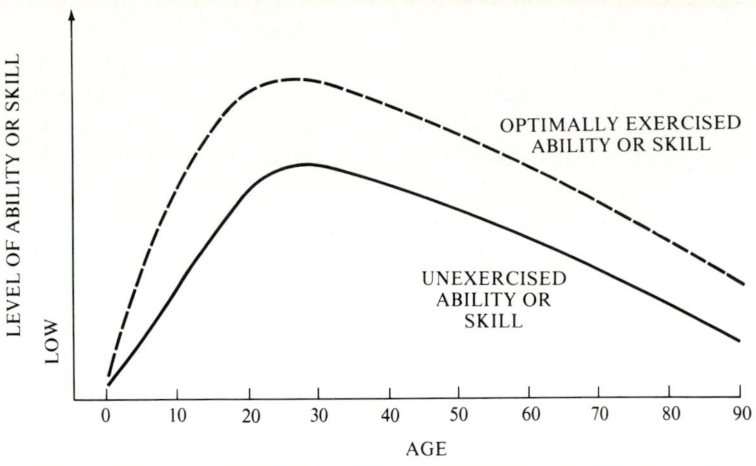

Figure 4–11 Nancy Denney has proposed this general model of age changes in "unexercised" and "exercised" activities. We might also use the term "base rate" instead of "unexercised." This lower curve is intended to represent the normal pattern of aging for any body function (or mental skill) without any special training or effort. The upper curve shows what the pattern of changes might be like for the same function or skill if special training or effort are applied. (Source: N. W. Denney, "Aging and Cognitive Changes" in Handbook of Developmental Psychology, *B. B. Wolman, Ed., copyright 1982, p. 819. Reprinted by permission of Prentice-Hall, Inc., Englewood Cliffs, NJ.)*

Bortz sums up nicely:

> It is wrong to suggest that exercise might halt the fall of the grains of sand in the hourglass. It is proposed, however, that the dimension of the aperture may be responsive to the toning influence of physical activity, and consequently the sand may drain more slowly. A physically active life may allow us to approach our true biogenetic potential for longevity. (1982, p. 1206)

HEREDITY We each also inherit specific genes that help to shape the pattern of our physical aging. Patterns of balding, for example, run in families as does the tendency to premature graying of hair (a gene I inherited).

If you have had a complete physical exam in which a full medical history is taken, you'll also realize that susceptibility to some specific diseases runs in families as well. Most physicians will ask you about the disease history of your parents, your grandparents, even your aunts and uncles. In particular, they are likely to ask you about the family patterns of heart disease, diabetes, and cancer (particularly breast cancer), each of which has been shown to be genetically influenced. Some other diseases that may have similar genetic components are ulcers, kidney disease, and perhaps Alzheimer's disease (Smith, Bierman & Robinson, 1978; Upton, 1977).

A propensity for alcoholism is also inherited (Schuckit, 1984). This is most clearly shown in studies of adopted children: Children of alcoholics who are adopted in early infancy and raised in nonalcoholic families are still about four times as likely to become alcoholics themselves in adulthood as are comparable adopted children born to nonalcoholic parents (Goodwin, 1984).

Interestingly, longevity seems to be partially inherited, which may mean that whatever body processes control the overall rate of aging are themselves controlled by specific genes or combinations of genes. If your grandparents and your parents have lived to ripe old ages, the chances are very good that you will as well, barring accidents or infectious diseases (McClearn & Foch, 1985).

You can add up many of these factors in making a prediction of your own longevity using the list in Table 4.5. As you do this, you'll notice that while many of the items are factors over which you have no control, many of the most significant items *are* controllable, or partially controllable, such as smoking and body weight.

TABLE 4.5. Calculating Your Own Longevity.

Respond to each item honestly, and sum the various positive and negative factors to arrive at the approximate number of years more (or less) than average you are likely to live.

Heredity	
For each grandparent who lived past age 80, add 1 year.	——
For each grandparent who lived to 70 but not 80, add 1/2 year.	——
If your mother lived past 80, add 4 years.	——
If your father lived past 80, add 2 years.	——
For each grandparent, parent, or sibling who died of any type of heart disease before age 50, subtract 4 years.	——
For each such relative dying of heart disease between age 50 and 60, subtract 2 years.	——
For each grandparent, parent, or sibling who died of diabetes or ulcers before age 60, subtract 3 years.	——
Women: for each sister or mother who died of breast cancer before age 60, subtract 1 year.	——
If your intelligence is *superior*, add two years.	——
Health History	
If your mother was younger than 18 or older than 35 at your birth, subtract 1 year.	——
If you are the first born in your family, add one year.	——
Women: If you have had no children (or plan no children) subtract 1/2 year.	——
If you have an annual physical exam, add 2 years.	——
Current Health	
If your weight is 10–30 percent above ideal weight shown in standard tables, the amount you must subtract depends on your age and gender. For women: subtract 5 years if you are between 20 and 30; 4 years if you are between 30 and 50, and 2 years if you are over 50. For men: subtract 10 years if you are between 20 and 30, 4 years if you are between 30 and 45, and 2 years for any age over that.	——
If your weight is more than 30 percent above standard tables: Women subtract 6 1/2 years if you are between 20 and 30, 5 years if you are between 30 and 50, and 4 years thereafter. Men subtract 13 if you are between 20 and 30, 6 if you are between 30 and 40, and 4 years thereafter.	——
If your diet is genuinely low in fat and sugar, and you never eat past the feeling of fullness, add 1 year.	——
If you smoke 2 or more packs a day, subtract 12 years; if you smoke 1–2 packs a day, subtract 7 years; if you smoke less than 1 pack a day, subtract 2 years.	——

If you never drink, neither add nor subtract; if you are a heavy drinker, subtract 8; if you are a moderate drinker *add* 3; if you are a light drinker, *add* 1 1/2.	____
If you do some aerobic exercise at least 3 times a week, add 3.	____
If you sleep more than 10 or less than 6 hours per night, subtract 2.	____
If you have intimate sexual relations once or twice a week, add 2.	____
If you have a chronic health condition (e.g. high blood pressure, diabetes, ulcer, cancer) or are frequently ill, subtract 5.	____
Your Current Life	
If you have 4 or more years of college, add 3; if you have 1–3 years of college, add 2; if you have completed high school and gone no further, add 1; if you have less than 8th grade, subtract 2.	____
If your occupation is at a professional, technical, or managerial level, add 1 year; if you work at unskilled work, subtract 4.	____
If your family income is above average for your education and occupation, add 1 year; if it is below average subtract 1.	____
If your job is a physically active one, add 2; if it is sedentary, subtract 2.	____
If you now live in an urban area and have lived in urban areas most of your life, subtract 1; if you have spent most of your life in a rural area, add 1.	____
If you are married and living with your spouse, add 1.	____
If you are separated or divorced, subtract 9 if you are a man, 4 if you are a woman.	____
If you are widowed, subtract 7 if you are a man, 4 if you are a woman.	____
If you are a never-married woman, subtract 1 year for each decade unmarried past age 25.	____
If you are a never-married man and living with family, subtract 1 year for each decade unmarried past 25; if you live alone, subtract 2 years for each decade unmarried past 25.	____
If you have at least two close friends in whom you can confide, add 1.	____
If your personality is noticeably aggressive and hostile and you feel regularly under time pressure, subtract 2–5 depending on how much the description fits.	____
If you are a calm, relaxed, easy-going person who adapts well to whatever happens, add 1–3 depending on how well the description fits.	____
If you are a basically happy person and have a lot of fun in life, add 2 years.	____
If you have had an episode of being depressed or very tense, guilty, or worried that lasted as long as a year or more, subtract 1–3 depending on how severe the depression was.	____
If you take a lot of risks, or live in a high crime neighborhood, subtract 2 years; if you use seatbelts regularly, and generally avoid risks, add 1 year.	____
TOTAL:	________

SOURCE: Adapted from Woodruff-Pak, 1988, pp. 145–154.

A Final Word

There is a fine line to be tread here between the overly optimistic and the overly pessimistic views of physical changes over adulthood. The sands *do* run through the hourglass and cannot be permanently stayed. And certainly many older adults, crippled by chronic disease or restricted by loss of physical skill or function, find their older bodies painful, uncomfortable, or distressing. But it is also true that, within limits, there are *choices* we can each make—beginning in early adulthood—that will delay or ease these changes, and there are attitudes or strategies to adopt that make the adjustments easier.

Summary

1. While the average life expectancy has been increasing steadily over the past decades, now reaching approximately 78 years for women and 71 years for men in the United States, the maximum life span appears to have remained the same, at about 100 or 110.
2. Body changes in adulthood include changes in external appearance such as loss of height, redistribution of fat, loss of hair, loss of elasticity in skin and other organs.
3. Loss of acuity in the senses also occurs, so that by age 65 or 70, 70 percent of adults have some visual loss, and 30 percent or more have significant hearing loss. Taste buds decline in number, and both taste and smell are reduced in acuity.
4. A loss of muscle tissue is another body change, as is a loss of bone marrow and a loss of calcium in the bones (osteoporosis).
5. The cardiovascular system shows a steady decrease in maximum oxygen uptake and in cardiac output under work conditions, but no changes when the body is at rest. Blood pressure increases with age under either work or resting states.
6. The nervous system shows little loss of cells, but it does show significant loss of dendritic connections and neurotransmitter sites. Nerve conductive speed declines.
7. The immune system declines in efficiency with age as the thymus gland decreases in size and in ability to support the growth of T cells. Older adults become more susceptible to disease and are more likely to develop autoimmune disorders.
8. Both men and women experience a loss of reproductive capacity in middle and old age through a series of changes in hormones and reproductive organs collectively called the climacteric. In men, there is a reduced production of sperm, some loss of genital tissue, and greater difficulty in achieving and sustaining an erection. In women, menstruation ceases at about age 50 (on average), and this change is accompanied by other physical changes in the genitals. Many women also experience hot flashes during the years leading up to menopause.
9. The physical changes listed also affect daily behavior, most generally by slowing speed for many activities but also affecting sleep/wake cycles and sexual activity.
10. Two categories of explanation of physical aging are currently offered: Those emphasizing the cumulative effect of random external insults (such as radiation) and the other focused on basic, internal, genetically-programmed changes in cells or organ systems.
11. One cellular factor is the ability of the body to repair breaks in DNA strands. Accumulated genetic errors from unrepaired breaks may eventually produce what we know as aging.
12. Another genetic argument is based on the observation that cells from each species have a particular capacity to reproduce themselves, thus limiting the life span.

13. Still other internal/developmental theories are based on changes in specific organ systems, such as the cardiovascular system, the immune system, or the nervous system.
14. Not all changes in the physical body that we associate with aging are gradual over the adult years. Some only begin late in life; some start early but have an impact on behavior only much later.
15. At least some of the changes we associate with "aging" may be due to disease, environmental influences, or interactions between basic physiological changes and environment, such as in the impact of noise on hearing loss.
16. Individual differences in rate and pattern of aging are extremely large, affected not only by differing heredity but by differing experiences, including exercise.
17. Exercise or physical activity has been linked to slower aging processes in several systems, lowered risk of disease, and greater capacity for physical exertion. At least some of the body changes normally thought of as "aging" may be, instead (or in addition), the result of disuse.

Suggested Readings

BRECHER, E. M. (1984). *Love, sex, and aging.* Boston, MA: Little, Brown. This book reports on the results of a very interesting survey of over 6,000 adults over the age of 50 who described their sexual behavior over their life span. The sample is not altogether representative, but the report is still fascinating.

HORN, J. C. (1988, DECEMBER). The peak years. *Psychology Today,* pp. 62–63. A brief report on the Schulz and Curnow study of the relationship between age and peak performance in sports of various kinds.

OSTROW, A. C. (1984). *Physical activity and the older adult. Psychological perspectives.* Princeton, NJ: Princeton Book Company. Ostrow has not written this book for the beginning student; it is written for psychologists, so is densely filled with research references and analyses. But it is a very readable, current, complete discussion not only of physical changes in aging, but of the impact of exercise on those changes.

SEKULER, R., & BLAKE, R. (1987, December). Sensory underload. *Psychology Today, 21,* pp. 48–51. As we age, senses become less acute. This readable paper discusses these changes and talks about some of the ways in which adults compensate for the loss.

The following two articles originally appeared in relatively unaccessible places, but have been reprinted in Readings in Adult Development and Aging, *(Little, Brown, 1982) edited by K. Warner Schaie & James Geiwitz. Both are excellent and not too complex.*

HAYFLICK, L. (1975). Why grow old? *The Stanford Magazine,* 3 (1) 36–43.

ROSSMAN, I. (1980). Bodily changes with aging. In E. W. Busse & D. G. Blazer (Eds.), *Handbook of geriatric psychiatry.* (pp. 135–158). New York: Van Nostrand Reinhold.

CHAPTER 5

Changes in Health and Health Habits in Adulthood

One of the myths about adult life is that retirement is a real bummer. Certainly among my well-educated friends the word is out that people wither up when they retire. But that's *not* what the research tells us: The research says that it is only when people retire *in ill-health* that they are likely to have a bad experience. We also know that adults who experience some health limitation or chronic disease are much less satisfied with their lives than are those who are in better health (Campbell, 1981). I'll have a lot more to say about life satisfaction and about retirement in later chapters. My point for now is that if we are going to understand the experience of physical aging it is not enough to chart changes in nervous system or arteries or reaction time. We also have to look at changes in health and disease in adulthood and at the impact of health or ill-health on our daily lives (and vice versa).

Overall Age Patterns in Health and Disease

Let's begin at the simplest descriptive level: What do adults of various ages die of? What kind of nonfatal diseases do they have?

Mortality: Causes of Death

Figure 5–1 condenses some of the key information about deaths and their causes at various ages. The upper part of the figure shows the probability of dying in any one year, for all adults in that age range. You can see that less than one-tenth of one percent of adults aged 15 to 24 die in any given year, whereas over 15 percent of adults over 85 die each year. The fact that older people are more likely to die is surely no great surprise (although you may be comforted to see how flat the curve is as late as 55 to 64). More interesting are the causes of death at each age.

If you examine the figure closely, you'll see that when young people die, they do not typically die of disease but of accidents, suicide, or homicide. Nearly 60 percent of deaths in the United States among adults aged 25 to 34 are from one of these three causes. In contrast, heart disease and cancer—the two leading causes of death at present—do not account for a significant percentage of deaths until the 35 to 44 age range, after which they account for the preponderance of deaths.

Morbidity: The General Pattern of Physical Illnesses with Age

Chronic and Acute Diseases

You might assume that a similar age pattern would emerge for illnesses, too, with older adults suffering from more of all types of diseases. But as you can see from Figure 5–2, that's not quite true. The chance that you will have an "acute" illness (a short-term disease, lasting from a few days to no more than three months) is actually higher in young adulthood. The expected rise in risk with age occurs only for "chronic" illnesses (a continuing disorder, such as heart disease, or arthritis, or high blood pressure). In your 20s and 30s, you catch more colds, have the flu more often, and have more minor

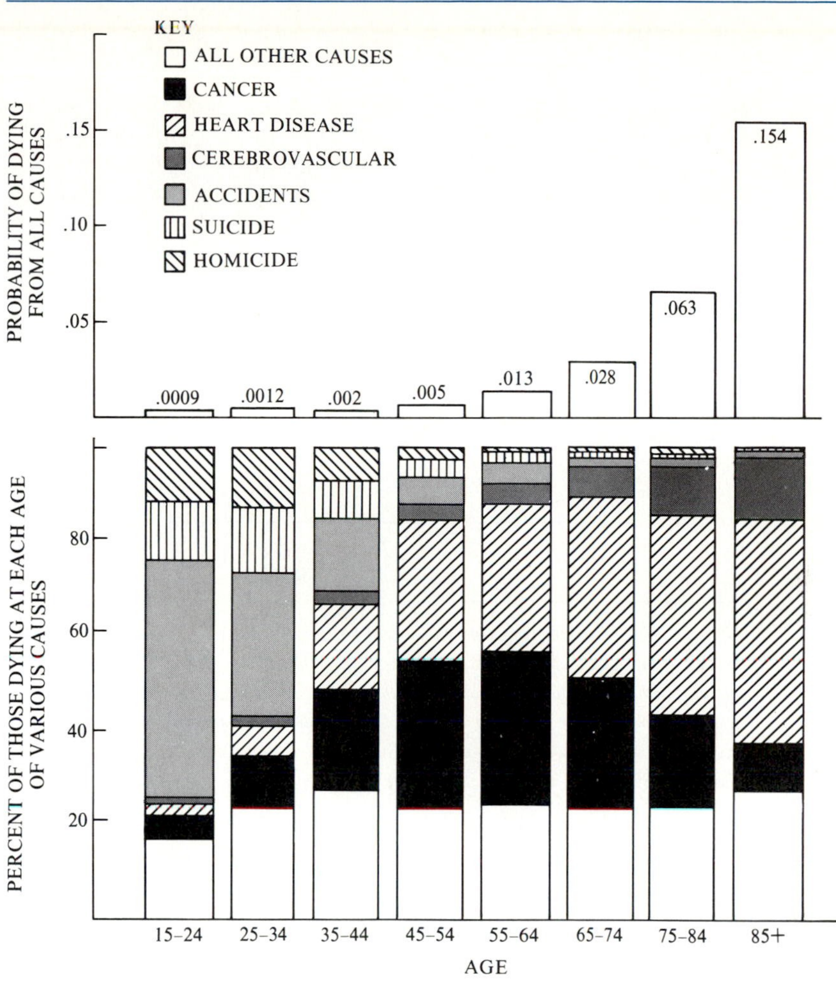

Figure 5–1 The upper part of this figure shows the probability of dying, for adults in each of a series of age groups, in the United States in 1983. The lower part of the figure shows, for each age group, the percentages who died from each of several types of disease or other cause. Proportionately, many more young people die of accidents, suicide, and homicide, whereas beginning in the 45 to 54 age group, cancer and heart disease are the major causes of death. (Source: U.S. Bureau of the Census, 1984, 32(13).)

accidents that limit your activity for at least a day. But you have a much lower risk of having a diagnosed chronic disease. In contrast, post-retirement age adults have fewer acute illnesses but a high rate of chronic disorders. And because a person is more likely to see a physician for a chronic than for an acute problem, doctor visits more than double between early and late adulthood (U.S. Bureau of the Census, 1989a).

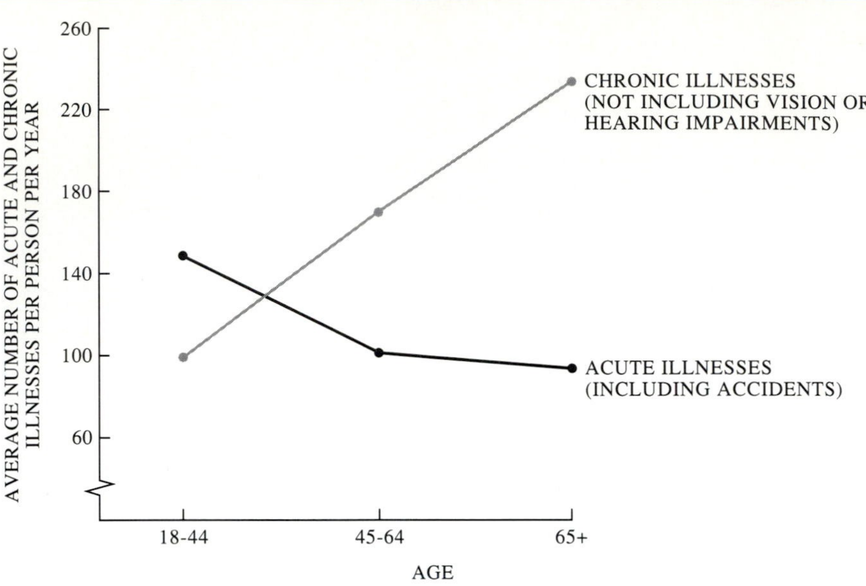

Figure 5–2 The number of acute (short-term) illnesses tends to go down with age, while the number of chronic illnesses goes up. In this particular figure, the number for acute problems includes those caused by accidents, so you might think that the number for acute illnesses is high for young adults simply because they are more often in accidents. But in fact, the pattern is precisely the same shape when one excludes accidents from the numbers. (Source: U.S. Bureau of the Census, Statistical Abstracts of the United States: 1989. Tables 182 and 183, page 114.)

Furthermore, when young adults do have chronic disorders they aren't the same ones you see in older adults, as you can see in Table 5.1. Among those under 45, the single most common chronic illness is chronic sinusitis, with hay fever or allergies also common. Both these problems remain frequent in older adults but become proportionately much less significant. In these older groups, it is

TABLE 5.1. Incidence (percentage) of Selected Chronic Illnesses for Different Age Groups In the United States in 1986.

Chronic Condition	18–44	45–64	65+
Heart conditions	3.9	12.3	28.4
High Blood Pressure	6.7	25.1	39.7
Arthritis	4.8	28.5	49.2
Diabetes	0.9	6.4	10.0
Chronic Sinusitis	17.0	16.7	16.9
Allergies, Hay Fever	11.3	9.6	7.0

SOURCE: U.S. Bureau of the Census, *Statistical Abstracts of the United States, 1989*, Table 183, p. 114.

arthritis, high blood pressure, and heart disease that are the most common chronic illnesses—all problems with low rates among adults in their 20s and 30s.

One possible point of confusion: The rates listed in Figure 5–2 may give you the impression that virtually everyone has at least one chronic illness, but actually that is not true. Some people have more than one; many have none. Even among older adults, the presence of chronic disease is not inevitable. U.S. figures suggest that a fifth to a quarter of adults over 65 have no chronic disease at all (Guralnik, LaCroix, Everett, & Kovar, 1989).

DISABILITIES Furthermore, it is quite possible to have one or more chronic diseases without experiencing any significant disability. I have a chronic lower back problem that requires thought and good sense but restricts me very little; another adult may have mild arthritis that responds well to aspirin and requires no limitation in major activities. For most adults, the crucial issue is not whether one has a chronic ailment but whether that ailment or disease has an impact on daily living, requiring restriction in daily activities or reducing your ability to care for yourself.

Just how many older adults are limited in their abilities to do everyday things like climbing stairs, lifting a box, stooping, or kneeling? This is a difficult question to answer accurately since we must rely on the self-reports of adults whose definitions of disability or difficulty may vary considerably. But there are some relevant findings.

For example, results from one longitudinal study (the National Longitudinal Surveys of Labor Market Experience, NLS, Chirikos & Nestel, 1985) involving several thousand black and white men indicate that 26 percent of the white men and 34 percent of the black men between 60 and 74 had difficulty going up stairs. Lois Verbrugge has reported very similar findings from a separate national survey by the National Center for Health Statistics (Verbrugge, 1985). In this survey, 35 percent of women and 24 percent of men over 65 had difficulty with stairs. Nearly a quarter of all adults over 65 have problems doing "heavy housework" (although half of those adults do such housework anyway), 19 percent have difficulty walking, and nearly ten percent have difficulty bathing without assistance. Overall, Verbrugge finds that about 35 percent of women and about 43 percent of men over 65 have at least some limitation in a major activity.

Once acquired, disabilities tend to persist. But not invariably. Kenneth Manton (1988) has analyzed changes in disabilities for adults in one large, two-year longitudinal study, the National Long-Term Care Survey of adults over 65. Over 6,000 adults who had been identified in 1982 as having some form of disability in "activities of daily living" were interviewed at length about their disabilities; of these, those who had been identified as chronically disabled in 1982 were reinterviewed, as were a new sample of adults who had been identified as having no disability in 1982. This design enabled Manton to track the disability experiences of older adults over the two-year period.

Several general conclusions emerged from Manton's analysis: (1) The more different activities in which the adult was restricted at the first interview, the greater the likelihood that individual would still have some disability two years later;

(2) The older the adult, the more likely the disability was to persist. Despite these trends, however, roughly 10 percent of those who had only one restriction in an activity of daily living in 1982 and five percent of those who had had up to two such restrictions, had no restriction at all two years later. Thus, recovery is possible in some cases. It would be interesting to know whether still higher rates of recovery from disabilities are characteristic of adults in their early- or middle-adult years. It seems reasonable to suppose that they would be, but I know of no comparable data for younger subjects.

Self-Ratings of Health Your own sense of good or poor health is presumably some combination of all these factors—actual disease combined with degree (and persistence) of disability. Table 5.2 shows self-ratings of health for current national samples in the United States. Clearly, the number of adults who think of themselves as having poor health increases by a factor of about five between early and late adulthood. But at the same time, more than two-thirds of adults over 65 think of themselves as having good, very good, or excellent health. This does not mean, of course, that a 70-year-old who describes herself as in "very good health" has the same physical functioning as a 27-year-old who chooses the same overall description. We adjust our expectations of health as we get older, so when we are asked how good our health is we are answering not on an absolute scale but, to at least some degree, on a relative one ("My health is excellent for someone my age"), and this is more true as we get into old age. Nonetheless, it is still striking that so many older adults describe their health as good, very good, or excellent.

Ilene Siegler and her colleagues (Siegler et al., 1980) have suggested a very nice way to combine all these bits and pieces of information about age changes in health and disease. We can think of each age group as made up of three subsets: those who describe themselves as healthy and who really are; those who think of themselves as healthy but who have some beginning disease process that has not yet reached the level of symptoms (such as high blood pressure, or early stages of heart disease, or some minor or nondisabling chronic ailment); and those who have at least one diagnosed disabling health problems. If the percentage of each of these three groups is estimated for different ages, you end up with something like the representation in Figure 5–3.

In the early years, most adults are genuinely healthy, although a few may have the beginning stages of diseases that will become symptomatic at later ages;

TABLE 5.2. Ratings of Their Own Health Given by Adults in the United States.

Rating	25–44	45–64	65+
Excellent or Very Good	72.6	52.3	35.2
Good	21.0	29.1	32.3
Fair or Poor	5.0	12.4	21.5

SOURCE: Verbrugge, 1989, Table 2.13, p. 48.

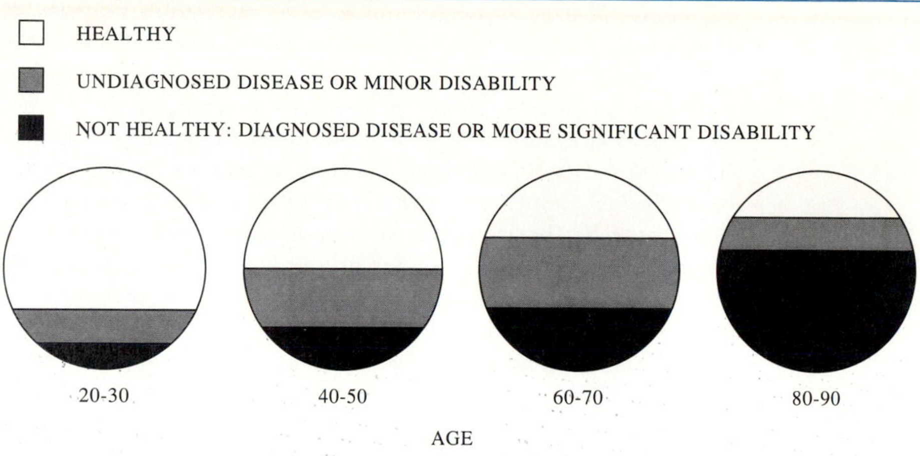

Figure 5–3 Each succeeding age group contains fewer people who are genuinely healthy and more who have diagnosed disease or substantial disability. In the middle years, there is also a substantial group of adults who may think of themselves as healthy but who have significant undiagnosed disease (such as CHD) or who have at least some minor disability. (Source: Siegler, Nowlin, & Blumenthal, 1980, Figure 43–1, page 601.)

in midlife, about half of adults have some kind of disease process present; at retirement age, the percentage with some kind of disease goes up, but at least half of that disease is still either undiagnosed or minor; in late old age, more than half have clearly diagnosed or major ailments. Such a sequence makes even more sense when you look at the age-related patterns for some of the major individual diseases.

Age Changes in Specific Diseases

Heart Disease

Although the death rate from **coronary heart disease** (which physicians normally abbreviate as CHD) has been dropping rapidly in the past two decades, (McGandy, 1988) it is still the leading cause of death in the United States and throughout the developed world (White, Cartwright, Cornoni-Huntley, & Brock, 1986). Although the phrase "coronary heart disease" covers a number of physical deteriorations, the key change is in the coronary arteries, which become slowly blocked with fibrous and calcified tissue, a process called *atherosclerosis.*

Given the amount of press coverage of heart disease, you may well assume that atherosclerosis is an inevitable part of aging. But it is not. It is a disease, and not everyone has it. For those whose genetic endowment or health habits put them at high risk for this disease, the beginning stages of arterial change actually occur as early as the teenage years or early 20s and typically proceed steadily thereafter (McGandy, 1988). These early changes appear to be at least somewhat reversible; changes in health practices can significantly reduce or reverse the actual physiological disease process and considerably reduce the risk of such overt signs of the disease as heart attack, stroke (which may occur when atherosclerotic change blocks brain arteries), or congestive heart failure. In contrast, those arterial changes that form the later stages of the disease—occurring in the 30s and 40s and later—are far less amenable to intervention. By changing health habits, it is possible to slow the process of the disease and thus to reduce one's risk of overt symptoms, but by fairly early adulthood, the disease changes themselves are difficult to reverse.

So just what health habits are important? What *are* the famous "risk factors?" Most of what we know about the risks contributing to cardiovascular disease comes from several longitudinal epidemiological studies, of which the most famous is the Framingham Study (e.g. Dawber, Kannel, & Lyell, 1963; Kannel & Gordon, 1980). The Framingham researchers began in 1948 with a sample of 5,209 adults, then aged 30 to 59, all residents of Framingham, Massachusetts. These adults have been reassessed roughly every two years for three decades, a process that enabled the researchers to track the long-term health of adults who had various physical characteristics or personal habits and thus to identify risk factors for heart disease. The risks they identified are listed in Table 5.3.

These risks are clearly cumulative. The more risk factors in your profile, the higher the chance that you have, or will develop, CHD. It seems clear that a tendency toward high blood pressure or high cholesterol (or obesity for that matter) has some genetic component. But it is also clear that all of the items

TABLE 5.3. Risk Factors of Cardiovascular Disease, Primarily from the Framingham Study.

Risk Factor	Specific Pattern
High Blood Pressure	Any elevated blood pressure increases risk; borderline high blood pressure ranges between 140–159 for systolic pressure. Any systolic pressure of 160 or higher is officially called "high blood pressure." Still higher risk of heart attack or other symptoms appear for blood pressure above 195. Elevated blood pressure is a risk factor for CHD even for adults with normal cholesterol who do not smoke.
Cholesterol	Elevated levels of cholesterol, but especially elevated levels of the component of cholesterol called low-density lipoproteins (LDL), are associated with increased risk. Currently, anything above the level of 250 is considered high risk. High levels of high density lipoproteins (HDL), the other component of cholesterol, are associated with *lower* risk of heart disease.
Obesity	Weight more than 30 percent higher than the normal weight charts increases risk. Since obesity also affects blood pressure, it is not entirely clear that obesity is an *independent* predictor of CHD, but that seems likely.
Cigarette Smoking	Any amount is bad; more than 20 per day is worse. If you quit smoking before age 65, your risk goes down; quitting after that seems to have little beneficial effect.

SOURCE: Kannel & Gordon, 1980: McGandy, 1988.

listed are modifiable to at least some degree. So there is a considerable opportunity for choice here.

So far, this is all pretty familiar stuff. What is less well known is that there may be some age differences in the risk factors. High blood pressure is a risk at every age; in fact, it becomes more risky the older you get. But there is some dispute about whether high cholesterol and smoking continue to be significant risk factors past age 65. In both the Framingham study and the Baltimore Longitudinal Studies of Aging, the risk associated with high cholesterol declined noticeably with age; in the Framingham sample, the impact of smoking also diminished with age, becoming insignificant after age 65 (Fozard, Metter, & Brant, 1990; Kannel & Gordon, 1980). But a recently reported epidemiological study in Hawaii (Benfante & Reed, 1990) shows a strong continued risk associated with high cholesterol and a weak but statistically significant risk associated with cigarette smoking, past age 65. To make the picture still more confusing, all three of these studies have focused primarily or exclusively on men; we know much less about risk factors for women, particularly among women over 65. While we're waiting for further research to clear up the confusion, most physicians are operating on the assumption that the risk factors listed in Table 5.3 are valid over the entire adult age range.

TYPE A BEHAVIOR One additional risk factor for CHD, which I did not list in Table 5.3 because it was not part of the Framingham study, is the **Type A personality** pattern. This personality pattern, first described by two cardiologists, Meyer Friedman and Ray Rosenman (1974; Rosenman & Friedman, 1983), includes several key elements: (1) competitive achievement striving (always wanting to win, to do better than others, to turn simple situations into contests); (2) a sense of time urgency (including packing your day with tightly scheduled activities, timing things, and trying to do them faster each time); and (3) hostility and aggressiveness, frequently expressed in chronic conflict with co-workers or family. Type A people hurry, press, and strive, but they also approach new tasks with confidence. Type B people are more relaxed, put less pressure on themselves, and take time to "stop and smell the flowers." Some people appear to show Type A behavior nearly all the time; some show it primarily under stress.

Friedman and Rosenman's own early research showed a link between blood cholesterol and Type A behavior. They found, for example, that accountants show a rise in cholesterol before the April 15 tax deadline, as the time pressure of their work increases, and then a sharp drop in cholesterol after the deadline. But whether there is a direct causal link between chronic Type A patterns of personality or behavior and increased risk of CHD is a matter of some dispute (e.g. Booth-Kewley & Friedman, 1987; Matthews, 1988). I can't give you details on the extensive (and contradictory) research findings on this question, but I can at least lay out a few conclusions that seem reasonable to me in light of the current data.

Among adults already at high risk for CHD because of high blood pressure, smoking, or high cholesterol, information about an individual's personality does *not* add to the accuracy of your prediction of an eventual heart attack or other overt manifestation of the disease. That is, given two adults both with high blood pressure and high cholesterol, the one who is also high in Type A personality characteristics is no more likely to have a heart attack than is the one low in Type A.

2. Over the population at large, however, there is a small but consistent link between Type A personality characteristics and heart disease. What this tells us is that among those adults who would be rated at low or medium risk on the basis of physiological functioning, those who are high in Type A behaviors or attitudes are slightly more likely to develop CHD than are those low in Type A behaviors. We do *not* know whether the link between Type A personality and CHD varies with age among adults.
3. Not all facets of the Type A personality, as originally described by Friedman and Rosenman, seem to be equally significant. The most critical aspects appear to be hard-driving competitiveness and hostility/aggressiveness. The sense of time pressure appears to be the least important aspect of the syndrome—although there is by no means complete agreement on this point (e.g. Wright, 1988).

All in all, it looks as if there is really something there, but it is not yet clear that we have identified (or accurately measured) the critical ingredients. A case in point: Stephanie Booth-Kewley and Howard Friedman analyzed over 80 studies on Type A personality and found that depression was actually a better predictor of CHD than was any aspect of Type A personality—a result that bears a good deal of future exploration.

Cancer

If you go back and look at Figure 5–1 you'll see that the percentage of deaths attributable to cancer rises to a peak in the 55 to 64 age range, and then declines. This does *not* mean that the incidence of cancer goes down; on the contrary, it continues to rise steadily from middle to late adulthood. The *proportion* of cancer deaths declines only because the rate of deaths from CHD goes up exponentially from midlife onward.

Aside from the steady rise in cancer mortality with age, there are only a few other age-related processes that seem to be at work. For example, women appear to become more prone to cancer (and to heart disease, for that matter) following menopause, when the apparent protection afforded by high levels of circulating estrogen is reduced. A second age-linked pattern occurs for survival rates from cancer: Five-year survival rates for cancers of various types remain fairly steady throughout adulthood but then decline after age 75 (List, 1988).

Like heart disease, there are some identifiable risk factors for various forms of cancer, including a family history of each specific type of cancer. Life style variations also make a difference. For example, smoking is clearly a major risk factor for lung cancer; low-fiber diets appear to increase the risk of colon cancer. Thus, as with heart disease, personal choices made in your 20s and 30s may either forestall or help set into motion disease processes that will become manifest only several decades later.

Senile Dementia

The term *dementia* refers to any general deterioration in intellectual abilities, typically gradual, typically involving significant impairment of memory, judgment, social functioning, and control of emotions. This set of symptoms can be caused by a variety of conditions, such as depression, metabolic disturbances, drug intoxication, Parkinson's disease, hypothyroidism, anemia, or alcohol abuse. Cerebrovascular disease is also implicated in a significant percentage of cases of dementia: As atherosclerosis of the arteries of the brain progresses, an individual may have a series of small strokes which produce cumulative brain damage and hence, dementia.

I give you this list of possible causes of dementia, not because I expect you to be able to make a differential diagnosis or even to remember the list, but to underline the point that dementia is a *symptom* that can be caused by many different kinds of diseases. When dementia occurs in an older adult it is usually described as **senile dementia,** and this too is a symptom, not a disease in and of itself. Furthermore, many of these types of dementias are reversible or treatable, such as those caused by depression or anemia. So merely because an older person begins to be noticeably forgetful and shows other signs of senile dementia does not necessarily mean that some irreversible brain decay has occurred. There may be some much simpler (and more optimistic) explanation.

The specific dementing disease you've doubtless heard most about is **Alzheimer's disease,** also often referred to by physicians and researchers as *senile dementia of the Alzheimer's Type* (SDAT). This disorder is a

> . . . common, chronic, debilitating mental disorder of later life involving a global deterioration of intellect in clear consciousness. Usually starting insidiously with recent memory loss, SDAT is characterized by progressive decline in all intellectual abilities. Failures in work, other role performance, and self-care activities follow sooner or later. (Sayetta, 1986, p. 271)

These signs of dementia are, in turn, caused by specific disease processes in the brain, including most specifically a kind of tangling of the nerve fibers, particularly in the area of the brain called the hippocampus. Since the hippocampus is heavily involved in memory processes, it is not surprising that the major diagnostic symptom of Alzheimer's disease is a loss of memory.

The incidence of senile dementia of the Alzheimer's type has been difficult to establish. We do know that any form of dementia, including SDAT, is extremely uncommon in adults younger than 65. After age 65 the rate rises steeply, but there is now a dispute about just how steeply it may rise. The conventional wisdom, based on a series of epidemiological studies in developed countries (United States, France, Great Britain, Sweden, Italy, and Japan), has been that the overall rate for adults over 65 is somewhere between 2 and 6 percent (Rocca, Amaducci,

& Schoenberg, 1986), with estimates of rates for those 65 to 75 averaging around 1 to 2 percent, and for adults over 85 ranging from 3 to 20 percent. A recent study in Boston, however, in which far higher figures were obtained, has called this conventional wisdom into question. In the Boston sample, chosen to reflect the demographics of a single community, 3 percent of those between ages 56 and 74, 18.7 percent of those age 75 to 84, and 47.2 percent of those over age 85 were classified as "probable Alzheimer's" based on extensive cognitive testing (Evans, Funkenstein, Albert, Scherr, Cook, Chown, Hebert, Hennekens, & Taylor, 1989).

Settling this empirical dispute is not just an issue for ivory tower epidemiologists. It is obviously of vital concern to us all, since it may affect national health policies and health insurance rates, as well as our own individual planning for old age. All I can say at the moment is that we do not yet know how common this disease may be, but the question is under vigorous research scrutiny.

We also do not yet know what causes dementias of this type, but there is no shortage of hypotheses. It seems clear that there is some genetic component, since various studies show that adults who have relatives with SDAT are 2 to 10 times more likely to develop the disease than are those with no family history (Rocca et al, 1986). Still, that cannot be all of the process, since over 60 percent of SDAT sufferers have no family history of the disease. Another intriguing possibility is that the disease results from some chromosomal instability. Among other things, the DNA repair capability in cells of patients with SDAT seems to be diminished (White, Cartwright, Cornoni-Huntley, & Brock, 1986)—an especially interesting finding in light of the current theories about the role of DNA repair in aging that I talked about in the last chapter. The possible role of chromosome instability is also suggested by the curious finding that patients with SDAT are more likely than the general population to have siblings with Down's Syndrome, a genetic disorder (present from birth) in which the individual has three copies of the #21 chromosome. Autopsies of Down's Syndrome adults also reveal brain changes that look very like the neurofibrillary tangles characteristic of Alzheimer's disease. Findings like this point to the possibility that Alzheimer's disease begins when some chromosomal deterioration takes place—although even this explanation only pushes the explanatory problem back one step. It doesn't tell us why chromosomal deterioration would occur at a higher rate in some adults than in others.

Other theories about the causes of this disease emphasize the possible role of the immune system, the possible impact of viral infections (such as the herpes simplex virus), the consequences of exposure to toxic agents such as aluminum, or head injuries. There are many intriguing leads, but we do not yet have a widely accepted theory.

Aging and Physical Disease: An Overview

Before I go on to other subjects, I need to underline yet again a key point about all I have said so far regarding both specific diseases and disease in general: While the risk of having *some* disease increases with age, no one of these specific diseases is an inevitable part of aging. It may be *common* to develop some atherosclerosis as you get older, but it is not a *normal* part of aging; Alzheimer's disease increases in frequency in the later years of life, but senile dementia (of any type) is not a *normal* part of aging in the same sense that puberty is a normal part of physical development in childhood or that menopause is part of normal aging in middle-aged women. That is, these diseases are not universally present during adulthood, even though they increase in frequency with age.

Of course, the physiological changes in the immune system, in the neurological system, and in the cardiovascular system that do appear to be part of normal aging obviously contribute to the increased vulnerability to disease as we get older. But that general statement does not explain why one person gets cancer, another heart disease, and another remains essentially disease-free into old age, finally dying of pneumonia.

Age Changes in Mental Health

In contrast to everything I have said so far about physical disease, which increases in probability with age, there is good reason to conclude that the likelihood of mental disease *decreases* with age, especially after age 65. This statement may surprise you, especially in light of the fact that the opposite view has been widely touted. For instance, a decade ago the President's Commission on Mental Health (1979) stated that "depression escalates decade by decade" (p. 3), and this is typical of statements in texts and government documents about the elderly. But if anything, the research evidence points to the opposite conclusion.

The best single source of information is an enormous study begun in the early 1980s by epidemiologists and gerontologists at five sites: New Haven, CT, Baltimore, St. Louis, Durham, NC, and Los Angeles (Regier, Boyd, Burke, Rae, Myers, Kramer, Robins, George, Karno, & Locke, 1988). In each area a sample of more than 3,000 households was selected, with one individual in each household interviewed at length. The sample was designed to represent the characteristics of the population of each area, except that both the elderly and minority group members (blacks and Hispanics) were deliberately oversampled to allow careful comparisons. The result is a total sample of 18,571 adults from rural as well as urban environments. Each was asked about the presence of specific symptoms over their whole lifetime, but the focus of the interview was on problems during the preceding month. The researchers ended up with *one-month prevalence rates* for each of a long series of disorders. They found that in every category of emotional disturbance they assessed, *except* for a measure of severe cognitive impairment (including Alzheimer's and other senile dementias), the rate for those over 65 was lower than the rate for all other age groups. Figure 5–4 gives a sampling of the findings.

You can see that both the overall rate of all emotional disorders (including dementias) and the rate for both alcohol abuse and depression is considerably lower in adults over 45 than in those younger. When Regier and his colleagues compared their findings to those from smaller studies in both London and Athens, they found confirmation of this central point: Those over 65 had markedly lower

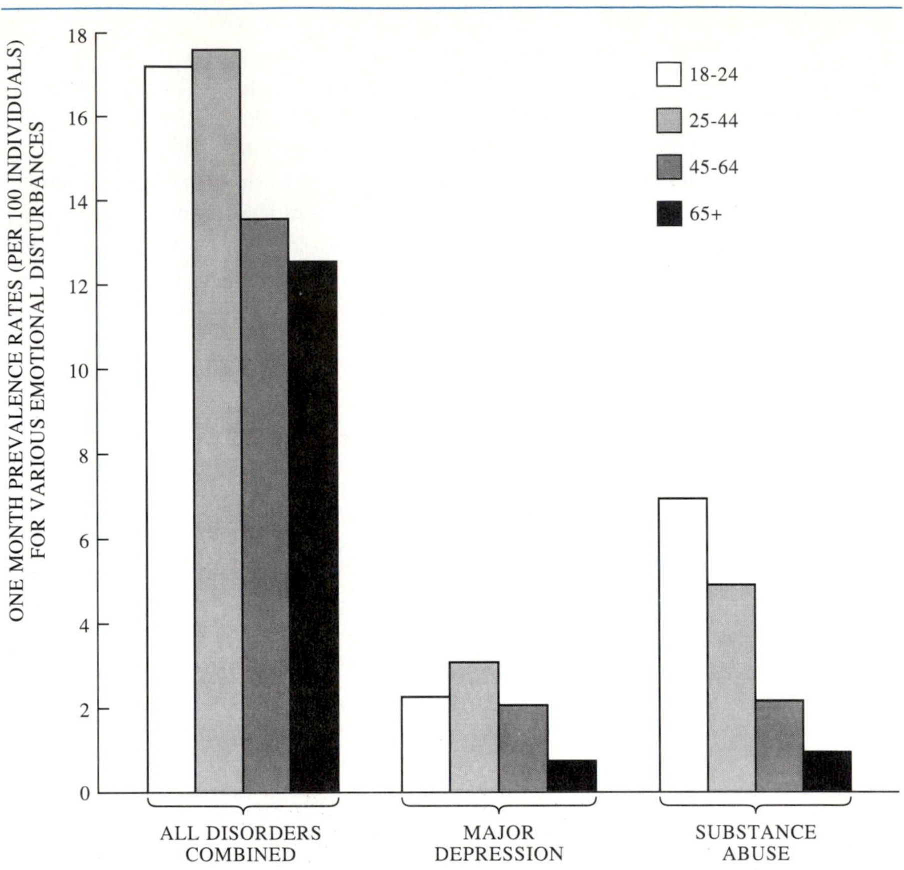

Figure 5–4 These results from an extremely large cross-sectional study show lower rates of emotional disorders among those past middle-age than among the young. This pattern is clear for all disorders combined (even though dementias were included in "all disorders," and dementias do show increases with age), as well as for depression and substance abuse. Except for dementias, this same pattern was found for all mental health problems assessed in this study. (Source: Regier, Boyd, Burke, Rae, Myers, Kramer, Robins, George, Karno, & Locke, 1988, Table 5, pp. 982-983.)

rates of all types of emotional disturbance, although in both London and Athens the patterns were more curvilinear, with higher rates among adults in the middle years of adulthood (between 25 and 50). Similar curvilinear patterns have been found in smaller studies in the United States as well, especially when the diagnosis of problems is done with an in-depth interview using standard clinical criteria for disturbance (Newmann, 1989). Overall, it looks as if the relationship between emotional disturbance and age among adults is either a general downward trend or a curvilinear pattern in which there is a rise in rate in middle adulthood and a drop past the age of 60 or so.

This conclusion seems well-buttressed by research, but there are at least three flies in this ointment.

A SAMPLING PROBLEM First, all of the studies I have been talking about include only "community-dwelling" adults. Older adults in nursing homes or other institutions have been specifically excluded from the samples. Thus, the very older adults who may be most prone to depression or other distress or who may be in an institution or nursing home precisely because they show some form of disturbance, are not counted in these statistics. To be sure, only about five percent of adults over 65 are in such institutions—a smaller figure than you might have guessed (Dolinsky & Rosenwaike, 1988). If we were to assume that all institutionalized elders show some form of emotional disturbance—a tenuous assumption at best—that would alter the picture considerably. Thus, what we know is that among those adults living in the community, those past the age of 65 have lower rates of disturbance than do younger adults.

CROSS-SECTIONAL VERSUS LONGITUDINAL DATA Second, some of you will have caught the fact that all of the research I have been describing is *cross-sectional*, so there may be cohort differences producing the pattern of results I've given you. For example, perhaps today's older generations, having grown up in a time of greater reticence about discussing personal problems, are simply less willing to disclose their emotional difficulties. Alternatively, perhaps today's younger generations are uniquely prone to disturbance. Martin Seligman has offered just such an argument (1988), suggesting that today's "Age of the Individual" is at fault.

He argues that baby boom generation adults (who are in the 25 to 44 age range in the cross-sectional studies shown in Figure 5–4) have grown up in an era in which expectations have soared. We not only expect to be able to buy a fancy car and live in a nice house, we also expect our jobs to be exciting and our marriages to be endlessly supportive. Since these are unrealistic expectations, Seligman argues, we are bound to be disappointed. The younger generations, more affected by these inflated expectations, will therefore show more depression and other signs of distress as reality fails to meet their dreams. As Seligman puts it, "Rampant individualism without commitment to the common good produces widespread depression and meaninglessness" (p. 55). Adults growing up in subcultures within our society in which expectations have not soared and traditional values have been maintained, such as the Amish, show much lower rates of depression at all ages.

Seligman clearly has a point, at least with regard to depression. But his argument does not account for the fact that the incidence of virtually every other type of emotional disturbance or serious mental illness is also lower among those over 65. It is not so clear that schizophrenia is a response to failed expectations. The cohort argument is also undercut to some degree by the fact that similar patterns are found in other cultures and in studies done in the 1970s as well as the 1980s.

Longitudinal evidence would be a better way to settle the question, and we do have a little. Carolyn Aldwin and her colleagues (Aldwin, Spiro, Bosse & Levenson, 1989) found that in their Boston sample of over 2,000 men studied over a period of several decades, psychological symptoms showed essentially no change over time, a pattern also found in a 20-year follow up of a group of

Manhattan adults (Srole & Fischer, 1986). In the latter study, the pattern of no change occurred both in those who had gone from age 50 to 70 in the 20 years of the study, and in those who had been 20 or 30 when the study began. Neither of these studies, of course, can tell us whether today's baby boomers will show the same high levels of depression and other emotional disturbances when they reach 65 or 70 that they now show.

SUICIDE Finally, there is one form of disturbance other than senile dementia that does indeed show an increase with age: suicide. In 1986 (the last year for which national figures are available), the suicide rate for adults over 65 was 21.5 (per 100,000 population) compared to 16.4 for those in the 45 to 54 age range and 15.8 for those 20 to 24. What's more, the rate stays high throughout the post-65 years.

Looking at these figures, you might well conclude that the reason we see overall declines in rates of emotional disturbances among adults over 50 or 60 is that the unhappy ones have killed themselves. But a bit of thought about the denominators involved will persuade you otherwise. In Figure 5–4, the rates I've given are incidence per 100 adults and are thus, basically, percentages. In contrast, the suicide rates are quoted per 100,000 adults; converted to percentages, these rates would barely make a blip on the graphs in Figure 5–4. Thus, the fact that suicide rates are higher among the elderly should not be allowed to sidetrack the more general conclusion that rates of emotional disturbance decline in the later years of adulthood. Nonetheless, the pattern of rising suicide rates with age is of great interest and needs explanation.

When we look at the figures more closely, the numbers become even more interesting. As you can see in Figure 5–5, the heightened suicide rates do not occur among all older adults. This particular pattern is carried almost entirely by a single sub group in the United States–white males–with black males showing a much smaller trend of the same kind. Women show no such rise with age.

What might account for such a pattern? Why is the rate so high among older men, especially older white men? The pattern has existed throughout this century in the United States, (although the absolute level of suicide has gone down considerably since the 1930s [McIntosh, 1985]), so this is not a temporary phenomenon. Yet I know of no good explanations. One fairly obvious possibility is that retirement is the key event. Perhaps adults whose work forms the core of their identity (which would be more likely true for men, perhaps especially for white men in the cohorts now older than 65), find retirement too traumatic. But if this explanation were correct, we should also find increases in depression or other signs of disturbance in adults over 65, especially in men. And we don't. Furthermore, as I pointed out earlier (and as I'll lay out more fully in Chapter 9), there is simply no indication that retirement itself causes any increase in emotional disturbance; on the contrary it is associated with increases in life satisfaction for the majority. Still, it may be that there is a minority of men for whom retirement is an experience to which they are unable to adapt.

Another possibility is that the figures partially reflect men's response to such stresses as being widowed. Because women live longer than men, on average, there

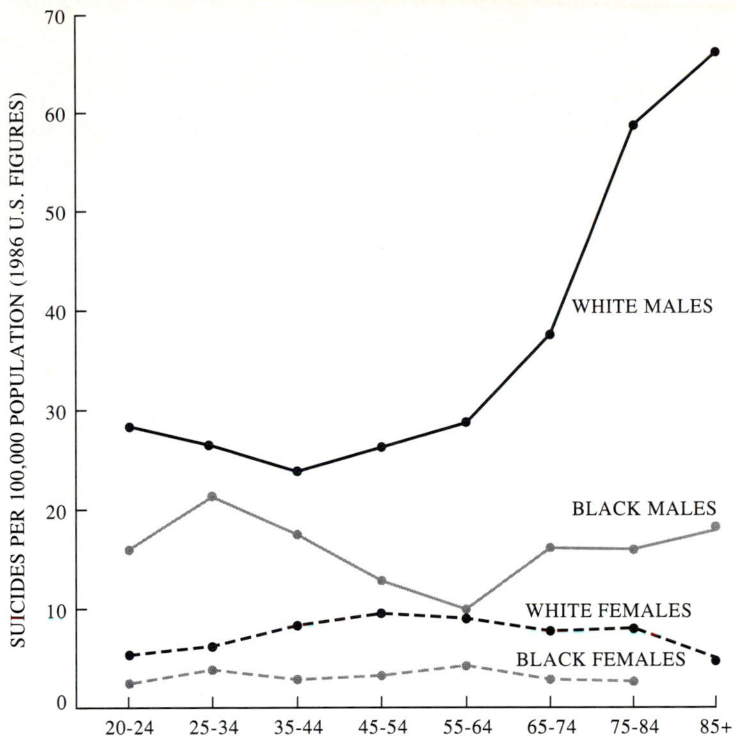

Figure 5–5 Suicide rates in the United States are markedly higher for white males than for any other group, and in this group (as, to a lesser extent, among black males) there is a sharp rise in rate of suicide past retirement age. Could this mean that retirement is a more difficult adjustment for white males? What other explanations occur to you? (Source: U.S. Bureau of the Census, Statistical Abstract of the United States: 1989. Table 125, p. 84.)

are proportionately fewer men who experience widowhood, but suicide rates *are* higher for widowed men than for widowed women (Stroebe & Stroebe, 1983). What I do not know is how much of the disproportionate level of suicide among older men may be accounted for by such a factor.

Overall, the age pattern of suicides is striking but remains to be explained.

Age Changes in Mental Health: An Overview

Taking all the evidence together, it looks to me as if the weakest statement I could make is that there is *no increase* in mental/emotional disturbance over the years of adulthood. The somewhat stronger statement, supported by the majority of evidence, is that there is a *decline* in emotional disturbance past age 65. Rates of depression appear to be lower, alcohol and drug abuse are lower, anxiety is lower. Such age changes *may* reflect cohort differences, but they may also reflect the fact that by 65 adults have well-developed coping skills and are facing fewer daily stresses. Their children are grown and gone, their own parents are likely to be no longer living, they are no longer working. And while their physical health is declining and they experience more disabilities or annoying physical limitations, their lives may be less stressful. The stresses and losses they do face, including the death of friends and perhaps of a spouse, as well as their own physical ailments, are (in Neugarten's terms) "on-time" or "expectable," and thus, perhaps easier to bear. Whatever the reason, what *is* clear is that there is no major *increase* in emotional disturbance in later adult life.

Individual Differences in Health and Disease

As usual, I have begun in this chapter by giving you overall age-linked patterns. But as was true of the basic processes of physical aging, there are widespread individual differences in health and disease in adulthood.

Sex Differences in Health

Women and men have quite strikingly different patterns of health and disease over the adult years.

- Women die of basically the same diseases of which men die, but they do so at older ages. Furthermore, when women do contract fatal diseases, they survive with the disease longer than men do.
- Women have more of almost every nonfatal chronic disease you can think of, and this is true beginning as early as midlife (Verbrugge, 1989). There are a few exceptions: Men have a higher incidence of hearing loss, visual impairment, and back problems. But women have higher rates of arthritis, sciatica, dermatitis, cataracts, gallstones, anemias, migraine headaches, bladder infection, varicose veins, and sinusitis—to name only a few. (As a woman, I find this list depressing!)
- Not surprisingly, given this higher rate of disease, women also have more daily health problems, such as muscle or joint pain, headache, cough, or fatigue. Here, though, there is an interesting interaction with age, as you can see in Figure 5–6. Before age 65, women report higher rates of daily health problems than do men. After that age, there are no differences.
- Women are more likely to seek medical treatment for their ailments (which may be one reason they live longer after some potentially fatal disease has been diagnosed).
- Virtually all types of mental/emotional disturbance are also more common in women (Nolen-Hoeksema, 1987). You can see some of the comparisons in Figure 5–7, taken from the results of the same major study of five communities from which I drew the findings in Figure 5–4. The one significant exception to the pattern of higher emotional disturbance in women is also shown in this figure: Men have higher rates of substance abuse at all ages studied.

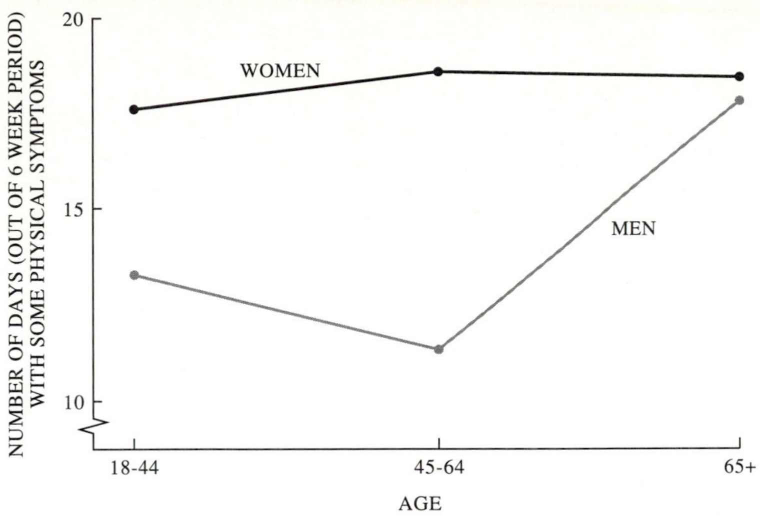

Figure 5–6 *Women not only suffer from more chronic diseases of virtually every kind, they also have more days when they experience some kind of physical symptom. When we look at this difference as a function of age, however, you can see that the difference disappears for adults over age 65. (Source: Verbrugge, 1989, Table 2.12, p. 47).*

Overall, what this means is that women have more "small" complaints—acute illnesses or chronic disease—and they have them over more years. But they simply don't contract the fatal diseases such as CHD or cancer until much later. Lois Verbrugge, who has been one of the major analysts of such statistics, says:

> It is a familiar picture in many families: Dad dies from cancer early in his retirement, and Mom lives to an advanced age but with incessant arthritis pain and circumscribed function. These pictures, writ large, become statistics of health, disability, and mortality. Individuals' own details get lost, but a more reliable view of life and death for middle-aged and older people emerges. (1989, p. 69-70)

At the same time, Verbrugge is careful to emphasize that despite these differences, older men and women encounter very much the same kind of health problems. It is the degree and the pace that differ.

Where might such differences come from? The explanations are partly biological, partly social. Most investigators agree with Verbrugge that the differences in longevity and in resistance to major disease are primarily biological: Women have some built-in greater robustness, whether produced by different genetic endowment which leads to slower physical aging or hormonal differences that give women some protection against major fatal diseases, such as heart disease. There are also probably differences in exposure to hazardous environments (such as very noisy workplaces)—although that difference is probably smaller in more recent cohorts as women have moved more into traditionally male occupations.

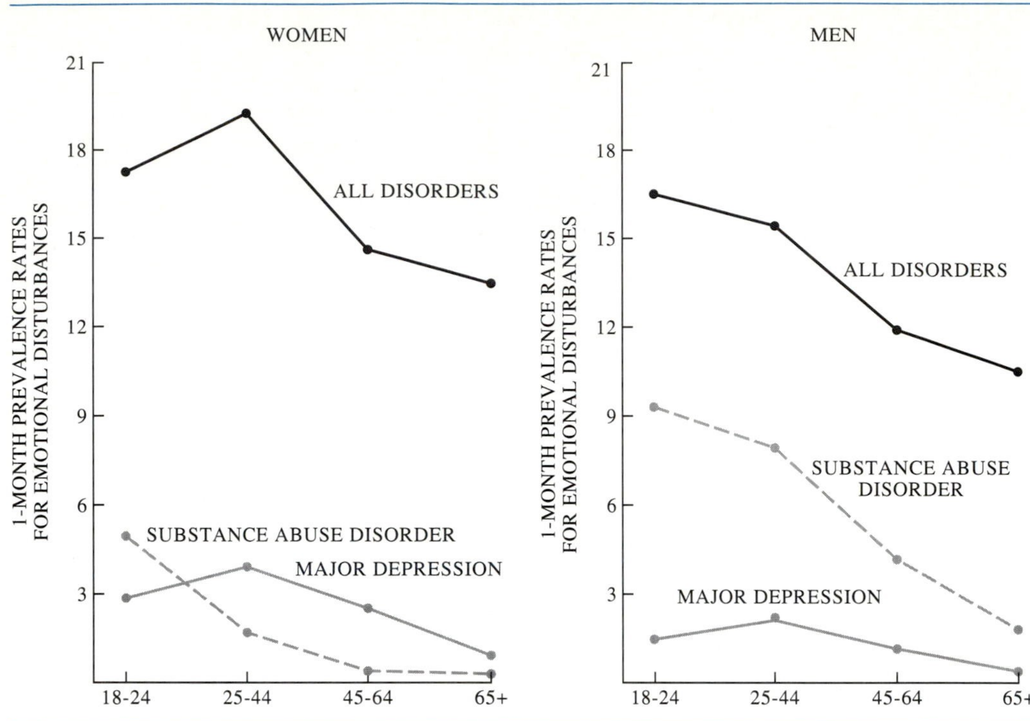

Figure 5–7 The data for this figure come from exactly the same study shown in Figure 5–4, except this time I have separated out the rates for men and women. You can see that overall, at every age, women have higher rates of emotional disturbances, and the same is true for virtually every subvariety such as the pattern for depression shown in this figure, which has been found at higher rates in women by every researcher. In this case, although the incidence rates are relatively low, women have roughly twice the rate of significant depression as do men at each age, as you can see in the figure. The one exception to the general pattern is in substance abuse, which is more common in men at every age as you can see in the figure. (Source: Regier, Boyd, Burke, Rae, Myers, Kramer, Robins, George, Karno, & Locke, 1988, Table 5, pp. 982–983.)

Women's higher rates of non fatal illnesses and of emotional disturbances are harder to explain. Hormone differences are an obvious possibility, although research on the link between hormone patterns and depression has not provided much support for this option (Nolen-Hoeksema, 1987). Women might also be more willing to *report* minor illnesses, depressions, or anxieties, although this possibility, too, is not well supported by research. There is little indication, for example, that women are more willing to acknowledge symptoms of depression than are men. Clearly, what we have here is another set of puzzles for future researchers and theorists.

Racial, Ethnic, and Social Class Differences in Health

Given everything I have said so far, you will not be a bit surprised that there are significant differences in the health patterns across adulthood for blacks, Hispanics, Native Americans, the poor, and middle class. In addition to differences in life expectancy, which I've already mentioned, there are differences in risks for specific diseases and in patterns of disability with age.

Blacks, for example, suffer from higher rates of all forms of cardiovascular disease, due in part to higher rates of high blood pressure among blacks than whites (Jackson & Perry, 1989). Alcohol abuse and its related health complications appear to be more common among Native Americans (Kunitz & Levy, 1989). We also know that black adults in middle and late adult life have higher rates of the kind of chronic disability that impairs functioning on daily tasks.

Aside from differences in the rate of specific diseases which may have genetic components, many of the ethnic differences in health over the adult years are really social class differences in disguise. It is the much higher rate of poverty among blacks, Hispanics, and Native Americans that is the critical ingredient in most of the poorer health and lower life expectancy of these groups. In the United States, the poor have higher rates of arthritis, heart conditions, and bronchitis—although there are no differences for diseases such as diabetes, varicose veins, or osteoporosis—and the middle class are more likely to have cancer (Longino, Warheit, & Green, 1989). The poor are also at greater risk for the types of chronic ailments that produce functional limitations, such as problems with preparing meals, doing housework, or bathing. They are also much more likely to retire due to poor health than is true of the more affluent, in no small part because the jobs held by the poor are likely to be much riskier or more physically stressful, with higher levels of noise and greater exposure to environmental hazards.

To some degree, then, the health experience of the poor (of whatever ethnic group) combines the worst features of the patterns for men and women: They have shorter life expectancy and higher risk of chronic disability at earlier ages.

We don't have to look very far for plausible explanations of such differences. First, and most obviously, adults with lower incomes are less able to afford reasonable medical care or even decent food (Davis, Randall, Forthofer, Lee, & Margen, 1985). The cumulative effect of medical neglect or undernutrition over the years of adulthood is likely to be shorter life expectancy and higher rates of both acute and chronic diseases. Second, the less well-educated adult may simply know less about good health practices, including good diet. And, of course, there are special strains associated with being poor, which may take a physical toll over time. All in all, it is not a pretty picture, and not one we have had much success in altering in recent years.

Personal Health Habits and Risk Behavior

The contributors to individual differences in health patterns I have been talking about so far—gender, ethnicity, social class, heredity—are all significant, but they are factors over which you have little or no control. What you *can* control are your personal health habits. I made this point in the last chapter (recall Table 4.5), but I want to emphasize it even more strongly here: Health habits play a major role in the rate with which you will experience the body changes of aging, the degree of good health you will have, and the length of your life.

The evidence supporting such a statement comes from a variety of sources. You've already seen some of it in my earlier discussion of research on the risk factors for heart disease. The Framingham study, among others, shows that among those adults who appear to have some genetic risk for CHD, those who control their risks through good health practices live longer, with fewer overt signs of disease.

A more striking and more general demonstration of the link between longevity and health practices comes from research by Nedra Belloc and her co-workers (Belloc, 1973; Belloc & Breslow, 1972). She identified seven good health practices, listed in Table 5.4, each of which has been shown to increase life expectancy. Belloc's basic question was whether combining these good health practices would increase life expectancy still more.

The evidence she gathered was from a large sample of 6,928 adults in Alameda County, California, who had completed a health survey. Five and a half years after the first contact, Belloc checked the county records for all deaths and was able to link the number of health practices initially reported to the probability of death over the five years. (Since she did not have information on the deaths of any of the sample who had moved from the county in the intervening years, the death rates are probably low; but the pattern of relationship between health practices and probability of death should not be affected by this limitation.)

You can see the results of Belloc's study in Figure 5–8. In early and midlife, it may appear that we can get away with poor health practices. But beginning at about 50 for men and perhaps 60 for women, poor health practices catch up with us, and the risk of death is considerably higher for those with poor practices. The same conclusion comes from the Duke longitudinal studies (Palmore, 1970). Adults who exercised less, smoked more, and were overweight died at an earlier age than one would predict from their age, sex, and race.

Data from the Duke longitudinal studies also show that poor health practices are associated with more frequent illnesses. Those adults who were relatively sedentary at the beginning of the study, six years later had more illnesses that forced them to stay in bed, visited the doctor more, and rated their own health as worse than did originally active adults.

TABLE 5.4. Good Health Practices Identified by Belloc.

1. Usually sleep seven or eight hours per night.
2. Eat breakfast almost every day.
3. Eat between meals once in a while, rarely, or never.
4. Weight for a man between 5% under and 20% over desirable weight for height. Weight for a woman not more than 10% over desirable weight for height.
5. Often or sometimes engage in active sports, swimming, or take long walks, or often garden, or do physical exercises.
6. Have not more than four drinks at a time.
7. Never smoke cigarettes.

SOURCE: Belloc & Breslow, 1972, p. 415. Reprinted by permission of Academic Press, Orlando, FL and the author.

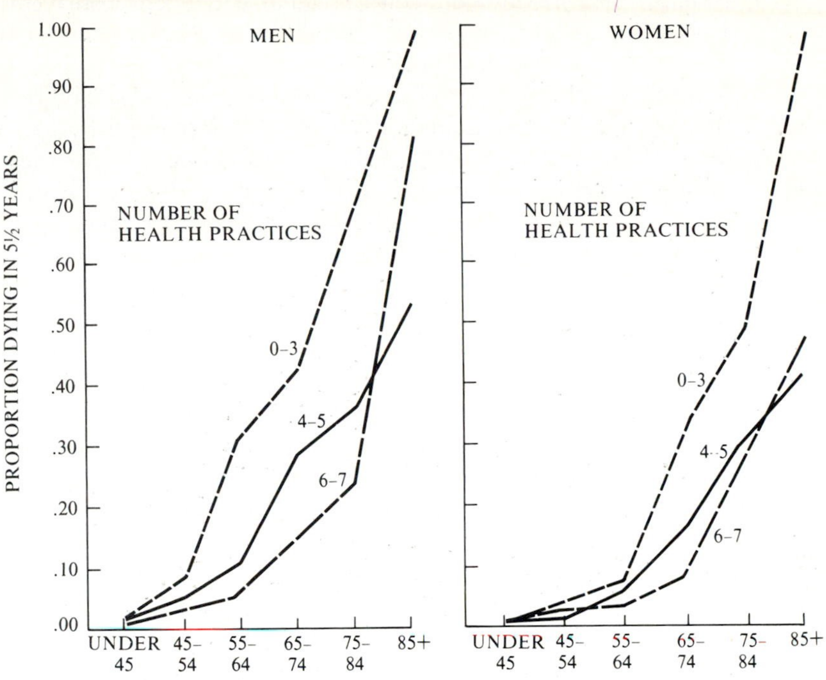

Figure 5–8 These findings from Belloc's study show clearly that the risk of death over a five-year period increased the fewer the number of good health practices a person followed. The effect is clearest among older adults, but that does not necessarily mean that you can get away with poor health practices in early adulthood. Other evidence suggests that the impact of such poor health practices as smoking or inactivity is cumulative. (Source: Belloc, 1973, p. 75. Reprinted by permission of Academic Press, Orlando, FL and author.)

Perhaps unsurprisingly, it is the young who have the least healthy lifestyle. Data from the U.S. National Center for Health Statistics (U.S. Bureau of the Census, 1989a) show regular declines with age in such poor health habits as skipping breakfast, snacking, drinking to excess, and smoking. Two exceptions to this pattern are obesity, which is most common among those 45 to 64, and getting too little sleep (6 hours or less), which is equally common at all ages.

Of course, one of the reasons the young follow a riskier health path is that they have a difficult time seeing or accepting a link between their current behavior and such long-term outcomes as decreased lifespan, or heart disease three decades later. Human decision making is not completely rational. Among other things, we tend to be more optimistic about our own situation than is warranted by the facts: "Other people become addicted, but I can handle it," or "It hasn't happened to me yet" (Jeffrey, 1989). We also tend to make decisions based on immediate rewards rather than on potential longer-term gains, so the immediate pleasure of overeating, alcohol, or smoking is likely to overwhelm any information we have about the long-term risks. As we get older, such optimism and such short-term hedonism may be more difficult to sustain as the poor health chickens come home to roost in the form of disease or disability. It becomes harder to deny the risks, and we change our behavior.

Public health information efforts have had some impact on this process. Nathan Maccoby and his colleagues (Maccoby, 1980; Maccoby, Farquhar, Wood, & Alexander, 1977), for example, have shown that intensive information campaigns in selected communities can lower heart attack incidence and risk in those communities by changing people's health habits—fewer eggs eaten per day, lower smoking rates, lower overall rates of cholesterol in the diet. What we do not know from these studies is whether the information campaigns were more successful with the middle-aged than with the young—a finding that would not surprise me in the least.

We also know that women follow better health practices than do men, a difference no doubt contributing to women's longer lifespans. William Rakowski (1988), in an analysis of national data, finds that at all ages except middle-age, women are more likely not only to follow those good practices Belloc identified, but they also see a physician and a dentist more often, floss their teeth more regularly, and eat less red meat. Intriguingly, Rakowski found that in the middle-aged group in this survey (age 42 to 53 in his study), this sex difference disappeared. In that group, it was education level and not gender that became the major predictor of good health habits, as if, having seen their impending mortality, men began to pay more attention and changed their behavior.

EXERCISE: A REPRISE I talked at some length about the impact of exercise on overall rates of physical aging in the last chapter. I could repeat almost the same words here. Certainly, the conclusion is the same: Those adults who exercise regularly also have better health. They have lower risk of heart disease (Lakatta, Goldberg, Fleg, Fortney, & Drinkwater, 1988), and—perhaps more importantly for everyday life—lower rates of physical disability. Roberta Rikli and Sharman Busch (1986) conclude from their studies of physically active and inactive women that "a chronically active lifestyle plays an important part in preventing age-related declines in motor performance" (p. 649). The 65-year-old women in this study who had maintained a level of regular vigorous activity for at least the past 10 years had better reaction times, better flexibility, and better balance than did less active women of the same age. In fact, the scores of the older active women were comparable to scores obtained by inactive women in their 20s.

What we do not yet know enough about is whether such benefits of exercise on health occur regardless of when one begins to exercise. Probably, the relationship is rather like what we see in the link between smoking and health: Not smoking at all is best; if you smoke, it is better to quit earlier in adulthood than later, but quitting is at least somewhat beneficial even in later years (although perhaps not after 65; the findings are conflicting). Similarly, maintaining fitness throughout adulthood by regular exercise is doubtless best, but improving your fitness at any age is likely to have some positive impact on your health, although the degree of benefit may well decrease with age.

Personality Differences and Health

Yet another kind of individual characteristic that seems to have some bearing on health is personality. I've already talked about the Type A personality and its possible link to heart disease. Other possible linkages have been suggested.

David McClelland (1989), a famous name in studies of human motivation, has assembled impressive evidence for the existence of connections between specific motive patterns and particular illnesses. For example, men who show high levels of what he calls the *need for power* are more likely to be problem drinkers. They are also more susceptible to infectious diseases, apparently because their motive pattern leads them into a lifestyle with more chronic stress, which in turn has the effect of suppressing the immune system. In McClelland's studies, those adults with the best health were those with higher levels of what he calls "affiliative trust" (which enables the individual to create cooperative, supportive, loving relationships) and a sense of "agency" (feeling as if you have some control over your life)—a finding supported by the work of Judith Langer, who has found in many studies of elderly adults that increasing their sense of agency or self-control led to improved health (Langer, 1989a).

Another health/personality connection has been reported by Paul Costa and Robert McCrae (1980b), researchers whose work on personality consistency I mentioned briefly in Chapter 2. They find that adults high in the personality dimension they call "neuroticism" (see Table 2.2) complain more about their health than do those low in this dimension. They are also more likely to smoke (and have more trouble quitting) and to have drinking problems. All of these findings point to potentially important links between personality and health. Personality apparently affects not only our health habits, and thus indirectly influences our current or later health; it may also have much more direct influences through impact on the immune system. This area of research, called *psychoimmunology,* has been burgeoning in the last few years; I am sure these connections will continue to become clearer.

A Review of Age Patterns of Health

As I did in the last chapter (and as I will do in each of the core chapters of the book), I want to summarize this mass of information for you in a table (Table 5.5).

Overall, most of us experience fairly robust health in the first decades of adulthood, although the early, non-symptomatic stages of disease may be present even then. Measurable symptoms of such diseases and loss of function or disability associated with those diseases are likely to appear for at least some adults in their 50s and 60s, which is reflected in the sharply increased rates of both illness and death in the decades past that. The good news in all of this fairly depressing stuff is that we each have some control over this process. Obviously, we cannot evade death. It comes to each of us. But there is a very good chance that we can improve not only our life expectancy but also the health we will experience

TABLE 5.5. Summary of Age Changes in Health and Illness.

Age 20–40	Age 40–65	Age 65+
Lowest death rate; deaths mostly from accident, homicide, or suicide.	Risk of death increases; most common causes of death are heart disease, with cancer a close second.	Highest risk of death; most common causes of death are still heart disease and cancer, with stroke, and diabetes also increasing in likelihood.
Highest risk period for acute illness; lowest risk of chronic illness.	Medium risk for both chronic and acute illness.	Lowest risk for acute, highest risk for chronic illness.
Negligible incidence of dementias of any type.	Still negligible risk of dementias of any type.	Beginning of increase in risk for senile dementia, including Alzheimer's disease.
Probably highest risk for depression and other mental illnesses; poorest health habits.	Risk for depression or other mental illness appears to decline; health habits improve.	Probably lowest risk for any type of mental/emotional illness; best health habits.

during our lifetime. I know that most of you reading this are young enough to still think yourselves invulnerable, (or immortal), and that it is difficult to adopt good health practices now when the payoff may be decades away, especially when the "good health practices" involve denying yourself something yummy or otherwise pleasurable. But the data seem clear.

Summary

1. The risk of death rises with increasing age, and the causes of death change systematically with age. Among young adults, death is most likely to be the result of accidents, suicide, and homicide. By midlife, cancer and heart disease are the largest causes of death.
2. The probability of acute (short-term) illness declines over adulthood, whereas the probability of chronic illness increases, particularly after midlife.
3. Disabilities, including those that interfere with tasks of daily living, also increase with age. Roughly, a third to a half of adults over age 65 have some such disability.
4. Self-ratings of health change with age in a pattern consistent with the findings on disease and disability: Young adults are most likely to rate themselves in good health or better; adults over 65 are the least likely to do so.
5. Coronary heart disease (CHD) is the leading cause of death in the United States and in other developed countries. It shows a geometric rise with age.
6. For those with a genetic (or environmental) tendency toward this disease, the underlying physical changes, such as atherosclerosis, begin in the teens and twenties and are irreversible by the 30s or 40s, even though the overt symptoms of the disease may not appear for some while after that.

7. Risk factors for CHD include high blood pressure, high cholesterol, obesity, and smoking.
8. The Type A personality may also be an additional risk factor for CHD, but this seems to be true only for those who would not otherwise be thought to be high risk for the disease.
9. Cancer rises in frequency across adulthood at a fairly steady (not geometric) rate; among women it increases in frequency especially after menopause.
10. Senile dementia, characterized by significant deterioration in mental abilities, may be caused by many disease processes, some of which are reversible. One common nonreversible cause is Alzheimer's disease, which occurs occasionally in adults younger than 60 but increases in frequency after that age. It is characterized by specific forms of brain degeneration.
11. Older adults are not more likely to show emotional disturbances such as depression, and may in fact have lower rates of such problems than do younger adults. Suicide, however, does rise in later life among some subgroups, most notably white men.
12. Women and men have different patterns of health changes with age. Women have more chronic ailments beginning at an earlier age but contract terminal illnesses at a later age.
13. In the United States, most minority groups have shorter life expectancies and higher rates of disease and disability than do whites. A good part of this difference is accounted for by higher levels of poverty (and thus, poorer health care and more risky environments) among minority groups.
14. Health habits associated with lower risk of disease and greater longevity include not smoking, getting regular exercise, not drinking to excess, eating three meals a day, getting sufficient sleep, and maintaining proper weight.
15. Young adults as a group have poorer health habits than do older adults, particularly those over 65.
16. Personality may also influence both general susceptibility to disease and the specific disease from which you may suffer. For example, there are some indications of a link between some personality characteristics and the functioning of the immune system.

Suggested Readings

FISCHMAN, J. (1987, February). Type A on trial. *Psychology Today, 21,* 42–50. If you are interested in the link between personality and health or particularly in Type A, this brief paper may give you some sense of the current controversy.

LANGER, E. J. (1989b, April). The mindset of health. *Psychology Today, 23,* 48–51. This is an excerpt from Langer's book, *Mindfulness,* that may give you at least a taste of her very interesting work. She is talking here about the impact of your thinking on your health, valid at any age.

NOLEN-HOEKSEMA, S. (1987). Sex differences in unipolar depression: Evidence and theory. *Psychological Bulletin, 101,* 259–282. A detailed, thorough, and clear analysis of all the evidence on sex differences in depression.

CHAPTER 6

Intellectual Changes in Adulthood

One of the most pervasive stereotypes about aging is that we all lose our intellectual powers as we age. The term "senile," which the dictionary defines merely as "of or pertaining to old age," has acquired a colloquial meaning of "stupid" or "mentally dense" or merely mentally slow. Most of us assume that as we age, we will lose our memory and our ability to reason or think clearly. When, perhaps in your 40s or 50s, you find you cannot remember the name of a familiar flower in your garden, or you go to the grocery store but forget to get the bottle of milk that was on your mental list, you may say to yourself, "Good grief, I must be getting old. I can't remember anything anymore." Or, if your work requires some element of creativity, you may worry that you will never again have a good idea after the age of 40.

This assumption of inevitable loss of mental ability with age is so much a part of our cultural view of aging that it does not occur to most people to question it. But we should question it. There is now a large and sophisticated body of research on intellectual stability and change with age, and *most* of the findings from that research show a much smaller, and much later, decline in mental abilities than the stereotype suggests.

In exploring this literature, it is probably easiest to begin by looking at consistency and change in the broadest measures of intellectual functioning—scores on IQ tests of various kinds—and then breaking that down into subvarieties of intellectual skills, such as verbal versus nonverbal tasks, memory, and problem solving.

Age Changes in IQ During Adulthood

Defining "intelligence" is one of the slipperier tasks in psychology. The typical definition goes something like this: Intelligence is "the aggregate or global capacity of the individual to act purposefully, to think rationally and to deal effectively with his environment" (Wechsler, 1939, p. 3).

Most psychologists assume that there is a central, general intellectual capacity, often called "g", which influences the way we approach many different tasks. The total score on an intelligence test, (usually labeled as "IQ," which is short for "intelligence quotient"), is intended to describe this general capacity. As you doubtless know from previous psychology classes, the average IQ score is normally set at 100, with scores above 100 reflecting above average performance and scores below 100 reflecting below average performance. The question to be addressed here is whether IQ changes systematically with age or remains constant. Before I can answer that question, though, I need to set the stage a bit more by talking about what is meant by "consistency and change."

Meanings of Consistency and Change

Psychologists use the term "consistency" to describe at least four quite different phenomena, which I've summarized in Table 6.1. In studies of intelligence, researchers and theorists have focused virtually all of their attention on the first two

TABLE 6.1. Alternative Types of Consistency.

1. Correlational	A characteristic is consistent in this sense if individuals retain the same *relative* position over time. For example, we would say that IQ is consistent in this sense if those adults who achieve the highest scores when they were 20 still have among the highest scores when they are 40 or 50, while those who originally had low scores still show low scores, *even if the average score of the whole group has gone up or down*.
2. Absolute Level	For this type of consistency, a characteristic is consistent if individuals show minimal change in the *absolute* level of that quality over time. Physical qualities like height show this kind of consistency in the early years of adulthood. We could say that IQ is consistent in this sense if the average IQ of a group of adults when they were 60 or 70 was the same as their average scores had been when they were 20.
3. Pattern	Several different qualities within an individual might retain their same relative strength within that individual over time; e.g., if your pattern of intellectual skills (such as better math than verbal skills) remains the same at 60 as at 20 this would show consistency of this type.
4. Trait	Consistency may exist at an underlying "trait" level even while external behavior has changed; e.g., an underlying trait of dependency might be manifested in a 20-year-old by behavior such as calling home a lot, or spending every vacation at home; 45-year-olds might show dependency by spending all leisure time with the same person (such as a spouse). Thus, the dependency may be the same, but the behavior might differ. Intelligence might show this type of consistency if those who score high on an IQ test in their 20s also scored high on tests of "wisdom" or practical intelligence at 65.

SOURCE: Based in part on classification scheme proposed by Kagan, 1980.

types of consistency: consistency (or change) in absolute level, and correlational consistency. Notice that these two types of consistency are at least theoretically independent of one another. One could have both, or neither, or only one type. The group average score might go up or down with age even while individuals stayed in the same relative positions. Or the average score might stay the same but individuals might shift around quite a bit, depending on their health or the stimulation of their lives at that time. As it happens, it is the first of these combinations that actually occurs: There is a predictable average change along with strong relative consistency.

Correlational Consistency in IQ

There is no way to study correlational consistency except with longitudinal data. Fortunately, there are several major, long-term longitudinal studies that have included measures of IQ or cognitive skill as part of their overall assessment (e.g. Herzog & Schaie, 1986, 1988; Eichorn, Hunt & Honzik, 1981). Results from this body of research have converged on quite a clear answer: IQ shows strong individual (correlational) consistency over the adult years. A typical finding is from the Berkeley Intergenerational Studies (Eichorn, Hunt & Honzik, 1981). In this sample, there was a correlation of .83 for men and .77 for women between IQ scores at age 17 and those achieved by the same adults between ages 36-48. Over shorter time intervals, the correlations are even higher. Christopher Hertzog and Warner Schaie, using data from the Seattle Longitudinal Study, have found that over seven-year intervals the correlations range from .89 to .96. Furthermore, they find the same high level of correlational consistency among those in their 60s and 70s as among those in their 30s and 40s (Hertzog & Schaie, 1986).

These are obviously very strong relationships. Still, there is some room for individual shifts within the range, especially over longer periods of time. In the Berkeley sample, for example, 11 percent of the subjects gained 13 or more IQ points over 20 to 30 years while another 11 percent showed losses of six points or more.

Overall, IQ scores at the start of adulthood are highly predictive of IQ scores at later ages, but psychologically significant individual change can and does occur. What this does not tell us, though, is what happens to the average score.

Consistency in Absolute Scores: Cross-Sectional and Longitudinal Results

Most of the early information on consistency or changes in absolute scores on IQ tests came from cross-sectional studies (e.g. Matarazzo, 1972). This research seemed to show that declines in IQ began about age 30 and continued steadily thereafter. This depressing conclusion was widely reported and widely believed by psychologists as well as laymen. But psychologists, at least, have changed their minds based on the longitudinal evidence.

The easiest way to show you the difference in results from these two strategies is to compare the cross-sectional and longitudinal findings from a single study. The best single example is the Seattle Longitudinal Study. Recall that Schaie (1983b, 1989a; Schaie & Hertzog, 1983) began in 1956 with a set of cross-sectional samples, seven years apart in age, ranging from age 25 to age 67. A subset of subjects in each age group was then retested at seven-year intervals for the next 28 years. In 1963, another set of cross-sectional samples covering the same age ranges was also tested, and a subset of these was retested 7, 14, 21, and 28 years later. In 1970, 1977, and 1984, third and fourth and fifth sets of cross-sectional samples were studied, with longitudinal follow-up of a subset of each.

The contrast between the longitudinal and cross-sectional analyses of IQ scores emerges very clearly from the results of this study, as you can see in Figure 6–1. The numbers in this figure are not traditional IQ scores with a mean of 100. Instead, Schaie calculated the mean of the IQ scores of all subjects on the first test each had been given when they entered the study. This average score was then set (arbitrarily) at 50 points on this scale, with a standard deviation of 10. Thus, two-thirds of all adults should fall between scores of 40 and 60 (one standard

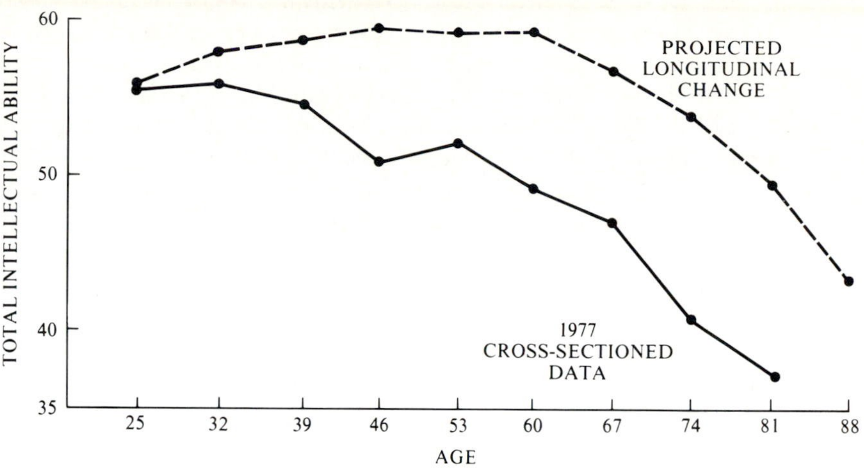

Figure 6–1 Age changes in total IQ based on cross-sectional comparisons and on longitudinal data. Cross-sectional comparisons clearly lead to the erroneous conclusion that mental performance begins to decline at about age 40; longitudinal analyses show that IQ is maintained until at least 60. (Source: Schaie, 1983b, Data from Tables 4.5 and 4.9, pp. 89 and 100.)

deviation on either side of the mean), and about 95 percent should fall between 30 and 70.

The lower line in the figure represents the average scores of adults of each age in the cross-sectional samples tested in 1977. The upper line is Schaie's estimate of the lifetime (longitudinal) pattern of change for someone born in 1952, who was thus 25 in 1977. Schaie arrived at this curve by calculating the average amount of change in IQ score for each age interval that he had observed for the subjects studied longitudinally. For example, the average longitudinal change between age 25 and age 32 (based on three separate longitudinal samples) was +2.0 points. The upper curve is thus, the smoothed sum of the observed seven-year longitudinal changes, projected for the group born in 1952 who began with an average score of 56 points at age 25.

When you compare the two lines in the figure, you can see that longitudinal and cross-sectional data yield very different answers to the question "Does IQ decline with age in adulthood?" The cross-sectional evidence, of which the lower curve is highly typical, seems to show a beginning decline in IQ starting somewhere between age 32 and 39. The longitudinal evidence does not show significant decline in total IQ until the period from age 60 to 67. But even that decline at age 60 to 67 does not bring the average score below the level observed at age 25. It isn't really until the period from 67 to 74 that total IQ scores in these samples dropped below that seen at age 25.

COHORT DIFFERENCES The obvious explanation for the difference between the cross-sectional and longitudinal comparisons is that there are very large cohort effects at work here. At least in this society, as years of education and health have increased in each successive cohort over the past century, average scores have generally gone up, especially on tests that measure skills that might be particularly influenced by education, such as vocabulary or verbal reasoning (Schaie, 1989b; Willis, 1989). In the Seattle study, Schaie has found that the scores of those born in the 1920s are roughly a half a standard deviation higher than those who were born in 1900. Despite these differences in the *level* of scores, though, Schaie has found that the *shape* of the curve is very similar for all cohorts. Thus, each successive generation appears to follow a pattern of maintenance of intellectual skill through early and middle adulthood, with a decline appearing only at age 60 or later.

Since this pattern has also been found by other researchers (e.g. Sands, Terry, & Meredith, 1989; Siegler, 1983), there is good support for the temptingly optimistic view that intellectual ability remains stable through most of adulthood. But before we accept it fully, let me point out some wrinkles.

Age Changes in Sub-Varieties of Intellectual Performance

The first and most substantial wrinkle is evident as soon as we look at subscores instead of total IQ scores. Although there is a general or "g" factor involved in virtually all measures of intellectual functioning, it is still useful to distinguish among more specific skills, such as verbal abilities, mathematical skill, spatial visualization, reasoning, or the like. In research on adult intelligence, such subskills have been grouped in at least three ways.

Some researchers (e.g. Cunningham & Owens, 1983; Jarvik & Bank, 1983) emphasize the difference between **speeded tasks** and **unspeeded tasks.** On any IQ test, some subtests require the subject to perform some actions within a stated period of time in order to receive credit. On the Wechsler Adult Intelligence Scale (WAIS, a widely used test), for example, there is a time limit for solving the problems on the arithmetic subtest. On other subtests, a fast response earns more points than a slower one, such as a test on the WAIS requiring the subject to arrange pictures in correct serial order (picture arrangement) or put together jigsaw puzzle-like pieces (object assembly) or copy geometric designs using colored blocks (block design). Other subtests, such as measures of vocabulary, typically have no time limits. The general finding is that performance on speeded tests begins to decline earlier in the adult years than does performance on unspeeded tests.

An overlapping distinction is between **verbal** and **performance** subtests. For example, the WAIS is divided into verbal tests (vocabulary, describing similarities, information, arithmetic, and comprehension) and performance tests (block design, coding, object assembly, picture arrangement, and the like). Performance tests generally involve manipulation of objects in some fashion, whereas verbal tests involve manipulation of words or ideas. Most verbal tests are untimed and most performance tests are timed, so you will not be surprised to know that verbal abilities generally show increases or stability through the adult age span, up to as late as the 70s, while performance tests show much earlier decline (Denney, 1982; Matarazzo, 1972).

A third distinction, between **fluid** and **crystallized** intelligence, has been proposed by Raymond Cattell and John Horn (Cattell, 1963; Horn, 1982; Horn & Donaldson, 1980) and has been widely influential among researchers studying adult cognition. Crystallized intelligence is heavily dependent on education and experience. It consists of the set of skills and bits of knowledge that we each learn as part of growing up in any given culture, such as verbal comprehension, vocabulary, the ability to evaluate experience, the ability to reason with real-life problems, and technical skills you may learn for your job or your life (balancing a checkbook, making change, finding the salad dressing in the grocery store). In Nancy Denney's model, which I described in Chapter 4, crystallized abilities are close to "optimally exercised" abilities. On standardized tests, crystallized abilities are usually measured by vocabulary and by verbal comprehension (e.g. reading a paragraph and then answering questions about it).

Fluid intelligence, in contrast, is thought to be a more "basic" set of abilities, not so dependent on specific education and more dependent on the efficient functioning of the central nervous system. (In Denney's model, these are the "unexercised" abilities.) A common measure of this is a "letter series test." The subject may be given a series of letters like A C F J O and must figure out what letter should go next. This demands abstract reasoning rather than reasoning about known or everyday events. Most tests of memory are also part of fluid intelligence, as are many tests measuring response speed and those measuring more difficult or abstract kinds of mathematics. Horn has concluded that crystallized abilities generally continue to rise or show stability over adulthood (until age 70 or so, at least), while fluid abilities begin to decline much earlier, beginning perhaps at 35 or 40 (Horn & Donaldson, 1980).

Whatever label we apply to these two broad categories of intellectual tasks (speeded versus unspeeded, verbal versus performance, crystallized versus fluid, or exercised versus unexercised), it seems clear that performance of one group (the unspeeded, verbal, crystallized tasks) is maintained into old age while performance on the other type of task (speeded, nonverbal, fluid) shows signs of decline in middle age.

I can illustrate the difference again with results from Schaie's longitudinal study (1983b), as I have done in Figure 6–2. The figure shows the findings for both the total "intellectual ability" score and for two subscores—vocabulary and number skills. The latter was a timed test involving simple addition problems which were either correctly added or incorrectly added. The subject had to decide if the sum was right or wrong. The vocabulary test was in a form you've seen on many tests: A word is given and then a series of alternate meanings are provided. The subject has to pick out the correct meaning.

In Figure 6–2, I have shown the average *change* in scores on these three measures for each group of subjects who had been studied over 14-year intervals. The units are tenths of a standard deviation. Thus, a score of -2.0 means that the subjects

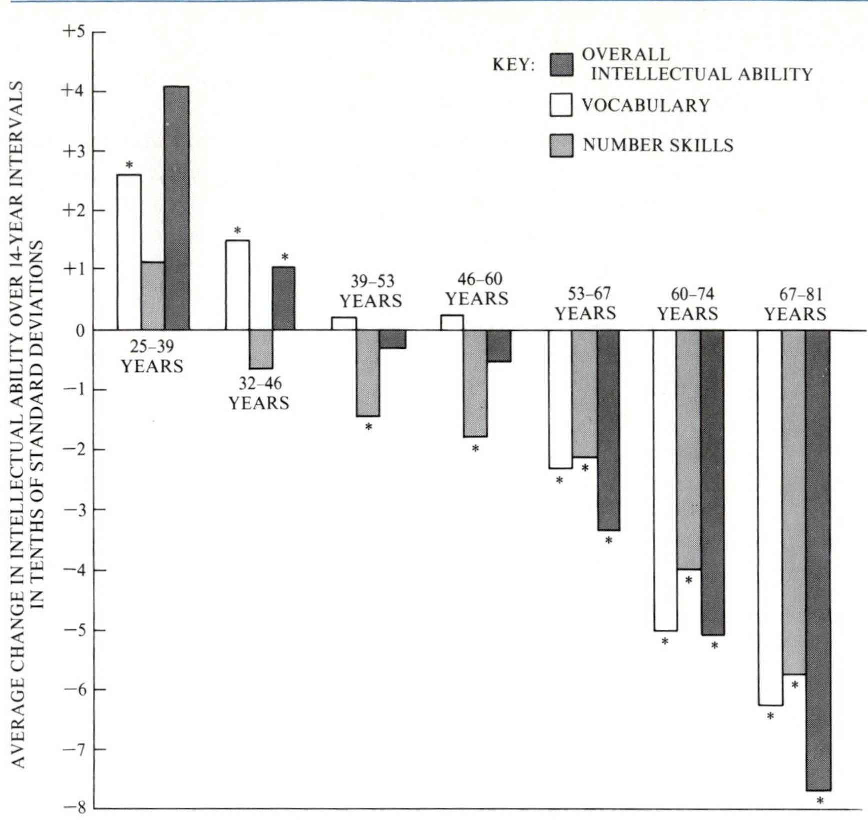

Figure 6–2 *Longitudinal changes in total intellectual ability, vocabulary, and number skills show somewhat different patterns, with number skills showing declines at earlier ages than vocabulary or total score. Each bar in this graph represents the average number of points of increase or decrease over that 14-year interval for all subjects who were tested longitudinally at those ages. An asterisk (*) at the end of a bar means that the average change for that group, for that test, was significantly different from zero. (Source: Schaie, 1983b, data from Table 4.10, p. 101.)*

studied during that particular 14-year age interval declined on that measure 2/10 of one standard deviation. Vocabulary, for example, shows increases during each age period until the 53 to 67 period. Subjects tested from age 53 to 67 showed a decline of 2.36 points (.236 of one standard deviation), those studied between 60 and 74 showed a decline of 5.0 points (half a standard deviation), and so forth. I have marked with an asterisk each bar that represents a change that is significantly different from zero, so you can see that for the number score, significant decreases began in the 39 to 53 age range, while for the vocabulary score, a significant decrease was not seen until the 53 to 67 age interval.

What this tells us is that the optimistic conclusion based on the longitudinal line shown in Figure 6–1 is not altogether accurate. On some kinds of tests, adults appear to show some decline beginning as early as their 40s. Typically, the tests that show this early decline pattern are those that are timed, that involve abstract reasoning or memory, or that require speedy response. On tests that do not make such demands, particularly those that involve often-used skills such as language, decline occurs much later.

Furthermore, even the decline in speeded/performance/fluid test skill, while *statistically* significant, may not represent psychologically significant loss until at least late middle age. Schaie concludes:

> . . . at the risk of possible overgeneralization, it is my general conclusion that reliably replicable age changes in psychometric abilities of more than trivial magnitude cannot be demonstrated prior to age 60, but that reliable decrement can be shown to have occurred for all abilities by age 74. (Schaie, 1983b, p. 127)

Schaie's conclusion fits the data quite well, but again there are further subtleties. Paul Baltes and his colleagues (Baltes, Dittmann-Kohli, & Dixon, 1984, 1986) have pointed out, for example, that psychologically or functionally relevant decrements may show up at earlier ages when adults are faced with highly complex or difficult tasks—tasks that stretch the individual's skills to the limit. Adults in their 40s, 50s, and 60s can maintain their habitual level of intellectual

Figure 6–3 The ability to read a road map is mostly dependent on what Horn calls crystallized intelligence. It requires specific map-reading experience and, once learned, is likely to be retained well into old-age. (Photo © Renee Lynn. Reprinted with permission.)

performance under ordinary, everyday conditions, but when they are asked to maintain a high level of effort over a long period of time, to do several things at once, to work at high speed, to switch gears rapidly or frequently from one task to another, or to perform under major competitive stress, their performance goes down more than is true for younger adults in the same circumstances. One of the ironic implications of this effect is that adults whose occupations require them to function regularly at these more taxing levels are likely to notice some loss of skill earlier in adulthood than do those whose life circumstances make less stringent intellectual demands.

One Last Caution

Even Baltes' point about earlier loss of performance under high demand conditions does not alter very much the basically rosy conclusion about maintenance of intellectual skills over most of the years of adult life. Decline seems to come much later than psychologists had concluded several decades ago, certainly much later than current folklore would have you believe. But once again a caution is in order. Recall the point I made in Chapter 1 about the *attrition problem* in longitudinal research. All longitudinal researchers have found that those adults who survive the longest had higher IQ scores to begin with (e.g., Jarvik & Bank, 1983; Siegler & Botwinick, 1979). This leads us to minimize the amount of decline that may be experienced by less capable or less healthy adults in their 60s or 70s, or earlier. What does seem clear, however, is that broad decline in intellectual ability in middle-age and early old-age is not an *inevitable* accompaniment of aging. Just what factors predict decline for some and maintenance for others is an issue I'll talk about in more detail later in the chapter. First, though, let me turn away from measures of global IQ and standardized test scores and look at age changes in several other aspects of intellectual functioning.

Changes in Memory over Adulthood

Complaints about memory loss are one of the common accompaniments of aging, at least in our culture. (As I write this, I can hear in my mind the sound of one 75-year-old friend making small noises of frustration as he struggles to recall the name of a familiar person or a book he read the week before. "Damn! I can't remember things anymore. What *was* the name of that book?") But how accurate is this widely shared perception of memory loss? Just how much memory do we actually lose, if any, as we get older?

There is a great deal of research touching on these questions, so you might suppose that the answers are clear-cut. But as is often true, the more deeply researchers have explored the question, the more we have seen the complexity of the process. In addition, we are hampered by the fact that the majority of research has been cross-sectional rather than longitudinal, often comparing only a group of 20-year-olds and a group of "old" adults, with little coverage of the ages of middle adulthood. Even worse, the 20-year-olds are nearly always college students, while most of the older adult subjects did not attend college. Timothy Salthouse, one of the major figures in studies of memory change in adulthood, has shown that this method of choosing subjects clearly exacerbates the cohort problem and makes the age differences look much larger (Salthouse, Kausler, & Saults, 1988). When he compared scores for young students, young nonstudents, and older adults he found that while both younger groups performed better than the older adults, the students performed better than the young nonstudents on many tests. Keep these limitations and design flaws in mind as we go along.

Some Terms

Before I describe the findings, I need to define some terms. Several sets of words have been used to describe memory processes. One set of distinctions, still widely used, is between **encoding, storage,** and **retrieval.** Encoding refers to the processes by which information is committed to memory, which may include rehearsal, organizing the material into chunks, making mental pictures of it, or the like. Storage simply refers to what happens (if anything) to the memory over time, regardless of how it was encoded, whereas retrieval describes the processes by which you get information out of memory again when you need it. Of the several types of retrieval, **recognition** is easier than **recall.** If I showed my 75-year-old friend a list of book titles, he could probably quite readily pick out the one he is trying to remember. That is, he recognizes it. What he has trouble doing is recalling it spontaneously.

The distinctions are a bit like what you do when you put food in your refrigerator. Encoding is like what you do when you put it in the refrigerator in the first place. You organize all the vegetables together, all the cheese together, and put all the meat in a special drawer. Storage is what happens to the food over time if you don't eat it. Some of it just sits there, staying essentially the same, like commercial mayonnaise, which will last virtually forever. Some of it decays, like the cheese in the bottom drawer which grows green furry stuff. Retrieval is the process of finding the stuff you want when you need it and taking it out of the refrigerator.

A second way of describing the processes of memory that has dominated more recent research is an information processing model. Again three aspects are typically defined: **sensory memory, short-term memory** (also sometimes called **primary memory**), and **long-term memory** (sometimes called **secondary memory**). In this model, memory is seen in terms of a flow of information through the system. Think of what you do, for example, when you look up and then try to recall a phone number. When you first actually see the number you have a very brief visual impression. This is a sensory memory. If you do nothing more, you will not be able to recall the number even a second later. But if you pay attention to the number in some fashion you transfer it to short-term memory. So, for example, if you say the number to yourself once you can usually remember it long enough to dial without having to check the number again. But short-term memory, too, decays. If I asked you to remember the number a few minutes later, probably you couldn't do so. You had put the number into short-term memory but not into long-term memory. Further processing is required in order to store something in long-term memory—more rehearsals, writing the number many times, or creating some further associations such as noting that the prefix is the same as some other number you know, or noting some pattern in the numbers.

(A perfect example: A mathematician friend pointed out to me that a number I called fairly often but had to look up each time, 256-4444, was easy to remember because 256 is the arithmetic result of 4 x 4 x 4 x 4. I have remembered this number easily ever since.)

Obviously, these two ways of talking about memory are not mutually exclusive. Both sets of terms are useful in understanding what happens to memory with age.

Evidence on Memory Changes

Whether we conclude there is a memory loss with age depends very much on which of these several facets of the memory process we study.

Sensory Memory You might think that sensory memory would get less efficient as you get older. But there is no evidence for a systematic decline in the ability to hold information for a fraction of a second in this sort of sensory memory. Of course, older adults have poorer vision and poorer hearing, so there are some things they simply do not perceive as well. But assuming that something (like the numbers in the phone book) has been perceived, older adults seem to have as good a sensory memory as do younger adults (Craik, 1977; Labouvie-Vief & Schell, 1982).

Short-Term Memory In contrast, there do appear to be slight declines in short-term memory with age. For example, if you read subjects a list of numbers, words, or letters and then ask them to repeat them back in the order given, younger subjects can repeat longer strings than can older adults. As you can see in Figure 6–4, the difference is not large—on the order of one digit or one word fewer for someone in her 70s compared to someone in her 20s (Botwinick & Storandt, 1974)—but it is found quite consistently in cross-sectional studies. (Regrettably, we have no comparable longitudinal evidence). You can also see in the figure that, as with total IQ and measures of crystallized intelligence, declines in memory span appear only in one's 60s.

The effect of age on short-term memory is much larger, however, if the person is asked to do anything with the information—to rearrange it, to recall it in some order other than the one in which it was given, or to repeat back only the words of a particular type. So, for example, if you read off a list of words and then ask the subject to repeat them in backwards order, the discrepancy between the performance of older and younger subjects is larger than when the words are recalled in the order in which they were given. Thus, on simple short-term memory tasks, there is only a small age difference, but as soon as the task is made more complex in almost any way, older subjects are at a greater disadvantage (Craik, 1977).

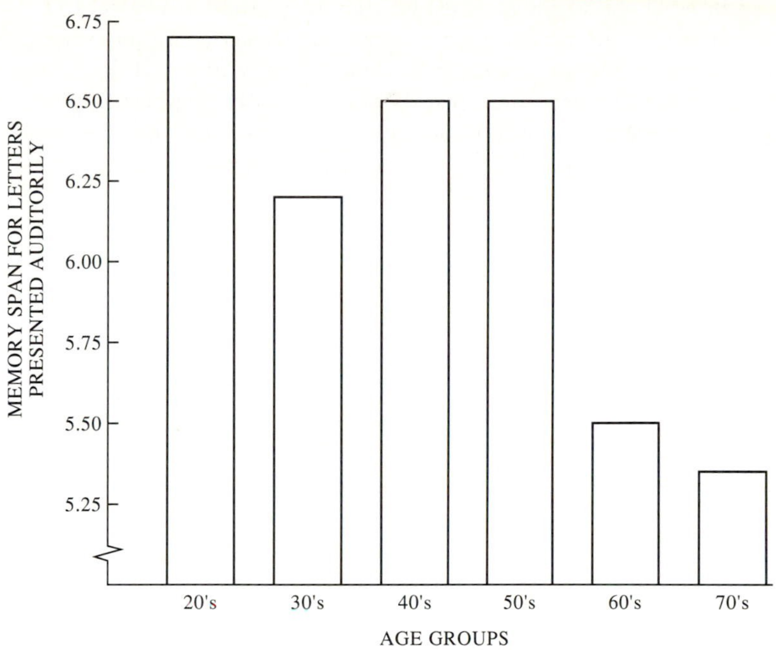

Figure 6–4 In this study, adults of various ages listened to someone reading off a series of letters at a rate of one per second. The subject then had to try to repeat the letters back in the order they had been given. The scores here are the maximum number of letters that could be recalled correctly for each age group, and you can see that adults in their 60s and 70s recalled roughly one letter less. We need to be careful about interpretation here, though, since these are cross-sectional data. (Source: Botwinick & Storandt, 1974.)

LONG-TERM MEMORY Still larger age differences appear when we look at long-term memory (Poon, 1985). Once you exceed the capacity of the short-term storage system, you must either transfer the information to long-term storage, or you will forget it. Somewhere in this process, the older adult seems to run into difficulty. What researchers are still arguing about is just where in the system the difficulty may lie. In particular, does it lie at the point of getting things *into* long-term storage (an encoding process), or does the problem lie at the point of retrieval? Are the memories "in there," but you just can't get to them as easily as you get older? Or do you have trouble getting them "in there" in the first place? As is often the case in disputes of this kind, the answer seems to be "both."

Some of the problem does seem to be in the retrieval process. Perhaps most noticeably, retrieval becomes *slower* with age (e.g. Cerella, 1985; Madden, 1989). But more than just speed seems to be involved here. Older adults generally do about as well (although slower) as younger adults on tasks demanding *recognition* but much less well on tasks demanding *recall.* If you give subjects a list of words to learn, for example, and ask them later to tell you merely whether particular words were in the list, older adults do quite well. But if you ask them to recall as many of the words as possible, they have more difficulty (Labouvie-Vief & Schell, 1982). So long-term memories become less accessible as we get older. Findings like these reinforce the impression of many older adults that they often "know" things that they cannot readily or quickly bring to mind. If they are given a hint, or reminded of the item at some later time, the memory comes back.

But it is in encoding rather than retrieval that the largest decrement with age seems to occur. Older adults appear to use less efficient or less effective strategies for organizing new material for learning. For example, in the standard experimental procedure, subjects are given a list of words to learn, either seeing the whole list at once or being shown each word in sequence for a brief interval. Several strategies have been shown to be effective memory aids on such a task, such as associating an image with each word, making up a sentence with each word in it, or grouping the words into clusters that have some common element (such as having the same first letter or belonging to some similar meaning class, like animals or tools). Least effective is just reading the words over and over to yourself or rehearsing them in the same order they were given to you. Extensive research shows that older adults are much less likely to use any of the more effective strategies spontaneously, even if they are given unlimited time.

In one fairly typical study, Jan Rabinowitz (1989) compared 15 older (ages 61 to 74) and 15 younger (ages 18 to 25) adults on memory for such word lists. In an especially helpful feature, Rabinowitz made sure that the two groups did not differ in overall vocabulary knowledge nor did they differ in education, since the older adults were mostly graduates of the same college from which the young adult sample was drawn. Rabinowitz asked each subject to learn and later recall four lists of 24 words each, two under standard conditions in which each word in the list was presented on a computer screen for five seconds, and two under unlimited study conditions in which the subjects controlled the speed of presentation, could take notes, and were encouraged to use any and all strategies that they thought would help. You can see in Figure 6–5 that having extra study time helped both the younger and the older adults to remember more of the words, but it helped the younger adults proportionately more. The younger subjects in this study did not spend more extra time studying than did the elders, but they appeared to derive more benefit from the study time, presumably because they were better able to use the extra study time to mobilize various strategies for encoding the list of words—a conclusion further bolstered by the fact that in this sample, those young subjects who took the longest times to study the words had the highest recall scores; but that was not true among the older subjects.

If older adults are given some hints about what strategies will work or if the task is organized in such a way that the adult is aimed at a good strategy, their performance typically improves, but the age difference does not disappear (e.g. Brigham & Pressley, 1988; Craik & Rabinowitz, 1985).

Some experts have concluded that what the older adult suffers from is what has been called a *production deficiency*. That is, the individual possesses the requisite skills or strategies but does not produce them spontaneously when they might be helpful (Perlmutter, Adams, Berry, Kaplan, Person, & Verdonik, 1987). This notion was originally proposed by John Flavell (1970) in his studies of young

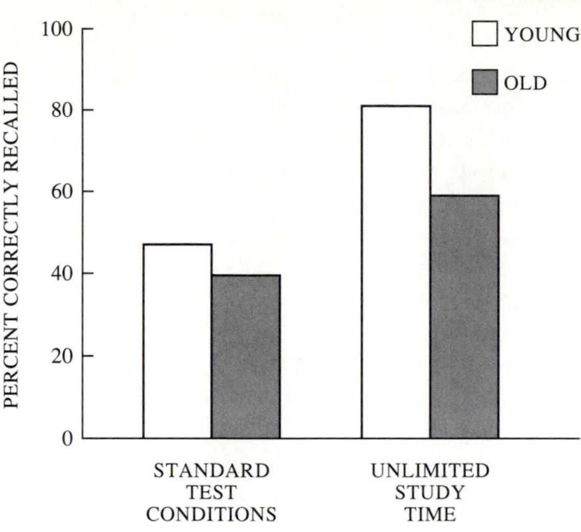

Figure 6–5 In Jan Rabinowitz' study, older adults had poorer recall of lists of words in both the standard condition, when a new word in the list was shown on the screen every five seconds, and with unlimited study conditions, when the subject controlled the rate of presentation. Both older and younger adults were helped by having more study time. But younger adults were helped more, suggesting that older adults are less good at thinking up or using good encoding strategies. (Source: Rabinowitz, 1989, from Table 1, p. 379.)

children's memory processes. He found that five- and six-year-olds could use quite elaborate strategies and therefore remember better if they were reminded to use those strategies, but they didn't use such techniques spontaneously. Two or three years later, children begin to use complex strategies without being reminded. There may well be a parallel here with what happens in old age; older adults may simply not use all the skills they actually possess. But it isn't clear that such a production deficiency can account for all the differences in memory skills, since the age differences don't disappear even when both young and old adults are using optimum encoding strategies.

Familiar versus Unfamiliar Material Another possibility is that older adults can remember just as well but that they are simply less motivated to play researchers' games with highly artificial tasks like memorizing lists of words. If we tested adults with memory for more ordinary things, perhaps we would find no age differences.

Yes and no. On the plus side is the typical finding that older adults do just as well as younger adults at remembering the basic points of some narrative passage they have read, such as a newspaper article (e.g. Tun, 1989). Older adults also seem to be as good (or maybe even better) at remembering to do things they have promised to do, such as calling someone at some agreed upon time (Poon

& Schaffer, 1982), and they are equally good at remembering items of experience that were highly salient at the time, such as whether they voted in an election four years earlier (Hertzog & Rogers, 1989).

In one study of this kind of everyday memory, Jan Sinnott (1986) tested a group of adults aged 23 to 93 who were part of the Baltimore Longitudinal Study. During the regular two-day testing session at the labs, each subject was asked to recall various bits of information about the labs themselves, about the daily routine, or about the other tests they had been given (e.g. "When does the hospital cafeteria stop serving dinner?" "Describe one problem you worked on during the problem solving test." "Which of this list of things was on the table when you were solving problems at the lab?"). Some of these items were highly salient for the subjects' daily life (such as the cafeteria serving times); others were not. Sinnott then called up each subject 7 to 10 days later, and again 18 to 21 *months* later, and asked the same questions. What she found was that the older adults did just as well at remembering the highly salient material but much less well at the less salient information, such as what items had been on the test table. Results like this suggest that what the older adult does is to focus her attention and encoding capacity on the really crucial every day stuff and ignore the rest. The younger adult, who may have greater encoding or memory storage capacity, picks up a wider range of information.

On the other side of this balance scale are studies that show that older adults are less good than younger ones at remembering whether they had performed some task—such as remembering whether you turned the stove off before you left the house (e.g. Kausler, Lichty & Freund, 1985)—and studies that show that older adults have a poorer spatial memory even for familiar places. In one fairly typical study, Evans and his colleagues (Evans, Brennan, Skorpanich, & Held, 1984) asked old and young adults (*not* college students) to list and place on a grid the major buildings in the downtown area of their own town—a town they had lived in for many years. The older adults recalled fewer buildings and were less accurate in placing them on the street grid.

There is also some indication that older adults are less good at remembering *where* they learned something—an issue of some practical relevance for such tasks as eyewitness testimony. In one study, Gillian Cohen and Dorothy Faulkner (1989), following a common procedure for studies of eyewitness accuracy, showed subjects a videotape of an ostensible crime. Half the subjects then read a short matching written description of the same events, while half the subjects read a misleading written version in which there were several key mistakes. Ten minutes later the subjects were all given a multiple-choice test about the content of the *film* and told specifically to cast their mind back to what they saw on the film. Cohen and Faulkner compared the performance of young adults (ages 25 to 45) and older adults (ages 62 to 82), with the two groups matched for education and social background. Figure 6–6 shows the key findings. Notice that the older subjects remembered less of what they'd seen in the film under both conditions, but the biggest difference occurred when the written version did not match the film. In this case, the older subjects had much poorer memories.

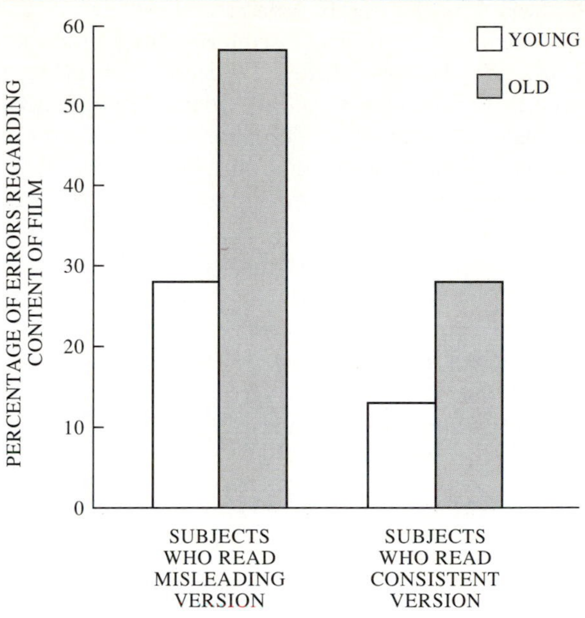

Figure 6–6 The results of Cohen and Faulkner's study of eyewitness recall are very similar in form to those Rabinowitz found in studying memory for lists (Figure 6-5): Older subjects recalled less accurately under both conditions. Both older and younger adults recalled the film more accurately when they had read a written version that matched the film, but the misleading version had a bigger negative effect on the older than the younger adults, suggesting that the ability to monitor one's memories and keep track of sources of information declines with age. (Source: Cohen & Faulkner, from Table 5, p. 16.)

Overall, then, the findings are decidedly mixed. On some kinds of everyday memory tasks, older adults seem to do about as well as younger ones, but on many others the familiar age deficit appears in adults in their 60s or older.

Summing up What We know about Age Changes in Memory

Before going on to talk about other aspects of thinking, let me pull the threads together on this diverse body of findings about memory.

First, it seems incontrovertible that there is some decline in memory as we get older. Because most of the research has involved comparisons of "young" and "old" subjects, we can't be very precise about when this decline begins, but it is clearly present by the 60s. Marion Perlmutter (1986), another of the key theorists and researchers in this area, estimates that over 40 years of adulthood the deficits are roughly 5 to 20 percent on encoding tasks and roughly 15 to 20 percent on retrieval tasks.

The biggest change appears to be in the speed of the whole memory process. It takes longer to register some new information, longer to encode it, longer to retrieve it—all of which undoubtedly reflects many of the physiological changes I described in Chapter 4, such as the slowing of neural processes.

What is still a matter of intense theoretical debate is whether there is also some loss of basic capacity. To go back to the refrigerator analogy, does the refrigerator get smaller as we age? We could also compare the whole process to a computer (a common analogy). Those of you who work with computers know that it is important to distinguish between the amount of memory capacity on the hard disk (equivalent to long-term memory) and the random access memory (RAM), which is the basic working memory capacity of the machine. This "short-term" memory has to hold whatever program you are currently using, along with whatever data you are adding in. What we do not know is whether, as we age, either our 'hard disk' memory or our RAM capacity declines, or whether the differences in memory performance that we see can be accounted for only in terms of speed or in less efficient use of strategies (Salthouse, 1990).

Changes in Problem Solving Ability over Adulthood

I could write a very similar summary about changes in problem solving skill over the adult years: On laboratory tasks there are consistent age differences; on more practical or everyday tasks the differences are smaller but not eliminated; and there is a production deficiency.

"Problem solving" refers to the complex set of processes that you use to figure out a solution to something, or as Rainer Kluwe (1986) puts it, it is "the search for means in order to reach a desired goal state" (p. 509). If your car doesn't start in the morning, the procedures you go through to figure out why or to call for help are all forms of problem solving. To pursue the computer analogy yet again, problem solving skills are the software, the programs.

Laboratory tasks of problem solving are varied, but a typical one requires the subject to figure out which combination of button pressings are needed to turn on a light. On such tasks, younger adults are not only more likely to be successful, they also appear to use more optimal strategies. As was true for memory tasks, this age difference is found even when the subjects are encouraged to take notes and keep track of each of the combinations they have already tried. Older adults in such studies take fewer and apparently less effective notes (Kluwe, 1986).

A slightly more real-life task, modeled after the game of "Twenty Questions" has yielded similar results. The experimenter thinks of some real-life object, and the subject has to figure out what it is by asking questions that can be answered "yes" or "no." In this case, the subject has two problems: to think up the questions and then to evaluate the answers to arrive at a solution. The kinds of questions a person asks can be divided into two main types, one of which is much more efficient and helpful than the other. Following the early labels proposed by Mosher & Hornsby (1966), the less effective question is called a *hypothesis* and consists of a specific guess ("Is it your red hat?" "Is it a gazelle?"). A *constraint question,* on the other hand, asks about a whole category of possibilities ("Is it living?" "Is it blue?" "Is it larger than a breadbox?").

Nancy Denney has used this game in a whole series of studies of problem solving in adults and consistently finds that in cross-sectional comparisons older adults use fewer constraint questions than do younger adults, as you can see in Figure 6–7. Since asking constraint questions is more informative and is thus, a better strategy, it also takes older adults more questions to arrive at the solution.

This rather striking change with age could have several explanations. It could, of course, be at least partially a cohort effect. As usual, the older groups in this study have had less education than the younger groups, and education may have an effect on the kinds of strategies people know how to use. The one longitudinal study of problem solving I know of, by Arenberg (1974; Arenberg & Robertson-Tchabo, 1977), lends some support to this possibility. Studying subjects aged 24 to 87 who were part of the now-familiar Baltimore Longitudinal Study, Arenberg tested each subject twice, six years apart. He found that declines in learning and

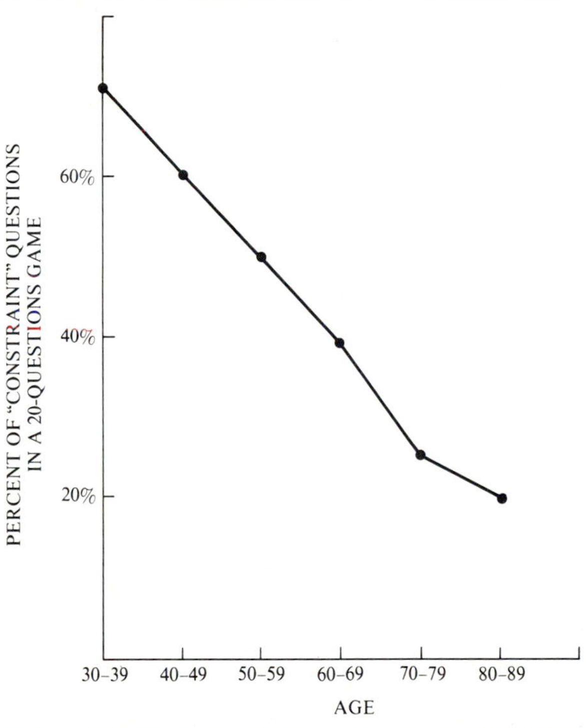

Figure 6–7 When adults of various ages were asked to play 20 Questions, older adults used fewer "constraint" questions than did younger adults. (A constraint question is one that eliminates or confirms a whole group of possibilities, such as asking "Is it larger than a breadbox?") These differences are quite striking, but they could reflect either cohort differences or differences in familiarity with the task, rather than real "decline" in problem-solving skills with age. (Source: Denney & Denney, 1982, from Table 2, p. 192.)

problem solving occurred only in subjects of 70 and older. Thus, the apparent earlier decline in problem solving ability, like the apparent decline in cross-sectional comparisons of IQ scores, may reflect cohort differences and not real loss.

The pattern of change shown in Figure 6–7 could also reflect the artificiality of the tasks used in experiments. Perhaps older adults are just as skilled as younger adults at solving real-life problems—the kind they encounter every day in their own lives—but are both less familiar with and less interested in the problems that researchers dream up.

Denney has attempted to discover whether familiarity and problem relevance play a part in the apparent decline of problem solving skill by asking a group of over-65-year-olds to help her identify a series of real-life problems that older adults might typically encounter, such as:

> Let's say that a 67-year-old man's doctor has told him to take it easy because of a heart condition. It's summertime and the man's yard needs to be mowed but the man cannot afford to pay someone to mow the lawn. What should he do? (Denney & Pearce, 1989, p. 439)

She then posed the 10 problems identified in this way to groups of adults of various ages from 20 to 79, scoring their answers according to the number of safe and effective solutions proposed. Denney found, as she had in previous studies, that the highest scores were found among the middle-aged, with the older subjects scoring the lowest, even when she controlled statistically for differences in educational levels among the various age groups. Thus, even when the problems to be solved are clearly relevant to older adults, their problem solving ability appears to be lower.

But as with studies of memory, there are signs of a production deficiency among the elderly. That is, they are less likely to use good problem solving strategies spontaneously, but if you remind them to use them or train them in some strategy, their performance improves—though still not to the level seen in younger adults (e.g. Hartley and Anderson, 1986).

There is not yet enough research on problem solving to draw firm conclusions, but as with the research on memory, there appears to be some decline or loss of skill in old age. As Kluwe puts it, in old adults' problem solving behavior, "The solution search, given well-defined problems, is not very well organized, it is inefficient, redundant, and finally not very successful" (1986, p. 519).

Changes in Intellectual Structure over Adulthood

All of the measures of intellectual ability I have talked about so far emerge from the tradition within psychology that defines intelligence in terms of *power* or *skill.* IQ tests are designed to tell us how well someone can do something or how quickly. But there is another way to think about intellectual changes with age, typified by Jean Piaget's theory of cognitive development (1952; 1964; Piaget

& Inhelder, 1969). Piaget was interested in changes in cognitive *structure* with age rather than in individual differences in intellectual power. What kind of logic does the child or adult use? How does the form of logic, the way of going about solving problems, change over the course of development? Piaget's work was almost entirely focused on cognitive development in children, but his theory has also influenced some of the work on cognition in adulthood and old age.

Piaget proposed that there are four major stages of cognitive development, which I've sketched in Table 6.2. Shifts from one stage to the next occur gradually rather than suddenly, but each stage is thought to represent a general pattern of thinking. In Western cultures, virtually all adults think easily at the concrete operational level; perhaps half of adults think at the formal operational level at least some of the time.

TABLE 6.2. Piaget's Stages of Cognitive Development.

Stage	Age	Description
Sensorimotor	birth–2 years	The baby interacts with the world, and understands the world around her, through senses and actions. Until at least age 1, according to Piaget, the infant does not represent objects internally. She "knows" objects only by what she can do with them or how she experiences them directly.
Preoperational	2–6 years	Preoperational children are still tied to their own view ("egocentric" in Piaget's terms), but they can represent things internally, using words or images, they can engage in fantasy play, and they begin to be able to classify objects into groups. There is a primitive form of logic at this stage.
Concrete Operational	6–12 years	The school-age child moves into a kind of intellectual third gear, discovering a whole series of powerful mental actions, which Piaget calls "operations," such as addition, subtraction, serial ordering, and the like. Children in this stage are capable of inductive logic (arriving at general principles by adding up specific experiences), and they are better able to understand others' points of view; but they are still tied to their own experience, and cannot yet imagine things they have not known directly.
Formal Operational	12 years and into adulthood	Formal operations represents intellectual high gear. Those teenagers and adults who achieve this level of thinking (and not all do) are capable of deductive logic ("if . . . then" reasoning, for example); can approach problems systematically, examining all possible combinations or possibilities; and can think about ideas as well as about objects. This is vastly more abstract than concrete operations, although concrete operations are sufficient for most everyday experiences.

When researchers studying adults have used some of the tasks Piaget devised to measure the structure of thought, the common result has been that older adults appear to "think like children." For example, Piaget was interested in the ways children grouped and classified objects. Young children in the preoperational stage often make stories or pictures out of objects and shapes (e.g. "The pipe and the matches go together because you use the matches to light the pipe.") Older children typically put objects together based on some more abstract similarity, such as shape or function. Nancy Denney (Pearce & Denney, 1984) gave a standardized version of this task to groups of children and adults and found that the adults over 65, like the younger children, most often grouped things based on "complementarity", while the young and middle-aged adults based their groupings on more abstract similarities.

Other research using Piaget's tasks has yielded similar findings (Denney, 1982). But we have to be very careful about assuming that these findings reflect "regression" to earlier levels on the part of older adults. Denney has found, for example, that older adults are quite capable of making groupings based on similarity if they are told that is what is wanted. So the analytic skill is there, but the older adult normally chooses to approach the task in a different way. Perhaps this is merely yet another illustration of a production deficiency. Alternatively, perhaps the necessity of dealing with the practicalities of every day adult life pushes adults away from the logic of formal operations into other ways of thinking, other structures.

A number of theorists have made precisely this argument. Among them is Gisela Labouvie-Vief (1980), who has argued that we should not make the mistake of assuming that formal operations is the highest and best form of thought in all situations. Formal operations, with its emphasis on the exploration of all logical possibilities, is highly adaptive in early adulthood when the young person is exploring options, establishing identity. But adult responsibilities require reasoning that is tied to specific concrete contexts. Adult thought thus becomes *specialized* and *pragmatic.* The adult learns how to solve the problems associated with the particular social roles she occupies or the particular job she holds and discovers how to meet the specific difficulties or challenges. In the process, the deductive thoroughness of formal operations is traded off for contextual validity. In Labouvie-Vief's view, this trade-off does not reflect a regression or a loss but a necessary structural change.

In her more recent writing (1990) Labouvie-Vief has also emphasized a theme that is common to many of the newer structural ideas—that in adulthood we begin to turn away from the purely logical, the purely analytic approach, toward a more open, perhaps deeper mode of understanding that deals more in terms of myth and metaphor, paradox instead of certainty. Michael Basseches (1984; 1989) calls this new adult type of thinking **dialectical thought.** He suggests that while formal thought "involves the effort to find fundamental fixed realities—basic elements and immutable laws—[dialectical thought] attempts to describe fundamental processes of change and the dynamic relationships through which this change occurs" (1984, p. 24). Adults do not give up their ability to use formal reasoning, but they acquire a new ability to deal with those fuzzier problems that seem to make up the majority of the problems of adulthood—problems that do not have a single solution or in which some critical pieces of information may be missing. You might be able to make a decision about what kind of car to buy using formal, logical thought processes. But such forms of logic will not be so helpful in making a decision about whether to end a marriage, whether to place your aging parent in a nursing home, or even something apparently more straightforward such as whether to take a new job in another city. Such problems demand a different kind of thinking—not a "higher" kind of thinking, but a different one.

There is little empirical evidence to support (or refute) these theories about special structures of adult thought. But the ideas are extremely interesting and may help to move us away from the dominant (but limited) view of adult thinking which focuses primarily on the gain or loss of specific skills.

Age Changes in Creativity and Productivity

While all of the changes I have been describing are of considerable interest, you may find the issues rather abstract. For many of us, the more compelling question is whether the cumulative changes in intellectual speed, power, or structure have any effect on our ability to do productive mental work as we get older. Do scientific breakthroughs—those rare, creative achievements—come mostly in early adulthood? Are older lawyers less effective advocates than younger ones? Do business executives have more difficulty solving problems later in life?

There is remarkably little research on questions of this kind, in part because in most areas of adult work there are no clear, agreed-on measures of skill or productivity. How do we judge the quality of a business person's solutions or the quality of an architect's plans? What little we do know about productivity and quality of work over adulthood comes primarily from studies of academic careers, where there are standard measures available, namely number and quality of publications.

Early research by Lehman (1953), widely quoted since then, indicated that major scientific discoveries over the past several hundred years were achieved primarily in early adulthood. That is, if you start by selecting scientific or theoretical breakthroughs and ask how old the researcher or theoretician was when he or she made that particular discovery, you find that most were quite young, especially in science and mathematics. Einstein was 26 when he developed the special theory of relativity; the theory of natural selection was proposed by Darwin when he was 29.

But there is another way to ask the question that seems to me to be more relevant for those of us who are not in the same class as Einstein or Darwin: Over the adult life of the ordinary scientist or mathematician (or lawyer or businessperson or artist), does productivity or quality of work peak in the early years and then decline?

There is not a vast amount of evidence, but the answer seems to be that *quantity* of work declines but the quality is maintained at a reasonably even level until fairly late in one's productive life, perhaps age 60 or so. One of the best of the current crop of research is a cross-sequential study of the productivity of psychologists from four different cohorts: those born in 1909 to 1914, 1919 to 1924, 1929 to 1934, and 1939 to 1944. Karen Horner, Philippe Rushton and Phil Vernon (1986) examined the publication records of the more than 1,000 academicians, with the results shown in Figure 6–8. Peak productivity occurred in midlife (35 to 44) and then dropped fairly steadily after that—a finding corroborated by other researchers (Cole, 1979; Over, 1989). This drop in the number of articles published could reflect loss of creativity or skill, although other interpretations are possible. Arthur Diamond (1986) points out that older scientists have more competing demands made on their time, including supervision of students, administrative work, peer review, and the like.

Perhaps more importantly, measures of publication quality do not show a decline in the middle years of adulthood. Articles written by mathematicians, psychologists, physicists, and other scientists in their 40s and 50s are cited just as often as are articles written in their 20s or 30s. Among musicians and other creative artists, the quality of work may be maintained far longer. Dean Simonton (1989), in a particularly interesting study of the quality of the work of the 172 most often performed musical composers, found that while late-in-life works showed lower

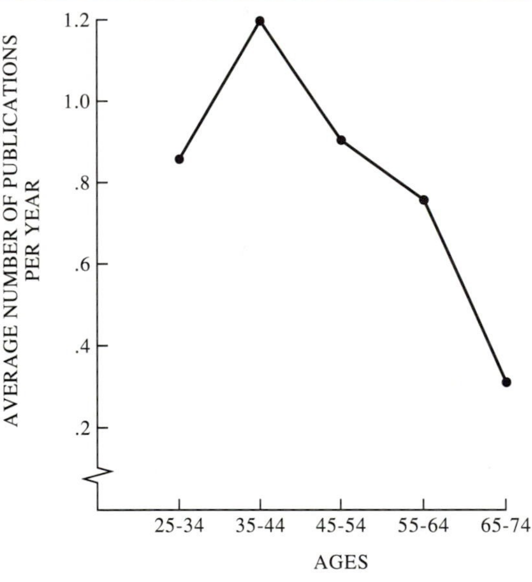

Figure 6–8 Horner and her colleagues, in this cross-sequential study of more than 1,000 academic psychologists born between 1909 and 1944, found that the number of publications per year peaked in early adulthood and then declined. But other evidence in this same study shows that the quality of work—at least as measured by the number of citations of the various papers—did not decrease. (Source: Horner, Rushton, & Vernon, 1986, Figure 1, p. 321).

melodic originality, the "aesthetic significance" of the late works was actually higher. Judges were more likely to rate these "swan songs" as being masterpieces than was true of earlier works by the same composers.

Although there are many possible interpretations of these findings, one conclusion seems fairly clear: At least among those adults who remain intellectually or creatively active, the possibility of significant, creative, powerful work remains well into late middle-age and perhaps much later. For those of you who thought you were (or would be) intellectually over the hill at 40, this may be a comforting conclusion.

Terminal Drop

Perhaps equally comforting is the concept of "terminal drop" or "critical loss" (although certainly these labels sound depressing enough!). The general idea, first proposed by Kleemeier (1962), is that intellectual power and skill is maintained virtually unchanged through adulthood until approximately 5 to 7 years before death, at which point there is a fairly rapid decline. Since each older cohort in a cross-sectional study and each subsequent testing in a longitudinal study contains a larger and larger percentage of adults who are within five years of their eventual death, an average pattern of decline emerges. But perhaps we would not find the same declines if we measured "time until death" instead of age.

The only way to study this is in a longitudinal study in which it is possible to track backwards after the death of each subject and determine whether there was either steady decline or stability followed by rapid decline. Exactly this sort of analysis has been done in several studies (e.g. Johansson & Berg, 1989; Siegler, McCarty & Logue, 1982; White & Cunningham, 1988). In one fairly typical study, Palmore and Cleveland (1976) examined the pattern of earlier test scores in a group of 178 deceased men who had participated in the Duke longitudinal studies. They found no indication of terminal drop on tests of physical functioning (which showed steady declines) but did find a pattern of terminal drop for the total IQ score. For these men, IQ remained relatively stable until a few years from death, at which point it dropped rather sharply.

On the whole, it appears that a sudden loss of performance on a nonspeeded or crystallized test, particularly vocabulary, is particularly predictive of impending death. Declines in performance on fluid/speeded tests are more gradual and seem not to show the pattern of terminal drop.

Summary of Age Changes in Intellectual Performance

I've given you myriad pieces of the puzzle. Now I need to try to create an overall picture, particularly in light of the long-standing (and sometimes acrimonious) debate between those theorists who have seen decline and those who have seen maintenance of intellectual abilities over the adult years. I think that we are reaching a point of empirical convergence in this debate, although there is still clearly a vast amount we do not yet understand. Here are the key points as I see them:

1. Most intellectual abilities are well maintained through early and middle adulthood, beginning to decline only in the 60s. The exceptions to this rule are some "fluid" abilities, especially those that require speed, which begin to decline earlier than this, and highly learned, well-rehearsed abilities, such as vocabulary, which decline later—perhaps not until five years before death.
2. Although the declines are measurable in our 60s, they are initially small enough in most cases to have relatively little impact on our daily functioning. By our 70s and 80s, however, the declines have reached a sufficient magnitude that they may affect our ability to solve daily problems, to learn new things, to recall ordinary bits of information.
3. When intellectual decline occurs, it is characterized by at least two key features: We get slower, and we get less efficient. We do not yet know whether there is some basic loss of processing *capacity* underlying these changes—some reduction in the power of the computer—or whether there are other forces at work here.
4. When we see deterioration in intellectual performance at ages younger than 60, it is likely to be either because of some disease process (such as Alzheimer's disease) or because the individual is confronted with an especially difficult, stressful, or complex task. It is at the limits of our ability that earlier deficits are apparent.
5. Whether there are new forms of intellectual activity unique to adulthood, such as practical or pragmatic intelligence or wisdom, is simply not yet known.
6. All of the above statements are true only of the average. There are *wide* individual variations in timing and speed of intellectual decline—a subject I now need to explore in more depth.

Individual Differences in Rate of Intellectual Changes in Adulthood

To give you some sense of the magnitude of this variation, let me show you (in Figure 6–9) the scores on a vocabulary test for four different individuals who were tested five times each, over 28 years, as part of Schaie's Seattle Longitudinal Study (Schaie, 1989b). It does not take more than a glance at this figure to see that both the timing and the rapidity of the drop in vocabulary skill varied enormously.

Schaie doesn't tell us much about these individuals, but he does give a few broad brushstrokes. Subject A is a woman who has been a homemaker all her adult life; her husband is still alive and in good health. Subject B, in contrast, is a woman who worked as a teacher for a good portion of her life. After she turned 60, she was divorced, retired, and began to experience significant health

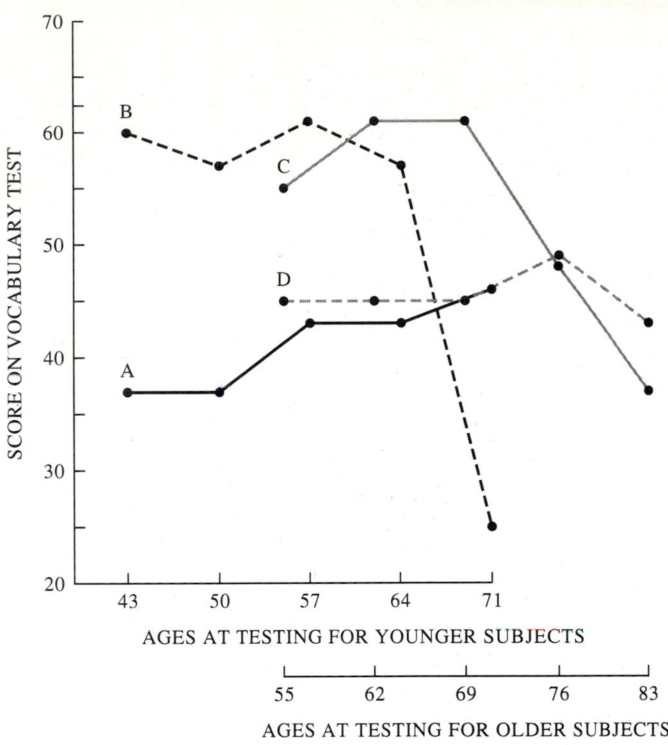

Figure 6–9 *These four adults were all participants in the Seattle Longitudinal Study, and all had been tested five times, at seven-year intervals. Obviously, there was wide variation in the pattern of maintenance or loss of verbal abilities among these adults. (Source: Schaie, 1989b, Figures 5.13 and 5.14, pp 82-83).*

problems. Subject C is a man with a high school education who did clerical work most of his life. He showed essentially no change until his seventies and again poor health may be implicated in this decline, since the final testing, at age 83, was only a year before his death. Finally, subject D is a man with a grade school education who had worked in a white-collar job. When he retired, his score on this test actually increased; it has gone down only at the latest assessment, at a time when he had recently become a widower and was experiencing health problems.

These brief profiles certainly point to health as a potentially major element in the individual differences equation. Other results from the Seattle study, as well as other longitudinal evidence, points to "exercise"—including mental activity of various kinds as well as physical exercise—as an important element as well.

Health Effects on Intellectual Aging

When I talk about the role of health in mental aging, there is a distinct echo from my earlier discussion of the link between health and physical aging. You'll remember from Chapter 4 that one of the key problems is to identify those aspects of physical change with age that are "real" aging—inevitable in everyone—and those that are a result of disease. The same question returns here: How much of the average decline in mental abilities that I've been documenting is inevitable and linked to age, and how much is the result of disease?

The answer is similar, too: There is some of both. In general, unusually early or rapid decline in mental abilities is nearly always associated with serious health problems. You can see an example of such a connection in Table 6.3, based on a survey of a representative national sample of over 14,000 adults aged 55 and older. It's clear from the table that those adults who report that their health has worsened also report that their memory has worsened. But you can also see in the table that a health improvement wasn't associated with any improvement in memory. In general, within the range of fair to good health, there was not a great deal of difference in reported memory problems. In other words, really poor health or a recent rapid decline in health seems to be associated with poorer mental performance. But other variations in health are less critical.

Further support for this general conclusion comes from a 14-year longitudinal study of 90 of the parents of subjects who participated in the Berkeley studies. Dorothy Field and her colleagues (Field, Schaie, & Leino, 1988) found that knowing about an individual's health in 1969, when the subjects were aged 59 to 79, did not predict that individual's mental test scores 14 years later *except* for those at the extremes of the distribution. Extremely poor health at the first test was associated with more mental decline over the 14 years.

It looks to me as if both the observed decline in mental skills and the increasing likelihood of poor health are reflections of the same basic, underlying aging processes I described in Chapter 4. When a particular individual shows better than average maintenance of both mental skill and good health, it may well reflect slower underlying physical aging processes for that person. An individual could also show normal or better-than-normal maintenance of mental skill in his 60s and 70s and still suffer from one or more chronic illnesses, so long as he does not contract any of the specific diseases that appear to have a direct effect

TABLE 6.3. Relationship Between Self-Reported Health and Self-Reported Memory Problems.

Self-reported health compared to a year ago	Frequency of trouble remembering things compared to a year ago	
	More often	*Same/less often*
Better	15.7 %	84.3 %
Same	13.1 %	86.9 %
Worse	42.9 %	57.1 %

SOURCE: Cutler and Grams, 1988, Table 1, p. S85. Reprinted with permission from *Journal of Gerontology: Social Sciences, 43*, pp. S82–90, 1988.

on intellectual functioning. Two groups of diseases are particularly implicated in intellectual loss: senile dementias of all types, and cardiovascular disease.

SENILE DEMENTIAS I talked about these diseases at some length in the last chapter and need to comment here only on the specific impact of dementias on mental functioning. The most noticeable effects are on speed of performing any mental operation and on memory. The memory function does not disappear all at once. Short-term memory goes first. The patient loses the ability to learn new things since they can't be kept in memory long enough to get them into long-term storage (e.g. Vitaliano, Breen, Albert, Russo & Prinz, 1984; Whelihan, Lesher, Kleban, & Granick, 1984). As the disease progresses, the patient eventually loses long-term memories as well, such as names and faces, how to use a fork, how to tie her shoes, the date, even where she lives. Simple commands can still be followed fairly well in the early stages, but that ability, too, is lost as the disease continues.

CARDIOVASCULAR DISEASE (CVD) This general label is applied to a whole family of diseases including coronary artery disease (CAD) and high blood pressure. We know that at any given age, adults with significant CVD have slightly lower scores on various tests of mental ability, and longitudinal studies indicate that those who suffer from such diseases show significantly earlier declines. In the Seattle Longitudinal Study, Schaie (1983b) has found that those subjects with CVD showed greater declines with age in both total intellectual ability and in number ability than did non CVD subjects. Even adults whose high blood pressure is controlled by medication appear to show earlier declines than do those with normal BP (Schultz, Elias, Robbins, Streeten, & Blakeman, 1986). But Schaie makes two critical points about these findings: (1) the size of the effect is quite small, and (2) the effect may be indirect rather than direct. That is, adults who are diagnosed as having some form of cardiovascular disease may change their lifestyle, perhaps becoming less active. It could then be the lifestyle changes, rather than the disease, that is the causal factor in the slightly greater intellectual decline.

"Exercise" Effects on Intellectual Aging

I am using the word "exercise" rather broadly to describe a second major category of influences on intellectual abilities in adults. Obviously, physical exercise is one part of this category. But so is mental exercise of any form, including going to school, doing crossword puzzles, playing chess, reading the daily paper, doing complex work. The basic hypothesis suggested by gerontologists and psychologists is that any intellectual ability that is used regularly will be maintained at a higher level, just as physically exercised bodies remain fitter. ("Use it or lose it" strikes again!). If that is true, then individual adults who are more physically and intellectually active should show better maintenance of intellectual skill than should less active adults.

There are several threads of information that support this hypothesis.

Education Effects

The most indirect evidence comes from the repeated finding that better educated adults not only perform intellectual tasks at a higher level but maintain their intellectual skill longer in old age (Jarvik & Bank, 1983; Palmore, 1981; Schaie, 1983b).

There are several possible explanations of this correlation between education and maintenance of intellectual skill. The most obvious possibility is that it may not be education at all that is involved here but underlying intellectual ability, leading to both more years of education and better maintenance of intellectual skill in old age.

A second explanation may lie in the fact that better educated people remain more intellectually active throughout their adult years. It may thus be the intellectual activity ("exercise" in the sense in which I have been using that term) which helps to maintain the mental skills. Education may influence lifestyle and intellectual activity, which in turn may help maintain intellectual skill.

The Effects of Intellectual Activity

There is at least *some* evidence to support this possibility. In three separate longitudinal studies involving adults past the age of 60 (Schaie, 1983b; Jarvik & Bank, 1983; Busse & Wang, 1971), a link between activity levels and intellectual maintenance has been found. Adults who read books and take classes seem to do better intellectually over time. It is the more isolated and inactive adults (whatever their level of education) who show the most decline in IQ. In the Duke studies, for example (Busse & Wang, 1971), those adults who reported that they participated in many "sedentary activities," which included reading, playing games, hobbies, and the like, actually showed a small but statistically significant increase in verbal skills over a six-year period, whereas those who were inactive showed a significant decline.

Cross-sectional studies show much the same thing. Let me give you just one example. Elizabeth Rice and Bonnie Meyer (1986) asked young, middle-aged, and older adults to read and recall in writing two brief prose passages—similar to the sort of article one might read in a newspaper or magazine. They also asked each person about how much and what kind of reading he or she did in everyday life. What they found was that those who reported the most real-life reading also had better recall of the passages. The correlations were not large (on the order of .20 or .25 for the different age groups), but they were statistically significant.

My hunch is that there is a real causal link between intellectual activity and maintenance of intellectual skill in old age, but at this point I can't argue for much more than a hunch. The evidence is neither extensive nor particularly strong. Intellectual activity is not usually measured very precisely, and in every case, level of activity is correlated with years of education. As I already pointed out in Chapter 2, better educated adults are more likely to continue their education through adult education classes or seminars and to read more—newspapers, novels, non-

Figure 6–10 It makes sense that the older adult in the lower photo, who is still mentally active, will stay alert and have better mental functioning longer than the less active adult in the upper photo. Longitudinal research supports this hypothesis, but of course it is possible that the causality is complex: Those adults who are initially more intellectually able are likely to remain mentally active longer and have generally had more education as well. Still, mental "exercise" seems like a useful (as well as interesting) activity throughout life. (Photos © Joel Gordon, 1990. Reprinted with permission.)

fiction. What we have, then, is a complex interactive process. As Schaie puts it:

> it appears that there are substantial relationships among social status, life-styles, and the maintenance of intellectual ability. But these relationships seem to be interactive rather than causal. . . . early, favorable life experience may be implicated in attaining high levels of intellectual functioning in young adulthood; their maintenance into old age, however, may be related to an engaged life-style, but that life-style may also be a function of a high level of ability. (Schaie, 1983b, p. 119)

Physical Exercise and Intellectual Abilities

The case for a causal link between physical exercise and intellectual skill is a bit better. The fundamental argument, of course, is that exercise helps to maintain cardiovascular (and possibly neural) fitness—which we know is linked to mental maintenance. And when researchers have compared mental performance scores for highly active and sedentary older adults, they have consistently found that the more active have higher scores. For instance, in one recent study, Louise Clarkson-Smith and Alan Hartley (1989) compared 62 highly physically active and 62 inactive adults, all between the ages of 55 and 88. These active adults reported an average of more than five hours of strenuous exercise or activity each week, including gardening and heavy housework as well as traditional aerobic exercise. In contrast, the low activity group reported zero hours per week of such strenuous pastimes. The high activity group scored consistently higher on tests of reasoning, short-term memory and reaction time, and this was true even when the comparisons included only those subjects who were exceptionally healthy and the two groups were matched for education.

Of course (as many of you will have figured out yourselves), there is a difficulty built in to any study like this, despite the researchers' care in matching the active and inactive groups for education and health. These groups are self-selected rather than randomly assigned. The active group *chose* to be active, and it remains possible that those adults who are already functioning at higher intellectual levels are simply more likely to choose to maintain their physical fitness. A better test would be an experiment in which healthy, sedentary adults are randomly assigned to exercise and nonexercise groups and then tested over a period of time.

Results from such experimental studies of exercise are somewhat mixed. Some find that the exercise group improves in mental test scores (e.g. Elsayed, Ismail, & Young, 1980) while others do not (e.g. Madden, Blumenthal, Allen, & Emery, 1989; Emery & Gatz, 1990). In most of these studies, the exercise program lasts no more than 8 to 16 weeks, which is long enough for such *physical* effects of exercise as increases in VO_2 max to be detectable, but it may not be long enough to generate a consistent effect on mental performance. It may be that exercise has a beneficial effect on raising or maintaining intellectual skill only when it is a long-term part of one's life.

Environmental Complexity and Intellectual Maintenance

A fourth piece in this interactive puzzle comes from the work of Melvin Kohn and Carmi Schooler (Kohn, 1980; Kohn & Schooler, 1978; Schooler, 1990), who have shown in a series of studies that the more complex the environment an individual lives in or works in, the greater the intellectual flexibility that person develops.

In one study, they interviewed a group of men twice, over a 10-year interval, each time assessing each subject's intellectual flexibility as well as the complexity of the work the man was then doing. Work complexity was measured by asking each subject to describe precisely what he does with written materials or data, what he does with his hands, and what he does with people. The complexity of each of these facets of each job was then rated and given weights, depending on the amount of time the worker spent in each of the three kinds of activity. (Incidentally, this is very similar to the kinds of analyses that are now being used as a basis for "comparable worth" scores for different jobs).

They found that both intellectual flexibility and job complexity were highly stable over the 10-year period. A man who had been high in intellectual flexibility at the first interview was likely to be high at the second interview as well, and a man with a complex job at Time 1 was likely to have a complex job 10 years later. But there were also some fascinating connections between the two measures.

First, greater intellectual flexibility led to higher job complexity. That is, men who were high in flexibility in 1964, when the first interview was completed, had more complex jobs 10 years later than did those men whose initial intellectual flexibility was lower. But second, those men who were employed at complex jobs became more intellectually flexible. So job complexity helped to *foster* intellectual flexibility. And greater intellectual flexibility then led to more complex jobs. In subsequent studies, Kohn and Schooler have found the same kinds of links for women, both those who work in the home and those who work outside the home (Schooler, 1990).

If we add these findings to what I have already said about individual differences in intellectual performance in adulthood, an intricate chain of influences is apparent. The starting points are a key part of the equation (recall Chapter 2): Adults who begin with high levels of intellectual flexibility (or who are better educated or who have higher intellectual ability) are likely to end up in more complex, intellectually demanding jobs. They may continue their education in order to advance in those jobs. The complexity of the job, in turn, stimulates or maintains intellectual flexibility, so the adult reads more, discusses issues more, thinks more about options and possibilities. These adults, barring significant disease, have a good chance of maintaining their intellectual power well into old age.

In contrast, those who begin their adult years with lower levels of education or intellectual flexibility are funneled into less complex and demanding jobs. Such jobs do not provide much mental challenge, so there is little growth of mental flexibility or skill, and in later years, perhaps less maintenance of intellectual abilities.

At any point along the way, however, it looks as if the trajectory can be altered by increasing the complexity of one's overall environment, such as by increasing physical or mental exercise, by moving into a more complex job, or by going back to school. I do not think that there is infinite flexibility here, nor that the "fall of the sands through the hourglass" can be totally halted or reversed simply by reading the newspaper every day, or teaching yourself a foreign language, or memorizing telephone numbers. But there is at least suggestive evidence that all of these activities help to maintain intellectual abilities in the later years of adulthood.

A Theoretical Model

Much of what I have said in this chapter both about the modal pattern of intellectual decline through adulthood and about individual differences in maintenance of intellectual skill can be combined by using Nancy Denney's model of exercised and unexercised abilities (1982, 1984). I described the general outlines of this model in Chapter 4, referring there to the potential effects of physical exercise on physical aging. But the model was originally proposed to describe age changes in mental abilities. The general propositions are as follows:

1. The basic pattern of age change in mental abilities involves a rise until perhaps age 20 or 30, followed by a gradual decline (see Figure 4–11). The precise shape of this "basic" curve is yet to be determined by research. The research I have reviewed in this chapter suggests that there may be a longer, flatter top to the curve than Denney proposes. But some decline does occur.
2. We can differentiate between "unexercised abilities" and "optimally exercised abilities." Unexercised abilities are those untrained or unpracticed abilities that are thought to reflect the basic functioning of the nervous system and/or the effects of standard environmental experience. Many traditional laboratory tasks, such as those used to test memory ability would fall in this category, as do most measures of "fluid" intelligence and many nonverbal tests of IQ. Optimally exercised abilities reflect the maximum ability that a normal healthy individual can attain with extensive practice and training. Of course, many abilities will fall in between these two curves. As you can see in Figure 6–11, Denney suggests that the ability to solve practical problems falls in between, as does verbal ability for most adults.
3. The curve for the optimally exercised abilities represents an upper boundary of ability or performance at any one age. Training or exercise will thus help to raise the level of performance toward that maximum. Since exercised abilities like vocabulary or practical problem solving are already closer to the maximum than are unexercised abilities, we should find that training has the largest effect on measures of fluid intelligence or on nonverbal tests, all of which are less fully exercised. Improvement in any unexercised ability should be possible at any age, but since there is also an underlying "decay" curve operating, training or exercise should not eliminate age differences entirely. Furthermore, if you look

carefully at the figure, you'll see that Denney assumes that the discrepancy between unexercised and exercised abilities narrows somewhat with age, so that the degree of gain one can make in some skill from training or exercise may decline.

4. There are individual differences in the level of these curves (both in the optimum that can be reached and in the lower boundary of unexercised abilities), reflecting differences in heredity, physical intactness, or early environmental stimulation. There are probably also individual differences in the trajectories, although that remains to be demonstrated. That is, some adults may be moving along a much slower "decay" curve than others are.

If you think about the various facts I have provided in this chapter, you'll see that they fit this model reasonably well. Semi-exercised abilities such as verbal skills show essentially the pattern that Denney has sketched in Figure 6–11: There

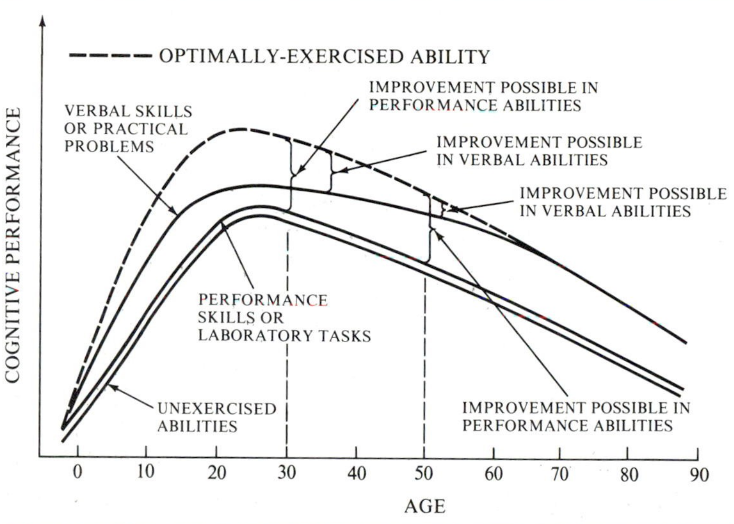

Figure 6–11 Figure 4-11 showed the simplest version of Nancy Denney's model of unexercised and optimally exercised abilities. Here you can see some of the further complexities of the model. The center curve represents an approximation of the age changes for what we might think of as "semi-exercised" abilities, such as verbal skills or problem solving with practical problems. The hypothesized pattern of age change for performance skills or for laboratory tasks, however, follows the line of unexercised abilities. Also shown here are the estimated amounts of improvement possible, with training or exercise, for these two categories of skills. Since performance and laboratory task skills are typically less exercised (or less familiar), there is much more room for improvement there than is the case for the "semi-exercised" abilities such as vocabulary. Still, according to this model, there is at least some room for improvement in unexercised abilities even late in life. (Source: N. W. Denney, "Aging and Cognitive Changes" in Handbook of Developmental Psychology, B. B. Wolman, Ed., C. 1982, p. 822. Reprinted by permission of Prentice-Hall, Inc., Englewood Cliffs, NJ.)

is no practically significant decline until about age 60 or 70. Fluid abilities, such as many memory functions, show an earlier decline, following a pattern more like that of the unexercised abilities.

Furthermore, evidence from training studies does show that it is possible to raise the level of intellectual performance of middle-aged and elderly adults by providing training, especially on measures of fluid ability such as inductive reasoning or spatial orientation. Both Paul Baltes and his colleagues, and Sherry Willis and Warner Schaie and their associates, have reported on the findings of a whole range of training studies (e.g. Baltes & Lindenberger, 1988; Schaie & Willis, 1986) that leave little room for doubt that there is intellectual plasticity well into late old-age. Some of Schaie and Willis's studies have involved older adults from the Seattle Longitudinal Study, so we have the added advantage of knowing the previous intellectual history of these adults. Schaie and Willis have found that both those who had shown a decline and those who had remained stable in some ability, such as inductive reasoning, were able to benefit from training. For many adults whose inductive reasoning skill had declined over the years, the training produced gains that were large enough to bring the individual's performance back to the level they had shown 14 years earlier (Willis & Schaie, 1986)—a finding that fits nicely with Denney's model.

Denney's model is also supported by the finding that training does *not* typically eliminate age differences: Young adults with training still perform better than older adults with training, as we would expect from this model (Denney, 1982; Denney & Heidrich, 1990). In fact, as I mentioned earlier, there is some indication that training *increases* the size of the age difference, since young adults often benefit more from training than do older adults, just as Denney's model proposes (Kleigl, Smith & Baltes, 1989).

Finally, the model explicitly predicts that more mentally active adults will maintain higher levels of skill later into old age, which is confirmed by the findings on activity I just discussed. Denney suggests, however, that the effect of exercise is quite specific to a particular task. Reading the newspaper every day exercises certain kinds of verbal skills, but it doesn't provide much exercise for your memory. Memorizing phone numbers, Bible verses, or poetry may help maintain memory skills but does little for your problem solving ability. In other words, there does not appear to be any mental activity that increases basic mental "fitness" in the same way that aerobic exercise increases physical fitness. Rather, to maintain any given intellectual skill, one must practice or exercise that skill.

Obviously, Denney's model is only a preliminary statement. Over the next decades as good research data become more plentiful, we will see whether this theoretical approach continues to offer both a good summary description and a heuristic basis for future work.

A Review of Age Patterns

As in the last chapter, I have summarized the various age changes in intellectual functioning in a table (Table 6.4). Unlike the pattern of physical changes sum-

TABLE 6.4. Summary of Age Changes in Intellectual Skills.

Age 20–40	Age 40–65	Age 65 and older
Peak intellectual ability between about 20 and 35 in both crystallized and fluid intelligence.	Maintenance of skill on measures of verbal, unspeeded, or crystallized intelligence; some decline of skill on measures of performance, speeded, or fluid IQ; decline is usually not functionally significant until age 60 or later.	Some loss of verbal or crystallized IQ, but this is most noticeable in adults with major health problems, lower levels of activity, and less education. Continued loss of skill on fluid IQ measures.
Optimal performance on memory tasks.	Little change in performance on memory tasks except perhaps some slowing later in this period.	Slowing of retrieval and all other memory processes; less efficient use of encoding strategies.
Peak performance on laboratory tests of problem solving.	Peak performance on real-life problem-solving tasks.	Decline in problem-solving performance on both laboratory and real-life tests.
Peak in quantity of creative output.	Lessening of quantity of creative output, but no loss of quality.	Further lessening of quantity of creative output; may be some decline in quality.

marized in Table 4.4, in which some decline or change is measurable in many dimensions in the years of midlife, there is little indication of intellectual loss until later life. Just how these two sets of changes may be linked together remains the subject for further study.

Summary

1. Correlational consistency of IQ is very high throughout adulthood. That is, an individual's relative position in an array of IQ scores remains very much the same over time.
2. Cross-sectional comparisons of total IQ scores across the adult years show a decline beginning in the 30s or 40s; longitudinal studies show maintenance of IQ until approximately age 60 or 65, after which there is a decline.
3. Analyses of subscores of IQ tests suggest that performance on speeded, or nonverbal, or "fluid" tests declines earlier, perhaps as early as age 45 or 50, whereas performance on nonspeeded, verbal, "crystallized" tests shows little decline until perhaps age 65 or 70.
4. Age changes in memory are observed in both short-term and long-term memory but are stronger in the latter. Both the encoding and retrieval processes are slower and less efficient. Older adults appear to suffer from a "production deficiency:" They do not spontaneously use effective memory strategies but will use them if reminded or taught.

5. Age differences in memory are generally smaller when recall of familiar material is tested, but even with familiar material, older adults typically remember somewhat less, or somewhat less rapidly. Whether there is also a decline in actual memory capacity is still being debated.
6. Problem solving performance also shows changes in the 60s or 70s, with older adults using less effective strategies. The difference is smaller when familiar, real-life problems are used but does not disappear. A production deficiency again is seen.
7. Changes in intellectual structure with age are more difficult to determine. Older adults are often found to approach tasks using strategies that are similar to what we see in quite young children, but whether this represents a real "regression" or rather a more practical or even a dialectical approach is not clear.
8. Studies of real-life intellectual or artistic productivity suggest that quantity declines but quality does not, at least through the years of the normal working life.
9. Some evidence points to a "terminal drop," that is a maintenance of intellectual skill until perhaps five years before death, at which point there is a fairly rapid drop. This seems particularly true for such crystallized skills as vocabulary.
10. In all the research, there are large individual differences in the timing and extent of intellectual maintenance or loss. Physical health and mental "exercise" appear to be key elements in such variations.
11. Markedly poor health is nearly always implicated in very early or very rapid declines in intellectual functioning. Within the more normal range of health, the link is less clear.
12. Two specific diseases are associated with earlier or more substantial decline in intellectual skill: senile dementia (e.g. Alzheimer's disease) and cardiovascular disease (CVD). Patients with senile dementia show very substantial loss of memory. CVD is associated with a slightly faster rate of decline in IQ and other measures of intellectual performance, perhaps because it is associated with a reduction in oxygen to the brain.
13. Those adults who maintain higher levels of physical and mental activity (who "exercise" their minds) show slower rates of intellectual decline in old age. Since mentally active adults tend also to be better educated and higher in IQ in early adulthood, the causal links are not yet clear. Work complexity, however, appears to have a causal effect on intellectual flexibility.
14. Denney's theoretical model, contrasting the pattern of gain and loss in performance of "optimally exercised" and "unexercised" abilities, appears to be a useful description of our current knowledge about intellectual changes in adulthood.

Suggested Readings

DENNEY, N. W. (1982). Aging and cognitive change. In B. B. Wolman (Ed.), *Handbook of developmental psychology.* Englewood Cliffs, NJ: Prentice-Hall. This is not a simple article but it is well worth the effort. Denney not only reviews much of the information I have described in this chapter, she also presents her theoretical model of exercised and unexercised abilities.

MEER, J. (1986, June). The reason of age. *Psychology Today, 20*, pp. 60–64. A good popular article covering changes in mental functioning with increasing age, focusing particularly on the question of the degree of impact such change may have on everyday life, noting that experience may substitute for quickness.

SCHAIE, K. W. (Ed.) (1987). *Annual review of gerontology and geriatrics*, (Vol. 7). New York: Springer. All of this series of annual review volumes are excellent, but the 1987 volume contains an especially good collection of papers on aspects of intellectual change with age, including a paper on aging and memory by Marion Perlmutter et al., one by Timothy Salthouse on the impact of experience on cognitive aging, and one by Sherry Willis on the effects of training on maintenance or increase in intellectual functioning in old age.

SCHAIE, K. W. (1990). Intellectual development in adulthood. In J. E. Birren & K. W. Schaie (Eds.), *Handbook of the psychology of aging*, (3rd ed.). San Diego, CA: Academic Press. In this current and relatively brief review of the literature, Schaie covers many of the issues I have talked about in this chapter. If you are interested in a deeper exploration of this subject, this would be an excellent source of further references.

CHAPTER 7

Sex Roles and Family Roles over the Adult Years

One of the things I remember most clearly about the transition from being single to being married was that "wives" were treated very differently from "college professors." At academic gatherings, I had found that new acquaintances routinely asked each other "What do you do?" But at PTA meetings or at gatherings where married couples meet for the first time, no one ever asked me that. What I "did," clearly, was to "be a wife," and since everyone knew what that job involved, no one needed to ask. I was at first offended, and then amused, by the widely shared and totally unspoken assumption that wives didn't "do" other things, despite the vast evidence to the contrary. Of course, my passage through this transition occurred 20 years ago, and times have changed since then—but not completely.

Parenthood—a role I acquired simultaneously with marriage, which isn't the normal pattern, to be sure—involved its own huge changes in roles. Not only was I now cooking and doing the laundry for four people instead of one, I was cleaning a house that got messy at a most astonishing rate and finding that getting ready to go anywhere took at least five times as long as when I had been single. I was also suddenly in the business of listening to after-school tales from children, dealing with teachers and school problems, providing transportation to and from basketball games or friends' houses, and worrying about the prospective bad influence of some playmates.

All of these changes involve changes in *roles,* a concept I discussed in Chapter 3. We can think of the patterns of change in physical and mental functioning which I have been talking about in the past three chapters as aspects of the march of physical time; role changes with age involve the march of *social time.* Over the years of our adult life, most of us fill a common sequence of socially-defined positions, each with its attendant role. In this chapter, I want to examine two particularly significant sets of such adult role sequences: sex roles and family roles. I'll explore the personal relationships within those family and sex roles in the next chapter and then return to the description of adult roles patterns in Chapter 9, where the topic of work roles will be the central focus.

Sex Roles in Adulthood

Some Definitions

There is a multitude of terms that get used rather imprecisely when people talk about sex roles. If I don't define these terms at the outset, we will find ourselves in a tangle later on.

SEX ROLE

The definition of a **sex role** is much like the definition of any other role. Any role is a *job description*, a socially-defined collection of behaviors and traits that a person occupying that role is expected to display. Thus, a sex role is the set of behaviors and personality traits that go with the social position of "woman" or "man." The role describes what women and men are expected to do and how they should think or behave.

SEX ROLE STEREOTYPES When the job descriptions for men and women become not only widely shared but highly fixed or inflexible, we can speak of **sex role stereotypes**. The presence of stereotypes is particularly evident when we make assumptions about the characteristics or behavior of an unknown individual based solely on his or her gender. When we do this, we move from descriptions of what men and women typically do, to assumptions about what men and women *are* or are *supposed* to be. In the process, we exaggerate both the similarities within each gender group and the differences between them.

SEX TYPING The third concept, **sex typing**, refers to the extent to which any individual's behavior or attitudes *match* the sex role for his or her gender. A person who behaves in a way that is highly consistent with the sex role for his gender would be described as "highly sex typed."

MASCULINITY, FEMININITY, AND ANDROGYNY Finally, there are three terms now widely used to describe each person's perception or self-description of his own sex-role-stereotyped qualities, **masculinity, femininity,** and **androgyny.** Typically, these personality traits or self concepts are measured by giving individuals lists of adjectives and asking them the extent to which each adjective describes themselves. Some of the adjectives describe male stereotyped qualities (such as assertiveness, independence, dominance, or self-confidence), and some describe female stereotyped qualities (such as gentleness, emotionality, kindness, excitability, or passivity.) (Spence & Helmreich, 1978; Bem, 1974, 1977).

Until the early 1970s, most psychologists thought of masculinity and femininity as opposite ends of a single dimension. One could be one or the other but not both. But the current measures of these traits or self concepts allow separate measurement of masculinity and femininity. You could, for example, describe yourself as *both* gentle and independent, both kind and assertive. Such a mixture of high levels of both masculine and feminine qualities is called androgyny. In contrast, adults who describe themselves as high in masculine traits, but low in feminine traits are labeled masculine, while those with the reverse pattern are labeled feminine. An individual who describes himself or herself as low in both masculine and feminine qualities is described as **undifferentiated.**

The Content of Sex Role Stereotypes

We know a good deal more about the content of the sex role stereotypes than we do about actual sex roles, in part because the roles themselves are changing rapidly while the stereotypes have remained remarkably stable over the past decades, even in the midst of the women's movement. Since the stereotypes form the basis of what most of us think men and women *ought* to be, let me start there.

SEX ROLE STEREOTYPES IN ADULTS The most extensive research on sex role stereotypes has been done by Inge and Donald Broverman and their colleagues (Broverman, Vogel, Broverman, Clarkson, & Rosenkrantz, 1972; Rosenkrantz, Vogel, Bee, Broverman, & Broverman, 1968). They asked subjects to go through long lists of traits (such as independent, talkative, optimistic, grumpy, and many others), each of which was a label for a scale that ran from high to low. For each trait, the subjects placed the "typical male" and the "typical female" somewhere on the scale. For some traits, the researchers found that there was a consistent difference in the placement of men and women on these scales. They also found that if they asked other subjects to go through the same traits and pick out the "good" or "desirable" end of the scale, many more of the typical masculine qualities were identified as good or desirable. Some of the highly valued masculine traits were aggressiveness, independence, objectivity, dominance, competition, ability to be leaders and to make decisions easily, ability to separate feelings and ideas, adventurousness, low levels of excitability in major crises, business skill, and logicalness. Some of the highly valued feminine traits were talkativeness, tactfulness, gentleness, neatness and quietness, awareness of others' feelings, and the ability to express tender feelings easily. Since this research was done roughly 20 years ago, you may think that these stereotypes have changed. Surprisingly, limited evidence suggests that these stereotypes have persisted, despite the women's movement and major changes in women's labor force participation (e.g., Williams & Best, 1982; Deaux & Lewis, 1984).

However, these stereotypes are not either/or statements. When adults are asked to state a *probability* that men and women could have certain qualities, certain roles, and certain physical characteristics, the two stereotypes are much less sharply differentiated, as you can see in Table 7.1. As the Broverman group had found, the data in the table show that the pervasive male stereotype centers around qualities of competence and instrumentality, whereas the female stereotype centers around qualities of affiliation and expressiveness; but we both observe and expect that there will be a good deal of overlap.

Such overlap does not mean, however, that the stereotypes are not powerful. They are. Among other things, Broverman and her colleagues (Broverman, Broverman, Clarkson, Rosenkrantz, & Vogel, 1970) have found that the male qualities are more highly valued and are considered "healthier" by psychotherapists than are the female qualities. Further, jobs that women perform are also typically rated as less difficult than are those that men do (Deaux, 1984), and men and women who cross role lines and fill the opposite sex role (such as men who become primary caregivers for their children) experience a considerable amount of strain. Thus, although there is overlap in our conceptions of male and female roles, the stereotypes nonetheless shape our thinking about men and women in general, and about individual men and women.

Age Changes in Sex Role Stereotyping We can detect sex role stereotypes in children as young as five or six, and stereotyping is at its strongest among elementary school children (Best et al., 1977; Ullian, 1981). By adolescence, there is some softening of the stereotypes, some recognition that while these are the qualities or activities of the *average* male or female, there are many exceptions. Among adults, older people are more likely to hold traditional (more stereotyped) views about sex roles than are younger adults (Huston-Stein & Higgens-Trenk, 1978), but this seems more likely to be a cohort difference than a true

TABLE 7.1. Sex Role Stereotypes: The Probability That the Average Man or Woman Will Show a Particular Trait, Behavior, or Physical Characteristic, According to Adult Raters.

Characteristic	Judged Probability	
	Men	*Women*
Trait		
Independent	.78	.58
Competitive	.82	.64
Warm	.66	.77
Emotional	.56	.84
Role Behaviors		
Financial provider	.83	.47
Takes initiative with opposite sex	.82	.54
Takes care of children	.50	.85
Cooks meals	.42	.83
Physical Characteristics		
Muscular	.64	.36
Deep voice	.73	.30
Graceful	.45	.68
Small-boned	.39	.62

SOURCE: Deaux, F. From individual differences to social categories: Analysis of a decade's research on gender. *American Psychologist*, 1984, 39, 105–116. Copyright holder is American Psychological Association. Reprinted by permission of author.

age-linked developmental change. The current cohort of older adults grew up in an era when sex roles were much more clearly differentiated than they are today, and their own life patterns were likely to have followed the traditional pathways. Until cohort-sequential studies are completed, we won't know whether there are any genuine developmental changes in sex role stereotypes over the adult years.

The Content of Sex Roles

CHANGES WITH AGE IN SEX ROLE CONTENT

Although the sex role stereotypes are quite distinct and have remained remarkably stable over the past years, the actual job descriptions of the male and female role have been much more flexible. I should emphasize very strongly that what I can say about sex roles over the adult years is *highly* culture- and cohort-dependent. Sex roles have probably changed faster in the United States than in other countries—in no small part because of the massive, rapid change in labor force participation by women over the past decade—so what is true for the United States may well not be true elsewhere. And what is true for current cohorts in the United States may well not be valid for later groups.

What *is* true in every culture is that sex roles do not remain constant over the years of adult life. As Paul Secord says, "sex roles are really age-sex roles" (1982, p. 37). We have different expectations for a 25-year-old woman than

TABLE 7.2. Present Content of Male and Female Roles at Different Ages.

Age Group	Female Role	Male Role
18–30: Role Differentiation	Marry; bear children; be primarily responsible for childbearing, housework, and cooking	Marry; father children; have small role in caring for and rearing children; be secondarily responsible for cooking and housework
	Provide nurturance for all family members	Make major decisions in family
	Maintain kin and friend contacts	Make progress in career or work
	Be secondary breadwinner (after children enter school particularly)	Be primary breadwinner
	Share in financial management	Manage family finances
	Be sexual partner; be recreational partner	Be sexual partner; be recreational partner
	Listen to others	Talk more
30–45 Continued Role Separation	Continue rearing of children, including links with schools, other families with children, etc.	Minimal role in rearing of children.
	Continue major responsibility for housework and cooking; Continue provision or nurturance for children and husband	Minimal responsibilities for house or cooking; Continue role as decision maker; provide strength and firmness
	Maintain friend and kin contacts	Make major progress in work or career
	Be secondary breadwinner	Be primary breadwinner
	Share in financial management	Manage finances
	Sexual and recreational partner	Sexual and recreational partner

45–65 Possible Cross-over	Continue major role as rearer of children; help to launch children into independent life; continue major housekeeping role	Increase role with children, providing financial support for launching; increase role in housekeeping
	Enter work force if have not already done so; increase levels of achievement and competence	Continue work or career; focus on training younger workers; (mentoring role)
	Assume primary role as caregiver or support for aging parent(s)	Assume secondary role as support for aging parent(s)
	Share financial management	Primary financial manager
	Continue major responsibility for kin contacts; become grandmother	Continue major family decision making role; become grandfather
	Sexual and recreational partner	Sexual and recreational partner
65+ Role Decline	Continue as primary kin link, including link to children and grandchildren; provide physical assistance to children	Secondary role with children and grandchildren
	Retire from paid employment	Retire from paid employment
	Be in charge of, but share more in, household management	Share more of household tasks
	Continue major role of support to aging parents, if they are still living	Secondary role with aging parents
	Share more in finances	Be in charge of finances
	Sexual and recreational partner	Sexual and recreational partner.

SOURCES: Atkinson, 1987; Dobson, 1983; Gutmann, 1987; Katz, 1979.

for a 55-year-old woman, for a 30-year-old man than for an 80-year-old man. Table 7.2 lists some of the current features of the male and female roles in different age groups in our society. You can see from the table that the male and female roles are differentiated both behaviorally and emotionally. Women not only bear and (primarily) rear children; they are also expected to provide the main source of nurturance and caring for both husband and children. Men are primarily responsible for the financial support of the family.

One middle-aged husband interviewed by Philip Blumstein and Pepper Schwartz for their fascinating book, *American Couples,* (1983) described the difference eloquently:

> She complains sometimes that I'm not nice enough to her, that I don't think of her enough, forget birthdays, that sort of thing. And I always apologize because I think there is some truth in that, but not because I don't love her or appreciate her. I am out there taking my lumps earning a living and a lot of times I don't have room to think about anything but earning a living. (pp. 169–170)

You can also see in the table that the largest differences in sex roles appear in early adulthood, after the birth of children. Before marriage and childbearing, men and women have much more similar roles; after marriage and children, there is a bifurcation of roles. This role separation continues until middle life (perhaps until age 45 to 50) when there are signs of a "crossing over," or of a reuniting of the two roles. Let me talk a bit more about each of these transitions.

THE INTENSIFICATION OF SEX ROLE DIFFERENCES IN EARLY ADULTHOOD There is now a good deal of evidence that the effect of marriage is to magnify the division of labor between men and women (e.g. Hoffman & Manis, 1978; Feldman & Aschenbrenner, 1983; Gutmann, 1987). Women become much more clearly the nurturers, the ones responsible for maintenance of the relationship. They take on a larger share of the housework, and they become less powerful in family decision making. The man turns more outward, toward the world of work, and his power within the family increases. In sum, egalitarianism declines.

Anthropologist David Gutmann points out that this division of labor in the man/woman relationship has an ancient (and honorable) history. In the days when tribal warfare was the rule, it was far more critical that the women be protected than the men. The women bore the children and thus, bore the future of the tribe or group. So the women were literally placed "in the center." The men, with their greater physical strength, protected the borders and drove off invaders. Women were turned inward, men outward; women were in charge of care, men of protection.

Even though the need for physical protection from marauders is long gone, we still retain the sense that the woman's proper place in an intimate relationship or within the family is "at the center." She is the hearth, the heart; the man is the power, the strength. To be sure, there has been some change in this pattern in recent years, but the ancient history of men's and women's roles within relationships is not easy to abandon—as anyone who has attempted an egalitarian relationship can tell you.

When the first child is born, this sex role difference is magnified still more, a process Gutmann describes as the **parental imperative.** He argues that this pattern is "wired in," that because human children are so vulnerable, parents *must* meet both the emotional and physical needs of the child, and it is very difficult for one person to do both. Because the woman bears the child and nurses it, Gutmann argues that it is natural for the division of role responsibility to fall along the traditional lines. Here's another illustrative voice, that of a man named Joe:

> The baby's coming was a good thing, because it drove home to me that I had to have a better job. And I knew I'd need an education to get one. I transferred to the evening shift so I could go to college during the day. The hours were hard, I was under a lot of pressure, and I missed my family, but it was something I had to do. (Daniels & Weingarten, 1988, p. 38)

Whether Gutmann is correct about such a role division being wired in or not is a matter of debate, but there is at least some confirming evidence for the empirical pattern: Male and female roles do get more separate after the birth of the child. Gutmann finds such a pattern in the several cultures he has studied (including the Navaho, the Mayan, and the Druze [Gutmann, 1975]), and there have been similar findings in studies of U.S. families (e.g. Hoffman & Manis, 1978).

Another facet of this accentuation of sex role differences after the birth of a child may be a change in the way new parents perceive their own masculinity and femininity. You can see the results of one study by Barbara Abrahams and her colleagues (Abrahams, Feldman, & Nash, 1978) in Figure 7–1. In this research, four separate groups of (white, middle class, U.S.) adults were compared: cohabiting pairs, newly married pairs without children, couples expecting their first child, and couples with a first child between 6 and 12 months old. As you can see in the figure, masculinity scores were highest for males (and low for females) in the group of parents, while femininity scores were highest for women (and low for men) among parents. In a later replication of this analysis with a different set of cross-sectional samples, Nash and Feldman (1981) found the maximum sex differences in self descriptions on such dimensions as leadership, autonomy, compassion and tenderness occurred among young parents and those expecting their first child, with lower differentiation among single adults or more mature parents.

Other researchers have not invariably found this same pattern. For example, Feldman and Aschenbrenner (1983), in a short-term longitudinal study of a group of highly educated, philosophically egalitarian couples, found that women became more feminine and men more androgynous (rather than more masculine) after the birth of a child. And in a study done in Australia, Cunningham and Antill (1984) found that working women had consistently lower femininity scores than did non working women, regardless of whether they were married or single, parents or non parents. At the moment, it appears that there is strong evidence for an

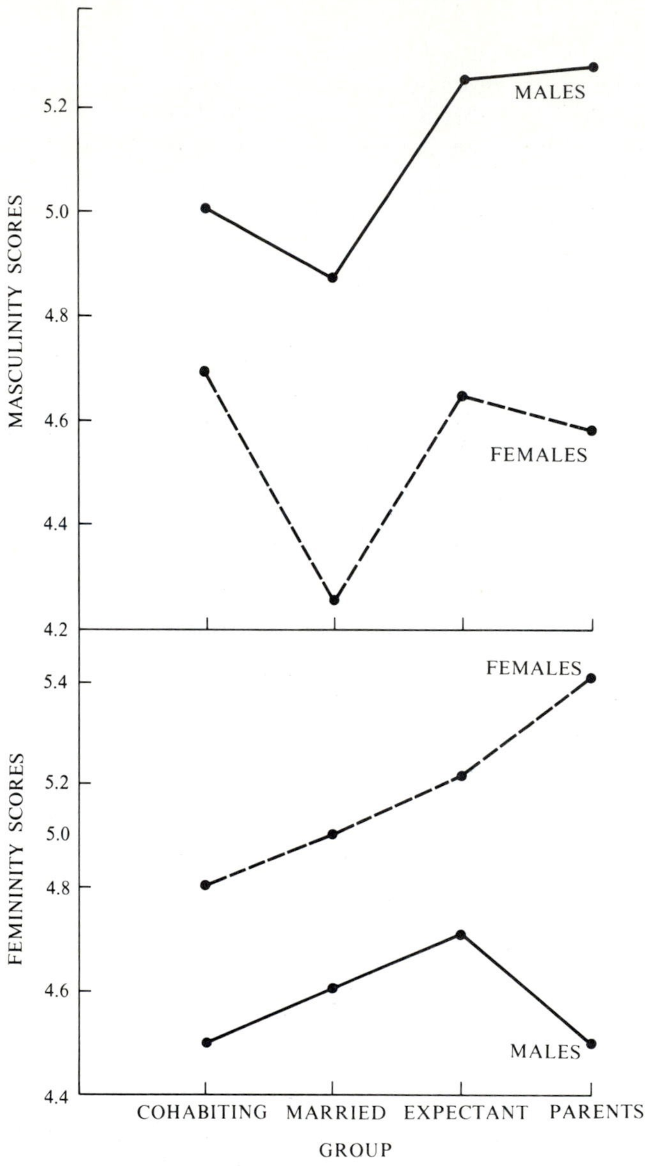

Figure 7–1 *In this cross-sectional comparison, young adults in various stages of family formation were tested for their self-described masculinity and femininity. You can see that masculinity was highest for men who were new parents and femininity was highest for women who were new parents, illustrating the intensification of traditional sex roles that appears to occur after the birth of the first child. (Source: Abrahams, Feldman, & Nash, 1978, Figure 1, page 397. Copyright holder is American Psychological Association. Reprinted by permission of author.)*

intensification of sex role *behaviors* and suggestive but not conclusive evidence about parallel changes in adults' self-perceptions of masculinity and femininity after the birth of a child.

THE CROSS-OVER OF SEX ROLES AT MIDLIFE Equally suggestive but not conclusive is the evidence that sex roles may converge once again, perhaps even crossing over, at midlife (Giele, 1982b; Rossi, 1980). The data are fragmented but intriguing. In their cross-sectional study of adults at various stages of the family life cycle, Sharon Nash and Shirley Feldman (1981) compared self-reported aspects of sex roles. As you can see in Figure 7–2, they found that men in later stages of the family life cycle described themselves as more compassionate, while women at later stages described themselves as more autonomous. In general, the findings point to a lessening of gender differences at midlife, particularly after the children have left home.

Some suggestion that such a cross-over at midlife may actually be psychologically healthier comes from several studies of current cohorts of middle-aged women, among whom an increase in traditionally masculine role patterns in midlife is associated with lower rates of anxiety or depression and higher levels of life satisfaction. So, for example, middle-aged women who work outside the home are less likely to show psychiatric symptoms, than are women who remain strongly family oriented (Powell, 1977; Lowenthal, Thurnher & Chiriboga, 1975).

Another fragment comes from the work of Alice Rossi (1989) who has been studying three generations of a group of Boston families, with the middle generation ranging in age from 20 to 70. She finds that both men and women in their 50s show a drop in what she calls "drive," but that the men show a much larger drop. (Drive, in this case, was made up of self-ratings on the qualities of "energetic," "hard-working," and "easily aroused sexually.")

Two theorists whose work I discussed in Chapter 3 have also suggested a sex role cross-over for men. George Vaillant, in his longitudinal study of Harvard men (1977), found that the men became more "feminine" in middle-age. In particular, they became more introspective, more concerned with feelings, more able to express emotions. Other researchers have found that men increase their involvement in housework after the children leave home (Model, 1981), although that is not a universal finding (e.g. Geerken & Gove, 1983). The role of "mentor," which Levinson (1986) describes as a common element in the midlife life structure, also involves many of the nurturing and supportive aspects of the traditional female role, although we have very little data on just how common this role may be for men or for women.

Finally, there is the cross-cultural evidence from David Gutmann's studies (1975; 1977; 1987) that a typical pattern in many societies is for men's roles to become more nurturing and less achievement oriented in old age, whereas women's roles come to involve greater assertiveness, greater power. Gutmann summarizes:

> . . . men who were once adversarial, whether as warriors, slash-and-burn agriculturalists, passionate pioneers, *politicos,* or trial lawyers, routinely become more pacific

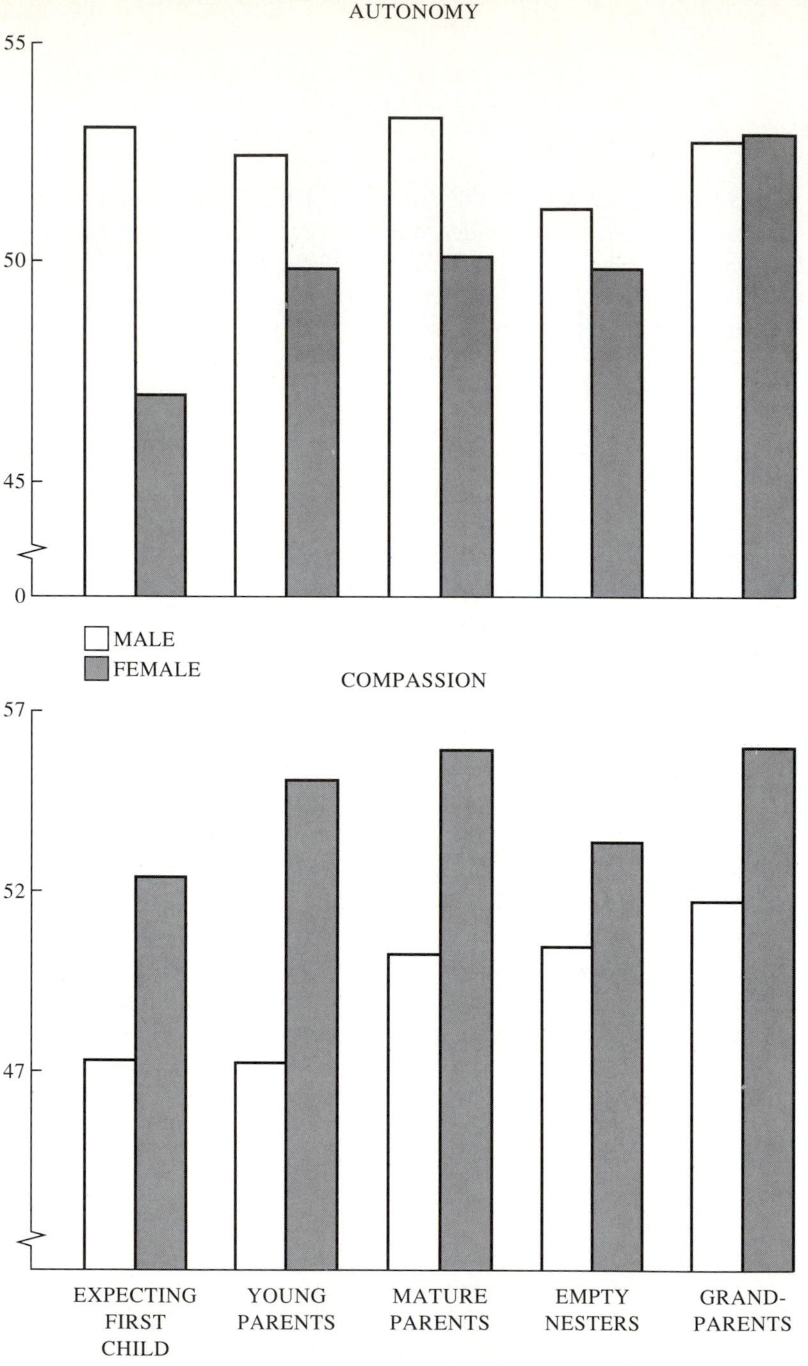

Figure 7–2 Like the findings in Figure 7–1, these data come from a cross-sectional study comparing adults in various stages of the family life cycle. Sex differences in both compassion and autonomy were smaller during the empty nest stage than at earlier ages, which suggests the possibility of a sex role cross-over (or at least a lessening of difference) at midlife. But because these are cross-sectional data, we have to be cautious about concluding that this pattern reflects genuine developmental changes. (Source: Nash & Feldman, 1981, Table 1–2, p. 20.)

> in later life; they turn to preserving life rather than killing, to maintaining social stability rather than fomenting ardent rebellion. In some cases, these transformations involve more than a drift away from flamboyant aggression, but an actual shift in gender distinctiveness, from univocal masculinity to sexual bimodality, or even implicit femininity. (1987, p. 94)

In women, Gutmann finds that the transition is from an interior to an exterior focus, from nurturance to a kind of virility.

I find the idea of sex role cross-over at midlife appealing, possibly because it fits with my own biases. But I should emphasize again that the data base is thin, and nearly all the evidence is cross-sectional. We simply do not know whether it is common, let alone universal, for individual adults to move toward more androgynous self-perceptions or toward more egalitarian sex roles in relationships, as they move into middle- or old-age. Until we have decent longitudinal data, over several cohorts, we cannot be sure if this is a consistent developmental pattern.

Sex Roles in Adulthood: A Brief Summary

I want to emphasize several points from this mixture of theory and research about sex roles and sex role stereotypes in adult life. First, as I pointed out earlier, adult life patterns are not totally fixed by gender. The sex role definitions overlap. When we say that men are expected to be "instrumental" in their role, this means primarily that men are expected to be *more* instrumental than are women, not that women show none of this quality. In fact, most of us appear to learn *both* male and female roles, so that we are able, at least minimally, to fill the cross-sex role if the situation demands it. Women who find themselves unexpectedly needing to support their family financially are frequently able to take on the more assertive male role; men are quite capable of the nurturance and expressiveness involved in being the major caregiver for a child or an elderly adult. When both men and women do fill the same job role, they are very similar in their personal qualities (Deaux, 1984), which suggests that the role itself shapes our behavior as much or more than the reverse.

Second, sex roles appear to have their largest effect on the adult life course by influencing the *choices* that men and women make at crucial points in their lives. And those choices, in turn, typically set men and women on somewhat different pathways through adulthood.

The sequence of family roles operates in much the same way, influencing choices. Once the sequence of family roles has begun, it creates a predictable rhythm in the life pattern of the adult over a period of 20 or 30 years or more.

Family Roles over the Adult Years

Just as individuals have roles, so the family, too, has a role or a set of tasks. Evelyn Duvall (1971, 1988) lists the following family tasks: allocation of resources, division of labor, reproduction, recruitment, and release of family members, maintenance of order, placement of members in the larger society, and maintenance of motivation and morale. Both the extent to which any one task dominates and the way the tasks are completed changes from one phase to the next in the *family life cycle,* a concept I described briefly in both Chapters 1 and 3. You'll recall that for families that remain together and have at least one child, eight steps in family composition are customarily distinguished by family sociologists: (1) newlyweds with no children, (2) families with one infant, (3) families with the oldest child of preschool age, (4) families with the oldest child at elementary school age, (5) families with the oldest child an adolescent, (6) families with the oldest child gone from home (to college, to marriage, or to single but independent living), (7) families with all children gone from the home ("empty nest"), and (8) aging families, in which one or both spouses has retired. Paul Glick (1989), another of the early and continued proponents of the family life cycle concept, suggests that we also need to look at a pre-family stage in young adulthood, before marriage. Since the ages at which adults begin this sequence vary considerably from one couple to the next, these stages do not describe chronological time. Rather, they describe social time or the "family career."

Each of the transitions involves one or more changes in roles. As Terkelsen (1980) points out, some of the role changes involve changes in things you *do,* (such as driving your kids to after school lessons or sports when they get to be of school age or going to PTA meetings) and some require that the adult *be* something new (such as being a wife or husband or being a parent, or becoming more self-sufficient at midlife). The former involve changes in mastery or adaptation; the latter involve changes in status or meaning and are more profound and difficult.

Secular Trends in the Family Life Cycle

Before I go on to describe some of the ways in which life experiences and attitudes are affected by this family life cycle sequence, I want to explore some of the very large cohort differences in the timing of that cycle that have occurred in the United States during this century. In part, this is designed to remind us all of the impact of cohort on the experiences of adulthood. But I also want to underline the cumulative effect of these changes for current cohorts and for our understanding of adult life.

Figure 7–3 shows the average age for three key events in the lives of women born in each of four decades, based on 1985 Census Bureau data on over 40 million women (Norton & Miller, 1990). All the women included in this graph had been married at least once. As you can see, the average age for a first marriage declined over these cohorts, as did the average age at the birth of the first and last children. These trends appear to have reversed in more recent cohorts, although I cannot give you a matching set of data, since women born in 1950 and later have not completed their childbearing years. What we know is that the average age at first marriage has risen abruptly. In 1988, the age at first marriage had reached 23.6 for women and 25.9 for men (Glick, 1989), with the age at first birth going up as well. Indeed, for a growing number of women, childbearing is also being delayed into their thirties. In 1987, 31.8 percent of all births were to

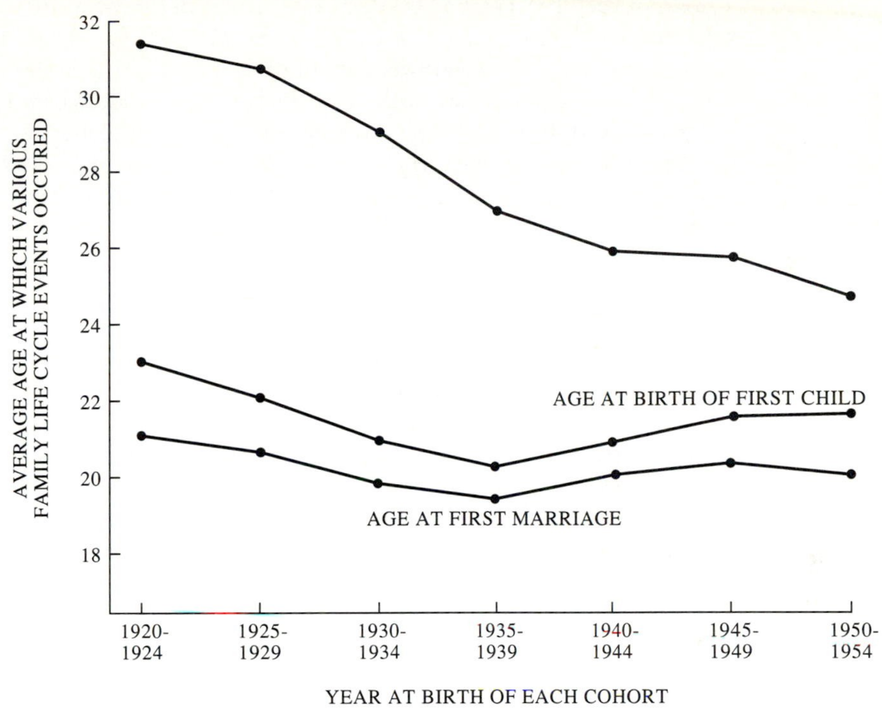

Figure 7–3 *Until quite recently, the trend in the United States during this century has been for women to marry at younger and younger ages, and to have both their first and last children at younger ages as well. Changes such as this, especially when combined with the lengthening of life expectancy, have had the effect of increasing significantly the total number of years in the postparental stage for women (and men) born in the 1930s and 1940s. Cohorts born in the 50s and 60s, however, have been marrying later and having first (and last) children later, which reverses this trend. (Source: Norton & Miller, 1990, Table A, p. 2).*

women 30 and over compared to only 23 percent in 1980 (U.S. Bureau of the Census, 1989a).

Demographers can only guess whether or not these recent patterns are the beginning of a long-term trend. My point in giving you this information is not to debate the causes or even the specific pattern of demographic trends but to emphasize the impact such changes in timing of life cycle events have on the adult life experiences of individuals in different cohorts.

For example, compare the experience of a woman born in the 1910 to 1919 cohort to one born between 1940 and 1949. Those in the 1910 cohort not only had their last child much later; They also had shorter life expectancies, a combination that means that these women have experienced many fewer child-free years at the end of their lives than will be true for those born in 1940, who had their last children at much younger ages and could expect to live much longer. Glick (1977, 1979) estimates that since 1900, 14 child-free years have been added to the life of the average adult, mostly in the postparental phase.

Many other life pattern changes flow from the same shifts in the timing of marriage and childbearing. For example, women in the 1910 to 1919 cohort were much more likely to be widowed before their last child left home. Widowhood was thus a quite different state than it is likely to be today, when a woman is likely to be widowed 10 or 15 years after her last child has grown and gone. Similarly, you can also deduce from Figure 7–3 that women in the 1910 to 1919 cohort were likely to complete menopause while there were still children at home. In contrast, the cohort born in 1940 was likely to experience menopause at about the time the last child was leaving home—a combination that may be more stressful simply because it combines two major changes.

In like manner, the pattern of delayed marriage and childbearing among today's young men and women will have predictable consequences for the timing and confluence of events downstream in their adult lives:

- The departure of the last child from home will be delayed, thus reducing the number of years in the postparental stage.
- There will be an increased likelihood of experiencing a midlife squeeze in which financial and emotional demands from both children and aging parents will coincide.
- Grandparenthood will come later, which may have implications for the quality of the relationship between grandparents and grandchildren.

The delay of marriage in the current cohort of young people has also had an impact on the family life cycle experiences of their *parents'* cohort, since the nest is not emptying as fast as many parents had expected. Census Bureaus show that in 1988 roughly 20 percent of men and 10 percent of women aged 25 to 29 were still living with their parents. Fifteen years earlier those numbers had been 10 percent and 5 percent respectively.

For me, two key points emerge from these analyses of secular trends. First, the timing of early family life cycle events has a significant impact on the whole pattern of an adult's later life (or even on the life of the parents' generation). Second, because the typical timing of such events changes from one cohort to the next, definitions of "on-time" or "off-time" are inevitably cohort specific. Some timing patterns may be inherently more difficult or stressful over the full adult life, but the general principle Neugarten proposes holds as well: If your own timing matches that of your cohort, you will have lots of company in facing whatever stresses may be encountered as you move through the decades. If you buck the trend, in whatever direction, it is likely to be more difficult.

Life Experiences and the Family Life Cycle

With that general point in mind, I need to look in much more detail at just how an adult's life is shaped by each of the family life cycle steps or stages. Let me begin by looking at some trends across the full set of stages and then focus on several specific stages more intensively.

MARITAL SATISFACTION, LIFE SATISFACTION, AND MENTAL HEALTH OVER THE FAMILY LIFE CYCLE Sociologists and psychologists who have studied the family life cycle have primarily focused their attention on the impact of the stages on three groups of dependent variables: marital satisfaction, overall life satisfaction or happiness, and aspects of mental health, such as depression.

I have already described some of the major findings on family life cycle stages and marital satisfaction in Chapter 1, as part of the illustration of cross-sectional research designs. You will want to go back and look at Figures 1–10 and 1–11 to refresh your memory. The general finding has been of a curvilinear relationship between marital satisfaction and family stage (Rollins & Galligan, 1978). The most well documented and reliably observed aspect of this curve is the decline in satisfaction that occurs with the birth of the first child, which has been demonstrated both longitudinally (e.g. Ryder, 1973) and cross-sectionally (e.g. Harriman, 1983). The rest of the curvilinear pattern has been shown only cross-sectionally, but it has reappeared in a number of studies, covering several different cohorts, so there is at least some reason to have confidence in the generality of the pattern.

However, as I pointed out in Chapter 1, we also have evidence that this curve is more likely to appear in some subgroups than in others. Recall that Anderson and his colleagues (1983) did not find such a curve for spouses high in "marital conventionalization." In other research, Estes and Wilensky (1978) have found that couples with low levels of financial worry showed roughly the same levels of marital satisfaction across the life cycle curve, while those who were experiencing financial strain showed the typical curve. And Abbott and Brody (1985) have found that, in a group of wives, a decline in marital satisfaction after the birth of children occurred primarily for those with two or more children, or those with only sons. These findings lead fairly naturally to the hypothesis that marriages which enjoy highly positive (or less stressful) circumstances, such as low levels of discord, secure finances, and fewer children, are less likely to be disrupted by the presence of a child. When there are stresses present, however, then children add to those stresses. One of the consequences is then a lower level of marital satisfaction.

A somewhat different curvilinear relationship appears if we look at overall happiness instead of marital satisfaction. Figure 7–4 shows some representative findings from the results of an analysis by Toni Antonucci and her colleagues (1980) of data from a time-sequential study, the Michigan Survey Research Center study of mental illness and health. Recall from Table 1.1 that in this study the same survey questions were used with two independent samples of over 2,000 adults each, interviewed nearly two decades apart (1957 and 1976). Comparison of the results in the two samples allows us to check whether the pattern is purely a cohort effect or not. In general, although more women described themselves as happy in 1957 than in 1976, the shape of the curves is quite similar. In each sample, there was a higher level of happiness reported among those recently married, and a lower level of reported happiness among those who had preschool children in the family. The pattern at later stages was less clear, but there is only a very weak indication of higher rates of reported happiness among those

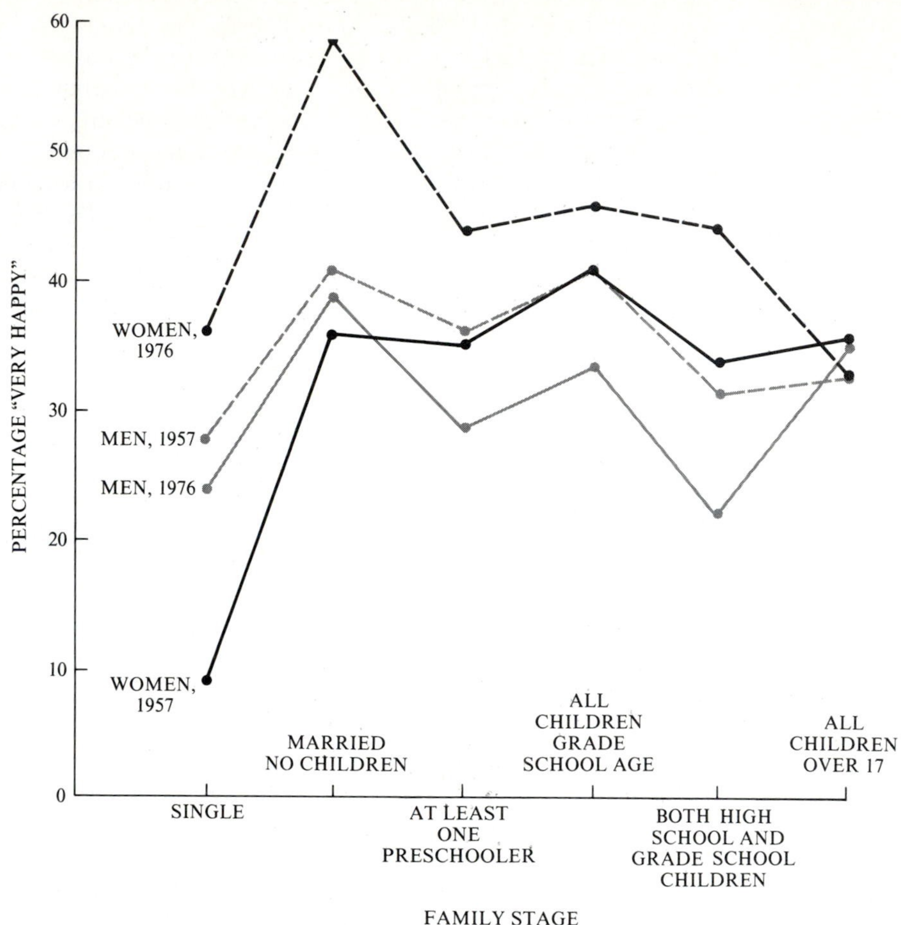

Figure 7–4 Two large national samples of adults, one in 1957 and 1976, were asked the following question: "Taking all things together, how would you say things are these days—would you say you're very happy, pretty happy, or not too happy?" This figure shows the percentage who said they were very happy, as a function of family life stage. Single adults obviously reported less happiness than did married adults; among married adults, those with children reported lower happiness than did those without children. (Source: Antonucci, Tamir, & Dubnoff, 1980, data from Table 1, p. 40.)

whose children had left home. In other research, however (e.g., Campbell, 1981), there are stronger signs of an upturn in overall life satisfaction in the postparental stage. It seems that older people are less likely to describe themselves as either very happy or very distressed, but the balance between the two (sometimes called *affect balance*) is more strongly positive in the postparental stage than at earlier stages.

Finally, there is similar evidence of a family life cycle pattern in depression and other measures of mental health (consistent with the age-related pattern I gave you in Figure 5–4). Several studies have shown that women with preschool children are more prone to both depression and anxiety than is true for women with older children (Gove & Geerken, 1977; Brown and Harris, 1978), and this is true whether the woman also works or not. In Brown and Harris's study of a sample of British women, however, (1978) the link between depression and age of children was apparent only for working class women. Middle class women, who have a greater range of options to deal with the role strains they experience, do not show elevated psychiatric symptoms when their children are small. In contrast, neither middle class nor working class men seem to show any change in depression or anxiety as a function of family life cycle stage.

These overall trends suggest that of the various transitions that are part of the family life cycle, three may be particularly critical: (a) the transition from singlehood to marriage, (b) the transition to parenthood, and (c) the transition to the postparental (or "empty nest") stage. Let me explore each of these stages more fully.

The Transition from Being Single to Marriage

Getting married marks one of the largest role changes that occurs over the adult years. An entirely new role is added, that of husband or wife, each with its own prescriptions. You already know from the data in Figure 7–4 that being married is associated with higher levels of happiness or well-being for both men and women. The statistical relationship is not huge, but it has been found again and again in different cohorts and different ethnic subgroups (Broman, 1988; Haring-Hidore, Stock, Okun, & Witter, 1985). There is also abundant evidence that, compared to single adults, married adults are physically healthier and less prone to depression or other forms of psychiatric disturbances (Gove, 1972; Williams, 1988). Such a difference could be the result of self-selection processes. If mentally and physically healthier adults are more likely to get married, then the least healthy and poorest functioning adults would be left in the "single" group. There is some indication that self-selection processes work in this way for men but probably not for women. Since in this culture men tend to marry "down" the social class ladder and women tend to marry "up," unmarried women are likely to be relatively well educated, with above average IQs and white collar jobs, while unmarried men are likely to have more average IQs and to be less well educated. In fact, unmarried men do have higher rates of physical and mental illness than do unmarried women (Spreitzer & Riley, 1974).

An alternative explanation of the relationship between marriage and health focuses on the role of **social support,** defined as the combination of affect, affirmation, and aid that a person receives from those around her (Kahn & Antonucci, 1980). We know that high levels of social support are associated with lower rates of physical disease and emotional disturbance (a relationship I'll discuss more fully in Chapter 12). Since getting married increases the available social support for most individuals, we should expect that married adults would be healthier than unmarried adults, which they are. We should also expect that married adults with more supportive relationships with their spouses would have better mental health than those who receive less support, a pattern confirmed in a recent large study by Dorie Williams (1988), based on the same 1976 sample represented in Figure 7–4.

Finally, if social support is the critical ingredient in making marriage a healthier state than singleness, we should expect quite high rates of physical and mental illness among divorced adults, who experience a marked loss in social support, and lower rates among those single adults who have an alternative source of social support. Researchers have found precisely these patterns. In general, rates of physical and mental illness are higher among the divorced than among the never married (Cargan & Melko, 1982; Doherty & Jacobson, 1982; Weingarten, 1985), and among the single, they are lower for those adults who have some other (nonspouse) adult living with them, whether that second adult is a roommate, a parent, a grown child, or some other person (Anson, 1989).

The emotional and physical benefits of the spouse role, however, do not seem to be evenly divided between men and women. In the majority of studies, married men are found to have better physical and mental health than married women. Walter Gove (1972, 1979) has suggested that this difference arises because the roles of husband and wife (in Western cultures, at least) are unequal in support, burdens, or gratification. For example, part of the wife's role is to provide nurturance and emotional support to all other family members, but the husband's role includes a much smaller expectation of support toward the wife. (If you go back and reread comments of the man I quoted on page 210, you'll see that although he was aware that his wife wanted him to give her more support, he didn't consider the provision of such support to be part of his role). In addition, the wife role is lower in status and higher in the number of unpleasant or routine jobs than is the husband role. Thus, men find marriage to be a better buffer against the slings and arrows of normal life than do women.

This difference in the two spousal roles is highlighted still further in the results of a study by Rosenfield (1980), who found that the typically higher levels of depression and physical illnesses for wives versus husbands occurred only for those wives who did not work outside the home. Working wives, who do less housework and have potential sources of emotional support and gratification in their work, had about the same levels of depression and sickness as did their husbands.

Overall, given the existing role definitions of male and female roles and of spousal roles, the transition to marriage appears to be particularly beneficial for men: Married men show the lowest rates of illness or disturbances, while unmarried men (never married or divorced) show the highest. Married and unmarried women fall in between. But as role definitions change, these sex differences may change as well.

The Transition to Parenthood Major role changes also occur at the birth of the first child. I have already talked about the changes in sex roles that seem to accompany this transition, but there are also major changes in the marriage relationship. Unlike the transition to marriage, which seems to be accompanied by an increase in happiness, initially the new role of parent brings a decrease in happiness and in marital satisfaction. Table 7.3 shows one fairly typical set of findings from a study by Jay Belsky and his colleagues (Belsky, Lang, & Rovine, 1985). They studied a group of 61 parents during pregnancy and then three months and nine months after the birth of the baby. Each partner was asked

TABLE 7.3. Changes in Marital Relationships Before and After the Birth of the First Child.

Measure of Marital Interaction	Time of Measurement		
	Pregnancy	*3 Months after birth*	*9 Months after birth*
Conflict	20.8	20.4	20.7
Relationship Maintenance*	31.1	29.7	28.9
Satisfaction with relationship*	62.8	60.3	58.3
Expressions of love*	78.4	76.5	75.5
Expressions of ambivalence*	11.6	12.1	13.3

* Those measures marked with an asterisk show statistically significant changes from before to after the birth of the infant

SOURCE: Belsky, Lang, & Rovine, 1985, *Journal of Marriage and the Family,* Table 1, p. 859. Copyrighted 1985 by the National Council on Family Relations, 3989 Central Ave, N.E., Suite #550, Minneapolis, MN 55421. Reprinted by permission.

a whole set of questions about the way his or her marriage relationship functioned, types of interactions with their spouse, and satisfaction with the relationship. For example, relationship conflict was measured by the responses to items such as "How often do you and your partner argue;" an item like "How much do you tell your partner what you want or need from the relationship" was a measure of relationship maintenance, while "love" was measured with items like "To what extent do you have a sense of 'belonging' with your partner?" You can see that every one of these aspects of the relationship except conflict got worse after the birth of the child. Other researchers have found very similar patterns (e.g. Roosa, 1988).

The source of the difficulty seems to be the major increase in both *role conflict* and *role strain* that is likely to occur when an infant is added to the family system. Recall that role conflict occurs when two or more roles are physically or psychologically incompatible with one another; role strain occurs when an individual does not have the skills to fulfill some role. Sociologists have argued, with considerable empirical support, that when you have too many jobs (roles) to do, you don't do *any* of them very well (e.g. Rollins & Galligan, 1978).

Since the role of major caregiver and the role of spouse are at least partially in conflict, it should not be surprising that role conflict occurs. The new baby demands time, attention, and nurturance, leaving less of all of these for the spouse. There are not enough hours in the day for the same kinds of recreational activities, for sex, or for quiet companionship between husband and wife as there were before. There is also less time for friends and less time alone. It is precisely this sense of not enough time, particularly affectionate or nurturant time with one's spouse, that marks this transition (Belsky, Spanier & Rovine, 1983; Myers-Walls, 1984).

For some parents there is also a sense of role strain, since caring for a child is a new and unfamiliar task. As you might expect, any factor that tends to increase the role conflict or strain is likely to make the marital satisfaction decline more. So, for example, couples that experience high levels of interference from their work, such as overtime demands or the need to bring work home, show more strain after the birth of a child than do couples with less work interference (Belsky, Perry-Jenkins, & Crouter, 1985). Similarly, more negative effects on marital satisfaction are seen when the newborn has a particularly difficult temperament (Sirignano & Lachman, 1985).

Before I persuade you that having children is an unmitigated disaster, I should hasten to add two things. First, despite the drop in happiness and marital satisfaction at this point in the family life cycle, having a child also brings profound satisfactions, including a greater sense of purpose, worth, or life meaning, a sense of being "grown up," and a shared joy between husband and wife (Hoffman & Manis, 1978; Umberson & Gove, 1989). In Hoffman and Manis's large sample of subjects, 80 percent said that their lives had been changed in positive ways by the arrival of children.

Second, the role conflict and role strain of the transition to parenthood can be significantly mitigated in several ways, particularly by being very clear about the roles that husband and wife will fulfill with the child, by choosing priorities (which may mean giving up some other roles for a while), and even by changing your standards for other roles. That is, you can reduce the role conflict by redefining some roles (not vacuuming the living room every day, or eating convenience foods more often, for example), and by eliminating others. Those couples who apply these good coping strategies to the transition to parenthood experience less distress and more satisfaction (Myers-Walls, 1984).

THE DEPARTURE OF THE CHILDREN: THE "EMPTY NEST" We have much less information about the role changes and their effects that occur when all the children have left home. Extrapolating from data in Figure 7–3, and assuming that the majority of young adults leave home by the age of 23 or 24 (an assumption which has become more dubious in recent years), we can estimate that women in the 1930 to 39 cohort will be about 52 to 54 years old when the last child leaves home. Since women typically marry men older than themselves by several years, the men will be roughly 54 to 56 when the last child has left.

This stage is sometimes called "postparental," as if the role of parent stopped when the last child walked out the door, suitcase in hand. Clearly it does not. Adults who have reared children go on being a parent until they (or their children) die. But the content of the role clearly changes, becoming less demanding, less time consuming. As a result, other roles within the family system change as well. Most importantly, the spousal roles become more central, with more time available for companionship. Of course the content of the husband and wife roles may have changed if some sex role cross-over has occurred, and either husband or wife may also take on new roles (new work roles, for example, or community roles), but the complexity of the entire role repertoire generally declines at this point.

Folklore would have it that this "empty nest" stage is a particularly unpleasant and stressful period, especially for a woman, since she loses what may have been the most central role of her early and middle adulthood, namely that of mother.

As a result, she may lose a powerful sense of her own worth. The research findings, however, do not altogether support such a gloomy picture.

On the one hand, Marjorie Lowenthal and her colleagues (Lowenthal, Thurnher & Chiriboga, 1975), in an often-cited cross-sectional comparison of newlyweds, middle-aged and pre-retirement adults, found that the women in the middle-aged group, all of whom were on the verge of the postparental transition, were consistently the least happy, the most "desperate" with their lives.

Another sign of an increased problem at this age comes from the data on suicides, which you have already seen in Figure 5–5. There is a slight rise in the suicide rate for white women between ages 30 and 55, with the peak at around age 50. And there is evidence that alcohol use or abuse also increases among women in those same years from 30 to 50, as you can see in Figure 7–5.

The other side of the argument, however, seems to me to be more persuasive. First, note that both the rise in suicide and in heavy alcohol use (and the high levels of "desperation" in Lowenthal's middle-aged subjects) occurs primarily in the years when children are still in the home, rather than postparentally. Second, although it is true that many women experience a major transition at this point in the family life cycle, many of the changes women report are positive rather than negative.

Such a pattern emerges from an especially interesting study by Rochelle Harris and her coworkers (Harris, Ellicott, & Holmes, 1986). They interviewed 16 women from each of a series of cohorts, aged 45, 50, 55, and 60, asking not only about family and employment history, but also about each woman's experiences of significant transitions over the course of her adult life. Virtually all the major transitions these women selected for emphasis had occurred at one of three points in the family life cycle: when her children were very young, when the children began leaving home, and after the children had left. And while most of the transitions at either of the first of these two points were characterized by turmoil and difficulty—marital problems, coping with children, feelings of restlessness—the transitions described in the postparental phase were much more likely to be positive. Women at this age more often reported an increase in life satisfaction, inner stability, a general mellowing. Of course, we can't be sure that the experiences of this sample of 64 middle class, well educated women are typical of their cohort or of women in different cohorts. What we can say is that the findings from this study are not consistent with the more pessimistic view of the empty nest stage that has been prevalent for some while in both the popular and professional literature.

Further support for a more optimistic view of the postparental period is not hard to find. Recall that marital satisfaction typically goes up at this stage and that emotional disturbances such as depression show no sign of rising at this age. On the contrary, adults in this life stage report fewer worries, fewer anxieties than do those with young children (Antonucci, Tamir & Dubnoff, 1981).

Those women who do experience heightened distress at this role transition—and there clearly are some—appear to be primarily those who attempt to maintain their old homemaking/parenting role, especially those who do not work outside the home.

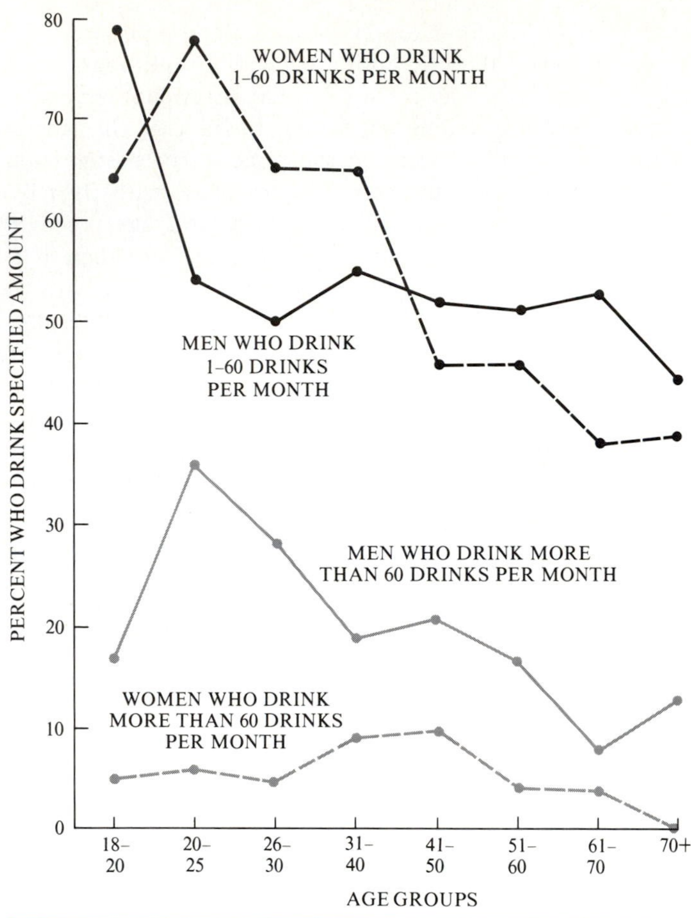

Figure 7–5 *These figures, based on a national survey in 1979, don't tell us about rates of alcoholism, but they do say something about self-reported high levels of alcohol use. High use is most common in men in their 20s and in women in their 30s and 40s. Self-reports of alcohol use are somewhat unreliable, so these figures may underestimate the amount of alcohol dependence or alcoholism, but there's no reason to suppose that the unreliability would vary as a function of age. So the basic age-related pattern is probably valid. (Source: U.S. Bureau of the Census, 1984, Table 192, p. 119.)*

I am not trying to suggest here that for most adults the 'postparental' period is a continuous idyll, devoid of problems, any more than the advent of children ushers in continuous difficulties. Rather, I am trying to suggest that as a general rule, filling more roles is more stressful and difficult than filling fewer. To be sure, multiple roles can also be a strength, since self-esteem or satisfaction can then have multiple sources. But there is no escaping the added conflicts and strains involved in multiple roles, perhaps particularly the role of parent. When this

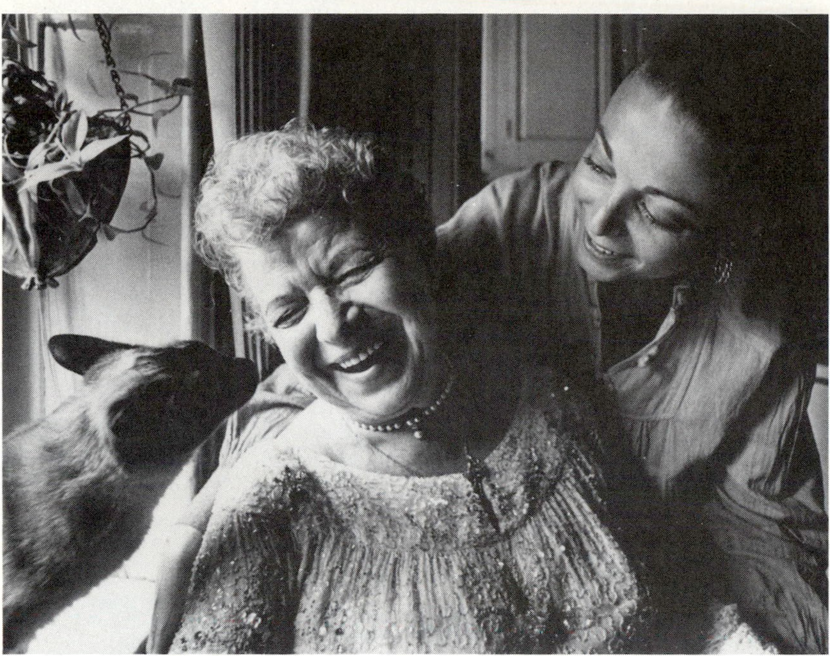

Figure 7–6 A minority of adults in middle-age take on the role of major caregiver to an aging parent, as this woman has done for her mother. Daughters are far *more likely to take on this role than are sons, even when the daughters are working full time. (Photo © Joel Gordon, 1976. Reprinted with permission.)*

role is added in early adulthood, it brings inevitable new role conflicts or strains; when the role is partially shed at midlife, those conflicts and strains are reduced.

CARING FOR AN AGING PARENT At the same time, many adults at midlife take on a new role, namely caring for (or arranging the care of, or worrying about) aging parents. Recent popular as well as professional articles have described such care of the elderly as a normative aspect of midlife, likely to become virtually universal as older generations live longer and longer. But the research data paint a rather different picture. When researchers have interviewed representative samples of middle-aged and older adults they have found that only 10 to 20 percent of those in their forties provide as much as three hours of help per week to a parent or parent-in-law, with even lower rates for adults in their 50s or 60s (e.g. Spitze & Logan, 1990). Equivalent levels of assistance given to adult children is actually more common than is regular care of an aging parent. Thus, despite gloomy statements about the inevitability of this added role at midlife, for current generations it is clearly not a normative experience.

When this role *is* added, it is far more often added to women's lives than to men's. In the United States at present, roughly three quarters of adults performing significant care of elder parents are women. In our culture, men become central caregivers to their aging parents only if they have no available sister, or if their own wives are unable to take on the task (Coward & Dwyer, 1990). Even in middle-aged couples in which both spouses work full time at equally prestigious jobs, the task of caring for the elders falls more on the woman (Finley, 1989).

When this role is added to the other role demands of midlife, it is not uncommon for adults in their late 40s and 50s to find themselves in what Reuben Hill calls a "middle generation squeeze." One's children may be out of the home, but they still need financial assistance, babysitting, and emotional support, even while one's parents become more needy. Hill's own research on this squeeze (1965), while not recent, is still the most complete.

Hill studied three generations in 100 families. Each family included a set of grandparents over the age of 60, a set of parents aged 40 to 60, and a set of married children, aged 20 to 40. He asked each member of the family how much help he or she gave to the other generations, and how much was received from them. As you can see from Figure 7–7, the middle generation gave the most help and received the least.

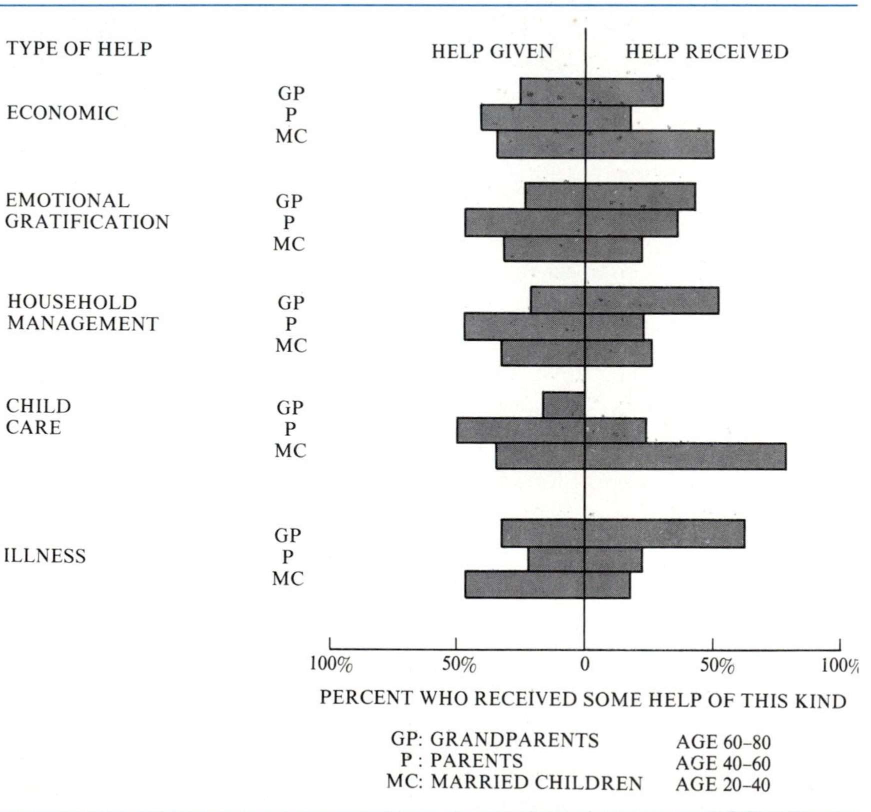

Figure 7–7 Middle-aged adults often find themselves in a kind of squeeze, still providing major assistance to their children at a time they may also be giving more and more help to their own aging parents, as you can see in these results from Hill's study of three generations of 100 families. (Source: Hill, 1965, data from Table 3, p. 125.)

The extent to which any one adult will experience role strain or conflict because of these overlapping roles will depend very heavily on the luck of the draw or on timing. For example, in current cohorts, those who delay childbearing are much more likely to find themselves in such a squeeze. Those who had their children when they were quite young, especially if their parents are healthy and long-lived, are likely to have a period of a decade or more at midlife when the demands of both parent and child roles are at low ebb. And of course many, perhaps most, adults will never need to fill a major role of caring for an aging parent at all.

Roles and Role Losses in Late Adulthood

One of the weaknesses of using family role stages as a basis for examining role changes in adult life is that old-age tends to get short shrift. The final stage in Duvall's system is simply listed as "aged parent," and there is usually little said about the role changes involved at this point. But, in fact, there are myriad role changes in later life which have a profound effect on the life experiences of older adults.

There are two key points about the role changes of late life. First, most of these changes involve role *loss* rather than role gain. At earlier time points, adults add roles—spouse, parent, worker, etc. In old-age, adults shed roles. The role of worker is given up at retirement (which I'll discuss fully in Chapter 9); the role of spouse is given up at widowhood for a great many adults. Friends die, children move away from the hometown, positions in volunteer or community organizations, such as the Lion's Club or the school board, are turned over to younger adults.

Second, as Irving Rosow has so cogently pointed out (1985), the roles that do remain in later life have less content. There is a social position or a label for the role, but there aren't as many duties or expectations as there were earlier in life. This was already apparent in Figure 7–7, where it was clear that the aging parent had fewer family responsibilities than had been true at earlier times. But it is also true in whatever work or organizational roles may remain for the older adult. There are honorific titles and jobs in organizations but few actual duties. In this culture at least, the role of "being old" is a role with few prescriptions. "Enjoying yourself" or "taking it easy" may be the role dictates, but these are highly amorphous role prescriptions. Rosow puts it this way:

> Although freedom from responsibility may sound heavenly to the young, it actually demands strong personal interests and motivation. In earlier periods, life is mainly structured by social duties. People's social positions and role obligations largely govern their general activities and time budgets. This is not true in old-age for, *within objective constraints*, life is essentially shaped by individual choice and personal initiative. (1985, p. 72)

Whether this loss of roles and role content means that older adults are less content with their lives is not so clear. I will be coming back to this issue in later chapters. But it is clear that simply labeling older adults as "aging family" is not adequate to describe the role experience of this age group.

GRANDPARENTHOOD One exception to the pattern of role loss in old age is the role of grandparent, which is typically added some time in the postparental period and retained throughout old-age. About three quarters of adults over 65 in the United States have at least one living grandchild; nearly half are great-grandparents (Hagestad, 1988). Furthermore, most grandparents see or talk to their grandchildren regularly, often as frequently as every week or two. (My own grandfather would have written that often had I answered his letters more promptly!).

Despite the frequency of contact, however, the content of the grandparent role has the same fuzziness that characterizes many other roles in later life (Hagestad, 1985). To put it more formally, there are few normative expectations associated with the role of grandparent. There are many ways to be a grandparent. Which pattern a given adult follows will depend on gender, on ethnic group, and on personal preference.

For example, in a study of white, black, and Mexican-American grandparents and grandchildren, Vern Bengtson (1985) has found that Mexican-American grandparents see their grandchildren more often, provide more help with their grandchildren, and report greater satisfaction with their relationships with their grandchildren. And Gunhild Hagestad (1985), in a study of three-generation families in Chicago, found that the role of grandmother seemed to be both broader and more intimate than the role of grandfather. The grandfathers gave advice, particularly about work or the world at large, and particularly to grandsons. The grandmothers gave advice about personal relationships as well.

But even within an ethnic group, or within groups of grandmothers and grandfathers, there are differences in the way the role is defined. Neugarten and Weinstein (1964), in one of the early studies of grandparenting style, identified five subsets: (1) Formal, which involves clear separation between grandparent and grandchild, with occasional treats or a gift or infrequent babysitting; (2) Fun-seeker, which involves informality and playfulness; (3) Surrogate Parent, a pattern in which the grandparent cares for the child part time; (4) Reservoir of Family Wisdom, which is a largely authoritarian pattern in which the grandparent (nearly always the grandfather) is seen as the source of clear knowledge or authority; and (5) Distant, a pattern in which the benevolent grandparent emerges "from the shadows" occasionally and fleetingly, such as at birthdays and holidays. Neugarten's data, and more recent studies (e.g. McCready, 1985) indicate that young grandparents are more likely to fall in the fun-seeker or distant patterns. Older grandparents are more likely to follow a formal pattern, or perhaps (for a few grandfathers) a reservoir-of-family-wisdom pattern. There are also some signs that grandparents in their 40s, for whom grandparenthood is "off-time" to some degree, like the role less than do those in their 50s and 60s.

Perhaps the key point in all of this is that whatever style one adopts, for most adults the grandparenting role appears not to be emotionally central. Life satisfaction in the elderly is not greatly influenced by the frequency of contact with grandchildren (Palmore, 1981). Still, for many there may be considerable satisfaction from seeing one's family continue into the next generations.

Figure 7–8 The big majority of adults become grandparents; as life expectancy increases, many more of us will become great-grandparents, or even great-great-grandparents. Being a grandparent is more likely to be a pleasant experience if it is "on-time" rather than "off-time," so adults in their 50s and 60s are more satisfied with this role than are those in their 40s. Those in their 70s and 80s also like the role less, perhaps because it becomes more of a strain. (Photo courtesy of Nancy Perry. Reprinted with permission.)

The Family Life Cycle in "Atypical" Families

Except for a few paragraphs on the unmarried, everything I have said so far in this chapter describes the life patterns of adults who follow a particular life course: They marry, have children, and remain married to the same spouse throughout adulthood. In fact, fewer than half of adults in the United States today follow such a life course. Approximately 6 to 10 percent never marry, and that has been rising rapidly in the past decade. And an increasing number have no children. As one example, in 1980, 10.1 percent of women 40 to 44 had no children; in 1987, the number was 14.2, including 10.2 percent of all married women in this age group (U.S. Bureau of the Census, 1989a, 1989b). And of course 40 to 50 percent of those who marry today will eventually divorce (Glick, 1984; Glick & Lin, 1986).

By the time we add in remarriages, redivorces, and extended families, the number of permutations and combinations of family structures and family life cycle sequences in these "atypical" families is boggling. I recall some years ago spending several hours with research colleagues trying to write a small set of questionnaire items that would clearly show the precise marital history and present family composition of each of our subjects. After we had found what we thought was a solution, I burst out laughing, realizing that the questions we were proposing would not have described my own family composition! Where in the normal descriptions of family constellations does an adoptive former step mother fit?

If you simply take a random sample of families, dozens of different combinations occur. In one study of black families in a poor black Chicago neighborhood 20 years ago, Shep Kellam found *86* different family structures (Kellam, Ensminger, & Turner, 1977), including combinations with four and five generations in one household, aunts and uncles, mothers and boyfriends, fathers and girlfriends, step-parents and stepchildren, and so forth. Such extended family structures are far more common among black families, but they are not uncommon among whites. National longitudinal data (Beck and Beck, 1989) suggest that roughly 30 percent of all middle-aged white women have lived in an extended household at some time in the past 15 years, while roughly two thirds of black women have had the same experience.

Out of all this diversity, space allows me to focus further on only three subtypes: (1) married but childless adults, (2) adults who marry and have their children very early, or very late, and who thus alter the timing of the family life cycle, and (3) divorced adults. Each of these groups is extremely interesting in its own right, and whole chapters could be written about them. (In fact I will have more to say about divorce, and its effects, at several later points). My interest at this point is quite selective: What is the impact of these deviations from the "normal" family life cycle on the roles and life experiences of an adult over the adult years?

Childless Adults

Childlessness clearly alters the family life cycle experience of any adult. The rhythm of the child's developmental timetable is simply not there to structure the adult's life experiences.

- Without the presence of children, there is no dip in marital satisfaction in the 20s and 30s (Anderson, Russell, & Schumm, 1983; Houseknecht, 1979, 1987; Ishii-Luntz, & Seccomb, 1989). Childless adults in this age range consistently report higher marital adjustment, particularly higher cohesion within the couple, than do adults with children—not surprising, in view of the fact that childless couples are able to put more emphasis on the role of spouse. But if you compare postparental adults with childless adults of the same age, as Sharon Houseknecht has done in one study, (Houseknecht & Macke, 1981) marital satisfaction is *higher* among the parents. Thus, childlessness seems to be associated with an essentially flat curve over age, in contrast to the U-shaped curve common among couples with children.
- Without children, there is far less barrier to a woman's pursuit of a full time career. Whether women who have made a commitment to a career choose not to have children or whether those who do not have children subsequently make a stronger career commitment is simply not completely clear. Some of

both may well occur. What is clear is that childless women are more likely to work throughout their adult lives, to have somewhat higher level jobs, and to earn more money (Houseknecht, 1987; Hoffman & Manis, 1978). Such work patterns are accompanied by a much higher investment in the work role among childless women. In Hoffman and Manis's study of over 1,500 married women under age 40, 23 percent of the childless women who had been married 6 to 10 years chose "a sense of accomplishment" as their most important life value, compared to 7.0 percent of women with preschool children and 13.5 percent of those with both teenagers and younger children. Overall, it appears that the adult lives of childless women have fewer transitions, fewer shifts in and out of the work force, fewer shifts in roles.

- Lacking children, the middle-aged childless adult is not going to experience a midlife generational squeeze, although the role of primary caregiver for an aging parent may be *more* likely to fall to a childless adult (particularly a childless woman) than to her childbearing sister.
- Lacking children, we might expect that childless adults would lack adequate emotional support in later life. Surprisingly, the research shows quite a different pattern. There are several studies that show that among post-retirement adults, happiness or life satisfaction is *not* related to the amount of contact the adult has with children or grandchildren (Lee & Ellithorpe, 1982; Lee & Ihinger-Tallman, 1980; Seccomb, 1988). Childless adults, at this life stage, appear to be as happy as are those with extended families (Glenn & McLanahan, 1981).

Two points stand out for me in this collection of findings. First of all, the research does not paint a picture of persisting sadness or distress among adults without children. On the contrary.

Second, despite a more steady-state quality to the lives of childless adults during the early and middle adulthood periods, an argument can be made that in important respects the shape of adult role patterns is still highly similar. For the childless, as for those with children, early adulthood is the time when roles are added—spousal roles, work roles. Middle adulthood is the time when those roles go through systematic changes. For the childless adult, there may be fewer such changes, but work roles do change in predictable ways (as I'll describe in Chapter 9), and marital relationships may also move through stages. Finally, late adulthood is a time when roles are shed, or when their substance declines, and that is just as much true for the childless as for those with children. One has the sense, reading about the lives of childless adults, that these lives may be more bland, but at the most fundamental level there is a common shape to the patterns of roles in adult lives.

Early and Late Marriage or Parenthood

I've already talked somewhat about the effects of cohort differences in the timing of family life cycle events such as marriage and childbearing. Here I want to look at variations *within* a cohort. Being off-time carries a price. Marrying and bearing children very early, or very late, seems to have a particularly marked effect.

In this case there is some decent longitudinal research to help sort out the effects of timing, although nearly all of it has focused on adults who marry and have their children very early. We know much less about those who delay childbearing until their 30s or 40s (although no doubt we will know more in the decades to come, as researchers focus their attention on this expanding group).

Marrying and/or having a first child before the age of 18 has several distinct consequences, each of which helps to set the adult's life on a particular trajectory. For both men and women, both blacks and whites, both poor and middle class, early marriage and early childbearing are associated with (1) more children, more closely spaced together, (2) fewer years of education, (3) lower levels of occupational success, (4) lower income, and (5) a higher probability of divorce (Hofferth, 1987; Furstenberg, Brooks-Gunn, & Morgan, 1987; Teti, Lamb, & Elster, 1987). These negative consequences are larger for those adults who were doing poorly in high school, or who come from families with low levels of education, and markedly larger for those who have several children while still teenagers.

Let me give you some sample data from an eight-year longitudinal study of approximately 5,000 families who participated in the Panel Study of Income Dynamics (Moore, Hofferth, Wertheimer, Waite, & Caldwell, 1981). Figure 7–9

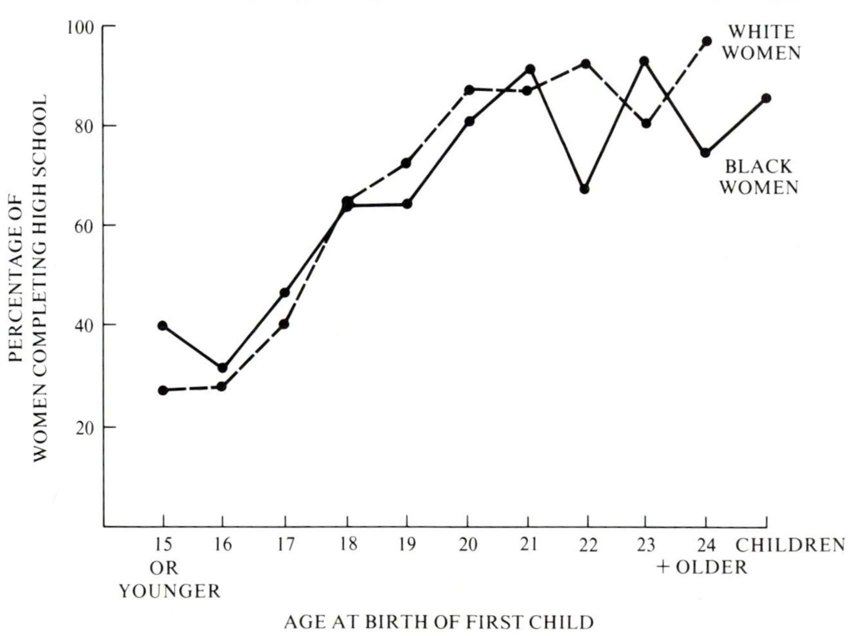

Figure 7–9 Women who bear their first child under the age of 18 have a much smaller chance of completing high school. The particular group of women represented in this figure had been studied longitudinally over a period of eight years, so we know that most of the early-birth women did not go back to school at later points. (Source: Moore, Hofferth, Wertheimer, Waite, & Caldwell, 1981, data from Table 1, p. 39.)

shows the percentage of women in this study who completed high school by the time they were aged 22–35, as a function of their age when the first child was born. You can see very clearly that in both black and white samples, those women who had their first child while still in high school were much less likely to complete high school. Given what we know about the effect of educational attainment on the life patterns of adults (recall Chapter 2), you can see that early marriage and/or early childbearing has a long-term effect on the adult life course.

Being "off-time" or atypical in other ways also seems to exact a price. Hogan (1978), for example, has done an extremely interesting analysis of Census Bureau data for over 35,000 men aged 20 to 65. He argued that men who followed the expected or normal sequence of finishing school, getting a job, and then marrying, should have lower divorce rates than should men who deviated from this sequence, and this is precisely what he found. The highest divorce rates were for those who married before they finished school, regardless of their age or the level of school they completed; the lowest rates of divorce were for those who had followed the normative sequence.

In all of these studies, marriage or first births at ages of 18 or 20 or older are lumped together and considered as "normal." But for the cohorts now in their 40s or older it was just as atypical to marry for the first time or to have a first child in your 30s or even 40s. If the "off-time is riskier" theorem holds, we should find that such adults also pay a price. There are some supporting data. Divorce rates are higher, for example, among adults who marry after age 30 than they are for those who marry between 20 and 30 (though not as high as among those who marry before age 20) (Kitson, Babri, & Roach, 1985.) Beyond this, there are some obvious implications for family life among those who marry late, some of which I've already sketched. Given that the postparental period is one in which many adults experience heightened marital and life satisfaction, delayed childbearing may reduce the pleasures of middle life. On the other side of the equation is the possibility that late childbearing may be associated with greater pleasure in the parental role. Financial security may be higher, so that some of the role conflicts can be reduced by hiring assistance, and there may be greater willingness (on the part of fathers, particularly) to spend the time to create closer emotional bonds to their children.

At the moment, all of this is speculation. Until we have some data from studies of couples who significantly delay marriage and childbearing, we will not be able to determine the consequences of this form of "off-timeness."

Divorced and Remarried Adults

There are myriad ways in which we might explore the effect of divorce or remarriage on adult development. But since I will be talking about the personal and emotional impact of divorce on adults in Chapter 12, when I discuss stresses of various kinds, let me focus here on the much narrower question of the impact of divorce or remarriage on family roles and the family life cycle.

Of the 40 percent to 50 percent of today's young adults who will eventually divorce, approximately 80 percent will eventually remarry, with an average unmarried interval of about three years (Glick & Lin, 1986). Men are more likely to remarry than are women, in part because they are likely to remarry a younger, never-married woman. Remarriage rates are also linked to age: The younger you are when you divorce, the greater the likelihood that you will remarry. Not surprisingly, the remarriage rates are also higher for those who have no or fewer children from the first marriage, although the difference is not very large: Among young divorced women with three or more children nearly 70 percent remarry. Among all those who remarry, about half will divorce a second time.

Although these patterns of marriage and remarriage produce an enormous array of family types, one of the really surprising facts is that divorce and remarriage patterns have a remarkably small effect on the *timing* of some of the important points in the family life cycle, such as a woman's age at the birth of her last child or the number of children she will eventually have. As illustration, look at the findings in Figure 7–10. What I have shown in this is Arthur Norton's analysis of 1980 census data, describing the cohort of women born between 1940 and 1949 (Norton, 1983). Norton divided this cohort into subgroups based on the women's marital history and then compared these subgroups on the timing of significant

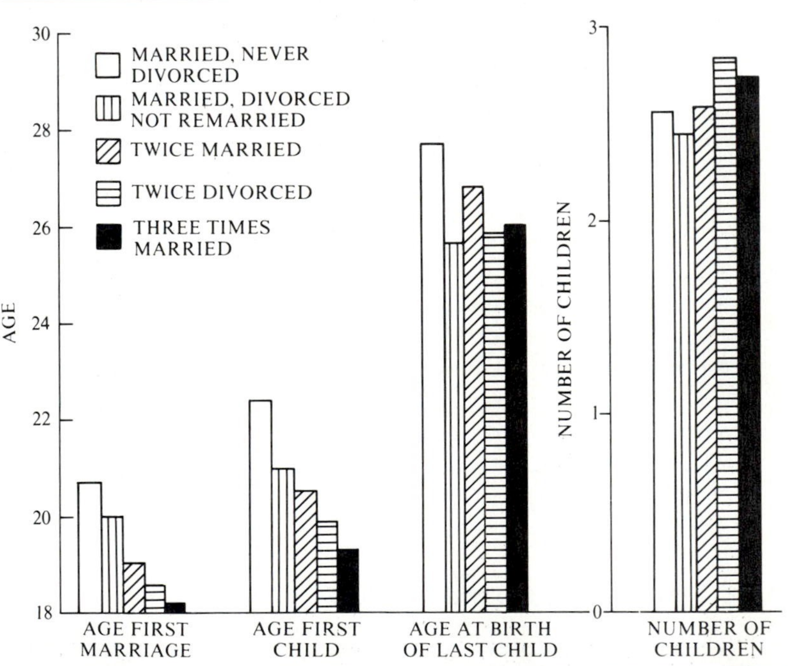

Figure 7–10 Surprisingly, there are only quite small differences in key family life cycle events between women who have remained married and those who have been divorced and remarried. These numbers are for the cohort of women born between 1940 and 1949, but similar patterns hold for women born in earlier cohorts as well. (Source: Norton, 1983, data from tables 2, 3, 4, 5, and 6, pp. 269–270.)

family life cycle events. What I find surprising in these findings is that the total number of years in childbearing does not differ a great deal from one marital status group to the next, ranging from 4.6 years for the group married and divorced once, to 6.7 years for the group married three times. Obviously, most women who remarry do not start over with a new round of childbearing, which means that this aspect of family life cycle is not expanded a great deal because of divorce or remarriage.

At the same time, the years of child*rearing* may be increased for many divorced and remarried adults. This is especially true for men whose second marriage is to a woman much younger than themselves, who then have a second family, or who help to rear the new wife's young children. For some, this sequence of marriage and remarriage shrinks or even eliminates the postparental stage of the family life cycle. But for most, the effects of divorce on family life cycle events is far smaller than you might suppose.

After analyzing the impact of varying combinations of marriage or widowhood on adult life paths, Reuben Hill (1986) concludes that the presence of children imposes a basic life cycle pattern on the adulthood of any person who must care for them, since the children—willy-nilly—are moving through a clear developmental sequence. Regardless of whether the parents remain married to each other, the custodial parent still will have predictable shifts in roles when the children begin school, when they become adolescents, and when they leave home. Stages are *added* to the traditional sequence, however, whenever there is a remarriage, especially if there are step-siblings or subsequent half-siblings added to the family. Each time there is such an abrupt change in the family membership, a new period of adaptation has to occur, much as a couple must adapt to the addition of a new baby. The family life cycle experience of divorced/remarried adults thus has shorter periods of stability and more periods of transition.

Divorce also brings with it a larger and more complex set of roles to fill. The single parent must now fill all of the adult family roles except spouse: breadwinner, emotional supporter, housekeeper, childcaregiver, activities director, chauffeur, and the rest. For the adult without child custody, there are also new roles to be learned, including whatever roles the former spouse had been filling.

On remarriage, another set of roles is added. Spousal roles once again enter the repertoire, along with that of step-parent, or step grandparent, and those charmingly ambiguous role relationships with the former spouse of one's spouse, and with the spouse's former in-laws who remain the grandparents of your new step children. (If you think this sounds as if I am speaking from painful experience, you are quite correct! I've done this twice now, and it's enough to make strong women (and men) weep.)

Such increases in the range of roles filled almost invariably increases both role conflict and role strain. In the short run, the effect of such role overload is to lower the quality of all role performances and to lower marital satisfaction in remarried couples.

Finally, there are large economic effects of divorce, especially for women, who typically experience a precipitous drop in income. Lenore Weitzman, a sociologist who has been a key chronicler of this effect, has estimated from her studies in California that the standard of living of divorced women with minor children drops 73 percent in the first year after the divorce (Weitzman, 1985, 1988). In contrast, their ex-husbands find their standard of living rising an average of 42 percent. National studies do not paint quite as gloomy a picture. Weiss, (1984) for example, found in a study of a large cross-section of American families that among the middle class, income after divorce dropped by about a third, for the poor it dropped by about a fifth. Still, it is clear that divorce is not an economically beneficial experience for women—a fact that will have long-term consequences for a woman's adult life experience.

Overall then, while divorce and remarriage have smaller effects on the *timing* of various key family life cycle events than you might suppose, they have major consequences for the frequency of life transitions, for the range of roles to be learned and fulfilled, and for long-term economic experiences.

Match or Mismatch Between Personal Qualities and Role Demands

So far I have been talking about the pattern and sequence of roles each of us is likely to fill over the years of adult life as if everyone reacted to these roles in the same way. But just as it is true that not everyone moves through the "typical" sequence of family life cycle roles, it is also true that any given role will "fit" some people better than others.

The possible impact of a good or poor match between the roles one fills and one's own personal qualities is a much neglected area of research. So we do not have a great deal of evidence to work from. But the basic point seems to me to be so important for our understanding of the experience of individual adults that it is worth exploring. The most complete and provocative study comes from Florine Livson, who has analyzed data from the Berkeley Intergenerational Studies (Livson, 1976, 1981).

Livson has focused her attention on a group of men and women who, at age 50, were rated by the researchers as having particularly healthy and successful patterns of development. They were rated as having a high capacity for work and for satisfying interpersonal relationships, a realistic perception of themselves, and a sense of moral purpose. All of these adults had also been rated for overall emotional/mental health when they were about 40, so Livson was able to identify some who had been consistently healthy (the "stable" subjects), and some who had looked less integrated and healthy at 40, but looked good at 50 (the "improver" subjects).

When Livson then went back and looked at the information about each of these groups from assessments when they had been adolescents and young adults, she found that for both men and women, those who had shown a pattern of stable, positive emotional health were those whose personal qualities matched the sex and family roles prevailing for that cohort. In other words, both the men and women in this stable group were highly sex typed. The men were focused on work achievement and supporting their families; the women were focused on providing nurturance to their families and on an array of friendships. By temperament, these women appeared to be high in extraversion and low in neuroticism. They liked staying at home and raising a family, and even at midlife, when the children were gone, they were quite content with their lives. The "improver" men and women, in contrast, had tried to fit themselves into the prevailing sex roles but the match had never been good. These groups included women who had been more strongly intellectually oriented as teenagers (not so acceptable in this cohort as it is now), but who had married at the expected time and followed the usual pattern of the family life cycle. By age 40, they were unhappy, thin-skinned, irritable. But by age 50, when they had reached the postparental stage, most had branched out into jobs or had returned to school.

Similarly, the "improver" men had been unconventional teenagers but had tried to fit themselves into the gray-flannel-suit male role expectations of their generation. They too, at 40, were unhappy, with their emotions under tight rein. But by 50, they had allowed their artistic interests and humor to bloom.

Livson does not describe the life patterns of men and women who' were less healthy at 50. But if the concept of "match" between personal qualities and role demands has any validity, we might expect to find that for this group an even greater mismatch occurred in the early life stages, or that they were unable to recover in midlife from the mismatches they had experienced at an earlier point.

I think that the concept of match or mismatch between cohort-specific role demands and personal qualities points us in a very important direction in our thinking about the impact of roles on adult lives. It is far too simple to think of a role as simply something that "shapes" the adult who occupies it. Rather, we might think of a role as similar to a piece of clothing that one puts on: It is bound to fit some people better than others. So it is the interaction between the demands and the flexibility of the role on the one hand, and the adult's qualities on the other, that may be crucial in determining the effect of the role. Thinking of roles in this way obviously makes the job of describing adult development far more complicated. But in my view it also brings us closer to the reality of adult developmental patterns.

An Age Summary

As in earlier chapters, I have pulled together the various patterns of change with age in a summary table, (Table 7.4) so that you can begin to build up composite pictures of the qualities and experiences of adults in different age groups. Several key summary points are also worth making:

1. The largest number of *new* roles are acquired in early adulthood; in middle adulthood these roles change in structure to some degree, but the basic repertoire of roles remains relatively constant until late adulthood, when roles

TABLE 7.4. Summary of Age Changes in Sex Roles and Family Roles.

Age 20–40	Age 40–65	Age 65 and Older
Maximum sex role differentiation, particularly after birth of first child	Some sign of sex role crossover in this age range	Further indications of sex role crossover, with men becoming more emotional and expressive, and women more assertive
Role of spouse added	Spousal role changes after children leave home, when spousal roles become central	Spousal role changes further after retirement; role may be lost entirely at widowhood
Role of parent added	Role of parent changes after children leave home, becomes more distant, although assistance still provided	Role of parent changes significantly as the direction of assistance is reversed
Role of child to one's own parents continues, with young adults receiving more aid than they give	Role of child to one's own parents shifts toward more caregiving, less help received	Role of child to one's own parents lost when parents die
Grandchild role continues, but is usually not highly significant	Role of grandparent added	Role of grandparent continues, but becomes less central with increasing age

begin to be shed. This basic shape of the curve of role accumulation and loss seems to me to be the same for virtually all adults, although the number of roles to be acquired or learned is clearly greater for those who marry than for those who don't, for those who have children than for those who don't, or for those who are divorced and remarry, compared to those who remain in a single marriage. Thus, each of the three periods in the table is characterized by a different basic role-related task or problem: In early adulthood, one must cope with learning new roles; in middle adulthood one must cope with changing definitions of existing roles; in late adulthood one must cope with the loss of roles.

2. For those adults who are involved with the rearing of children (and this includes a considerable majority), the children's own developmental timetable creates a framework, a rhythm, that shapes the adult's own adult life experience.
3. The timing of various key family life cycle events has varied quite sharply from one cohort to the next, and these variations have significant effects on the pattern of adult life by lengthening or shortening various life periods, such as the postparental phase. Being off-time *for your cohort* seems to exact a price, just as being off-time in other adult life experiences is more stressful than is following the normative pattern.

Summary

1. Sex roles, family life cycle roles, and work roles all show sequential changes over adulthood. Each sequence helps to shape the pattern and the rhythm of adult life for those who follow it.
2. Sex roles refer to the "job descriptions" for male and female behavior and qualities. Sex role stereotypes refer to the shared, excessively generalized beliefs about what men and women should be like. Sex typing refers to the extent to which any one adult's behavior or qualities matches the sex role for his or her gender. Masculinity, femininity, and androgyny describe aspects of the personality, or aspects of the self-concept, of individuals.
3. Sex role stereotypes are strong and have had a consistent content for at least several decades in the United States. The male stereotype centers around qualities of competence and instrumentality; the female stereotype centers around qualities of affiliation and expressiveness.
4. Stereotypes are not absolute; there is overlap between the expected behavior for men and women.
5. The content of sex roles changes over the adult years, with an intensification of traditional, differentiated sex roles apparent particularly in early adulthood, especially after marriage and after the birth of the first child. In midlife, there may be a cross-over of sex roles, with women expected to become more independent and assertive, and men becoming more affiliative and expressive.
6. Family roles also change in a sequence usually marked by the progression of the oldest child through a series of age-stages. This sequence is typically referred to as the family life cycle. Each transition from one stage to the next involves addition, alteration, or deletion of roles.
7. Marital satisfaction, life satisfaction, and mental health all show some decline after the birth of the first child. Marital satisfaction rises again in midlife, after the departure of the last child.
8. The transition from singlehood to marriage, for most adults, involves an increase in happiness and a decline in the rate of physical and mental illness. In general, married men show the lowest rates of illness, with single men showing the highest. Married and single women fall in between.
9. The arrival of the first child ushers in a marked increase in the number of roles each adult must fill, with attendant increases in role conflict and role strain. The degree to which this disrupts the marital relationship depends on the extent to which the individuals can systematically reduce the role conflict or strain.
10. In midlife, the "postparental" period is marked by some increase in marital satisfaction for many adults, but it is also a time when adults may have increased role responsibilities with their own aging parents. Midlife adults give the most aid to both the older and younger generations.
11. The most marked change in roles in late adulthood is a decline in the number of roles filled combined with a reduction in the content or the clarity of the roles still occupied. One new role of middle and late adulthood, grandpar-

enthood, is a role filled by about three quarters of older adults. The content of this role varies widely from one adult to another.

12. Childless adults do not experience the rhythm of role change that accompanies a child's development, but they nonetheless follow the basic pattern of adding roles in early adulthood, changing the basic roles in middle adulthood, and shedding roles in late adulthood. Childless women are more likely to have jobs outside the home and more likely to devote themselves to a career. Childless couples report higher marital satisfaction and in old-age do not report lower life satisfaction than do adults who reared children.
13. Very early marriage and parenthood also alters the life pattern. For both men and women, but more strongly for women, marriage or parenthood under the age of 18 is associated with fewer total years of education, lower work success, lower income, larger families, and higher probability of divorce.
14. The timing of basic family life cycle events is not greatly changed by divorce or remarriage, but the number of roles occupied and the number of transitions from one set of roles to another is increased. Divorce is also associated with significant economic decline for women.
15. In understanding the impact of sex roles and family roles on adult lives, it may also be helpful to examine the degree of match or mismatch between an individual's personal qualities and the demands of the roles she or he must fill. Where the match is poor, the adult may experience higher levels of stress and lower levels of physical and mental health.

Suggested Readings

BLOCK, M. R., DAVIDSON, J. L., & GRAMBS, J. D. (1981). *Women over forty. Visions and realities.* New York: Springer. This is a very readable, brief, interesting book that addresses some of the questions I have been raising in this chapter.

DEAUX, K. (1984). From individual differences to social categories: Analysis of a decade's research on gender. *American Psychologist, 39,* 105–116. This is a very good, moderately current review of the topic. It deals less with sex roles than with other aspects of gender but is an excellent source.

GLICK, P. C. (1989). The family life cycle and social change. *Family Relations, 38,* 123–129. Paul Glick has been one of the major contributors to the literature on family life in the United States for many decades. In this brief paper, he looks at the statistics on some of the current social trends—such as delay of marriage and childbearing and divorce—and explores some of the social consequences of the numbers.

LYELL, R. (1980). *Middle age, old age: Short stories, poems, plays, and essays on aging.* New York: Harcourt Brace Jovanovich. There are several short stories in this collection that will convey to you far better than I the actual *experience* of being young or old or middle-aged. You might particularly enjoy Winslow's story "Grandma," or Ferber's story "Old Man Minick," or Anderson's "I Never Sang for My Father."

WEITZMAN, L. J. (1988). Women and children last: The social and economic consequences of divorce law reforms. In S. M. Dornbusch & M. H. Strober (Eds.), *Feminism. Children and the new families*. New York: The Guilford Press. Weitzman's analysis of the impact of divorce on women is a real eye-opener. This is her most recent paper; if you want a longer version, or cannot find this paper, her 1985 book (*The Divorce Revolution: The Unexpected Social and Economic Consequences for Women and Children in America,* Free Press) covers the same information in greater detail.

CHAPTER 8

Development of Relationships in Adulthood

Take a moment and think about some of the most joyous and some of the most painful moments in your life. Perhaps graduating from high school or college, getting promoted, or becoming a parent are on your list of joys. Your list of painful moments may include getting fired from your job or that day you got your first really bad grade in school. Certainly, many of life's highs and lows have to do with school or work experiences. But I will wager that most of the joys and pains you thought of first were connected to a few key relationships—with your parents, with your partner, with your friends. In particular, the processes of attachment and detachment, of creating and breaking bonds with others, lie at the heart of many of the turning points in our lives.

In the last chapter, I talked about some of the key roles that involve family and relationships, focusing primarily on the form and timing of those roles. Here I want to look inside the roles, at the quality of the relationships themselves. Are there age-linked changes in the quality or quantity of relationships over adulthood? Are there typical changes in the number or type of friends we have over adulthood? Does the relationship between partners (spouses or lovers) go through predictable changes over time or over age? Do relationships with our parents or our growing children change in specific ways over the adult years?

A second theme—as usual—will be individual differences in relationships or relationship patterns. What differentiates satisfying or lasting marriages from dissatisfying marriages? What are the differences between adults who have many friends and those who have fewer?

The Underlying Nature of Adult Relationships: Some Theory

If you think about your own relationships—with your parents, your friends, your partner/lover/spouse, your coworkers—it's clear immediately that they are not all the same, either in intensity or in quality. But how can we describe those differences more precisely? What set of terms can we use to talk about the array of relationships we each create?

Theoretical interest in the qualities of adult relationships is really quite recent, so there are many new ideas, new concepts, and no clear agreement on the best framework. The disagreement is exacerbated by the fact that theorists have started from at least three different places: from studies of **attachment**, from analysis of **love**, and from research on **social support**.

Attachment

The concept of attachment has been most commonly used to describe the strong affectional bond formed by an infant to her major caregiver. (e.g. Ainsworth, Blehar & Waters, 1978; Bowlby, 1969, 1973, 1980). John Bowlby and Mary Ainsworth, two of the major theoretical figures in this area, have both made a clear distinction between the attachment itself, which is an invisible, underlying bond, and **attachment behaviors**, which are the ways in which an underlying attachment is expressed by the individual. Since we cannot see the attachment, we have to infer it from behavior. In infants, we see it in their crying when their favored person leaves the room, in their clinging to the favored person when they are frightened, in their use of the favored person as a safe base for exploring some new situation. The three key underlying features are: (a) association of the attachment figure with feelings of security, (b) an increased likelihood of attachment behavior when the child is under stress or threat, and (c) attempts to avoid or to end any separation from the attachment figure (Weiss, 1982).

In adults, of course, many of these specific attachment behaviors are no longer seen. Most adults do not burst into tears if their special person leaves the room; adults maintain contact in a much wider variety of ways than what we see in children, including the use of letters, phone calls, and fantasy and imagery. But if we allow for these changes in the *form* in which the attachment is expressed, it does appear that the concept of attachment is a useful way to think about many adult relationships. We appear to form strong new attachments in adulthood, particularly to a spouse or partner, and we may maintain our attachment to our parents as well. As Weiss says,

> In all these instances individuals display need for ready access to the attachment figure, desire for proximity to the attachment figure in situations of stress, heightened comfort and diminished anxiety when in the company of the attachment figure, and a marked increase in discomfort and anxiety on discovering the attachment figure to be inexplicably inaccessible. (1982, p. 173)

A personal experience brought this final point home to me very clearly. Several years ago, I was separated from my partner under circumstances that made it impossible for me to contact him even by phone. Given the dictates of our separate careers, we have been apart many times. Separation itself is not anxiety provoking. But I found his inaccessibility quite surprisingly uncomfortable. I was plainly relieved when he was once again available, if only by phone.

Given that the concept of attachment accurately describes at least some adult relationships, it is still not at all clear that it makes sense to think of *all* relationships between adults as forms of attachment. Are casual friendships merely "weak" attachments? Is your relationship to your grandparents or your aunts or uncles a kind of attachment? Probably not. Most theorists in this area, including both Weiss and Ainsworth, have begun to differentiate between attachments and several other forms of relationships.

Mary Ainsworth suggests that the more general category is that of an *affectional bond*, which she defines as "a relatively long-enduring tie in which the partner is important as a unique individual and is interchangeable with none other. In an affectional bond, there is a desire to maintain closeness to the partner." (1989, p. 711). In Ainsworth's view, an attachment is one subvariety of affectional bond in which, as an added ingredient, the person receives a sense of security and comfort from the presence of the partner. Relationships with friends are rarely attachments in this sense of the term, although they certainly may be affectional bonds. In contrast, the relationship an adult has with his partner/spouse usually is an attachment, as is his relationship with his own parents—as demonstrated by the nature of the grief and sense of profound loss an adult feels at the death of a parent. The most difficult relationship to categorize in this system is the bond between a parent and his or her adult child. Clearly, parents experience profound grief at the death of a child, but it is not so clear that parents of adult children regularly feel more secure or comforted when in the presence of the child, or feel uncomfortable or anxious when the child is absent. Obviously, there is some kind of affectional bond involved here, but whether it is an attachment in Ainsworth's sense is not completely clear.

Robert Weiss (1982, 1986) agrees with Ainsworth that the key ingredient in an attachment that makes it different from other forms of bonds is the sense of comfort and security that is part of being with the favored person. But Weiss goes beyond Ainsworth to identify several subvarieties of nonattachment bonds, which I've listed in Table 8.1.

Distinctions like the ones Weiss is proposing have not yet had much impact on research on adult relationships, but the direction of this newer thinking about attachments in adulthood seems very fruitful to me. We need to distinguish between the small set of key relationships properly called attachments, which are different not just in intensity but also in quality, and the many other varieties of friendships or personal connections. And we will need to know how each of these types of relationships may wax or wane over the adult years, how individuals may differ in the types of relationships that make up their personal networks, and how such differences may affect their life experiences.

Love

Another group of theorists has approached the question from a different direction but has arrived at a similar place. Rather than generalizing from the parent-child relationship, social psychologists such as Zick Rubin (1973) and Elaine Walster

TABLE 8.1. Six Types of Adult Social Relationships Proposed by Robert Weiss.

Attachment	Key feature is a feeling of enhanced security in the presence of the special person and a sense of loss or distress when apart.
Affiliation	Feelings of mutuality, affection, respect, and loyalty based initially on recognition of shared interests or shared life circumstances.
Nurturance	A sense of commitment to, or investment in, the care of someone seen as weak or needful.
Collaboration	A feeling of shared commitment to reaching some goal. A relationship of colleagues or partners, usually accompanied by sense of mutual respect.
Persisting Alliance	Feelings of identification or overlapping identities, independent of goals or aims, accompanied by sense of obligation to help the other if needed. Characteristic of many kinship ties but also of marriage.
Help Obtaining	A bond to someone seen as wiser who is looked to for guidance—perhaps an aspect of the bond of younger worker with a mentor.

SOURCE: Weiss, 1986, pp 96–97.

(Walster & Berscheid, 1974) began by trying to understand the difference between loving and liking, between passionate and companionate love. As Rubin defined it, liking includes the feelings of respect and affection, while loving includes caring and intimacy.

Robert Sternberg (1987) has taken this basic distinction a step further, much as Weiss has gone beyond the distinction between attachment and affectional bonds. Sternberg proposes that love has three key components: (1) intimacy, which includes feelings that promote closeness and connectedness, (2) passion, which includes a feeling of intense longing for union with the other person, including sexual union, and (3) commitment to a particular other, often over a long period of time. If these three components are combined in all possible ways, you end up with the subvarieties listed in Table 8.2.

Weiss' categories and Sternberg's are clearly not the same. Weiss's system is broader, encompassing more types of intimacy and commitment than Sternberg suggests. Still, there are some obvious overlaps. "Affiliation" and "Liking" seem similar. And some combination of what Sternberg would call intimacy and commitment seems to be the minimal ingredient for what Weiss would call an attachment. Which of these two approaches (or some other) will eventually dominate the thinking and the research on adult relationships is not yet clear. What is clear is that both of these conceptualizations are advances over our earlier thinking, and each can help to create a framework for our understanding of relationships across the years of adult life.

TABLE 8.2. Eight subvarieties of love suggested by Robert Sternberg.

Nonlove	When none of the three components are present, there is no love. Most casual relationships are of this type.
Liking	Intimacy is present, but passion and commitment are not. Many enduring friendships have this quality.
Infatuated love	Passion without intimacy or commitment.
Empty love	Commitment without passion or intimacy. May characterize some stagnant, long-term marriages or "friendships" that have gone on for years but have lost mutual involvement and mutual attraction.
Romantic love	Both passion and intimacy are present but no commitment. May be characteristic of the early stages of a relationship.
Companionate love	Both intimacy and commitment are present, but passion is not. May describe long-term committed friendships, or relationships with parents or other kin, or with a partner with whom passion has waned.
Fatuous love	Passion and commitment but no intimacy, as in a whirlwind courtship; the commitment is based on passion rather than on intimacy, though intimacy may come later.
Consummate love	All three components are present. The attainment of consummate love is no guarantee that it will last.

SOURCE: Sternberg, 1989.

Social Support: A Third Approach

The third term currently used to talk about relationships among adults is *social support.* Unlike attachment or love, however, both of which describe the quality or quantity of a person's link to some other individual, social support describes one of the forms of exchange in a relationship. Although we also give support to those we love, like, or are attached to, most of the literature on support has focused on what we receive from such relationships.

Kahn & Antonucci (1980) suggest that social support has three elements, **affect**, **affirmation**, and **aid**. We receive social support to the extent that we receive affection, warmth, and love (affect), expressions of agreement or acknowledgement (affirmation), and direct assistance, such as money, advice, information, and time (aid).

In this chapter, I want to spend most of my time looking at the quality of the relationships themselves rather than on the supportive effects of relationships. I'll be returning to the question of social support in Chapter 12, when I talk about stress and the ways we handle it. The key point for the moment is that it is clear that the amount of social support available to an adult has a powerful effect on nearly every facet of adult life and development. Since such support comes from the network of relationships one has established, we have to start by understanding the relationships and how they develop over the life course. Let me begin with that most central of those relationships, the link with one's spouse or partner.

Intimate Partnerships

I have quite purposely chosen to use the term "partnership," rather than "marriage," since I also want to include here both long-term committed homosexual relationships and unmarried but committed heterosexual relationships. Of course, the vast majority of the research has focused on marital relationships, which will make this discussion somewhat lopsided. However, limited recent research on cohabiting heterosexual and homosexual couples reveals that many of the same processes occur in them as are found in marriages.

Finding a Partner

The process of mate selection preoccupies most of us in our teens and twenties; for many adults it becomes a preoccupation again after a divorce. We are searching for a partner with whom we hope to spend the rest of our lives. Just what attracts one person to another? How does a couple move past passion or intimacy to commitment? Why do some early combinations break up, while others become stable? Social scientists have tried very hard to answer these questions, but despite the efforts, understanding still largely eludes us.

The most widely accepted theories describe mate selection as a series of "filters" or steps (Perlman & Fehr, 1987). One example: Bernard Murstein (1970, 1976,

1986) suggests that when you meet a prospective partner, you first check for the degree of match on basic "external" characteristics, such as appearance, or manners, or apparent social class. If this first hurdle is passed, you then check for a match on attitudes and beliefs, such as politics, sex, or religion. Finally, if you are still interested in one another, the degree of "role fit" becomes an issue: Do your prospective partner's expectations fit with your needs or inclinations? Is there sexual compatibility, or agreement on sex roles?

There is some support for filter theories of courtship, but the filtering process probably occurs very early in the courtship process rather than over a period of months or years as Murstein originally suggested and may not follow a strict sequence. The one thing that is clear is that we choose our partners more on the basis of similarity than on any other single basis—a process sociologists refer to as *assortive mating* or *homogamy*. We are far more likely to choose someone who is similar in age, social class background, race or ethnic group, religious preference or involvement, interests, attitudes, and temperament than someone who differs from us in these respects. Furthermore, long-term partnerships based on such similarity are more likely to endure than are those in which there are wide differences between the partners (Murstein, 1986).

Several studies of couples who eventually marry also show that there are distinct changes in facets of the relationship as the couple moves from casual dating to greater commitment to marriage (Huston, et al. 1981). Feelings of belongingness and attachment (what Sternberg would call intimacy) increase over time as do "maintenance behaviors," such as disclosing feelings, trying to solve problems, and being willing to change in order to please the partner. Both ambivalence and conflict also increase early in relationships, with the peak just before a commitment to marriage is made, after which they decline. Ted Huston and his colleagues also found a sex difference in these patterns: Women appeared to be more cautious about forming an attachment or making a commitment, but once it was made, they took on more of the task of relationship maintenance—a standard female sex role task in this culture.

MARRIAGE VERSUS COHABITATION Once a commitment has been made, today's couples face another choice: cohabitation or marriage. In 1985, nearly two million couples—roughly four percent of all couples—were cohabiting, a fourfold increase since 1970 (Buunk & van Driel, 1989). Cohabiting couples come from all age groups and social backgrounds, although the pattern is most common among two rather disparate groups: those who dropped out of school before finishing high school and those with a college education or more. It is least common among those who have a high school degree but no further education. Cohabiting women are more likely to be working than are married women and on average have somewhat higher level jobs—in large part because there is such a liberal sprinkling of highly educated women among the cohabiting group (Spanier, 1983).

Most couples who live together conceive of cohabitation as a final "filter," a sort of "test" before marriage. Can we really get along together? Are we sexually compatible? In Sternberg's terms, it is a test of the commitment element of love. The assumption is that relationships that pass this test will end in marriage and

Figure 8–1 Despite many years of research, psychologists don't know much about how couples choose one another and why some relationships lead to commitment and others do not. But there is certainly no doubt about the fact that finding a partner is a key task of early adult life nor about the fact that infatuation is an amazing and wondrous state! (Photo © Susan Lapides, 1988, c/o Design Conceptions. Reprinted with permission.)

that such marriages will be more satisfying and more durable. Interestingly, the current evidence, if anything, shows exactly the opposite. Some researchers have found no differences in the eventual marital quality of cohabitors and noncohabitors, but when a difference has been found it is consistently in the direction of poorer marital quality among previously cohabiting couples. Cohabiting couples who eventually marry, in comparison to married couples who did not live together before marriage, are *less* satisfied with their marriages, have poorer communication (e.g., Booth & Johnson, 1988), and are more likely to divorce (Trussell & Rao, 1989; Watson, 1983).

The most likely explanation of this surprising set of findings is not that cohabiting somehow spoils people for marriage but that adults who choose to live together before marriage are systematically different in key ways from those who reject such an option. DeMaris and Leslie (1984), for example, found that cohabitors are less traditional in sex roles, less likely to attend church, and less likely to agree that one should stick with a marriage no matter how bad it is. Whatever the explanation, these preliminary research findings do not support the idea that cohabitation is a good "training period" for marriage.

Development of Partnerships over Adulthood

Of greater interest to me as a developmental psychologist is the nature of change in partnerships over time, or over age. Are there predictable changes in the quality or content of the relationship as adults pass through various steps and stages? Is there some kind of systematic shift from one of Sternberg's categories of love to another? Do partnerships move from consummate to companionate love or even to empty love?

I have already talked about one set of answers to such questions, namely the curvilinear relationship between marital satisfaction and family life stage (recall Figures 1–10 and 1–11 and the discussion in Chapter 7). But such results only skim the surface.

The best way to delve deeper would be to study the same marriages over long periods of time, measuring the various aspects of the relationship, such as Sternberg's intimacy, passion, and commitment, at each of various time points. The only research I know of that approximates this design draws on data from the Berkeley Intergenerational Studies. Sylvia Weishaus and Dorothy Field (1988) studied 17 couples, all parents of children who participated in the main study and all interviewed four different times, once in their young adulthood (1929), once in middle-age (1946), once in young-old age (1969) and once in old-old age (1983). These 17 were the only pairs who had both survived that long and were still married to each other. The researchers found no common pattern of change or stability among these 17 marriages. The single most frequent pattern—found in seven of the couples—was the now-familiar curvilinear change, with high satisfaction in the early years, a drop in the middle years, and then a rise in later life. The descriptions of their marriages by these seven couples sound as if they moved through a time of 'empty love' to a deeper attachment or to a companionate or consummate love in Sternberg's terms. They said things like, "Our love has grown."

The remaining 10 pairs had much more stable patterns: Five expressed high levels of satisfaction and positive emotion throughout the years (perhaps an example of consistently consummate love), three were largely neutral at every time point (perhaps an example of empty love), and two were consistently negative.

Of course, we have no way of knowing whether these 17 couples are at all typical, either of their cohort or of couples as a whole. Still, the study is intriguing, suggesting as it does the highly plausible hypothesis that there is not one but many different potential pathways through the marriage relationship. It is also plausible that the particular pathway one follows will depend a good deal on the kind of love or attachment that was present at the beginning.

The only other longitudinal data we have come from short-term studies of the first year of marriage, such as the work of Ted Huston and his colleagues (Huston, McHale & Crouter, 1986). They have documented some of the specific experiences that may contribute to the commonly reported drop in marital satisfaction after the honeymoon period is over.

In this study of 168 couples, mostly young adults all in their first marriages, each partner was interviewed at some length within the first 3 months of the marriage and then again after 1 year. In addition, in the weeks surrounding each of these time points, each couple was called nine different times and asked to describe in detail what they had done over the previous 24 hours. Thus, Huston has information not only about feelings and attitudes but about actual activities. He found that over the first year there was a decrease in satisfaction with both the quantity and the quality of interaction. These couples reported lower levels of love after one year, and that was true whether they had had a child or not. Furthermore, their activities had changed. In the early months, they spent a lot more time in joint leisure activities; after one year when they did things

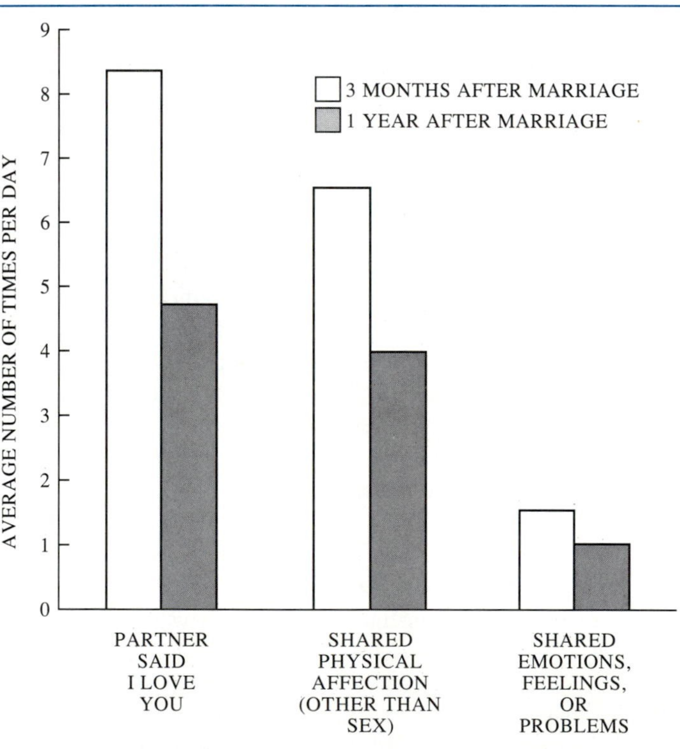

Figure 8–2 Most couples report that they become less satisfied with their marriages during the first year, whether they have children or not. They say fewer positive things to one another, express affection less often, and disclose their feelings less. (Source: Huston, McHale, & Crouter, 1986, from Table 7.4, p. 124).

together, it was more likely to be on "instrumental tasks" (grocery shopping, errands, housework, and the like). They also talked to each other less. Perhaps most importantly, the husbands and wives both described a sizeable drop in the frequency with which the partner did pleasing things for them. Huston did not find any increase in negative interactions, but there was a clear decline in positive interactions, a pattern you can see in the results I've shown in Figure 8–2. In Sternberg's terms, there was a decline in the intimacy aspect of love as well as in the passionate aspect—a combination that may lead directly toward an empty or devitalized marriage, at least for those couples who do not find ways to counteract the trend.

Signs that such a devitalization of marriage may be quite common comes from one of my favorite cross-sectional studies. Clifford Swensen and his colleagues (Swensen, Eskew, & Kohlhepp, 1981) studied a sample of 776 adults that spanned the spectrum of family life cycle stages. Each subject was asked to describe aspects of both loving and problematic marital interactions from which Swensen developed two scales: a "love scale" that describes the expressions of affection, self-disclosure, moral support and encouragement, material support, and toleration of the less pleasant aspects of the other person; and a "marital problems" scale that describes the degree of problems experienced in six areas: problem solving and decision making, child rearing and home labor, relationships with relatives and in-laws, personal care and appearance (Does your partner leave more mess than you like? Has your partner gained too much weight? etc.), money management, and expressions of affection. You can see the relationship between the scores on these two scales and family life cycle stages in Figure 8–3.

In this sample, expressions of love were lower with each succeeding age group, whereas problems peaked among those with young children. If we measure overall marital satisfaction by taking the difference between these positive and negative elements, we would end up with precisely the curvilinear relationship that has been reported so often. But such a net score doesn't tell us very much. Swensen points out that although the older couples have relatively high net scores—that is, they describe their marriages as satisfactory overall—these are nonetheless *devitalized* or *empty* marriages. The high net satisfaction is bought at a price of low levels of love and lower levels of problems.

The same kind of increased devitalization showed up in a time-sequential study by Joseph Veroff and his colleagues (Veroff, Douvan, & Kulka, 1981)—a study I have mentioned before. Recall that Veroff studied two sets of cross-sectional samples, one set in 1957 and one set in 1976. At both time points, the cross-sectional comparisons show lower levels of marital problems for each succeeding age from age 21 to 65+. At the same time, the frequency of physical affection also declined with age.

In attachment theory terms, then, it may be that one of the patterns of change in marriages over the adult years is a decline in frequency of certain classes of attachment behaviors. In Sternberg's terms, both intimacy and passion tend to decline over the years of a long-term partnership, leading to more empty kinds of love. The underlying attachment, however, certainly seems to persist, even in such devitalized unions. Long-married older adults continue to turn to one another in times of stress and show marked distress at the death of the spouse—both signs

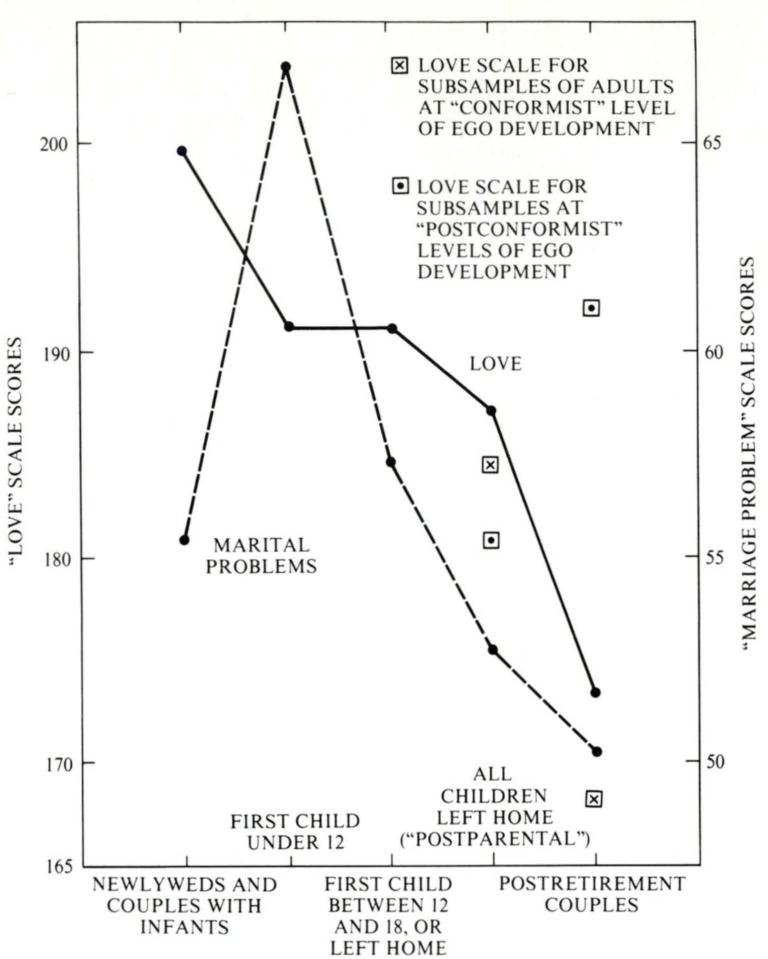

Figure 8–3 When these researchers measured expressions of love and marital problems in couples at various stages of the family life cycle, they found a pattern that helps to explain the typically found curvilinear relationship between marital satisfaction and life stage. Satisfaction may be low when children are young because marital problems are high; satisfaction may rise later in life because problems decline, although expressions of love also decline. This late-life decline in expressions of love did not *occur, however, for those postretirement-age adults who scored at postconformist levels of ego functioning on Loevinger's scale. (Source: Swensen, Eskew & Kohlhepp, 1981,* Journal of Marriage and the Family, *Figure 1, p. 848, and data from Table 3, p. 849. Copyrighted 1981 by the National Council on Family Relations, 3989 Central Ave. N.E., Suite #550, Minneapolis, MN 55421. Reprinted by permission.)*

Figure 8–4 If you watch other couples in restaurants you will often see pairs like this, who seem to have little to say to one another and rarely exchange glances. You might guess that they have been married a long time—a guess supported by the research on marital devitalization in midlife and beyond. (Photo © Joel Gordon, 1986. Reprinted with permission.)

of an enduring attachment. But attachment behaviors in the absence of stress may become less common, just as they do in children over the early years of life.

But while this trend may describe the average pattern, it certainly does not describe changes in all relationships, as witness the five consistently positive long-term marriages in the Berkeley longitudinal study. Swensen and his colleagues give us a hint about one factor that may make a difference. For at least some of the two oldest groups of subjects shown in Figure 8–3, Swensen had obtained scores on Jane Loevinger's measure of ego development (see Table 3.2 for a review). He then divided the sample into those adults who scored at the conformist level and those who scored at the postconformist level, and looked again at the love scores. I've shown those scores in boxes in Figure 8–3. Among those in the postparental stage, there was no difference in love scores between those at the conformist and those at the postconformist level. But among postretirement couples there was a very large difference, with the postconformist adults reporting much higher expressions of love in their relationship. Swensen says:

> . . . post-conformists are able to transcend role expectations and form relationships based more upon the reality of needs, feelings, wishes, and aspirations of

> the individuals. They are more capable of coping with conflict through discussion rather than avoidance, and so form relationships in which vitality, as measured by the expression of love, may increase over time." (Swensen, Eskew, & Kohlhepp, 1981, p. 850)

Further confirmation of this basic point comes from a study by Mark deTurck and Gerald Miller (1986), who measured the extent to which adults perceived their spouse as a unique human being as opposed to perceiving the spouse primarily in terms of the set of roles he or she occupies. deTurck and Miller did not use Loevinger's scale to measure this, but the parallel seems clear since perceiving and responding to others on the basis of unique individual characteristics is one of the features of the postconformist stages. deTurck and Miller found that marital satisfaction and cohesion were highest in those couples in which both individuals perceived their mate in this more individualistic way and lowest in couples in which both responded primarily on the basis of roles.

Studies like this seem to me to be a major step forward. They tell us something about the kinds of individual skills or qualities that may promote or alter the commonly reported U-shaped pattern. But even studies like this are only a bare beginning. We need to know a great deal more about the nature of changes in relationships over time and over age, not just in marital satisfaction, but in communication skills, values, empathy, humor. And we need to know far more about the links between the individual development of each partner and the quality of the relationship. To take just one example, I would like to know whether the often-reported rise in marital satisfaction in late middle age occurs in part because many more adults by that time have moved toward less stereotyped responses to the world in general. Could it also reflect some sex role cross-over? I not only want to understand the typical age-related patterns of change, I want to understand how those changes interact with the changes going on within each individual in the partnership.

A Word of Caution You've heard this song before but let me sing it again: It is wise to remember that virtually all of the information we have on age-related patterns of marital interaction comes from *cross-sectional* comparisons. In this case, in addition to the usual problems of interpretation of developmental trends from cross-sectional data, there is another serious problem: length of marriage, age, and stability of marriage are totally confounded in virtually every study. If we compare the marriages of adults in their 30s with marriages of adults in their 60s, the older group is not just older, they have also been married longer, and their marriages have survived. Adults the same age who are divorced are simply not included in the study, nor have we studied groups of older couples who have been married only a short period of time. Longitudinal data can help sort out some of this problem, but not all of it, since age and length of marriage are still going to be confounded. Thus we do not know whether the curvilinear pattern I have been talking about is related to age, or to length of marriage, or appears only in stable marriages.

Good and Bad Marriages

A second window through which we can look at partnerships is through the study of good and bad or stable and unstable marriages. This very large body of research is *non*developmental. To my knowledge, no one has asked whether different elements contribute to marital breakdown or success at different points in the adult life cycle. But we may nonetheless glean some insights into the workings of this key relationship by a brief journey through this literature. I have summarized some of the main conclusions from this research in Table 8.3, giving recent references for each.

As you look at the items in this list, you may be struck by some of the same points that stood out for me as I read this literature. When a marriage begins, some couples have a lot of good things going for them. Others start out with a few strikes against them. In general, the more "resources" a couple has—such as more education, more communication skill or problem solving ability, better physical and emotional health, and greater individual self-confidence—the better their

TABLE 8.3. Some Differences Between Satisfying or Lasting Marriages and Dissatisfying or Unstable Marriages.

Personal Characteristics of Individuals in More Successful Marriages
They married between age 20 and 30 (Kitson, Babri, & Roach, 1985; Booth & Edwards, 1985).
They come from high social-class families and have more education (Lewis & Spanier, 1979).
They have greater communication skill and greater cognitive complexity (Bruch, Levo, & Arisohn, 1984).
They are more likely to be highly involved in religion (Wilson & Filsinger, 1986) or to be of the same religious background (Heaton & Pratt, 1990).
They have higher levels of self-esteem (Schafer & Keith, 1984).
Qualities of the Interaction of Couples in More Successful Marriages
They have high agreement on roles (including sex roles) and high satisfaction with the way the spouse is filling his/her roles (Bowen & Orthner, 1983).
They are roughly matched on levels of self-disclosure (high, medium, or low in both partners) (Davidson, Balswick, & Halverson, 1983; Hansen & Schuldt, 1984).
They have high levels of "nice" interactions and low levels of "nasty" ones (Filsinger & Thoma, 1988; Gottman & Levenson, 1984; Halford, Hahlweg, & Dunne, 1990). In particular, there is more reciprocation of negative behavior in poor marriages.
They have lower levels of stereotyped or highly predictable behavior patterns; in dissatisfied couples, behavior patterns are more strongly routinized (Gottman & Levenson, 1984).
They have better conflict resolution strategies, with low levels of both criticism and problem avoidance (Gottman & Levenson, 1984).
They are more symmetrical in their skill at reading each other's signals. In dissatisfied marriages, the husband appears to "read" the wife less well than she reads him (Gottman & Levenson, 1984; Gottman & Porterfield, 1981).
They like each other and consider their spouse their best friend (Lauer & Lauer, 1985).
They spend more leisure time together (Hill, 1988).

chances of forming a satisfying intimate relationship (Lewis & Spanier, 1979). In the case of self-esteem, there are even some supportive longitudinal data. Using data from the Berkeley Intergenerational studies, Arlene Skolnick (1981) has compared the self-concepts at adolescence and early adulthood of three groups of middle-aged adults: happily married, unhappily married, and divorced. She found that those with satisfying marriages had the highest self-esteem at both the earlier measurement points, in adolescence and early adulthood. Those with unsatisfying but enduring marriages had the lowest self-esteem, with the divorced group falling in between.

If we use the language of Erikson's theory, then it looks like those young adults who have successfully completed the step of forming a clear (and positive) identity have a much better chance of creating a lasting and satisfying intimate partnership.

Important as these initial skills are, though, they are clearly not the whole picture, nor even necessarily the most critical ingredient. Far more important is the pattern of interaction the partners create together. Obviously, the skills each partner brings to the relationship affect the interaction pattern in some important ways. In particular, the ability to communicate clearly seems to be an especially important skill that some adults bring to their marriages and which enhances their interaction. But any partnership is a dynamic system, not merely the sum of the individual personal skills or qualities. Each couple works out its own ways of dealing with conflict, of expressing affection, of handling day-to-day encounters.

The most consistent interactional difference between happy and unhappy couples is simply the "niceness" or "nastiness" of everyday encounters. In one typical finding, the ratio of pleasing encounters to displeasing ones was about 30 to 1 for happy couples, but about 4 to 1 for distressed couples (Birchler, Weiss & Vincent, 1975).

Differences between happy and unhappy marriages are also clear when researchers have looked at more complex chains of interaction. John Gottman's research on conflict resolution is particularly fascinating (e.g., Gottman & Levenson, 1984). He has found distinct differences between satisfied and dissatisfied couples at every stage in the conflict resolution process, from the "agenda-building" stage, through the "arguing" phase, to the "negotiation" phase. For example, in the agenda-building phase, dissatisfied couples are more likely than satisfied couples to engage in what Gottman calls "cross complaining," such as:

> WIFE: I'm tired of spending all my time on the housework. You're not doing your share.
>
> HUSBAND: If you used your time efficiently, you wouldn't be tired.

Throughout a difficult discussion, satisfied couples are also more likely than are unsatisfied couples to acknowledge the partner's comments—even with something so simple as "that's true but. . ." or "Yeah"—before offering their own arguments or solutions. If one listens to prolonged sequences, the striking thing is the way in which satisfied couples continually deescalate any build-up of negative feelings, while the dissatisfied couples allow (or encourage) such negative emotion to build.

Figure 8–5 Every couple fights at least once in a while. It is when the ratio of such angry exchanges compared to more positive expressions gets high that couples are likely to report serious dissatisfaction with their marriage. (Photo © Joel Gordon, 1983. Reprinted with permission.)

Fortunately, the patterns are not immovable. Therapists who work with couples have found that marital satisfaction can be significantly increased by teaching couples how to solve conflicts, how to talk to one another, how to increase their positive interactions. So couples whose interactions have moved slowly toward stereotyped, negative, escalating discord, can acquire new skills, or relearn earlier patterns of interaction.

The direction of causality has been difficult to determine in all this. Do couples develop negative, stereotyped, and insensitive ways of interacting because they are already dissatisfied, or do they become dissatisfied because their interactions are so negative? Probably it is both, but the fact that overall satisfaction can be increased by teaching couples how to interact more positively suggests that it is the interaction style that primarily affects the satisfaction and not the other way around. To a considerable degree, couples seem to be unhappy because they are negative, not negative because they are unhappy.

The final point that comes to my mind when I look at this research is the parallel between descriptions of interactions of satisfied couples and descriptions of interactions of "securely attached" infants with their caregivers. A securely attached baby is readily comforted by his mother when he's distressed and can easily use her as a safe base for exploring the environment. She, in turn, responds to the baby's signals, picking up on the infant's needs and reacting contingently. In such interactions, there is a feeling of atunement, a mutual rhythm, a smooth turn-taking. When this rhythm is disrupted in childhood—such as when an infant can't give good signals, or when the parent is not engaged or consistently available—then we see a pattern of insecure attachment, often characterized by alternating clinging and rejection or unconsolable distress. Similarly, in adults with good marriages there is an atunement and smooth turn-taking. They adapt to one another. If one or both partners comes to the relationship lacking the needed personal skills, or if one or both partners withdraws emotionally from the relationship, or if the particular combination of interaction patterns in the partnership meshes poorly, then the relationship never develops the rhythm of a secure attachment. Then the interactions become less and less positive, with the partnership spiraling toward disruption.

Obviously, there are important differences between the relationship of an infant with her mother or father and the relationship of two adults in a marriage or a long-term committed relationship. But I find the parallel a helpful one in my own thinking about marital satisfaction. What I would like to see now is some exploration of the *development* of satisfying or dissatisfying relationships over time. How does a couple shift from smooth, positive interactions to more conflicted ones? More generally, do satisfying and dissatisfying relationships differ in the same ways in couples of all ages, or at all stages of the family life cycle, or at all points in the length of a marriage? Only when we have research dealing with such questions will we be able to approach a truly developmental look at intimate partnerships in the adult years.

Homosexual Relationships

Accurate numbers are virtually impossible to obtain, but perhaps two to five percent of adults in the United States are exclusively homosexual, with another three to five percent typically, but not exclusively, homosexual (Paul & Weinrich, 1982). Virtually all surveys show higher rates of homosexuality for men than for women, but it is not clear whether this reflects greater willingness to report gay experiences among men or a genuine difference in frequency.

All summary statements I can make about gay relationships must be taken with great caution. Since this group is a "hidden" minority, a large percentage is unwilling to participate in research or even to acknowledge their sexual orientation openly. Inevitably, what we know about adult homosexuals and their relationships comes from studies of a subset, primarily those who are fairly well educated and those who are "out" about their homosexuality. Whether this subgroup is at all typical of the larger group of gays, researchers do not know.

A number of recurrent findings have emerged from this research, however, which I can summarize briefly:

1. Long-term committed relationships are very common among homosexuals, particularly among lesbians. Estimates vary, but perhaps 70 percent of lesbians are in committed relationships, in most cases living together (Buunk & van Driel, 1989). Among gay men, the percentage is lower, perhaps 45 to 50 percent (Larson, 1982). Among lesbians, monogamy within a long-term relationship is about as common as in heterosexual relationships (marriage or cohabitation), but monogamy is much less commonly a feature of gay male relationships. In one large national study, for example, sociologists Philip Blumstein and Pepper Schwartz (1983) found that 72 percent of lesbians in long-term relationships had been monogamous, compared to 79 percent of married women. In contrast, only 18 percent of gay men had been completely

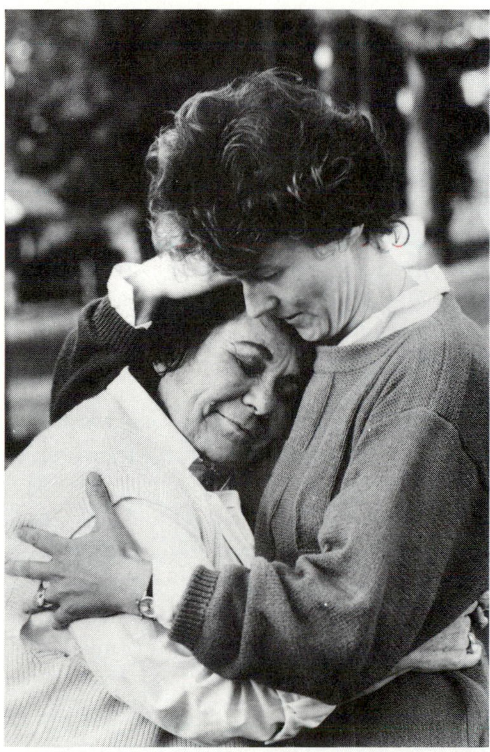

Figure 8–6 Long-term committed relationships, largely monogamous, are the rule rather than the exception among lesbian couples. (Photo © Joel Gordon, 1987. Reprinted with permission.)

monogamous within their current relationship, compared to 74 percent of married men.

2. Homosexual relationships are, on the whole, more egalitarian than are heterosexual relationships, with less sharp role prescriptions. It is quite uncommon for homosexual couples to have one partner occupy a "male" role and the other a "female" role (Buunk & van Driel, 1989). Instead, power and tasks are more equally divided. Again, however, this is more true of lesbian couples—among whom equality of roles is frequently a strong philosophical ideal—than for gay males. Among male homosexual couples, the man who earns the most money is likely to have greater power within the relationship (Blumstein & Schwartz, 1983). One gay male in the Blumstein & Schwartz study who was the more economically successful of the pair, said for example:

   > I'd like him to come up with some ideas for free time together. But then he can't come up with ideas for free time that require spending money, which he doesn't have. Like theater, plays, travel. If he made those decisions, he wouldn't have the money to do it . . . So we do those things when I suggest it and feel like doing it. (p. 60)

3. Satisfying and dissatisfying homosexual relationships differ in essentially the same ways as do relationships in equivalent groups of heterosexual couples (Peplau & Amaro, 1982). Like marriages, gay relationships are more likely to persist and be satisfying if the two individuals are similar in background and interests and equally committed to the relationship. I know of no research that has explored the specific interactional patterns in satisfied and dissatisfied gay couples, but I would be surprised if the key dimensions of communication patterns were substantially different from what I have listed in Table 8.3.
4. At least one cross-sectional study shows that both gay and lesbian couples move through the same early stages of relationship described for married couples, with a drop in satisfaction in the early years (Kurdek & Schmitt, 1986).

In sum, homosexual relationships are far more like heterosexual relationships than they are different. While long-term committed intimate pairings are less common among gay men than among other groups, when such commitments are made, they involve love and strong attachment. Many last a lifetime. Since homosexual relationships by definition involve two people who have both been socialized toward the *same* sex role, there are some differences in the dynamics of gay male and lesbian relationships. But the human urge to form one close, intimate, central attachment is evident in gay relationships as it is in heterosexual relationships.

Relationships with Other Family Members over the Lifespan

With so many adults living longer and with high divorce rates and remarriages, the term "family" these days may describe a far more complex set of relationships than was true even a few generations ago. At any one time, a "family" nearly always includes three generations and many include four or even five.

With more generations, the sheer number of people with whom one is linked by family ties goes up, including not only children, grandchildren and great-grandchildren, but their spouses and in-laws. When there have been divorces and remarriages, the combinations can become quite intricate. My own family may be an extreme example, but makes the point clearly: Three succeeding generations in my lineage have been divorced and remarried (both sets of grandparents, my parents, and my sister and myself), which creates patterns so complex that I have to draw genealogical charts to explain the relationships to others. There are stepgrandmothers, step-stepuncles, and many stepcousins. As Matilda Riley points out (1983), when the "family" is so broad, personal relationships within the family group cease to be based entirely on obligation or fixed kinship roles, and become more and more determined by choice. One can pick and choose among the array of relatives those with whom one wants a closer, more intimate relationship. I have, for example, very friendly relationships with two of my stepbrothers and their families and with the natural maternal grandmother of my two adopted children.

Research on family relationships in adulthood has not yet caught up to this complexity. Most research attention has been directed toward parent-child relationships, with a lesser emphasis on sibling relationships or grandparent-grandchild links. There is essentially no information available on relationships between step-siblings, or even with in-laws (let alone ex in-laws). Certainly, parent-child relationships are among the most enduring and the most central for many adult lives. In the future, though, I hope we will see explorations of a broader array of "family" connections and their effects on adult pathways.

General Patterns of Family Interaction in Adulthood

One of the persistent findings in research on family interactions in adulthood is the remarkable consistency with which nearly all of us maintain contact with our parents and siblings. Findings from a large study by Geoffrey Leigh (1982) show this very clearly.

Leigh interviewed a total of about 1,300 adults, spanning the full set of family life-cycle stages. Each adult reported how frequently he or she saw, spoke with, or wrote to parents, brothers and sisters, cousins, and grown children. Figure 8–7 shows the major findings for parents, siblings, and children. There is no real sign here of any variation in contacts with family members as a function of life-cycle stage except for a slight decline in frequent contact during the "new parent" stage. In this study, virtually all adults, whatever their age, reported at least some kind of contact with their parents at least monthly, and the majority also had regular contact with siblings.

Not surprisingly, the amount and type of contact is strongly affected by physical proximity. When parent and child live within one or two hours travel of one another, face-to-face contact and phone calls are common; as distance increases, letters and phone calls become the most frequent form of communication, with

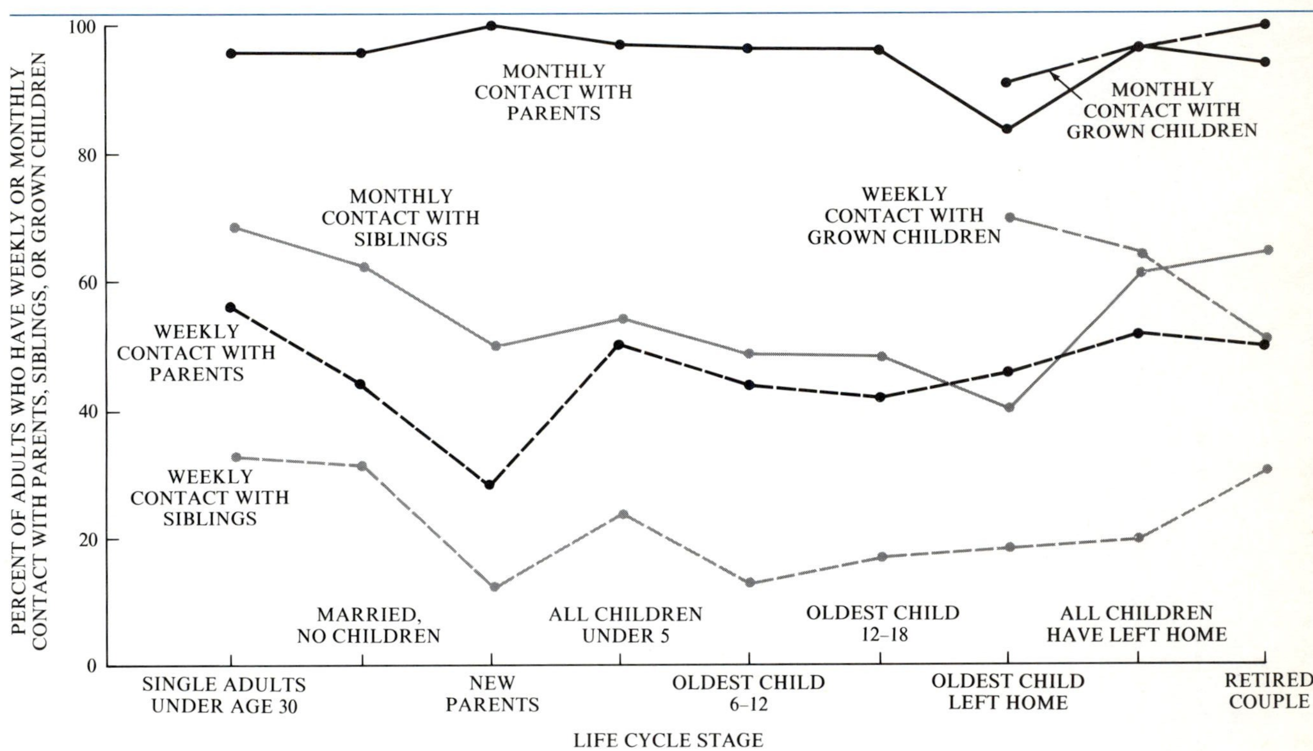

Figure 8–7 *Contact between adults and their parents, siblings, and grown children seems to remain remarkably constant over adulthood, judging from these (and similar) results from a 1976 survey. Virtually all adults have at least monthly contact with their parents; about half talk to, write to, or see their parents at least weekly. Contact with siblings is less frequent, but is still steady over the life span. (Source: Liegh, 1982, data from Table 2, p. 202.)*

the occasional overnight visit thrown in (Dewit, Wister, & Burch, 1988; Moss, Moos, & Moles, 1985). Equally unsurprising is the consistent finding that it is women who are primarily responsible for the contacts with other family members. "Kinkeeping" is clearly part of the female role in our culture (Rosenthal, 1985); women make more of the phone calls, write more of the letters (to their in-laws as well as their own parents), and plan or encourage the visits.

As usual, these are cross-sectional results. We cannot be sure that today's 20-year-olds will still have regular contact with their parents when they are 50 or 60, for example. But the consistency of such findings, in studies of several different cohorts, points to the stability of the pattern. Family relationships are a part of our lives throughout adulthood.

What is the emotional quality of those relationships? Are they attachments, or affiliations, or persisting alliances (to use Weiss's category system)? And when we make contact, what is the content of our interactions? Let me amplify.

Parent-Child Relationships in Adulthood

Attachments Between Adult Children and Their Parents

You'd think it would be fairly straightforward to figure out whether adult children are still attached to their parents. But it isn't. The answer obviously depends in part on how we define attachment. More importantly, it may depend on the age of the "adult children." In early adulthood the attachment to Mom and Dad *must* be weakened. Robert Weiss puts it this way:

> If children are eventually to form their own households, their bonds of attachment to the parents must become attenuated and eventually end. Otherwise, independent living would be emotionally troubling. The relinquishing of attachment to parents appears to be of central importance among the individuation-achieving processes of late adolescence and early adulthood. (1986, p. 100)

I do not agree with Weiss that the attachment to the parent is totally relinquished. It seems clear that at least *some* kind of attachment remains between adults and their parents. Not only do we typically maintain regular contact, we also show signs of deep grief and loss at the death of that parent. And in times of severe stress or need, most of us would be glad to have our parents on hand as support—all signs that an attachment is present. Yet Weiss is quite correct in emphasizing that it is only when this central attachment to the parent has weakened somewhat that the young adult can make a genuine commitment, a deep attachment, to a partner. So there has to be a pulling back, a separation. Later, perhaps a deeper, more reciprocal form of attachment toward the parent can be expressed. One recent study, for example, (Frank, Avery, & Laman, 1988) shows that among adults in their late 20s and early 30s, those who have moved through a successful process of individuation are more empathetic toward their parents, more able to see and accept their parents as they are, warts and all.

Overall, it looks to me as if the adult child's attachment to the parent is attenuated but not typically abandoned totally; furthermore, it seems highly likely that the extent or depth of an attachment to one's parents will change in predictable ways over the adult years. Some findings from Alice Rossi's three-generation study give us at least a first hint of such variations (Rossi, 1989).

Rossi has studied nearly 1,400 men and women of varying ages who are all the "middle generation" in their family lineages: They all have at least one living parent and at least one child. A subset of the older parent generation and some of the grown children were also interviewed. Each of the middle generation subjects was asked, among many other things, to rate the current affective closeness of their relationship to each of their parents on a seven-point scale that ranged from very close and intimate to very tense and strained. In addition, they rated their *previous* levels of closeness, recalling the time when they were 10, 16, and 25. You can see the results in Figure 8–8.

Overall, men reported less closeness to either parent than did women, and both men and women reported that they were closer to their mothers than to their

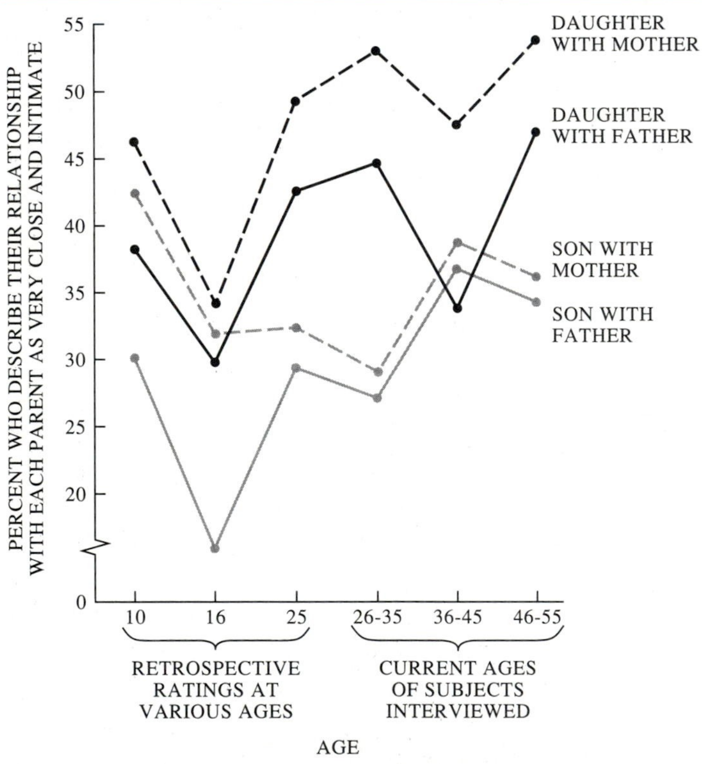

Figure 8–8 In this study, Alice Rossi interviewed over 1,000 adults of varying ages about their current relationship with each parent and about their recall of their past relationship with their parents when they were 10, 16, and 25. You can see a clear drop in recalled closeness at 16, which may be part of the attenuation of the attachment to parents that is necessary for adult independence to be achieved. Note too that the mother-daughter bond is consistently described as the most close. (Source: Rossi, 1989, Figure 6.3, p. 225.)

fathers—still further evidence that women are the central figures in maintaining kin relationships. Further, both men and women remembered a major drop in closeness in their late teens and early 20s, when the individuation process was presumably going on; but that was followed by a rise in closeness in their 20s and 30s, a pattern especially notable for women with their mothers, perhaps because as women bear and rear their own children, their empathy with their mothers increases. In adulthood, the figure shows somewhat different kinds of changes with age for men and women, with women in their late 30s and early 40s reporting markedly less closeness to either parent, and men in the same age range reporting somewhat more than at either of the other age periods—a finding that is consistent with the idea of sex role cross-over at midlife.

Attachments Between Parents and Their Adult Children

On the parents' side of the equation, as I pointed out earlier, the picture looks a little different. While the young adult is trying to negotiate a separation from the parent, the parent generation is trying to sustain a connection, not only because of their own bonds of nurturance and love for the child, but also because of what Vern Bengtson calls the *generational stake* the parent group has in the relationship. For the adult parents, their children and prospective (or actual) grandchildren represent continuity, even a kind of immortality.

Yet important as this relationship obviously is to the parents, it is not clear that it typically represents an attachment in the sense in which Ainsworth or Weiss have used that term. In particular, it is not clear that the presence of one's adult children brings with it that sense of security and comfort that is the central feature of an attachment. There is now abundant research evidence, for example, that among adults over 50 (on whom most of this research has been done), life satisfaction and happiness are simply not predicted by the amount of contact the individual has with his grown children (e.g. Lee & Ellithorpe, 1982; Seccombe, 1987; Markides & Krause, 1985). The adults in these studies did have regular contact with children and grandchildren and said they enjoyed it. But family interaction was not necessary for, nor did it enhance, their sense of well-being.

Cicirelli's (1983) summary captures the somewhat ambivalent quality of this relationship well:

> While the [parent-child] relationship is not one of day-to-day contact or close personal intimacy, neither is it one of mere obligation, pseudo-intimacy, and estrangement. . . . Instead it is characterized by closeness of feeling between parent and child, an easy compatibility between them, a low degree of conflict, and a good deal of satisfaction. (p. 45)

Overall, this sounds more like what Weiss would call an affiliative relationship than an attachment, although there are clearly many parent-child pairs with strong attachment-style bonds. When a strong attachment does exist—either from parent to child, or child to parent—it is more likely to involve a mother-daughter relationship than any other combination. But even mother-daughter relationships vary markedly. Two interesting studies by Linda Thompson and Alexis Walker

(Thompson & Walker, 1984; Walker & Thompson, 1983) give us some insight into the elements in mother-daughter relationships that may affect attachment.

They have studied three-generational families of women, each with a grandmother, a middle-aged mother, and a college student granddaughter. In general, whenever the pattern of assistance or support in these pairs is uneven—such as when a middle-aged mother is providing high levels of assistance to her aging mother or to her college-daughter but is not receiving assistance in return—intimacy and attachment are lower. The best predictor of high attachment in these women was a high level of *reciprocal* assistance or contact. Findings from studies of middle-aged adults (primarily women) who take on major caregiving responsibilities for an elderly parent underline the same point: The affection and attachment to the parent *weakens* as the interaction becomes less and less reciprocal or more and more a burden (Cicirelli, 1983). Since the probability of reciprocal relationships between parents and their grown children varies over their (and their children's) lifetimes, the attachment too is likely to strengthen and fade.

Another general point about parent-child attachments, at least in women, is that they appear to be somewhat stronger among unmarried than married women (Baruch & Barnett, 1983). Whether this is so because the unmarried woman has more time to create a pattern of reciprocal interaction with her parents, or whether the parent-child attachment in single adults in some sense takes the place of a central marital attachment, I do not know.

Patterns of Aid Between Adult Children and their Parents

Whether the underlying emotional bond between parents and their adult children is accurately described as an attachment or not, it is perfectly clear that between the two generations there is an intricate system of assistance, advice, and aid. I have already talked about the key elements of this aid system in Chapter 7 and need only summarize here: The middle-aged generation gives the most assistance both "upward" and "downward" through the generations and receives the least.

Influence Attempts Between Parents and Children Parents and children not only provide affection and assistance to one another, they also give each other advice, try to change each other's opinions, and attempt to influence each other's behavior. You may try to get your parent or your child to stop smoking, or to eat more oat bran or skim milk. You may give advice about investments, or jobs, or how to handle money, or try to persuade your parents or children to vote in a particular way. Advice and influence attempts, in fact, make up a large percentage of the interactions within families. Gunhild Hagestad (1984), who has done some of the most interesting research on family interactions, has interviewed three generations of adults in 150 families, asking each family member about the ways in which he or she had tried to influence the others, which other family members had tried to influence them, and how successful those influence attempts had been.

In these families, advice "up" the generational chain from middle-aged child to older parent dealt most often with health or with practical matters such as where to live, how to manage the household, money, uses of time. Middle-aged adults also tried, but had less success, influencing their parents' attitudes on current social issues and on internal family dynamics. Older parents gave advice to their middle-aged children on subjects such as health, work, and finance. The youngest generation in these families tried to influence their own middle-aged parents as well, particularly regarding health, social attitudes, and the uses of free time. These younger adults helped their parents "keep up with the times."

Two other suggestive patterns emerged from Hagestad's research, both of which gave me food for thought about my own family and other families I know. She observed that in these three-generation families, parents were more likely to try to influence their children than the reverse, and this was true in both generational pairs (grandparents/parents, and parents/grown children). Interestingly, though, the influence attempts from children to parents were more likely to be *successful.* Only about a third of the advice or influence attempts from parents to children seemed to be effective, while about 70 percent of the influence attempts in the other direction found their mark. As parents, we don't seem to give up trying to influence our children, even when our children are in their 50s or 60s.

Figure 8–9 As we each move through the generational positions within a family, our relationships to parents and to our own grown children are renegotiated in various ways. Probably the oldest and middle generation women in this picture are still busily trying to influence their daughters; probably the youngest woman is not listening much to all the advice she is getting—although she is likely to feel much closer to her own mother after her first child is born. (Photo © Joel Gordon, 1987. Reprinted with permission.)

But our children listen quite selectively! Perhaps in the process of emancipation from parents in the late teens or early twenties, most young adults learn to tune out many kinds of parental advice, and this pattern persists. But as our children become adults, we begin to tune them in, listening more openly to their suggestions.

Another of Hagestad's observations was that each family seemed to have a certain set of themes or topics that acted like a kind of glue, holding the family together. Different members in the same family tended to talk about the same things, describing the same types of advice or influence. Some families talked about their relationships and spent a lot of time giving each other advice about or trying to change each other's behavior in those relationships. ("Don't you think you should write to your brother?" "I wish you and Dad wouldn't argue so much about money.") Other families almost never talked about relationships but talked instead about money or jobs. Generational chains of men (grandfather, father, grown son) were more likely to focus their advice and influence on such practical matters, whereas generational chains of women spent more time on relationships; but each family also had a characteristic "agenda," and this agenda seemed to be a powerful force for cohesion across the generations. (On my mother's side of my own family, one of the common themes has been music, a passion shared in three generations. When we are together, we sing, which not only strengthens our bonds by creating mutual pleasure, it helps us avoid talking about all the subjects about which we disagree!)

All in all, family interactions have layers of subtlety and depth that researchers have only begun to plumb. Some parent-child links seem not to be characterized by extremely strong emotional attachments, but most are characterized by strong patterns of habit, family tradition, assistance, and influence. The most complex positions in the family chain appear to be the ones in the middle—the generations that have both parents and grown children. Over a lifetime, each of us moves through these generational positions, acquiring new roles, and learning the changing "rules" of relationships at each step.

Relationships with Brothers and Sisters

Emotional bonds with brothers and sisters seem rarely to be attachments in the sense Weiss uses that term, but they may well be strong affiliations, or at the least a persisting alliance. The link to siblings is generally weaker than the one to one's parents, but it nonetheless persists over the entire lifetime for most adults. For most of us, a relationship with a sibling will be the longest single family connection we will experience in our lives.

About 85 percent of current adults, including those in old age, have at least one living sibling (Cicirelli, 1982). Current younger cohorts who come from smaller families may be less likely to have living siblings in their later years, but most of today's elders still have living brothers or sisters.

Descriptions of sibling relationships in every day conversation range from exceptional closeness, to mutual apathy, to enduring rivalry. While rivalry and apathy certainly both exist, the research suggests that some kind of physical and emotional closeness is the most common pattern (Cicirelli, 1982; Goetting, 1986; Scott, 1983). If you go back to Figure 8–7, you'll see that the majority of adults have fairly frequent contact with siblings. It is really quite rare for a person to lose contact completely with brothers and sisters. Most write or call fairly regularly and see one another on family occasions or for brief visits, with the closest relationships generally found between siblings who were close as children; it is unusual for adult siblings to *become* close for the first time in adulthood (Ross & Milgram, 1982; Dunn, 1984).

Yet even those who describe their links to their siblings as close say that they do not often talk over important decisions or discuss intimate questions with their brothers or sisters. Mutual assistance is also fairly rare among siblings at any age. For example, in a study of sibling relationships in a group of older adults (aged 65 to 90), Jean Scott (1983) found that 72 percent of her subjects received no help at all from siblings.

Nonetheless, there are signs that the sibling relationship becomes more important in old age. Older siblings can and often do provide a unique kind of emotional support for one another, based on shared reminiscences and companionship. But it seems once again to be especially sisters who are valued in old age. In one recent study, Victor Cicirelli (1989) found that within a group of elderly men and women, it was those who described themselves as close to a sister who had the lowest levels of depression, with higher depression among those with poor relationships with sisters. The quality of relationships with brothers was unrelated to depression.

The impression I get from all these facts and figures is that many sibling relationships are pleasant and affectionate but not terribly intense. There is an enduring relationship, maintained across many decades, but it does not appear to be a central one for most adults. The only point in the adult life span when the sibling relationship seems to be more likely to play a significant role is in old-age. There may be something about being the oldest living generation in a family that intensifies feelings of closeness. No one else knows all the old stories, all the family jokes, the names and history of former friends and neighbors. Those shared memories form a solid basis for the continuing bond.

Friendships in Adulthood

If you made a list of the significant people in your life, the list might well include your partner, your parents, your children, your brothers and sisters, or your boss or a significant co-worker. For most of us, the list would also include a number of friends. When Toni Antonucci and Hiroko Akiyama (1987) asked a nationally representative sample of 718 adults, aged 50 to 95, to list the 10 people they felt closest to, beginning with those they could not imagine living without and moving outward to those who were important but not quite that close, the majority of those listed were family members, but nearly a fifth were friends, as you can see in Figure 8–10. In this study, friends did not very often appear in the 'inner circle' of relationships, but they nonetheless made up an

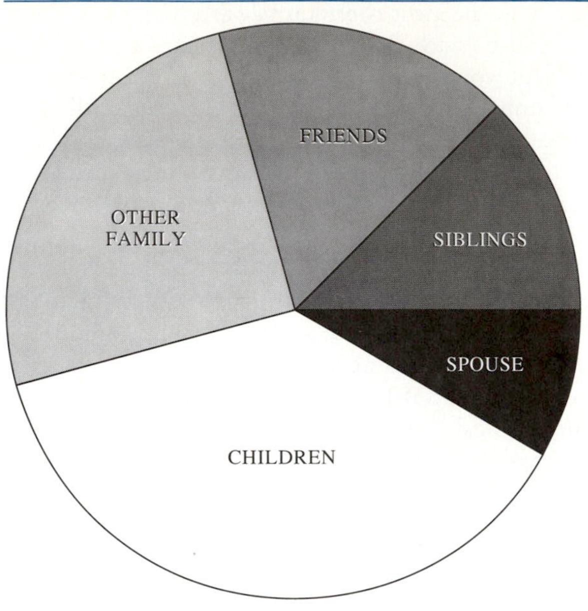

Figure 8–10 The figure reflects the answers older adults gave when Antonucci asked them to list the 10 people closest to them. Obviously, each respondant could have only one spouse, so the spouse category could not represent more than 10 percent of the choices; but the family and friends categories are more open-ended. You can see that all family choices combined represent roughly eight out of the ten choices, with friends filling the remaining two positions on the lists. (Source: Antonucci & Akiyama, 1987, from Table 2, p. 524.)

important segment—a segment that seems to have a significant role in our adult lives.

What Is a Friend?

But how shall we define friendship? Psychologists and sociologists who have studied friendship in adulthood have used many different definitions, which makes it extremely difficult to add up the findings. If you think about your own friendships for even a moment, it will be clear that they run the gamut from close confidants to rather casual pals with whom you share particular activities. John Reisman (1981) divides this continuum into two parts, which he calls **associative friendships** and **reciprocal friendships**. The latter may be similar to what Weiss calls an *affiliative* relationship, while the former may reflect any one of a number of different types of relationships—collaboration, help-obtaining, or some other. In some few cases, friendships may reflect genuine attachments: That friend's presence gives you a sense of security and comfort; their absence leaves you with a feeling of loss or emptiness.

The stronger, more intimate, reciprocal friendships involve mutual feelings of affection, loyalty, and emotional disclosure. Such friends seek each other out, desiring and enjoying one another's company (Hartup, 1975; Reisman, 1981). In a talk on friendship I once gave to a group of middle-aged professionals, I suggested two somewhat homelier "tests" of a genuinely intimate friendship: A good friend is one who does not "keep score" of who owes whom a favor or time, and a good friend is someone you are always glad to see, no matter what the circumstances—your hair in curlers, or while sick with the flu, or when the baby has just spit up all over your shirt.

In a great deal of the research on friendship in adulthood, such a distinction between casual and reciprocal friendships has not been maintained. Most often, subjects have merely been asked to say how many friends they had, without being told just how "friend" should be defined.

Despite this serious limitation, and despite the (usual) lack of longitudinal information, there are still some consistent and interesting patterns.

Choosing Your Friends

We do not choose our friends randomly. There are some well-established principles that seem to apply, many of them very similar to the principles of partner-selection I discussed earlier.

The most general statement is that we chose people as friends whom we see as like ourselves: in age, in gender, in social class or education, in interests or attitudes, in family life-cycle stage (Dickens & Perlman, 1981; Norris & Rubin, 1984). This does not mean that all of your friends are your own age or your gender. Perhaps 30 to 40 percent of adults have cross-gender friendships; older adults (more than younger adults) are also likely to have friends from other generations than their own. Still, similarity is a powerful first filter. Propinquity is also part of the equation. Our friends come from among those who live near us, such as those who live on the same floor in a dorm, or those who live on the same block or in the same neighborhood as your family home. Work colleagues—who share both similarity and frequency of contact—are also a pool from which friends are drawn, as are the parents of your children's playmates.

Past the point of first acquaintance, as with potential mates, a second filter seems to be the willingness of the other person to be open about feelings. Particularly in the early stages of friendship, and particularly for women, such intimacy is a key ingredient in those friendships that move beyond acquaintance to closeness. Other key qualities enhancing friendships are loyalty, warmth, affection, and supportiveness (Parlee, 1979).

Friendships over the Adult Years

These "rules" for making new friends seem to apply at every age, but most of us make more new friends in adolescence and early adulthood than we ever will again. The general pattern is of a fairly steady decline in the numbers of friends adults have from early adulthood at least through late middle age. There *may* be an increase in number of friends later in life, but the evidence here is simply contradictory. Some researchers find that the decline continues through old age (e.g., Fischer & Phillips, 1982). Others find an increase in the 50s or 60s (e.g., Lowenthal, et al. 1975). I suspect that the differences may lie in the way "friendship" is defined. My own hypothesis is that the sheer number of friends, counting both associative and reciprocal relationships, probably does decline steadily over all of adulthood. But the number of intimate friends, or the average level of intimacy of all friendships, may increase in the postparental or retirement periods.

You can see some of these trends in Figure 8–11, which shows the results of a study of 500 men aged 25 to 48 in the Boston area (Farrell & Rosenberg, 1981). These men were describing close friendships, and as you can see, they didn't have many. But the older men had fewer than the younger men. Frequency of contact and intimacy of the relationship also declined through about age 40 or 45, after which there is at least a hint of an increase.

There's also a hint of an increase in the number of friends among the 10 closest relationships listed by Antonucci and Akiyama's older subjects. Those between age 65 and 74 had proportionately more friends than did either the pre-retirement group or the group over 75—an age at which one's friends begin to die off.

It would be a mistake to read these (and comparable) data as saying that the older you get the lonelier you will be. While personal networks do contract with increasing age, and 12 to 13 percent of adults over 65 report that loneliness is a serious problem for them (Harris, 1981), fewer older than younger people describe themselves as lonely (Peplau, Bikson, Rook, & Goodchilds, 1982). As Peplau and Perlman define it, loneliness arises when there is a discrepancy between the amount of social contact you *want* and the amount you have. So although older adults have a smaller set of friends and kin with whom they interact, they apparently either want less or are more satisfied with the interactions they do have.

The age differences in reported loneliness are very striking. In one survey, 79 percent of young adults 18 to 24 years old said they felt lonely sometimes or often, compared to 60 percent of those 35 to 40 years old, and only 37 percent of adults over 55 (Parlee, 1979). These differences may mean that older people simply have more realistic expectations or enjoy their own company more. But the decline in loneliness could also be the result of higher quality of friendships and family relationships over the adult years. In support of the latter interpretation is the fact that the older you get, the longer you are likely to have known your good friends (Dickens & Perlman, 1981).

If I can go beyond the data here, my sense of the developmental pattern is that in early adulthood, we make many friends and have a wide circle of acquaintances. In Weiss's terms, we seek out and establish many affiliative bonds. Within a few years, however, most young people's attention shifts from affiliative to attachment bonds—they begin to seek out that one person who might be a life partner, and to focus on deepening their relationships with a few close friends who will become part of what Antonucci has called a relationship *convoy*—a "protective layer . . .

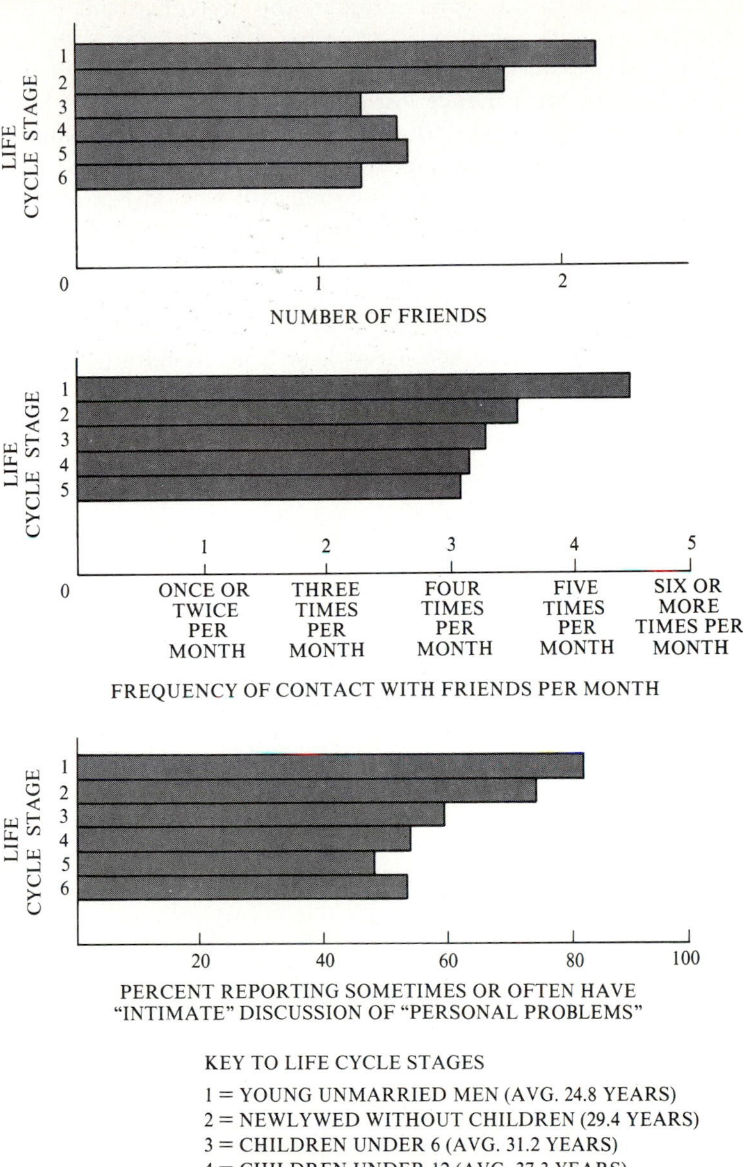

Figure 8–11 *This group of working class and middle class men in the Boston area reported on the number of their friends, how often they had contact with them, and how often they discussed personal problems with their friends. All three scores were lower among men at later stages of the family life cycle, although there is at least a hint of an increase in intimacy in the oldest group. (Source: Farrell & Rosenberg, 1981, from Tables 9–3 and 9–4, pp. 195–196.)*

of family and friends, who surround the individual and help in the successful negotiation of life's challenges" (Antonucci & Akiyama, 1987, p. 519).

The convoy is not totally static, of course. Membership in your convoy changes over the years with friends lost or gained, parents lost to death, losses or gains from marriage or divorce. But most of us have some continuing members of this group who follow us through life. Although we do not have the longitudinal data to test this hunch, it looks to me as if we add relatively few new members to our convoy during the years from our mid-20s to perhaps 50 or older, years in which we are mostly so focused on learning and performing the various key roles of marriage, parenthood, and work that there is little time to establish new friendships. In late middle age, however, when work and family roles ease, there may be time to extend the network of close friendships and to deepen existing friendships. In late old age, our convoys begin to shrink again, as spouses and old friends die.

Some Individual Differences in Friendship Patterns

This general developmental picture differs in important ways, though, for several subgroups of adults. Most notably, there are consistent sex differences in friendship patterns observed in both childhood and adulthood. Men have larger networks of friends (counting both "associative" and "reciprocal" friendships), but women's friendships are more intimate, involving more mutual self-disclosure, more exchange of emotional support. When men interact, they are more likely to compete, less likely to support or agree with one another (Ginsberg & Gottman, 1986; Maccoby, 1990; Reisman, 1981). Another way to describe the difference is to say that men do things together while women talk—usually about feelings (Bell, 1981).

One of my favorite quotes, from a 38-year-old male executive interviewed by Robert Bell (1981), makes the point clearly and poignantly:

> I have three close friends I have known since we were boys and they live here in the city. There are some things I wouldn't tell them. For example, I wouldn't tell them much about my work because we have always been highly competitive. I certainly wouldn't tell them about my feelings of any uncertainties with life or various things I do. And I wouldn't talk about any problems I have with my wife or in fact anything about my marriage and sex life. But other than that I would tell them anything. [After a brief pause he laughed and said:] That doesn't leave a hell of a lot, does it? (pp. 81–82)

I do not mean to imply that men have no close friends, nor even that men are necessarily less satisfied with their friendships. But these differences in the content or style of friendship may reflect a more fundamental sex difference. Dan McAdams (1985) has proposed that one of the central human motives is the motive for *intimacy*, which is defined as "a recurrent preference or readiness for interpersonal experiences of warmth, closeness and communication" (p. 92). On his measures, McAdams finds that women simply have more of this motive than men do—at least in our culture.

Both men and women meet their intimacy needs primarily through relationships with women. As one example, in a study of college students who were asked to keep detailed daily records of the nature of each of their social interactions, Harry Reis (1986) reports that the least "meaningful" interactions were reported for friendship encounters between two men, the most between two women, with the cross-sex friendships lying in between. Once again, then, we find that attachment and intimacy are carried or created by women much more than by men. Women have more intimate connections with each other, with men, with their children, with their own parents.

Whatever the source of such sex differences in motives—a subject that goes beyond the scope of this discussion—it is clear that there are some important long-term implications of this difference in relationship patterns for the experiences of adult life. Women's role as kinkeeper within the family is undoubtedly linked to this difference. But the man's relative lack of skill in creating intimate relationships has consequences as well. We know, for example, that having at least one intimate relationship with a confidant is associated with better physical and mental health (a relationship I'll talk about further in Chapter 12). Thus, if men's friendships are less intimate, it means that men may be at greater risk for finding themselves in stressful situations without a confidant.

Friendships in adults also differ by social class. In general, working class adults (and most of this research is on men) appear to have fewer close friends than do middle class adults (e.g. Bell, 1981; Farrell & Rosenberg, 1981). In contrast, kin relationships (parents, children, siblings, etc.) seem to be closer in working class families than in the middle class (Dickens & Perlman, 1981). In other words, the total size of the social network may be about the same for adults from different social strata, but the network is composed differently. Just what the causes or consequences of such differences in network compositions may be for adult development, I do not know. But such a difference is definitely worth further study.

Relationships in Adulthood: An Overview

Table 8.4 summarizes the myriad age-linked patterns in relationship I have talked about so far. Some of these are curvilinear patterns, some reflect increases, and some reflect declines in relationships. On the face of it, there seems very little consistency. Erikson's theory, however, may help to make sense of these patterns.

In the very early years of adulthood, perhaps 18 to 25, it looks as if virtually all relationships are highly significant. This is the period that Erikson describes as the stage of intimacy versus isolation, and that label seems to capture the flavor well. Adults in their early twenties are searching for and forming intimate partnerships and typically are highly satisfied with their marriages. They also have large networks of friends, creating that "convoy" of relationships that will travel with them through the years. But a sense of isolation is also common. More young adults report feelings of loneliness than is true for any other age

TABLE 8.4. Summary of Age Changes in Relationships.

Age 29–40	Age 40–65	Age 65 and older
Marital satisfaction typically at peak in early part of this period, then declining; marital problems are high, but so are expressions of affection.	Marital satisfaction often increases in the 50s and 60s; relationship includes fewer problems but also fewer expressions of affection: "devitalized".	Marital satisfaction appears to remain relatively high in this period, but there may be continued "devitalization" in many relationships.
Contact with parents remains steady and high, but some kind of attenuation of the basic attachment must be negotiated if the young person is to achieve independence. At all ages, women are the kinkeepers within the family.	Relationship with parents may again become more central, perhaps more empathetic; level of assistance to aging parents also increases for many in the middle generation.	Contact with parents ends when parents die; contact with children continues and is satisfying but does not appear to be critical for overall life satisfaction.
Contact with siblings remains relatively high and steady.	Contact with siblings continues relatively high and steady, although there is little sign of significant attachment.	Some indication that relationship with siblings becomes more significant in later years.
Friendships are most numerous in early adulthood, then decline in the 30s. Women's friendships are more intimate.	Friendships are lower in number and probably lower in intimacy; women continue to have more intimate friendships.	Friendships probably decline slightly in number but may become more intimate.

group. In other words, relationships *matter* very much at this age, and any lack in relationships is felt keenly.

In the years from 25 to 40, the period Erikson calls generativity versus stagnation, two things seem to happen. First of all, even though marital satisfaction is often at its lowest point, this is nonetheless clearly the key relationship of these years. Relationships with one's parents, even relationships with friends, seem to be at lower ebb. Energy is devoted to the immediate family and to work. The convoy is still there, but young adults spend little energy expanding or working on that convoy.

From 45 to 65, as the adult moves into Erikson's period of integrity versus despair, the quality of relationships once again seems to become an issue. Marital relationships seem to improve, at least for many couples, perhaps as a result of new attention devoted to the interactions. Friendships, too, may become somewhat more intimate, although not more frequent. These are also the years in which many adults find themselves the "sandwich" generation in their own family lineage; they have heightened family responsibilities both "upward" and "downward" in the chain.

Finally, in the years past retirement, the convoy continues to shrink in size but is highly valued. Relationships with siblings may be renewed or revitalized; relationships with friends form an important part of older adults' social networks.

Beyond this general Eriksonian description of the age changes in relationships, I want to emphasize several points.

First, the changes in our relationships over time occur not just because time passes but because we engage in active renegotiation. This renegotiation process is clearest in the case of the relationship with one's parents but occurs in other relationships as well, such as those with siblings, grandparents, partner, in-laws, and many others. In the parent-adult child relationship, the young adult first must negotiate a separation from her parents, staking out her own territory (literally as well as figuratively). Gunhild Hagestad (1979) talks about the *demilitarized zones* that are often created in this process: "silent mutually understood pacts regarding what not to talk about" (p. 30). Or there may be no taboo subjects, but there may be boundaries past which neither parents nor young adult offspring dare to go (Greene & Boxer, 1986). In later years, many of these DMZs disappear and the boundaries become much more permeable. And still later, as the older generation requires more and more assistance, there may be new terms to be negotiated.

Second, the *reciprocity* of any given relationship seems to be a key feature, affecting a person's sense of satisfaction with that relationship or with life in general. If you receive more than you can give, or give much more than you receive, you are likely to be less satisfied with a relationship. And when an ongoing relationship shifts from being reciprocal to being less so, adults report that they become less satisfied, less emotionally supported by that relationship. This may help to explain why relationships with friends and siblings become more central to life satisfaction in old age, since relationships with peers are far more likely to be reciprocal than are those with one's children.

Finally, there is a general point I have only touched in passing that I think is central to our understanding of relationships in adult life. We each bring to our adult relationships what Bowlby calls an *internal working model* of attachments and interactions. Based on our early relationships, primarily with our parents, each of us creates a model of how relationships work: Do others respond when you need them? Are love and affection contingent on being "good"? Are you likely to be abused or mistreated unless you are careful? The internal working model is thus not only a description of previous relationships, it is a template for future relationships.

The secure and insecure attachments Ainsworth and others have described in infants and young children are one example of such internal working models. What is now clear is that these early models are carried over into adult life and affect our relationships not only with our children but with other adults. Mary Main and her colleagues (Main, Kaplan, & Cassidy, 1985) have been able to measure the security or insecurity of adults' own internal working model of attachment and have shown that adults with insecure models are more likely to recreate such a relationship with their own infants. That is, mothers who are insecurely attached to their *own* mothers are more likely to have infants who are insecurely attached to them. Taking this idea one step further, Rogers Kobak and Amy Sceery (1988) have found that among college students, those with a less secure attachment model are less skillful in social relationships, including dating relationships.

The general point is that in our central convoy relationships, we each tend to recreate the patterns from our family of origin, as we understood them and translated them into our internal working models. Glen Elder and his colleagues (Elder, Caspi, & Downey, 1986) have shown how this works longitudinally in yet another remarkable analysis of the Berkeley Intergenerational Study subjects. Those subjects who described their own parents as most irritable and unstable were much more likely to have unstable marriages and to be less affectionate and more hostile toward their own children. Their own children, in turn, were more likely to show problem behavior and higher rates of divorce in their own marriages. Undoubtedly, secure attachments, too, are transmitted from one generation to the next.

Each of us, then, begins adulthood not only with some amount of the specific skills needed to form and maintain relationships; we also begin adulthood with deeply embedded expectations about patterns of interaction. These internal models affect our choices of partners and friends as well as the quality of the relationships we create. These models can be changed, of course. A "healing relationship"—to use a phrase George Vaillant introduced to describe some of the men he followed in the Grant Study—can alter an insecure model. Growing personal maturity can lead to the self-awareness needed to alter the patterns. But lacking such intervention or personal effort, the basic template will remain, shaping our relationships throughout our adult life.

Summary

1. The term "attachment" is now quite commonly used to describe relationships between adults as well as between infants and caregivers. The key feature of an attachment is a sense of security or safety or comfort in the presence of the other and a sense of loss when apart. Not all adult relationships involve attachment. Others may reflect affiliation, nurturance, collaboration, or persisting alliances.
2. Love and liking need also to be distinguished. Love includes intimacy, passion, and commitment. Liking typically involves only intimacy.
3. The relationship with an intimate partner is typically the most central relationship in adulthood. Selection of a partner is influenced initially by perceived similarity and by propinquity. As relationships develop, both love and conflict increase, until the point of commitment is reached; then conflict declines.

4. Cohabitation does not appear to improve the quality or durability of later marriage relationships; if anything, it is associated with lower rates of later marital satisfaction.
5. Satisfaction in marriage typically follows a U-shaped trend, with satisfaction high both before children arrive and after children leave home. But not all couples follow such a pattern; some show consistent satisfaction, others consistent dissatisfaction or neutrality.
6. Some couples, in middle and old age, can be described as "devitalized," with low levels of expression of affection, but also low levels of reported problems. This pattern may be more common among those who do not progress past the conformist stage of ego development.
7. Satisfying and unsatisfying marriages differ on a number of key dimensions, such as niceness/nastiness, degree of role agreement, and adequacy of conflict resolution strategies.
8. Long-term partnerships are also common in homosexual couples, especially in lesbian pairs. Such partnerships appear to be more egalitarian in role allocation and power than are heterosexual partnerships.
9. Interactions with parents and siblings occur at high and relatively constant levels throughout adulthood. Nearly all adults have at least some contact with their parents at least once a month.
10. For a young adult to achieve independence, the initially strong attachment to his parents must be attenuated, although some level of attachment typically remains throughout adult life. Stronger attachments to parents are typical for daughters and for unmarried adults.
11. The relationship of parents with their adult children is clearly a strong affectional bond, but whether it should be considered an attachment is open to debate.
12. Patterns of mutual aid between parents and adult children remain strong throughout adulthood. Typically, the middle generation of adults provides the most assistance to both adult children and aging parents.
13. Parents and children also to try to influence each other. More influence attempts are directed from parents to children than the reverse, but influence is more successful from adult child to parent.
14. Relationships with siblings, while constant over the lifespan, and perhaps intensifying in old age, appear to be less central to most adults than is the relationship with a partner.
15. Friendships, in contrast, appear to be quite central in early adulthood, and perhaps again in middle age and beyond. The number of friends declines with age, but the intimacy of friendships may rise in midlife.
16. Loneliness, however, does not rise as the number of friends goes down. Older adults are less lonely than younger adults.
17. Women's friendships are typically more intimate than are men's, perhaps because women have a higher motive for intimacy. And working class adults typically have fewer friends than do middle class adults.

18. These patterns of relationships can be partially understood by using the framework of Erikson's theory of developmental stages.
19. The concept of internal working models of relationships may also be helpful in understanding the ways in which each adult recreates the patterns of relationship that he or she understood to exist in his or her own family of origin.

Suggested Readings

BLUMSTEIN, P., & SCHWARTZ, P. (1983). *American Couples.* New York: William Morrow. This book was intended for both a professional audience and for the general public, so it is written much less technically than is usual. They report on the findings from their research but also include a series of lovely case studies of heterosexual and homosexual couples. I found it fascinating reading.

BRUBAKER, T. H. (1985). *Later life families.* Beverly Hills, CA: Sage. This brief text covers many of the topics I have included in this chapter, though emphasizing families at middle-age and beyond rather than covering the full adult life span. It is not too technical and is more complete and detailed than I have been able to be.

GILMOUR, R., & DUCK, S. (1986). *The emerging field of personal relationships.* Hillsdale, NJ: Lawrence Erlbaum Associates. A nice collection of semi-technical papers by some of the major researchers and theorists in this area.

LAUER, J., & LAUER, R. (1985, June). Marriages made to last. *Psychology Today, 19* (6), 22–26. Like all articles that appear in *Psychology Today,* this is written for a nonprofessional audience, so it is perhaps more lively reading than some other sources I have suggested. In this case, it reports on the responses of 351 couples who had been married 15 years or more.

REISMAN, J. M. (1979). *Anatomy of friendship.* New York: Irvington Publishers, Inc. This is a very clear, interesting, nontechnical book on friendship over the entire lifespan, from infancy through old-age.

RUBIN, L. B. (1985). *Just Friends. The role of friendship in our lives.* New York: Harper & Row. If you are interested in understanding your own friendships better, I can suggest no more provocative book. Rubin explores the role of friendships through a series of interviews with adults of various ages and walks of life. You will see yourself here too.

CHAPTER 9

Work and Work Roles in Adulthood

"I'm probably the youngest general foreman in the plant, yes, sir. I'm in the chassis line right now. There's 372 people working for us, hourly. And thirteen foremen. I'm the lead general foreman" (Terkel, 1972, p. 249). The speaker, Wheeler Stanley, was just 30 when Studs Terkel talked to him in 1972. Stanley had started at the Ford plant when he was 20, fresh out of the paratroopers. His goal in life was to be a "utility man"—the man in the plant who can do all the assembly-line tasks and who spot-relieves other workers.

> I thought that was the greatest thing in the world. When the production manager asked me would I consider training for a foreman's job, boy! my sights left utility. I worked on all the assembly lines. I spent eighteen months on the line, made foreman, and eighteen months later I made general foreman. (p. 250)

Now Wheeler Stanley's goal is to be superintendent and then maybe production manager. He likes his work, likes the company but hopes his son will do something better.

Ray Wax has had a very different working life. He sold cakes in an outdoor market when he was 12, caddied at a golf course at 14, and as an adult tried a whole range of jobs, all at least partially successful: He exported cars to South America, speculated in land, built houses, built and ran a hotel, and now in his 50s is a stock broker. The restlessness that has been part of his work life all along is once again visible.

> I can't say what I'm doing has any value. This doesn't make me too happy. . . . When I built the houses, I hired a bricklayer, I hired the roofer, I determined who put the goddamned thing together. And when I handed somebody a key, the house was whole. I made it happen. I can't do that in the market. I'm just being manipulated. . . . (Terkel, pp. 446–447)

Not everyone gets promoted or shifts from job to job. Dolores Dante has been a waitress for 23 years, working in the same restaurant. She started working when her marriage broke up, and she had three young children to support. Waitressing was a way to make good money from tips without a lot of training or schooling. She has stayed with it because she's very good at it and enjoys it.

> When somebody says to me, 'You're great, how come you're *just* a waitress?' *Just* a waitress. I'd say, 'Why, don't you think you deserve to be served by me?' It's implying that he's not worthy, not that I'm not worthy. It makes me irate. I don't feel lowly at all. I myself feel sure. I don't want to change the job. I love it. (Terkel, p. 391)

But it's tiring work. Her feet hurt, she aches, she doesn't eat right, and at the end of a day's shift, at 2:00 a.m., she's drained and nerve-racked. But she wouldn't want to give up working. "I won't give up this job as long as I'm able to do it. I feel out of contact if I just sit at home" (p. 395).

Sigmund Freud was reportedly once asked to define maturity. His answer was that maturity was determined by one's capacity for work and love. I would probably add a few things to that list, but no one would argue about the centrality

Figure 9–1 Work outside the home has always been central to men's lives; in recent years it has also become central for women. Most of us will spend 30 to 40 years of our adult lives working. (Photos © Joel Gordon, 1983 & 1986. Reprinted with permission.)

of both love and work in adult life. I talked about love in the last chapter; now I need to talk about work.

For Wheeler Stanley, Ray Wax, and Dolores Dante, as for most of us, work is one of the most time-consuming, significant, identity-defining aspects of adult life. An occupation, a "career," probably consumes a third to a half of a man's waking hours over a period of 40 years. One specific example: The men in the Berkeley intergenerational studies—mostly white collar workers and professionals—reported in their 40s that they were working an average of 48 hours per week; the older professionals and top executives in this group were working an average of 51 hours per week (Clausen, 1981). And that doesn't count the time spent lying awake at night worrying about the report you're supposed to write, or the promotion you didn't get, or hours getting to and from work, or taking special classes.

Women have not typically spent as many years focused on a career, but that situation has been changing rapidly. Current projections tell us that those women born in 1980 will spend an average of 29.4 years working outside the home, compared to an average of only 12.1 years of work for those born in 1940 (my generation) (Spenner, 1988).

I do not mean to imply by this that child rearing or homemaking (or unpaid volunteer work) are not "work." They are. I have talked about these roles and their effect on adults in Chapter 6, and I'll turn later in this chapter to the question of combining work and family roles. But here I want to focus on paid employment, on "jobs" or "careers."

It will not surprise you to hear that most of what we know about work and its effects over adulthood comes from studies of men. Only in quite recent years have large percentages of women been in the labor force, and even now, when roughly 70 percent of women between the ages of 20 and 64 are in the work force, most women do not work continuously through adulthood. Since sociologists, economists, and organizational psychologists who have studied work patterns have mostly been interested in continuous work patterns, women have largely been omitted from the research. Even our knowledge of men's work patterns is drawn primarily from studies of middle class occupations—business executives, lawyers, doctors, professors. We know a bit about men like Wheeler Stanley, who is in a job with a clear "career ladder," a sequence of steps or promotions from entry level jobs on up. But we know almost nothing about the Dolores Dantes of the world—the waitresses, garbage collectors, meter readers, artists, flight attendants and many others who work at jobs that don't have steps or clear promotion sequences, or who have little chance for advancement. What we know, then, is incomplete, but nonetheless fascinating.

Choosing an Occupation

Most of us think of the process of choosing an occupation as something one does only once, in early adulthood. The concept of a "career"—a lifelong sequence of jobs in a particular field or area—implies just such a permanent or long-term choice. But in fact, most of us make a series of minidecisions over a period of time: choosing what to study in school, picking summer jobs, choosing a first job after high school or college, later perhaps being promoted to a different task within the same occupation, or shifting to another occupation altogether. It is the exception rather than the rule for a given adult to remain in precisely the same job throughout adult life. Most job changes are promotions or slight sideways shifts within a single job field, but more substantial career changes are common. Donald Super, one of the major figures in research on careers, found that of a group of 100 men studied longitudinally from high school to their mid-thirties, 30 percent had shifted from one field of work to another (Super, 1985). Robert Havighurst (1982) estimates that as many as 10 percent of men over 40 make radical shifts in careers. Obviously, one is not stuck forever with the first job chosen as a young adult. Nonetheless, the initial choice is a significant one, and that first choice is influenced by most of the factors I talked about in Chapter 2, including gender, race, intelligence, personality, family background, and education. These qualities of a young person affect the range of jobs that may be "open" to him or her, as well as the attitudes or goals the young adult may have.

The Effects of Gender on Job Selection

For example, despite enormous changes in the work roles and opportunities available to women, it is still true in the United States (and in other developed countries) that many jobs are clearly labeled as "women's jobs" or "men's jobs." Male jobs are more numerous and are typically higher in both status and income (e.g. doctor, lawyer, business executive, carpenter, electrician) than are traditional women's jobs. "Women's jobs" are fewer in number and concentrated in the lower-middle class or working class levels (e.g. nurse, waitress, librarian, receptionist, elementary school teacher, and secretary) (Betz & Fitzgerald, 1987; Blau & Ferber, 1985). One third of all working women are in clerical jobs, another quarter are in health care jobs (excluding physicians), teaching, or domestic service.

The force of sex role socialization, beginning in early childhood and operating through the family, TV, books, and schools, is such that young women are steered into traditional female jobs and men into traditional male jobs (Betz & Fitzgerald, 1987). The impact of these sex roles appears to be more powerful for young adults who grow up in working class families, where sex role ideology is more traditional. Among adults now in their 30s and 40s and older, cross-sex typed occupational choices were more common in middle class families, particularly if the fathers were highly educated, if the mother had had a long-term work commitment, and if both parents supported the daughter's unconventional career choice (Betz & Fitzgerald, 1987; Fitzpatrick & Silverman, 1989). As more and more women enter the work force, at least some of this pattern may change: Since the majority of adults in current young cohorts will have grown up with working mothers, a mother's work history may be less significant in predicting cross-sex typed career choices.

What is likely to remain important is the young woman's own self-perception of femininity, masculinity, or androgyny. There is abundant research evidence that young women who perceive themselves as more androgynous or more masculine are more likely to chose unconventional occupations. They are also more likely to be committed to a career and to work continuously throughout their adult lives (Betz & Fitzgerald, 1987). Overall, then, the sex typing of occupations, combined with family and personal sex role attitudes, strongly channels men and women into different sets of potential occupations and different levels of occupational commitment.

Family Influences on Occupational Choice

Families not only help to create the sex role socialization, they also influence occupational choice in at least two other ways. First, as I pointed out in Chapter 2, family background has a profound effect on educational attainment. Middle class parents are far more likely to encourage their children to attend college and to provide financial support for such further education. This social class difference in college attendance is not just an ability difference in disguise, either. Even when you compare groups of high school students who are matched in terms of grades or test scores, it is still true that the students from middle class families are more likely to go on to further education. The family's encouragement and support is a significant factor, above and beyond the young person's own intellectual ability. Since a college degree, in turn, is a required credential for many entry level jobs in better paying and higher prestige occupations, particularly jobs in business, children from middle class families are much more likely to end up in such occupations.

Families also push their children toward some specific careers and away from others, through both inculcation of specific values and through direct modeling. Both sons and daughters are more likely to chose their parents' occupations than some other, with sons more likely following in Dad's footsteps and daughters in Mom's (Stevens, 1986). Jeylan Mortimer (1974, 1976), for example, has found that college men are likely to match their father's actual occupations or to choose occupations with similar values or rewards. In her studies, sons of professionals were likely to choose occupations that had similar levels of autonomy and work complexity; sons of businessmen were likely to choose occupations that were high in extrinsic rewards. These connections were stronger in families in which the relationship between father and son was particularly close.

The Role of Personality in Job Selection

The family also has an impact on occupational choices in a less direct way, through shaping the young person's personality. The chief figure in the study of personality/occupational connections has been J. L. Holland (1973; 1985). His basic argument has been that people tend to choose and to be most satisfied with and successful in jobs that have requirements or features that match the individual's own personality. More specifically, Holland proposed six basic personality types and six parallel work environments, which I've listed in Table 9.1.

These six personality types can be measured using any one of several tests on which you are asked to say whether you like, dislike, or are indifferent to a whole range of jobs, school subjects, activities, amusements, situations, and people. From your answers, scores on each of the six dimensions are derived, and these scores can then be used not only by researchers who might be interested in the effects of matched or mismatched personality and careers, but by counselors who use the scores to advise young people on suitable occupations.

Research on Holland's category system lends a good deal of support to his basic thesis, not only in Western cultures but also among adults in developing countries (Eberhardt & Muchinsky, 1984; Kahn, Alvi, Shaukat, Hussain, & Baig, 1990). Among both men and women, for example, ministers score highest on the social scale, car salespersons on the enterprising scale, and engineers and doctors score highest on the investigative scale (Benninger & Walsh, 1980; Walsh, Horton, & Gaffey, 1977).

The match is not always quite as predicted, however, and may differ by sex. For example, Benninger & Walsh (1980) found that women police officers scored

TABLE 9.1. John Holland's Six Personality Types and Six Work Environment Types.

Type	Personality	Work Environment
Realistic	Aggressive, masculine, physically strong, low in verbal or interpersonal skills. Prefer mechanical activities and tool use, choosing jobs like mechanic or electrician or surveyor.	Demand for explicit, ordered, or systematic manipulation of tools or machines or objects or animals.
Investigative	Thinking, organizing, planning, particularly abstract thinking. These people like ambiguous, challenging tasks, but are generally low in social skills. They are often scientists or engineers.	Demand for observation, creative symbol investigation of physical, biological, or cultural phenomena.
Social	Similar to extraverts (see chapter 2). Humanistic, sociable, need attention. Avoid intellectual activity, dislike highly ordered activity. Prefer to work with people.	Demand for training, caring for, enlightening of, informing, or serving others.
Conventional	Prefer structured activities and subordinate role; like clear guidelines. See themselves as accurate and precise.	Demand for systematic, ordered, precise, manipulation of data, such as keeping records, filing, bookkeeping, organizing written material, following a plan.
Enterprising	Highly verbal and dominating, like organizing and directing others; persuasive, high in leadership.	Demand for manipulating others, such as in sales of all types, or other manipulation to further organizational goals.
Artistic	Asocial, preference for unstructured, highly individual activity.	Demand for ambiguous, free, unsystematized activities to produce art or performance.

SOURCE: Holland, 1973.

highest on the social scale, while policemen were highest on the realistic scale. In general, however, among occupations that are open to a young person—given her or his gender, intellectual skill, education and family background—personality characteristics appear to play a significant role in the choice.

Once the choice is made, the degree of match between personality and job qualities is also predictive of the individual's satisfaction with his or her job. The correlation between the two is not large. Combining the results of 41 separate studies, Assouline and Meir (1987) report an average correlation of .20 between job satisfaction and broad measures of match between personality and occupation. The correlation is considerably stronger, however, (.42) if a narrower measure of match is used, such as by looking at subspecialties within occupations. (Among physicians, for example, surgery and pediatrics are very different in job qualities and may attract and satisfy adults with quite different personalities). Interestingly, job *success* is only very weakly related to the match between personality and job requirements. Clearly, adults can and do succeed at jobs that match their own skills or qualities poorly. But they are more satisfied with jobs that offer a good fit.

These insights into some of the processes of choosing a first occupation are helpful, but they obviously do not tell the whole story of work roles in adulthood. We also need to know what happens over the next 40 years of work life. Are there consistent patterns? Are there stages or steps in occupational life? With due regard to the wide variability, the answer is a cautious "yes."

General Age Trends in Work Experience

Research by sociologists and industrial psychologists shows several well-replicated patterns of change in work related attitudes and behaviors over the adult years, most of which appear to hold for women as well as for men (Rhodes, 1983).

Age Changes in Job Satisfaction

The facet of work life that has been most frequently studied is overall job satisfaction. Cross-sectional comparisons show a consistent and clear pattern: Work satisfaction increases quite steadily throughout the work life, from age 20 to at least age 60, for both college-educated and noncollege-educated adults. Figure 9–2 shows some fairly typical findings from Norvall Glenn and Charles Weaver's (1985) analysis of the combined results of a series of annual surveys between 1972 and 1982, each of a representative national U.S. sample of roughly 800. Each respondent was asked to rate her or his overall satisfaction with work on a four-point scale that ranged from very dissatisfied to very satisfied. For the data in Figure 9–2, a "very satisfied" reply was assigned a score of 3, a "very dissatisfied" reply was given a score of 0.

It seems clear from the figure both that the average level of satisfaction was quite high and that older workers reported higher satisfaction than did younger ones. Still, these are cross-sectional data. Is it possible that this is all just a cohort effect? Maybe current younger cohorts will continue to be less satisfied throughout their working lives; maybe current older cohorts were more satisfied at every age. We do not have longitudinal evidence to allow us to sort this out, but Glenn and Weaver's data do allow a time-sequential analysis. Since they have new samples for each year over a ten-year period, we can look at each cohort as it moves through that ten-year interval. It is not the same *people* being measured at each time point, but it is a sample from the same *cohort*. Figure 9–3 shows what happens when we look at this set of findings in this fashion.

Each line in this figure represents workers from a single birth cohort measured at two time points ten years apart. So, for example, the left hand lines represent samples of women and men born between 1943 and 1952 (part of the baby boom generation), who were 20 to 29 in 1972 and 30 to 39 in 1982; the pair of lines on the far right represent samples born between 1913 and 1922 who were aged 50 to 59 at the first assessment and 60 to 69 at the second. You can see that

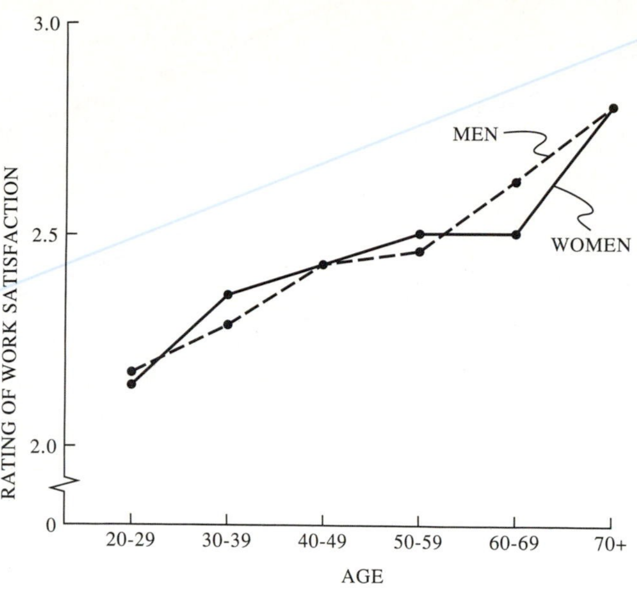

Figure 9–2 These cross-sectional data, averaged over separate samples interviewed each year from 1972 to 1982, show a clear rise in work satisfaction with age for both men and women in the United States. However, since these are cross-sectional comparisons, it is always possible that the data reflect cohort differences rather than some more basic age-linked change (Source: Glenn & Weaver, 1985, Table 1, p. 92).

while the overall pattern is similar to what appeared in Figure 9–2, there are also some signs of cohort effects. In particular, those who were between 30 and 39 in 1972, at the time of the first testing (who were thus born between 1933 and 1942) consistently reported more positive attitudes toward their work than did the youngest cohort. One possible explanation of this apparent peculiarity is that the 1933 to 1942 birth cohort was particularly small, so these adults have had fewer competitors for available jobs. The baby boomers, in contrast, are part of a very large cohort, with greater competitiveness and fewer job choices available to them. Even with this cohort variation, however, it is still true that seven of the eight lines in this figure move upward, indicating that for each cohort work satisfaction was higher at older ages than at younger ages.

Why would work satisfaction rise with age? Partly, the shift is caused by changes in extrinsic factors: Older workers have better pay and more job security. But intrinsic satisfaction also rises: Older people like the actual work they do better than younger workers do (Rhodes, 1983). To some degree, this is an accurate reflection of differences between "young jobs" and "older jobs." Jobs held by younger workers tend to be physically harder and dirtier, and/or less complex and less interesting (Kunze, 1974; Spenner, 1988). Jobs held by older workers are likely to have more authority (more "clout," to use Tamir's word),

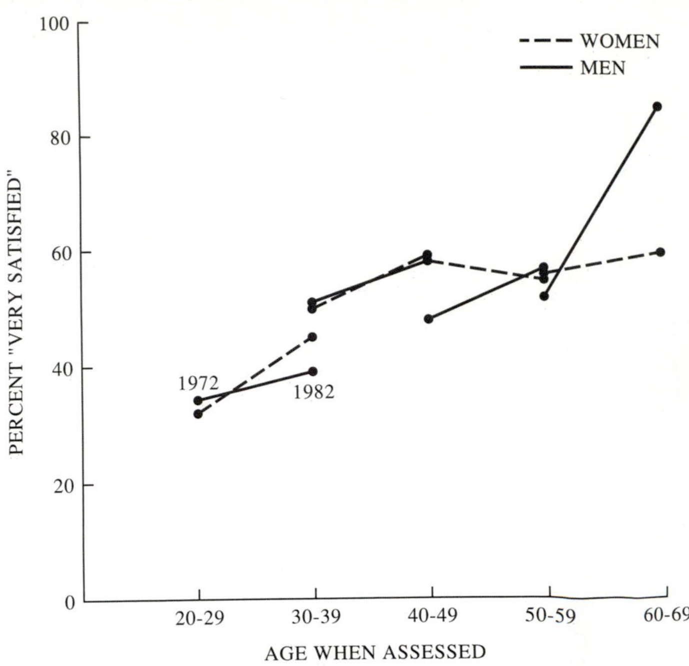

Figure 9–3 *Glenn and Weaver's cross-sequential analysis of work satisfaction can take us a step beyond the cross-sectional information in Figure 9–2. Each line in the figure represents the percentage* from a given cohort, *sampled in 1972 and again in 1982, who said they were "very satisfied" with their work. It is not the same people at both time points for each line, but it is a sample from the same cohort. There are clearly some cohort differences revealed here, but it is nonetheless true that seven of the eight lines go up, suggesting that there is also a basic age-linked change occurring. (Source: Glenn & Weaver, 1985, Table 3, p. 95).*

more prestige. It is not a great surprise, then, when we find that older workers like their jobs better.

There is undoubtedly some self-selection operating here too: Workers who really dislike some line of work don't stay in it. Older workers in any given occupation are thus likely to be people who sought out or chose to stay in that line of work because it gives them a good match to their personality or their interests (White & Spector, 1987).

Age Changes in Job Involvement and Motivation

Researchers have also observed an increase with age in commitment to or involvement with work. Over time, workers become more and more committed to their specific job or their specific employer and more involved with the work itself (Rhodes, 1983). Men in their 40s and 50s are less likely to change jobs than are younger men; they see their current job as something they are likely to keep on doing until retirement; they show lower levels of avoidable absenteeism

(Martocchio, 1989). All of these are indications of greater commitment to the job. Older men, in other words, take their work more seriously and find things about it that they like. Younger men are still experimenting, still searching for the right job or occupation, so they may be focused more on what is *wrong* with the current job than what is right about it.

Another reflection of this same age change is a general increase in what is often called the Protestant Work Ethic—the belief in the moral value of hard work. Older workers place greater emphasis on this value than do younger workers—although once again this is a cross-sectional difference and could well result from cohort changes in the centrality of such a value.

Age Changes in Job Performance

The one major feature of jobs that does *not* appear to change systematically with age is job performance. Older workers are as good as younger workers by most measures (Rhodes, 1983; McEvoy & Cascio, 1989). The major exceptions to this generalization are those occupations in which physical strength or speedy reaction time are critical elements, such as longshoremen, air traffic controllers, truck-drivers, professional athletes, and the like. In these jobs, there is a performance decline beginning in midlife or later (Sparrow & Davies, 1988). Many adults in such occupations change jobs at midlife in anticipation of, or because of, such declines.

To sum up: In most occupations, age does not influence work performance or productivity in systematic ways, but age is related to most aspects of job satisfaction and job values. Older workers like their jobs better and are more committed to them.

Career Ladders or Career Mobility

A quite different way of looking at overall work experience over time is to focus on the career pathways of individual adults in particular occupations. The metaphor of a *career ladder* is a pervasive one. Most of us think of our adult work life in terms of a series of definable steps or rungs on a ladder. In the academic world, this is very clear: You move from instructor to assistant professor to associate professor to full professor. In the Ford assembly plant where Wheeler Stanley worked, there is an equally clear ladder, from assembly line worker, to foreman, to general foreman, to superintendent, to pre-delivery manager, to production manager, and on up the line. Clearly, not all occupations have such sharply defined promotion steps. But most jobs have at least some features that distinguish beginners or low level workers from advanced or high level workers.

Just how does one move up this ladder or through this sequence? Are the steps equidistant? Can you skip steps? Does everyone move along them at the same rate?

Answering such questions requires either retrospective reports from individuals about their work history or, preferably, longitudinal data. As usual, there is only a small amount of evidence that fits this prescription. A particularly helpful study is James Rosenbaum's (1984) analysis of the work histories of a group of 671 adults who entered a large company (called ABCO by Rosenbaum) between 1960 and 1962 and were still employed by the company in 1975. Since company policy specified that all workers should enter the company at the submanagement level, Rosenbaum was able to trace career paths for a large group of individuals who had begun at roughly the same point. A second helpful study is the American Telephone and Telegraph study of managers over a 20-year period (Bray & Howard, 1983). The AT&T researchers have focused less on sequences of individual career moves and more on factors that affected career success, but the results are illuminating nonetheless.

Several generalizations are possible from these and equivalent studies. First, as I pointed out in Chapter 2, a college education makes a very large difference in the pathway an individual worker follows. Even with measures of intellectual ability held constant, a college degree is associated with earlier and more career advancements.

Second, those who are promoted early go further. Sample results from Rosenbaum's study in Table 9.2 illustrate this. Eighty-three percent of those workers who received their first promotion (to foreman) within three years of joining the company had moved up to at least the first level of management within 13 years, but only 33 percent of those who took that first step to foreman at a later time made it to the management level. College-educated workers were more likely to be promoted early, so these are not independent bits of information. But even among the noncollege-educated, early promotion was associated with greater overall advancement.

A related finding is that (in our culture at this point in history) most work advancement occurs early in adult life. By age 40 or 45, most adults have gone as far as they will go in their career ladder. Again, data from Rosenbaum's study of ABCO employees are illustrative (Figure 9–4). For this analysis, Rosenbaum has used data for all the workers in this company in the period from 1962 to 1965. Workers at the nonmanagement level had a very low probability of promotion after the age of 45; for promotion to foreman the pattern is even more striking.

TABLE 9.2. The Relationship Between Earliness of First Promotion and Achievement of Middle-level Management in Managers in the ABCO Company Studied by Rosenbaum.

	Number Promoted to at Least Lower Management			
	Yes	*No*	*Total*	*Percentage*
Period During Which Worker Was First Promoted:				
During the first three years	56	11	67	83%
Later than first three years	42	86	128	33%

SOURCE: Rosenbaum, 1984, adapted from Table 2.4, page 56. Reprinted by permission of Academic Press, Orlando, FL and author.

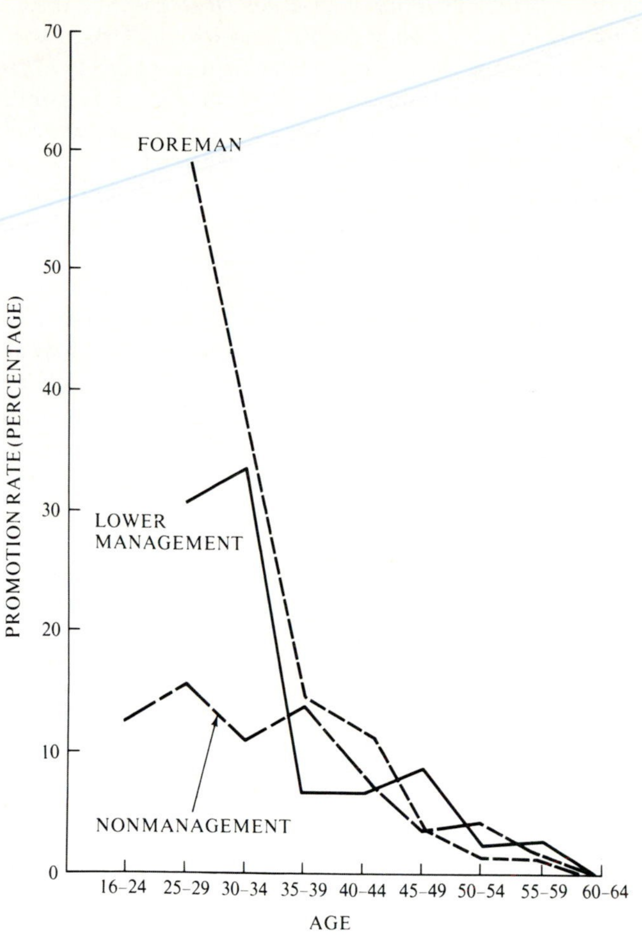

Figure 9–4 Results from Rosenbaum's study of promotions in a large corporation show that the promotions come early in workers' careers. Promotions are comparatively rare past about age 40, in part because the number of positions decreases at each successively higher level. (Source: Rosenbaum, 1984, Figure 3.1, p. 80. Reprinted by permission of Academic Press, Orlando, FL and author.)

There was a high probability of promotion until about age 30 or 35, and then a very sharp drop. This general pattern has also been found in other occupations, such as in Kenneth Spenner's analysis of career moves among accountants (Spenner, 1988), so it appears not to be unique to business career ladders, although all of these studies have focused on adults who entered some occupation in their 20s and remained in it throughout their 20s, 30s, and 40s. There are some suggestions in the research findings, however, that it may be time-in-profession as well as age that is critical for rate of advancement—a point I'll return to shortly.

Rosenbaum uses the metaphor of a *tournament* to describe the entire process. Career paths are marked by decision points at which you either "win" (get promoted, get a raise, receive some bonus or new responsibility) or "lose" (are considered for but fail to receive a promotion, a raise, or increased responsibility). If you win, you are still in the tournament until the next decision point, and so on until you lose and thus remain at whatever level you had reached at that point.

This metaphor describes the data reasonably well but needs several supplements. First, it seems to make a difference just what sort of new responsibilities or skills the worker is given at the next higher level of the system. In the AT&T studies, for example, the degree of challenge of the individual's job had a significant impact on later advancement: Workers at any given level who had more challenging jobs were more likely to be promoted (Bray & Howard, 1983). Given Kohn and Schooler's work on the impact of work complexity on intellectual flexibility (which you may remember from Chapter 6), this link makes very good sense. A complex job increases your intellectual flexibility, which in turn makes you a better prospect for further advancement. Since most promotions move a worker into more complex and challenging jobs, promotions themselves will tend to increase a worker's skills and capacities. The "fast track", then, is not just a reflection of entering skills; it *creates* skills.

The tournament model also needs to be modified to take account of the fact that "losing" does not put you totally out of the game, particularly at early steps in the career. Many individuals make slower or later progress in their careers; a few fail many times and then succeed spectacularly. Sports metaphors are risky; life is not really much like a tournament. But the metaphor does capture some of the features of career mobility patterns in at least some occupations. What it fails to show is that there are many games in this system. If a worker "loses" in one profession with one company, he can try another. And that is precisely what most people do, especially during their 20s and early 30s, when most steps up the career ladder are taken.

All of what I have described so far appears to be roughly valid for both men and women. Women's job satisfaction increases with age, as does men's, and is influenced by roughly the same job characteristics (Weaver, 1978); job success in a company like AT&T can be predicted as well for women as for men, using essentially the same predictors (Ritchie & Moses, 1983); personality characteristics predict job choice about equally well for men and women. But there are clearly a great many ways in which the life-time work patterns of men and women differ—differences I now need to explore.

Men's Work Patterns

Unlike women, who tend to go in and out of the labor force several times, the majority of men work continuously from early adulthood until retirement. If there is a break in a man's work history, it is most likely to happen only once, such as when he goes back to school, changes careers, or is temporarily unemployed. Table 9.3 illustrates this point with data from the Panel Study of Income Dynamics,

TABLE 9.3. Patterns of Continuous and Interrupted Work for Black and White Men Participating in the Panel Study of Income Dynamics.

Work Pattern	Percentages	
	White Men	*Black Men*
Continuous work	55	61
Nonwork followed by work	11	15
Work/nonwork/work	29	22
Nonwork/work/nonwork/work	3	1
At least five periods of alternating work and nonwork	3	1

SOURCE: Corcoran, 1978, Figure 2.3, pp. 59-62. Reprinted by permission of John Wiley and Sons, Inc. and author.

which you may remember is a study of 5,000 families interviewed repeatedly over a period of years. In this particular analysis, Corcoran (1978) shows the frequency of various forms of continuous and noncontinuous work for men in the 1970s. As you can see, 66 percent of white men and 76 percent of black men had worked continuously once they began their work careers; only a very small minority had more than one break.

Stages in Men's Work Patterns

The typically continuous period of work in a man's life can nonetheless be fruitfully divided up into a series of steps or stages, each with its own character.

The Trial or Establishment Stage: Up to Age 30 In the first stage, the young man must decide on a job or career, searching for a fit between his interests and personality and the jobs available. Young men particularly value jobs that are intrinsically interesting and challenging; neither salary nor job security is as critical in the job choice at this stage as is challenge. There is some trial and error involved in the whole process. Jobs may be tried and rejected, and new jobs tried. Perhaps because many jobs available to young men are relatively low in challenge, and because many young men have not yet found the right fit, job changes are at their peak during this period.

Once he has chosen a job or career, though, the young man must learn the ropes. You may remember from Chapter 3 that at least one theorist, Daniel Levinson (1978), argues that a relationship with a mentor may be an especially important aspect of this phase of the work career, since a mentor can not only teach the young man the job and smooth the way to advancement, he can also provide a key transitional relationship in the young worker's shift from dependence on parents to complete independence.

There is not a great deal of research on the significance or centrality of the role of mentor in men's work life. We do not know how common such mentoring relationships may be, nor whether they are specific to particular professions.

Interestingly, in Levinson's own research, relatively few men described mentors. In contrast, several studies of business executives suggest that having a mentor is a fairly common experience. In one recent study, 83 percent of 140 male and female middle and upper level executives in a variety of business firms said that they had mentors, although only 43 percent listed their mentor as one of the most significant helpers in their career (Shapiro & Farrow, 1988). There are also some hints that those who have a mentor are more successful in their later careers (Roche, 1979), but this has not been observed consistently. (Nor, of course, is it clear which way the causality would run in such a case. It may be that more effective young workers are more likely to attract the attention and interest of potential mentors rather than that having a mentor brings about greater career success.)

In lines of work other than business, we have very little evidence one way or the other. Still, it is an intriguing concept, one I hope researchers will continue to explore in the future.

Levinson suggests that this trial stage also has another key feature, the creation of the Dream. Young scientists dream of winning the Nobel prize; Wheeler Stanley dreamed initially of being a "utility man" and later modified his dream to being a production manager. Young businessmen may dream of being the company president. Each young man, according to Levinson, has such a secret ambition, a private fantasy of eventual success. The first career stage is one in which the young person takes the first steps toward realizing that dream.

THE STABILIZATION STAGE: FROM 31 TO 45 In the next stage, the man strives hard to fulfill his Dream. In the early years of this period, the striving often pays off with promotion or improvement; toward the end of this period, there is a substantial slowing of progress, as I have already documented. But satisfaction with the job is usually higher during this period than earlier, in part because the work itself is typically more complex and interesting than it was in the early stages.

THE MAINTENANCE STAGE: FROM 45 TO 60 Somewhere around age 45 or 50 a change seems to take place, although the content of that change appears to contain some contradictions. On the one hand, cross-sectional studies like Lois Tamir's excellent research (1982) show that midlife is the peak time for men's sense of clout in their jobs. Job satisfaction is also high at this age. At the same time, most men have by then gone as far as they will go in their work; promotion or other advancement after midlife is quite unusual. Tamir says of this rather odd combination of midlife work characteristics:

> . . . it is likely that job satisfaction and clout are expressed by [men at midlife] for one of two reasons; (1) success and status actually have reached a satisfying peak by middle age or (2) at middle age the man becomes resigned to the fact that further advancement is unlikely and therefore needs both to convince himself of current satisfaction and to convince himself and others that he indeed has achieved high status at work. (1982, pp. 81–82)

Some men have come close to their Dream and are satisfied; others realize they will not achieve their Dream, but they handle this disappointment by changing the way the game is played, by changing their expectations or values. Tamir's own analyses provide further evidence for just such an internal shift, as you can see in Table 9.4. For men under the age of 40 in this nationally representative sample, job satisfaction was quite strongly related to overall life satisfaction, to a sense of zest for life, and to self-esteem; for men at midlife, there was *no* such relationship. To put it another way, for a young man, being successful at his job is one of the key elements in self-esteem or overall satisfaction. For a middle-aged man it is not—despite the fact that this is the time in his life when a man is likely to be maximally successful and to have the greatest clout in his work.

Other research also points to redefinition of work values at midlife, along with a deemphasis on the centrality of work for self-esteem or life satisfaction. For example, in an analysis of information from the middle-age interviews with men in the Berkeley longitudinal sample, John Clausen (1981) found that men younger than 45 valued their jobs primarily in terms of the intrinsic interest of the job and whether the job used their skills; men older than 45 evaluated their jobs by these same standards but *also* judged their jobs in terms of income, job convenience, and job security—all extrinsic factors that seem to be less important to younger workers. What we see in this midlife work stage is a

> . . . disengagement from work as a source of personal fulfillment, or at minimum a reconsideration of the place work has in one's life. Perhaps this is due to the fact that nearly all that is attainable has been reached by middle age and the challenge of work has diminished. Other sources of fulfillment now must be sought to take its place. (Tamir, 1982, p. 95)

ADJUSTMENT TO RETIREMENT: 60+ A final stage involves the transition to retirement, a subject I'll explore in detail later in this chapter.

TABLE 9.4. Relationship Between Job Satisfaction and other Aspects of Life Satisfaction for Men of Different Age Groups in Tamir's Cross-Sectional Study.

	Age Group	
	Young (25–39)	*Middle Aged (40–49)*
Correlation between Job Satisfaction and:		
Overall Life Satisfaction	.31**	.04
Zest*	.43**	.09
Self esteem	.26**	-.02

* These correlations are for college educated men only.

** Indicates that this correlation is significant at the .001 level, which means that if there were really no link between the two variables, such a correlation could occur by chance only once in every 1000 samples of this size.

SOURCE: Tamir, 1982, Tables 4.14, 4.15, and 4.16, pp. 91 & 92.

It is important to note once again that although I have given approximate ages for each of the four stages, it is probably time-in-job rather than age that is the more critical variable. Despite Levinson's insistence that the steps are strongly age-linked, the research findings simply don't fit that model terribly well. New workers in any field, whatever their age, have certain characteristics in common. A man coming to a new career at 40 will go through a trial period and a period of stabilization before reaching a maintenance/reassessment stage. For those of us interested in women's careers, this is an important point, since the ages at which women enter (and leave) jobs and careers are frequently quite different from what we see in men's career patterns. If time-in-career is more helpful than age for predicting men's job-related attitudes and behavior, this suggests that women could successfully enter careers at later ages and still follow similar career paths. Research on women's career patterns lends at least some credence to this possibility.

Women's Work Patterns

It is not going to be news to you that women's work patterns have been changing radically over the past several decades. More and more, women's adult work histories have come to resemble men's, as more women work for more years in adult life. You can see the current state of affairs, as well as the change since 1970, in Figure 9–5.

Several points need to be made about this figure. Most obviously, there has been an increase since 1970 in the percentage of women in every category who are in the labor force. But note that the *largest* increases have occurred among married women living with their husbands, especially among those with young children. In 1960, only 18.6 percent of married women with preschool children were employed; this had risen to 30 percent by 1970 and to 57 percent by 1988. That is an enormous change in a very short time. The changes are not nearly so vivid among separated and divorced women who have been working in large numbers for some time.

Another curious point about this figure is the relatively low rate of work for women with no children under 18. The explanation lies in the fact that the numbers include a great many older women, from cohorts for whom work outside the home was simply less common. If only women between the ages of 16 and 44 are counted, more than 80 percent of married women with no children under 18 are in the work force.

Counting the number of women who are working at any given time, however, does not tell us much about the life-time work patterns of women. How many of those working women have worked continuously? How many leave the work force when they marry or have children? The limited answers I can give you apply primarily to those cohorts who moved through the years of early and middle adulthood in the 1960s and 1970s. Whether similar patterns will hold for current 20- or 30-year-olds as they move through childbearing and peak work years, I simply cannot say, not only because we do not yet have longitudinal data

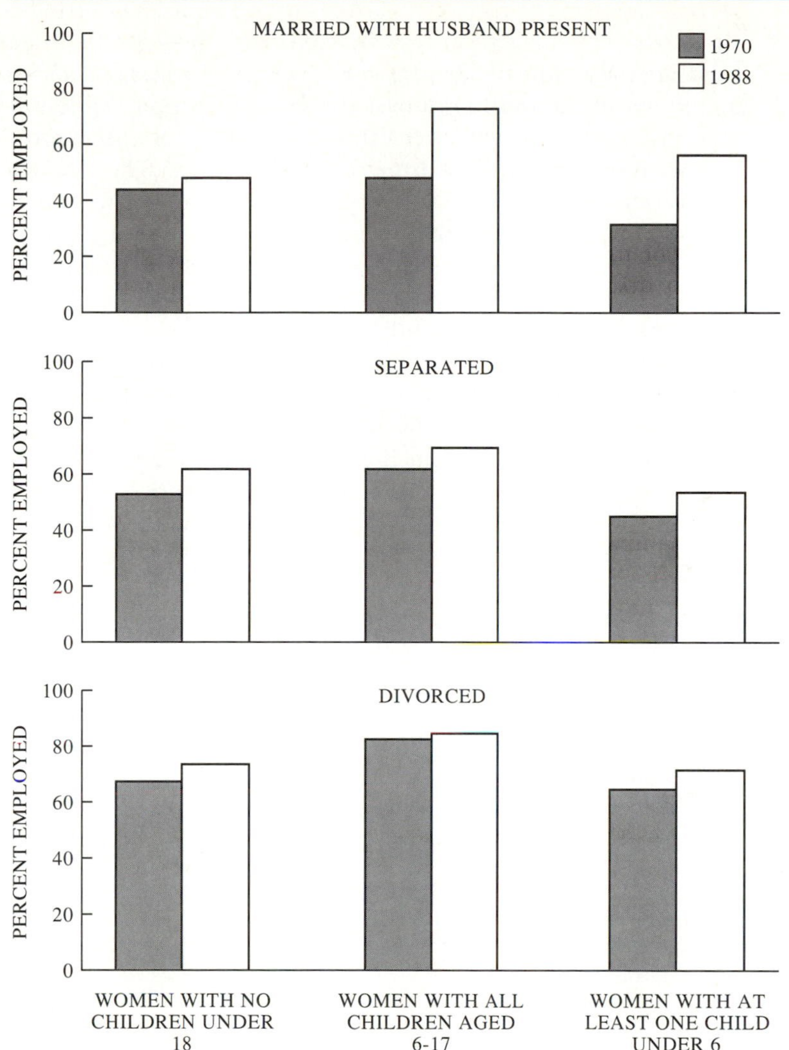

Figure 9–5 The percentage of women in every category who are in the work force has increased from 1970 to 1988, but the change has been especially marked among married women with children. (Source: U.S. Bureau of the Census, Statistical Abstract of the United States: 1989, Table 639, p. 386.)

describing these younger cohorts, but of course because their work patterns are not yet history. We simply do not know, for example, how many of the women who are now working continuously through their 20s will decide to take some time out to bear and rear children when they are in their 30s. The best I can do at this point is to tell you what we know about earlier cohorts.

One particularly helpful set of data is the Panel Study of Income Dynamics, some of whose findings for men you have already seen in Table 9.3. Phyllis Moen

(1985) has analyzed the work patterns of 3,586 women included in this sample, all of whom had been interviewed repeatedly between 1972 and 1976. Because these are longitudinal data, Moen has been able to track each woman's movement in and out of the work force over the five-year period. Table 9.5 shows the work patterns for women who were at various stages of the family life cycle at the beginning and end of the five-year study period. The data show quite clearly that the majority of women moved out of the labor force when they had young children. They also show that many women in these cohorts used part time work as an intermediate step, especially when their children were young.

Moen's study is extremely helpful, but of course it covers only a five-year period. It doesn't tell us about the full sweep of women's work patterns over 30 or 40 years. Annemette Sørensen's research helps to fill the gap (1983), although her subjects represent an older cohort, those who graduated from high school in 1958. She has examined the employment history of a group of over 3,500 women, all 1958 graduates of Wisconsin high schools, all married at least once, who gave retrospective reports of their work and family histories in 1975, when the women were in their middle to late 30s. Approximately a quarter of these women had worked continuously. Twenty percent had left the work force after their first child was born and went back to work after the last child was born; another 18 percent left after the first birth and had not returned to work as of the 1975 interview.

A more recent source is a 1979 Census Bureau Survey (U.S. Bureau of the Census, 1984b) of a representative sample of over 9,000 U.S. families. As in Sørensen's study, women were asked to describe their work histories. They found that among those women who had ever worked, 28 percent had worked continuously without a single work interruption of six months or more. Among those women aged 30 to 44, 22.5 percent had never had such a work interruption.

TABLE 9.5. Percentage of Women with Various Work Patterns Among Women in the Panel Study of Income Dynamics Between 1972 and 1977.

Work Pattern	Family Status Between 1972 and 1977			
	*No child any year**	*First child born after first interview in 1972*	*At least one preschool child throughout the 5 years*	*Pre-school child in 1972; school age in 1977*
No paid work in any year	0.8	12.8	27.5	23.4
Part time all years	0.9	1.1	2.9	2.5
Full time all years	54.4	20.7	10.6	23.4
Part time and full time	31.2	13.3	7.8	5.7
No work and part time work	1.6	4.6	19.1	19.8
No work and full time work	5.9	27.9	17.4	11.8
No work, part time, and full time work	5.2	19.6	14.7	10.5

* To make the comparison more comparable, this subgroup contains only women who were less than age 38 and thus still potentially in their childbearing years

SOURCE: Moen, 1985, Table 4.3, page 132.

There is a surprising degree of unanimity in these findings, despite the varying cohorts being studied and the huge social changes that have occurred in the past few decades: While the percentage of women who work at least *some* time has risen dramatically, along with the percentage of women working at any given time, only 20 to 25 percent of women appear to work *continuously* through their adult lives; and this continues to be true even for the most recent cohorts studied. The remainder of women in the United States move in and out of the work force at least once, often many times.

Continuous work patterns are more common in some subgroups of women than others: among black women (Corcoran, 1978); those in nontraditional or "masculine" jobs (Betz, 1984); those who are philosophically committed to the idea of women's work (Greenstein, 1986); those whose husbands strongly approve of the woman's employment (Moen, 1985); those with strong commitments to work or career (Betz, 1984; Rexroat, 1985); and among the unmarried or those with no children (Sørensen, 1983). Highly educated women, who one might expect to have a high likelihood of continuous employment, are in fact divided into two distinct groups. Some stop work when they marry and remain homemakers (presumably in part because they marry men who are able to provide good incomes); others pursue a continuous work pattern. Interrupted patterns are less common in this group (Sørensen, 1983).

Impact of Differential Work Patterns on Women's Lives

Given the enormous variability of work patterns for women, it's not surprising that there has been little systematic attempt to describe common stages of work life for women. Once a woman begins a long period of continuous employment, it may make sense to think of her work life in terms of trial, establishment, stabilization, and maintenance stages (e.g. Ornstein & Isabella, 1990). But such a sequence of stages doesn't help us at all in describing the in-and-out years, when women work part time, full time, or not at all in alternating periods. Might we think of this in-and-out period as a stage in itself? If we think of it as a stage, then we can ask whether it makes any difference when in the sequence it occurs—whether before or after the trial period, or before or after the establishment stage.

This may sound like a fairly esoteric theoretical question, but it has immense practical importance for today's cohorts of young women. The practical version of the question goes something like this: If you want to have a successful career *and* a family, is it better to establish the career before you have children, or is it better to rear your children first and then pursue your career, or can you do both at the same time? I wish I could give you a clear answer, but I can't. The research is both relatively new and scarce. And with circumstances changing so rapidly, I am not confident of the generalizability of the results from one year to the next, let alone from one cohort to the next. So take what I am about to say with due caution.

If work achievement is one of your goals, continuous work patterns appear to be most successful. Van Velsor and O'Rand (1984), for example, have examined work success in a large seven-year longitudinal study of a national sample of women, all of whom were between age 30 and 44 at the start of the study. In this group, the women who had worked continuously had the highest salaries. Another longitudinal study, by Ellen Betz (1984), covering the first 10 years since graduation of a group of 1968 college graduates, lends further support to this general conclusion. The women in Betz's sample who had the highest work commitments (most of whom had worked continuously) were much more likely to have moved upward in their jobs or careers than were less work-committed women. The latter group showed more horizontal job movement or change, shifting from one job to another at about the same level.

Studies of extremely successful women also show that high success is achieved primarily by those women who worked continuously (e.g. Hennig & Jardim, 1976). In other words, the best way to succeed in the world of work is to follow an essentially "male pattern" of continuous work and high work commitment.

For those women who do *not* work continuously, two strategies seem to be associated with higher earnings: (1) remaining in the same field or along the same career path rather than switching from one type of job to another each time you return to the labor force (Van Velsor & O'Rand, 1984), and (2) returning to the labor force regularly, rather than remaining out of work for one long period and then going back to work after all the children are gone from home (Gwartney-Gibbs, 1988). Even when the total months or years of nonwork is the same, women who have had several short bursts of work in the midst of a nonwork period do better economically than do those who are continuously unemployed for one stretch, perhaps because in the former case, work skills are regularly regained or updated. The use of part time work as an in between step, as many women in Moen's study had clearly done (Table 9.5), thus appears to be a highly rational strategy for many women *if* work success or higher earnings are among their goals or needs.

All of this research no doubt makes clear something you already knew: The trade-offs are extremely difficult to judge, the decisions hard to make.

The Effects of Work on Men and Women

I have been focusing so far on work itself and its role in adult lives. But an equally important issue for a developmental psychologist interested in adults is the effect of work on other facets of adult functioning or development. Very little of the research on this topic is really developmental in nature. Researchers have not asked, for example, whether certain kinds of work have more or less impact on personality change or growth at different points in the adult years. But there are several sets of studies that yield some interesting fragments.

Effects for Men

I've already given you one set of relevant data in Table 9.4. Tamir obviously found that for men under the age of 40, those who were satisfied with their work were also likely to be more satisfied with their lives as a whole. Averaging across many studies and across all ages, Marianne Tait and her colleagues (Tait,

Padgett, & Baldwin, 1989) find a correlation of .31 between work satisfaction and life satisfaction among men, which is exactly the result Tamir's reports for younger men. This is not an overwhelmingly large correlation, but the result is consistently found: Men who like their work like their lives better.

The picture is different, though, if we look at *success* in work instead of work satisfaction. I can find little evidence that men who are more successful in their careers are a great deal happier or better adjusted than those who are less successful (e.g. Korman, Mahler, & Omran, 1983). In the most interesting study in this area, the 20-year longitudinal study of AT&T managers, Bray and Howard (1983) found that the men who had moved furthest up the corporate ladder at midlife were more satisfied with their *jobs* than were the less successful men, but they were *not* happier or better adjusted overall, nor did they have higher marital satisfaction. The Berkeley intergenerational studies, like the AT&T studies, suggest that successful men and well-adjusted men are distinctly different types. Contrasting these two groups of men—the successful, and the best adjusted—Bray and Howard write:

> . . . the most successful and best adjusted were worlds apart. The most successful were cognitively astute; the best adjusted scored lower than others on cognitive tasks. The most successful were worldly Enlargers, had more general knowledge, and expanded themselves physically and intellectually; the best adjusted were less cynical, less oriented to heterosexual pleasures, and more religious than those who rated lower on life satisfaction. The most successful were less nurturant and deferential and more aggressive than their age peers; the best adjusted had steadier temperaments and were less selfish. (1983, p. 303)

The causality seems to run both ways. Some of these differences were already present at the beginning of the men's careers and influenced the men's work commitment and behavior. But to some extent, success and strong work commitment bring about changes in personality or values, just as Kohn and Schooler have shown that intellectual flexibility increases with high levels of work complexity. The moral seems to be that work success (or lack of it) does have an effect on men, but the effect is not primarily on overall happiness or life satisfaction.

Effects for Women

For women, as for men, satisfaction with work is moderately associated with life satisfaction. In Tait's combined analysis of many studies, the average correlation for women was .22, but if only those studies reported after 1974 were included, the correlation was the same as that found for men: .31. This pattern of results suggests that as more women have worked, the quality of their work experience has begun to make more difference in their overall life satisfaction, although that conclusion can obviously be only tentative, since we are working with correlational data here.

Most of the research on the impact of work on women's lives, however, has been focused not on the effects of variations in work experience but on the effects of *work itself*. That is, the question has been whether women who work *at all* are better off or worse off psychologically or physically than women who do not work.

Research comparing the life satisfaction of working women and homemakers is highly inconsistent, in part because of the rapid changes in women's work roles in recent years. Recent research generally shows that working women are slightly more satisfied with their lives and have somewhat better mental and physical health than housewives (Betz & Fitzgerald, 1987; Coleman & Antonucci, 1983), although this difference is less clear for working class women than for the middle class. Several longitudinal studies of older cohorts of women, however, do not show this general positive effect of work. Eleanor Willemsen (1980), for example, studied aspects of work commitment in a group of highly gifted women who have been part of a famous longitudinal study, Terman's study of a group of gifted children who have now been followed for over 50 years. Examining the data up to the time the women were 60, Willemsen could find no indication that those women in this group who had had strong work commitments saw their lives any more positively than did women who had been primarily homemakers. The one difference between the two groups was that the strongly work-committed women were more likely than the less committed women to see their lives as something they had shaped themselves rather than having been shaped by external forces.

Stroud's analysis (1981) of work histories of the women in the Berkeley intergenerational studies also showed no overall benefit in life satisfaction for the working women. Among college-educated women, those who had been homemakers for all their adult lives had the highest morale and self-esteem at midlife, followed closely by those with a strong commitment to work. The lowest levels of esteem and morale occurred among women who had uneven or interrupted work histories and who had had only a moderate level of work commitment.

It appears that in the generations of women born from 1900 to about 1930, high life satisfaction could be found either through commitment to family or through commitment to work. Subsequent generations have increasingly tried to combine the two, assuming that women, like men, need to mature in both "love and work." Studies of these more recent cohorts do show higher morale, life satisfaction, and self-esteem for women who work than for those who do not. But the effect is not a large one, nor is it shared by all subgroups of women. Whether a woman finds that work helps to foster higher self-esteem or greater life satisfaction appears to depend at least in part on the way in which she combines work and family roles—a subject to which I now turn.

Combining Work and Family Roles

In Chapter 7, and so far in this chapter, I have largely talked about family roles and work roles as if they were quite separate. For most adults today, these two sets of roles are inextricably intertwined. I want to explore the connections by looking at the relationship from two directions: the effect of family roles on work experiences and the effect of work on family.

The Impact of Family Roles on Work Experiences

Family roles clearly have different effects on men's and women's work lives. Joseph Pleck, a psychologist who has been especially interested in men's changing roles, suggests that the boundaries between work and family are "asymmetrically permeable" for the two sexes (Pleck, 1977). For a woman, family roles intrude on work, not only in the sense that she is much more likely to leave the workforce entirely when her children are young, but in the sense that she is more likely to stay home with a sick child or be the one to rearrange her schedule so that she can go to a teacher's conference or a PTA meeting. Women's greater relationship focus within the marriage is also more likely to lead to job changes because of the husband's relocations. So for women, family roles spill over into work life, and they experience greater role conflict and strain between the two roles (Scott & Alwin, 1989). For men, the two roles are more separate, and they experience less role strain. If any spillage occurs, it is likely to be work roles that spill over into family life as the family adapts to a father's long work hours or to his job changes.

Another way to think of the same process is that for women who work, work and family tasks create two *simultaneous* roles while for men they are *sequential* (Hall, 1972; Nieva, 1985). The man is a worker during the day and a husband/father at night and on weekends. The woman is a mother/wife all the time whether she works or not—a point nicely made in a panel of my favorite comic strip in Figure 9–6.

Still, even for men there are clearly links between the two roles. I mentioned in Chapter 7 that married men are healthier and more satisfied with their lives than single men. It is also true that as a general rule, married men are more successful in their jobs than are men who remain single (Aldous, Osmond, & Hicks, 1979). Some of this difference may be self-selection: Healthier and brighter men may simply be more likely to marry. But some of the difference undoubtedly reflects the impact of family life on the men. The responsibility of earning a living for

Figure 9–6 (Source: For Better or for Worse. Copyright 1984 by Universal Press Syndicate. Reprinted with permission. All rights reserved.)

his family motivates the man to strive (the "parental imperative" that Gutmann describes), and the assistance of a wife who provides emotional and logistical support frees the man to devote more attention to his work.

If the latter argument holds, then we ought to find that the most successful men are those with wives who do not work and who thus can devote more time and attention to supporting their husbands in their careers. There are several bits of data to support this hypothesis. As one example: In one large national survey completed in 1977 (Stanley, Hunt, & Hunt, 1986), men in dual-earner households reported lower job satisfaction and lower overall life satisfaction than did men who were the single earners, and this was even more true at higher status levels and when the wife was strongly committed to her career. Of course, this may have changed since 1977. But perhaps not. In role-theory terms, a man can most readily fulfill the demands of his work role when he has low conflict or strain between work and family roles. Since in a two-earner household the man's family roles may become more demanding, two-job or two-career family patterns may exact a career price for men, even while they add career success for women.

The Impact of Work on Family Roles

With the exception of studies of *un*employment, we know surprisingly little about the impact of variations in men's work on family life. When a man is laid off from his job, there are clear stresses on the family, including a higher risk of divorce, physical abuse, and child neglect. Even when these very serious negative consequences do not occur, there is typically a loss of marital satisfaction, apparently caused by a sharp increase in hostile and negative behavior by the now unemployed husband (Conger, Elder, Lorenz, Conger, Simons, Whitbeck, Huck, & Melby, 1990). Consistent with all the research on marital quality, as the negative interactions increase, marital satisfaction goes down.

But we have only fragments of information about the impact of variations in the man's job success or satisfaction on his family life. We know that women's marital satisfaction is higher if the husband is successful at his work, although wives of *highly* work committed men have somewhat lower marital satisfaction (Aldous et al., 1979), presumably because such men simply have less time or energy for their family lives. We also have some fascinating hints from Kohn and Schooler's research on the substantive complexity of work that men in less complex jobs, particularly jobs that are embedded in authoritarian hierarchies, become less flexible in their thinking and bring that lack of flexibility home with them. As just one example, such men are more likely to emphasize obedience and discipline with their children than are men in more complex or less authoritarian jobs (Kohn, 1980; Kohn & Schooler, 1983). If we are to understand the interface between work and family life, we need more research of this kind.

We know a great deal more about the impact of women's work on family life, but as with studies of the impact of work on women's own development, the emphasis has not been so much on the quality of the woman's work experience as simply on whether she works or not. There are hundreds of studies comparing family lives for working and nonworking wives or mothers. Let me try to summarize the findings by focusing on three issues: how the wife's employment affects the way decisions are made in the family, the way household labor is allocated, and the sense of overall marital satisfaction.

Effect of Wife's Work on Decision Making and Power Most (but not all) of the research on two-worker couples suggests that in such families, the wife has more power than in families in which the husband is the only wage earner. Employed women, compared to housewives, have more say in important family decisions and more control of finances (Spitze, 1988). The general rule is that whoever earns the money has the largest say in how it is spent. When both partners earn money, there is greater equality in decision making, and the more equal the earnings the more equal the power (Blumstein & Schwartz, 1983).

Effect of Wife's Work on Division of Family Labor In this, as in so many areas, we are in a period of transition. Ten or 20 years from now I may write a very different summary statement. But today, despite the enormous increase in women's employment, despite the women's movement, despite an increase in egalitarian attitudes about childrearing and housework, it is still true that women have the major responsibility for both rearing children and keeping house, *whether they work or not.*

The research findings tell us several intriguing things about the ways that families take care of the endless chores of family life. First, they tell us that when a woman works, especially if she works full time, she does spend fewer hours in housework or child care than do her homemaker peers (e.g. Berardo, Shehan, & Leslie, 1987; Geerken & Gove, 1983; Shelton, 1990). The slack is partially picked up by husbands and by children, but mostly by simply letting things slide (I remember what a shock it was to me to realize that the living room rug really didn't *have* to be vacuumed every day). However, the data also show clearly that a working woman remains *in charge* of housework, cooking, cleaning, and childrearing. She is still the one who must organize, monitor, and supervise the work. Figure 9–7 shows some fairly typical data from a large sample of working wives (Maret & Finlay, 1984). It shows the percentage of women who describe themselves as "solely responsible" for each of several household jobs. If I added the percentages of women who describe themselves as "primarily" responsible (those who organize the work but have some help doing it), the figures would add to nearly 95 percent for every category, whether the woman works or not. A lovely illustration of how this responsibility can affect a woman's life comes from Anne Seiden (1980):

> A distinguished woman professional, about to give a scientific paper, suddenly is distracted as she sits on the podium by the thought, 'Oh, my God, I forgot to buy toilet paper.' [These researchers] did not find male professionals of similar rank who as often felt a sense of personal responsibility for remembering, scheduling, and orchestrating the purchase and maintenance of routine or unusual domestic supplies. (p. 171)

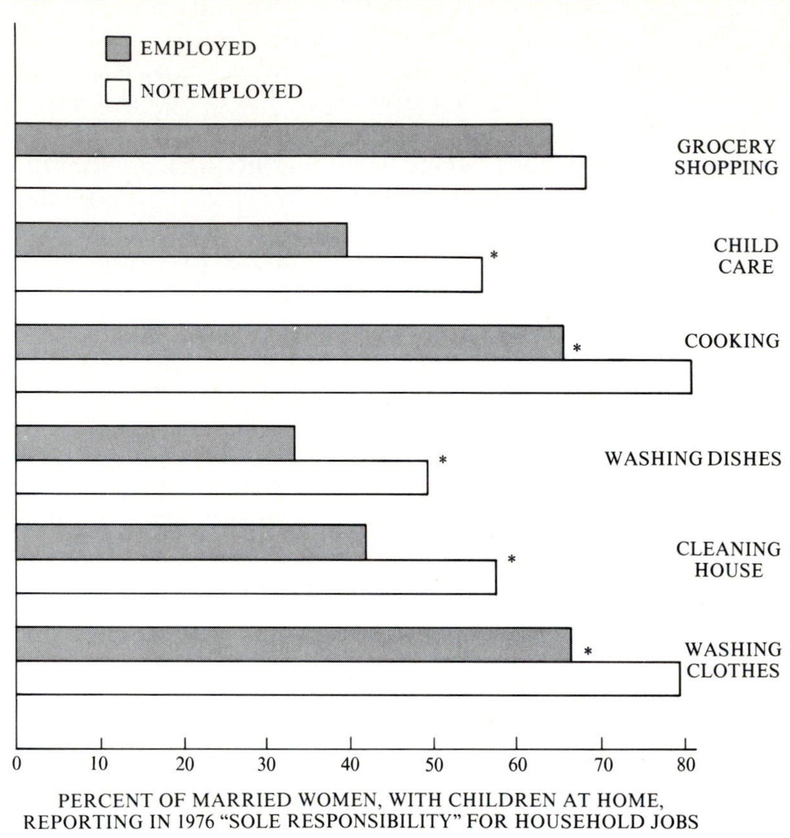

Figure 9–7 Working women share more of the household responsibilities with husbands or children than do full time homemakers but still bear the brunt of the responsibility, as you can see from these results from over 1,000 working wives. The numbers represent the percentage of women, working or not working, who indicated they had sole and full responsibility for each task. An asterisk (*) indicates that for that measure, the difference between working and nonworking women was statistically significant, at least at the .05 level. (Source: Maret & Finlay, 1984, data from Table 1, p. 360).

Husbands of working women "help" with the housework when "asked," but most of the research shows only a small or moderate increase in the number of hours per day or per week that husbands of working wives spend in household tasks, compared to the household contribution of husbands with wives who are full time homemakers.

Several studies also show a link between household labor allocation and stage of the family life cycle. Cynthia Rexroat and Constance Shehan (1987) asked men and women who were part of the Panel Study of Income Dynamics how many hours a week they spent on housework, not including child care. When they divided the subjects up according to their stage in the family life cycle, they found a

U-shaped curve describing men's time spent doing housework at various points in the family life cycle: Household work was highest among newlywed men, men with young children, and retired men, lowest among men with teenage children or for those in the "empty nest" stage. The curve for women was precisely the opposite: Household work was highest among those with children of any age, peaking when children were in elementary school and dropping among those whose last child had left home.

Those of you committed to the idea of egalitarian family life may find these data depressing. In reply, let me offer two potentially comforting points. First, there is now good evidence that the best predictor of a husband's involvement in housework and childcare in two-worker households is his own sex role ideology. Men with more egalitarian attitudes provide more household help (e.g. Perry-Jenkins & Crouter, 1990; Seccombe, 1986b). If such egalitarian ideology becomes more prevalent, we may well begin to see a change in the average data as well.

Second, it is easy to blame men for the lack of a greater shift toward equality of household labor in two-worker households, but it's not so clear that this is either fair or correct. There is also some resistance on the part of women to having their husbands take on more family/household responsibilities. One woman, whose husband was very involved in their care of their infant, said:

> I love seeing the closeness between him and the baby, especially since I didn't have that with my father, but if he does well at his work *and* his relationship with the baby, what's my special contribution? (Cowan & Cowan, 1987, p. 168)

To the extent that a woman derives an important part of her sense of identity from her role as wife and mother, she may be reluctant to give up her central responsibility for home care—a point again illustrated wonderfully by a recent cartoon (Figure 9–8).

The Effect of Wives' Work on Marital Satisfaction and Stability

Given what I've said so far, you might expect that husbands of working wives would be less satisfied with their marriages. The men have lost some power in the relationship, and they are expected to provide more assistance around the house and with the children. And I've already reported that men with working wives have somewhat lower satisfaction with their work. So it is somewhat surprising to find that on average men whose wives work are neither more nor less satisfied with their lives or their marriages than are men whose wives are housewives (Fendrich, 1984; Spitze, 1988). It is only in selected subgroups that we see the expected increase in men's dissatisfaction or distress when their wives work: among high income or professional men and among those whose wives have salaries competitive with their own (Cotton & McKenna, 1988). Divorce rates are also higher among couples in which the woman earns more than half of the family income (Greenstein, 1990).

The general rule suggested by Blumstein & Schwartz in their book *American Couples* (1983), is that for a relationship to be satisfying and lasting, at least one member of the pair must be "relationship-centered" rather than "work-centered."

Figure 9–8 *Source:* Sally Forth, © *1986. (Reprinted with special permission of King Features Syndicate, Inc.)*

In the vast preponderance of cases, it is the woman who is relationship-centered. That is part of the job description for the role of "woman" in this culture. When the woman does not work, she can be strongly relationship-centered. But even when she does work, the woman normally continues in the role of keeping the home fires burning. So long as she does so, or if the husband and wife are both relationship-centered, satisfaction is reasonably high. It is when both husband and wife are strongly work-centered that difficulties arise. Divorce seems to be higher in such couples (e.g., Philliber & Heller, 1983), and marital satisfaction is lower.

If Blumstein & Schwartz are right, and I think they are, there are some troubling implications for women who are strongly motivated to achieve high level success in a career but who also want marriage and children. Such a "superwoman" combination has become the ideal for many young women in recent years. It is well to keep in mind that the research tells us this is an extremely difficult combination to carry off. A successful career virtually requires continuous employment and a strong work commitment. But a strong work commitment by a wife, especially if there are children, is likely to decrease marital satisfaction, increase the risk of divorce, and certainly increase overall role conflict and role strain. This does not imply that there is a conspiracy of some kind to prevent women from achieving both work success and family satisfaction. It does mean that our society has not yet evolved good methods to deal with such combinations of roles. Individual couples have worked out accommodations, but these are still exceptions. The difficulty at the moment is that large numbers of young women are aiming for something that is far harder to achieve than they may realize, especially in view of the sex role definitions still extant.

Coping with the Conflict and Strain

There is no perfect way to eliminate all of the overload and role conflict that come from attempting to combine two paid jobs with complex family roles. But there are some strategies that help.

1. Improving management skills, especially time management. Couples who sail these reef-strewn waters successfully need to be remarkably good at organizing their time. These are skills that can be learned (Seiden, 1980).
2. Redefining or restructuring the family roles. In several studies, Douglas Hall (1972, 1975) has found that women who find ways to distribute tasks to other family members, or simply give up doing some tasks, experience less stress. The living room rug does not have to be vacuumed every day, men *can* clean toilets, teenage children can cook. And of course, given enough economic support, help can be hired.
3. Changing your ideas about what you *ought* to be. Sex role definitions are not written on stone tablets for all eternity. Each of us learned those sex role job descriptions as children and teenagers, and they are strongly ingrained. But it is possible to change the way one thinks about family roles and work roles. Women who undertake this kind of cognitive restructuring report lower levels of role conflict (Elman & Gilbert, 1984).

One strategy that does *not* help is simply trying harder to do it all. Superwomen report high levels of strain. But those who become skillful in using any or all of the three more helpful strategies are able to reduce their role conflict and achieve a reasonable balance of work and family life. Still, the balance is quite fragile, easily disrupted by unexpected demands such as a child's illness, or a car breakdown, or any of the myriad other small crises of everyday life. The simple fact is that there is no way to combine these roles that will completely eliminate the conflict or the strain. That may sound discouraging, but it is realistic.

Retirement

I have talked so far about working and its effects. But what about the cessation of work at the time of retirement? What effect does it have on adult lives?

Two distinctly different images of retirement are part of our cultural lore. On the one hand, there is the vision of rest and relaxation, time at last to do as you please, release from the daily grind. Move to Florida and sit in the sun; get up at noon if you feel like it; stay up and watch the late movie on TV without worrying if that will make you too tired the next day; have time at last for your hobby or to donate hours to your favorite charity.

The other vision of retirement is nicely captured by some comments I read recently in a one-page reprint making the rounds among faculty in a large university. "There is no way to describe adequately" it said, "the letdown many people feel when they retire from a responsible executive post." It went on to predict that retirees would undertake a desperate and doomed search for other sources of meaning and satisfaction, followed by depression and illness.

Which of these visions is valid? Does retirement bring large increases in satisfaction or happiness, or does it bring illness, depression, loss of a sense of self-worth, or something in between? In general, research on retirement supports the sunnier of these two visions.

The Preparation for Retirement

Retirement is not something that just happens the day you turn 65. Barring an unexpected illness, disability, or job layoff as the cause of retirement, the vast majority of adults who retire do so after some period of planning and expectation.

Adults prepare for retirement in various ways, beginning perhaps as early as 15 or 20 years before the anticipated time of retirement (Evans, Ekerdt, & Bosse, 1985). They talk with their spouse, with relatives and friends, read articles, do some financial planning, begin an IRA account. These activities seem to increase fairly steadily as the expected retirement date draws closer.

Such preparatory activities are not equally likely in all middle-aged workers, however. Linda Evans and her colleagues, in a panel study of 2,000 men in the Boston area (Evans, Ekerdt, & Bosse, 1985), found that men over 45 were more likely to report retirement-planning behavior if they were looking forward to retiring, if they enjoyed hobbies and pastimes, thought their pensions would be adequate, were dissatisfied with their jobs, or had a good friend who had retired. Those who dreaded retirement did the least preparation, but even in this group, those closest to retirement age showed more preparation than those more distant from it.

The Timing of Retirement

Just as planning varies, so too does the actual timing of retirement. The age of 65 is probably stuck in most of our minds as the "age of retirement." And as recently as 1970 in the United States, 65 was the most common retirement age for men. But no longer. In the past several decades, there has been a rather rapid shift toward earlier retirement for men (Clark, 1988). You can see the year-by-year work force participation rates for the U.S. population in 1986 in Figure 9–9—the most current year for which we have such complete data. It's obvious that men are retiring in large numbers in their late 50s and early 60s, with the biggest drop in employment between age 61 and 62.

The curve for women in Figure 9–9 has much the same shape, although it is not so clear that it has the same meaning: Since women in each succeeding cohort represented in this figure have been more and more likely to work outside the home, it is hard to be sure whether the figure is telling us about retirement ages or simply that younger women are more likely to work. Many researchers interpreted trends in the 1970s as saying that women were retiring at later and later ages, even while men were retiring earlier and earlier. Current evidence no longer points to such a conclusion. Among employed women, retirement patterns now look much like men's, with retirement ages at earlier and earlier points (Clark, 1988; Hayward, Grady & McLaughlin, 1988).

The Reasons for Retirement

Our knowledge about how people choose when (or whether) to retire has been greatly augmented by a remarkable analysis by Erdman Palmore and his colleagues of a group of seven large longitudinal studies of adults before, during, and after

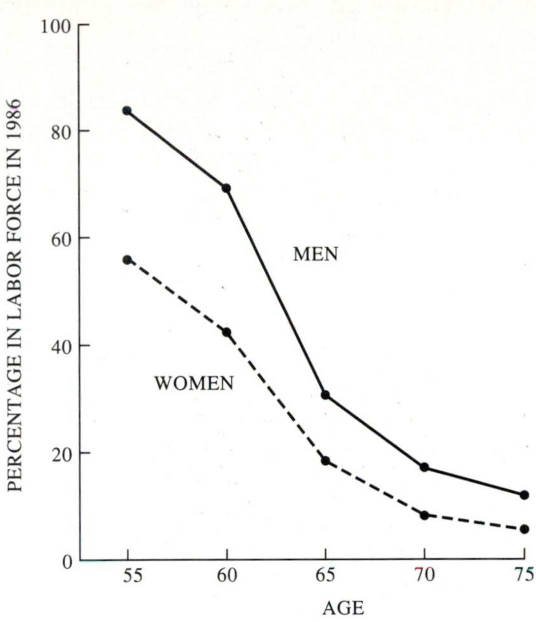

Figure 9–9 This information from the Bureau of Labor Statistics for 1986 shows that 65 is no longer the most common age of retirement for men or for women. These days, 61 and 62 are the most common retirement ages. Note, though, that a small percentage continue working well into old-age. (Source: Clark, 1988, data from Table 3, p. 174).

retirement (Palmore, Burchett, Fillenbaum, George, & Wallman, 1985). Included in this set of studies is not only the now familiar Duke longitudinal studies and the Panel Study of Income Dynamics, but major studies by the Department of Labor (the National Longitudinal Surveys) and the Social Security Administration (the Retirement History Study), and several others. In all, over 7,000 adults of retirement age participated in these studies, each interviewed at least twice, typically three or four times over a period of six to ten years. The evidence from all of these studies taken together points to a few key factors that influence retirement decisions.

AGE For any given cohort there is a certain normative time to retire—which used to be 65 but now may be 62 or even younger. Each of us is aware of those norms, and the norms tend to push us toward common retirement ages. Mandatory retirement ages also have an influence, although the big majority of older adults report that they retired not because they were forced to but because they chose to.

HAVING CHILDREN STILL AT HOME Whatever the adult's age, those with children still at home are much less likely to retire. Men with late-life children tend to stay in the work force until their children are launched even if this takes them past the normative retirement age.

HEALTH Those in poor health are likely to retire earlier than those in good health, and this is particularly so for those who retire before age 65. For example, one third of the men who participated in the National Longitudinal Surveys who retired between 1966 and 1981 did so because of poor health, and the majority of them retired before age 62 (Parnes, Crowley, Haurin, Less, Morgan, Mott, & Nestel, 1985). Thus, to a significant degree people retire early because they are no longer able to work or are unable to work to their previous levels of proficiency.

PENSION PROGRAMS Not surprisingly, availability of adequate financial support during retirement makes a big difference in individual decisions. Those who belong to a private pension program (who will thus have income in addition to Social Security) retire earlier than do those who lack this economic support during retirement.

SOCIAL CLASS OR INCOME You might assume that because adults in higher social class groups are likely to have good private pension programs, they therefore retire sooner. But that is not the case. Better educated and higher social class adults retire somewhat *later*, presumably because they are likely to have less physically demanding jobs or they are more interested in their jobs.

WORK CHARACTERISTICS The self-employed and the highly work-committed retire later than do those who work for others or who are less committed to their work, a pattern that suggests the not surprising conclusion that those who find greater gratification in their jobs are more likely to continue working past the normative retirement age. In an interesting supplementary analysis of the results of the National Longitudinal Survey sample, Mark Hayward and Melissa Hardy (1985) have found that those in more substantively complex jobs retire later. For this group, ill health, or a particularly good pension program, are the major pushes toward retirement. Among those in less complex jobs, it is the timing of availability of pensions that is a key ingredient. Thus, men with low level, repetitive jobs are highly likely to retire as soon as they are eligible for private pensions; those in more challenging jobs are likely to put off retirement until either pushed by ill-health or attracted by some special financial inducement.

In any individual case, these factors will interact in complex ways. For example, many workers with low incomes also have no pension program. Under these conditions, workers retire somewhat later. Furthermore, all of the effects I have listed appear to be less significant predictors of retirement in women than in men (George, et al. 1984). In women, the only really consistent predictor of retirement is age. Just why there should be this sex difference in the predictability of retirement is not at all obvious. It may reflect the effects of the changing status of women which has been accompanied by an increase in work participation by women in their 50s and 60s. This social change may work against the influence of other forces moving women toward retirement.

The Decision Not to Retire

Before I go on to talk about the impact of retirement on late adult life, I need to say a word about the interesting minority of adults who choose not to retire at all. This subgroup actually includes two types of people: (1) those who never retire from their previous line of work but continue to work at their normal occupation until they die, such as college professors who become emeritus professors and maintain an active research life into their 70s and 80s, or legislators like the late Congressman Claude Pepper of Florida, champion of causes of the elderly, and (2) those who retire from their regular occupation but then take up other lines of work, part time or full time, in their 60s, 70s, and 80s. Of course, for many of the people in both these groups, the amount of work done gradually declines, perhaps dwindling to nearly nothing over a period of many years. Still, it is not unreasonable to describe them as having "shunned" retirement.

We know almost nothing about women who choose not to retire, but we do know something about men who shun retirement. Some of them are men with very low education, poor retirement benefits and thus very low incomes. These men continue working out of economic necessity. A larger fraction of the retirement shunners are highly educated, healthy, highly work-committed professionals. Before retirement age, men in the National Longitudinal Surveys were asked "If, by some chance, you were to get enough money to live comfortably without working, do you think that you would work anyway?" Nearly three quarters of those who later shunned retirement had answered this question in the affirmative (Parnes, et al. 1985). Men who believe that retirement is likely to be an unpleasant state are also more likely to keep on working. Overall then, those who shun retirement do so either because economic necessity gives them little choice or because their work continues to provide more satisfaction than they expect retirement to offer.

What Are the Effects of Retirement?

Such a negative expectation of retirement might well be valid for some—a point I'll come back to in a moment. But the striking fact is that for most adults, retirement itself has remarkably few effects on income, health, activity, or attitudes. What is more, any negative effects of retirement have declined over recent decades, as retirement benefits and health care have improved and as cultural acceptance of retirement has increased (Haring, Okun, & Stock, 1984).

EFFECTS ON INCOME

The largest single effect of retirement is a reduction in income. The longitudinal evidence from the seven major studies that Palmore and his colleagues have analyzed suggests that incomes drop an average of about 25 percent upon retirement. But because expenses, too, are typically lower in retirement years (the mortgage may be paid off, the children are out of school and on their own, etc.) the *adequacy* of income does not drop by so much as 25 percent (Clark & Sumner, 1985). For some subgroups, spendable income may actually increase after retirement. Several analyses by Palmore show that such an increase may occur for the working poor, since the combination of Social Security and Supplemental Security Income (SSI) may be more than they were able to earn in their working lives.

The financial status of the elderly has improved a good deal in the past several decades as Social Security benefits, SSI, and private pension income have increased sharply, raising the base income for most retired adults significantly. For example, in 1959, 35 percent of adults over 65 lived below the poverty line; in 1987 it was only 12.2 percent (U. S. Bureau of the Census, 1989b). Today, the elderly are no more likely to be poor than is true for any other age group (Schulz, 1988).

This description of the greatly improved economic condition of the retired, while accurate in the average, masks the existence of some significant subgroups who suffer extreme financial hardship in the retirement years. Women living alone represent the highest level of poverty among the elderly: Roughly 30 percent of such women were living below the poverty line in 1987 (U.S. Bureau of the Census, 1989c). And within this group, black and Hispanic women are markedly worse off, with as many as 70 percent living in poverty. ("Poverty," by the way, was defined as an annual income of $5,393 for one individual in 1987). Put another way, over 70 percent of elderly poor are women (Minkler & Stone, 1985). Many of these women did not, in fact, "retire" since they never worked. Because they never worked, they have no private pensions, and their Social Security benefits are tied to, but lower than, their spouse's. When their husband dies, their incomes drop sharply, often into poverty (Burkhauser, Holden, & Feaster, 1988). Some of this sex difference in poverty may diminish in succeeding cohorts, since many more women will have higher earned incomes and more private pension benefits.

For the majority of adults, then, retirement does not bring as large a change in income as the common stereotype would suggest. But there is still a significant minority whose financial needs are not being met by any existing retirement programs.

EFFECTS ON PHYSICAL HEALTH The effects of retirement on physical health, too, are smaller than you might expect. Summing across a number of studies, the best conclusion is that retirement itself has little direct effect on health. That is, people do not get sicker *because* they retire. Some retire because they are ill; those in good health at retirement age show about the same levels of illness over the succeeding years whether they continue to work or not (Streib & Schneider, 1971; Palmore, et al., 1985).

EFFECTS ON ATTITUDES AND MENTAL HEALTH The case for the effects of retirement on mental health is not quite so clear cut, in part because many of the large longitudinal studies did not measure such mental states as depression or inquire about the use of mental health facilities. One large study that did include a self-report of psychological symptoms, the Normative Aging Study, does show that adults reported more such symptoms after they retired than before (Bosse, Aldwin, Levenson, & Ekerdt, 1987). And in the Duke longitudinal studies, men showed both increases in self-worth and increases in perceptions of uselessness after they retired. On the other side of the scale is the more extensive body of research that points to little or no change in overall life satisfaction or "subjective well-being" after retirement. Palmore's own conclusion is that "there is certainly no clear evidence . . . that retirement tends to make people depressed or dissatisfied with life" (Palmore, et al., 1985, p. 48).

EFFECTS ON ACTIVITY LEVEL The findings on changes in activities are also mixed, but as a rule, retired adults increase the amount of time they spend in various nonwork activities compared to preretirement levels. They spend more time with friends, more time with hobbies or volunteer work.

Given these consistent research findings, it is interesting to speculate about why the belief persists in our society that retirement causes an increase in the risk of ill-health and unhappiness. Partly this myth is nourished by anecdotes about poor fellows who quit working and died a year later. Part of the problem may lie in our tendency to attribute any change in our mental or physical health to some big event in our lives—a tendency no doubt magnified in recent years by all the emphasis on the stressful effects of life changes (Ekerdt, 1987). In fact, what the research tells us is that retirement is *not* a stressful life change at all, perhaps because it is a *scheduled* change rather than an unscheduled one. As Leonard Pearlin has repeatedly reminded us, it is the unscheduled life changes that are associated with major negative consequences. Since most of us can prepare for retirement and plan its timing, for most of us it is a highly scheduled and nonstressful event.

Who Adjusts Best to Retirement?

Nevertheless, this relatively rosy picture of retirement does not hold for everyone. For some, retirement does bring real adjustment problems. Those who adjust most easily are those who are healthy, have an adequate income, are better educated, remain active or add new activities, have an extended social network of friends and family, think of themselves as "middle-aged" rather than "old", and were generally satisfied with their lives before they retired (Palmore, et al., 1985; Szinovacz, 1982; Block, 1982). A small percentage of well-educated, highly work-committed adults find retirement particularly difficult, but this is *not* a general experience of well-educated, high-status workers. Such people retire later, as a general rule, but normally make a good adjustment to retirement. Nor is it the case that single adults, who may have had greater work commitments, have more difficulty with retirement (Keith, 1985).

The least satisfied retirees are those with inadequate income and ill health, or those who must *simultaneously* cope with retirement and other major life changes, such as widowhood (Stull & Hatch, 1984) or an unexpected or unplanned for loss of income. Yet even for these adults it is not the loss of the work role that is the problem but the inadequacy of pension programs or the debilitating effects of ill health.

On the whole, what predicts life satisfaction in later adulthood is not whether a person has retired or not but whether he or she was satisfied with life in earlier adulthood. We take ourselves with us through the years; grumpy, negative young people tend to be grumpy, negative old people, and satisfied young adults find satisfactions in retirement as well. The consistency in this is quite striking and provides very good support for consistency theories of adulthood (Palmore, 1981). Work does shape our daily lives for upwards of 40 years of our adulthood; but our happiness or unhappiness with life, our growth or stagnation, seems less a function of the specifics of the work experience than it is a function of the attitudes and qualities we bring to the process.

A Review of Work Roles in Adulthood

As before, I have summarized the age-related changes described in this chapter in a table (Table 9.6). The pattern here is strongly reminiscent of the pattern of family and sex role changes I talked about in Chapter 7. Early adulthood is

TABLE 9.6. Summary of Age Changes in Work Roles.

Ages 20–40	Ages 40–65	Age 65 and Older
Trial or establishment stage: first choice of occupation, influenced by personal qualities; formation of the Dream; finding a mentor	Maintenance stage of career, during which there is not likely to be further career advancements; may take the role of mentor	Retirement for most workers accompanied by loss of income, but not marked reduction in health or satisfaction; some increase in social or volunteer activities
Stabilization stage (from 30 to about 45) after career is chosen, try to succeed at that path; most promotions and other advancements occur during this period	May be redefinition of importance of work in adult life	
Job satisfaction begins low and rises; job satisfaction tied in early years more to intrinsic work qualities than to extrinsic qualities	Job satisfaction at its highest, as is job involvement; job values shift somewhat, however, with greater emphasis on extrinsic values	
For women, this period has the greatest shifting in and out of the work force, with marriage and the birth of children	For those women who work, this is a more stable work period, with continuous work patterns more common than at earlier ages	
	Women who work at this age are generally more satisfied with their lives than are women who do not work	

marked by the acquisition and mastery of new work roles. A job must be found, and after each promotion or job change, the new job must be learned. In middle adulthood, in contrast, there are few totally new work roles, but the existing roles undergo redefinition. Emphases change, work values change, the relative importance of work changes. And in late adulthood work roles are lost, just as is true of many family roles.

Each of these tasks—acquisition of roles, redefinition of roles, and loss of roles—has its own set of issues, problems, and stresses. Different adults are likely to find particular periods difficult or easy, depending on their temperament or circumstances. So for some, the heavy dosage of role acquisition in early adulthood may be particularly stressful, especially if many complex roles must be mastered simultaneously. For others, the redefinitions at midlife are more stressful, perhaps particularly for those who are low in openness to experience or who lack the cognitive skill or intellectual flexibility to reassess or redefine. For still others, the loss of roles in late life is most difficult. Thus, while we can identify a general pattern of role change over adulthood that seems to be common for the vast majority of adults, in many cultures, the experience of that pattern will vary markedly from one individual to another.

Summary

1. We know more about men's work patterns than women's and more about middle class than working class work histories.
2. While selection of an occupation occurs primarily in early adulthood, many adults change jobs and careers quite often over the 40 years of a working life.
3. Occupational choices are affected by gender, family background, and personality.
4. Traditional "men's jobs" are more varied and higher in status than traditional "women's jobs." The impact of sex role ideology on job choice is more marked among working class youth than in the middle class.
5. Families affect job choice through influencing educational attainment and by steering children toward occupations similar to those of their parents.
6. Adults also tend to select occupations whose demands match their own personality characteristics or values. Six personality/job types have been suggested by Holland: realistic, investigative, social, conventional, enterprising, and artistic.
7. Cross-sectional research generally shows job satisfaction and job commitment to be lower among young workers, higher among older workers. Some cohort effect seems to influence this pattern, but some genuine age effects remain.
8. Job performance is generally unrelated to age, except for those jobs requiring high levels of physical strength or speed. Performance of the latter jobs declines in middle-age.
9. Individual movement up a career ladder is facilitated by higher education and by early promotion. Most adults achieve whatever upward movement

they are likely to experience within the first 15 to 20 years in an occupation.

10. Most men follow a pattern of continuous work through adulthood. The continuous flow can, however, be divided into stages.
11. In the establishment stage, the young man selects an occupation through trial and error and learns his work. In the stabilization stage, men pursue their career goals vigorously, striving to move as far as possible within the occupation. In the maintenance stage, men come to terms with their level of success and may reduce the emphasis they place on work success as a mark of personal value.
12. Women's work patterns are far more variable. In present midlife cohorts, roughly a quarter of women have worked continuously, another 50 percent have moved in and out of the work force, depending on family responsibilities, and the remainder have remained at home full time.
13. Occupational success has been greater for women who have followed continuous work patterns and for those who pursue the same field of work during interrupted work histories.
14. Men who are satisfied with their work generally report higher life satisfaction in general, although work success is not similarly linked to life satisfaction or better adjustment. For women, having a job is generally associated with higher life satisfaction than is full time homemaking.
15. When both husband and wife work, role conflict and role strain increase, especially for women. In two-job families compared to one-job families, women have more power, remain responsible for homemaking tasks and childrearing, but spend fewer hours actually doing housework.
16. Marital satisfaction is unrelated to wives' employment, except in select subgroups. Lower satisfaction is found among men with high income, or those with wives who are very highly work-committed, or who earn salaries competitive with their husbands.
17. The conflict and strain of a two-job family can be reduced by improving management skills, redefining or reassigning the tasks, and rethinking and restructuring internal concepts of sex and work roles.
18. Among men in the United States, retirement has been occurring at earlier and earlier ages; 62 is now modal. For women, there are signs of a similar lowering of retirement ages in recent years.
19. Most adults begin to prepare mentally and emotionally for their retirement some years before retirement age. Those who retire early, compared to those who retire later, tend to be in poorer health, are lower in social class, are less committed to their work, and have decent pension programs.
20. The impact of retirement on individual lives is far smaller than folklore suggests. Income does go down somewhat and daily routines change, but neither health nor life satisfaction declines as a result of retirement.
21. The largest negative economic effect of retirement is found among single women, particularly minority group women. The largest negative psychological effect is found among the least educated, those with poor financial

support, with limited and/or unsupportive social networks, and those who were dissatisfied with their lives before retirement.

Suggested Readings

BETZ, N. E., & FITZGERALD, L. F. (1987). *The career psychology of women.* Orlando, FL: Academic Press. This is a splendidly detailed, thorough book covering all aspects of women's careers, the impact of women's work on family functioning, and many other topics I've touched on in this chapter. If you want more detail on women's work lives, this is a first-rate source.

BLUMSTEIN, P., & SCHWARTZ, P. (1983). *American couples.* New York: William Morrow. This book describes a series of extensive interviews with a broad range of couples about money, work, and sex. Included are married couples, cohabiting couples, and both gay and lesbian couples, which gives the study a unique richness. The book is written for a lay audience and includes a number of fascinating case studies.

SCHULZ, J. H. (1988). *The economics of aging.* (4th ed.). Dover, MA: Auburn House. This is the most detailed, up-to-date book I know of on this subject. Schulz covers not only the current financial situation of retirees but describes various pension systems and financial planning for retirement.

TERKEL, S. (1972). *Working.* New York: Avon. If you want to know what work feels like to Americans across an enormous range of occupations, read Studs Terkel's fascinating book.

THOMPSON, L., & WALKER, A. J. (1989). Gender in families: Women and men in marriage, work, and parenthood. *Journal of Marriage and the Family, 51*, 845–871. This is an excellent current review of the literature on the links between family and work roles.

CHAPTER 10

Changes in Personality and Motives in Adulthood

One of the remarkable things about our sense of self over the years is that we simultaneously see ourselves as staying the same and as changing. The sense of sameness is easy to identify. Think about yourself when you were 18 or 20, and then think about yourself as you are now and see if that isn't true (Of course, this will not be so helpful an exercise if you are now only 20, but bear with me). Your sense of who you are is composed in large part of a set of traits or qualities that are the same over time.

There are dozens of ways in which I am the same person I was at 20. I was then, and still am, talkative, assertive, friendly, definite, uncoordinated, somewhat rigid (my family might argue that the term "somewhat" is a slight understatement!), well organized, unorthodox, and strongly solitary. I liked things to be predictable when I was 20 and still do. Time alone was something I greatly valued as a child, as a young adult, and now. It is no accident that I have chosen an occupation that lets me work alone, nor that I make my living with words. It is also no accident that I have ended up on the board or as the manager of virtually every organization I have ever joined, nor that when I wanted to get in better physical shape I chose running rather than a team sport, aerobics classes, or a competitive sport like tennis.

A particularly wonderful example of consistency comes from David McClelland (1981), a Harvard psychologist who has been one of the major figures in personality research. McClelland describes his encounters over a 25-year period with a man originally known as Richard Alpert—a man I also knew briefly when I was a graduate student at Stanford when he was a visiting professor.

In the early 1960s, Richard Alpert was a psychologist at Stanford and Harvard, very verbal, charming, successful. He could hold classes or audiences spellbound. McClelland, who was Alpert's colleague at Harvard, also describes him as having been ambitious, interested in influencing others, and with a strong need for power, accompanied—so McClelland reports—by guilt about wanting such power. Then, when he was a young faculty member at Harvard, Alpert got involved with Timothy Leary, another Harvard professor who was experimenting with LSD and who advised young people of that time to "turn on, tune in, and drop out." Alpert did all three. He left Harvard, drifted about for a few years, then went to India for some years where he stayed at the ashram (study center) of a guru. Eventually Alpert came back to the United States with a new name—Ram Dass—and a new philosophy. McClelland says:

> When I first saw Ram Dass again in the early 1970s he seemed like a completely transformed person. His appearance was totally different from what it had been. He was wearing long Indian style clothes with beads around his neck; he was nearly bald but had grown a long bushy beard. He had given away all his possessions, refusing his father's inheritance, carried no money on his person, and for a time lived as a nomad in a van which was all he had in the world. He had given up drugs, abandoned his career as a psychologist, no longer wanted even to save the world and talked all the time as if he were "nobody special," although previously it had been clear to himself and others that he was somebody special . . . yet after spending some time with him, I found myself saying over and over again "It's the same old Dick," . . . He was still very intelligent . . . he was still verbally fluent.

Figure 10–1 *Almost forty years separate these two photos—of me, as you may have guessed. I was seven in the top picture, forty-four in the lower picture. The differences are obvious. In the more recent picture I have more wrinkles, white hair, am fully grown. But I still feel like the same person in many respects, despite the maturing. (Source: Helen L. Bee, author.)*

> . . . And he was still charming. . . . At a somewhat less obvious level, Alpert was very much involved in high drama, just as he had always been. . . . I would certainly conclude that he continues to have a strong interest in power. . . . Furthermore he still feels guilty about being so interested in power. [McClelland, 1981, pp. 89–91]

Last year I had a chance to hear Alpert/Ram Dass speak and came away with the same impression, both from watching him and from listening to his words. In some ways, he was still the same man I knew 30 years ago. He still held the audience spellbound, he still had a wonderful self-deprecating form of humor, he still seemed pleased to be admired—although now he was aware of this and made fun of himself. He said quite explicitly that the same neuroses, the same foibles are still there. In some sense, they define him. That's who Dick Alpert (or Ram Dass) is.

Yet in the midst of all this continuity, all this sameness, there is clearly change as well. I am not the same as I was at 20, just as Dick Alpert is not. He has lost the restlessness of mind and body that I remember and now radiates an inner quiet and calm. At 50, I am still comparatively rigid, but I am a lot *less* rigid than I was at 20, a lot more forgiving, more able to laugh at myself, less intense, more confident, less anxious—or perhaps more accurately, anxious about fewer things.

In this chapter, I want to explore both parts of this system, both the consistencies and the changes. What aspects of personality tend to stay the same and why? What kinds of changes do we see and can those changes be thought of as growth or inner development, as Loevinger or Erikson might say, or are they more in the way of adjustments to changing circumstances, as Levinson suggests?

Consistency in Personality Across Adulthood

What Kinds of Consistency Are We Talking About?

Go back and look at Table 6.1 to review the various types of consistency that psychologists have studied. Nearly all of the research on consistency I'm going to talk about here belongs in the category I have called *correlational consistency.* Just as was true of those studying consistency in IQ, psychologists studying consistency of personality are most often asking whether each individual's relative position on some constant measure has remained the same over time. Typically, the researcher uses the same personality-measuring procedure at two or more times and looks at the correlation between the two sets of scores.

In the personality literature, there has also been some attempt to measure both *pattern* and *trait* consistency, particularly by researchers associated with the Berkeley intergenerational studies. Their primary measure of personality has been based on a procedure called a **Q-Sort** (Block, 1971), a technique that is unusual enough to require some elaboration.

A Q-sort consists of a large number of words or phrases that might describe an individual, such as "socially poised" or "feels guilty" or "satisfied with self." A highly skilled rater, using all the information available about a subject including interview responses, observations by other psychologists, and test scores, sorts the many statements into nine separate piles, with those statements that seem to be most true of the subject placed in pile #9, and those least true of the subject placed in pile #1. The sorting is restricted, however: The number of items that can be placed in each pile is specified ahead of time, forcing the rater to create a normal distribution of items in the nine piles. Pile #9 and pile #1 are each allowed only a few statements, piles #2 and #8 can have a few more, but the bulk of the statements must be placed in the middle piles. For each subject, each item in the set is then assigned a score that corresponds to the pile it was placed in. Clusters of items, such as those that may reflect extraversion, or openness, or some other basic trait, can then be summed and those scores compared from one time point to the next.

For the subjects in the Berkeley studies, five separate Q-sorts have been completed for each subject, each by a different rater, each based on information at a single age. It is important to understand that, given this type of measurement, change or continuity from one age to the next represents change or consistency in *intra*individual patterns. We are asking whether the internal structure or distribution of qualities has remained the same or changed. A Q-sort is also a measure of trait consistency (or change), since the rater is searching for underlying traits, not surface behavior. Quite different behaviors at each age might lead a rater to decide to place a particular item in the #8 or #9 pile for that individual. Of course, it is still possible to examine these types of consistency using correlation coefficients, since we can correlate each subject's cluster scores from one age to the next, much as we would correlate scores on some standardized test.

Evidence for Consistency in Personality

The strongest evidence for consistency of personality or temperament in adulthood comes from the work of Paul Costa and Robert McCrae (1980a, 1984; Costa, McCrae, & Arenberg, 1983), some of whose work I described briefly in Chapter 2. Recall that they propose three basic personality dimensions—neuroticism, extroversion, and openness (see Table 2.2)—each of which shows stability over relatively long periods of adulthood. In their Baltimore Longitudinal Study of Aging, they have studied men who range in age from 20 to 90, testing and retesting each man every six years. (Recently, they have also begun to study women but do not yet have any longitudinal results for women). Table 10.1 shows the correlations between self-reported personality characteristics over 12-year intervals for men in three different age groups. These correlations are quite remarkably high, suggesting strong consistency, at least over periods of a decade and for this type of measure of personality. In separate analyses, they found somewhat lower consistency for their domain of Openness, with 10-year correlations ranging from .44 to .63 (Costa & McCrae, 1980a).

As further support for the basic point, Costa & McCrae have also shown consistency in absolute level: In a cross-sectional study of a nationally representative sample of over 10,000 adults (Costa, McCrae, Zonderman, Barbano, Lebowitz,

TABLE 10.1. Correlations Between Scores on Several Personality Dimensions Obtained 12 Years Apart on a Large Group of Men of Different Ages.

	Age Groups			
	22–44	*45–59*	*60–76*	*Entire Group*
Personality Dimensions Relating to Extraversion:				
General Activity	.77	.82	.78	.77
Ascendance	.61	.74	.76	.83
Sociability	.64	.81	.66	.74
Dimensions Relating to Lack of Neuroticism				
Emotional Stability	.63	.76	.71	.70
Objectivity	.66	.76	.59	.69
Friendliness	.74	.68	.87	.74
Personal Relations	.78	.64	.73	.68

SOURCE: Costa, P. T., Jr. McCrae, & Arenberg, 1983, adapted from Table 7.5, p. 247. Reprint by permission of the Guilford Press, New York.

& Larson, 1986), the researchers found only very small changes with age in the average scores on any of these three dimensions.

Other researchers have also found high levels of correlational consistency on similar measures. For example, in a six-year longitudinal study in Australia, Bruce Headey and Alexander Wearing (1989) found that a measure of extraversion was correlated .60 over the six years, whereas a measure of neuroticism was correlated .74.

However, researchers who have studied adults over longer periods, using other types of measures, have generally reported lower levels of consistency. Let me give you two examples, both shown in Table 10.2.

Ravenna Helson and Geraldine Moane (1987) (in a study I will refer to frequently) have studied a group of 132 women who graduated from Mills College in California in 1958 or 1960, retesting and reinterviewing them when they were roughly 27 and again at age 43. The scores shown in the table are from a standardized personality assessment called the California Personality Inventory, which was filled out by each subject at each time point. You can see in Table 10.2 that there was considerable individual consistency in scores, especially over shorter periods of time. Over the longest interval studied, the 22 years from age 21 to 43, the consistency was less but is still striking for several scales, especially dominance, which measures the person's confidence and initiative in social undertakings, and self control, which measures the individual's ability to control the expression of emotions, especially anger.

The second set of data shown in the table is drawn from the now familiar Berkeley studies. Norma Haan and her colleagues (Haan, Millsap, & Hartka, 1986) have reduced the Q-sort information to six clusters. Scores on each of

TABLE 10.2. Consistency in Personality over Long Periods of Adulthood in Two Separate Studies.

Helson & Moane's study of Mills College Women				Norma Haan's study of Berkeley Intergenerational Study Subjects			
Personality Measure (California Personality Inventory)	*Consistency Between Ages:* 21 & 27	27 & 43	21 & 43	*Personality Measure (from Q-Sorts)*	*Consistency Between Ages:* 30 & 40[a] 37 & 47	40 & 55 47 & 62	5 & 55 5 & 62
Dominance	.61*	.67*	.50*	Self-confident/victimized	.44*	.49*	.26
Independence	.52*	.40*	.28	Assertive/submissive	.52*	.65*	.24
Responsibility	.60*	.59*	.36*	Cognitively committed	.60*	.47*	.34*
Self-control	.72*	.70*	.58*	Outgoing/aloof	.52*	.56*	.37*
Psychological Mindedness	.55*	.44*	.33	Dependable	.54*	.60*	.25
Femininity	.51*	.62*	.41*	Warm/hostile	.33*	.44*	.14
Flexibility	.56*	.50*	.37*				

[a]Different pairs of ages are included in each set, since the subjects in the two separate studies that make up the Berkeley intergenerational studies were not assessed at precisely the same ages. For each study, one age was designated as 'early adulthood,' one as 'middle adulthood' and one as 'late adulthood.' The correlations shown are thus between early and middle, and between middle and late, and then finally for the entire life span studied in this research, from age 5 to age 60.

* Statistically significant at $p < .001$ or better.

Sources: Helson & Moane, 1987, from Table 1, p. 180; Haan, Millsap, & Hartka, 1986, from Table 2, p. 225.

these clusters show significant consistency over the adult years; some even show consistency over periods of more than 50 years, from early childhood to nearly retirement age—an amazing finding. Remember that what you are looking at in Haan's results is consistency of individual pattern or trait, rather than consistency in some absolute score on a standard instrument. What we know from this is that these qualities remained at roughly the same level of centrality or peripherality in the personalities of these subjects over time.

One of the real frustrations about the research evidence in this area is obvious from Tables 10.1 and 10.2: Researchers have used such different measures of personality that it is next to impossible to specify just which dimensions of personality are stable and which are not. My own view is that Costa & McCrae's three dimensions, which are distillations of scores from many different personality inventories, come closer than any other such list to capturing the stable qualities. You can see some aspects of these dimensions in Haan's Q-sort data as well: The cluster of outgoingness versus aloofness seems to capture some aspect of extraversion; the warm/hostile cluster may tap some aspects of neuroticism.

But Costa and McCrae's list does not include all the stable dimensions. In particular, the stable cluster Haan calls "cognitively committed" seems to be omitted from Costa and McCrae's list. It describes an "intellectual, achievement orientation accompanied by a degree of innovativeness" (p. 223). It may have elements of openness, but it also describes a personal bias toward using intellectual means to solve problems, which is not a part of any of Costa and McCrae's dimensions.

Costa and McCrae conclude from all of this evidence that "personality dispositions are extraordinarily stable in adulthood" (1984, p. 149). Norma Haan (1981) comes to a more cautious conclusion, perhaps because she has studied adults over much longer periods of time: "The implication seems to be that people change slowly, while maintaining some continuity" (p. 128).

Explaining Personality Consistency

Where might such personality consistency come from? The two obvious possibilities are that old familiar dichotomy, heredity and environment.

GENETIC INFLUENCES ON PERSONALITY CONSISTENCY

As many of you know, one of the standard ways to look for genetic influences on behavior is to compare the degree of similarity of identical and fraternal twins. Since identical twins are genetically identical and fraternal twins are not, if the identical twins are more like one another than are fraternal twins on some trait, you can be reasonably sure that there is some genetic component in that trait. Two recent studies of personality in twins point to just such a genetic component for the dimensions that Costa and McCrae have identified.

Robert Plomin and his colleagues (Plomin, Pedersen, McClearn, Nesselroade, & Bergeman, 1988) have studied personality characteristics in 700 pairs of Swedish twins born between 1886 and 1958, including 328 pairs who were not brought up together. The inclusion of pairs who were reared apart makes the design of this study even stronger, since if identical twins reared apart are still more like one another in personality than are fraternal twins reared together, the role of heredity is more conclusively shown.

Plomin measured three dimensions of personality: emotionality (which is somewhat similar to Costa and McCrae's neuroticism), activity level, and sociability (similar to Costa and McCrae's dimension of extraversion/introversion). On all three dimensions, the identical twins (even those reared apart) were more alike than were same-sex fraternal twins. This was particularly true for the several measures of emotionality.

A second study of more than 7,000 twin pairs in Finland, by Richard Rose and a group of Finnish colleagues (Rose, Koskenvuo, Kaprio, Sarna, & Langinvainio, 1988), points to the same conclusion. In this case, they measured both extraversion and neuroticism directly and found that for both, identical twins were more like each other than were fraternal twins. The basic findings are in Table 10.3.

Rose went a step beyond merely determining whether the twins had been reared together or not and compared groups that varied in the amount of time they spent together, as children and as adults. He found that identical twins actually spend more time together as adults than do fraternal twins, and those who spend most time together are most like one another in personality. But there is still a genetic component involved as well, as evidenced by the fact that among those twins with little or no contact, the identical twins are still more like one another than are fraternal twins. The same point is strengthened still further by the finding that pairs of genetically unrelated adopted children, reared in the same family, have essentially *no* similarity in personality (Loehlin, 1989). So similarity of environment cannot account for the findings from studies of twins.

These studies and others like them do not tell us that all of the consistency in personality that we see over adult years is caused by some inborn trait. But *some* degree of genetic influence is clear, especially for extraversion and neuroticism.

Environmental Influences on Personality Consistency

Important as the genetic influence on personality may be, it is clearly not the only force moving us toward consistency. Avshalom Caspi, Daryl Bem, and Glen Elder (1989) describe two ways in which the environment also has a profound effect, which they call *cumulative continuity* and *interactional continuity.*

TABLE 10.3. Correlations Between Scores on Neuroticism and Extroversion for Identical and Fraternal Twins in Finland.

	Twin Brothers		Twin Sisters	
	Identical	*Fraternal*	*Identical*	*Fraternal*
Extraversion	.46	.15	.49	.14
Neuroticism	.33	.12	.43	.18

SOURCE: Rose, Koskenvuo, Kaprio, Sarna, & Langinvainio, 1988, from Table 4, p. 164.

Cumulative continuity refers to the fact that our actions produce results; those results then accumulate over time, moving us along specific trajectories. Once on a particular trajectory, we tend to stay on it, which produces continuity. There is a good deal of choice involved in all of this: We each choose environments that fit our own peculiar characteristics and avoid those that demand things we think we cannot deliver, just as I avoid learning how to play tennis because I assume I could not ever perform skillfully, or a shy person avoids applying for a job that would require outgoing interactions.

But cumulative continuity is not all a product of conscious (or even unconscious) choice. There are also consequences for our actions that accumulate and tend to keep us in a particular pattern over time. Among other things, we learn specific strategies, specific patterns of interaction that work for us. Faced with new situations, we first try what we already know. If that works, we seek no further (Atchley, 1989).

Interactional continuity refers to the patterns of interaction between any individual and those around her or him that tend to reinforce habitual personality qualities. A man (or a woman) high in neuroticism is likely to have difficulty getting along with bosses or co-workers. He may lose his job more often or quit more often because of his personality. But having lost his job regularly merely reinforces his neuroticism and maintains the basic pattern. We also tend to set things up so that our expectations will be confirmed. There is research with children, for example, that shows that highly aggressive boys expect more hostility from others than do less aggressive boys. When such a boy behaves aggressively, he does, in fact, elicit hostility, thus confirming his expectations. In this way, preexisting patterns are strengthened, and continuity is reinforced.

Both of these types of continuity are illustrated by Caspi and Elder's own research, which you have already encountered in Chapter 2. Recall that they found that among the subjects in the Berkeley studies, those who began adulthood with high levels of either ill-temper or shyness had different life histories than those who were less extreme on these dimensions. Ill-tempered men did indeed end up at lower occupational levels than did less ill-tempered men, and ill-tempered women were more likely to divorce and to be critical and ill-tempered with their own children.

Helsen and Moane (Helson, Mitchell, & Moane, 1984) also have provided some evidence illustrating the impact of cumulative continuity, particularly the process of self-selection into different environments, from their 22-year study of the Mills College women. For this particular analysis, they divided the group into those who had followed a "feminine social clock" (marrying and having their first child before 28 and never being highly committed to a career) and those who had followed a "masculine social clock" (marrying late, or not marrying at all, with a strong commitment to work). Those women who most consistently followed the masculine social clock had already been distinctly different from their peers in their early twenties. They were more dominant, more sociable, had the greatest self-acceptance, independence, empathy, and "social presence." In contrast, those women who most closely followed the feminine social clock were described, at 20, as seeking to follow the social norms. These young women had been quite well-adjusted and content with themselves but perceived that achievement could best be reached through conforming. Each group chose a life path that would tend to reinforce their preexisting qualities and thus to produce the very personality consistency illustrated in Table 10.2.

In the face of such powerful forces moving each of us toward consistency, it is impressive that there is also significant change in personality over the years of adulthood. Not only do individuals shift from one relative position to another on measures of personality, but adults show at least some *shared* patterns of personality change over the years.

Changes in Personality over Adulthood

Stronger folk than I have quailed in the face of the task of summarizing the evidence on personality changes in adulthood. You have already seen that many different measures of personality have been used in different studies, which already creates problems for any kind of summing of the results. Furthermore, despite the fact that there are a number of theories of personality change in adulthood (many of which you met in Chapter 3), most of the research has been essentially atheoretical, so the measures chosen are frequently ill-adapted to exploring specific theoretical ideas. Add to that the usual difficulty of combining longitudinal and cross-sectional findings in some coherent fashion, and you have a situation rather like trying to put together a jigsaw puzzle only to find that you have pieces from three or four different puzzles, none of which add up to a complete picture. The task is easier now than it was a few years ago since more long-term longitudinal evidence is now available, but it is still formidable.

In trying to create some order out of this chaos, rather than simply list the various findings and thus risk leaving you with no sense of the patterns that may be there, I am going to err in the direction of oversimplification and focus on what I see as common threads. And because we know more about the changes that seem to take place from early to middle adulthood than we do about changes from middle to late adulthood, I'm going to discuss these two sets of changes separately.

One more caveat before we move on: I have said this before but need to reemphasize the fact that virtually all the evidence we have comes from studies of adults reared in the United States, during a particular time in history. We do have some cross-cultural evidence, most notably Gutmann's studies, but any statements I may make about general developmental patterns of change in personality should be taken with a good deal of caution until we have comparable findings from longitudinal studies in other cultures.

Changes from Early to Middle Adulthood

A case can be made for three different clusters of shared changes in personality between early adulthood and midlife: (1) an increase in confidence/self-esteem/independence/achievement-striving, with a parallel decrease in affiliation,

(2) a greater openness, particularly to previously unexpressed parts of the self, and (3) an increase in the maturity of defense mechanisms.

INCREASES IN CONFIDENCE/SELF-ESTEEM/INDEPENDENCE/ACHIEVEMENT I am including a lot of seemingly disparate things in this cluster, but I think there is an underlying theme that links the separate items in this list. The biggest shift in personality in the years from 20 to 45 seems to be an increase in what one might think of as *self-centeredness*. The young adult seems to move from a more dependent reliance on others (such as the parents) toward an independent definition of the self, from an emphasis on doing for others to an emphasis on defining the self. One might also summarize this shift as an increase in what David Bakan (1966) has called an *agenic* orientation: an emphasis on achieving, on doing, on succeeding, on making one's mark in the world.

Evidence for this shift comes from a number of excellent longitudinal and sequential studies, covering several different cohorts, so I am reasonably sure about the generality of this change—at least within our own culture. Let me give some examples:

Norma Haan's analysis of the Q-sort scores on the Berkeley subjects gives us the longest-term look at changes in this area of personality. Figure 10–2 shows the scores on two relevant clusters, one describing self-confidence versus a sense

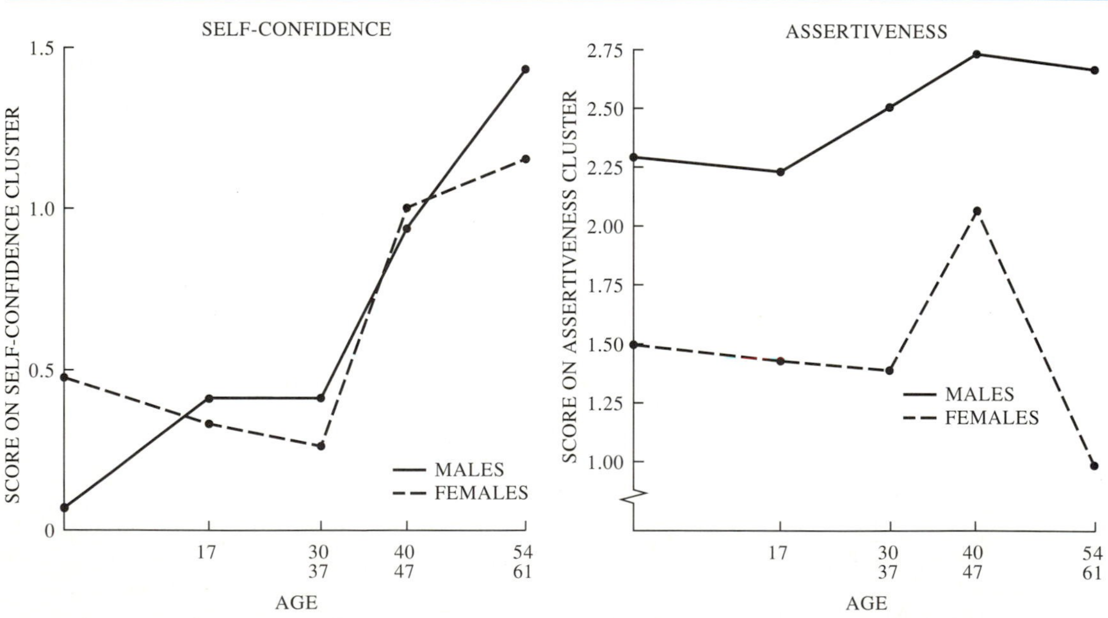

Figure 10–2 These data from the Berkeley Longitudinal Studies show two aspects of the general increase from early to middle adulthood in achievement/independence/autonomy/self-confidence. For both men and women in this study, self-confidence and assertiveness became more prominent parts of their personalities at midlife, with particularly clear increases in the 30s and early 40s. (Source: Haan, Millsap, & Hartka, 1986, Figures 1 and 2, p. 228).

of being victimized and the other describing assertiveness versus submissiveness. You can see that for both measures there was a general rise to midlife, with some indication that the rise was more rapid in the 30s and early 40s than in the 20s.

Results of Helson and Moane's longitudinal study of the Mills College women (1987; Helson, Mitchell, & Moane, 1984) add another piece to the puzzle. Remember that they assessed these women once at age 21, once at age 27, and once at about age 43. They found relatively few changes between 21 and 27 but many and significant changes between 27 and 43. Most centrally, between 27 and 43 these women increased in dominance (which includes aspects of confidence) and independence (which includes aspects of competence and self-reliance). The increase in dominance was particularly large; the average score rose almost one full standard deviation from age 27 to 43.

You will remember from Table 10.2 that scores on both dominance and independence also showed some stability over these same years. So we are seeing both continuity and change in the same sample, on the same measures of personality, just as we do in the Berkeley sample. That is, those women who were higher in dominance than their peers when they were 21 were still likely to be higher than their peers at 43, but the whole group has increased in dominance over those same years.

Studies of changes in motives, beginning with Bray and Howard's study of the AT&T managers, paint a similar picture. The 422 men included in this study had been born between 1927 and 1936, so they represent a slightly more recent cohort than the one included in the Berkeley studies. They had all entered AT&T as low level managers between 1956 and 1960 and were then studied for 20 years. Each subject completed a standardized personality assessment called the Edwards Personal Preference Schedule (EPPS), and each was rated by observers on scales such as Need for Superior Approval and Need for Peer Approval. Bray and Howard found that there was a decline over the 20 years in several measures of dependency, including both Need for Superior Approval and Need for Peer Approval and a clear increase in something called the Need for Autonomy, a change I have shown in Figure 10–3. You can see that the pattern of change was the same for both college-educated and noncollege-educated men. Furthermore, to check to see if such an increase in autonomy with age was unique to the original cohort, in 1977 Bray and Howard also tested a new group of young managers (including both men and women) whose scores on this measure are also shown in Figure 10–3. This 1977 cohort, born in roughly 1952, scored at the same approximate levels as had young managers in 1956, a finding which lends support to the assumption that this is an age-related or developmental change and not merely a pattern characteristic of a single cohort.

Changes on other measures included in the Bray and Howard study provide additional insights into the nature of this increased push toward independence and away from dependence. "The men showed a decline in motivation to make and enjoy friends, to understand others' motives or feelings, and to conform to authority and regulations" (1983, p. 293). Overall, Bray and Howard suggest that these men have become "harder" over the 20-year period.

This increase in autonomy is replicated in yet another longitudinal study in which (happily) the same personality measurement was used. David Stevens and

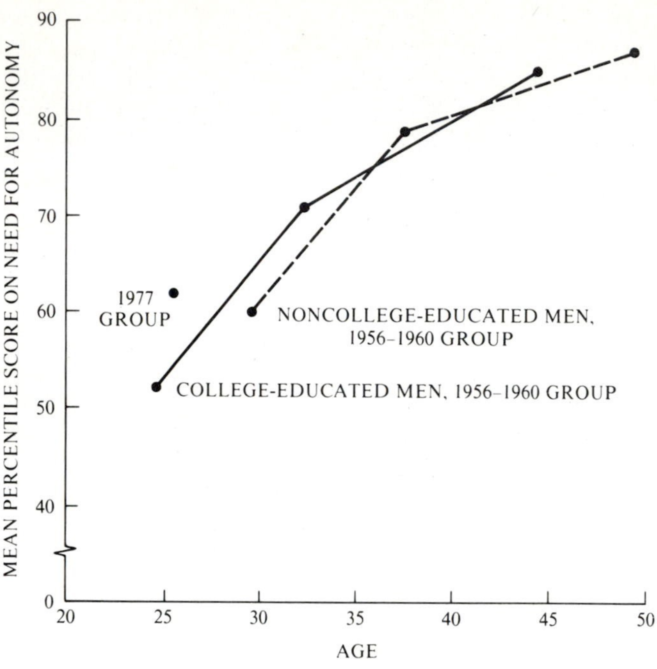

Figure 10–3 In the AT&T managers studied by Bray and Howard, the need for autonomy rose from early to middle adulthood in both college-educated and noncollege-educated groups. Twenty years later, another group of young managers reported a level of need for autonomy that was similar to that of the young managers in 1956 to 1960, which tells us that this pattern is not typical of just a single cohort. (Source: Bray & Howard, 1983, Figure 8.5 adapted.)

Caroll Truss (1985) tested three groups of adults in 1978: (1) a group of 40-year-olds who had first taken the EPPS as college students in the late 1950s, (2) a group of 30-year-olds who had first taken the EPPS as college students in 1965, and (3) a group of current college students, aged about 20. Like Bray and Howard, they found that both the male and female subjects in their samples had increased in autonomy between 20 and 40, and that the 20-year-olds in 1978 had low autonomy scores, just as did the 1977 cohort in the Bray and Howard study. Stevens and Truss also found that scores on achievement increased in early adulthood, as did a measure of dominance.

These changes in motives are confirmed still further by results from Joseph Veroff's major time-sequential study. Recall that Veroff and his colleagues (Veroff, et al., 1981; Veroff, Reuman, & Feld, 1984) have compared results from two large national cross-sectional samples, one drawn in 1957 and one in 1976. In this study, motives were measured with the Thematic Apperception Test (TAT), which is a widely used projective test requiring the subject to tell stories based on somewhat ambiguous pictures. The pictures are specifically selected so that they might trigger stories reflecting several major motives, including *affiliation* (the disposition to seek out or retain emotional relationships), *achievement* (the disposition to perform activities in competition with a standard of excellence), *fear of weakness* (the desire to avoid being controlled by others), and *hope for power* (the desire to have an impact on the world, often by focusing attention on the self). Two of the patterns Veroff found are shown in Figure 10–4. Among women, he found that the affiliation motive declined consistently over age, whereas in men, the hope of power increased from early adulthood to midlife and then declined. Neither of these changes occurred for the other sex, but in both cases virtually identical age-changes were found in the 1957 and 1976 samples, which makes the generality of the findings more credible.

Collectively, these various results seem to me to point to a basic shift in personality in early adult life—a shift toward greater autonomy, greater achievement striving, greater self-confidence, greater personal assertiveness. For women, the change seems to be accompanied by a decrease in the motive to affiliate; for men it is accompanied by an increase in the push for power. That these same general changes are found by researchers using widely different research designs and widely different measures of personality only strengthens the general point.

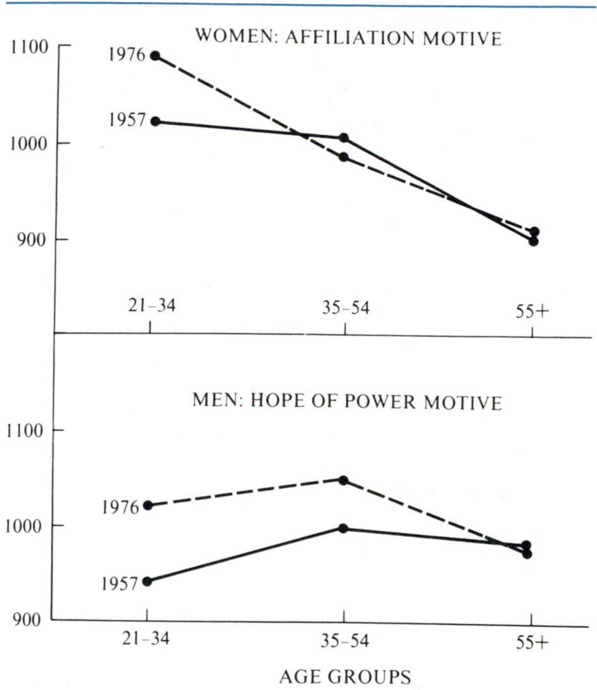

Figure 10–4 Data from two large cross-sectional studies, two decades apart, show the same patterns of decline in affiliation motive with age in women, and a peaking in power motive in middle-age among men. (Source: Veroff, Rueman, & Feld, 1984, from Table 1, p. 1148).

Increased Openness to Self A second cluster of changes seems best described as increased openness. The middle-aged adult seems more willing to acknowledge and explore the previously unexpressed parts of herself, to acknowledge inconsistencies, to examine her assumptions critically. Research touching on this aspect of change is much scarcer, so I can be less confident about this shift. But there are at least fragments.

One piece of information comes from the Berkeley study. In her 1981 analysis, Norma Haan (1981) looked at age changes on a cluster of Q-sort items she referred to as "openness to self," which included high placement of such items as "insightful," "introspective," and "think unconventionally" and low placement of items like "conventional," or "self-defensive." She found that the scores on this cluster rose from early to middle adulthood, with a particularly clear increase in the late 30s and early 40s.

Another fragment comes from Helson & Moane's study of the Mills College students. The authors found that when the women were in their 40s, compared to their 20s, they were much more likely to say spontaneously that they were discovering new parts of themselves or that they had an intense interest in their inner life.

The hypothesized sex role cross-over at midlife, which Gutmann observed in a number of other cultures, might also be thought of as an example of increased openness to expression of previously un- or under-expressed parts of the self. To the extent that a woman has focused in early adulthood on traditional feminine qualities such as nurturance or affiliation, or a man on traditional masculine qualities, any exploration of the less-expressed qualities would look like a crossing over of sex roles. As I pointed out in Chapter 7, there is at least some evidence for cross-over, or at least for increased androgyny at midlife. Norma Haan finds that in the Berkeley sample, women became more masculine and men more feminine at midlife, and all the evidence I've just described showing that midlife women are more assertive and dominant than young women would support the same point. Yet not all the evidence fits this interpretation, a point already clear from my earlier discussion of cross-over. Marjorie Lowenthal and her colleagues (Lowenthal, Thurnher, & Chiriboga, 1975), in a cross-sectional study, found that masculinity was higher for women at midlife than at any other age but did not find a parallel peak in femininity for men. And Carol Erdwins and her colleagues (Erdwins, Tyler, & Mellinger, 1983) found that the highest masculinity scores in their study were recorded by a group of college-age women and the lowest by a group of older homemakers (aged 40 to 75).

One possible explanation for these diverse findings is that the trend toward androgyny in the 40s and 50s noted by several authors is evident particularly in those cohorts born around the 1920s who reached midlife at the time the women's movement was beginning to be strongly felt. For these adults, one could argue that a shift toward expressiveness in men and assertiveness in women reflects social changes and not shared developmental processes. Yet I think even such a cohort difference is consistent with my more basic point that at midlife adults become more open to exploring and expressing whatever aspects of themselves have been previously less expressed. The particular facets of personality that have been less expressed will change from one cohort to the next, from one individual to the next, and from one culture to the next, depending on sex roles, the particular pathway chosen in early adult life, and the temperament or personality with which one begins adulthood. For each person, then, as well as each generation and each culture, the specific manifestations of "increased openness to self" at midlife will differ, even while this basic developmental change may be shared by many adults.

Intriguing as these bits of evidence may be, I cannot leave this discussion without pointing out a strong piece of counter evidence. Schaie (1983b) has found in his cross-sequential Seattle study a fairly steady increase with age in personal rigidity as measured by a standardized test (the rigidity scale of the California Psychological Inventory). Helson and Moane have observed a similar increase: The Mills College women described themselves as less flexible at 43 than they had at 27. It is hard to reconcile "increased openness" with "decreased flexibility," although Helson and Moane found signs of both in the same subjects. The resolution of this apparent paradox will have to await further research.

Increases in the Maturity of Defense Mechanisms The third shift in personality that seems to occur between early and middle adulthood is an increase in the use of what Vaillant would describe as "mature" defense mechanisms. One could argue that this shift is just another facet of increased openness to self, since more mature defense mechanisms generally involve less self-deception, more conscious awareness of one's anxieties and fears. But I list this separately because of the theoretical importance placed on this change by Vaillant and others.

Vaillant's own data provide one set of supportive evidence for such a change. He has drawn upon data from the Grant Study, which included 268 men originally studied when they were Harvard sophomores between 1936 and 1942 (and who were thus born between approximately 1917 and 1922). The men chosen were all thought to be relatively "healthy" and successful as undergraduates, so the sample includes few men who had any serious emotional problems. The men later completed questionnaires annually or biennially and were interviewed at length in 1950 to 1952. Vaillant then interviewed a subsample of 100 men 30 years after they had entered the study, when the men were then in their late 40s or early 50s. The analysis of changes in defense mechanisms was based on scores given by judges who read transcripts of interviews and responses to open-ended questions on the questionnaires. As you can see in Figure 10–5, Vaillant found that with increasing age there was a shift toward more mature defenses and away from immature defenses.

Such a change is replicated in both Haan's assessments of the Berkeley longitudinal subjects and in Helson and Moane's study of the Mills College women. When Haan (1976) analyzed changes in individual Q-sort items rather than in clusters of items, she found decreases with age in self-defensiveness, fantasizing, and projection. Similarly, Helson and Moane (1987) report that the women in their study increased between age 21 and 43 in "coping" skills such as objectivity and intellectuality and decreased in the use of denial and primitive defenses. Thus, we have three quite different studies reporting similar declines in immature defensive patterns between early adulthood and midlife. Both men and women

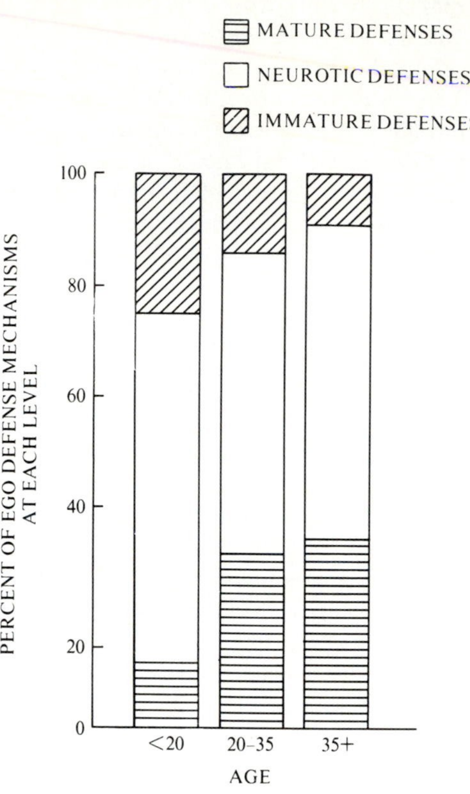

Figure 10–5 These scores on the three categories of defense mechanisms come from analsyses made by Vaillant of the interviews and questionnaires of 100 men in the Grant study who had been followed from college-age to age 50. Immature defenses declined, and mature defenses increased over those years. (Source: From Adaptation to Life by George E. Vaillant. Copyright 1977 by George E. Vaillant. By permission of Little, Brown and Company.)

show this change, and it occurs in adults born in several different cohorts, all of which makes it appear that this is a fairly basic developmental process.

ADDING UP THE PERSONALITY CHANGES FROM EARLY LIFE TO MID-LIFE Taken together these three changes describe a basic shift from a position of conformity to parental or societal expectations toward an exploration of the limits of the self. We see increasing insistence on independence or autonomy, increasing emphasis on personal achievement, increasing self-confidence. To accomplish this change, an adult must become more open to himself, must shift from repression and denial as basic defenses to less distorting defenses such as suppression. The middle-aged adult thus typically has a more complex personality, more individual, more hard-edged.

Changes from Middle to Late Adulthood

From midlife to old age, if there is any common change, it seems to involve a softening of those hard edges, a shift away from the intense preoccupation with achievement and autonomy. What is much less clear is just what the older adult's personality is shifting *toward.* One suggestion comes from Bernice Neugarten (1977), who argues for a shift toward *interiority* in old age. In her view, older adults are less focused on trying to change the world, less "outer directed," more focused on interior processes. Precisely the opposite change has also been argued, namely a shift toward greater concern for others.

Which of these two views (if either) is correct is simply not clear from the available research. We have much less evidence to work with here, especially less longitudinal evidence, and the findings are less consistent. One possibility is that with increasing age, there is simply more and more variability in pathways, so that there is no common set of changes but only individual patterns of coping. Let me give you a sampling of the findings.

Reductions in Achievement/Autonomous Orientation One of the sets of evidence that points to a lessening of emphasis on achievement and autonomy is the data from the Berkeley longitudinal study that you have already seen in Figure 10–2. The figure shows scores not just at midlife but also beyond. You can see that while self-confidence continued to increase, assertiveness peaked at midlife with a subsequent decline, a pattern also clear in Figure 10–4 in Veroff's analysis of men's hope for power motive. Haan has found similar peaks at midlife for a cluster she calls *cognitively committed,* as you can see in Figure 10–6. This cluster seems to tap both aspects of openness and aspects of achievement/independence. It includes high placements of such descriptors as "wide interests," "ambitious," "introspective," "values intellect," and "values independence" and low placement of items such as "conventional" and "submissive." The very clear rise from early to middle adulthood for both men and women on this cluster reinforces the points I have already made about that period. But note that in this cluster, as with the assertiveness cluster, there is decline in the centrality of these qualities after midlife.

There is also some cross-sectional evidence that points in a similar direction—at least for women. For example, in two studies comparing middle-aged and older women, Carol Ryff (Ryff & Baltes, 1976; Ryff, 1982) has found a significant shift from "instrumental" to "terminal" values. Instrumental values relate to desirable modes of conduct (*being* something), such as "ambitious," "capable," or "courageous." Terminal values describe desirable end states of existence (*having* something), such as a sense of accomplishment, freedom, or happiness. In both her studies, Ryff found that women in their 40s and 50s were more likely to select instrumental values, whereas women in their 60s and 70s were more likely to select terminal values. However, Ryff found no such difference in men.

Collectively, (although not uniformly), this evidence points to a peak in "instrumentality" or "agenic" orientation at midlife, with a decline thereafter.

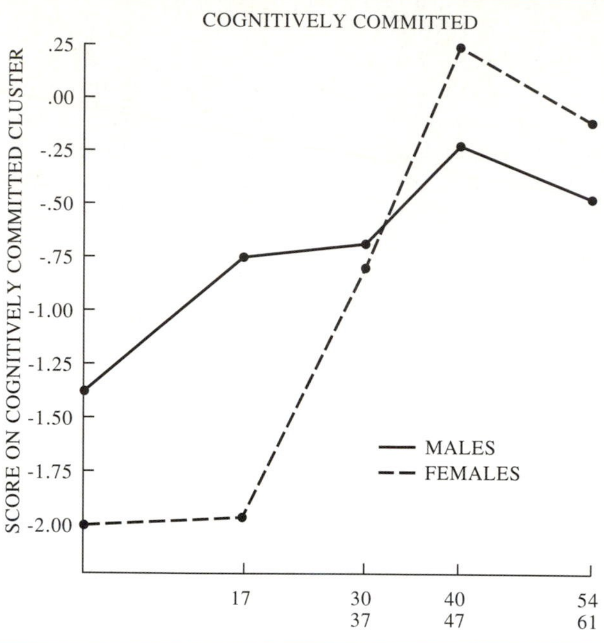

Figure 10–6 *Signs of the reduction in centrality of autonomy and assertiveness come from these data from the Berkeley studies. Those who scored high on the cluster Haan calls cognitively committed were ambitious and introspective, valued intellect and independence, and were low in conventionality and submissivness. These qualities peaked in prominence at midlife and then declined. (Source: Haan, Millsap, & Hartka, 1986, Figure, page 229).*

INCREASED CONCERN FOR OTHERS There is also limited evidence for a shift away from preoccupation with the self and toward concern for others. One bit of information comes from Schaie's major cross-sequential study. Schaie's central concern has been changes in intelligence, as you'll recall from Chapter 6. But Schaie also included some measures of personality in this study, including one he calls *humanitarian concern*. Scores on this measure declined slightly between early and middle adulthood, and then rose steadily from middle to late adulthood. This pattern was found in two separate cross-sectional comparisons and over a seven-year longitudinal interval (Schaie & Parham, 1976).

Consistent with this finding is the fact that older adults are also more generous in contributing to worthy causes—although here the evidence is entirely cross-sectional. In one experiment (Midlarsky & Hannah, 1989), researchers solicited donations for a charity devoted to the welfare of infants with birth defects. Half the time the solicitor was visibly pregnant, half the time she was not. Adults of all ages were more likely to contribute if the solicitor was pregnant, but proportionately more older than younger adults donated under either condition. And when the researchers adjusted for the incomes of the contributors, they found that older adults also gave proportionately more. A 1988 survey by the Gallup organization (Hodgkinson & Weitzman, 1988) shows the same trend: The percentage of household income donated to charity increases steadily with age. Figure 10–7 shows the results from both studies, so you can see the strong similarity in the shape of the curves.

Striking as they are, some caution is in order in interpreting these findings. First and most obviously, these are all cross-sectional comparisons. We can't be sure whether this apparent age-linked pattern reflects some underlying developmental change, or whether it reflects changes in society such that current older adults are more likely to have grown up placing a high value on generosity. It may also reflect greater disposable income among older adults.

There are some other flies in this ointment as well. The Gallup survey did *not* show that older adults were more likely to do volunteer work; the peak of

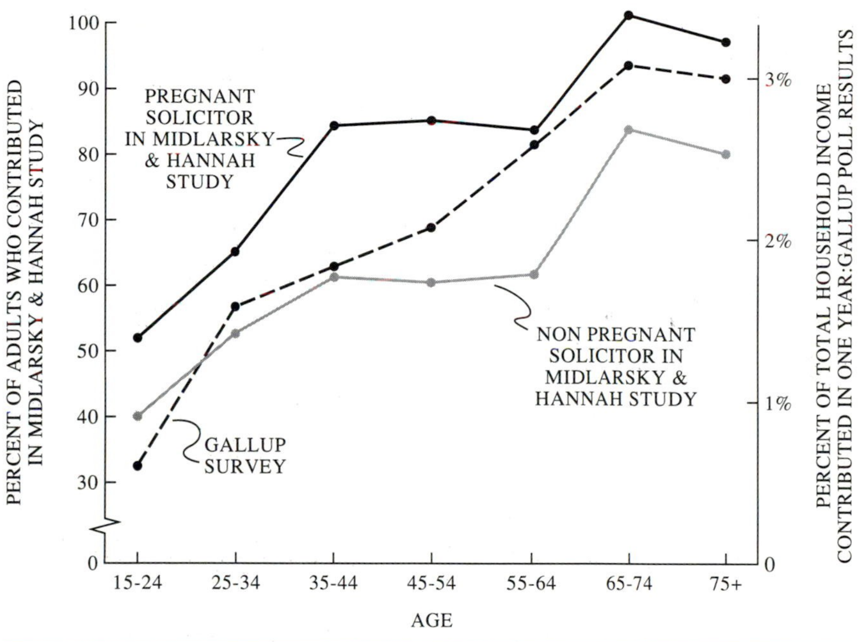

Figure 10–7 *Financial generosity is higher among older adults, a pattern confirmed by two separate sets of data shown in this figure. The two lines marked "pregnant solicitor" and "nonpregnant solicitor" represent findings from a study by Midlarsky and Hannah in which adults of various ages were approached for donations for an organization devoted to fighting birth defects. Half the time the solicitor was pregnant, half the time not. The line marked "Gallup Survey" shows the average percent of charitable contributions per household as a function of the age of the head of household, based on a nationally representative sample interviewed in 1987. In both cases, there is a clear increase in contributions with age. (Sources: Midlarsky & Hannah, 1989, Table 1, p. 349; Hodgkinson, Weitaman, and the Gallup Organization, reported in U.S. Bureau of the Census, 1989a, Table 615, p. 371).*

volunteer work occurred among those aged 35 to 44. So if older adults are more "other-oriented," it is not reflected in all aspects of their behavior.

Further counterevidence comes from a study by Carol Ryff (1989), who interviewed middle-aged and older adults at length about their current life, their past life experiences, and their ideas about what made up a good life. *Both* age groups emphasized an orientation toward others, including being a compassionate, caring person and having good relationships as being central to their sense of well-being. At the same time, Ryff found that the middle-aged but not the older subjects emphasized self-confidence, self-acceptance, and self-knowledge as important aspects of their sense of well-being. So in this study, there was a difference between the two age groups that is consistent with the peaking of achievement/confidence qualities in midlife, but there is little indication here that older adults place more value on compassion or caring for others than do the middle-aged.

Given this mixture of findings, the best I can say is that the jury is still out on the hypothesis that in later adulthood there is a shift toward greater concern for others.

INCREASE IN INTERIORITY The jury is similarly still out on Neugarten's hypothesis of increased interiority in old age. In support of the hypothesis is the finding from several cross-sectional studies that introversion increases slightly over the adult years (e.g., Costa, et al., 1986; Leon, Gillum, Gillum, & Gouze, 1979). On the other side of the scale is once again research by Carol Ryff (Ryff, 1984; Ryff & Heincke, 1983). She asked young, middle-aged, and old adults to describe their current selves, and to describe themselves as they had been at earlier points. She could find no age differences at all on her measures of interiority, either in the subjects' descriptions of their current selves, or in their recollections of themselves at earlier ages.

Adding to the confusion is a set of studies, both cross-sectional and longitudinal, all using standardized pencil and paper instruments as assessments of personality, that show no age differences in personality at all. Schaie and Parham, for example (1976), found no differences on 18 of the 19 measures they used; only the measure of humanitarian concern showed changes with age. Similarly, Ilene Siegler and her coworkers (Siegler, George, & Okun, 1979) found no changes in personality over the eight years of the Duke longitudinal study on a measure called the Cattell 16 Personality Factor test. These adults were 46 to 69 at the start of the study, 54 to 77 at the end, so the relevant age range is certainly being sampled. Other investigators have found no changes with age in an individual's tendency to attribute events to internal versus external controls (Pitcher, Spykerman, & Gazi-Tabatabaie, 1987).

Explaining the Changes in Personality over Adulthood

Making sense of this patchwork of findings is no small task. I need to try to explain both the patterns that do seem to exist and to account for the ones that do not.

Three types of explanation are available. First, I can appeal to methodological differences or flaws in the various studies. Second, I can examine the potential impact of role changes on personality. And third, I can go back to the theories I described in Chapter 3 and see if any of them does a decent job of encompassing the various research findings.

Methodological Explanations

TYPES OF MEASUREMENT As I look over the array of evidence, I note that those studies showing no change with age (e.g. Siegler, George, & Okun, 1979) and those reporting the most discrepant findings (e.g., Leon et al., 1979; Schaie, 1983b) are those in which personality has been measured with standardized pencil and paper tests. In contrast, studies in which researchers have derived scores from open-ended written comments or from extensive interviews have generally shown systematic and reasonably consistent age effects. Since part of what I am searching for in these data is some indication of whether or not the basic *structure* of personality changes rather than simply whether some traits have increased or decreased, I am inclined to place greater faith in those studies that have tested both broadly and deeply, including (for example) Haan's study of the Berkeley samples, the AT&T studies, Vaillant's analysis of the Grant study sample, and Ryff's research on self-perceived change. The Q-sort data, for example, tell us something about changes in structure of personality, as may Vaillant's analysis of changes in defense mechanisms. My preference for these more depth-oriented studies is obviously a matter of taste. Other psychologists may wish to place much greater weight on those studies in which reliable, standardized instruments were used and may thus conclude that there is little evidence for age changes in personality.

COHORT DIFFERENCES The other obvious methodological point is one that has surely occurred to you. The differences between one study and the next, and the reported age differences themselves, may reflect basically cohort differences rather than shared developmental patterns. I cannot reject this explanation out of hand, but I think a good case can be made for the more general validity of at least some of the changes I have described, particularly the increase between early adulthood and midlife in achievement/independence/autonomy. My argument rests on two facts: First, we now have a number of longitudinal studies involving cohorts born over nearly a 40-year period, including both men and women, both working class and middle class. Samples of adults from each of these cohorts have shown similar changes. Second, if cohort differences were the key factor, then the sorts of social changes we have seen in recent years, with women moving into the labor force and into high achievement jobs more and more, should create precisely the opposite pattern from the one we observe: Current *young* women should show *higher* levels of achievement and independence striving than current middle-aged women, since the latter groups are part of a cohort that placed much less emphasis on independent work.

This is not to say that some specific findings may not be particularly vulnerable to a cohort-differences explanation. The age difference in generosity is one obvious example. But I am not persuaded that cohort differences can explain the pattern of findings I have described to you.

Role Changes as Explanation of Personality Differences

If, then, we assume that there are some real age changes in personality left to account for, what are the alternative explanations? The most obvious possibility is that the horse pulling this particular cart is the set of changes in sex, work, and family roles I described in Chapters 7 and 9. Avshalom Caspi and Glen Elder say:

> Successful transitions to age-graded roles are the core developmental tasks faced by the individual across the life course. The corresponding agenda for personality psychology is to examine how individuals confront, adapt, and make adjustments to age-graded roles and transitions. (1988, pp. 120–121)

Several lines of argument can be mustered in support of role changes as the driving force in personality change in adulthood. First, there are some obvious parallels between the overall shape of the pattern of role acquisitions that I talked about in Chapter 7 and in Chapter 9 and the shape of changes in personality I have been discussing here. In early adulthood, we must learn and combine a series of hugely complex roles—adult sex roles, worker, spouse, parent. We try to fit ourselves into those roles, to conform to their demands. The emphasis is thus less on individuality or personal achievement and more on adapting to external expectations. The power of that external set of definitions seems to wane as we learn the roles themselves and discover the flexibilities in them, the ways we can bend the rules to fit our own situations. By our 30s, certainly by our early 40s, our own individuality is more dominant, hence the shift on measures of personality toward greater individual achievement motivation, greater independence and autonomy, greater emphasis on personal mastery. One woman of 41, an interior designer interviewed by Amia Lieblich (1986) put it this way:

> I never did anything that wasn't the thing to do. I feel I have not developed due to the limitations . . . which I have accepted for myself—female limitations, personal limitations, and being married limitations. Now, I will take the freedom to pursue whatever job I want to pursue, and if we can set it up being married, fine, and if I can't set it up being married, also fine. (p. 307)

A friend of mine, a man now 51 whose four children are finally all out of college and more or less launched, described a similar thought:

> This is really the first time in my life that I have felt I could choose what I wanted to do. Once I got married and the kids were born I really didn't have many choices. Sure, I chose this particular job, but not because it was the very best job I could have had. We moved here because my wife hated where we lived and said that either we moved or she would. Now I feel I can really do some things because *I* want to.

As the roles are learned and as the demands of the various roles of early adulthood diminish, there is simply more room for individuality.

If this argument is valid, then we ought to find that the types of changes in personality I have been describing are linked to role transitions or role statuses and not to age. Several sources of data point to just such a conclusion.

One particularly interesting bit of evidence comes from a study by Rochelle Harris, Abbie Ellicott, and David Holmes (1986) of 60 women, aged 36 to 60, each of whom provided detailed retrospective descriptions of their lives, their feelings, their inner experiences, over the period from their early 30s to the present. Raters then searched the transcripts for evidence of major personal transitions—major changes in life structure in Levinson's terms. Eighty percent of the women reported at least one such transition, nearly all of them linked to some particular stage in the family life cycle rather than to age. Table 10.4 summarizes the results. What is especially interesting here is not only that these transitions were linked to role changes, but that the content of the transitions at the launching and postparental stages sounds so much like the personality changes at midlife I have already described. Since, on average, these two life cycle stages are likely to occur at roughly midlife, these findings suggest that, for women at least, the shift toward greater individuality, greater assertiveness, greater achievement orientation may be caused by changes in family roles that accompany grown children's departure from home.

Another way to separate out the effects of age and role changes as they affect personality is to look at groups of adults of roughly the same age who occupy

TABLE 10.4. Link Between Family Life Cycle Stages and Personal Transitions in Harris, Ellicott, and Holmes' Study of Middle-Aged Women.

Family life cycle stage	Percentage of women who described a major personal transition during that phase	Reported content of the transition
Newborns/preschoolers development	28%	Reduced personal life satisfaction; reduced number of friendships
Launching period stability	48%	End of period of increased introspection; inner change; increased assertiveness
Postparental phase	33%	General personality change; ending period of stability; increased introspection; increased assertiveness.

SOURCE: Harris, Ellicott, & Holmes, 1986.

different roles, such as women who work outside the home and those who do not. In one set of studies of this type, Carol Erdwins (Erdwins & Mellinger, 1984; Erdwins, Tyler, & Mellinger, 1983) has found that a woman's employment status is a better predictor of personality or motivation than is age. Full time homemakers in these studies had higher affiliation motives than did married or single working women, regardless of age. The working women, of all ages, tended to be higher on self-acceptance, autonomy, and achievement via independence.

Further evidence that work status, or work commitment, is a critical variable in personality comes from Joseph Veroff's study of motives (Veroff et al., 1984). Recall that he found that affiliation motives declined from early to middle adulthood among women but not among men. To try to understand that pattern, Veroff looked in more detail at two subgroups: women in his samples who were highly work-committed, and men who were weakly work-committed. In contrast to the patterns for the samples as a whole, Veroff found that the work-committed women showed no change in affiliative motivation over age, while the low work-committed men showed the "feminine" pattern of declining affiliation with age.

Veroff's explanation of these findings is that the traditional woman's role sequence is associated with maximum role uncertainty and anxiety in the 20s and early 30s, when women are struggling to juggle several conflicting roles—to learn to become a good mother, to be a wife at the same time, often to be a worker, too. When anxiety or uncertainty is high, people turn to their family or to friends, thus showing high affiliation. As women move through adulthood, however, the uncertainty and the anxiety decline as they learn the roles and as some of the roles are subtracted, such as the day-to-day care of infants or young children. Women's affiliation needs would thus go down with age. For men, in contrast, role uncertainty and anxiety remain at about the same level throughout the working life, so we should not see any age-related pattern in affiliation for most men. The fact that work-committed women show this "male" pattern thus makes sense. Men low in work commitment, on the other hand, may be affected by their nonwork roles in the same way as are most women.

The need for power, in contrast, may peak at midlife precisely because this is the point in most men's careers when they experience a loss of authority or power in their jobs—the point when the career has reached a plateau, and they doubt their effectiveness. If this argument is correct, then we should find that men whose careers peak earlier than this show a peak in the power motive at that same earlier point, while men whose careers continue to be more and more successful into their 50s and 60s should show no reduction in the power motive. Veroff's data are not detailed enough to allow him to test this possibility. It would make an interesting subject for future research.

Other differences in roles or life experiences, such as divorce, may also have a major impact on personality, as Helson has been able to demonstrate in the Mills study. She compared the personality patterns of two groups of women who had both followed a feminine social clock: those who were later divorced, and those who stayed in unrewarding marriages. Women in the former group appeared to have been pushed into a new personality organization by the divorce. They increased in self-control and in psychological mindedness (a tendency to introspect and analyze their own and others' behavior) after the divorce. Those women who stuck with bad marriages—who remained in the same basic roles, ungratifying as they might have been—showed a loss of poise, confidence, empathy, sociability, and sense of well-being over time.

Have I convinced you? Certainly, all of this evidence makes a strong case for the primary causal effect of role changes and role sequences in shaping the personality changes we see over the adult years. But there is another side to the argument too.

First of all, it is clear that roles alone do not impose personality patterns on adults. The very fact that there is strong consistency in personality in at least some traits tells us that much. Furthermore, I already pointed out that one reason for such consistency is that individuals *choose* roles and role patterns that are consistent with their existing personality. Recall, for example, the finding from Helson's study of the Mills women (Helson, Mitchell, & Moane, 1984) that shows that those who followed the feminine social clock differed in initial personality from those who followed the masculine social clock. The latter group, at 21, was more dominant, independent, and sociable. Taken in this light, Carol Erdwin's research does not necessarily prove that the working role pushes women toward greater assertiveness; equally likely is that more assertive women choose to work. If the latter is true, then we are left with no obvious explanation for the average rise in assertiveness and autonomy with age among women (or men). Similarly, if it is the reduction in the potency or demand of the various key social roles that allows the flowering of individuality in midlife, then why isn't there still further flowering of the same kind of independence/autonomy/achievement-orientation in late life, when social roles become markedly less prominent? What role change produces the *decline* in autonomy and assertiveness after midlife? One could appeal to work roles as key ingredients in this second change, much as Veroff has based his explanation of the change in power motives in men on the peaking of work status. But it is difficult to account for the findings from the Berkeley study in that way, since the women in the cohorts included in this study mostly did not work outside the home and certainly experienced no "peak" of work accomplishment at midlife. Yet they, too, showed a drop in assertiveness and cognitive commitment after middle age.

Even more striking are the results of a second study by Harris and Holmes and their coworkers (Reinke, Holmes, & Harris, 1985) of a group of women aged 30 to 45. Detailed retrospective interviews with these women revealed that in this group, unlike the older women in the parallel Harris, Ellicott, and Holmes study I already described, it was age and not family life cycle stage that predicted personal transitions. Seventy-eight percent of these women reported a transition between the ages of 27 and 30. Such a transition was more common among those women who worked outside the home than among those who did not, but was equally common among those with and without children and did not vary as a function of the age of the children.

> For many women this time of life [age 30] was characterized by disruption of one's previous sense of self, altering one's aims and seeking something for self, and

> finally the emergence of increased feelings of personal competence and confidence. (p. 1359)

This basic finding of a widely shared transition at roughly age 30 is replicated in an analysis by Priscilla Roberts and Peter Newton (1987) of the lives of 39 women who had been interviewed in depth as part of several unpublished smaller studies. Of those women who were over 30 at the time of the interview, all but one described a major transition between 27 and 32, typically characterized as a process of "individuation."

Of course, these findings do not tell us that there is something inherent in being biologically 30 that causes a change in personality. It may well be that in our society, at this time in history, age 30 has been invested with a particular kind of social significance that causes adults to rethink their priorities at that age. We may perceive that "over 30" is a different state, even a different role, than "under 30." In that sense, these two studies might be seen as consistent with a role-change explanation of personality change. Yet it is still true that in these two studies, family role changes in these young adult women were not associated with changes in personality, while age was.

If I take all this evidence together, there seems little doubt that differences in role patterns, in the specific sequence and the timing of the sequence of role changes, have an impact on personality and motivation. Most adults enter several role "streams" in their early 20s and are carried along those streams for at least the next 30 or 40 years. The fact that many of us are in the same streams means that there are likely to be shared changes in personality or motives roughly correlated with age. All of this is important. But I am not convinced that it is the whole story. There seem to me to be deeper changes going on, changes that may be triggered by role changes for some adults or may trigger role changes in others. It is just such deeper change that is hypothesized by various theories of personality development.

Theoretical Explanations

Aside from Vaillant's basic theoretical proposal that (at least some) adults become more psychologically mature as they get older—a proposal supported by the research results I have reported—there are three theories we need to take a look at. Two you have met before; one I have not yet described.

Erikson's Theory of Identity Development Certainly, the most familiar theory of adult personality change is Erikson's. You will remember that he proposes three basic stages in adulthood: intimacy versus isolation in the early years of adulthood, generativity versus stagnation in the middle years, and ego integrity versus despair in late life. Erikson suggests that the central issues of each of these stages are brought to the fore by essentially universal experiences of adulthood: the need to create a lasting central relationship with a mate, the need to bear and rear children and to take one's place—and make one's mark—in adult society, and the need to come to terms with one's own mortality.

If you think about the various patterns of personality change in adult life that I've been describing, you'll see that there is at least a rough correspondence between those changes and Erikson's three stages. At the very least, there is some sign that there may be three basic steps or stages involved, one in early adulthood, one in middle adulthood, and one in late life. But it is not so clear to me that the specifics of Erikson's stages, particularly his stage of generativity, are a very good match to the data. As I pointed out in Chapter 3, Erikson does talk about generativity not just in terms of bearing and rearing children but also of generating ideas or products. But the quality of "passing on the flame" that is central to the stage of generativity does not seem to me to be quite the same as the intensification of individuality at midlife that is most consistently shown in the research findings. Generativity, as Erikson has described it, has an outward-directed quality that is quite opposite to what we see in studies of early and middle adult life.

On the other hand, Erikson's description of the final stage of ego integrity seems to capture many of the contradictions in the findings; both interiority or increased concern for others can be encompassed in the concept of integrity.

Abraham Maslow's Hierarchy of Needs

A quite different approach comes from Abraham Maslow (1968, 1970a, 1970b, 1971), a psychologist who traces his theoretical roots to Freud and other psychoanalytic thinkers and who has offered some highly original insights.

Maslow's most central concern has been with the development of motives or needs, which he divides into two main groups: **deficiency motives** (also called D-motives) in contrast to **growth motives** or **being motives** (also called B-motives). Deficiency motives involve instincts or drives to correct imbalance or to maintain physical or emotional homeostasis, such as getting enough to eat, satisfying thirst, or obtaining enough love and respect from others. Deficiency motives are found in all animals. Being motives, in contrast, are distinctly human. Maslow argues that humans have unique desires to discover and understand, to give love to others, and to push for the optimum fulfillment of their inner potentials.

In general, the satisfaction of deficiency motives prevents illness, or cures illness, or recreates homeostasis (inner balance). In contrast, the satisfaction of being motives produces positive health. The distinction is like the "difference between fending off threat or attack, and positive triumph and achievement" (Maslow, 1968, p. 32).

But being motives are quite fragile and do not typically emerge until well into adulthood, and then only under supportive circumstances. Maslow's widely quoted needs hierarchy (Figure 10–8) reflects this aspect of his thinking. The lowest four levels all describe different deficiency needs, while only the need for self-actualization is a being motive. Further, Maslow proposes that these five levels emerge sequentially in development and tend to dominate the system from the bottom up. That is, if you are starving, the physiological needs dominate. If you are being physically battered, the safety needs dominate. The need for self-actualization only emerges when all four types of deficiency needs are largely satisfied.

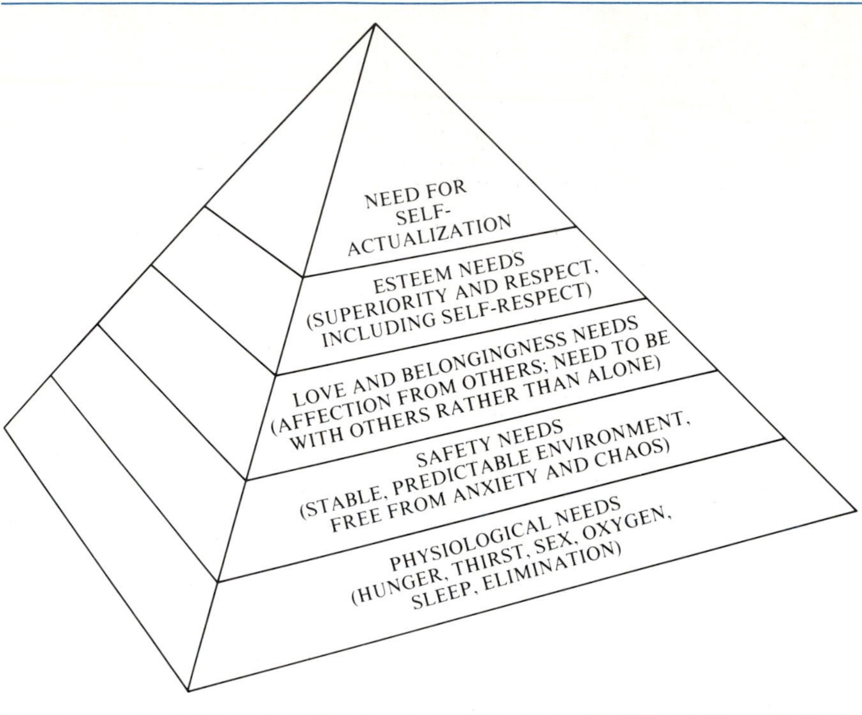

Figure 10–8 Maslow's Need Hierachy. Maslow proposed that these needs dominate the system from the bottom up, with higher level needs only becoming prominent later in life and only when (or if) the lower needs were largely satisfied. (Source: Maslow, 1968, 1970b).

To understand Maslow's theory you need to have a fuller sense of his concept of self-actualization and of the self-actualizing person. His interest was in positive health, in genuine growth, not simply in the avoidance of illness or the creation of stability. So he sought to understand the personality and characteristics of those few adults who seemed to have risen to the top of the need hierarchy and to have achieved significant levels of self-understanding and expression—individuals like Eleanor Roosevelt, Albert Schweitzer, Albert Einstein, or Thomas Jefferson. Some of the key characteristics of such individuals, as Maslow saw them, are listed in Table 10.5.

As you read this list, you may wonder whether anyone—short of sainthood—is really like this! In fact, Maslow thought that complete self-actualization was quite rare and likely to occur only quite late in life. But he believed that many adults, as they move into their middle years, may come to display at least a few of these characteristics, gradually adding more and more as lower level needs are satisfied and as the need for self-actualization comes to dominate the motive system. Yet those adults whose environments or relationships do not adequately satisfy their lower level needs rarely experience the press of the need for self-actualization and may show few of these qualities.

TABLE 10.5. Some of the Characteristics of the Self-Actualizing Person As Proposed by Maslow.

Accurate perception of reality	The person is relatively free of defensive distortions or self-delusion and sees others and the environment clearly.
Acceptance of self and others	The person is more tolerant of both himself and others, accepting frailty as well as strength, generally lacking shame or anxiety about himself.
Spontaneity and self-knowledge	These individuals are quite "natural," perhaps even eccentric in their behavior and life style, since they are not constrained by fear of what others will think of them. They know themselves well and follow that understanding.
Problem centering	Despite their high level of self-knowledge, self-actualizing persons are typically not very introspective or "self-centered." Rather, they are typically involved in external problems and may have a consuming mission in life involving wide philosophical or ethical issues.
Freshness of appreciation and richness of emotional response	Self-actualizers live rich emotional lives and have the capacity to see things freshly, to experience again and again the wonder and joy of existence or the intensity of pain.
Peak experience	A peak experience, in Maslow's language, is a brief (or prolonged) mystical moment, a sense of perfection or a momentary loss of the sense of separate self, a submersion in a sense of unity. It may occur during sex, during creativity, in profound insight such as a scientific discovery, or in meditation or prayer.
Social interest	Self-actualizing individuals have deep sympathy and compassion for their fellow beings and a strong desire to help others.
Deep, loving personal relationships	Personal relationships with spouse and close friends tend to be extremely deep and not motivated by deficiency love needs. Sex is seen as meaningless without love; they are attracted to others who display goodness and considerateness.
Need for privacy	Paradoxically, self-actualizing adults also have stronger than normal needs for time alone, for solitude. There is a kind of emotional detachment that characterizes these individuals, even while their relationships are extremely loving.
Creativity	Every self-actualizing person Maslow studied displayed some unusual form of creativity, whether artistic or otherwise.
Sense of humor	These adults dislike humor that involves making fun of others. Their humor may take the form of anecdotes, but does not involve sarcasm.

SOURCE: Maslow, 1968.

Maslow's theory of motives has had little scientific testing, in part because it has not been stated with great precision, and he developed no methods of assessing the dominance of the various motives he proposed. The theory has nonetheless been widely influential, perhaps because there is a certain ring of truth to it—a ring of truth reinforced by the correspondences between the sequence of motives Maslow proposes and the research findings I have described in this chapter. Collectively, these findings could be interpreted as showing that love and belongingness needs dominate in early adulthood, esteem needs dominate up to and through midlife, and self-actualizing needs become prominent for at least some adults in late life. On the whole, I think that describing the personality changes that seem to occur in one's 30s and 40s in terms of dominance of esteem needs comes closer to the mark than describing them in terms of increased generativity.

Even better, in my view, is Loevinger's theory.

LOEVINGER'S STAGES OF EGO DEVELOPMENT. Go back and look at Table 3.2, which summarizes Loevinger's proposed stages. She argues that each of these stages involves a basic structural change, a fundamental shift in the way the individual experiences and understands his relationships and his world. Unlike Erikson, who thought that all adults eventually face all the key developmental dilemmas whether they have successfully worked out the earlier ones or not, Loevinger does not assume that all adults move through the sequence of stages she describes. What she proposes instead is that *if* an individual's personality changes, it will change in a particular sequence, moving from dominance by social roles and conventionality to increasing individuality and autonomy, and then toward increasing awareness of inner complexities.

In early adulthood, most adults are at the *conformist* stage, characterized by an external definition of what is good or right, and a desire to live up to the expectations of the group to which one belongs. Note that Loevinger is not saying that all conformist behavior is the *same*. Rather, she is saying that each of us goes through a period in which we understand ourselves and experience ourselves in relation to group norms. If all your peers are going to college and then combining work and motherhood, that may be the norm to which you conform. But if your peers (and parents) value the role of full time homemaker, you will be likely to follow that path and derive your values and your motives from that role pattern.

Some adults remain in this pattern for all of their lives. But others, because the roles do not fit, or because some kind of trauma shatters the system, or because of some inner push toward greater self-understanding, gradually move away from this external definition of self toward what Loevinger calls the *conscientious* and *individualistic* stages. Adults who make this transition struggle to find some internal definition, to discover who they are and what they can do independent of others' expectations and definitions. In the process, adults often become focused on success or on striving, because these are ways of asserting and exploring their own individuality. At this stage, being uncomfortable with the dependence involved, many adults also show some turning away from relationships.

Daniel Levinson (1978) uses the term *detribalization* to describe this same underlying shift from external to internal definition of the self. At midlife, he says, the adult

> . . . becomes more critical of the tribe—the particular groups, institutions and traditions that have the greatest significance for him, the social matrix to which he

> is most attached. He is less dependent upon tribal rewards, more questioning of tribal values, more able to look at life from a universalistic perspective. (p. 242)

The 41-year-old designer I quoted a few pages ago is describing a kind of detribalization when she talks about rejecting the limitations of her earlier life and striking out for the job she really wants.

Loevinger proposes that there are still further stages, such as the autonomous stage, in which some adults reach a degree of security and comfort in their own independence/autonomy that allows them to turn outward, toward helping others, toward "humanitarian concern."

To me, this theoretical model comes closer than any of the others to encompassing the various research findings I have described. In particular, the transition from conformist to conscientious or individualistic stages sounds very like the basic shift toward greater individuality, autonomy, and self-confidence that seems to occur between early and middle adulthood. The hints of greater openness to inner feelings and more mature defense mechanisms would also be consistent with the shift Loevinger describes.

Depending on the role patterns they have chosen or have been thrust into, men and women may display this change quite differently. Individuality for the man, or for the woman who has initially conformed to a masculine social clock, may be expressed in high achievement strivings or a motive for power; for women who began by conforming to a more traditional female role sequence, the midlife individuality may be expressed in changing patterns of interaction within the family, such as reduced nurturance, or in reduced reliance on friendships. A woman need not abandon her family roles in order to become more individualistic, but she may redefine them.

In later life, too, we find some confirmation for Loevinger's model in the signs of a move away from this heightened individuality and toward a broader set of concerns. These patterns make at least some sense if we think of the midlife period, when the conscientious stage and the individualistic level are likely to be achieved, as one in which the person attempts to *do* things, to have an effect on the world, be it in work or in family life. For those who make the transition to the autonomous stage, the later life period is more focused on *being*, on acceptance of the self, on what Erikson calls ego integrity.

Since Loevinger does not think that all adults move all the way through this sequence of stages, relatively few adults will reach the level of an autonomous ego structure. In this theory, age is only a very rough correlate of the kind of personality and motivational changes Loevinger is describing. Given that assumption, then, the older the group you study the more variability there should be in the stages or levels represented in the sample. Thus, while the transition from conformist to individualistic stages should be fairly widespread, the later shift toward autonomy should be much more difficult to detect. The lack of consistency in the results for older adults is thus to be expected. Whether a particular pattern is found or not will depend very heavily on the particular subjects studied.

Loevinger's theory can also help us to understand some of the processes of self-selection of roles and pathways. As one example, Helson (Helson et al., 1984) offers the hypothesis that those women in her study who followed the masculine social clock were already, at 20, beyond the conformist stage. Those women who chose to follow the most traditional feminine social clock, in contrast, appeared to be very much in the conformist stage and tended to remain there unless forced out of that position by some major life change such as divorce.

I do not want to suggest that every piece of evidence on personality change and continuity in adulthood can be fitted tidily under the umbrella of this or any other single theory. There remain some glaring contradictions, most notably the increase in personal rigidity with age that Schaie found for both men and women (Schaie, 1983b). Erikson, Maslow, and Loevinger would all doubtless predict the opposite, at least for some older adults. I am suggesting that theories such as Loevinger's may provide some insight into the underlying pattern of personality change that lies behind the surface diversity. Changes in family roles, gender roles, or work roles, and major life changes such as divorce or the death of a spouse can all be catalysts for change. But what theory can suggest to us is the *direction* or *sequence* such change is likely to follow.

I am also suggesting that it would be extremely fruitful if theoretical models like these were more often used as a basis for research designs. Simply using a standardized pencil and paper test of personality on adults of varying ages, without taking varying role patterns or personality structure into consideration, is not going to lead to much insight. We might, as one example, look at the later life personality changes in adults who are at varying stages at midlife. Do middle-aged adults at the conformist stage have different experiences of later life than do those at the conscientious or individualist stages? We might also ask what sorts of life experiences are likely to trigger a transition to a new stage. Are normative role transitions enough? Or does it take some more dramatic or traumatic event to stimulate a change? Perhaps the sort of mismatch between personality and role demands that Florine Livson studied in the Berkeley subjects (and that I described in Chapter 7) is enough to trigger change. Certainly in Livson's study, those who experienced such a mismatch not only went through a time of upheaval, they seemed to come out on the other side with a different structuring of personality.

I could multiply these examples at length, but I hope the basic point is clear: In the study of personality, as in many other areas of the study of adult development, we need a better marriage between theory and research if we are to understand the basic processes.

Summary of Age Changes in Personality and Motivation

As usual, I've summarized the age changes in a Table (10.6). It is clear from the table that in early adulthood, age is a fairly decent predictor of the personality changes we see, perhaps because the timing of major role changes is more widely shared in early adulthood than later, or simply because many more adults make the basic transition from conformist to individualist perspectives than is true for

TABLE 10.6. Summary of Age Changes in Personality and Motivation.

Age 20–40	Age 40–65	Age 65+
Over these years, an increase from low to higher levels of autonomy, achievement orientation, independence, self-confidence, cognitive commitment, assertiveness	Peak levels of assertiveness, cognitive commitment, achievement, autonomy reached in midlife, after which a decline begins in these traits	Declines in assertiveness, cognitive commitment, achievement, autonomy, etc. from the midlife peak
Increase from low to higher levels of openness to self	High levels of openness to self	No evidence on whether such openness remains or increases in later years
High levels of immature and low levels of mature defenses	Increase in mature defenses, decrease in immature defenses	No evidence on whether there is continued increase in maturity of defenses, although such an increase would be suggested by theory
Low levels of humanitarian concern; lower levels of generosity toward others	Medium levels of humanitarian concern and generosity, although peak in volunteering time for charity	Highest levels of humanitarian concern and generosity
Lowest levels of personal rigidity	Medium levels of rigidity	Highest levels of personal rigidity

later transitions. Whatever the reason, there are far fewer widely shared changes in personality past midlife.

One of the possible changes in old-age, to which I have given little attention in this chapter, is an increased emphasis on issues of meaning. Do adults in their later years become sufficiently freed of the constraints of individual roles or circumstances to allow them to become concerned with wider-reaching metaphysical issues, with the nature of personal integration (as Erikson suggests) or the meaning of life?

It is precisely to this question of the development of meaning or wisdom over the adult years that Chapter 11 is addressed. So read on.

Summary

1. As we move through adulthood, each of us has both the sense of self-continuity and a sense of personal change. We both stay the same and develop.

2. Virtually all the information we have about consistency in personality or motives concerns correlational consistency, although there is also limited evidence about both pattern and trait consistency.
3. Clear evidence for stability of personality over the years of adulthood is available for the traits of extraversion and neuroticism. Consistency on other traits has also been reported in individual studies, such as the cluster of "cognitively committed" from the Berkeley studies.
4. At least some of the observed personality consistency appears to have a genetic basis. Twins studies show that identical twins are more like one another than fraternal twins on measures of extraversion and neuroticism.
5. Consistency is also fostered by the fact that the consequences of individual actions accumulate over time and by the fact that each adult tends to choose situations and create patterns of interaction that will tend to support her or his existing qualities.
6. Personality change over the adult years has also been demonstrated, although both the amount and the nature of the change seem clearer in early than in late adulthood.
7. Between early adulthood and middle life, adults show three types of changes: (a) an increase in a cluster of behaviors related to individuality, including achievement strivings, autonomy, independence, confidence, and self-esteem, (b) an increase in openness to self, and (c) an increase in mature defense mechanisms and a decrease in immature forms. Of these three, the evidence is clearest for the first, least clear for the second.
8. Evidence demonstrating these changes comes from several longitudinal studies describing adults from several different cohorts, so there is some reason to have confidence in the generality of the findings.
9. Between midlife and old age the changes in personality are less clear. There are signs that individuality peaks in midlife and declines thereafter, and some indications that older adults may be more altruistic, more concerned for others. Paradoxically, there are also signs of greater interiority.
10. Several explanations of these patterns of change in personality are available. They may be due to methodological problems with the research, such as imprecision of measures based on interviews, or cohort differences, although these possibilities seem largely unpersuasive.
11. Personality change may also be caused (and explained) by changes in family, work, and gender roles. Some research suggests that personality differences are more strongly related to variations in role occupancy than they are to age, although the reverse has also been found. The shift from the primacy of roles in early adulthood to a midlife state in which roles are both looser and better learned is certainly consistent with the observed changes in personality, although which is cause and which is effect is not clear.
12. Some explanation of the observed changes may also be found in theory, such as particularly Jane Loevinger's model of personality change. In her terms, the changes involve a fairly widespread shift from a conformist to an individualistic model between early and middle adulthood, followed by a much less common shift to an autonomous stage in later life.

Suggested Readings

There are a great many popular books that touch on this subject (including Sheehy's Passages), *but few seem to me to be worth recommending, other than Vaillant's* Adaptation to Life, *and Gould's* Transformations, *which I recommended in Chapter 3. For those of you interested in more personal accounts of some of these transitions, Bender's book (listed below) might be an intriguing place to start. In the other direction lie a great many more technical and methodologically complex sources, of which the Eichorn et al. and Schaie books listed below might be useful next steps.*

BENDER, S. (1989). *Plain and simple. A woman's journey to the Amish.* San Francisco: Harper & Row. I found this book deeply touching, not only as a highly personal description of one person's struggle with the transition from an individualistic to a more integrated perspective but also in its descriptions of life in an Amish family. The book is like its title: plain and simple—short, clear, highly provocative.

KOGAN, N. (1990). Personality and aging. In J. E. Birren & K. W. Schaie (Eds.), *Handbook of the psychology of aging* (3rd ed.). San Diego: Academic Press. This current, brief review of the research on personality change and continuity over adulthood covers many of the same points I have made in this chapter, albeit in more technical language. It would be an excellent source of current references if you wish to pursue this subject.

EICHORN, D. H., CLAUSEN, J. A., HAAN, N., HONZIK, M. P., & MUSSEN, P. H. (Eds.). (1981). *Present and past in middle life.* New York: Academic Press. This book contains the bulk of the most current reports of the findings from the Berkeley and Oakland longitudinal studies through the midlife measurement point. It assumes some knowledge of statistics but most chapters are quite clearly written. If you want information about the measurements at age 55 to 60, take a look at Norma Haan's 1986 paper cited in the bibliography at the end of this book.

SCHAIE, K. W. (ED.). (1983c). *Longitudinal studies of adult psychological development.* New York: Guilford Press. Included in this book are reports of many of the most complete and interesting longitudinal studies covering intellectual and personality change in adulthood. Schaie's own study is described here, as is the AT&T study, the Duke study, and several others.

CHAPTER 11

The Growth of Meaning

Why a Chapter on the Growth of Meanings?

In the last chapter, I talked about changes in personality and self-actualization, which is certainly one aspect of inner development or growth in adulthood. But there is another aspect to inner development—perhaps more speculative but certainly no less vital to most of us—that touches on questions of meaning, of purpose, of human potential. As we move through adulthood, do we interpret our experiences differently? Do we attach different meanings, understand our world in new ways? Do we become wiser, or less worldly, or perhaps more spiritual?

Certainly a link between advancing age and increasing wisdom has been part of the folk tradition in virtually every culture in the world, as evidenced by fairy tales, myths, and religious teachings (Chinen, 1987; Clayton & Birren, 1980). Wisdom, in such sources, has been understood to mean not only an increased storehouse of worldly knowledge and experience but also a different perspective on life, different values, a different world view, often described in terms of some kind of self-transcendence. What I am interested in knowing is whether such an increase in wisdom, such changes in world view or meaning, such potential for self-transcendence, is part of the normal process of adult development.

You may well think that the answers to such questions lie in the province of religion, not psychology. Despite the increasing numbers of psychologists interested in the psychology of religion, in wisdom, and in adult's ideas of life's meaning (e.g., Clayton & Birren, 1980; Frankl, 1984; Koplowitz, 1990; Reker & Wong, 1988), you are not likely to find any discussion of this subject in any other text on adult development. So perhaps my first task here is to explain to you why I think this is important. Why talk about meanings? There are three reasons.

It Is the Meaning We Attach, and Not the Experience, that Matters

Most fundamentally, psychologists are beginning to understand that individual experiences do not affect us in some automatic way; rather, it is the way we interpret an experience, the meaning we give it, that is really critical. A fairly trivial personal example may make the point:

After a 30-year hiatus, I have recently begun taking singing lessons again. Over the many years when I sang mostly at campfires, accompanying myself on a guitar, I got away with pitching songs in a range that was easy and comfortable for my very low voice. But now that I am singing with a good choir, I have discovered that the regular alto register takes me up into the twilight zone of my vocal range. So I went to a voice teacher to see if she could help me learn how to sing those higher notes again. Of course, since the whole purpose of the lessons has been to learn to sing those high notes, we spend a lot of time on it, and a lot of the time the noises coming out of my mouth are less than attractive.

The objective fact, then, is that I have technical difficulties singing notes in a particular range. But it is not that fact that is most significant to me; rather, it is the *meaning* I attach to those difficulties that is critical. There are obviously several different possibilities. I could see them purely as technical problems. That's the meaning my voice teacher would like me to attach to the situation. Or I could conclude that those notes just aren't "in there" and stop worrying about it. But as you can probably guess by now, neither of those is the meaning I have attached to this experience. Instead, I experience this difficulty as a personal failure. I feel that I ought to be able to conquer this problem easily, that once my teacher has explained the problem to me, I should be able to soar to the note and sound like a gorgeous opera singer. When I can't do that, I am incredibly frustrated.

My distress arises not from the objective situation but from my interpretation—from the meaning I attach to the event. Furthermore, the meanings I give to events are not random. There are certain basic assumptions I make about the world and my place in it, about myself and my capacities, that affect my interpretations of many experiences. Such a system of meanings is sometimes referred to as a "world view" or an "internal model." I've touched on other aspects of this same point in earlier chapters without labeling it in quite this way. For example, we can think of an "internal working model" of attachment relationships (a concept I touched on in Chapter 8) as a meaning system. If my internal model includes the assumption that "people are basically helpful and trustworthy," that assumption is clearly going to affect not only the experiences I will seek out, but my interpretation of those experiences. I will see helpfulness and trustworthiness where another person, with a different internal model, might see manipulativeness or self-interest. The objective experiences each of us has are thus filtered through various internal models, various meaning systems. I would argue that the ultimate consequence of any given experience is largely (if not wholely) determined by the meaning we attach and not the experience itself.

To the extent that this is true, then, it is obviously important for us to try to understand the meaning systems that adults create.

Adults Say that Meaning Is Important to Them

A second reason for exploring this rather slippery area is that if you ask adults what issues are of central concern to them, questions of meaning loom large in the answers. For example, Milton Yinger (1977) asked a group of college students in Japan, Korea, Thailand, New Zealand, and Australia the following question:

> What do you consider the one most fundamental or important issue for the human race; that is, what do you see as the basic and permanent question for mankind, the question of which all others are only parts?

Sixty percent of the answers touched on some aspect of life's meaning as being the fundamental question for the human race—what is the meaning of suffering or injustice? What is the purpose of existence?

This theme finds echoes in the writings of many clinicians and theorists. Erich Fromm listed the need for meaning as one of the five central existential needs of human beings; Victor Frankl (1984) argues that the "will to meaning" is a central human motive. James Fowler, a theologian and developmental psychologist, has made a similar point: "One characteristic all human beings have in common is that we can't live without some sense that life is meaningful" (1983, p. 58). Thus, not only do we interpret our experiences and in this way "make meaning," it may also be true that the need or motive to create *meaningfulness* may be a central one in adult (and perhaps children's) lives. If this is so, then we cannot ignore this subject if we are to understand adult lives.

Changes in Meaning Systems with Age

Finally, there is a developmental argument as well: There are a number of theories and at least some data (consistent with the message from myths and fairy tales) pointing to the possibility that there may be shared or potential changes in our meaning systems as we move through the adult years, just as there may be shared changes in personality. In fact, the personality changes I talked about in the last chapter may be embedded in a broader shift in meaning systems. If so, then it is obviously important for us to try to understand meaning systems and their potential developmental changes.

How Can We Study Meaning Systems and Their Possible Change with Age?

Assuming that I have persuaded you that this subject is worth exploring, we then come to the equally sticky/tricky question of method. How do we explore something so apparently fuzzy?

One way, of course, is to look for some outward sign of adults' meaning systems. Since one of the key functions of religion is to provide answers to fundamental questions about the meaning and purpose of life and about human beings' relationship to the universe, one obvious place to look would be at adults' involvement with religious observances of various kinds. Are there particular points in adulthood when people become more, or less, involved in religious practices such as church attendance? Does prayer (or meditation, or equivalent) play a larger role in life at some ages than at others? One group of researchers has pursued this line, and I'll look at this evidence in a moment.

Many theologians and developmental psychologists, however, have been dissatisfied with this approach. Involvement in organized religious activities may or may not change with age, but in any case such change or stability does not tell us about any changes in the *purpose* of religion in adults' lives nor about adults' more basic meaning systems. To understand these, we need to go beyond or behind observable behavior and ask people about their lives and their understanding of their own lives, often using very open-ended interview techniques. Then we have to categorize or analyze their answers, looking for some kind of orderliness. Personality researchers have used such open-ended techniques for many years, often very fruitfully as you have seen in the results from the Berkeley studies (among many others). Similar strategies have now been used in the study of meaning systems, not only by Lawrence Kohlberg and his many colleagues in their studies of the development of moral reasoning, but by Fowler in his studies of faith development and Robert Kegan (1982) in his exploration of "the evolving self." With the striking exception of research on moral reasoning, which is extensive, the amount of empirical evidence is distinctly limited, but the basic research strategy is at least familiar.

More controversial is the use of individual case studies drawn from biographies or autobiographies—personal reports by well-known adults (politicians, saints, philosophers, mystics) about the steps and processes of their own inner development. Collections of such independent reports have been analyzed, perhaps most impressively by William James (a distinguished early American psychologist) in his book *The Varieties of Religious Experience* (James, 1902), and by Evelyn Underhill (1911), in her book *Mysticism.*

Even detailed analyses of such personal reports do not fit with our usual concept of "scientific evidence." Only those few adults who have chosen to write about their inner "journey" can be included–hardly a random sample. Yet information from such sources has had a powerful effect on theories of potential changes in meaning systems. At the least, they tell us something about what *may* be possible, or about the qualities, meaning systems, or capacities of a few extraordinary adults who appear to have plumbed the depths of the human spirit. Yet even if we accept such descriptions as valid reports of inner processes, it is a very large leap to apply the described steps or processes to the potential experiences of ordinary folks. I am going to take that leap in this chapter. You will have to judge for yourself whether it is justified.

A Caveat

I need to make one further preparatory point: It is surely obvious (but nonetheless worth stating explicitly) that I bring my own meaning system to this discussion. Of course, that statement is true about this entire book (and about anyone else's book, too). I cannot report "objectively." Inevitably, I select, place emphasis, integrate information in a way that is influenced by my basic biases, my assumptions about human nature. Such bias, although always present, is less troublesome in areas in which there is an extensive body of empirical evidence, such as in the study of physical or mental development. But it becomes far more troublesome when I talk about the development of ideas about life's meaning itself. So let me at least make my biases clear.

I approach this subject with a strong hypothesis that there are "higher" levels of human potential than most of us have yet reached, whether that is expressed as the potential for wisdom, in Maslow's terms as self-actualization, in Loevinger's concept of the integrated personality, or in Fowler's concept of "universalizing faith." When I describe the various models of the development of meaning systems, I am inevitably filtering the theories and the evidence through this hypothesis. There is no way I can avoid this, any more than you can avoid filtering this chapter through your own assumptions, your own meaning system. Keep it in mind as you read further.

Religious Participation over Adulthood

Let us begin at the level of overt behavior, with research on religious participation. Most of the data are cross-sectional, as usual, but there are at least a few longitudinal studies of older adults. The findings can be summarized quite briefly.

Cross-sectional studies show a slight increase in church or synagogue attendance with age. National Gallup poll data collected in 1987, for example, show that 62 percent of 18 to 29 year-olds attended a religious service within the past seven days, compared to 68 percent of those aged 30 to 49 and 76 percent of those over 50 (U.S. Bureau of the Census, 1989a). Linda Chatters and Robert Taylor (1989) have provided confirming evidence from a more detailed study of a nationally representative U.S. black sample of several thousand adults. The results in Figure 11–1 are based on a five-point scale on which a 5 meant the respondent reported

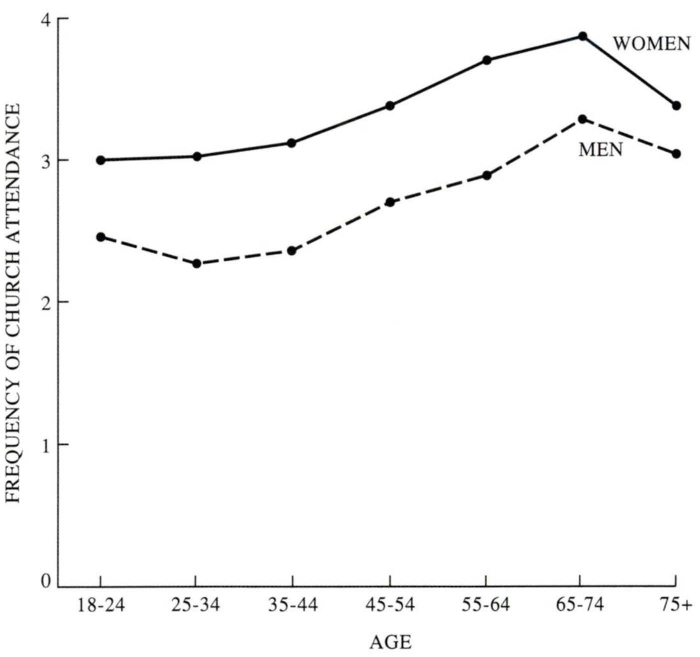

Figure 11–1 The figure shows findings from a nationally representative black cross-sectional sample. Subjects were asked how often they attended some kind of formal religious service and given a five-point scale on which to answer. A 5 indicated "daily" attendance, a 4 indicated at least weekly attendance, and so on. You can see that church attendance was higher among the middle-aged and older adults than among the young but dropped off past age 75. (Source: Chatters & Taylor, 1989, Table 1, p. S186.)

attending a religious service daily and a 1 indicated attendance less than once a year. Church attendance obviously rises steadily until late life, with a drop only after age 75.

Such a drop in church attendance in old age has been replicated in other research, including longitudinal studies. For example, participants in one of the Duke longitudinal studies, who were age 60 to 90 at the start of the study, collectively showed a decline in religious participation over the next 14 years (Blazer & Palmore, 1976).

It would be a mistake, however, to interpret this late-life drop in church participation as a sign of decreased interest in religion. Rather, it seems to reflect decreased mobility or energy. On measures of other types of personal religious practices, such as private prayer, reading religious books, or listening to or watching religious programs, there is essentially no decline in old age (Ainlay & Smith, 1984; Chatters & Taylor, 1989; Hunsberger, 1985; Mindel & Vaughan, 1978).

Overall, then, there is some hint here of an increase in religious participation in middle and old age. We can't be entirely sure of this because we have no longitudinal evidence covering the years of early and middle adulthood, but we can find some supportive evidence in the finding that as adults age they become more concerned with issues of personal morality or spirituality. The longitudinally observed increase with age in "humanitarian concern" that I reported in the last chapter (Schaie & Parham, 1976) is one example of such a change.

Additional evidence consistent with this trend comes from two cross-sectional studies. Savage and his colleagues (Savage, Gaber, Britton, Bolton, & Cooper, 1977), in their study of a large group of elderly adults in Britain, found that the older the individual, the more likely she was to select items that reflected moral qualities as key elements in her self-concept (e.g., "I am an honest person."). Similarly Veroff and his colleagues (Veroff, Douvan, & Kulka, 1981), in both their 1957 and 1976 national samples, found that older adults were more likely than younger ones to use moral or virtuous qualities as self-descriptions (e.g., "I lead a clean life," or "I'm unselfish," or "I don't go to church as often as I should."). Veroff, et al. conclude:

> It is as though older people refocus identity from interpersonal relationships to broader social concerns. Older people indicate less need of social acceptance, and they less often feel inadequate in social roles. While we can interpret this as a diminishing energy for role performance and interpersonal relationships, we can also think of these results as reflecting the fact that older people are more at peace with themselves and more invested in moral and spiritual values. (pp. 378–79)

These findings are suggestive, especially those from Veroff's studies of values, but to my taste they do not go deeply enough. They tell us little about possible changes in the role of religion in adults' lives as they age or about other changes in meaning systems that may be taking place. To explore this, we need to look at some broader theory and data.

The Development of Meaning Systems over Adulthood

For several reasons, I want to start this exploration with a look at Lawrence Kohlberg's theory of the development of moral reasoning—reasoning about what is right and wrong and how to judge the rightness or wrongness of some act. Although the questions Kohlberg has addressed touch on only a corner of the subject I am examining, his basic theoretical model has been the foundation of much of the current thinking about adults' evolving world views or meaning systems. Kohlberg's theory has also been extensively tested with empirical research and has been widely accepted among developmental psychologists, so it provides a relatively noncontroversial jumping off point.

Kohlberg's Theory of the Development of Moral Reasoning

Faced with conflict between different values, on what basis does a child or an adult decide what is morally right or wrong, fair or just? Kohlberg argued, as an extension of Piaget's theory of cognitive development, that children and adults move through a sequence of stages in their moral reasoning, each stage growing out of, but superceding, the one that came before. Each stage, in this view, reflects a meaning system or model, an internally consistent and pervasive set of assumptions about what is right and wrong and how it should be judged in others (Colby, Kohlberg, Gibbs, & Lieberman, 1983; Kohlberg, 1958, 1964, 1973, 1976, 1981, 1984; Kohlberg & Kramer, 1969).

Kohlberg made an important distinction between the *form* of thinking and its *content*. The issue is not whether the child or adult thinks, for example, that lying is wrong, but *why* they think it is wrong. Kohlberg searched for developmental changes in the form of thinking about moral questions, just as Piaget searched for developmental changes in broader forms of logic (recall Table 6.2).

The Measurement Procedure Kohlberg assessed an individual's level or stage of moral reasoning by means of a "moral judgment interview" in which the subject is asked to respond to a series of hypothetical moral dilemmas. In each dilemma, two different potential principles are in conflict. For example, in the now famous Heinz dilemma, the subject must grapple with the question of whether Heinz ought to steal a drug to save his dying wife, if the only druggist who can provide the drug is demanding a higher price than Heinz can pay. In this instance, the conflicting principles are the value of preserving life and the value of respecting property and upholding the law.

The Stages Based on many subjects' responses to such dilemmas, Kohlberg concluded that there were three basic levels of moral reasoning, each of which could be divided further into two stages, resulting in six stages in all. Kohlberg's own descriptions of these stages are given in Table 11.1.

The **preconventional level** is typical of most children under age nine, but is also found in some adolescents and in some criminal offenders. At both stages of this level, the child sees rules as something outside himself. In Stage 1, what is right is what is rewarded or what is not punished; in Stage 2, right is defined in terms of what brings pleasure or serves one's own needs or what is negotiated with others. So at this stage, children insist that rules of games must be followed precisely and that fairness is a crucial value for any kind of human interaction. (Parents who have elementary school age children will recognize this stage immediately; children in this stage of moral reasoning make a big point about fairness in the family and "That's not fair!" becomes a commonly heard cry.) Stage 2 is sometimes described as a position of "naive hedonism," a phrase which also captures some of the flavor of this stage.

At the **conventional level,** which is characteristic of most adolescents and most adults in our culture, the individual internalizes the rules and expectations of her family or peer group (at Stage 3), or of society (at Stage 4). In early presentations of the stages, Stage 3 was sometimes called the "good boy, nice girl" orientation, while 4 was sometimes labeled as the "law and order" orientation, both of which may be helpful mnemonics.

The **principled level,** which is found in only a minority of adults, involves a search for the underlying reasons behind society's rules. At Stage 5, which Kohlberg calls the "social contract" orientation, laws and regulations are seen as important ways of insuring fairness, but they are not perceived as immutable nor do they necessarily perfectly reflect more fundamental moral principles. Since laws and contracts are usually in accord with such underlying principles, obeying society's laws is reasonable nearly all the time. But when those underlying principles or reasons are at variance with some specific social custom or rule, the Stage 5 adult argues on the basis of the fundamental principle, even if it means disobeying or disagreeing with a law. Civil rights protesters in the early 1960s, for example, typically supported their civil disobedience with Stage 5 reasoning. Stage 6 is simply a further extension of this same pattern, with the individual searching for and then living in a way that is consistent with the deepest set of moral principles possible, such as the ultimate value of all life.

Another way to look at the shifts from preconventional, to conventional, to principled levels of reasoning is as a process of *decentering,* a term Piaget used to describe cognitive development more generally. At the lowest level, the child's reference point is herself—the consequences of her actions, the rewards she may gain. At the second (conventional) level, the reference point has moved outward away from the center of the self to the family or society. Finally, at the principled level, the adult searches for a still broader reference point, namely some set of underlying principles that lie behind or beyond social systems. Such a movement "outward" from the self is one of the constant themes in writings on the growth or development of meaning systems in adult life.

Kohlberg argued that these forms of moral reasoning emerge in a fixed sequence and that the stages are hierarchically organized. That is, each new stage grows from and eventually replaces the one before it, and each successive stage is more

TABLE 11.1. The Six Stages of Moral Development Proposed by Kohlberg.

Level and Stage	What is Right	Reason for Doing Right	Social Perspective of Stage
LEVEL 1: PRECONVENTIONAL			
Stage 1: Heteronomous morality	To avoid breaking rules backed by punishment, obedience for its own sake, and avoiding physical damage to persons and property.	Avoidance of punishment, and the superior power of authorities.	*Egocentric point of view:* Doesn't consider the interests of others or recognize that they differ from the actor's; doesn't relate two points of view. Actions are considered physically rather than in terms of psychological interests of others. Confusion of authority's perspective with one's own.
Stage 2: Individualism, instrumental purpose and exchange	Following rules only when it is to someone's immediate interest; acting to meet one's own interests and needs and letting others do the same. Right is also what's fair, what's an equal exchange, a deal, an agreement.	To serve one's own needs or interests in a world where you have to recognize that other people have their interests, too.	*Concrete individualistic perspective:* Aware that everybody has his own interest to pursue and these conflict, so that right is relative (in the concrete individualistic sense).
LEVEL 2: CONVENTIONAL			
Stage 3: Mutual interpersonal expectations, relationships, and interpersonal conformity	Living up to what is expected by people close to you or what people generally expect of people in your role as son, brother, friend, etc. "Being good" is important and means having good motives, showing concern about others. It also means keeping mutual relationships, such as trust, loyalty, respect, and gratitude.	The need to be a good person in your own eyes and those of others. Your caring for others. Belief in the Golden Rule. Desire to maintain rules and authority which support stereotypical good behavior.	*Perspective of the individual in relationships to other individuals:* Aware of shared feelings, agreements, and expectations which take primacy over individual interests. Relates points of view through the concrete Gold Rule, putting yourself in the other person's shoes. Does not yet consider generalized system perspective.

Level and Stage	What is Right	Reason for Doing Right	Social Perspective of Stage
Stage 4: Social system and conscience	Fulfilling the actual duties to which you have agreed. Laws are to be upheld except in extreme cases where they conflict with other fixed social duties. Right is also contributing to society, the group, or institution.	To keep the institution going as a whole, to avoid the breakdown of the system "if everyone did it," or the imperative of conscience to meet one's defined obligations.	*Differentiates societal point of view from interpersonal agreement or motives:* Takes the point of view of the system that defines roles and rules. Considers individual relations in terms of place in the system.
LEVEL 3: POSTCONVENTIONAL OR PRINCIPLED			
Stage 5: Social contract or utility and individual rights	Being aware that people hold a variety of values and opinions, that most values and rules are relative to your group. These relative rules should usually be upheld, however, in the interest of impartiality and because they are the social contract. Some nonrelative values and rights like life or liberty, however, must be upheld in any society regardless of majority opinion.	A sense of obligation to law because of one's social contract to make and abide by laws for the welfare of all and for the protection of all people's rights. A feeling of contractual commitment, freely entered upon, to family, friendship, trust, and work obligations. Concern that laws and duties be based on rational calculation of overall utility, "the greatest good for the greatest number."	*Prior-to-society perspective:* Perspective of a rational individual aware of values and rights prior to social attachments and contracts. Integrates perspectives by formal mechanisms of agreement, contract, objective impartiality, and due process. Considers moral and legal points of view; recognizes that they sometimes conflict and finds it difficult to integrate them.
Stage 6: Universal ethical principles	Following self-chosen ethical principles. Particular laws or social agreements are usually valid because they rest on such principles. When laws violate these principles, one acts in accordance with the principle. Principles are universal principles of justice: the equality of all human rights and respect for the dignity of human beings as individual persons.	The belief as a rational person in the validity of universal moral principles, and a sense of personal commitment to them.	*Perspective of a moral point of view from which social arrangements derive:* Perspective is that of any rational individual recognizing the nature of morality or the fact that persons are ends in themselves and must be treated as such.

SOURCE: Kohlberg, 1976. Reprinted by permission of the author.

differentiated and integrated than the last. Of course, during the transition from one stage to the next, a person will use reasoning reflecting more than one stage, but eventually, according to this argument, the lower levels of reasoning will drop out and be replaced by the more complex, more integrated system of reasoning. This is the strictest form of a stage theory. In contrast, Erikson's stages are sequential but not hierarchically organized. That is, in Erikson's system, each new stage ushers in a new set of issues, but the old issues do not vanish, and there is no assumption that the new stage involves some new internal model, some integration and reorganization of an old way of thinking.

THE DATA Only longitudinal data can tell us whether Kohlberg's model is valid. If he is correct, then not only should children and adults move from one step to the next in the order he proposes, they should not show regression to earlier stages. Kohlberg and his colleagues tested these hypotheses in three samples, all followed longitudinally: (1) Eighty-four boys from the Chicago area first interviewed when they were between 10 and 16 in 1956, some of whom were then reinterviewed up to five more times. The final interview was in 1976 to 1977, when they were in their 30s (Colby, et al. 1983); (2) a group of 23 boys and young men in Turkey, (some from a rural village and some from large cities) followed over periods of up to 10 years into early adulthood (Nisan & Kohlberg, 1982); (3) sixty-four male and female subjects from kibbutzim in Israel (intentional collective communities), who were first tested as teenagers and then retested once or twice over total periods of up to 10 years (Snarey, Reimer, & Kohlberg, 1985).

Figure 11–2 gives two kinds of information about the findings from these three studies. In the top half of the figure are total "Moral Maturity Scores" derived from the interview. These scores are based on the stage scores and can range from 100 to 500. As you can see, in all three studies the average score went up steadily with age, although there are some interesting cultural differences in speed of movement through the stages. In the bottom half of the figure are the percentages of answers reflecting each stage of moral reasoning for subjects at each age. These data are for the Chicago sample only, since that sample has been studied over the longest period of time. As we would expect, the number of Stage 1 responses drops out quite early, while Conventional Morality (Stages 3 and 4) rises rapidly in the teenage years and remains high in adulthood. Only a very small percentage of answers, even of those in their 30s, show Stage 5 reasoning (principled reasoning), and none show Stage 6 reasoning.

Both analyses show the stages to be strongly sequential, a pattern even more strongly suggested by the fact that in none of these three studies was there a single subject who skipped a stage, and only about 5 percent showed regressions—a percentage that would be consistent with scoring errors. Each subject also showed a good deal of internal consistency at any one testing, using similar logic in analyzing each of several quite different moral problems.

Using a questionnaire method of measuring moral judgment, rather than the more open-ended interview, James Rest and his colleagues have also shown longi-

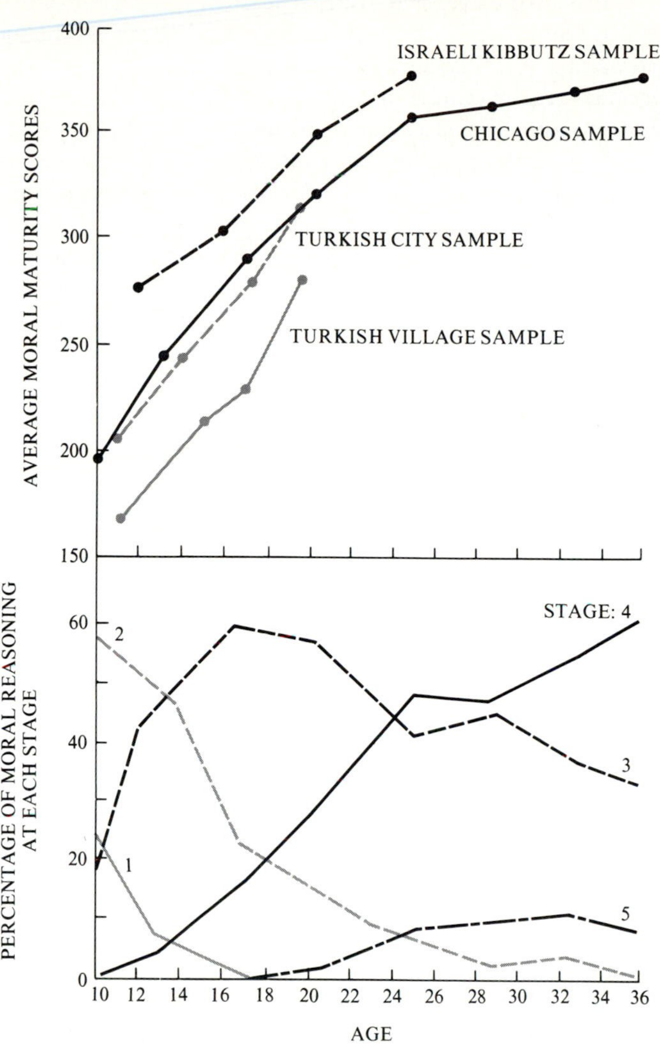

Figure 11–2 The upper half of this figure shows Moral Maturity scores, which reflect level of reasoning on Kohlberg's moral dilemmas. Included are findings from teenagers and young adults in three countries. The lower half of the figure shows the percentages of answers to moral dilemmas among subjects in the Chicago study rated at each stage of reasoning at each age in the longitudinal study. As you can see, overall scores go up as age increases. It is also clear that principled reasoning (Stage 5 or 6) is relatively rare, even in adulthood. (Sources: Colby, et al. 1983; Nisan & Kohlberg, 1982; Snarey, Reimer, & Kohlberg, 1985. Colby, et al. reprinted by permission of copyright holder, The Society for Research in Child Development, Inc. and author.)

tudinal changes of the expected kind, at least in the years from the teens through the early 20s (Rest, Davidson, & Robbins, 1978; Rest & Thoma, 1985).

Unfortunately, no equivalent longitudinal data exist for any adults past midlife. Cross-sectional results (Lonky, Kaus, & Roodin, 1984; Pratt, Golding, & Hunter, 1983) show no age differences in overall level of moral judgment between young, middle-aged, and older adults. Such findings might be taken to mean that the level of reasoning achieved in early adulthood remains relatively stable throughout adulthood. But the longitudinal data do not support such an assertion—at least not through the middle 30s. Among Kohlberg's sample were quite a few individuals who shifted from stage 3 to stage 4 while in their 20s, and a few who moved to stage 5 while in their 30s. At least some adults may thus continue to develop through Kohlberg's stages throughout adulthood. The only way to know this for sure will be to assess moral reasoning longitudinally over the full years of adult life.

Stage 6, and the Possibility of Stage 7 In his early work Kohlberg suggested that a fair number of college students reached Stage 6. In his later writings, however, he argued that this universalistic stage is extremely uncommon. The longitudinal data suggest that Stage 5 may be the typical "end point" of the developmental progression. Adults who reach Stage 5 (about 15 percent of those in their 30s in Kohlberg's samples) do indeed operate on some broad, general principles. What they lack, however, is

> . . . that which is critical for our theoretical notion of Stage 6, namely, the organization of moral judgment around a clearly formulated moral principle of justice and respect for persons that provides a rationale for the primacy of this principle. (Kohlberg, 1984, p. 271)

In other words, at Stage 5 one develops some broad principles that go beyond (or "behind") the social system; at Stage 6, the rare individual develops a still broader and more general ethical system in which those principles are embedded. Among those individuals Kohlberg lists as apparent Stage 6 thinkers are Martin Luther King and Gandhi.

Kohlberg also speculated about the existence of a still higher stage, Stage 7 (Kohlberg, 1973; Kohlberg, Levine, & Hewer, 1983), which he thought might emerge only toward the end of life, after an adult has spent some years living within a principled moral system. It is the confrontation of one's own death that can bring about this transition. As they ask the fundamental questions—"Why live?" and "How to face death?"—some individuals transcend the type of logical analysis that typifies all the earlier forms of moral reasoning and arrive at a still deeper or broader decentering. As Vivian Clayton and James Birren (1980) describe it,

> The individual shifts from seeing himself as the center of the universe to identifying with the universe and seeing himself from this perspective. What results is that the individual senses the unity of the universe in which he is but one element . . . [it is a] nondualistic, nonegoistic orientation. (p. 122)

Kohlberg himself put it this way: "Generally speaking, a Stage 7 response to ethical and religious problems is based on constructing a sense of identity or unity with being, with life, or with God" (Kohlberg, Levine, & Hewer, 1983).

EVALUATION AND COMMENT The body of evidence that has accumulated concerning the development of moral reasoning provides strong support for several aspects of Kohlberg's theory:

1. There do appear to be stages that children and adults move through in developing concepts of fairness and morality.
2. At least up to Stage 5, those stages appear to meet the tests of a hierarchical stage system: They occur in fixed order, each emerging from and replacing the one that preceded it and forming a structural whole.
3. The stage sequence appears to be universal. The specific *content* of moral decisions may differ from one culture to the next, but the overall form of logic seems to move through the same steps in every culture in which this has been studied, including Taiwan, Turkey, Mexico, Kenya, India, Israel, and the Bahamas.
4. The stages have some relevance for real life, as well. As one example, Edward Lonky and his colleagues (Lonky, et al. 1984) have found that adults who reason at the principled level are more able than are those at the conventional level to deal positively and constructively with significant losses in their lives, such as the death of a family member or the breakup of a relationship.

At the same time, a number of critics have pointed out that Kohlberg's theory is relatively narrow, focusing almost exclusively on the development of concepts of justice or fairness. Other aspects of moral/ethical reasoning, other facets of meaning systems, are omitted.

The most eloquent of the critics has been Carol Gilligan (1977, 1982), whose approach I mentioned in Chapter 3. She argues that Kohlberg was interested in concepts of justice and not concepts of care, so his theory and research largely ignore an ethical/moral system based on caring for others, on responsibility, on altruism or compassion. In particular, Gilligan proposes that women more often than men approach moral and ethical dilemmas from the point of view of responsibilities and caring, searching not for the "just" solution, but for the solution that best deals with the social relationships involved. She argues that men more often than women use a morality of justice.

This aspect of Gilligan's argument has not been supported by research findings. In studies in which males and females have been compared on stage of moral reasoning using Kohlberg's revised scoring system, no sex differences are typically found (e.g., Pratt, Golding, & Hunter, 1984; Walker, 1984). That is, girls and women can and do use moral reasoning based on principles of justice when they are presented with dilemmas in which that is a central issue. Still, Gilligan's more basic point seems clearly valid: Kohlberg's approach does focus only on a narrow range of aspects of moral judgment or meaning. But it is possible to take the basic structure and assumptions of Kohlberg's theory and use that reasoning to explore not only ethics based on relationships and caring, such as Gilligan has described, but also religious beliefs and more general facets of personal meaning systems, as James Fowler has done in his theory of faith development.

Fowler's Theory of Faith Development

In talking about stages of faith development, James Fowler (1981, 1983) goes beyond questions of moral reasoning to search for the emergence of each individual's world view or model of her relationship to others and to the universe. He uses the word "faith" to describe such a personal model—a somewhat confusing usage since the word faith more commonly refers to any specific set of religious beliefs. In the language I have been using in this chapter, Fowler's model might be called a theory of the development of meaning systems, but I will use his own term—faith—to be true to the original formulation.

In Fowler's view, each of us has a faith whether or not we belong to any particular church or organization. Moral reasoning is only a *part* (perhaps quite a small part) of faith. Faith is broader. In my terms, it is a set of assumptions or understandings, often so basic that they are not articulated, about the nature of our connections with others and with the world in which we live. At any point in our lives, he argues, each of us has a "master story" which is "the answer you give to the questions of what life is about, or who's really in charge here, or how do I live to make my life a worthy, good one. It's a stance you take toward life" (Fowler, 1983, p. 60).

Like Kohlberg, Fowler is interested not in the specific content of one's faith but in the structure or form of that faith. A Christian, a Hindu, a Jew, or an atheist could all have faiths that are structurally similar, even while they differ sharply in content. Thus, when Fowler talks about the development of faith, he is not talking about specific religious beliefs or about conversions from one religion to another. He is searching for the underlying *structure* or logic that is common to many different specific beliefs or creeds.

And like Kohlberg, Fowler hypothesizes that each of us develops through a shared series of faith structures (or world views, broad internal working models, meaning systems, or whatever we might choose to call them) over the course of childhood and adulthood. Two of the six stages he proposes occur primarily in childhood, and I won't describe them here; the remaining four can be found among adults.

THE STAGES OF FAITH The first of the adult forms of faith, which Fowler calls **synthetic-conventional faith,** normally appears first in adolescence and then continues well into early adulthood for most of us. Like Kohlberg's level of conventional morality, conventional faith is rooted in the implicit assumption that authority is to be found outside of oneself. Although the teenager does go through a process of creating a new identity, a process that normally includes reexamination of old beliefs, this process still goes on against the backdrop of the basic external-authority assumption. The young person chooses some set of specific beliefs from among those that are "out there."

Many adults remain within this form of faith/meaning throughout their lives, defining themselves and interpreting their experiences within the meaning system of some group or specific set of beliefs. Let me give you two concrete examples from Fowler's own interviews that may make the point clearer.

Mr. D., a 63-year-old retired teamster, talked about his beliefs this way:

> My views are quite the same as those of any teamster, or any working man. . . . I'm not now a religious man, never was, and never will be. Religion is just a lot of nonsense as I see it. As I see it, we are born, we live here, we die, and that's it. Religion gives people something to believe in, that there's something more, because they want there to be something more, but there isn't. So . . . you see, I'd rather put some money down on the bar and buy myself a drink, rather than put that same money into a collection plate! (Fowler, 1981, pp. 165–166)

Mr. D. is rejecting formal religion, but there is still an external authority here—working men or other teamsters. In fact, he defines himself as "one of the boys."

In contrast, the external authority for Mrs. H. is very definitely a specific set of religious beliefs. A 61-year-old Southern woman who grew up on a tenant farm, at the time Fowler interviewed her she had recently rededicated herself to the Baptist church after many years away from church activity. At one point she said:

> I feel very sad and ashamed for the way I have wasted my life. I do know that God has forgiven me for every wrong that I've done, and that He loves me. I feel very close to God most of the time, now that I am active in the work of the church again. Of course there are times that I don't feel as close to Him as I'd like to, but I know that I am the one who moves away, not He. I've learned that we all have so much to be thankful for, if we only stop and count our blessings. (Fowler, 1981, p. 172)

It is precisely this reliance on external authority that changes when an adult moves to the next proposed stage, which Fowler calls **individuative-reflective faith.** "For a genuine move to Stage 4 to occur there must be an interruption of reliance on external sources of authority . . . a relocation of authority within the self" (Fowler, 1981, p. 179). In making this shift, many adults first reject or move away from the faith community to which they had belonged. Often there is also a rejection of ritual or myth and an embracing of science or rationality. But the transition can occur without such rejections. The key is that the individual not only reexamines old assumptions but takes responsibility in a new way.

It is hard to convey just how profound a change this is. The metaphor I have found most helpful is one I have adapted from mythologist Joseph Campbell's writings (1986). It is as if in the stage of conventional faith, we experience ourselves as like the moon, illuminated by *reflected* light. We are not ourselves the source of light (or knowledge) but are created by outside forces. In the stage of individuative faith, we experience ourselves as like the sun, radiating light of our own. We are no longer defined by the groups to which we belong; rather we choose the groups, the relationships, based on our self-chosen beliefs or values. Thus, even if the specific beliefs we choose at this point are the same ones with which we have grown up, the underlying meaning system is changed.

Rebecca, a woman in her mid-30s interviewed by Robert Kegan in another context, seems clearly to have made this transition:

> I know I have very defined boundaries, and I protect them very carefully. I won't give up the slightest control. In any relationship I decide who gets in, how far, and when. What am I afraid of? I used to think I was afraid people would find out who I really was and then not like me. But I don't think that's it anymore. What I feel now is—'that's me. That's mine. It's what makes me. And I'm powerful. It's my negative side, maybe, but it's also my positive stuff—and there's a lot of that. What it is is me, it's my self—and if I let people in maybe they'll take it, maybe they'll use it—and I'll be gone.' . . . This 'self,' if I had to represent it I think of two things: either a steel rod that runs through everything, a kind of solid fiber, or sort of like a ball at the center that is all together. . . . " (Kegan, 1982, pp. 240–241)

The next stage in Fowler's model, **conjunctive** faith, requires an opening outward from the self-preoccupation of the individuative level. There is an openness here to paradox, a moving away from fixed truth toward a search for balance, not only of self and other but of mind and emotion, of rationality and ritual. Not typically found before midlife, the individual who lives within this meaning system accepts that there are many truths, that others' beliefs, others' ideas, may be true for them—a point of view that not only brings far greater tolerance toward others but also very commonly brings the individual to an interest in service or commitment to the welfare of others.

Here's one illustrative voice, that of Miss T., a 78-year-old woman who had been variously a Unitarian, a Quaker, and a follower of Krishnamurti and other Eastern teachers. When asked if there were beliefs and values everyone should hold, she said:

> If somebody asked me that and gave me just two minutes to answer it, I know what I'd say. It's a line from George Fox, the founder of Quakerism. It's old-fashioned English and it seems to me to have the entire program of anybody's life. It's a revolution, it's an enormous comfort, it's a peace maker. The line is: "There is that of God in every man." Now, you can start thinking about it. You can see that if you really did believe that, how it would change your relationships with people. It's far-reaching. It applies nationally and individually and class-wise; it reaches the whole. To anyone that I loved dearly I would say, "Put that in your little invisible locket and keep it forever." (Fowler, 1981, p. 194)

Other statements by Miss T. make it clear that the content of her faith at this point involves a kind of return to some of the elements of her earlier religious teachings, but she has reframed it, casting it in language that has meaning to her now and that focuses on finding fulfillment in service to others—all of which are significant elements of conjunctive faith.

The final stage Fowler proposes he calls **universalizing faith.** Like Kohlberg's Stage 6, reaching this stage is a relatively rare achievement, but Fowler argues that it is the next logical step. To some extent, it involves a step beyond individuality. In the stage of conjunctive faith, the individual may be "open" and "integrated" but is still struggling with the paradox of searching for universality while still attempting to preserve individuality. In the stage of universalizing faith, the individual *lives* the principles, the imperatives, of absolute love and justice. Because such individuals live their lives based on such basic outward-oriented principles, they are heedless of their own self-preservation, much as Mother Theresa goes on caring for the dying even when her own health is frail. They may even be seen by others as subversive to the structures of society or traditional religion, since they do not begin with the assumption that society or religion is necessarily correct in its institutions or customs. So Mahatma Gandhi, who based his later life on the basic principle that injustice should be eradicated from the world, was profoundly disruptive of the established social order.

Some Basic Points about Fowler's Stages

Some key points need emphasis. First, like Kohlberg, Fowler assumes that these stages occur in a sequence but that the sequence is only very roughly associated with age, especially in adulthood. Some adults remain within the same meaning system, the same faith structure, their entire lives; others make one or more transitions in their understandings of themselves and their relationships with others.

Second, Fowler nonetheless contends that each stage has its "proper time" of ascendancy in an individual's lifetime—a period at which that particular form of faith is most consistent with the demands of life. Most typically, Stage 3 (conventional faith) is in its ascendance in adolescence or early adulthood, Stage 4 (individuative-reflective faith) in the years of the late 20s and 30s, while a transition to Stage 5 (conjunctive faith), if it occurs at all, may occur at approximately midlife. Finally Stage 6, if one can reach it, would be the optimal form of faith in old age, when issues of integrity and meaning become still more dominant. Each stage at its optimum time has the "potential for wholeness, grace and integrity and for strengths sufficient for either life's blows or blessings" (Fowler, 1981, p. 274). But remaining at a particular stage of faith, past the "proper" time or age, may bring problems. This is a potentially testable assertion, but one which has not yet been studied systematically.

Third, Fowler says that "each stage represents a widening of vision and valuing, correlated with a parallel increase in the certainty and depth of selfhood, making for qualitative increases in intimacy with self-others-world" (1981, p. 274).

Research Findings

No longitudinal data have yet been collected to test the sequential aspect of Fowler's theory. However, Fowler has reported some cross-sectional data that show the incidence of the stages of faith at each of several ages (see Figure 11–3). The data included in this figure came from several different studies in both the United States and Canada, all of which involved extensive open ended interviews with teenagers and adults. The assignment of an overall stage of faith was based on raters reading the entire interview.

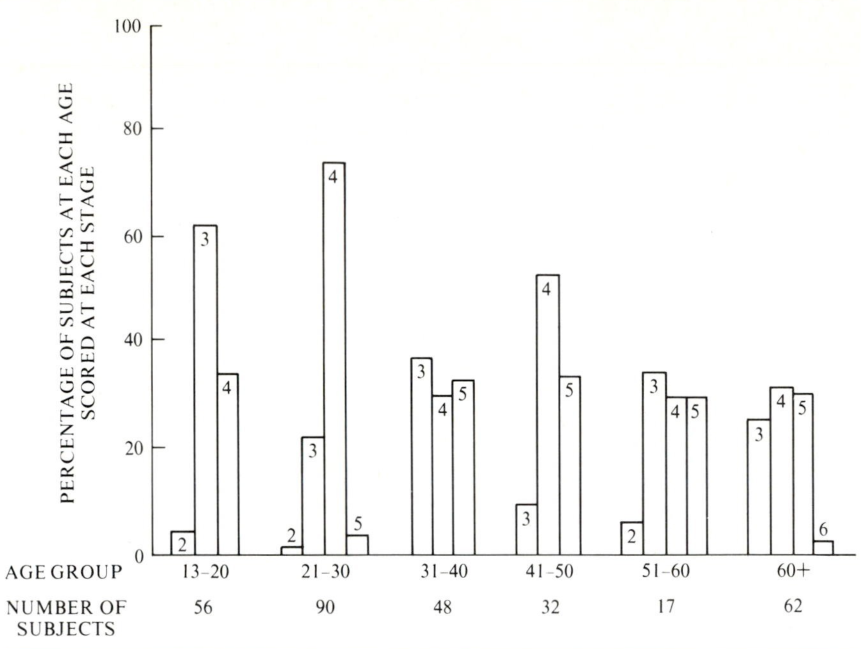

Figure 11–3 Cross-sectional information about stages of faith from studies in several cities. Fowler actually scores interview responses in half steps. To simplify, I have combined each half step with the stage above it, so included in the bars reflecting Stage 4 are responses scored as both 3 1/2 and 4. The findings suggest that Stage 3 is modal in the teenage years with Stage 4 emerging strongly in the 20s. Stage 5 does not appear frequently until the 30s, all of which is consistent with Fowler's theory. (Adapted from Fowler, 1981, Table B.3, p. 318.)

Since these are cross-sectional rather than longitudinal data, they do not tell us whether each individual has moved through the proposed stages in the sequence Fowler describes. But the findings fit the theory reasonably well. Stage 3 (conventional) faith is most common in the teenage years, Stage 4 (individuative) peaks among those in their 20s, while Stage 5 (conjunctive faith) only really emerges in the 30s. Only one adult interviewed in any of these studies was placed at Stage 6, and he was a man in his 60s. Thus, the stages appear to emerge in the order and at the approximate ages that Fowler suggests. Further, these data are consistent with the idea that not all adults continue to shift from one stage to the next. Among adults of 30 or older, Stages 3 and 4 are as common as Stage 5 faith.

A Preliminary Assessment Theories like Fowler's supplement our thinking about adulthood in important ways, if only to help us focus on the importance of meaning systems and their possible sequential change with age. But it is still very early in our empirical exploration of this and related theories. The greatest immediate need is for good longitudinal data, perhaps initially covering the years that are thought to be transitional for many adults but ultimately for the entire adult age range.

Integrating Meaning and Personality: A Preliminary Theoretical Synthesis

No doubt some of the parallels between these several theories and those I discussed in Chapters 3 and 10 have already struck you. The surface similarities are obvious, as you can see in Table 11.2.

- Loevinger's conformist stage certainly sounds a great deal like both Kohlberg's conventional morality and Fowler's conventional faith. There seems to be agreement that in adolescence and early adulthood individuals tend to be focused on adapting to the demands of the roles and relationships society imposes on them and that they assume the source of authority is external.
- Loevinger's conscientious/individualistic stages sound a great deal like Maslow's layer of esteem needs, Kohlberg's early principled reasoning, and Fowler's individuative faith. All four theorists agree that the next step involves a shift in the central source of meaning or self-definition from external to internal, accompanied by a preoccupation with the self and one's own abilities, skills, potentials.
- Loevinger's autonomous stage and Fowler's conjunctive faith have an equivalent similarity, possibly related to self-actualization needs as described by Maslow. All speak of a shift away from self-preoccupation toward a search for balance, a shift toward greater tolerance toward both self and others.
- Finally, there seems to be agreement about some still higher stage which involves some form of self-transcendence—Kohlberg's Stage 7, Fowler's stage of universalizing faith, Maslow's peak experiences.

TABLE 11.2. Synthesis and Summary of Stages of Personality, Moral, and Faith Development.

General Stage	Loevinger's Ego Development Stages	Maslow's Needs Hierarchy	Kohlberg's Stages of Moral Development	Fowler's Stages of Faith
Conformist or culture-bound self	Conformist; self-aware.	Belongingness & love needs.	Conventional morality.	Synthetic-conventional.
Individuality	Conscientious; individualistic.	Self-esteem needs.	First stage of principled morality (Stage 5).	Individuative.
Integration	Autonomous & integrated.	Self-actualized.	Stage 6: universal ethical principles.	Conjunctive.
Self-transcendence	—	Some peak experiences.	Stage 7: ethics based on unity.	Universalizing.

SOURCES: Fowler, 1981; Kohlberg, 1984; Loevinger, 1976; Maslow, 1954.

Of course, we are not dealing with four independent visions here. These theorists all know of each other's work, have been influenced by each other's ideas. This is particularly true in the case of Fowler and Kohlberg, since Fowler's theory is quite explicitly an extension of Kohlberg's model. So the fact that they all seem to agree does not mean that we have uncovered "truth" here. My confidence in the validity of the basic sequence all these theorists describe is bolstered by three additional arguments:

First, although they have influenced one another, there are still three quite distinct theoretical heritages involved. Kohlberg's (and Fowler's) work is rooted in Piaget's theory and in studies of normal children's thinking; Loevinger's work is rooted in Freud's theory and in clinical assessments of children and adults, including those with emotional disturbances; Maslow's theory, while influenced by psychoanalytic thought, is based primarily on his own observations of a small number of highly unusual "self-actualized" adults. The fact that one can arrive at such similar views of the sequence of emergence of meaning systems from such different roots makes the convergence more impressive.

Second, in the case of both Kohlberg's and Loevinger's models, we have reasonably strong supporting empirical evidence, especially concerning the first step in the commonly proposed adult sequence, the move from conforming/conventional to individualistic. The transitions beyond that are simply much less well-studied, in part because longitudinal studies have not yet followed adults past early midlife, and perhaps in part because the later transitions are simply less common. Still, this is not all totally speculative stuff. We can anchor at least part of the commonly proposed basic sequence in hard data.

Finally, this basic model seems plausible to me because the sequence makes sense in terms of a still more encompassing developmental concept proposed by Robert Kegan (1982).

Kegan's Synthesizing Idea: The Alternation of Independence and Union

Kegan proposes that each of us has two enormously powerful and equal desires or motives built in. On the one hand, we deeply desire to be included, to be joined, to be integrated with others. On the other hand, we desire equally to be separate, independent, differentiated. No accommodation between these two is really in balance, so whatever "evolutionary truce" (as Kegan calls each stage) we arrive at, it will lean further toward one than toward the other. Eventually, the unmet need becomes so strong that we are forced to change the system, to change our understanding. In the end, what this creates is a fundamental alternation, a moving back and forth of the pendulum, between perspectives or meaning systems centered around inclusion or union and perspectives centered around independence or separateness.

The child begins life in a symbiotic relationship with the mother or mother figure, so the pendulum begins on the side of connection and union; by age two, the child has pulled away and seeks independence, a separate identity. The conformist or conventional meaning system that we see in adolescence and early adulthood (if not later) is a move back toward connection, toward the group, while the transition to the individualistic meaning system is a return to separation and independence. The term "detribalization" that Levinson uses to describe one facet of the midlife transition fits nicely with Kegan's basic model. In taking the source of authority inward there is at least initially a pushing away of the tribe and all its rituals and rules. If the model is correct, then the step after this ought to be another return toward union, which seems to me to be precisely what most of the theorists I have described have proposed. As I see it, most of them talk about two substeps in this shift of the pendulum, with Fowler's conjunctive faith or Kohlberg's Stage 6 being intermediate steps on the way toward the more complete position of union or community represented by universalizing faith or Kohlberg's Stage 7.

Although I have talked here as if the process were one of a pendulum moving back and forth, clearly Kegan is not proposing that movement is simply back and forth in a single groove. Instead, the process is more like that of a spiral in which each shift to the other 'side' of the polarity is at a more integrated level than the one before.

If such a basic alternation, such a spiral movement, really does form the underlying rhythm of development, is there any reason we should assume that it stops even at so lofty a point as Kohlberg's Stage 7? When I first understood this aspect of Kegan's theory I had one of those startling *ah ha!* experiences when I realized that the descriptions of the stages of the mystical "journey" given by Evelyn Underhill and by William James could be linked seamlessly with the sequence Kegan was describing.

I am well aware that describing such mystical experiences here will seem to some to be going very far afield, perhaps totally outside the realm of psychology. But to me the risk is worth it, not only because in this way perhaps I can make a case for my own basic assumption regarding the immense potential of the individual human spirit, but also because the pattern that emerges fits so remarkably well with Kegan's model.

Stages of Mystical Experiences

The stages I am describing here are those suggested by Evelyn Underhill (1911) in her book *Mysticism,* based on her reading of autobiographies and biographies and other writings of the lives of hundreds of individuals from every religious tradition, all of whom described some form of self-transcendant experience. Not everyone described every one of the steps or stages listed, but Underhill reports that there was a remarkable degree of unanimity about the basic process, despite huge differences in historical period and religious background.

Step 1 in this process, which Underhill calls *awakening,* seems to me to correspond to the usual end point in theories such as Kohlberg's or Fowler's. It involves at least a brief self-transcendant experience, such as the peak experiences Maslow describes. In Kegan's model, this step is clearly represented on the "union" end of the polarity; it is an awakening to the possibility of stepping outside one's own perspective and understanding the world from a point of deep connection.

Step 2, which Underhill calls *purification,* is clearly a move back toward separateness. The individual, having "seen" herself from a broader perspective, also sees all her own imperfections, fruitless endeavors, and flaws. As St. Teresa of Avila, one of the great mystics of the Christian tradition puts it, "in a room bathed in sunlight not a cobweb can remain hidden" (1562/1960, p. 181). To understand and eliminate those flaws, those cobwebs, she must turn inward again. Many individuals at this stage are strongly focused on self-discipline, including special spiritual disciplines such as regular prayer or meditation, fasting, or the like.

Step 3 clearly moves us back toward union. Underhill calls this the stage of *illumination.* It involves a much deeper, more prolonged awareness of Light, or greater reality, or God and may, in fact, encompass some of what Kohlberg refers to as Stage 7. In Plato's metaphor of the cave, this is the step in which the individual, after realizing that the figures on the wall of the cave are only shadows, and after struggling to find the mouth of the cave, finally steps outside into the sun. This is accompanied by deep joy.

But even this illumination is not the end of the journey. Underhill finds two other steps described by many mystics that appear to lie beyond. The first of these, often called "the dark night of the soul," involves a still further turn inward, back toward separateness. At the stage of "illumination," the individual still feels some personal satisfaction, some personal pleasure or joy, in having achieved illumination. According to mystics who have described these later stages, if one is to achieve ultimate union even this personal pleasure, too, must be abandoned. And the process of abandonment requires a turning back to the self, to awareness of, and exploration of, all the remaining ways in which the separate self has survived. Only then can an individual achieve the end point, that of "union"—with God, with Reality, with Beauty, with the Ultimate, however this may be described within a particular religious tradition.

I cannot say, of course, whether this sequence, this spiral of inner human progress, reflects the inevitable or ultimate path for us all. I can say only that the developmental analyses of stages of morality or stages of faith or personality that have been offered by many psychologists, for which we have at least some preliminary supporting evidence, appear to form a connected whole with the descriptions of stages of mystical illumination. At the very least, we know that a pathway similar to this has been trod by a long series of remarkable individuals, whose descriptions of their inner journeys bear striking similarities. There may be many other paths or journeys. But the reflections of these remarkable few point the way toward the possibility of a far vaster potential of the human spirit than is apparent to most of us in our daily humdrum lives.

The Process of Transition

Coming down a bit from these lofty levels but still assuming for the moment that there *is* some basic rhythm, some developmental sequence, in the forms of meaning we create, let me turn to the question that may be of special personal importance: What is the process by which transitions or transformations from one stage to the next take place? What triggers them? What are the common features of transitions? How are they traversed?

Most developmental psychologists who propose stages of adult development have focused more on the stages than on the transition process. But there are some common themes in the ways transitions are described.

A number of theorists have described transitions in parallel terms, with each shift from one "level" or "stage" to the next seen as a kind of death and rebirth—a death of the earlier sense of self, of the earlier faith, of the earlier equilibrium (James, 1902; Johnson, 1983; Kegan, 1980). The process typically involves first some glimpses, precursors, or premonitions of another stage or view, which are then followed by a period (which may be brief or prolonged) in which the individual struggles to deal with these two "selves" within. Sometimes the process is aborted and the individual returns to the earlier equilibrium. Sometimes the individual moves instead toward a new understanding, a new equilibrium. There is, as William Bridges (1980) puts it simply and clearly, first an ending, then a middle, and then a beginning.

The middle part of this process, when the old meaning system has been partially given up but a new equilibrium has not yet been reached, is often experienced as profoundly dislocating. Sentences like "I am beside myself" or "I was out of my mind" may be used (Kegan, 1980). And like the transitions I described in the last chapter, the process of equilibration may be accompanied by an increase in physical or psychological symptoms of various kinds, including depression.

Kegan perhaps best summarizes the potential pain of the process:

> Development is costly—for everyone, the developing person and those around him or her. Growth involves a separation from an old system of meaning. In practical terms this can involve both the agony of felt meaninglessness and the repudiation of commitments and investment. . . . Developmental theory gives us a way of thinking about such pain that does not pathologize it. (1980, p. 439)

Such transitions may emerge slowly or may occur rapidly; they may be the result of self-chosen activities, such as therapy or exercise, they may result from the happenstances of ordinary life, or from unexpected experiences. In Table 11.3 I have suggested some of the stimulants for such transitions, organized around what appear to be the three most frequent adult transitions: (1) from conformity to individuality, (2) from individuality to integration or conjunctive faith, and (3) from integration to self-transcendence. I offer this list quite tentatively. We clearly lack the longitudinal evidence that might allow us to say more fully what experiences may or may not stimulate a transition.

You can see in the table that I am suggesting that somewhat different experiences may be involved in each of these three transitions. Attending college or moving away from home into a quite different community seem to be particularly influential in promoting aspects of the transition to individuality. For example, in longitudinal studies, both Kohlberg (1973) and Rest & Thoma (1985), have found a correlation between the amount of college education completed and level

TABLE 11.3. Transitions from One Stage to Another: Some Possible Triggering Situations or Experiences that May Assist in Passing Through a Transition.

Specific Transition	Intentional Activities that may foster that Transition	Unintentional or Circumstantial Events that may foster a Transition
From Conformist to Individualistic	Therapy; reading about other religions or faiths	Attending college; leaving home for other reasons such as job or marriage; usual failures or reversals while "following the rules"; development of personal or professonal skills.
From Individualistic to Integrated	Therapy; introspection; short-term programs to heighten self-awareness (e.g., Gestalt workshops).	Illness or prolonged pain; death in the family or prolonged crisis; peak experiences.
From Integrated to Self-Transcendent	Meditation or prayer; Various forms of yoga; Self-disciplines.	Near-death experience; transcendent experiences such as peak or immediate mystical experiences.

of moral reasoning. Principled reasoning was found only in those who had attended at least some college. This transition, then, seems to be precipitated by exposure to other assumptions, other faiths, other perspectives. Such a confrontation can produce disequilibrium, which may be dealt with by searching for a new, independent, self-chosen model.

I have also suggested that therapy may play some role in triggering or assisting with either of the first two transitions. In fact, helping a client to achieve full integration is the highest goal of many humanistically oriented therapies, such as those based on the work of Carl Rogers or Fritz Perls. But my hypothesis is that traditional forms of therapy do little to assist the transition from integrated person to a level of self-transcendence. This transition, I think, requires or is assisted by a different form of active process, such as meditation or other forms of yoga or systematic prayer (LeShan, 1966).

Both painful experiences and transcendant ones can also be the occasion for a new transition. The death of a child or of a parent may reawaken our concern with ultimate questions of life and death. A failed marriage or discouragement at work may lead to questioning or to a loss of the sense of stability of one's present model. Peak experiences, too, by giving glimpses of something not readily comprehensible within a current view, may create a disequilibrium. Most adults who have had a "near death experience," for example, report that their lives are never again the same. Many change jobs or devote their lives to service in one way or another. Other forms of peak experiences or religious "rebirth" may have the same effect.

I have been consistently using the word "may" in the last few paragraphs to convey the fact that such life changes do not invariably result in significant reflection or decentering. Patricia Gurin and Orville Brim (1984), in an argument reminiscent of the concept of scheduled and unscheduled changes, have offered an interesting hypothesis to explain such differences in the impact of major life changes. In essence, they argue that widely shared, age-linked changes are not likely to trigger significant reassessments of the sense of self precisely because expected changes are interpreted differently than are unexpected ones. Shared changes are most often attributed to causes outside of oneself, for which one is not personally responsible. In contrast, unique or off-time life changes are more likely to lead to significant inner reappraisals precisely because it is difficult to attribute such experiences to outward causes. If everyone at your job has been laid off because the company has gone out of business during a recession, you need not reassess your own sense of self-worth. But if you are the only one fired during a time of expanding economy, it is much more difficult to maintain your sense of worth.

Some shared experiences, such as college, may commonly trigger reappraisals or restructuring of personality, moral judgment, or faith. But most age-graded experiences can be absorbed fairly readily into existing systems. It may then be the unique or mistimed experiences that are particularly significant for changes in meaning systems. This hypothesis remains to be tested but raises some intriguing issues.

Commentary and Conclusions

For me, one of the striking things about the information I have presented in this chapter is that it is possible to find such similar descriptions emerging from such different traditions. But let me say again that the fact that there is a great deal of apparent unanimity in the theoretical (and personal) descriptions of development of moral judgment, meaning systems, motive hierarchies, and spiritual evolution does not make this shared view true.

It does seem fair to say that most adults are engaged in some process of creating or searching for meaning in their lives. But this is not necessarily—perhaps not commonly—a conscious, deliberate process. Some adults appear to engage in a conscious search, and their descriptions of the process are remarkably similar. But, as I pointed out earlier, this may or may not mean that such a search, or even a nonconscious, or nonintentional, sequence of faiths, is a "natural" or essential part of adult development.

Furthermore, it is important to realize that all of what I have said, and all of what these various theorists have said, is based upon a single metaphor of development, the metaphor of "life as a journey" (a kind of Pilgrim's Progress). We imagine the adult trudging up some hill or along some road, passing through steps or stages as she moves along. Implicit in this metaphor is the concept of a goal, an end point or *telos* (a Greek word from which our word "teleological" comes, meaning having purpose or moving toward a goal). This is a journey *going somewhere.* As Sam Keen says (1983), "If we use the idea of stages and journey we are obliged to follow the logic of our metaphors and ask where we are going and why. If life is a journey, the end of life may be death but it cannot be its telos" (p. 30). Thus, if the purpose of the journey is thought of as "growth" or "evolution," then we must have some concept of "highest growth."

The linearity and teleology of this journey metaphor may well limit our thinking about changes in adult meaning systems. Keen suggests several other ways in which we might think of the process, two of which I find particularly appealing: (1) "When we think of this eternal dimension of our being, the circle is more appropriate than the line. If life is a journey, then, it is not a pilgrimage but an odyssey in which one leaves and returns home again" (p. 31). Each step may be a circling back, a remembering of the "still point" within (to use T. S. Eliot's phrase). Progressively, we understand or "know" ourselves and our world differently with each movement of the circle, but there is no necessary end point. (2) We could also think of the entire process as "musical themes that weave together to form a symphony; the themes that are central to each stage are anticipated in the previous stage and remain as resonant subthemes in subsequent stages" (p. 32). Still another possible metaphor is that of life as a tapestry, in which one weaves many colors. An individual who creates many different meaning systems or faiths may thus be weaving a tapestry with more colors, but it may be no more beautiful or pleasing than a tapestry woven intricately of fewer colors.

The basic point I am trying to make here is a simple one, although often hard to absorb thoroughly: Our theories are based in part on metaphors. We begin our search for understanding of adult development with such a metaphor, and it colors all of what we choose to examine and all of what we see. The journey metaphor has dominated most of the current thinking, but it is not the only way to think about the process.

If we are to understand this process further, if we are to choose among these several metaphors, what we need is a great deal more empirical information to answer questions such as the following.

First, is there a longitudinal progression through Fowler's stages of faith or through equivalent sequences proposed by others, such as Loevinger's stages of ego development? I pointed out in Chapter 10 that Loevinger's theory is at least roughly consistent with some of the evidence from existing longitudinal studies. But more direct tests are needed.

Second, what are the connections, if any, between movement through the several sequences described by the various theorists? If we measure a given individual's moral reasoning, his stage of ego development in Loevinger's model, and his type of faith, will that person be at the same stage in all three? And when a person

Figure 11–4 The metaphor of the journey, often depicted as a movement up an apparently endless flight of stairs, is at the root of many theories of adult development focused on either the growth of meaning or changes in personality. But the journey metaphor is not the only one we might adopt and may be misleading in its strong emphasis on both linearity and on a clear goal. (Photo courtesy of Richard Hutchings/Photo Researchers, Inc. Reprinted with permission.)

shifts in one area, does he shift across the board? Alternatively, might integration occur only at the final steps, at the level of what Loevinger calls the integrated person? Just as was proposed in the timing models I described in Chapter 3, each sequence may develop somewhat independently. Disequilibrium may be created when two or more sequences are significantly out of synchrony, thus triggering further moves toward overall integration.

We do not yet have the evidence that would allow us to choose among these alternatives, but several existing studies point to at least some consistency across the sequences. For example, measures of Loevinger's ego development and Kohlberg's moral reasoning are typically found to be correlated moderately, in the range of $r = .50$ (Sullivan, McCullough, & Stager, 1970; Loevinger, 1984), although several studies of adults in their 20s show much lower correlations (e.g., Commons,

Armon, Richards, Schrader, Farrell, Tappan, & Bauer, 1989; King, Kitchener, Wood, & Davison, 1989). Similarly, Leean (1985) reports a moderate relationship between scores on a measure of stage of faith development and on a measure of extent of completion of Erikson's stages. Data from still another recent study suggest a link between principled moral reasoning (Stage 5 in Kohlberg's system) and "openness to experience," which we might take as an aspect of the shift to' individualistic/integrated stages (Lonky, Kaus, & Roodin, 1984). But these are merely the first whiffs of evidence. Much more is needed.

Third, assuming that longitudinal data confirm that there are stages of meaning-making, we need to know what prompts a shift from one to the next. What supports a transition? What retards it?

Finally, we need to know if there is any relationship between stages of faith (or models of meaning, or constructions of the self) and a sense of well-being, or greater physical health, or greater peace of mind. For example, it seems at least plausible that adults might experience greater happiness or satisfaction with their lives when they exist within a meaning system that lies at the 'union' end of the dichotomy than when they are embedded in any of the more self-oriented stages. To check this hypothesis, it is not enough to look at changes with age in life satisfaction (although that is interesting for other reasons). Rather one must measure stages of faith or stages of ego development (preferably longitudinally) and examine life satisfaction at the same time.

No longitudinal study fits this bill but one cross-sectional study goes part way. Costa and McCrae (1983) measured ego development stages using Loevinger's sentence completion test, assessed extraversion, and neuroticism, and asked each of nearly 1,000 men about his feeling of well-being. Among these men aged 35 to 85, the researchers found no overall correlation between ego development and a sense of well-being, but they did not check for the possibility of alternating higher and lower levels of well-being.

Answers to some of these questions may be forthcoming in the next decades, as researchers devise better ways to measure and explore these elusive dimensions of adult lives. For now, much of what I have said in this chapter remains tantalizing and intriguing speculation–but speculation that nonetheless points toward the potential for wisdom, compassion, even illumination within each adult.

Summary

1. In addition to studying inner development by examining personality change over adulthood, we can also ask about any changes in meaning systems or faith or spirituality.
2. It is important to study personal meaning systems for several reasons, including the fact that the impact of any given experience is mediated by the meaning we attach to it and the fact that adults place the search for meaning high on their list of life goals.
3. Changes in formal religious participation with age may be one way to assess changes in meaning systems or values. Church attendance appears to rise

steadily through adult life, with a decline only in late old age. That late life decline is, however, compensated by an increase in private religious practices, suggesting that the overall increase in religiosity with age continues throughout adulthood.

4. Older adults also appear to have higher levels of humanitarian concern and to place greater emphasis on the importance of morality or virtue in their self-concepts.
5. Theories of the development of systems of meaning have been strongly influenced by Kohlberg's theory of the development of moral reasoning. Kohlberg describes three sequentially achieved levels of moral reasoning, with two stages at each level. Level 1 is preconventional reasoning, in which right is understood as that which brings pleasure or approval. Level 2 is conventional reasoning, in which right or justice is defined by the rules or mores of the family, and later of society. Level 3 is principled reasoning, in which right or justice is defined by appeal to a set of principles that lie behind social customs or laws.
6. Kohlberg also proposes a final stage, Stage 7, which involves a form of self-transcendence, a sense of unity with being or life.
7. Longitudinal data show that teenagers and young adults do move through these stages, without skipping, and with little indication of regression. In adults, conventional reasoning is most common. The sequence has been found in every culture thus far studied.
8. Fowler's theory of faith development is broader in concept than Kohlberg's model, encompassing the ways in which adults explain to themselves the purpose of life. Fowler proposes six stages, of which the final four are characteristic of adulthood: (3) synthetic-conventional, marked by external sources of authority, (4) individuative-reflective, in which the source of authority is seen as within the self, (5) conjunctive, which involves an integration of mind and emotion, and (6) universalizing, which goes beyond individuality to a sense of universal connectedness.
9. Cross-sectional data are consistent with Fowler's theory, with stages 3, 4, and 5 first found at approximately the points in adult life that he proposes. Among adults, however, stages 3, 4 and 5 are all about equally common.
10. Integration of Kohlberg's and Fowler's theories with those of Loevinger and Maslow suggests a common set of stages, moving first from conformity to external authority and external self-definition toward individuation, and then toward universalizing or self-transcendant meaning systems.
11. This sequence can be understood in terms of Kegan's proposal that the underlying rhythm of development is a basic alternation between the motive for union and the motive for separateness or individuality.
12. Descriptions by mystics of the stages of inner illumination appear to follow the same underlying rhythm.
13. Transitions from one stage to the next in this progression are frequently experienced in terms of loss or "death" of the old self or the old view. Transitions may thus be profoundly dislocating.

14. Transitions may be triggered by unique life changes, by suffering, by peak experiences, by intentionally pursued self-knowledge, or by self-disciplines.
15. To move beyond the speculative aspect of these theories, additional longitudinal and cross-sectional data will be required.

Suggested Readings

Given my obvious interest in this area, you will not be surprised that I have a long list of books to recommend to you. Any of these would be provocative; none is too technical since they were all written for a lay audience as well as for professionals.

FOWLER, J. (1981). *Stages of faith.* New York: Harper & Row. You may find the case material he gives as fascinating as the theory.

FOWLER, J. (1983, November). Stages of faith. PT Conversation with James Fowler. *Psychology Today,* 17, 56–62. If you want a briefer look at Fowler's theory, try this short article.

FRANKL, V. E. (1984). *Man's search for meaning* (3rd ed). New York: Simon & Schuster. Frankl is a psychiatrist who came to the conclusion that an understanding of a patient's model of meaning was the key to any successful therapy. The roots of this conclusion came from his own experience in a concentration camp. He describes both in this book.

JAMES, W. (1958. Originally published 1902). *The varieties of religious experience.* New York: Mentor. I find this a delightful book, remarkably free of the convoluted style that otherwise seems to be common in this area.

KEEN, S. (1983). *The passionate life: Stages of loving.* New York: Harper & Row. Like most current writers in this area, Keen's views have been influenced by Kohlberg, so this is not totally new stuff. But his focus on the emotional/loving side of the developmental process makes this book particularly relevant for most of our lives.

KEGAN, R. (1982). *The evolving self.* Cambridge, MA: Harvard University Press. Kegan too has been influenced by Kohlberg. You may find the case material particularly interesting in this book.

PECK, M. S. (1978). *The road less travelled.* New York: Simon & Schuster. In this book, Peck offers a highly original, very readable, provocative theory of love and spiritual growth in adulthood and of the potential role of therapy in promoting that growth.

ST. THERESA OF AVILA (1960). *Interior castle.* (E. Allison Peers, Trans.) Garden City, NY: Image Books. (Original work published 1577). Many experts consider St. Theresa's several descriptions of her inner spiritual journey to be the most complete and comprehensible available. I found it astonishing: delightfully written, thought-provoking, and stimulating.

UNDERHILL, E. (1961). *Mysticism.* New York: E. P. Dutton. (Original work published 1911). This book is a scholarly tour de force. She has combined and distilled the essence of the reports of hundreds of mystics and other religious teachers, from all religious traditions, into a single coherent account. Her style is clear and straightforward.

CHAPTER 12

Dealing with the Stresses of Adult Life

There may be a few exceptionally lucky people in this world who rarely face major crises, upheavals, or loss. But most of us encounter these experiences regularly. I consider my own adult years to have been comparatively crisis-free; but in the 31 years since I turned 20, I have gone through the usual failed love affairs, a divorce, sixteen moves, seven or eight job changes, assorted minor car accidents, assorted small surgeries and the usual collection of illnesses, the death of a close friend and of two grandparents, and I have twice been the victim of a crime. Most people have doubtless had to cope with far more.

As I have pointed out all along, some crises and upheavals are predictable and are quite widely shared by adults as they move through the various normative roles and stages. But many such experiences, or their timing, are unique to each individual. If we are to understand the various pathways through adulthood that may be taken by an individual, we need to take a look at the effect of such stresses on adults. We also need to look at those qualities of adults, or their environments, that may soften or shorten the effect of stress.

Fortunately, the study of stress has been a hot research topic in recent years, so there is an extensive literature. Less fortunately, very little of the research is developmental in conception or design. Nonetheless, some extremely interesting concepts and provocative findings have emerged that expand our understanding of adulthood.

Definitions of Stress

Let me begin be defining the term "stress." Writing a definition would be a simple task if there were agreement among stress researchers. But at this stage in the evolution of theory and research on stress, there are still at least three types of definitions, each associated with a different body of theory and research: response-oriented theories, stimulus-oriented theories, and interactionist theories.

Response-Oriented Theories The one name most prominently associated with response-oriented theory is Hans Selye, who is really the "father" of modern stress research (1936; 1976; 1982). Selye defines stress as "the nonspecific (that is, common) result of any demand upon the body, be the effect mental or somatic" (1982, p. 7). That is, stress is the body's *response* to demand. The more demands there are on a person—demands from roles, from environmental hazards such as heat or noise, from time pressures, and so on—the more stress the person experiences.

According to Selye, the body's stress reaction occurs in three stages, which he calls collectively the **general adaptation syndrome** (GAS). First comes the *alarm reaction,* which has two phases. In the "shock" phase there is an initial, immediate effect of some noxious stimulus on the body's tissues, marked by such indicators as a drop in both body temperature and blood pressure. Then there is a "countershock" phase in which some kind of physiological defenses are mounted. The adrenal cortex enlarges and secretes higher levels of hormones, and the body temperature and blood pressure move back toward normal levels. If the stressor continues, these alarm reactions fade and are replaced by a stage Selye calls *resistance*, in which the body strives to achieve homeostasis. Three physiological changes are particularly notable in this stage: enlargement of the adrenal gland, shrinkage of the thymus gland, and gastrointestinal ulceration. The shrinkage of the thymus gland is especially critical since the thymus is centrally involved in immune responses, as you'll recall from Chapter 4. Thus, in this phase the individual is able to control the initial alarm reaction to the stressor but does so in a way that lowers resistance to other stressors or stimuli. If the stressor continues long enough (and many chronic stressors do continue over very long periods of time), the somewhat fragile adaptation of the resistance phase breaks down, and the person reaches the stage of *exhaustion,* when some of the alarm-stage responses reappear. If the stressor is severe enough, exhaustion is accompanied by physical illness or even death.

These three stages are analogous to what happens when you exercise. When you first begin a several-mile run or an aerobics class or some equivalent, your body may initially feel tired, and it may be difficult to keep moving. But then you achieve some level of homeostasis as you get into a physical rhythm; for a while, you feel as if you could go on forever. Eventually, though, if you continue long enough you will reach the stage of exhaustion.

Physical illness, or even death, can be associated with any of the stages of the general adaptation syndrome, even the resistance stage in which some kind of balance is achieved. The catch is that some resistance patterns may themselves promote illness in the long run. For example, the Type A pattern of behavior I talked about in Chapter 5 is a kind of resistance pattern in which the individual responds to work demands by being extremely organized and pressing for ever more efficiency. Such an adaptation pattern is associated with increased risk of heart disease. The key point is that although the intermediate stage of response to stress is more stable than the initial alarm reaction or the ultimate exhaustion stage, the body's response to heightened physical or emotional demand is not perfect. Furthermore, Selye specifically postulates that the return to "rest" after the stressor has stopped and the GAS is terminated is never complete. One gets back *almost* to the old level but not quite. The process we call aging may thus be simply the accumulation of the effects of many GASs, each leaving a residue of effects on the hormone system, the cardiovascular system, the immune system.

Selye's definition of stress has prompted a great deal of useful research, primarily by physicians and physiologists who have attempted to identify the specific physiological patterns that are part of the stress response or GAS. In particular, much of the extremely interesting work in the area now called psychoimmunology can trace its roots to Selye's work. But I suspect that Selye's definition of stress does not match your own everyday use of the word. Normally, when we use this word in everyday conversation, as in "Joan has been under a lot of stress lately," or "I must have gotten this cold because I'm really stressed out," we are referring not to our body's reaction to some external event, but to the external event itself—to the stimulus and not to the response.

STIMULUS-ORIENTED THEORIES Most psychologists who have been interested in stress have used just such a stimulus-oriented approach, defining stress in terms of the degree of environmental demand for adaptation. For a researcher using such a definition of stress, the task is to specify just what classes of events are stressful and what the effects of that stress may be on the individual.

A number of different lists of stresses have been developed among which the most famous and widely used has been the Social Readjustment Rating Scale developed by Thomas Holmes and Richard Rahe (1967), which consists of the 42 "life change events" listed in Table 12.1. The basic idea is that any change, be it positive or negative, requires adaptation. The more changes, the more the adaptation. Because some life changes are more profound or severe than others, Holmes and Rahe had raters assign different numbers of points to each life change to reflect the degree of adaptation it appeared to require. A subject's score on this instrument is thus the sum of the points for all the changes he or she checks off as having occurred during the past 6 to 12 months. Holmes and Rahe hypothesized that the higher the score, the greater the likelihood that the person would become physically ill or emotionally disturbed within the next year. In particular, a score over 300 was thought to reflect a major life change crisis or stress.

There is a great deal of research evidence (which I'll describe shortly) supporting Holmes and Rahe's original hypothesis. At the same time, there have been serious questions raised about this definition of stress and this method of measurement (e.g. Cohen, 1988b; Dohrenwend & Dohrenwend, 1978). First of all, it is not so obvious that all kinds of life change are equivalent in their stress-producing effects. Are positive life changes and negative life changes really equally stressful? And even among life changes that may be classed as negative, are there some subvarieties that are more stress-producing or more likely to lead to illness than others?

With these questions in mind, several researchers have suggested subcategories of life changes or stress experiences that may prove to be more helpful predictors of illness than the original Holmes and Rahe list. For example, Pearlin (1980, 1982b) makes a distinction between chronic life strains and life changes. And among life changes, as you will remember from earlier chapters, he distinguishes between those that are scheduled and those that are unscheduled. Richard Lazarus and his colleagues (Lazarus & DeLongis, 1983; Lazarus & Folkman, 1984) similarly suggest that we will better understand the links between stress and illness if we count not just major life changes but also "daily hassles" and "daily uplifts." Hassles, which may be transient or chronic, include such familiar experiences as misplacing your keys, having to fill out forms, finding you've gained a pound when you step on the scales in the morning, or getting caught in a traffic jam on your way to an important meeting. Uplifts may include laughter, pleasant times with your family, or other joyous or satisfying moments. These newer expansions of the concept of life stresses, while not as thoroughly studied as life changes, have proven to be useful predictors.

A second major question raised about defining stress only in terms of major life changes is whether the same life change is equally stressful for all people. Perhaps, instead, it is the person's *subjective interpretation* (the *appraisal,* to use Lazarus's word) of an event that is critical and not the objective event itself. In the terms I used in the last chapter, perhaps it is the meaning we assign to some event, rather than the event, that determines both our psychological and physiological reactions to it. Questions of this kind have led to a third, interactionist, view of stress.

INTERACTIONIST APPROACHES Interactionist definitions of stress focus on the individual's perception of an event, or on the extent to which some experience exceeds the individual's adaptational capacity. For example, stress may be defined as "a (perceived) imbalance between demand and response capability, under conditions where failure to meet demand has important (perceived) consequences" (McGrath, 1970, p. 20), or as "a particular relationship between the person and the environment that is appraised by the person as taxing or exceeding his or her resources and endangering his or her well-being" (Lazarus & Folkman, 1984, p. 19).

Looked at this way, stress is neither located solely in the environment nor in the body; rather the physiological GAS is mediated by the individual's perception or appraisal of some situation. Thus, when a person says "I'm really under stress" this is not an objective statement about some amount of external pressure but a statement about that person's sense of strain or difficulty in coping with the pressures that she experiences. Only when a person feels unable to cope with a demand would we expect some potential stressor to be related to disease or emotional disturbance. Exactly the same environmental event might therefore be "stressful" to one person and not to another.

A COMBINED VIEW My own leanings are toward an interactionist approach, but I would add still further elements. I continue to think it is useful to attempt to identify specific experiences that are likely to be stressful for most individuals because they demand change or adaptation, as in Holmes and Rahe's list. But whether those experiences will trigger the physiological stress response (GAS) and thus increase the risk of illness, will depend not only on an individual's interpretation of the event, but also on that person's temporary or long-term vulnerability (such as might accompany a lack of social supports) and internal coping skills. Figure 12–1 shows this system schematically.

Note that age does not appear in this figure. But age or developmental stage may affect the stress response system at any one of several points. Adults of different ages may be exposed to differing numbers or types of potentially stressful experiences. Or, as they move through the life span and their meaning systems change, adults may interpret (appraise) such life changes differently. Or adults may become more skilled at coping with the stressful experiences they encounter as they get older. Most of the research I'll be talking about is not cast in such a developmental framework, but there are at least some bits and pieces that I will weave into the discussion as we move along.

Let me begin the exploration of the elements in this system by looking at the most studied portion of the figure, the link between potentially stressful experiences and illness.

TABLE 12.1. Life Change Events Included in the Holmes and Rahe Social Readjustment Rating Scale.

	Life Event	Points Assigned
1.	Death of spouse	100
2.	Divorce	73
3.	Marital separation from mate	65
4.	Detention in jail or other institution	63
5.	Death of a close family member	63
6.	Major personal injury or illness	53
7.	Marriage	50
8.	Being fired at work	47
9.	Marital reconciliation with mate	45
10.	Retirement from work	45
11.	Major change in the health or behavior of a family member	44
12.	Pregnancy	40
13.	Sexual difficulties	39
14.	Gaining a new family member (e.g., through birth, adoption, oldster moving in, etc.)	39
15.	Major business readjustment (e.g., merger, reorganization, bankruptcy, etc.)	39
16.	Major change in financial state (e.g., a lot worse off or a lot better off than usual)	38
17.	Death of a close friend	37
18.	Changing to a different line of work	36
19.	Major change in the number of arguments with spouse (e.g., either a lot more or a lot less than usual regarding child-rearing, personal habits, etc.)	35
20.	Taking out a mortgage or loan for a major purchase (e.g., for a home, business, etc.)	31
21.	Foreclosure on a mortgage or loan	30
22.	Major change in responsibilities at work (e.g., promotion, demotion, lateral transfer)	29
23.	Son or daughter leaving home (e.g., marriage, attending college, etc.)	29
24.	Trouble with in-laws	29
25.	Outstanding personal achievement	28
26.	Wife beginning or ceasing work outside the home	26
27.	Beginning or ceasing formal schooling	26
28.	Major change in living conditions (e.g., building a new home, remodeling, deterioration of home or neighborhood)	25
29.	Revision of personal habits (dress, manners, associations, etc.)	24
30.	Trouble with the boss	23
31.	Major change in working hours or conditions	20
32.	Change in residence	20
33.	Changing to a new school	20
34.	Major change in usual type and/or amount of recreation	19
35.	Major change in church activities (e.g., a lot more or a lot less than usual)	19

	Life Event	Points Assigned
36.	Major change in social activities (e.g., clubs, dancing, movies, visiting, etc.)	18
37.	Taking out a mortgage or loan for a lesser purchase (e.g., for a car, TV, freezer, etc.)	17
38.	Major change in sleeping habits (a lot more or a lot less sleep, or change in part of day when asleep)	16
39.	Major change in number of family get-togethers (e.g., a lot more or a lot less than usual)	15
40.	Major change in eating habits (a lot more or a let less food intake, or very different meal hours or surroundings)	15
41.	Vacation	13
42.	Christmas	12
43.	Minor violations of the law (e.g., traffic tickets, jaywalking, disturbing the peace, etc.)	11

SOURCE: Reprinted with permission from *Journal of Psychosomatic Research*, 14, Holmes, T. S. and Holmes T. H. Short term intrusions into Life-Style routine (pp. 121–132). Copyright 1970. Pergamon Press, Ltd. (Original publication of the Social Readjustment Rating Scale appeared in the *Journal of Psychomatic Research*, 11, 1967, pp. 213–218. Copyright 1967, Pergamon Press, Ltd.)

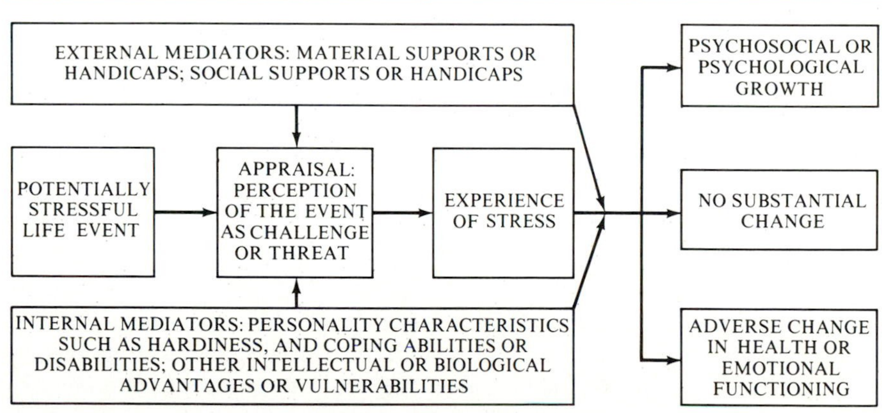

Figure 12–1 A first approximation of a model of the link between stress and adverse or positive changes during adulthood. Whether some potentially stressful life event, such as a major life change or an accumulation of daily hassles, will lead to illness or not depends on how a person perceives the event, whether that person has adequate support to help meet the stress, and the specific coping strategies the person uses. (Source: adapted and modified from a similar model by Dohrenwend & Dohrenwend, 1980, Figure 1.1, p. 2.)

Effects of Stressful Experiences on Adult Functioning

Physical Disease

Most of the early research examining the links between stress and disease was based on the original Holmes & Rahe scale (Table 12.1). Despite the limitations of this scale, a consistent finding emerged: The larger the number of life changes a person has experienced within the past 6 to 12 months, the greater the likelihood of physical illness, such as tuberculosis, diabetes, arthritis, cancer, heart disease, complications of pregnancy, accidents, and athletic injuries (Perkins, 1982). This does not mean that if your score on the scale is over 300 you will contract *all* these diseases, nor even that you will automatically get sick. It does mean that the risk of contracting *some* disease goes up. Similarly, high levels of life change are also associated with lowered resistance to pain or discomfort (Harney & Brigham, 1985).

Studies using more differentiated measures of life events or potential stressors show similar links. High rates of daily hassles, for example, are associated with increased risk of illness. Of course, major life changes usually bring with them an increase in daily hassles, but the more ordinary strains add up as well (DeLongis, et al. 1982; Holahan, Holahan, & Belk, 1984).

A number of investigators have now taken these findings a major step further and shown a link between life changes or potential stressors and actual physiological functioning, particularly immune system functioning. As one example, Janice Kiecolt-Glaser and Ronald Glaser (1988) have demonstrated such a connection in several studies of medical students whose immune systems were assessed one month before and then during final exams. These researchers found the immune systems of the students to be comparatively less effective at exam time, with lower levels of "natural killer" cells and markedly lower levels of interferon production. Lowered immune system functioning was also found by Lee Willis and colleagues (Willis, Thomas, Garry, & Goodwin, 1987) in a study of 15 elderly adults (age 68 to 86) who were part of an ongoing longitudinal study. Because these adults had been tested regularly, it was possible to obtain both physiological and psychological measures before, immediately after, and at least six months after some major life change that the subject described as a crisis, such as the death of a child or spouse, diagnosis of a major illness, divorce, or auto accident. What Willis found was that immune system function declined sharply in the month following the crisis. Six months after the crisis the level of immune system function had returned almost to the precrisis level.

Despite the consistency of these findings and the impressive new evidence showing the link between the stressful experience and immune system functioning, the size of the effect is nonetheless quite small. The correlation between subjects' scores on the Holmes and Rahe scale and illness, for instance, is typically only around .30. Such a correlation converts to the statement that global measures of stress can account for only about 10 percent of the variation in the presence or absence of disease (Dohrenwend & Dohrenwend, 1981). It is possible, of course, that the effect of stress is really much larger than this and that we will detect it better as our measures of stress become more refined and as we begin to take into account the other elements in the model in Figure 12–1. But it is important to emphasize that stress theorists are *not* saying that stress is the only cause of disease. People obviously get sick or have accidents for a whole lot of reasons other than stress.

Emotional Disturbance

A similar picture emerges when we look at the relationship between life change and emotional disturbance. There is a link, but the size of the effect is relatively small (Monroe & Peterman, 1988). Let me describe one study in some detail to give you some sense of the kind of effect I'm talking about.

E.S. Paykel (1974) has explored the connection between life change and depression. He compared a group of 185 patients being treated in psychiatric hospitals for depression with a nonhospitalized sample from the general population, carefully matching the two sets of subjects on age, sex, marital status, race, and social class. He then determined the number of life changes (out of a list of 61) each of these subjects had experienced during the six months prior to the depressive episode or during the equivalent period for the nondepressed subjects. Paykel found that the depressives had experienced more life changes than had the non-depressives in several categories: employment (beginning or ending a job, being demoted or fired, being promoted or retiring) health, and marital relationships (marriage, separation, divorce, or increase in arguments with spouse). There were no differences between the depressed and nondepressed subjects in the number of other family changes, such as a child marrying or being in legal difficulties.

When he analyzed the findings more closely, however, Paykel found that only *undesirable* life changes were really at work here, and among the undesirable changes, the key ones appeared to be what he called *exits*—loss of some relationship, such as the death of a close family member, divorce, or a child leaving home. You can see these results in Table 12.2.

These findings have been confirmed by several large studies in England of which the best known is a study of depression in women by George Brown and Tirril Harris (1978). They found that severe, negative events were common in the few weeks before the onset of a depression both in women who were actually being treated for depression and among those who had not sought professional help but who nonetheless reported depressive symptoms. Approximately 60 percent of depressed women had experienced at least one severe event within the three weeks just prior to their depression while only about 20 percent of the nondepressed patients had experienced an equally severe event during an equivalent three-week period. Like Paykel, Harris and Brown found that the key precipitating event was most often some loss or "exit."

But as was true in the findings on the link between life change or stress and physical disease, a high level of life change or loss does not guarantee depression or other emotional disturbance. It merely increases the likelihood. Paykel estimates

TABLE 12.2. Frequency of Undesirable, Desirable, "Exit," and "Entrance" Life Changes in the Recent Experiences of Depressed and Nondepressed Adults.

Category of Life Change	Percentage of Subjects Who Had Reported at Least One Such Change in the Past Six Months	
	Depressed Patients	*Controls*
Desirable life changes (e.g., engagement, marriage, promotion).	3.2%	5.4%
Undesirable life changes (e.g., death of family member, separation, demotion, serious illness of family member, jail, major financial problems, unemployment, divorce, business failure, stillbirth).	44.3%	16.8%
Entrances (engagement, marriage, birth of child, new person in home).	11.4%	9.7%
Exits (death of a close family member, separation, divorce, family member leaves home, child married, son drafted).	24.9%	4.9%

SOURCE: Paykel, 1974, adapted from Tables 2 and 3, p. 139–140. Reprinted by permission of John Wiley & Sons, Inc.

that only about 10 percent of the people who experience a significant exit in their lives become clinically depressed.

Positive Effects of Stress

To make the picture still more complex (and far more interesting from my perspective), there are a few studies suggesting that stressful life changes may be actually beneficial to some individuals—increasing life satisfaction, improving overall mental health, perhaps prompting the kind of inner changes I discussed in Chapters 10 and 11.

The best evidence for such growth-producing effects of stress comes from several longitudinal studies by David Chiriboga (Chiriboga, 1984; Chiriboga & Cutler, 1980; Chiriboga & Dean, 1978). This research is based on an interesting sample which included originally a group of high school seniors, a group of newlyweds, a group of adults around age 50 whose children were leaving home, and a group of older adults (about age 60) who were getting ready to retire. These adults were reinterviewed and retested 3, 5, 7 and 11 years later and completed lengthy assessments of life changes at the later contacts. Chiriboga has been interested in the relationship between particular subtypes of life changes and various outcomes for the individuals, including life satisfaction, depression, other psychological symptoms, and health.

Chiriboga's results parallel those of other researchers studying stress and life change: Negative life events were more likely to be related to later negative outcomes than were positive life changes, and life changes that involved changes in close personal relationships, particularly marital relationships (marriage, separation, divorce, death of a spouse, etc.), were more consistently related to negative outcomes than were other kinds of life changes.

But Chiriboga also found a few indications that some kinds of stresses may have led to *improved* functioning. For example, among the younger men those who dwelt on and worried about work and personal changes showed a *decline* in depression over several years. And among older men, a group of changes that Chiriboga calls "disharmony," which includes changes in political or religious beliefs, in hobbies, and in anticipation of impending stress, were associated with *lower* levels of reported emotional problems.

Some evidence from the Berkeley intergenerational studies confirms the possible positive effect of life changes. Haan reports that those subjects who had been hospitalized or physically ill more often over their adult lives were later rated as more empathetic and more tolerant of ambiguity than were those who had been physically healthier (Haan, 1982).

The amount of research suggesting such potentially positive effects of stress or life change is small, so I need to be careful about placing too much emphasis on these specific results. But the possibility obviously fits with the general view of personality and inner change I have proposed in the last two chapters. Major stresses or life changes, under some circumstances or for some people, may be the stimulus or the occasion for reassessment and transformation, and thus, for growth.

Developmental Differences in Stress Experiences and in Responses to Stress

When age differences in life change events or stress experiences have been examined, the consistent finding is that older adults experience fewer major life changes than do younger adults (Goldberg & Comstock, 1980; Murrell, Norris, & Grote, 1988). Figure 12–2 shows the average number of life changes reported by each age group in Chiriboga's studies, out of a maximum total of 138 events. Clearly, the total scores were higher among the younger groups.

But when such total life change scores are broken apart we discover (not surprisingly) that the age pattern we find depends very much on the particular type of life change or stress we look at. In several large surveys, such as one involving nearly 4,000 subjects in North Carolina (Hughes, Blazer, & George, 1988), researchers have found that adults over 65 are less likely to experience such life changes as getting married or divorced or changing jobs or moving, but they are *more* likely to be hospitalized for an illness, to retire, or to experience the death of a spouse.

This pattern makes perfectly good sense when we think about the kinds of role additions and losses typical in each age period that I talked about in Chapters 6

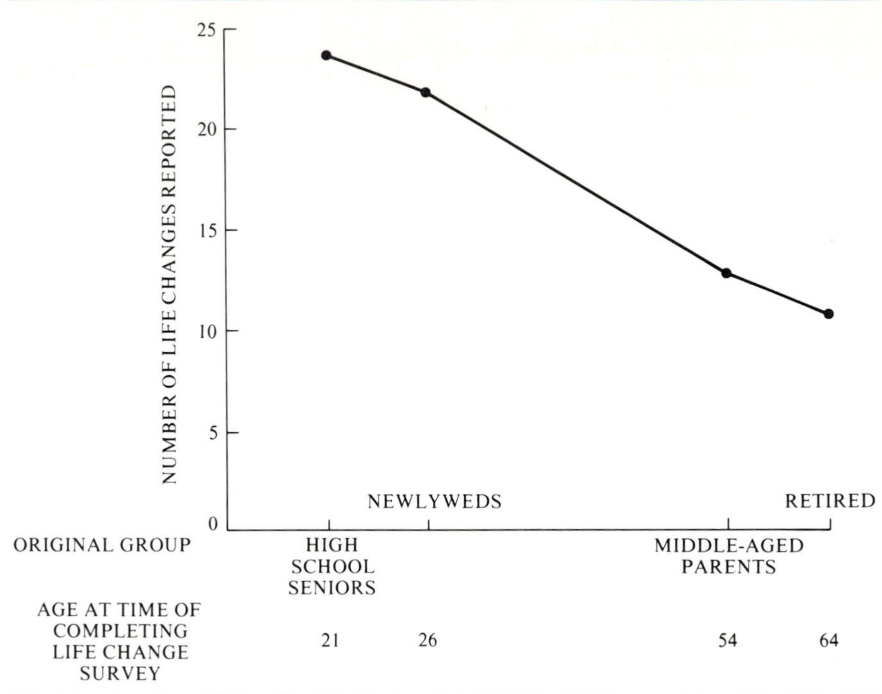

Figure 12–2 These findings are typical of the few studies that have looked at the relationship between age and the number of life changes adults encounter: The older you get the fewer life changes you are likely to have to deal with. (Source: Chiriboga & Dean, 1978, from data in Table 1, p. 50.)

and 8. It is almost inevitable that young adults will experience many major life changes as they add roles. Life changes in old age, in contrast, have more to do with role loss or with health deterioration.

What is not so clear is whether there is any change with age in the meaning or appraisal adults give to life changes. Chiriboga and Dean (1978) found that the younger adults in their longitudinal studies were more likely to be preoccupied with the stresses they were encountering (e.g., "I can't forget it," or "I think about it all the time.") Others have noted that older adults report less disruption from any given life change than do younger adults (e.g., Masuda & Holmes, 1978). Yet the North Carolina researchers, in their much larger study, found no age differences in the strength of adults' reported reactions to specific events or in the reported importance of those events in their lives. Furthermore, we have ample evidence that there is an apparently causal link between high levels of life change and poor health outcomes among older adults just as there is among the young. So we certainly cannot conclude that older adults are immune to the stress-producing effects of life changes even if they are able to interpret them differently or take them less seriously. The jury is clearly still out on this set of questions.

A Quick Summary

To summarize all of this, we have evidence that increased rates of life change, particularly life changes that involve emotional losses or losses of relationships ("exits"), are modestly predictive of physical illness and emotional disturbances such as depression. Daily hassles, too, accumulate and increase the risk of both physical and emotional illness. The absolute incidence of life changes appears to be higher in early adulthood than in later adulthood, but adults of differing ages encounter different sets of life changes as they move through the normative series of role acquisitions and losses. Finally, for some adults, life changes and hassles *may* led to emotional or personal growth, rather than disease or depression.

Resistance Resources

This summary leaves a great many questions unanswered. In particular, it does not explain why it is that different adults, faced with the same life change or potential stressor, do not all respond in the same way. To understand such individual variations, we must turn our attention to those personal and social resources that may buffer the individual from the potential impact of stress. Such resources may be collectively called **resistance resources.** Central among these are social support and coping responses.

Social Support and Response to Stress

I gave an initial definition of social support in Chapter 8, namely the receipt of affect, affirmation, and aid from others. Another way to think of it is as one of the properties of a **social network.** One's social network is the collection or web of relationships with family, friends, and colleagues that each of us has at any given time. Often a person's network is described primarily in structural terms, such as:

1. *Size.* How many people are there with whom you have any kind of regular contact?
2. *Composition.* Is your network composed mostly of family or mostly of friends? Does it include people you have known a short time or only those you have known a long time?
3. *Rate or frequency of contact.* Do you see network members often or rarely?
4. *Interconnectedness.* Do the people in your network know and interact with each other, or do you have separate groups of family and friends who do not have contact with one another?
5. *Duration.* How long have you known the people in your network?

These structural descriptions are helpful but they do not tell us much about the intimacy or supportiveness of the relationships involved. Whether larger or more interconnected networks provide more or less social support is an empirical question, but as a general rule, if we want to understand the role of social support, it is not enough just to ask people how many friends they have or how often they see their family. We need to ask much more specifically about the content of the interactions, such as receipt of affect, affirmation, and aid, or emotional, tangible, or informational support (Schaefer, Coyne, & Lazarus, 1982).

EVIDENCE ON THE BUFFERING EFFECT OF SOCIAL SUPPORT Research on the impact of social support on responses to stress has been confused by a lack of agreement on just how social support should be measured; very often, measures of network structure (such as how many friends a person reports having) are counted as measures of social support. Because of these difficulties, the research findings have been mixed. However, the bulk of the evidence suggests that those adults with high levels of social support:

- live longer, even when other potential causal factors such as social class, smoking, alcohol consumption, initial health risk, race, life satisfaction, and level of physical activity have been controlled or matched (Berkman, 1985);
- are less likely to be depressed and more likely to report high levels of life satisfaction or happiness (Cohen & Wills, 1985);
- are less likely to respond to some stressful experience with either physical illness or emotional disturbance (Cohen & Wills, 1985).

It is this final effect, usually described as the *buffering* effect of social support, that has been of particular interest to those who have studied the link between stress and physical or mental illness. Let me illustrate the process with some examples from research on various types of stress with adults of various ages.

In one of the early studies to show this buffering effect, Nuckols, Cassell and Kaplan (1972) found that, in a group of pregnant women, those with high levels of life change and low levels of what they called "psychosocial assets" also had the highest levels of complications of pregnancy. Women with equivalently high levels of life change who were supported by greater psychosocial assets were apparently buffered from the effects of the life changes. Similarly, in Brown and Harris' study of depression in women I described earlier (Brown and Harris, 1978), the link between severe life changes and depression was significantly weaker when the woman had a close, intimate relationship with her husband or boyfriend than when she lacked such a relationship. The key data from this study are shown in Table 12.3. The clearest contrast is between those women who had no confidant and those whose husband or boyfriend was an intimate confidant. As you can see in the table, the former group was four times as likely to become severely depressed following a major life change as was the latter group.

This buffering effect occurs for men as well. For instance, in a short-term longitudinal study of men who had been laid off work because their companies had gone out of business, Kasl and Cobb (1982) found that those men who felt that they had adequate social support from their wives and friends showed fewer physical and emotional symptoms than did those men with lower levels of perceived support.

TABLE 12.3. Percentage of Women in a Large British Study Who Experienced Significant Depression Following a Major Life Change as a Function of the Presence of an Intimate Confidant in Their Lives.

	Husband or Boyfriend Was Intimate Confidant (N = 281)	Family Member or Friend Other Than Boyfriend or Lover Was Confidant; Seen at Least Once a Week (N = 86)	Either No Confidant, or Confidant Seen Less Than Weekly (N = 52)
At least one severe life event within the past year	10%	26%	41%
No severe event in past year	1%	3%	4%

SOURCE: Brown, G. W. & Harris, T. Social origins of depression: A study of psychiatric disorder in women. Publishers Tavistock Publications, Ltd., London and the Free Press (division of Macmillan, Inc.), New York.

Social support also reduces the risk from stressful experiences among the elderly. Neal Krause has shown this particularly nicely in an elegant series of studies of a random community survey of more than 300 older adults in Galveston, Texas (Krause, 1986, 1987a, 1987b, 1987c; Krause, Liang, & Yatomi, 1989). In one analysis, Krause (1987a) has shown that chronic financial strain significantly increases the chances that these elderly adults will report depressive symptoms, but this effect is considerably weaker among those with adequate social support, particularly if they received adequate informational support.

These studies and others like them certainly confirm the common sense assumption that having supportive relationships helps you ride out the various storms of life. But the buffering effects of social support are not nearly so straightforward or so general as these findings may lead you to think. As researchers have gone beyond the mere demonstration of a buffering effect, they have discovered some complexities. Let me suggest a number of refinements.

THE IMPORTANCE OF INTIMACY First, for a buffering effect to exist, the most critical property of a social network appears to be its intimacy. Even very small networks can be helpful if the relationships are intimate. The smallest number of intimate relationships that seems to be absolutely necessary is one. To be sure, the majority of adults have at least one confidant. In one national survey, Campbell (1981) found that five out of six adults have at least one such intimate relationship; Gary Lee, in a Washington State survey of over 4,000 adults (1988) found that 85 percent of the women and 70 percent of the men reported having at least one confidant. So the majority of adults are at least minimally buffered against the most serious effects of stress. But there is a significant minority who do not have a confidant and who may thus be particularly vulnerable to the negative effects of stressful life experiences.

THE MATCH BETWEEN THE SOURCE OF SUPPORT AND THE TYPE OF STRESS Second, as Morton Lieberman points out, "it is not the total amount of help that is salient, but rather the fit between a particular kind of problem and the help provider" (1982, p. 771). Different types of crises may require different forms or sources of support.

The source of support that is most often critical is that of a spouse or lover. For example, women who are expecting or have just given birth to their first child suffer fewer physical and emotional effects if they have their husband's support. Other sources of support, such as from close friends or other family members, apparently do not do the trick or do not work as well (Lieberman, 1982). You can see just this effect in the results from the Brown and Harris study shown in Table 12.3. If you go back and look at the table again you'll see that an intimate relationship with a family member was better than no intimate relationship at all, but it was not as good a buffer against severe stress as was the support of a husband or lover.

The relationship with spouse or lover is not invariably the most helpful. For a life change like widowhood, (which I'll talk about in detail shortly) where it is precisely the *loss* of that central intimate source of social support that must be dealt with, the source of support associated with the greatest buffering effect

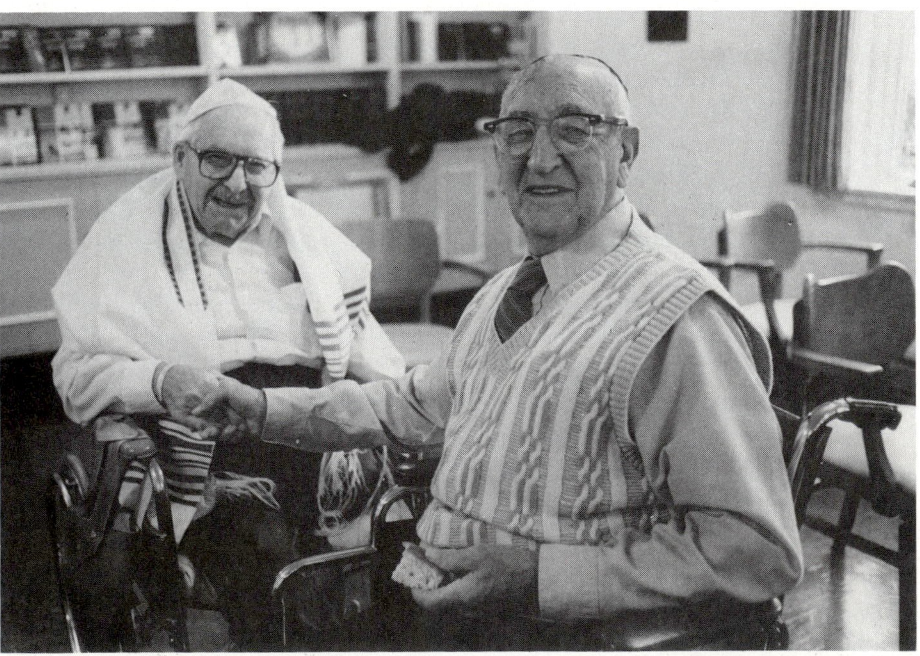

Figure 12–3 If you are facing a life crisis of some kind, having at least one good friend you can talk to like this seems to be critical in helping you weather the storm without too much ill-effect. (Photo © Susan Lapides, 1989, c/o Design Conceptions. Reprinted with permission.)

appeared in one study to be the widowed person's parents or other widowed friends (Bankhoff, 1983), especially during the early phases of mourning.

Morton Lieberman has taken this argument a step further by suggesting that "It may very well be that when the salient support person is available but does not provide needed [support], substitution becomes almost impossible; this may not be the case when the critical relationship no longer exists" (1982, p. 773). In Bankhoff's study of widows, for example, those widows who had the most difficult time were those whose parents were still alive but not providing help and emotional support. For these women, substitute support from friends did not appear to have a buffering effect. But those widows whose parents were deceased appeared to be able to use the support of widowed friends as a replacement. Similarly, one might guess that in Lieberman's study of women who have just given birth, the greatest risk of physical and emotional difficulties would be among those women whose husbands or lovers failed to provide the expected support.

Lee's Washington State study, although not specifically focused on the buffering impact of social support, is nonetheless consistent with Lieberman's hypothesis as well. As you would expect, he found that adults whose single most important confidant was their spouse had much higher marital satisfaction than did those whose spouse was not listed as a confidant. More surprising is the fact that adults who had a close confidant *other than* the spouse actually reported lower marital satisfaction than did those who had no confidant at all.

THE ROLE OF EXPECTATION I find Lieberman's hypothesis especially intriguing because it once again points to the importance of interpretation or meaning as a key variable. It begins to look as if the causal ingredient in the buffering effect of social support is the individual's *perception* that his support network is sufficient to aid him in critical ways (Cohen & Wills, 1985). Feeling let down by a key person alters that perception of support adequacy and limits or eliminates the buffering effect, even for an individual with an extensive network.

Krause has been able to show this causal connection unusually clearly in his study of older adults in Galveston since he followed this group longitudinally for a period of 18 months. Not only did he find that subjects' satisfaction with their level of social support was a better predictor of health than was the objective amount of support (Krause, 1987c), but when he traced the sequence he found that a decline in an adult's sense of satisfaction with his social support was likely to be followed by an increase in depressive symptoms, rather than the other way around (Krause, Liang, & Yatomi, 1989).

SOME NEGATIVE EFFECTS OF SOCIAL NETWORKS Lest I give the impression that there is nothing but sweetness and light in the world of social relationships, let me hasten to add that there are costs associated with social networks. Network systems are generally reciprocal. Not only do you receive support, you give it as well. And as I pointed out in Chapters 7 and 8, there are particular points in the life cycle when the giving side of the equation seems to be more heavily weighted than the receiving side, which may increase stress and daily hassles.

Everyday social interactions can also be a significant source of hassles. Most of us have at least some regular interactions with individuals we do not like or who irritate us to distraction: Your co-worker whose desk is constantly messy, your neighbor who stops by for a chat every time you have settled down for an hour of pleasant solitude, your mother who invariably tells you how to rearrange your living room furniture each time she comes to visit. Karen Rook (1984) argues that an adult's overall sense of well-being and happiness may be more affected by the presence of such irritating or problematic social ties than by the presence of positive and supportive relationships.

Rook interviewed a set of 120 widowed women in Los Angeles, ranging in age from 60 to 89, inquiring not only about their overall sense of well-being and their supportive social ties, but also about their more problematic social relationships, such as people who invaded their privacy, people who broke promises, or people who provoked conflicts or feelings of anger. Rook found that the number and frequency of positive social interactions was unrelated to overall life satisfaction, but negative interactions were predictive of lower life satisfaction.

Krause, too, has found some sign of negative effects of social support in his Galveston sample, although in this case it seems to be a function of 'too much of a good thing' rather than too many negative interactions. Krause (1987d) argues that social support operates to buffer the individual from the effects of life change by increasing the adult's sense of personal control over his own life. But the relationship between social support and the sense of control is not linear, it is an inverted U. Either too much or too little support, especially emotional support, is associated with a lower sense of control. So when you are facing a crisis and your friends and relations are hovering over you in an effort to be maximally supportive, you may feel less in control, and thus ultimately less supported, than if they had backed off a little.

Age Differences in the Effects of Social Support So far as I know, no researcher has looked specifically for a possible relationship between age and the buffering effect of social support. The research I've already described, of course, shows that it is possible to find examples of such buffering in each age group, but there is much that has not been explored. For example, we do not know whether some age groups are more skillful in using their social networks than are others, or whether definitions of the adequacy of support may change with age. Our developmental information is limited to comparisons of the properties of networks of adults of different ages, much of which I have already described in Chapters 7 and 8. Recall that contact with family members remains largely constant across adulthood. Young adults, however, appear to have the largest networks and to place the greatest emphasis on the importance of friends (e.g., Veroff et al. 1981). The number of friends adults report is usually lower among adults in their 30s and 40s than among those in their 20s and 50s, but there seem to be no major changes in the total size of adults' networks between middle age and old age (Antonucci, 1985).

The one change in the functioning of social networks that does appear to occur in the later years of adulthood is a reduction in the amount of support *given*. Once an adult leaves the years of the "sandwich generation," when maximum help is given in both directions in the generational chain, there is a gradual drop in the amount of help or other social support given to the members of one's network. This may imply a decline in the amount of reciprocal interaction that occurs between family members, or with friends. Since most adults report preferring reciprocal relationships, there may develop some reluctance to call on the assistance of the network in times of stress, which might result in some loss of the buffering effect of the support system. But such a possibility has not been tested empirically.

Personality and Coping Strategies

The second major category of resistance resources for dealing with stress are those personal qualities or skills that may help reduce the impact of the stress. Most researchers (e.g., Pearlin & Schooler, 1978) distinguish between two aspects of such personal responses: (1) psychological resources, which are enduring qualities each individual may have, including such things as intellectual skill, temperament, or personality, and (2) coping behaviors, which are the things a person does in the face of stress or potential harm. The two are clearly interconnected. Adults with particular personality patterns are more likely to use some coping behaviors than others, and certain kinds of coping behaviors require at least a minimal level of intellectual skill. But for initial clarity let me continue the distinction here.

PERSONALITY AS A MEDIATOR OF STRESS

A number of different dimensions of personality that might be significant in mediating the effects of stress have been suggested by various theorists. Martin Seligman has argued for the importance of one aspect of meaning-making or appraisal that he calls **explanatory style** (e.g., Seligman, Kamen, & Nolen-Hoeksema, 1988). In essence, he is saying that each of us develops a particular style of explaining to ourselves the good and bad things that happen to us. If an individual habitually explains such events to himself by assuming (1) that the cause is within himself (e.g., "It was my own fault"), and (2) that the cause is general and lasting (e.g., "I'm too stupid to know the difference," or "I've never been able to do that"), then the individual will tend not only to have low self-esteem but will feel helpless in the face of problems or life changes. Adults who explain the same events to themselves as being caused externally or as being narrow in application or brief in duration (e.g., "I screwed up that time but next time I can do it right,") are likely to feel much less helpless. These explanatory styles are not necessarily permanent, but Seligman's research suggests that they are relatively stable over fairly long periods of time.

Seligman has been able to link helpless explanatory styles with increased risk of disease, death, and depression in a number of studies, including one analysis of some of the longitudinal data from the Grant study of Harvard men—the same study that George Vaillant has used as the basis for much of his theorizing.

Seligman and Vaillant have found that those men who exhibited more helpless explanatory styles when they were in college were less healthy 36 years later than were those who had had a less helpless style (Seligman, et al. 1988).

Another dimension of personality that may mitigate the effects of stress is what Suzanne Kobasa (1979, 1982; Kobasa, Maddi, & Kahn, 1982) calls **hardiness**. Hardiness includes three facets:

1. Commitment: "the ability to believe in the truth, importance, and interest value of what one is doing, and the willingness to exercise influence or control in the personal and social situations in which one is involved" (Kobasa, 1982, p. 708). Adults high in commitment are likely to disagree with statements like "The attempt to know yourself is a waste of effort," or "Life is empty and has no meaning in it for me."
2. Control: a disposition to see oneself as in control of or influential over (rather than helpless) problems or tasks. This dimension is obviously similar to Seligman's dimension of explanatory style, as well as to the dimension of inner versus outer **locus of control** proposed by Rotter (1966, 1975).
3. Challenge: "the belief that change rather than stability is normal in life and that the anticipation of changes are interesting incentives to growth rather than threats to security" (Kobasa, Maddi, & Kahn, 1982, p. 170). People low in challenge are those for whom safety, stability, and predictability are higher values.

To my ear, there is a certain similarity between these descriptions of hardiness and some of the descriptions of the "individualized" or even the "integrated" stages of personality or spiritual growth. Perhaps what Kobasa is describing here is not just an enduring personality dimension but the achievement of a particular level of ego development. Be that as it may, the key point for the present discussion is that Kobasa has consistently found that adults who are high in hardiness are less likely to become ill in the face of high levels of stress than are adults low in hardiness (Kobasa, 1979, 1982; Kobasa, et al. 1982). The relationship also holds longitudinally. Hardiness measured at the beginning of a two-year study predicted the response of a group of business executives to subsequent stress or life changes. The initially hardiest subjects were least likely to respond to such later stress with illness (Kobasa, et al. 1982). Hardiness also seems to help stave off depression in the face of stress as well (Ganellen and Blaney, 1984).

James Crandall (1984) proposes a somewhat different personality dimension as a potential buffer against stress: **social interest.** Crandall defines social interest in terms of "valuing (being interested in and caring about) things that go beyond the self. It is the opposite of complete self-centeredness or self-preoccupation" (p. 164). It not only includes interest in and concern for others, it also covers an interest in nature, art, the cosmos. The nonself-centered, altruistic element in this description once again sounds rather similar to the descriptions of particular developmental stages I proposed in Chapters 10 and 11, in this case to the description of the integrated personality or even the stage of universalizing faith described by Fowler, both of which also contain a strong element of altruism.

Social interest is also related to hardiness. In particular, individuals high in social interest are also typically high in the control dimension of hardiness. And like hardiness, the quality of social interest appears to serve as a buffer. In one study of a group of undergraduates, those who were higher in social interest were less likely to become depressed, anxious, or hostile in the face of high levels of life change (Crandall, 1984).

In all of this research, the consistent finding is that the buffering effect of specific personality characteristics is only apparent when the individual is under high stress. Under low stress, there is no difference between hardy and nonhardy or socially interested or disinterested adults in the rate of depression or illness.

These studies, as well as the research on social support, point us toward an answer to one of the key questions about stress: Given the same level of life change or external threat, why do people react so differently? Part of the answer seems to lie in the way each individual defines or perceives the problem and the extent to which the individual feels in personal control of the solution. Another part of the answer, which we now need to explore, lies in the particular coping behaviors the person uses to deal with stress.

Coping Behaviors in the Face of Stress Suppose you have been trying for a particular promotion and find out that you didn't get it. Or suppose that your father has just died. How do you cope with these stresses? "Coping" is a very broad and fuzzy word to describe all the things you might think, feel, and do in response to such events in an effort to handle the stress. Lazarus and Folkman (1984) define it as "constantly changing cognitive and behavioral efforts to manage specific external and/or internal demands that are appraised as taxing or exceeding the resources of the person" (p. 141).

The number of different specific actions that might fall under this rubric is almost unlimited, so various theorists have attempted to categorize the possibilities. The most helpful category system, to my mind, is a combination of one proposed by Kobasa (Kobasa, 1982), who suggests two categories, *transformational* and *regressive* coping actions, and one offered by Moos and Billings (1982; Billings & Moos, 1981), who suggest a three-part division into *problem-focused* (what you *do*), *emotionally focused* (how you *feel*), and *appraisal-focused* (what you *think*) strategies. Table 12.4 shows the six combined categories.

There are some obvious parallels between this classification and Vaillant's categories of defense mechanisms (Vaillant, 1977a) I described in Chapter 3. Many of what are listed here as transformational coping strategies would be included in Vaillant's list of mature defenses, while regressive coping strategies overlap with the categories of immature or neurotic defenses.

In general, we ought to find that adults who use more transformational coping strategies deal with stress more effectively. They should be less likely to get sick, depressed, or anxious in the face of major life changes or chronic life strains. On the whole, that is what the research shows (Holohan & Moos, 1990; Lohr, Essex, & Klein, 1988), but there are some interesting exceptions.

For instance, Pearlin and Schooler, in their 1978 study of a representative sample of 2,300 Chicago-area adults, found that advice-seeking in the face of stress

TABLE 12.4. Types of Coping Strategies in the Face of Stress.

	Transformational	Regressive
Problem-focused Coping: DOING something	Seek information or advice. Take specific action, such as negotiation or compromise. Develop alternative rewards. Learn new skills. Make alternative plans.	Withdraw physically, such as taking time off, sleeping a lot, or moving to another place to avoid a problem.
Emotion-focused Coping: FEELING things	Postpone paying attention to impulses and feelings (suppression). Try not to be bothered or to worry too much.	Discharge emotion, such as by crying, increased drinking, smoking or eating. Show resigned acceptance. Show apathy. Keep things to yourself.
Appraisal-focused Coping: THINKING about the problem	Analyze the problem logically. Reassess priorities. Redefine the problem, such as with positive comparisons ("It could be worse"; "Other people are worse off").	Deny fear or distress. Try to forget it. Avoid thinking about the problem.

SOURCE: Kobasa, 1982; Moos & Billings, 1982.

was associated with *higher* rather than lower rates of distress. Self-reliance, rather than help-seeking, seemed to be a more effective coping strategy. They also found that selective ignoring (a regressive coping device) was actually effective if the stress was experienced in the area of finances but counterproductive if the stress was in marriage or family relationships. Among transformational strategies, too, particular coping devices worked better for some stresses than others. Negotiation appeared to be a particularly good strategy for a marital stress, while a reassessment of values or priorities worked when the problem was economic.

Thus, although it is roughly true that coping strategies from the transformational list are more likely to eliminate or alleviate the worst effects of stress, the best coping strategies will vary from one kind of stress situation to the next. Those adults who have a large repertoire of coping strategies are likely to be most successful in buffering themselves from the worst effects of potentially stressful life changes or daily hassles.

AGE OR DEVELOPMENTAL DIFFERENCES IN PERSONALITY OR COPING STRATEGIES As usual, most of the research I have just described has not been cast in a developmental framework. But there is now a growing, if confusing, body of research exploring age differences in coping strategies.

Some researchers have found absolutely no age differences at all, including Robert McCrae (1989) in a seven-year longitudinal study of a sample of nearly 200 adults of various ages. He found simply no sign of systematic change, at least over this period of years.

Longer-term longitudinal studies, on the other hand, do point to some changes in coping styles. I've already reported some of the relevant research to you in Chapter 10. Recall that Vaillant's data from the Grant study as well as Haan's analyses of the Berkeley data show a decline with age in various forms of immature defense mechanisms, including denial and repression, a pattern consistent with several recent cross-sectional studies (e.g., Feifel & Strack, 1989).

Other studies of age differences in coping have not been cast in these same terms, so it is difficult to add up the results. Still, the findings are intriguing. In particular, two cross-sectional studies using Richard Lazarus' measure of coping styles (Folkman, Lazarus, Pimley, & Novacek, 1987; Irion & Blanchard-Fields, 1987) show strikingly similar age changes. Both sets of researchers found that young and middle-aged adults, compared to adults over 65, reported using more active, problem-focused, interpersonal forms of coping, such as confrontive coping (e.g., "I stood my ground and fought for what I wanted"), planful problem-solving (e.g., "I made a plan of action and followed it"), and seeking social support (e.g., "I talked to someone who could do something concrete about the problem," or "I accepted sympathy and understanding from someone.") Adults over 65 reported that they used more passive, internal, emotion-focused forms of coping, such as positive reappraisal (e.g., "I found new faith"), and accepting responsibility (e.g., "I realized I brought the problem on myself"). In the category system I've suggested in Table 12.4, the younger adults are using more problem-focused strategies while the older adults are using more emotion-focused and appraisal-focused strategies.

These are not longitudinal findings, so we don't know if these results reflect only cohort differences, or whether there are real age-linked changes at work here. In addition, it would be very nice to know whether there is any link between any shift from more active/outward oriented forms of coping to more passive/internal forms and the broader changes in personality I talked about in Chapters 10 and 11. For now, we have to be content with the fragments of information we have available.

Other Resistance Resources

Social support and good coping strategies are not the only resistance resources that make a difference in adults' responses to stress. A decent income helps as well, as does good health and vitality. Specific beliefs may also help an individual cope with major life changes. For instance, any source of hope may be helpful, be it a belief in God, or in justice, or simply in the efficacy of a particular doctor, a particular program, a new diet, or whatever. Personal skills may also have an effect. An adult with a wide range of occupational skills may face divorce or relocation more easily; an adult with good social skills—including those skills that allow one to relate easily and well to others and to form close relationships—

may be able to form new networks if old ones are disrupted. All of these additional resources may affect the range of coping strategies or options that are available to the individual in the face of some stress, as well as affecting the individual's choice among the options that are available.

Responding to Stress: An Overview

All of these pieces can be put together, at least in a preliminary way, using the model I proposed in Figure 12–1. Stressful stimuli are most likely to result in illness or depression (or other adverse change) if a person appraises the potential stressor as a threat, has a low level of social support, particularly if he lacks a close confidant appropriate for that stress, and lacks suitable coping strategies. The opposite set of conditions seems to lead to at least some chance of growth or maturing in the face of stress.

To make all this more real to you, let me explore at least briefly the impact of a few particularly critical or interesting life changes or stress-experiences, in this case widowhood, divorce, and relocation in old age.

Application of the Basic Principles to Specific Life Changes

Widowhood

Approximately 12 million adults in the United States have lost a spouse by death, most commonly when they were in middle or late adulthood. Of these, 11 million are women. (This does not mean, by the way, that 11 husbands die for every wife. In fact, approximately one out of every five spouses who dies is a woman [Carter & Glick, 1976]. But since women live a lot longer than men do, more of the widows survive for many years. Thus in the population at large, 11 of 12 living adults who have lost a spouse are women.) Over half of all women over 65 in the U.S. today are widowed, compared to only 12 percent of men. Because of this sex difference in frequency, most of the research on widowhood describes the adaptation of women. When researchers have studied both men and women, however, the pattern of response to bereavement seems to be very similar. So for the following discussion, unless I say otherwise, assume that the findings hold for both sexes and that when I use the word widow I mean either gender.

The death of a spouse is itself a huge life change, and it triggers a whole string of other changes. It involves not only the loss of a relationship but also the loss of the support and assistance of the spouse and loss of the role of spouse itself. Justine Ball (1976-77) describes one widow as saying she "felt she had no name or label now. She was not a 'wife' or 'housewife' and with no job, it gave her no concept of who she was" (p. 329). For a man, or for a woman who has been employed regularly or who has some other source of identity, the loss of identity may be less severe, but the loss of the support from the spouse is still substantial, perhaps particularly for men, since they are less likely to have other close, supportive relationships outside of their marriage.

Consistent with the information I have already reported on the link between major life changes and physical illness or emotional disturbance, research on widowhood shows that in the year following bereavement, rates of death and disease rise, and depression becomes significantly more common than is found among adults the same ages who have not been widowed (e.g., Balkwell, 1981; Reich, Zautra, & Guarnaccia, 1989; Stroebe & Stroebe, 1986). Such a pattern has been found not only in detailed studies of small numbers of widowed adults, but also in very large, longitudinal, epidemiological studies. For example, in an enormous study in Finland, Kaprio and Koskenvuo (1983, cited in Strobe & Strobe, 1986) examined the mortality rates for a group of 95,647 widowed persons over the five years following the spouse's death. They found that compared to the population at large, death rates among widows went up during the first six months after bereavement, after which the mortality risk returned to normal. Similar results have been found in large studies in the United States.

Fortunately, these negative effects appear to last for only a relatively short time. The riskiest period seems to be the first six months, with lesser but still increased risk for an additional 18 months after the spouse's death. Studies that compare widowed and nonwidowed adults after this critical two-year interval generally find no differences in physical or mental health (e.g., McCrae & Costa, 1988).

Age Differences These effects appear to be much greater for younger men and women than for widowed adults in their 60s, 70s and 80s (e.g., Balkwell, 1985). Ball's results, shown in Figure 12–4, illustrate this age difference particularly well. She divided her sample into three age groups (18 to 46, 47 to 59, and 60 to 75), and then further subdivided it by the suddenness or unexpectedness of the death. As you can see, younger widows were much more disturbed by the death than were older widows, and this was particularly true if the death was unexpected.

This pattern of findings obviously fits nicely into Pearlin's model of the effect of scheduled and unscheduled changes (1980, 1982). The death of a spouse is rarely "scheduled," but for those over 65 or so, such a death is not altogether unanticipated. In contrast, having your spouse die when you are in your 30s or 40s is clearly unscheduled or off-time. Pearlin's general hypothesis would lead us to expect that such early widowhood should be associated with greater experience of stress and heightened physical and emotional effects. Furthermore, since a very sudden death is still less "scheduled" or anticipated than is a death after a more prolonged illness, we should find greater negative impact from a sudden than from a prolonged death. This is precisely what the findings in Figure 12–4 show. Certainly, the death of a spouse at any age is associated with at least some consequences. But the effects seem to be markedly more severe—both physically and emotionally—when the death is unanticipated and off-time.

Sex Differences One of the prevalent assumptions about widowhood is that men handle it less well than do women. Current research offers some support for

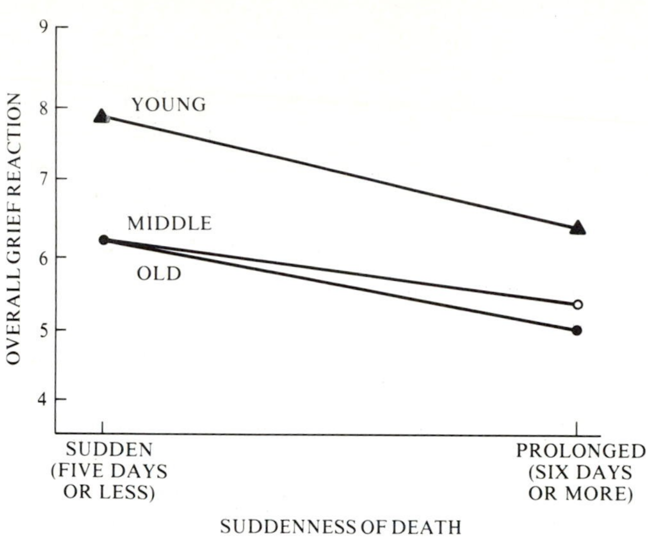

Figure 12–4 These results from a study of young and older widows are an illustration of the general principle that unexpected or unscheduled or nonnormative life changes are generally harder to deal with and more likely to lead to illness, than are scheduled or expected or normative life events. (Source: Ball, Justine F., 1976–77, Widow's Grief: The Impact of Age and Mode of Death. Omega—Journal of Death and Dying, *7(4), Fig. 1, p. 319. Reprinted by permission of Baywood Publishing Co., Inc.)*

this assumption although not in all areas. Epidemiological studies show quite convincingly that the risk of death from either natural causes or suicide in the months immediately following widowhood is significantly greater for men than for women (Stroebe & Stroebe, 1986), even when higher male death rates at most ages are taken into account. Thus, men's physical health appears to be more affected by this particular stress than women's.

Emotional health is another matter. The evidence on sex differences in depression following widowhood is confused, to say the least. Some investigators conclude that men are more likely to be depressed, others that women are, still others that there are no differences. One of the key difficulties here is that women as a group—widowed or not—have higher rates of depression than do men. So in order to tell whether widowhood increases depression more for men than for women, a researcher would have to do one of two things: (1) obtain measures of depression or distress before as well as after widowhood for some group of people, or (2) include comparison groups of nonwidowed adults. Virtually none of the studies of sex differences in depression following widowhood have used either of these designs, so we are still largely in the dark (Stroebe & Stroebe, 1983). The few studies that do include appropriate comparison groups suggest the possibility that men may be more affected than women, but this conclusion is not at all firm.

The most plausible explanation of men's heightened physical (and perhaps emotional) vulnerability is that men are more likely to be socially isolated at the death of their wife than are women at the death of their husband. As I have mentioned several times, men's social support networks are typically less extensive and less intimate than are women's. In particular, men are more likely to have only a single confidant, their wife. And when she dies, they are left without that key element of the social network.

SOCIAL NETWORKS, PERSONALITY, AND COPING SKILLS Such a sex difference is part of a more general pattern: Those widows who show the fewest physical and emotional symptoms following bereavement are those with the most supportive social networks. For example, Margaret Dimond and her colleagues (Dimond, Lund, & Caserta, 1987) studied a group of 192 recently widowed adults, all over the age of 50. They found that those adults who had more regular, intimate, and mutually helpful contact with the members of their social networks three weeks after the spouse's death showed significantly less depression two months later than did those whose networks were less supportive.

Even more persuasive is a set of findings from a longer-term longitudinal sample studied by Evelyn Goldberg (Goldberg, Comstock, & Harlow, 1988) in which information was available about social support systems before as well as after widowhood occurred. Goldberg and her colleagues had interviewed a group of over 1,000 women, all of whom had been between 62 and 72 in 1975. Of these, 150 were widowed in the several succeeding years, and Goldberg was able to interview them within six months of bereavement. Twenty-five of these reported needing help for an emotional problem during those postwidowhood months, and Goldberg could go back and see how those 25 women had initially differed from those who did not have significant emotional problems after widowhood. You can see in Figure 12–5 that among the widows, those who had fewer friends, smaller networks, and less closeness to their children before being widowed were more likely to have significant problems adjusting to widowhood.

But as I pointed out earlier, not all elements in a social support network are interchangeable. Recall Bankhoff's study (1983), which showed that the most buffering relationships were with the widow's parents or with widowed friends. Contact with children, interestingly enough, seems to provide less buffering against the negative effect of bereavement than does contact with friends (e.g., Ferraro, 1984), a difference apparent in Figure 12.5 as well. Helena Lopata, in several classic studies of widows (Lopata, 1969, 1973, 1979; Lopata, Heinemann, & Blum, 1982) does find that widowed women with children report less loneliness than do widows without children, but there is no indication that widows with children show lower rates of disease or depression than do widows without children.

Researchers studying widowhood have not explored personal dimensions such as hardiness or social interest nor the several types of coping strategies listed in Table 12.4. But extrapolating from Lopata's findings, there is some indication that those widows who tend to reach out to others, maintaining or even increasing social contacts (a transformational, problem-focused form of coping) show least loneliness and best adjustment. In addition, Lopata has found that those widows with

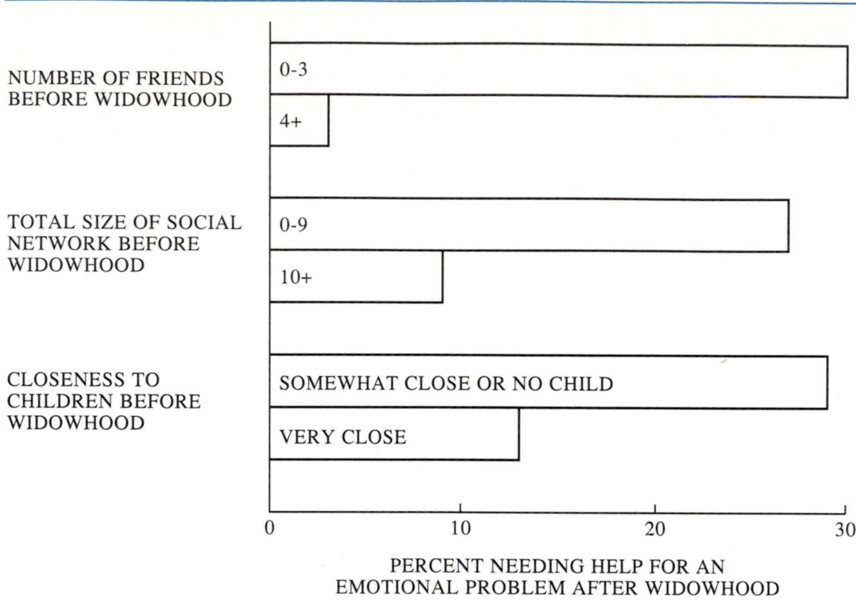

Figure 12–5 Among this group of widows who had been studied both before and after widowhood, those who had more friends, larger social networks, and closer relationships with their children before they were widowed were less likely to report a significant emotional problem after they were widowed. (Source: Goldberg, Comstock, & Harlow, 1988, from Table 1, p. S207.)

a positive attitude toward themselves and others report lower levels of loneliness and distress than do those whose self-concept and social interactions are more negative (Lopata, et al. 1982). Similar patterns emerge from studies of divorced adults.

Divorce

In Chapter 7, I talked about what may happen to family roles after a divorce, but I sidestepped the question that I want to address now, namely the impact of divorce on the individual's functioning. As I pointed out then, between 40 and 50 percent of adults marrying today will eventually divorce (Glick, 1984). Half of all divorces occur within the first seven years of marriage; most therefore occur when adults are fairly young. In 1985, for example, 74 percent of those receiving a divorce in the United States were under age 40; only 1.3 percent were over age 65 (Uhlenberg, Cooney, & Boyd, 1990). So to the extent that this is a "scheduled" life event, it is normative in early adulthood and not in late adulthood—at least in present cohorts.

Among life changes, divorce is one of the most stressful and difficult. But unlike widowhood, which is almost uniformly experienced as painful, reactions to divorce are more varied. Over the long term, divorce is even associated with significant improvements in quality of life for many. Perhaps the most widely quoted study has been Judith Wallerstein's (1986) longitudinal assessment of a group of 60 divorced couples. Ten years after the divorce, over half the women and a third of the men appeared to have a better emotional quality of life than they had before the divorce, whereas 40 percent of the women and nearly half the men were worse off than they had been.

Divorce is like widowhood in that both require a process of *de*tachment, a breaking or a giving up of that powerful affectional bond that formed the core of the initial partner relationship. But in the case of divorce, the emotional components of this detachment process are, if anything, more complex than for the widowed. A number of researchers have found that most divorcing adults continue to maintain an emotional attachment to the now departed spouse for some period of time after the separation, (Hetherington & Camara, 1984; Kitson, 1982; Tschann, Johnston, & Wallerstein, 1989) while at the same time experiencing anger and distress over the spouse's contribution to the dissolution.

As is true of widowhood, the period of maximum upheaval seems to last about two years, with the first six to 12 months being the worst time (Chase-Lansdale & Hetherington, 1990). Mavis Hetherington has provided us with an in-depth look at this period in a longitudinal study of a group of divorcing adults over the two years following the decree (Hetherington & Camara, 1984; Hetherington, Cox, & Cox, 1978). In those months, daily routines became chaotic with meals taken at irregular hours. Discipline of the children became erratic as well. The men in the study, most of whom had moved out of the family house, often felt rootless and without a clear identity. The divorced women felt unattractive and helpless. Both often felt isolated from their still-married friends. Divorce also causes financial upheaval. However, as I pointed out in Chapter 7, this effect is far more marked for women than for men.

EFFECTS OF DIVORCE ON PHYSICAL AND EMOTIONAL ILLNESS I already pointed out in Chapter 7 that married adults as a group are happier and healthier than are single adults, but among the single it is primarily the divorced rather than the never-married who show heightened levels of problems. As is true for widowhood, divorce is followed by a temporary rise in physical illness and emotional disturbance. Figure 12–6 shows two typical findings, one for the incidence of admissions to outpatient psychiatric clinics, and the other for the number of days a year that adults report they are restricted in activity because of illness (sick in bed or staying home recuperating). In each case, for comparison purposes, I have given not only the rates for separated and divorced adults but also the rates for never-married, married, and widowed adults. You can see that divorced and separated adults are more likely to seek psychiatric help and are physically sick more than are married or never-married adults. Interestingly, in this study widowed adults had low levels of psychiatric care, but levels of physical sickness comparable to those for the divorced.

Other research, both cross-sectional and longitudinal, shows that divorced and separated adults, compared to married (or never-married) adults, have more car accidents, are more likely to be the victim of homicide (Bloom, White & Asher, 1979), commit suicide more, (Stack, 1989), and are more likely to be

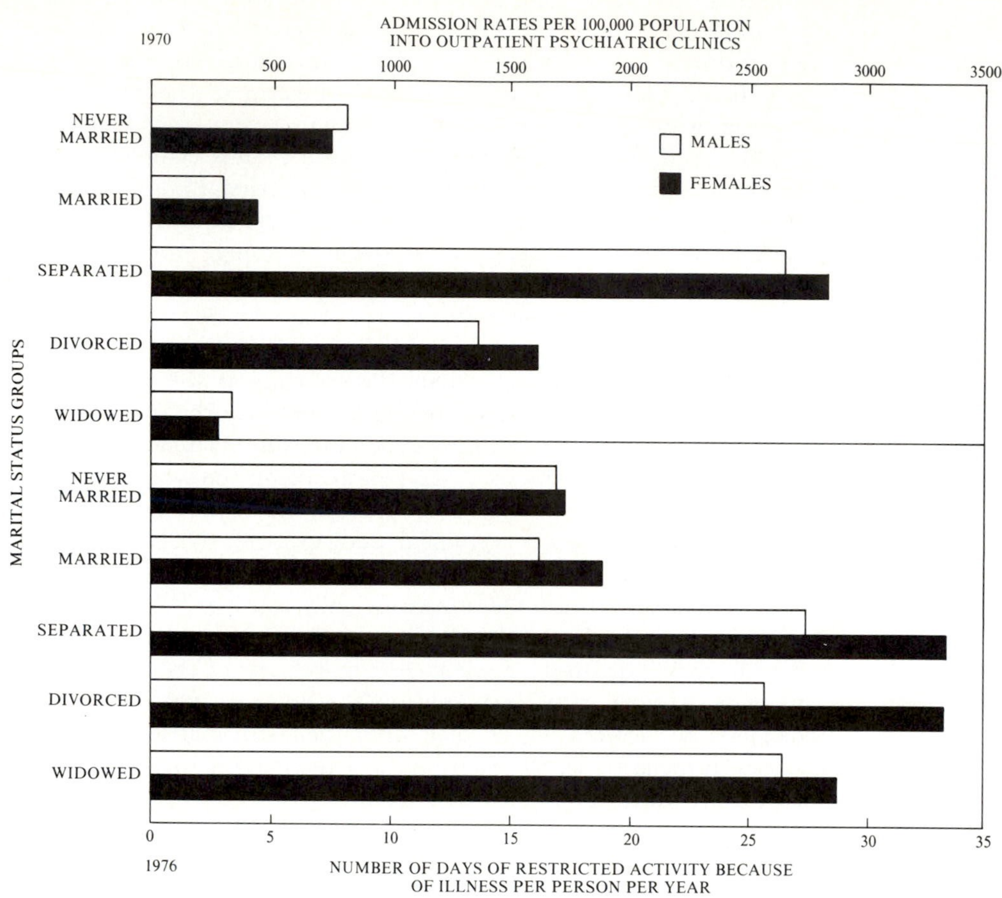

Figure 12–6 Divorced and separated adults compared to married, never-married, and widowed adults, are more likely to be seen in psychiatric outpatient clinics and are sick more days of the year. Since this is especially so for separated adults who have presumably experienced this stress more recently, these results suggest that the risk of illness is particularly high immediately following this life change. (Source: adapted from Bloom, White, & Asher, 1979, data from Tables 11–1 and 11–2, p. 186.)

depressed. One of the nicer studies illustrating the increase in depression is Elizabeth Menaghan and Morton Lieberman's panel study (1986) of a group of Chicago adults first interviewed in 1972 and reinterviewed four years later. Seven hundred fifty-eight of the subjects were married to the same spouse at both times, but 32 were divorced between the first and the second interviews. The married and the subsequently divorced had *not* differed significantly on a measure of depression when they were first interviewed, but the divorced were significantly more depressed after the divorce.

Obviously, there are several possible explanations for these heightened levels of sickness, death, and disaster among the divorced. One possibility, usually called the *selectivity* theory, is that people who eventually get divorced were less stable to begin with. No doubt, that is at least partially true. In one five-year longitudinal study, for example, Erbes and Hedderson (1984) found that on a measure of psychological well-being, those men who eventually divorced had had lower scores as many as five years before the divorce than had continuously married men.

But selectivity does not seem to account for all of the results, including the findings from Menaghan and Lieberman's Chicago study I just described. Because this was a longitudinal study, we can go beyond the usual correlational evidence. Recall that they found that those who subsequently divorced had not been more depressed before the divorce but became more depressed afterward. Selectivity also cannot readily account for heightened rates of illness, death, and emotional disturbance in widowed persons. Doubtless, a bidirectional effect is at work. Initial instability or unhappiness may increase the likelihood of divorce or other life changes. But the life change itself also increases the risk of later disease or disturbance.

AGE DIFFERENCES IN EFFECTS OF DIVORCE In the few cases in which age has been studied as a variable in epidemiological studies, researchers have consistently found that *older* divorcing persons have a more difficult time adjusting to this life change than do younger adults (Bloom, White, & Asher, 1979). This is the precise opposite of what is true for widowhood, but both patterns obviously make sense within Pearlin's theory of scheduled and unscheduled changes. Most adults have less difficulty adjusting to life changes that are normative or expectable than to those that are not, and divorce is more normative and expectable in early adult life, while widowhood is more normative in late life.

SEX DIFFERENCES IN THE STRESSFULNESS OF DIVORCE The differences in men's and women's responses to divorce are much less clear-cut even than in the case of widowhood. Women certainly suffer far greater economic upheaval, and most must deal with the complexities and stresses of single parenting. But there are hints that divorcing men may have slightly higher levels of emotional and health problems than do women. More divorced men end up as inpatients in psychiatric hospitals than do divorced women, for example (Bloom, et al. 1979), despite the fact that in the population at large there are more women psychiatric patients than men. Yet not every study shows such a pattern (e.g., Doherty, Su, & Needle, 1989). Once again, the jury is still out.

SOCIAL SUPPORT AND COPING STRATEGIES IN DIVORCE The one clear finding is that for *both* men and women, adequate emotional and social support from friends and kin helps to speed the process of recovery (Hetherington & Camara, 1984). Development of new intimate relationships also plays a significant role in the recovery process for both men and women. To the extent that men's friendships and kin relationships are less intimate, and thus possibly less supportive, men may have fewer social resources on which to draw.

Those personal qualities other than social support that appear to assist an adult in dealing effectively with the crisis of divorce are readily predictable from what I have already said about hardiness and transformational coping. Divorced adults who have higher self-esteem, stronger feelings of internal control, are open-minded and tolerant of change, show better or more rapid adjustment to the divorce (Hetherington & Camara, 1984). They are likely not only to weather the immediate crisis of the divorce without major symptoms but may also show real personal growth in the process.

Relocation in Old Age

The third life change I want to talk about, a change of residence in old age, is quite different from either widowhood or divorce primarily because it is normally far less stressful. If you take another look at Table 12.1, for example, you will see that death of a spouse and divorce head the list of stressful life changes, while a "change in residence" is 32nd on the list. My particular interest here, however, is not in all moves but in those moves that may occur after retirement, such as a voluntary move to a sunnier clime, a forced re-

Figure 12–7 *For those who move voluntarily to such retirement havens as Florida or Arizona or to special retirement communities, the relocation seems to be associated with low levels of stress and improvement in morale. The same is not true of involuntary relocations in old age, however, especially in those cases in which the individual has little or no control over her daily life. (Photo © Joel Gordon, 1982. Reprinted with permission.)*

location because the older person can no longer afford the housing she previously occupied, or a move to a nursing home or other special residence for the elderly. Current popular articles have painted highly romanticized pictures of the first of these and highly gloomy pictures of the latter two. But what does the evidence tell us?

First and perhaps most interestingly, there is really far less moving after age 65 than I (and perhaps you) had thought. In the United States, those over 65 are the least likely to move. For example, only 22.6 percent of older adults had moved during the five years from 1975 to 1980, compared to roughly three quarters of adults in their 20s. Only about 1 percent of older adults move from one state to another in any given year (Golant, 1987; Lawton, 1985). Among the elderly, such moves most often occur at the time of retirement or widowhood, prompted by the desire for a living situation that is more pleasant or less expensive, or by the wish to be closer to family members who may be able to provide care or support (Serow, 1987).

Second, those older adults who *choose* to move or have some clear control over their move or their destination, typically show *increases* in morale or life satisfaction and little sign of increased physical disease or other symptoms. The move itself is likely to be stressful (as any of you who have moved can surely understand!), but these effects are quite short-term.

It is the *involuntary* moves, including those to nursing homes, that are likely to cause the greatest stress—at least as indicated by rises in death and disease rates. On average, involuntarily relocated elderly adults show sharp increases in death rates compared to roughly equivalent groups who have remained at home. But this average statement masks some important variations in experience. Most importantly, the quality of the new care facility makes an enormous difference. Those elderly adults who move to institutions or other settings that are characterized by warmth, individuation, and an opportunity for the elder to have some control over her or his own life actually show improvement in morale and health (Lawton, 1985, 1990).

Two points emerge from these findings that are particularly relevant for the issues I have been discussing in this chapter. First, once again it is the *perception* or *appraisal* of the residential move that seems to be critical in determining any stressful effect. When the move is voluntary, the effects are positive rather than negative; even an involuntary move can be low in stress, if the move is perceived as positive.

Second, more generally, the ability of the individual to control his life circumstances appears to be a particularly significant element in determining the appraisal of some potential stressor. I have already pointed out in the discussion of personality characteristics and stress responses that adults who typically see themselves in control of their environments generally show smaller effects from potentially stressful events than do those who feel helpless in the face of circumstance. But even adults who are typically low in helplessness are likely to have difficulty dealing with circumstances in which actual control is reduced. The corollary of this statement is obviously that even in involuntary or low-control circumstances, the more a perception of individual choice and control can be built into the situation, the less likely we are to see negative consequences of that life change. Presumably, this same principle applies to life changes other than relocation as well. Looked at in this way, "on-time" life changes are low in stress precisely because by planning ahead the individual can control the timing or the circumstances to some extent. Off-time events, in contrast, are much less likely to be controllable.

This principle may be worth bearing in mind the next time you face a major life change or even an accumulation of daily hassles. To the extent that you can control your choices (a kind of transformational, appraisal-focused coping), your experience of stress can be reduced.

Summary

1. Stress is defined in at least three ways: as a physical response to demand, as an external stimulus, such as a life change or hassle that demands adaptation, or as the result of some interaction between a demanding environmental event and the individual's coping capacity.
2. Response-oriented approaches are typified by Selye's description of the General Adaptation Syndrome, which includes an alarm reaction, a resistance stage, and then exhaustion.
3. Stimulus-oriented approaches have commonly involved measurement of the number of major or minor life changes experienced by an individual in a given space of time. Current measures typically distinguish between positive and negative events; some also assess daily hassles.
4. Interactionist views of stress emphasize not only the demands of the environment and the body's response to that demand, but in predicting the consequences of such stress, these views stress the individual's interpretation of the event and the availability of such resistance resources as social support or a repertoire of coping responses.
5. A small but consistently observed increase in the risk of disease or emotional disturbance has been found to be associated with heightened levels of life changes or hassles. Undesirable life changes, particularly those involved in a loss of a relationship, appear to be especially likely to be associated with such disease states.
6. Life changes may also be associated with some positive outcomes, such as personal growth, although this is much less well established.
7. Older adults experience fewer major life changes and fewer daily hassles than do younger adults, but some specific life changes are more common in late life, including (of course) retirement, illness, and loss of spouse and friends to death.
8. The effects of stress may be mitigated ("buffered") in individuals by any of several resistance resources, including social support, certain personality patterns, and certain coping strategies.

9. Studies of social support in stressful conditions suggest that the intimacy of the relationships within a social network is a key variable. Adults with emotionally supportive, intimate relationships are less likely to respond to stress with illness than are adults without such support.
10. There are indications that the optimal supportive relationship may vary from one type of life change to another, with the central relationship with spouse or partner most often the key source of support.
11. Social networks also have some negative effects, since their maintenance may increase daily hassles, and they may include genuinely negative interactions.
12. Several personality characteristics have been linked to reduced impact of stress, including a nonhelpless explanatory style, hardiness, and social interest. Hardiness includes a belief in yourself and in your ability to control and influence the world around you as well as a perception of stress experiences in terms of challenge rather than threat. Social interest describes a quality of selfless interest in and caring about others.
13. Of the many varieties of coping strategies in the face of life changes or hassles, those described as "transformational" are generally (though not uniformly) more effective than those described as "regressive." Taking positive actions, rethinking priorities, evaluating alternatives are all transformational strategies; ignoring and emotional outbursts (including increased drinking, smoking, and eating) are regressive strategies.
14. Other resistance resources include adequate income, health or vitality, and a generally positive outlook on life.
15. These general principles can be applied to responses to such specific major life changes as widowhood, divorce, and relocation in old age.
16. Widowhood is associated with heightened rates of illness, depression, suicide, mortality from other causes, and auto accidents. The disease and death effects are larger for men, but it is not clear whether there are sex differences in the effect of widowhood on depression.
17. Divorce similarly is associated with heightened rates of depression and illness, with the effects most noticeable in the first year.
18. Divorce has a greater negative impact on older adults, while the effects of widowhood are generally larger for any adult widowed early in life or unexpectedly. This pattern of results suggests that any life event that is nonnormative for an age group or a cohort is particularly likely to lead to illness.
19. Relocation in old age has relatively little negative effect if the move is voluntary. An involuntary move may also have no negative effect if the move is to some setting or institution in which the individual has some personal autonomy or control. Involuntary moves to nonoptimal institutions are the only ones consistently associated with increased levels of mortality or illness.
20. Overall, in the face of some kind of potentially stressful experience, illness or emotional disturbance is most likely if the individual appraises the experience

as a threat, has a low level of social support, lacks options or control, and lacks suitable transformational coping strategies.

Suggested Readings

Bookstore shelves are full of books on "stress management." If you find yourself facing major life changes or accumulated hassles, one of these may be helpful to you. If you are interested in the more academic side of the question, I can recommend several excellent collections of papers on which I have drawn:

COHEN, L. H. (1988a). *Life events and psychological functioning. Theoretical and methodological issues.* Newbury Park, CA: Sage. Included here are papers on the measurement of life events, the relationship between life events and psychopathology, social support, and hassles, or other smaller stress sources.

GOLDBERGER, L., & BREZNITZ, S. (EDS.) (1982). *Handbook of stress. Theoretical and clinical aspects.* New York: The Free Press. Included in this collection are papers by nearly all of the big names in stress research, such as Hans Selye, Richard Lazarus, Rudolph Moos, Leonard Pearlin, Norma Haan, Barbara Dohrenwend, and many others. The papers are somewhat technical but most are quite clear.

CHAPTER 13

The Periods or Stages of Adult Life

In the past nine chapters, I have been describing age differences, or age changes, in each of a series of domains—physical functioning and health, mental functioning, roles, relationships, and so on. I've tried to point out some of the connections among these many different developmental tracks as I've gone along; but despite my best efforts, I'm sure that by now you have a rather fragmented view of adulthood. So now I need to put the adult back together by looking at the ways in which all the various threads come together in each age period.

In most of the earlier chapters, I summarized the major trends and age changes in a table, so one way to give you a look at the whole picture is to combine them all into a single giant table, like Table 13.1. You'll see that in this mega-table, I have subdivided the ages somewhat more than in the earlier summary tables, with both the early adulthood and the late-adulthood periods divided into smaller age ranges. Such a further subdivision helps to highlight several key points about age patterns.

Also note that the table describes the "average" or typical sequence of events for an adult who follows the culturally defined sequence of roles at the modal ages. I'll have a whole lot more to say about individual pathways in the final chapter (Chapter 15). For now, though, it is important to think about the typical or average. The normative pattern is clearly to marry in one's early 20s and begin having children before 25. The children then typically leave home by the time one is about 50. Each row of the table represents a highly condensed version of one facet of change we might see over the lifetime of an individual who follows such a modal pattern.

Of the eight rows in the table, four seem to me to describe genuinely maturational or developmental sequences. Clearly, the physical and mental changes summarized in the first two rows are strongly related to highly predictable and widely shared physical processes. While the *rate* of change is affected by lifestyle and habits, the sequences appear to be maturational. More tentatively, I have argued that the sequences of change in personality and in systems of meaning may also be "developmental" in the sense in which I have used that term throughout the book. These are not strongly age-linked changes, but there is at least some evidence that they are sequential and *not* merely a function of particular or culture-specific changes in roles or life experiences. The remaining four rows, describing roles, tasks, and relationships, seem to describe sequences that are common insofar as they are shared by many adults in a given cohort in a given culture. If the timing or the sequence of those roles or tasks changes, then the pattern described in the table changes as well.

A second way to look at the table is to read down the columns rather than across the rows. This gives some sense of the various patterns that may occur simultaneously—the meshing of the several "gears" in Perun and Bielby's timing model I described in Chapter 3 (recall Figure 3–4). Let me look at each of these periods in a bit more depth.

Young Adulthood: From 18 to 25

These days we are so indoctrinated with the idea of a "midlife crisis" that we may well assume that midlife is the time of greatest stress, but a good case can be made that it is young adulthood and not middle age that holds the honor as the most stressful period of adult life. Consider the following: Between 18 and 25 young adults

- complete the major part of their education, which requires intensive learning and remembering;
- must separate from their parents, establishing an independent existence;
- typically add more major roles than at any other time in their lives—a work role, marriage, typically parenthood;
- change jobs more frequently and move more frequently than any other age group, producing higher total numbers of "life changes" than at any other time in life;
- are likely to have the dirtiest, least interesting, least challenging jobs, and to like their jobs less well than any other age group.

The effects of such high levels of stress are not hard to find. Recall, for example, that rates of depression and self-reported loneliness are higher among adults in this age range than in any other group.

Fortunately, young adults have a number of striking assets to help them deal with these high levels of demand. Most obviously, these are the years in which body and mind are at their peak. Neurological speed is at its greatest, so reaction time is swift, not only physically but mentally; new information is learned easily and recalled easily; the immune system is at its efficient best so that one recovers quickly from disease or injury; the cardiovascular system is similarly at its peak, so that sports can be played with speed and endurance. One feels immortal.

Young adults also deal with the stresses by creating a network of friendships and other close relationships—part of what Erikson talks about as the task of intimacy. Friendships seem to be not only numerous but particularly important in these years; loneliness is high in these years precisely because relationships are felt to be so important. When one's relationships do not meet those high expectations, one is more vulnerable, more likely to feel alone than is true at other ages when the quality of relationships may not be so central.

Perhaps because the role demands are so powerful, the young adult's sense of himself, the meaning system with which he interprets all these experiences, seems to be dominated by rules, by conformity, by a sense that authority is external to the self. We think of these years as a time when the young person is becoming independent, but in becoming independent of their parents, most young adults are not becoming *individualized* in the sense in which I used that term in Chapters 10 and 11. Most are still locked into a conformist view, seeing things in black and white terms, looking to outside authority to tell them the rules. If midlife

TABLE 13.1. A Summary of Changes in Eight Different Domains of Adult Functioning Over the Years from 18 to Late Old-Age.

	Young Adulthood 18–25	Early Adulthood 25–40	Middle Adulthood 40–65	Late Adulthood ("young old") 65–75	Late Old-Age ("old old") 75+
Physical Change (Chap. 4–5)	Peak functioning in most physical skills; maximum health; optimum childbearing time.	Still good physical functioning and health in most areas; health habits established now create pattern of later risks.	Beginning signs of physical decline in some areas, e.g., strength, elasticity, height, cardiovascular functioning.	Physical decline continues but not yet at an accelerated rate. Risk of disability or disease increases; reaction time slows.	Acceleration of rate of physical and health decline.
Cognitive Change (Chap. 6)	Cognitive skill high on most measures; maximum synaptic speed.	Peak period of cognitive skill on most measures at about age 30.	Some signs of loss of cognitive skill on "fluid," timed, unexercised skills: high cognitive investment; little functional loss.	Small declines for virtually all adults on "crystallized" and "exercised" skills; larger losses on "fluid" skills. But rate of loss has not yet accelerated.	Again the approximate point of acceleration of cognitive loss, including areas of memory and both fluid and crystallized abilities.
Family and Sex Roles (Chap. 7)	Major role acquisition; marriage and family formation; clear separation of male and female roles.	Family roles strongly dominant, with continued differentiation of sex roles; women do most family and home work.	Launch children; postparental phase; begin care of elderly parents; possibly some sex role crossover.	Grandparent role; significantly less dominance of family and sex roles.	Family roles now relatively unimportant.

Relationships (Chap. 8)	Maximum emphasis on forming friendships and partnership; usually high marital satisfaction until birth of first child.	Lower marital satisfaction; fewer new friends made and lower contact with friends; continued contact with parents.	Increased marital satisfaction; possibly some increase in the importance of friends.	High marital satisfaction for those not widowed; some sign that friends and siblings become more important; Relationships with children are frequent but not central to well-being.	Majority are widowed; friends and siblings remain important, although relationships become less intense.
Work Roles (Chap. 9)	Choose career, often several job changes; low work satisfaction.	Rising work satisfaction; major emphasis on work or career success; most career progress steps.	Plateau of career steps but high work satisfaction.	Retirement for vast majority.	Work roles unimportant for virtually all.
Personality and Meaning Systems (Chap. 10–11)	Task of intimacy; typically conformist level of personality or meaning.	Increasing individuality, e.g., increasing self-confidence, independence, autonomy. Task of generativity.	Peak and then decline in desire for power, in autonomy; perhaps individualist and then autonomous level. Lower use of immature defenses.	Task of ego integrity; perhaps more interority; a few may reach integrated level.	Continuation of previous pattern.
Major Tasks	Separate from family; form partnership; begin family; find job; create individual life pattern.	Rear family; establish personal work/family pattern; strive for success.	Launch family; redefine life goals; achieve individuality; care for aging parent.	Cope with retirement; cope with declining body and mind; redefine life goals and sense of self.	Possibly reminiscence to come to terms with one's own life and with death.

is a time of *de*tribalization (to use Levinson's term), then these earliest adulthood years are a time of maximal tribalization. We define ourselves by our tribe and our place in that tribe.

Roger Gould, whose theory of adult development I mentioned very briefly in Chapter 3, has put it slightly differently. He has talked about a series of assumptions or myths that are the basis for our existence at each of a series of ages or stages. In this early adult period, one of the key assumptions Gould sees is that "rewards will come automatically if we do what we're supposed to do."

> We expect that if we do our part, life will pay off accordingly. Our dreams will come true. People will respond to us the way loving and decent people ought to respond; fair play is guaranteed, and we will be compensated for our efforts. (Gould, 1978, p. 59)

From society's point of view this is a highly adaptive world view since it keeps young people in the mold, nose to the grindstone. From the individual's perspective, too, a conformist inner model can be highly adaptive (perhaps especially for those young people whose temperament or personal qualities happen to match the then-current cultural expectations). Hard work *is* frequently rewarded; finding a mate and beginning a family in one's early 20s *is* associated with maximum marital stability over the long haul and has the advantages of being "on-time" rather than "off-time." Such a conformist or conventional world view is also adaptive precisely because this is a time in life when external role demands are so intense. The biological clock may be largely inaudible at this age, but the *social clock* is ticking very loudly indeed.

In the next period, from 25 to 40, the social clock remains louder than the biological clock (with the obvious exception of the childbearing clock for women), but most adults begin to respond to the social demands in new ways.

Early Adulthood: From 25 to 40

Like the young adulthood period I have just been describing, the years from 25 to 40 are blessed with peak or near-peak physical and mental functioning. You have the energy for the 50- or 60-hour work week or for keeping track of several small children, or both. It is also the age period within the total set of age strata in which adults have the highest status, at least in the United States culture, as Figure 13–1 shows.

The data in this figure are from a study by Paul Baker (1985), who asked adults (aged 17 to 35) to read a series of 28 profiles of fictional individuals who varied in age and gender and to rate each of the profiled individuals for overall status on a 7-point scale where a rating of 7 reflected status "far above average." The 28 profiles were created to span 14 different age levels from age 5 to age 90, with a male and a female profile written for each of the 14 ages. Each was intended to reflect the normative features of a person of that age and gender. You can see in the figure that there was a sharp increase in perceived status between 25 and 30, and that the peak status for both men and women was between 30 and 40.

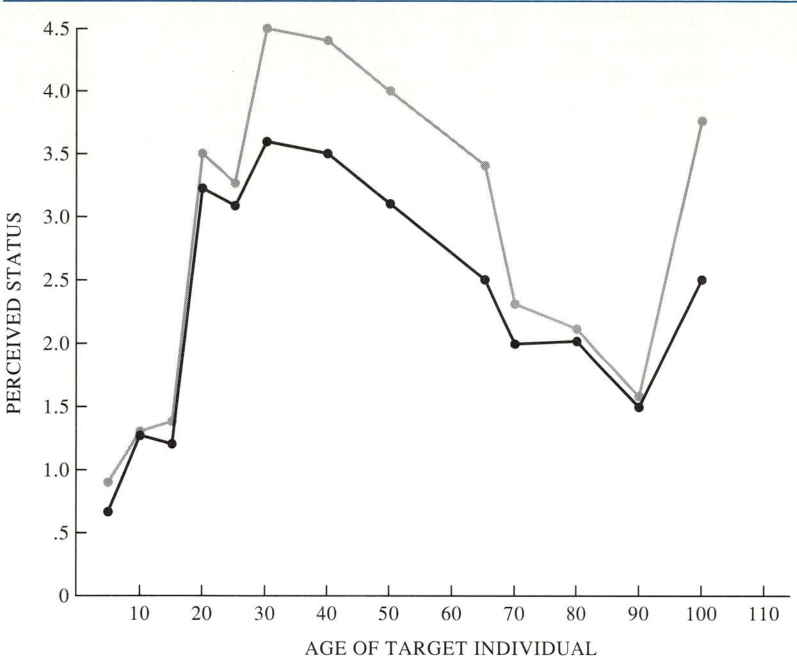

Figure 13–1 Ratings of the status of adults of various ages in this study by Baker suggest that (in Western culture at least) status may be highest in the years between 30 and 40. (Source: Baker, 1985, Fig. 1, p. 507).

There are some flaws in this study, among them the fact that the people doing the ratings were all relatively young. Baker found that the pattern of ratings was not affected by the age of the person doing the rating, but it is of course possible that middle age or old age would be rated as having higher status if middle aged or older raters were used. The study would also have been better if there had been several different profiles for each age/gender combination so that age and the specific features of the profile were not confounded, but the findings are interesting nonetheless and match other data on the status of different age groups.

Perhaps it is the "generative" quality of this age period that leads to such a high level of status. It is the time that Levinson describes as "settling down," in both work and family life. In our early 20s, we choose the role niches we will fill—the particular job, the particular spouse or partner, the number and timing of children. In our late 20s and our 30s, we set to work to fulfill the demands of those role niches, to achieve our Dream. In the work domain, this is the time when most adults experience their greatest or most rapid advancement. In family life, it is the time when children are borne and reared.

But it is also a time when the conformist or conventional world view begins to give way to a more individualistic approach. We can see this in all the personality changes I chronicled in Chapter 10: the increase in independence and autonomy, the peak of achievement motivation and the motive for power in men, the decline of nurturance in women.

This change seems to come about for several reasons. Among other things, we discover that following the rules doesn't always lead to reward, a realization that causes us to question the system itself. Neither marriage nor having children, for example, leads to unmitigated bliss, as evidenced by the well-replicated drop in marital satisfaction after the birth of the first child and while the children are young. For those who married in their early or middle 20s, that drop in satisfaction occurs in their late 20s and 30s, contributing to a kind of disillusionment with the entire role system. A second reason for the change in perspective, I think, is that this is the time in which we develop really individual skills. In conforming to the external role demand that we find work and pursue it, we also discover our own talents and capacities, a discovery that helps to turn our focus inward. We become more aware of our own individuality, more aware of the parts of ourselves that existing roles do not allow us to express. This change is reflected in the growing self-confidence noted by many researchers, as well as by the greater "openness to self" described by Norma Haan and others.

But while this individualization process begins in our 30s, it is still the case that this period of early adulthood, as in the period from 18 to 25, is dominated by the social clock. We may chafe more at the strictures of the roles in which we find ourselves; we may be less and less likely to define ourselves in terms of the roles we occupy, but the role demands are still extremely powerful in this period. This fact tends to make the lives of adults in early adulthood more like one another than will be true at any later point. To be sure, some adults do not follow the normative pattern, and their lives are less predictable. But the vast majority of adults do enter into the broad river of family and work roles in their 20s and are moved along with the common flow as their children grow older and their work status progresses.

One of the key changes as we move into middle adult life is that the power of those roles declines; the social clock begins to be less audible, less compelling.

Middle Adulthood: From 40 to 65

Although the change is usually gradual rather than abrupt, the period of middle adulthood is really quite distinctly different from the years that have come before. As Elizabeth Barrett Browning said in another context, "let me count the ways."

THE BIOLOGICAL CLOCK Most obviously, the biological clock begins to be audible, since it is during these years that the first signs of physical aging become apparent—the changes in the eyes that mean most adults require glasses for reading, loss of elasticity in the skin that makes wrinkles more noticeable, the diminished reproductive capacity, most noticeable for women but present for men as well, the heightened risk for major diseases such as heart disease or cancer, the slight but measurable slowing in reaction time or foot speed, perhaps some slowing in the speed of bringing names or other information out of long-term memory.

The early stages of this physical aging process normally don't involve much functional loss. Mental skills may be a trifle slower but not enough slower that you can't do your job or teach yourself something new like using a computer or a new language. Maintaining fitness may take more work, but it's still quite possible. If you've been out of shape, you can even improve significantly, running faster or doing more pushups than you could when you were 30. But as you move through these years toward retirement age, the signs of aging become more and more apparent and less and less easy to ignore.

David Karp (1988) has documented this growing awareness of physical aging in a series of interviews with 72 men and women between the ages of 50 and 60. This was not a representative sample; all these adults are white, all are in professional occupations. Karp's study doesn't tell us whether working class men and women would respond in the same way. Still, he has given us an in-depth look at the experience of a few. He says, "The fact of aging seems to be one of life's great surprises, a surprise that is most fully sprung in the fifties" (p. 729).

The reminders are both external and internal. The body itself sends you some messages. As one of Karp's subjects said:

> I do not see the signs of old age, but I can see some of the clues. I have arthritis. You can't deny that. To me that's kind of old age. I've been running for 20 years and I didn't run last year. My arthritis caught up with me and a couple of other things like that. So, I see myself fitting it [age], but I'm only on the threshold of what I would call becoming old. (p. 730)

And our culture sends messages as well. When I turned 50, I received in the mail an invitation to join the American Association of Retired Persons. "Hey," I said, "I'm not retired! I'm not old enough to belong to AARP!" But I am. Their membership begins at 50. And one of Karp's subjects told of hearing an insurance salesman on television inquiring, "'Do you know someone between 50 and 80 years old?' His response was, 'My God, he's talking about me'"(p.729).

There are also generational reminders, such as the increasing infirmity or death of one's own elderly parents, or seeing one's own children entering their late 20s or 30s. One professor who was part of Karp's study said:

> More recently, I would say in the last 5 years. . . When I meet the parents of students, it occurs to me that not only am I old enough to be their father, but I'm half way on the way to being their grandfather. (p. 732)

My father recently expressed an equivalent realization, albeit one stage later. On hearing that he was about to become a great-grandfather he said, "I don't mind so much being a great-grandfather; what I mind is being the father of a grandmother!"

The Social Clock at Midlife At the same time, the social clock becomes much less significant. To a considerable degree, of course, this is the result of the fact that by middle adulthood many of us have completed at least some of the key roles, as I described in Chapter 7 in some detail. If you had your children in your 20s, then by your late 40s or early 50s they are likely to be launched. And in your work life, you are likely to have reached the highest level that you will achieve, you know the role well, and the drive to achieve may peak and then decline.

But the softening or weakening of the social clock is also the result of the "detribalization" process that Levinson talks about, perhaps part of a deeper shift in personality or meaning systems toward a more individualistic view. The greater openness to self that emerges at this time includes an openness to unexpressed parts of the self, parts that are likely to be outside the prescriptions of the roles. The change is thus both external and internal.

If you think about the relationship of these two "clocks" over the years of adulthood, you might visualize them something like the pattern in Figure 13–2. The specific point of cross-over of these two chronologies is obviously going to differ from one adult to another, but it is most likely to occur some time in this middle-adulthood period.

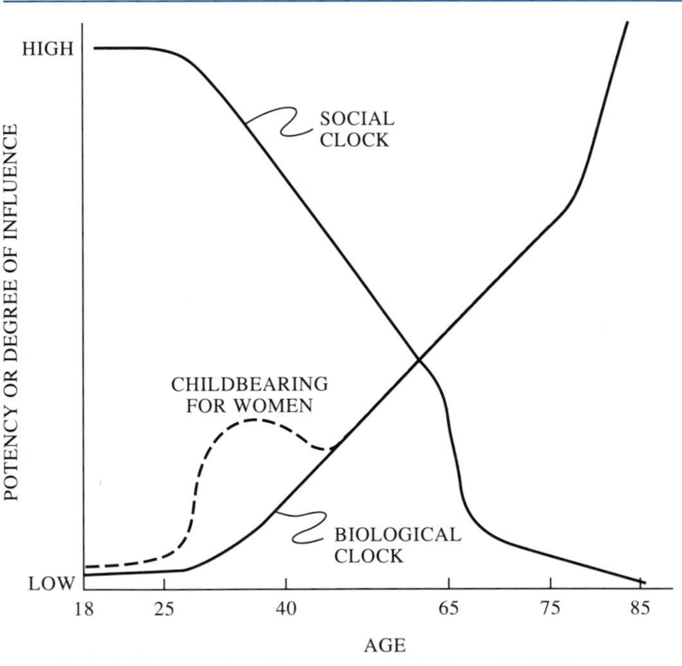

Figure 13–2 One way to think about the different phases or stages of adulthood is in terms of the relative potency or importance of the biological and social "clocks." Except for the issue of childbearing for women, the biological clock is relatively unimportant until some time in midlife, after which it becomes increasingly important. The social clock follows an opposite pattern.

Work and Marital Satisfaction One of the ironies is that the decline in the centrality of work and relationship roles in midlife is often accompanied by greater satisfaction with both work and relationships. You'll recall from Chapters 8 and 9 that both marital and work satisfaction rise in these years of middle adulthood. As always, there are undoubtedly many reasons for the rise, including the fact that the actual work one is doing in these years is likely to be objectively more interesting than was true in one's 20s or even 30s, and that once the children are grown and gone, one of the major strains on a marriage declines. But the improvement in satisfaction with both work and relationships may also be a reflection of the inner shift of perspective I have been talking about. An adult who experiences the world from a more individualist or conscientious perspective takes responsibility for her own actions, so she may find ways to make her work more pleasant and work on her relationships in a new way. Or she may choose to change work, or partners, in order to find what she needs elsewhere.

The Sense of Choice It is precisely this sense of choice that seems to me to be a key aspect of this age period. There are certainly still roles to be filled; one does not stop being a parent just because the children have been launched; one still has work roles to fill, relationships with one's own parents, with friends, with the community. But adults in middle life have more choices about how they will fill those roles, both because the roles of this age themselves have more leeway, and because we now perceive roles differently, as being less compellingly prescriptive.

Variability A related phenomenon is the increased variability of pathways that we see in midlife. In early adulthood, because of the power of the various roles and of our attitude toward them, there is a certain lock-step quality to development. Certainly, there are variations; I've talked about a lot of them. But if you followed the norm, or close to the norm, in your early adult life then the next 20 years are reasonably predictable. In an inner sense, too, there are signs that there is more commonality of psychological functioning in early adulthood than there is later. In Loevinger's terms, for example, virtually everyone reaches the conformist stage; many reach the individualist stage, but fewer and fewer will be found achieving each subsequent stage. In old age, physical aging will again impose some uniformity, but in personality and meaning systems the diversity should be even greater.

Research support for such greater variability in midlife has been accumulating in recent years (Dannefer, 1988). One example: Norma Haan (1981) has found that the range of scores on the dimension of "openness to self" in the Berkeley longitudinal sample was significantly larger at midlife than it had been when the subjects had been in their teens, 20s, or 30s. That is, not only did the average score on this dimension go up, the diversity also rose.

Is This Picture Too Rosy? The picture I've been painting is pretty rosy, isn't it? In midlife we have more choices, our work and marital satisfaction is likely to rise, there is a likelihood of some inner growth or transformation as well. To be sure, there is also the growing awareness of physical aging, but for most of us such an awareness is not dominant. We still feel pretty fit and capable. It sounds as if these years, when neither the biological nor the social clock is deafening us with its sound, are the best of all worlds.

But isn't this also the time when the famous midlife crisis is supposed to hit? In this more negative view of midlife, "midlife men [are seen] as anxious, conflicted, and going through a crisis. The women are menopausal, fretful, and depressed" (Hunter & Sundel, 1989, p. 13). Can these two views be reconciled? I've been sidestepping the question of whether there really is a midlife crisis for most of this book; now I need to face it more squarely.

The Midlife Crisis: Fact or Myth?

The notion that a personal or emotional crisis at midlife is an integral part of adult experience has been fed by characterizations in novels, plays, and films as well as by such popular books as *Passages* (Sheehy, 1974). The existence of some kind of crisis at this time of life is also part of several theories you have become familiar with already, including most notably Levinson's.

You'll remember from Chapter 3 that Levinson (1978, 1980) argues that facing the constellation of developmental tasks that confront us at midlife, including acceptance of death and mortality, recognition of biological limitations and health risks, restructuring of sexual identity and self-concept, reorientation to work, career, creativity, and achievement, and reassessment of primary relationships, guarantees some kind of significant reassessment and change of basic life structure in our early 40s, typically accompanied by depression, distress, and upheaval.

But is it really true? I realize that the concept of a midlife crisis has become so widely accepted that to raise doubts about it will align me against a good deal of popular culture. But doubts I do have.

Transition versus Crisis To make any sense out of the evidence and theory in this area, I must first distinguish between a *transition* and a *crisis*. Levinson, as well as other theorists, proposes that adult life is made up of a series of transitions—times when existing life structures are reassessed and may be altered. Transitions *may* be experienced as stressful or crisis-like, but they can also be relatively smooth. A "crisis" occurs, as Cytrynbaum and his colleagues suggest, "when internal resources and external social support systems threaten to be overwhelmed by developmental tasks that require new adaptive resources" (Cytrynbaum, Blum, Patrick, Stein, Wadner, & Wilk, 1980, p. 464).

With this distinction in mind, we have to ask two questions about midlife: (1) Do all adults experience a *transition* of some kind at midlife? (2) Is this particular transition likely to be experienced as a crisis, especially in comparison to other transitions in adult life?

Transition at Midlife? No researcher has yet developed a real measure of transitions, so it is difficult to answer this first question cleanly. Still, I have made some effort, both in this and in earlier chapters, to point out that some time in midlife most adults not only change roles but change inner perspectives as well. It seems fair to say that there is a transition of some kind for many if not most adults in these years. But is this transition usually experienced as a crisis?

IS IT A CRISIS? Opinions differ sharply. In one recent book on *Midlife Myths* (Hunter & Sundel, 1989), two respected researchers reading the same evidence came to opposite conclusions. David Chiriboga concludes that "there is mounting evidence from research studies that serious midlife problems are actually experienced by only 2 percent to 5 percent of middle agers" (1989, p. 117), while Lois Tamir not only argues that there is a significant transition at this age but that the transition is marked with "deep-seated self-doubts or confusion" (1989, p. 161).

My own reading of this set of evidence is more in line with Chiriboga's conclusion. Clearly, there are some adults who experience this transition as a crisis; it may even be possible that this particular transition is more likely to be crisis-like than are other adult transitions. But there is little evidence to suggest that crisis is a common feature of midlife, *except for* one particular subgroup: middle-class or professional white men. Several studies show that for this group (at least in this culture and for current cohorts), a crisis-like experience is relatively common.

Much of the evidence against the existence of a widespread midlife crisis seems to me to be compelling. For example, Costa & McCrae (1980a; McCrae & Costa, 1984) developed a midlife crisis scale which included items about a sense of inner turmoil, a sense of failing power, marital dissatisfaction, or job dissatisfaction. When they then used this scale in a cross-sectional study of over 500 men, aged 35 to 70, they could find no age at which scores were particularly high. Some men at each age reported feelings of crisis. Farrell and Rosenberg (1981), whose study of friendship patterns in men I mentioned in an earlier chapter, similarly found no age difference on a scale measuring midlife crisis, nor did Pearlin (1975) find a piling up of depression or anxiety at midlife in his cross-sectional study of life stresses. Epidemiological studies also do not show any clear rise or peak in midlife for such likely signs of crisis as divorce, alcoholism, or depression (Hunter & Sundel, 1989). As an example, go back and look at Figure 5–7 again: In this major study, serious depressions were more common in the period from 25 to 44 than in the 45 to 64 period (Regier, et al. 1988).

Of course, all of this is cross-sectional evidence. Studies like Costa & McCrae's may tell us that there is no specific age at which some kind of upheaval is common, but they don't tell us whether each individual, as he or she passes through the decades of midlife, is likely to have an upheaval at *some* time. Since the span of years we are calling "midlife" is fairly broad, it might still be that some kind of a crisis is common between 40 and 60, but that it happens at different times for different adults, depending on the timing of particular kinds of life changes, such as the topping out of one's career or the children leaving home.

Such a possibility is strengthened by the retrospective studies of Rochelle Harris and her colleagues (Harris, Ellicott, & Holmes, 1986) that I described in Chapter 10. You may remember that they studied a group of women aged 45, 50, 55, and 60, asking each to talk in detail about the years of their adult life. Their descriptions were then rated for the presence of transitions. Eighty percent of the 64 women in this study reported at least one such transition between the ages of 36 and 60, but the transitions were linked not to age but to some change in family life-cycle status. Not all these transitions were crisis-like; many involved uplifting feelings rather than depressions. But the findings at least raise the possibility that crises might be common but simply not detected by our usual cross-sectional techniques of study.

Longitudinal evidence is obviously the best antidote to this problem. Yet here, too, there is little support for the expectation of widespread midlife crises. For instance, Norma Haan (1981), in her analysis of the subjects in the Berkeley and Oakland longitudinal studies, found no indication of a widespread upheaval in midlife.

It is only for the subgroup of white, professional or middle class males that there is some support for the idea of a common life crisis, most compellingly from a cross-sectional study by Lois Tamir (1982) of a national sample of roughly a thousand men ranging in age from 25 to 69. She found that among college-educated men, the period from age 45 to 49 was characterized by lower levels of zest, more "psychological immobilization," drinking problems, and more turning to prescription drugs to relieve nervous tension. You'll also recall from Chapter 5 (Figure 5–5) that suicide rates among white men begin to rise in midlife, although they continue to rise for this subgroup well into old age, which does not suggest some uniquely crisis-like feature of midlife.

It may well be that for well-educated, successful men, in this culture and in current cohorts, the period of midlife is particularly stressful. Tamir's findings notwithstanding, however, my conclusion is in line with Costa and McCrae's summary: "These findings do not necessarily mean that there is no midlife crisis . . . They do, however, cast grave doubt on the claim that everyone goes through a crisis, or that there is any particular portion of the adult age span in which crises are concentrated" (Costa & McCrae, 1980a, p. 84).

In sum, it seems plausible that there is a psychological or role-related *transition* of some kind for many (perhaps even most) adults in this culture some time around midlife. The timing of this is quite variable, however, depending on the timing of various role changes, on the longevity of each adult's parents, or on such unexpected events as unemployment or divorce. But this transition is not routinely experienced as a crisis. Whether a crisis occurs probably depends on the specific personality or temperament of the individual and on whether there is a pile-up of role changes or other stressful life events within a short space of time. What we need now is much more research focused on the content of whatever transition occurs at this age, and much less emphasis on the "crisis" of midlife.

Late Adulthood: From 65 to 75

Bernice Neugarten (1974, 1975) has referred to those adults in the years from 55 to 75 as the "young old," in contrast to those over 75, whom she calls the "old old," a distinction that has been widely adopted by gerontologists. I have divided the years somewhat differently here, making the break at 65 rather than 55, but the point is still significant. In many ways, the young old are more like the middle-aged than they are like the old old. So why make a division here at all, whether at 55 or at 65?

From a physical point of view, there is nothing notable about age 65 that would suggest that some new stage or phase has begun. Certainly, some adults in this age range experience significant disease or chronic disability. But the norm is rather that small—albeit noticeable—physical changes or declines continue to accumulate at roughly the same rate as was true in one's middle years. Hearing loss is now more likely to become a problem, as is arthritis; one is likely to have an increased sense of being a bit slower. But for most adults (in Western countries at least) the rate of physical or mental change does not appear to accelerate in these years. What makes this 10-year period unique is the abrupt or at least rapid drop in role demands that accompanies retirement, a drop that once again changes the balance between what I have been calling the social clock and the biological clock, as I have tried to suggest in Figure 13–2.

There is certainly little evidence that this change is marked by any kind of crisis. As I pointed out in Chapter 8, research on retirement shows no increase in illness or depression or other distress that can be linked causally to the retirement itself. For those who retire *because* of ill-health, the picture is rather different; for this subgroup, retirement is linked with further declines in health and perhaps depression. But for the majority, and with the notable exception of the continuing rise in suicide among white males, every indication is that mental health is as good—or perhaps better—in this age group than at younger ages.

What does mark this change is the loss of the work role, which is of course accompanied by a continuing decline in the centrality of other roles as well. Irving Rosow (1985), who divides role positions into four types, describes the role position of the aged as *tenuous*: they have a social position, but it is a social position without clear roles. Spousal roles continue, of course, for those whose spouse is still living; there is still some parental role, although that too is less demanding and less clearly defined; the role of friend and of brother or sister to one's aging siblings may actually become more central. But even more than was true in middle life, these roles are full of choices.

Edwin Schneidman (1989), writing about the decade of one's 70s, puts it this way:

> Consider that when one is a septuagenarian, one's parents are gone, children are grown, mandatory work is done; health is not too bad, and responsibilities are relatively light, with time, at long last, for focus on the self. These can be sunset years, golden years, an Indian Summer, a period of relatively mild weather for both soma and psyche in the late autumn or early winter of life, a decade of greater independence and increased opportunities for further self-development. (1989, p. 684)

But what is it that adults in this period of early old age, of "Indian Summer," choose to do with their lives? Do they remain active and involved, or do they begin to withdraw, to turn inward toward self development or reminiscence? If there has been controversy about this age period, it has centered on some variant of this question. The issue is usually framed in the terms of the theory of **disengagement** in old age.

Disengagement in Old Age: Another Myth?

The term disengagement was first proposed by Cumming and Henry (1961) to describe what they saw as a key psychological process in old age. As restated by Cumming (1975), this process was seen as having three features or aspects: (1) Adults' social "life space" shrinks with age, a change especially noticeable in the period from 65 on. We interact with fewer and fewer others and fill fewer and fewer roles as we move through old age; (2) In the roles and relationships that remain, the aging individual becomes more individualized, less governed by the rules and norms; (3) The aging individual anticipates this set of changes and actively embraces them, disengaging more and more from roles and relationships. Furthermore, Cumming and Henry argue that such disengagement is not only natural but optimally healthy in old age, so that those who show such disengagement the most are going to be the happiest and least disturbed.

As with the data on midlife crisis, the evidence is mixed. In old age, most adults do show a decline in the number of social activities they engage in. They participate in fewer clubs or organizations, go to church less often, see friends less often. This has been found in both longitudinal studies, such as the Duke studies of aging (Palmore, 1981) and in cross-sectional ones (e.g., Morgan, 1988), so the pattern seems well established. But there is no indication that those who show the greatest decline in social activity (who "disengage" the most) are happier or healthier. On the contrary, the common finding is that the *least* disengaged adults report slightly greater satisfaction with themselves or their lives (e.g., Holahan, 1988; Palmore, 1981). The effect is not large but the direction of the effect is consistently positive: more social involvement is linked to greater satisfaction.

On the other side of the ledger is a significant body of work pointing to the conclusion that solitude is quite a comfortable state for many older adults. Note, for example, the finding I reported to you in Chapter 8, that among all age groups loneliness is least common among the elderly. Indeed, some older adults clearly find considerable satisfaction in an independent, socially isolated (highly disengaged) life pattern. Maas and Kuypers (1974), for example, in a study of some of the parents of the subjects in the Berkeley longitudinal studies, describe a group of satisfied men they call "hobbyists," whose lives revolved around some solitary hobby such as woodworking or birdwatching. Similarly, in studies in England, Savage and his colleagues (Savage, Gaber, Britton, Bolton, & Cooper, 1977) found some introverted, socially isolated elderly adults who seemed largely content with their lives. Clearly, then, it is possible to choose and to find contentment in a largely disengaged lifestyle in these older years. What these data do not say, however, is that such disengagement is necessary for mental health. On the contrary, most of the evidence says exactly the opposite: For most older adults, social involvement is both a sign of, and probably a cause of, higher levels of satisfaction. Those who do not have satisfactory contact with others, particularly with friends, are typically less satisfied with their lives.

So while our lives become less ruled by roles in this decade of the young old, we still maintain, even need, social contact with others.

Late, Late Adulthood: From 75 Until Death

The fastest growing segment of the U.S. population is the group of elderly adults Bernice Neugarten calls the "old old," those over 75. As just one example, between 1960 and 1980 in the United States the population over age 84 increased by 141 percent (Longino, 1988). As life expectancy increases, more and more of us are living well past the fabled "four score and ten." And as health has improved, it is not until these years of late late adulthood that the processes of physical aging, with the mental declines that accompany them, really accelerate.

I do not want to make too big a deal about the age of 75. The demarcation point between the period of the young old and that of the old old is more a function of health than it is of age. Some adults may be frail at 60; others may

Figure 13–3 *Even among those Neugarten would refer to as the old old, like these folks, there is still a lot of variability both in physical dysfunction and living circumstances. Still, there is no escaping the fact that in this age range, the biological clock becomes a potent factor in everyone's lives. (Photos {left} © Susan Lapides, c/o Design Conceptions, 1981; {right} © Joel Gordon, 1990. Reprinted with permission.)*

still be robust and active at 85. But if you look at the norms, as I have been doing in this chapter, it appears that age 75 is roughly where the shift takes place.

Our knowledge of the old old is not extensive; only in relatively recent years have there been large numbers of such adults; only quite recently has the Census Bureau begun to divide some of its statistics for the elderly into decades rather than merely lumping all those over age 65 into a single category. But we do have some information that points to a qualitative change that takes place at roughly this time.

Go back and look again at Figure 6–1, for example. You'll see that the acceleration in the decline in total mental ability scores starts at about 70 or 75. There is decline before that, but the rate of decline increases in the old old. Researchers testing the elderly subjects who participated in the Duke longitudinal studies also found sharp increases in some kinds of disability at roughly 75, such as the incidence of severe hearing impairments (Eisdorfer & Wilkie, 1972) and the prevalence of visual losses sufficient to be classed as legal blindness (Anderson & Palmore, 1974). Census data also tell us that over half of those over 85 have a disability that would make it impossible for them to use public transportation; many more have more limited disabilities (Longino, 1988).

As a result of the loss or reduction of mobility that now becomes common, elders in the years after 75 also show some further "disengagement" socially. You'll remember from Chapter 11, for example, that church attendance drops at about 75 not because elders are less religious but because getting to church becomes more of a strain. Since widowhood is also the norm in these years, those old old who still live independently are spending more time alone, although it would be a mistake to describe them as socially isolated. Most maintain regular, if reduced, contact with their children, with other family members, and with friends. They may go to fewer club meetings or other group gatherings, but they keep in touch.

Because so few of the old old have been studied, we know far less about what might be happening inwardly even than what we know about physical changes. Does reminiscence increase? Do elders in this final life period spend time trying to integrate the pieces of their past, to come to some acceptance? Certainly, Erikson suggests that some attempt to move toward "integrity" is the final stage of life.

Some years ago, Robert Butler (1963) attempted to take Erikson's idea one step further. He proposed that in old age, all of us go through a process he called a *life review*, in which there is a "progressive return to consciousness of past experience, and particularly, the resurgence of unresolved conflicts." Butler argued that in this final stage of life, as preparation for our now clearly impending death, we engage in an analytic and evaluative review of our earlier life.

This has been an attractive hypothesis. Unfortunately, the quality or clarity of the conclusions does not match the quantity of the research. There are some hints that a process of reminiscence may increase the life satisfaction or self-esteem of the elderly (e.g., Haight, 1988), but despite two decades of research we still know little about this process: Is reminiscence more common in the elderly than among the middle-aged? If so, is there some age at which it begins to be more noticeable? How much do elderly individuals vary in the amount of reminiscence they engage in? How much of reminiscence is really integrative or evaluative, rather than merely story telling for amusement or information? Is reminiscence a necessary ingredient in achieving some form of integration in late life?

Obviously, it remains to be seen whether life review or some other form of reminiscence is a significant part of the experience of the old old. What we do know for sure is that some kind of preparation for death is an inevitable, even central, part of life in these last years. While death may certainly come at earlier ages, adults in younger phases can continue to push the idea of death away; that's something for later. But in the years past 75, the imminence of death is inescapable and must be faced by each of us—a story I will turn to in the next chapter.

Summary

1. It is useful to look at the various ways in which the several threads of development interact in each of the major periods of adulthood.
2. The years from 18 to 25 appear to have the highest levels of stress, but also the greatest physical and mental assets. This period is also marked by the domination of the demands of various roles, which the young person typically experiences from a "conformist" perspective.
3. In the years from 25 to 40, the "social clock" continues to dominate, but there is increasing individualization both in day-to-day lives and in inner perspectives. These years also appear to have the highest status within our culture.
4. In middle adulthood, from 40 to 65, the social clock becomes less compelling while the biological clock begins to have a greater impact, as the first clear signs of physical aging appear. Social roles become less dominant not only because many young-adult roles are well-learned or even largely fulfilled, but also because the middle-aged adult perceives the roles differently, experiencing the world from a more individualist perspective.
5. Work and marital satisfaction are typically at high points in the midlife decades, as is a sense of choice. Variability in pathways or characteristics appears to increase as well.
6. There is little indication of a widespread midlife crisis, except among middle class white males.
7. Adults between 65 and 75 are sometimes referred to as the "young old." Although physical and mental aging continues in this age range, the rate does not normally accelerate and most adults in this age range are still independent and relatively fit. Because of retirement from work, however, the social clock becomes even less significant.
8. Some aspects of disengagement theory's description of these years have been supported: There is a reduction in the total number of social contacts of adults past age 65. But there is no indication that disengagement is central to mental health. If anything, the reverse is true.

9. Those past 75 are sometimes called the "old old." It is in these years that the rate of physical and mental aging accelerates, so that frailty becomes more common, disabilities more limiting.
10. Reminiscence or life review in these later years may aid some older adults to reassess and integrate the meaning of their lives, but this hypothesis remains to be adequately tested.

Suggested Readings

Gould, R. L. (1978). *Transformations. Growth and change in adult life.* New York: Simon & Schuster. I've recommended this book before. Even more than a decade later, I still find it has one of the most compelling descriptions of the inner issues of aging, particularly in the period of early adulthood.

Hunter, S. & Sundel, M. (1989). *Midlife myths. Issues, findings, and practice implications.* Newbury Park, CA: Sage. If you want to look at the alternative views of midlife crisis, this is a good recent source. Compare Tamir's paper with the one by Chiriboga. This book also has other useful chapters about the period of midlife, many written by authors whose names will be familiar from the pages of this book.

Karp, D. A. (1988). A decade of reminders: Changing age consciousness between fifty and sixty years old. *The Gerontologist, 28*, 727–738. Although Karp's sample is certainly not random nor representative, this is one of the few papers in which the actual voices of a particular age group can be heard, in this case adults between 50 and 60. The article is both absorbing and thought-provoking (perhaps particularly for me, since I am now in this decade!)

CHAPTER 14

The Final Stage: Death and Dying

In the last chapter, I talked about the various phases or stages of adult life, but there remains one stage left to discuss, the period of dying and death. In exploring this difficult subject, it is not enough merely to describe the last months or days of life. We have to start earlier. Just as we prepare mentally and physically for earlier stages of adulthood, such as by planning for retirement or by periodically reassessing our priorities and choices, so too do we prepare for our own death in various ways over many years. Each adult has attitudes about death, fears of death, and makes preparations for death long before the final confrontation with dying. So let me begin the story by looking at these attitudes, fears, and preparations over the adult years.

The Meaning of Death

> The one invariant of the meaning of death for both the individual and society is that death matters. And so does the process of dying. The event of death and the process of dying have immense impact on individuals and on the community, whether judged by emotional feelings, social relationships, spiritual well-being, financial stresses, or changes in daily living. (Kalish, 1985, p. 149)

Understandings of death change over the life span. Preschool children, for example, do not understand the irreversibility of death (perhaps aided and abetted by the tendency of adults, when explaining death to young children, to say things like "Grandma has gone to Heaven." In the child's experience, "going" implies "coming back.") Between about ages five and nine, children personify death—they may imagine a "death-man" of some kind who comes to take people away. Finally, beginning in adolescence, children begin to understand more fully not only that death is universal, but also that it is irreversible (Childers & Wimmer, 1971; Kastenbaum & Aisenberg, 1976; Nagy, 1948).

In adulthood, there are still some remnants of the earlier views, particularly various personifications of death such as "the pale horse" or "the Grim Reaper." But most adults have a far more complex conception of death. Kalish (1985) suggests four different meanings for death among adults, which are typically mixed in any individual's meaning system:

Death as an Organizer of Time Death defines the end point of one's life, so the concept of "time till death" may be an important one for an individual trying to organize his life. In fact, Bernice Neugarten (1968, 1977) suggests that one of the key changes in thinking in middle age is a switch in the way one marks one's own lifetime, from "time since birth" to "time till death." Her interviews with middle-aged adults frequently yielded statements like the following:

> Time is now a two-edged sword. To some of my friends, it acts as a prod; to others, a brake. It adds a certain anxiety, but I must also say it adds a certain zest in seeing how much pleasure can still be obtained, how many good years one can still arrange, how many new activities can be undertaken. (Neugarten, 1968, p. 97)

Such a change in time perspective, accompanied by a greater awareness of (and worry about) death, does not occur at midlife for every adult. Nor do all older adults think of their lives in terms of time till death. In one study of elderly adults, for example, Pat Keith (1981-82) found that only about half of her sample of 568 72- to 99-year-olds seemed to think about or precisely define "time remaining." But such a recognition of time remaining may be a useful (perhaps even a necessary) aspect of coming to terms with one's own death. In Keith's study, those adults who did talk about time remaining also had more favorable attitudes toward and less fear of death. Other research confirms this pattern: Older adults who continue to be preoccupied with the past, who avoid thinking about the future, are more likely to be fearful or anxious about death than are those who face the future (and their own deaths) more fully (Pollak, 1979–80).

DEATH AS PUNISHMENT Many religious traditions emphasize that death is a punishment for sins, and many adults believe that a "good" person will be rewarded with longer life.

DEATH AS TRANSITION Death involves *some* kind of transition, from life to some sort of life after death, or from life to nothingness. In one recent study, Daniel Klenow and Robert Bolin (1989–90) found that 70 percent of adults in a nationally representative U.S. sample reported believing in life after death. Women were more likely to believe in an afterlife than were men, and Protestants and Catholics much more likely than Jews to have such a belief, but there was no significant age difference in this belief. Adults in their 20s were just as likely to believe in life after death as were those older than 60.

DEATH AS LOSS Perhaps most pervasively, death is seen by most of us as a loss of some kind—loss of the ability to complete projects or carry out plans, loss of one's body, loss of experiencing, of taste, smell, touch, loss of relationships with people. No more hot fudge sundaes, no more delight in the reds and golds of autumn leaves making a pattern on the ground, no more caresses or kisses, no more Bach chorales, no more trips to exotic new places. Of course, some of these losses may occur during a person's lifetime. A loss of hearing will already cut out the Bach chorales; widowhood may deprive an adult of caresses. But death guarantees all of these losses.

Unlike beliefs in an afterlife, in this domain there are age differences. In particular, the specific losses that adults associate with death appear to change as they move through the adult years. Young adults are more concerned about loss of opportunity to experience things, and about the loss of family relationships; older adults may be more concerned with the loss of time to complete some inner work. These differences are reflected in the results of a study by Richard Kalish (Kalish & Reynolds, 1976). He asked a group of adults what they would do with their time if they were told they had a terminal disease and six months to live. (You may want to think about your own answer to this question before you read further.) The key results are in Table 14.1. Younger adults were clearly

TABLE 14.1. What Would You Do If You Knew You Were to Die in Six Months? Subjects in a Los Angeles Study Gave These Types of Answers.

	Age Groups		
	20–39	*40–59*	*60+*
Make a marked change in lifestyle, (e.g., travel, sex, experiences, etc.).	24%	15%	9%
Center on inner life (read, contemplate, pray).	14%	14%	37%
Focus concern on others, be with loved ones.	29%	25%	12%
Attempt to complete projects, tie up loose ends.	11%	10%	3%
No change in lifestyle.	17%	29%	31%
Other	5%	6%	8%

SOURCE: Kalish & Reynolds, 1976, p. 205. Reprinted by permission of University of Southern California Press.

more likely to plan to spend time either experiencing things or on relationships, while older adults much more often said they would read, contemplate or pray—more evidence, perhaps, for the greater "spiritual" preoccupation in later life I suggested in Chapter 11.

Fears of Death

The view of death as loss is strongly linked to the most studied aspect of death attitudes, namely the fear of death. If we fear death, it is in part the losses of experience, sensation, relationships that we fear. Fear of death may also include fear of the pain or suffering or indignity that may be involved in the process of death itself, fear that one will not be able to cope well with such pain or suffering, fear of whatever punishment may come after death, and a fundamental fear of loss of the self.

Pervasive as it is, fear of death is extremely difficult to study, in part because we defend ourselves against this fear in various ways, most typically with repression or denial. If you ask adults directly whether they are afraid of death, the majority will say no. If you approach the subject somewhat more indirectly, such as by asking about a person's feelings about the deaths of others, or about her expectation of or fear of pain, you will find somewhat higher levels of fear. And when researchers attempt to tap unconscious fear, virtually everyone shows signs of such fear. For example, Herman Feifel and Allan Branscomb (1973) gave several hundred subjects lists of words, printed in various colors. The subject's task was to read off the *color* of the word, not the word itself. Half the words in the series were death-related words, half were neutral words. If it takes subjects longer to read the colors of death words than neutral words, this implies some resistance to these words, and may reflect unconscious anxiety or fear about death.

Feifel and Branscomb found that 71 percent of their subjects, when asked directly, "Are you afraid of your own death?" said no. But it nonetheless took these subjects significantly longer to read off the colors of the death-related words than the neutral words.

Age Differences in Fear of Death

Using all these various types of measures, researchers have attempted to plot age changes in the strength of fear of death. Several possible age-related patterns seem plausible. On the one hand, I could make an argument for the hypothesis that young adults would be more fearful, since they have in some sense the most to lose—all those experiences not yet enjoyed, those relationships uncompleted. I could also make an argument for exactly the opposite hypothesis: Since older adults are on average much closer to death, they may be much more fearful of the impending pain or suffering and so fear death more.

As it happens, neither of these two possible hypothesis is supported by the data. Instead, the peak of fear of and worry over death seems to be at midlife rather than in early adulthood or later life.

Such a pattern emerges, for example, from a set of interviews with a large national sample by Matilda White Riley (unpublished, cited in Riley & Foner, 1968). Riley asked subjects to say if they agreed or disagreed with certain statements about death, such as "Death always comes too soon," or "To die is to suffer." Table 14.2 gives the percentages who agreed with the first of these statements, by age, for each of three levels of education. You can see that in all three education groups, the middle-aged adults were most likely to agree that death always comes too soon.

A higher level of explicit, conscious fear among middle-aged adults also appeared in a well-designed study by Vern Bengtson and his colleagues (Bengtson, Cuellar, & Ragan, 1977). Bengtson's sample, all between 45 and 74 years of age, was selected to be representative of adults in the Los Angeles area, and included approximately equal numbers of whites, blacks, and Mexican Americans. The measure of fear of death was quite simple (perhaps too much so, in fact). He

TABLE 14.2. Percent of Adults of Various Age Groups and Education Groups Who Agreed with the Statement, "Death Always Comes Too Soon".

Age	Education		
	Junior High School or Less	*High School*	*College*
30 and under	65	53	40
31–40	58	50	24
41–50	75	64	49
51–60	70	50	53
61+	58	59	29

SOURCE: From *Aging and Society. Volume One. An Inventory of Research Findings* by Matilda White Riley and Anne Foner. Copyright ©1968 by Russell Sage Foundation. Reprinted by permission of Basic Books, Inc., Publishers.

asked each subject "How afraid are you of death? Would you say you are: not at all afraid?/somewhat afraid?/or very afraid?" Only 37 percent said they were either somewhat or very afraid, but these were mostly the middle aged subjects, as you can see in Figure 14–1.

Bengtson's study only tells us that fear of death is higher in middle age than in old age; since he did not include adults younger than 45, we can't tell whether fear of death is lower or higher among those in early adulthood. But a more recent study by Gina Gesser and her associates (Gesser, Wong, & Reker, 1987–88) fills in the gap, showing precisely the same curvilinear relationship of age and fear of death as Riley had found several decades before. Gesser found the highest levels of fear of both death and of the dying process among middle-aged subjects, the

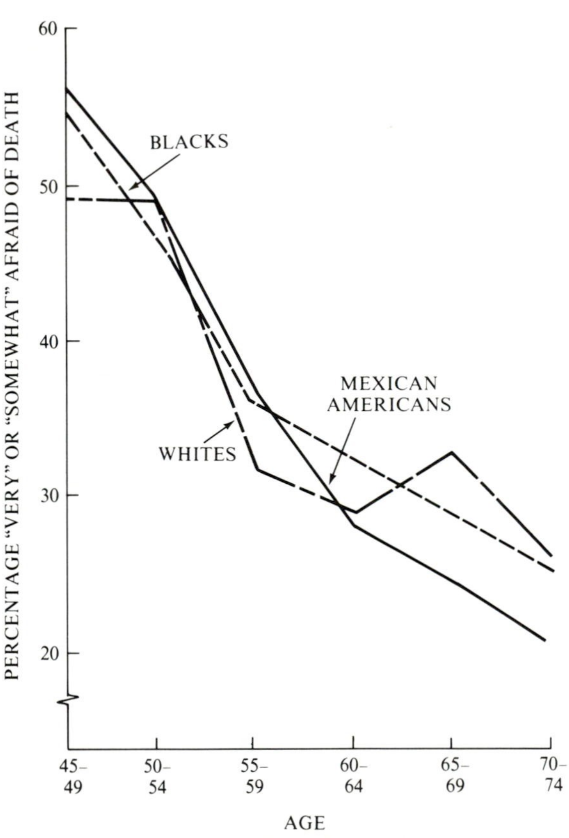

Figure 14–1 The remarkable similarity of the patterns of age change in overt fear of death in these three different groups lends credence to the view that older adults are less consciously fearful than are middle-aged adults. (Source: Bengtson, Cuellar, & Ragan, 1977, Figure 1, p. 80. Reprinted by permission of The Journal of Gerontology, *32(1), 1977.)*

lowest levels among those over 60, with intermediate levels among young adults. In this study, the over-60 group also showed more acceptance of death, agreeing with such statements as "I look forward to a life after death," or "I would neither fear death nor welcome it."

Collectively, these results are consistent with the suggestion made by Levinson (based on both Jung's theories and the work of psychoanalyst Elliott Jaques, 1965) that one of the central tasks of midlife is to come to terms with the inevitability of death. The greater awareness of body changes and aging that is part of this period, coupled, perhaps, with the death of one's own parents, combine to break down the defenses we have all erected against the knowledge of and fear of death. In particular, the death of one's parents may be especially shocking and disturbing, not only because of the specific loss to be mourned but because you must now face the realization that you are now the oldest generation in the family lineage and thus "next in line" for death. So in midlife we become more aware of the fear, more preoccupied with death and its imminence. In these years, many adults grope toward new ways of thinking about death, eventually accepting it in a different way, so that the fear recedes in old age. This does not mean, by the way, that older adults are unconcerned with death. On the contrary, they are more likely to talk about it and think about it than are younger adults (Kalish, 1985). But while death is highly *salient* to the elderly, it is apparently not as *frightening* as it was in midlife.

Other Correlates of Fear of Death

Age is not the only element in fear of death. Several other personal qualities, familiar from my discussions of resistance resources and personality in earlier chapters, appear to be related to conscious fearfulness.

First of all, the degree of religious feeling seems to make some difference. After reviewing the few studies addressing this link, Kalish (1985) concludes that, in general, adults who describe themselves as deeply religious or who go to church regularly are less afraid of death than are those who describe themselves as less religious or who participate less regularly in religious activities. In some instances, however, researchers have found a curvilinear relationship with both those who are deeply religious and those who are deeply irreligious being less fearful than those who may be uncertain about, or uncommitted to, any religious tradition.

Individual temperament or personality is another variable in the fear of death equation. Extraversion is not consistently related to fear of death, but measures of neuroticism are. A typical finding is Patricia Frazier and Deborah Foss-Goodman's (1988–89) reported correlation of .41 between a measure of neuroticism and a measure of anxiety about death in a group of college students. Since neuroticism is generally characterized by greater fear or negative attitudes toward many aspects of life, this pattern makes good sense.

More interesting, I think, is the link between fear of death and a sense of personal worth or competence. Several facets of this domain have been studied. Adults who feel they have achieved the goals they set out to achieve, or who think of themselves as not too discrepant from the person they wanted to be, are less fearful of death than are those who are disappointed in themselves (Neimeyer & Chapman, 1980–81). Adults who feel that their life has some purpose or meaning also appear to be less fearful of death (Durlak, 1972), as do those who feel some sense of personal competence (Pollak, 1979–80).

Such findings suggest at least the possibility that those adults who have successfully completed the major tasks of adult life, who have adequately fulfilled the demands of the roles they occupied, who developed inwardly, are able to face death with greater equanimity. Those adults who have not been able to resolve the various tasks and dilemmas of adulthood face their late adult years more fearfully, more anxiously, even with what Erikson describes as despair. Fear of death may be merely one facet of such despair.

In some sense, then, all of adult life is a process of moving toward death. An adult's attitude toward death and his approach to it are influenced by many of the same qualities that affect the way he approaches other life changes or dilemmas.

Preparation for Death

Despite the fear, and despite the frequent avoidance of the very subject, adults do make preparations for death, particularly as they get older. In her national survey, Matilda White Riley (Riley & Foner, 1968) found that 80 percent of adults of all ages thought that one *should* make plans for one's death, and most of us do take at least some steps. For example, 65 percent of all adults over 18 in the United States have life insurance (U.S. Bureau of the Census, 1989a). The older you are, the more likely you are to have such insurance, a pattern Riley also found when she asked her subjects if they had made out a will. Those over 60 years of age in this study were more than twice as likely as those under 40 to have made out a will or to have made funeral or cemetery arrangements.

Life Review

Another process that may be part of preparation for death may be the *life review,* which I talked about in the last chapter as possibly part of late old-age. Butler, in his original formulation of the concept of life review, quite explicitly linked it to awareness of death when he defined it as the "naturally occurring, universal mental process . . . prompted by the realization of approaching dissolution and death, and the inability to maintain one's sense of personal invulnerability" (1968, p. 487).

Intellectual and Psychological Changes Before Death

At a much less conscious level, adults seem to "prepare" physically and psychologically for death. In Chapter 6, I introduced the concept of *terminal drop:* The rather rapid decline in intellectual performance that seems to occur in the years immediately prior to death. Related kinds of terminal changes seem to occur in personality and in emotional patterns.

Morton Lieberman has provided one of the best descriptions of such changes based on a series of short-term longitudinal studies of elderly adults who were tested and interviewed regularly over a period of three years. At the end of the three-year study Lieberman continued to keep track of his subjects, identifying one subset of 40 who had died within one year of the final testing. These 40 were then matched in age, sex, marital status, and education with another 40 participants in the study who had all survived at least three years after the final testing. He was thus able to compare the earlier test scores and personal qualities of those who had been near death with those who had been further from death at the time of testing (Lieberman, 1965; Lieberman & Coplan, 1970).

Lieberman found that those nearer to death not only showed the expected lower performance on tests of memory and learning but also differed on measures of emotion and self-image. Near death subjects displayed fewer different emotions and were *less* introspective than were adults of the same age who were further from death (which doesn't sound like a "life review" was going on, does it?) Those near death also perceived or described themselves as less aggressive or assertive, more conventional and conforming, more docile and dependent, more warm, more responsible. Furthermore, these qualities emerged ever-more-clearly over the three years of the study. It was not that initially conventional, docile, unaggressive adults died sooner, but that these characteristics were accentuated as death neared.

Some of these changes are doubtless the result of (or influenced by) physiological processes occurring immediately prior to death. But some may be a reflection of a psychological preparation for death. Adults very near death become less active both physically and psychologically. They give up tilting at windmills, cease fighting the daily battles. In that sense they become more passive, more accepting, perhaps more inwardly turned.

The Process of Dying

A similar movement toward "acceptance" of death has been described by Elizabeth Kübler-Ross, based on her interviews with hundreds of terminally ill adults and children (1969, 1975). Kübler-Ross is a remarkable clinician, with enormous empathy and compassion for dying patients. Her observations and her proposed stages of dying have been enormously influential and have helped greatly to humanize the process of dying for millions.

Kübler-Ross's Stages of Dying

After watching and listening to many patients, Kübler-Ross suggested that the process of dying involves five steps or stages, occurring in a particular order: denial, anger, bargaining, depression, and acceptance.

DENIAL When confronted with a terminal diagnosis, the first reaction most patients report is some form of "No, not me!": "It must be a mistake." "The lab reports must have been mixed up." "I don't feel that sick, so it can't be true." "I'll get another doctor's opinion." All these are forms of denial, which Kübler-Ross argues is a valuable, constructive first defense. It gives the patient a period of time in which to marshall other strategies of coping with the shock. Some patients, of course, continue to use denial right up to the end. But for most, according to Kübler-Ross, the extreme versions of denial fade within a short time and are replaced by anger.

ANGER The classic second reaction, so Kübler-Ross argues, is "Why me?" The patient resents those who are healthy and becomes angry at whatever fate put her in this position. This may be reflected in angry outbursts at nurses, family members, doctors—anyone within reach. In part, this anger may be a response not just to the verdict of death but also to the typically dependent and helpless position of a patient. There is a "Hey, pay attention to me! I'm still here!" aspect to this anger.

BARGAINING At some point, Kübler-Ross saw anger being replaced by a new kind of defense. The patient now tries to "make a deal" with doctors, nurses, with God. "If I do what I'm told, and don't yell at everyone, then I'll be able to live till Christmas." Kübler-Ross (1969) describes one woman with terminal cancer who wanted to live long enough to attend the wedding of her oldest, favorite son. With help from the hospital staff, she learned how to use self-hypnosis to control her pain for short periods and was able to attend the wedding. As Kübler-Ross reports, "I will never forget the moment when she returned to the hospital. She looked tired and somewhat exhausted and—before I could say hello—said, 'Now don't forget I have another son!'" (1969, p. 83).

DEPRESSION Bargaining only works for so long, however, and as disease processes continue and the signs of the body's decline become more obvious, patients typically become depressed. This is a kind of mourning—for the loss of relationships as well as of one's own life. Often the dying person sinks into a sort of despair, which may last for a prolonged period. But Kübler-Ross argues that this depression is part of the preparation for the final step, acceptance. The dying person must grieve for, and then give up, all the things of the world. Only then can acceptance of death occur.

ACCEPTANCE The final step, according to this theory, is a quiet understanding, a readiness for death. The patient is no longer depressed, but may be quiet, even serene. In a widely quoted passage, author Stewart Alsop (1973), who was dying of leukemia, described his own acceptance: "A dying man needs to die as a sleepy man needs to sleep, and there comes a time when it is wrong, as well as useless, to resist" (Alsop, 1973, p. 299).

Kübler-Ross thought that a current of hope ran through all of these stages. Patients hope for a new form of therapy, a new drug, a miraculous cure. And patients hope that they can die "well," without too much pain and with some acceptance.

An Assessment of Kübler-Ross's Dying Stages

Kübler-Ross's description has been enormously influential. She has provided a common language for those who work with dying patients, and her highly compassionate descriptions have, without doubt, sensitized health care workers and families to the complexities of the process of dying. There are moments when what the patient needs is cheering up and moments when he needs simply to be listened to; there are times to hold his hand quietly and times to provide encouragement or hope. Many new care programs that arrange for terminally ill patients, such as the hospice programs I'll describe in a moment, are clearly outgrowths of this greater sensitivity to the dying process.

These are all worthwhile changes. But there has been perhaps too ready an acceptance of the theory of stages of dying. Kübler-Ross's hypothesized sequence was initially based on clinical observation of perhaps 200 patients, and she does not provide information about how frequently she talked with them or spent time with them, or over how long a period they continued to be observed. Other clinicians and researchers who have attempted to study the process more systematically have not found that all dying patients exhibit these five emotions at all, let alone in a specific order (Schulz & Aderman, 1974). Of the five, only some type of depression seems to be consistently present in dying patients. There is little support for the notion that all or even most dying adults move toward any kind of emotional disengagement or acceptance (e.g., Baugher, Burger, Smith, & Wallston, 1989–90). Some do, while others remain as active and engaged as possible right up to the end. Edwin Shneidman (1980, 1983), a major theorist and clinician in the field of "thanatology" (the study of dying), puts it this way:

> I reject the notion that human beings, as they die, are somehow marched in lock step through a series of stages of the dying process. On the contrary, in working with dying persons, I see a wide panoply of human feelings and emotions, of various human needs, and a broad selection of psychological defenses and maneuvers—a few of these in some people, dozens in others—experienced in an impressive variety of ways. (1980, p. 110)

Shneidman goes on to describe some of the many "themes" that can appear, disappear, and reappear in the process of dealing with death in any one patient: terror ("I was really frightened"), pervasive uncertainty ("if there is a God . . . "), fantasies of being rescued ("somebody . . . that maybe could perform this miracle"), incredulity ("It's so far fetched, so unreal . . . it is a senseless death"), feelings of unfairness, a concern with reputation after death, the fight against pain, and so forth.

Thus, instead of each person following a series of five fixed stages, each person moves back and forth, in and out of a complex set of emotions and defenses. Kübler-Ross herself would now agree with this view. In one later writing (1974) she says "most of my patients have exhibited two or three stages simultaneously and these do not always occur in the same order" (pp. 25–26). Given this variability, the term "stage" does not seem to be an appropriate label for these several emotions or themes. Certainly, those who work with the dying should not expect a tidy sequence of emotions.

Farewells

One aspect of the process of dying that is not reflected in Kübler-Ross stages or in most research on dying but which is clearly a significant feature for the dying person and his or her family is the process of saying farewell. A recent study in Australia by Allan Kellehear and Terry Lewin (1988–89) gives us a first exploration of such goodbyes. They interviewed 90 terminally ill cancer patients, all of whom had been told they were within a year of their death, and a smaller group of ten patients who were in hospice care and thought to be within three months of death. Most had known they had cancer for over a year before the interview but had only recently been given a specific short-term prognosis. Each subject was asked whether he had already said some goodbyes or intended future farewells to family or friends, and if so, when and under what circumstances. The minority (19 of the 100) said they did not plan any farewells at all. The rest had either already begun to say goodbye (22) or planned their farewells for the final days of their lives—deathbed goodbyes, if you will.

The early farewells had often been in the form of a letter or a gift, such as giving money to a child or grandchild, or passing on personal treasures to a member of the family who might especially cherish them. One woman made dolls that she gave to friends, relatives, and hospital staff. Another knit a set of baby clothes to give to each of her daughters for the child that neither daughter had yet had.

More commonly, both planned and completed farewells were in the form of conversations. One subject asked her brother to come for a visit so that she could see and talk to him one last time; others arranged with friends for one last get together, saying good-bye quite explicitly on these occasions. Those who anticipated saying farewell only in the last hours of their conscious life imagined these occasions to be times when loving words would be spoken or a good-bye look would be exchanged.

All such farewells, whether spoken or not, can be thought of as forms of gifts. By saying good-bye to some individual, the dying person signals that that individual matters enough to them to warrant such a farewell. They also serve to make the death real, to force the imminent death out of the realm of denial into acceptance by others as well as by the dying person. And finally, as Kellehear and Lewin point out, farewells may make the dying itself easier, especially if they are completed before the final moments of life. They may make it easier for the dying person to disengage, to reach a point of acceptance.

Individual Adaptations to Dying

So far I have talked about the dying process as if it were largely the same for every person. Yet clearly, it is not. The length of time varies enormously as does the degree of pain and debilitation. And the way each person handles the process also varies. Some fight hard against dying; others appear to accept it early in the process and struggle no further. Some remain calm; others fall into deep depression.

I should say at the outset that virtually all of the research we have on individual variations or adaptations to dying are based on studies of patients with terminal cancer. Not only is cancer a clear diagnosis, many forms of it also progress quite rapidly, and the patient not only knows that he is terminally ill but roughly how long he has to live. Some diseases, such as AIDS, have these same features, but most diseases do not. Most particularly, heart disease, which along with cancer is the leading cause of death in middle- and old-age, may exist for a long period, the patient may or may not know that he has significant heart disease, and the prognosis is highly variable. We simply do not know whether any of the conclusions drawn from studies of cancer patients can be applied to adults dying less rapidly or less predictably. And even in studies of cancer patients, the best I can say of the empirical evidence is that it is confusing.

The first task of researchers has been to figure out how to measure "adaptation" to some terminal illness. One strategy has been to compare those who die relatively rapidly to those who survive longer than expected given the diagnosis and stage of disease. In the case of studies of women with breast cancer, for example, this research approach typically involves comparing those who survived for five years after surgery to those who did not survive that long.

In one study using this general strategy, Weisman and Worden (1975) studied 46 cancer patients, varying in age and specific diagnosis. They found that those who survived longer than expected were those who had a history of good relationships with others and maintained those relationships quite well during their illness. They asked for, and received, emotional and medical support. They accepted the reality of their illness but actually showed a fair amount of denial of the inevitability of their death. They were seldom deeply depressed but did show anger or resentment at times.

Those who died sooner than expected were typically patients with a history of poor social relationships, often with early separations from parents or other family members. They did not have close friends and did not maintain good relationships with family during the illness. These patients became much more depressed, and the depression often deepened to the point that they wished to die.

Some of the same themes appeared in a study of breast cancer patients by Greer (Greer, Morris, & Pettingale, 1979). As you can see in Table 14.3, those who survived five years without any recurrence of disease were more likely than those who died or had a recurrence to have reacted initially with both denial and "fighting spirit." Stoic acceptance, or a feeling of helplessness or hopelessness, was more likely among those who had died within five years.

But not everyone has found such a pattern. Barrie Cassileth and colleagues (Cassileth, Lusk, Miller, Brown, & Miller, 1985), for example, could find no link between a combination of psychosocial measures and length of survival with breast cancer, although they did not measure quite the same variables as had Greer or Weisman and Worden.

Another approach has been to measure the degree of depression, anger, or anxiety the patient experiences. Carey (1974) had hospital chaplains rate each of a series of terminal patients on "emotional adjustment," which included ratings of the amount of anger, guilt, anxiety, depression, and the ability to verbalize feelings with family and friends, while Hinton (1975) made similar ratings based on interviews with patients, their spouses, and nurses.

TABLE 14.3. Relationship Between the Patient's Response to the Cancer Diagnosis and Surgery, and the Five-Year Survival Rate Among Women with Breast Cancer in Greer's Study.

	Outcome after 5 years			
Psychological Response 3 Months After Surgery	*Alive with no recurrence (28 cases)*	*Alive with metasteses (13 cases)*	*Dead (16 cases)*	*Total (57 cases)*
Denial	7	2	1	10
Fighting spirit	8	1	1	10
Stoic acceptance	12	10	10	32
Helplessness/hopelessness	1	0	4	5

SOURCE: Greer, Morris, & Pettingale, 1979, p. 786.

Results from these two studies suggest that there are several qualities that differentiate "better adjusted" patients from less well adjusted patients. Those who show the least persistent depression or anger appear to be those who:

- are in the least pain. Carey found that the patient's report of pain or discomfort was negatively related to adjustment (the more pain, the least "adjustment.")
- have had previous close contact with a person who was dying (Carey, 1974).
- have good marriages or supportive relationships with friends and family members during the illness (Carey, 1974; Hinton, 1975).
- have a previous history of coping well with life's problems and crises (Hinton, 1975).
- have a previous history of being satisfied with their lives. In Hinton's study, this is particularly predictive of the amount of depression and anger shown by the patient and may reflect a characteristically positive versus negative mood.
- describe their religious orientation as "intrinsic" rather than "extrinsic" (Carey, 1974). An individual with an intrinsic religious orientation is one who attempts to integrate beliefs into actual living, taking the specific tenets and ethical concerns seriously and personally. An extrinsically oriented person is more likely to focus on the forms of religious observance—church attendance, specific times of prayer, or the like—and on personal gains from religious observance, such as gains in social standing.

These studies of survivors and the studies of patient adjustment have each yielded somewhat consistent results, but the two sets of information don't go together very well. In the adjustment studies, for example, the *absence* of anger is part of the definition of a "good adjustment" to dying, while in survival research, anger or at least feistiness has been associated with greater longevity. The only common ground appears to be the importance of a significant intimate relationship, which is both linked to longer survival and to lower levels of depression.

Beyond that it is risky to go at this point, given the mixed types of research and the inconsistent results. Still, let me be a bit risky: My sense of the research results is that adults die very much as they live. Each of us brings to the process of dying the same personality, the same level of coping skills, the same degree of capacity for secure, satisfying relationships that we evinced throughout our lives.

It is also interesting that the list of characteristics of "well-adjusted" dying adults sounds so similar to the list of factors I mentioned as "resistance resources" to stress or life change in Chapter 12. And if we can take intrinsic religious orientation as a reflection of, perhaps, an individualistic or a conjunctive faith (in Fowler's sense), while an extrinsic orientation may reflect conventional faith, then Carey's results suggest that the process of personal growth, of inner development, affects the way we approach death as much as the way we approach life.

Where Death Occurs

The vast majority of people in our culture die in hospitals. But in part because of Kübler-Ross's work and the subsequent awakening of interest in the process of dying, a number of health professionals and other caring adults began to ask whether a traditional hospital setting was really the most supportive and compassionate place for a dying person to be cared for. If an "appropriate death" (to use Weisman's phrase, [1972])—a death according to the wishes of the dying person, with dignity—can most readily be accomplished when the individual has frequent contact with loving friends and family, in familiar surroundings, then hospital wards designed to maximize efficiency rather than contact will not be as supportive as would a home setting or a home-like setting.

Considerations like these have led to a movement generally known as **hospice care**. The original concept came from England (Saunders, 1977), where it emerged as an alternative form of care for the terminally ill patient. The idea spread rapidly to the United States, where it is now to be found not only in special wards within hospitals but also in supervised home-care programs. Today there are roughly 1,200 hospice programs in the United States, serving thousands of terminally ill patients and their families.

The philosophy that underlies this alternative setting or approach to the dying patient has several aspects (Bass, 1985): (1) that death should be viewed as a normal, inevitable part of life, not to be avoided but to be faced and accepted; (2) that the patient and the family should prepare for the death, by examining their feelings, by planning for their later life; (3) that the family should be involved in the care to as full an extent as possible, which permits each family member to come to some resolution of his or her relationship with the dying person; (4) that the control over the care and the care-receiving setting should belong to the patient and family; (5) that the medical care provided should be palliative rather than curative. Pain should be alleviated and comfort maximized, but a minimum of invasive or life-prolonging measures should be undertaken.

In home-based hospice programs there is typically one family caregiver (most often the spouse) who may spend as much as 19 hours a day caring for the patient. Other family members may help, but the central person has the organizational responsibility. This key person is then assisted and supported by one or more nurses or other hospice personnel, who visit regularly (often daily when death is

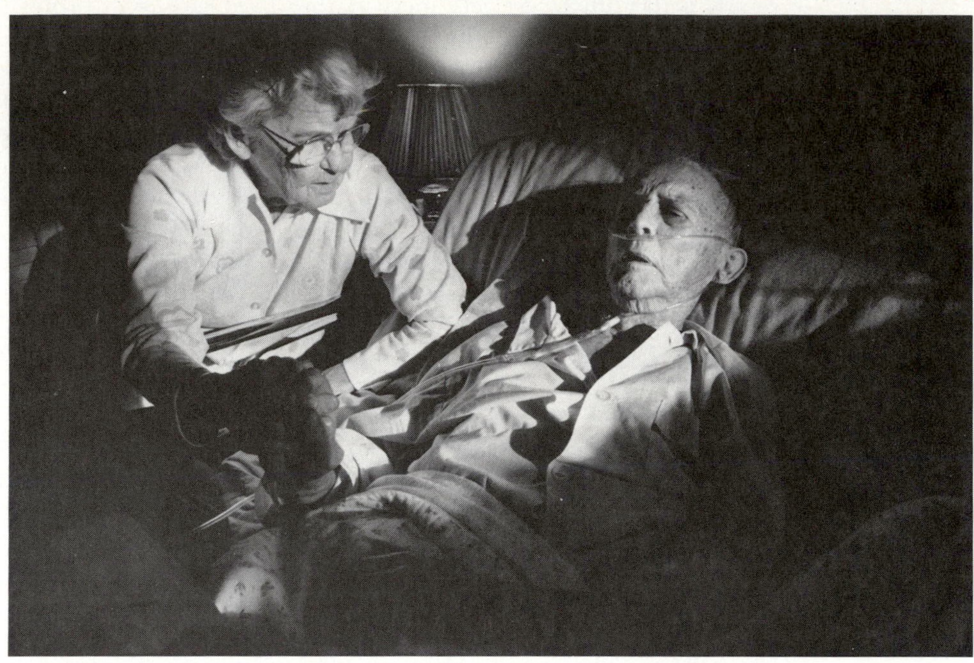

Figure 14–2 Hospice care, either in a special hospice unit in a hospital or at home as shown here, has become a widely available alternative in recent years. The emphasis in hospice programs is on palliative care rather than on prolonging life but also on helping each dying person to die with dignity.(Photo © Joel Gordon, 1990. Reprinted with permission.)

near), train family members in care procedures, help the family to prepare for the death, and provide emotional support throughout the process. In hospital-based hospice care the family continues to be important and involved in day-to-day care, although of course there is also 24-hour nursing support available.

Two major studies comparing hospice care with traditional hospital care have recently been completed, so we are now finally in a position to say at least something about the relative merits of these two approaches to dying and death. The National Hospice Study, headed by David Greer and Vincent Mor (Greer, Mor, Morris, Sherwood, Kidder, & Birnbaum, 1986; Morris, Mor, Goldberg, Sherwood, Greer, & Hiris, 1986), analyzed the experiences of 1,754 terminally ill cancer patients treated in 40 different hospices and 14 conventional hospital settings. Half the hospice programs studied were home-based, half were hospital-based. The researchers examined not only the quality of life, as reported by the patient and the central caregiver, but also the patient's reported pain and satisfaction with the care received. Each of these measures was obtained several times over the weeks preceding death. It is a remarkable study, although because the individual patients *chose* which form of care they received, there remains the possibility that any observed differences are the result of self-selection rather than effects of the type of care.

The second major study, by Robert Kane and his colleagues (Kane, Klein, Bernstein, Rothenberg, & Wales, 1985; Kane, Wales, Bernstein, Leibowitz, & Kaplan, 1984), solved this problem by assigning dying patients randomly to either hospice or regular hospital care. The hospice care was a combination of home-based and hospital-based; many of the hospice patients remained at home when possible but were in the hospital's hospice unit at other times. The drawback in this study is that only one specific hospice program and one specific traditional hospital program are being compared. Still, if the results from the two studies are consistent with one another, we can have some confidence in the conclusions.

As it happens, there is a fair degree of agreement in the findings. Both studies found *no* differences between hospice and regular hospital care in the patient's reported pain, in the patient's day-to-day functioning, or in length of patient survival. But they did find differences in the reported satisfaction with the care received. In Kane's study, the patients in hospice were consistently more satisfied with the quality of care they received and with their own involvement in that care. The caregivers in Kane's hospice program were also more satisfied with their own involvement in the patient's care than was true for family members of patients in standard care. The National Hospice Study did not show any difference in patients' reported satisfaction with care, but the family caregivers of patients in *hospital-based* hospice programs were more satisfied with the patient's care. Kane also found that anxiety was lower among the family caregivers in the hospice group, a finding not matched in the National Hospice Study.

Overall, then, the differences between hospice and regular hospital care appear to be small. When there is a difference, it is not in physical measures such as pain, or duration of survival, but rather in social/emotional measures. On some of these measures, but by no means on all, hospice patients and their families are slightly more satisfied. Still, hospice care is not an option to be undertaken lightly. The burden of care is enormous and may require skills that the caregivers do not have. In the National Hospice Study, those caregivers involved in the family-based programs did report a significantly greater feeling of burden. In another study, Bass (1985) has found that some families that initially chose hospice care later placed their dying relative in a hospital setting because they could no longer cope. But as with renewed health care options at the beginning of life, including the return of midwifery and home delivery, it seems to me to be a very good thing that in many communities today dying adults and their families have some choices about where and how the process of dying will occur. Since that sort of choice and control is one of the coping strategies that seems most effective in helping adults deal with other life crises, it is likely to have the same beneficial effect in the case of the ultimate life change—death.

After Death: Rituals and Grieving

Whether a death is sudden or prolonged, anticipated or unexpected, it leaves survivors who must somehow come to terms with the death and eventually pick up the pieces of their lives. I talked a bit about widowhood in Chapter 12 as part of the discussion of the impact of several major life changes. But my emphasis there was primarily on the epidemiological effects—the rate of illness, emotional disturbance, or premature death among the survivors. Let me turn here to a more general discussion of the process of grieving itself.

Ritual Mourning: Funerals and Ceremonies

Every culture has some set of rituals associated with death. Far from being empty gestures, these rituals have at least three clear and important functions. First, in these rituals the bereaved person is given a specific *role* to play. Like all roles, this one includes prescriptions and proscriptions, expected and prohibited or discouraged behaviors. The content of these roles differs markedly from one culture to the next, but the clarity of the role in most cases provides a shape to the days or weeks immediately following the death of a loved person. (I have an unreasoning bias, by the way, against the phrase "loved one," which sounds to me like unctuous funeral director language.) In our culture, the rituals prescribe what one should wear, who should be called, who should be fed, what demeanor one should show, and far more. Depending on one's religious background, one may need to arrange to sit shiva, or gather friends and family for a wake, or

Figure 14–3 Funeral rituals may sometimes seem overly elaborate or draining of the energy of the recently bereaved. But they serve important functions for the bereaved individuals and their friends.(Photo © Joel Gordon, 1978. Reprinted with permission.)

arrange a memorial service. There are a large number of details to be taken care of, all of which keep the grieving person busy during the first, numbing hours and days.

At the same time, the rituals provide less central but significant roles for friends, most particularly that of support-giver. Friends and family bring food to the home of the bereaved person, for example, or drop in to offer help, or send letters of condolence. (I shall never forget my gratitude to one friend who appeared, unasked, on my mother's doorstep the day after my stepfather had died. I had to pick up other family members at the airport but had not wanted to leave my mother alone. The friend appeared at precisely the right moment.)

Finally, the rituals, particularly the religious rituals, may give a sense of transcendant meaning to the death itself, at a time when the bereaved person very much needs an answer to the question "Why?"

Stages of Grief

But when the funeral or memorial service is over, what do you do then? How does a person handle the grief of this kind of loss, whether it be of a spouse, a parent, a child, a friend, a lover?

The short answer to that is "slowly and with difficulty." Grief over the death of someone to whom you have been strongly attached is not normally a quick process. The effects can ordinarily be detected at least a year after the loss; a minority of adults show much longer grieving, lasting several years (Wortman & Silver, 1989).

Some theorists and observers of the grief process have detected stages in the grieving process very similar to the stages of dying that Kübler-Ross proposes. And as with the stages of dying, there is a good deal of dispute about whether stage-like descriptions of grief are valid. But since the stage descriptions have had a good deal of influence on our thinking, you should be familiar with the proposals. John Bowlby (1980) has identified four phases of grieving, while Catherine Sanders (1989) proposes five. Combining the two systems yields the following:

Shock (Sanders) or Numbness (Bowlby). This stage may be very brief or may last weeks or months. Typically, it is operative during the ritual period after the death. There is disbelief, confusion, restlessness, feelings of unreality and of distance from others as if "wrapped in a blanket," a sense of helplessness, accompanied by a state of physiological alarm (the first phase of the General Adaptation Syndrome, as you may remember from Chapter 12). Bereaved persons in this phase say things like:

"I feel so vague. I can't keep my mind on anything for long."
"I'm afraid I'm losing my mind. I can't seem to think clearly." "You're just helpless you know. You just keep saying, 'Help me, somebody help me.'"
"It was so strange. I was putting on my makeup, combing my hair, and all the time it was as if I were standing by the door watching myself go through these motions." (Sanders, 1989, p. 47,48, 56.)

2. Awareness of Loss (Sanders) or Yearning (Bowlby). This period is one in which the bereaved person desires to recover the lost object. She or he may actively search for the dead individual or may wander around as if searching. Not infrequently, adults report that they actually do see the dead person in some familiar setting (Kalish, 1985; Kastenbaum & Aisenberg, 1976). But it is also a time in which the bereaved person is full of anxiety and guilt, weeps, is fearful, frustrated, has a hard time sleeping. Anger is also frequently part of this period, sometimes directed at the deceased, sometimes at oneself, sometimes at those thought to have contributed to his death ("The doctors didn't try hard enough," "His boss should have known better than to ask him to work so hard"). Bowlby suggests that this searching or yearning has some of the elements of what we see when a young child is temporarily separated from his mother. In the young child, such searching is a sign of a powerful attachment, so it is not surprising that we should see it in adults permanently separated from some object of strong attachment.
3. Conservation-Withdrawal (Sanders) or Disorganization and despair (Bowlby). The third phase, very similar to the period of depression described by Kübler-Ross, is one in which searching ceases and the loss is accepted. But with that acceptance comes despair. Depression, or a sense of helplessness, is common. Immense loneliness may be experienced, immune to the ministrations of kind friends or family members (Lopata, et al. 1982). Frequently, these symptoms are accompanied by incredible fatigue and a desire to sleep a great deal. A 45-year-old whose child had just died described this period this way:

   > I can't understand the way I feel. Up to now, I had been feeling restless. I couldn't sleep, I paced and ranted. Now, I have an opposite reaction. I sleep a lot. I feel fatigued and worn out. I don't even want to see the friends who have kept me going. I sit and stare, too exhausted to move. . . . Just when I thought I should be feeling better, I am feeling worse. (Sanders, p. 73)

4. Healing and Renewal (Sanders) or Reorganization (Bowlby). Sanders divides the final phase into two periods, the first she calls Healing and sees it as the turning point, and a final phase she calls Renewal. Bowlby combines these two into one period. However it is divided, this final step involves taking control again of one's life, accompanied by increased energy, better health, improved sleep patterns. There is some forgetting, some sense of hope, a search for the meaning of the loss. The person takes up his usual activities, finds new relationships. This is equivalent to the stage of acceptance in Kübler-Ross's system, although in the case of grief, there is less an element here of resignation than there is of constructive and active restructuring of one's life.

Bowlby and Sanders argue that these stages are not confined to the grief an adult shows at the death of a spouse or partner. You may recall from Chapter 8 that Robert Weiss suggests that any relationship in which there has been an attachment is one in which such grieving will occur (Weiss, 1988). So the loss of a partner, of one's child, or of one's parent are likely to trigger the emotions Sanders and Bowlby are describing, while the loss of a good friend, a sibling, or a grandchild, with whom we are not likely to have such a deep attachment, is less likely to trigger the full array of grieving responses. In fact, that is just what researchers have found (Murrell & Himmelfarb, 1989).

But whether these grieving responses invariably or even regularly occur in a sequence or not is not so clear from the research. Herman Feifel (1990) states the counter argument:

> We are discovering that just as there are multitudinous ways of living, there are numerous ways of dying and grieving. . . . the hard data do not support the existence of any procrustean stages or schedules that characterize terminal illness or mourning. This does not mean that, for example, Kübler-Ross's "stages of dying" and Bowlby's "phases of mourning" cannot provide us with implications and insights into the dynamics and process of dying and grief, but they are very far from being inexorable hoops through which most terminally ill individuals and mourners inevitably pass. We should beware of promulgating a coercive orthodoxy of how to die or mourn. (p. 540)

Some would argue that it would be better to think in terms of themes or aspects rather than stages, such as themes of anger, guilt, depression, anxiety and restlessness, and preoccupation with the image of the deceased. One way to reconcile these several views would be to think of each of these themes as having a likely trajectory, such as the pattern suggested in Figure 14–4 by Selby Jacobs and his colleagues (Jacobs, Kosten, Kasl, Ostfeld, Berkman, & Charpentier, 1987–88).

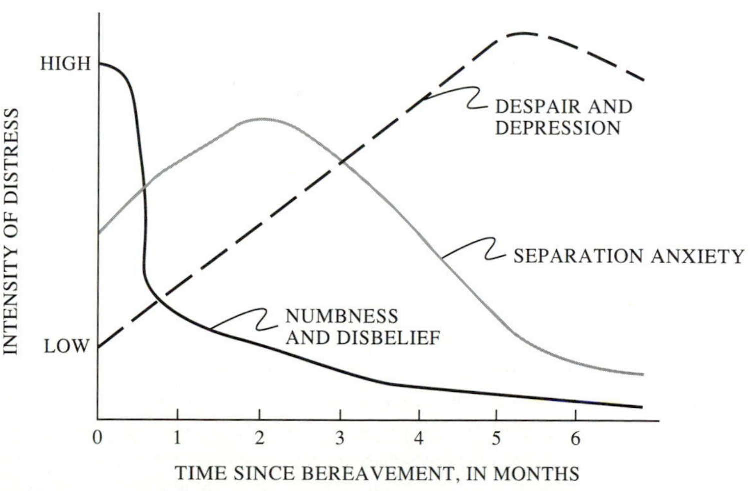

Figure 14–4 This model of the possible course of grieving takes us a step beyond simpler stage concepts. At any one time, several themes may be present, but each theme may still be likely to dominate at a particular time, thus producing a stage-like sequence in many individuals. (Source: Jacobs, Kosten, Kasl, Ostfeld, Berkman, & Charpentier, 1987–88, Figure 1, p. 43.)

Jacobs is not arguing that each and every person follows exactly this pattern; for different individuals these features may follow longer or shorter courses at higher or lower levels. The argument is rather that in the first period, numbness is likely to be the dominant theme, with separation anxiety or awareness of loss becoming dominant somewhat later, followed by despair and depression, producing a stage-like sequence, even though each theme may be present to some extent in each phase.

Dissenting Voices

In what I have said about the grieving process so far, I have implied that there is essential agreement about the key themes or ingredients, even if there is not agreement about the presence of stages. But that implication is incorrect. There are dissenting voices, most notably those of Camille Wortman and Roxane Silver (Silver & Wortman, 1980; Wortman and Silver, 1987, 1989). They take the position that depression or significant distress is not at all an inevitable, let alone a necessary, accompaniment of bereavement. They also point to research that shows that significant depression following a loss is not necessarily a sign of healthy "working through" of the loss; on the contrary, those adults who show the greatest depression in the months following bereavement are likely to be the ones who are still depressed several years later, which does not sound as if the depression is either temporary or a sign that the grief is being "worked through." Conversely, Wortman and Silver's analysis suggests that those who show little or no depression following loss are *not* more likely to have later difficulties; on the contrary, these adults seem to show the least long-term physical or emotional effects.

Based on the research evidence, Wortman and Silver suggest that rather than there being only one common pattern in response to loss, there are at least three distinct patterns: (1) the "expected" pattern, which involves distress followed by some kind of resolution, (2) a pattern in which there is little distress expressed, either immediately or in the longer term, and (3) a pattern of high prolonged distress, lasting many years.

This seems to me to be an important modification of the standard view of grief, not only because it opens the way to potentially better understanding of which individuals are likely to follow each of these grief pathways, but also because of the obvious practical implications. To the extent that our cultural norm for grieving includes the expectations of heightened distress, "working through" the grief, and then getting on with your life, any bereaved person who does not follow this pattern is likely to be perceived as deviant. In particular, the person who shows little despair or depression may be accused of "not dealing" with her grief, or of not having loved the deceased person. Of course, it *is* possible that such lower levels of distress are indicative of weaker attachments, but we have as yet little evidence to confirm (or reject) such a hypothesis. Meanwhile, Wortman and Silver's arguments should serve to make each of us more sensitive to the unique process of grieving we may see in friends or family members.

Those who seem deeply distressed or despairing may benefit from some kind of support group or therapy; certainly they are not likely to find it helpful or sensitive for you to urge them to get 'back in the swim' right away. Those who express little obvious distress, on the other hand, may not be repressing but may be coping in other ways. They may not take kindly to your suggestion that they should "Get it all out," or to "Be sure to take time to grieve." As usual, the best way to be helpful to a person dealing with such a loss is to be highly attentive to the signals you are receiving, rather than imposing your own ideas of what is normal or expected.

Living and Dying: A Final Word

If it is true that we die as we have lived, then it is also true that to some extent we live as we die. Our understanding of death and its meaning, our attitude toward the inevitability of death, the way in which we come to terms with that inevitability, affects not only the way we die, but the way we choose to live our lives throughout adulthood. David Steindl-Rast (1977), a Benedictine monk, makes this point:

> Death . . . is an event that puts the whole meaning of life into question. We may be occupied with purposeful activities, with getting tasks accomplished, works completed, and then along comes the phenomenon of death—whether it is our final death or one of those many deaths through which we go day by day. And death confronts us with the fact that purpose is not enough. We live by meaning. (Steindl-Rast, 1977, p. 22)

An awareness of death is thus not something we can put off until, one day, we hear a diagnosis of our own impending demise. It can, instead, help to define and give meaning to daily life.

Summary

1. Four different aspects to the meaning of death have been identified: death as an organizer of time, death as punishment, death as transition, and death as loss.
2. Anxiety or fear of death seems to peak in midlife. Younger adults are still partially convinced of their own immortality, and older adults have to some degree accepted the inevitability.
3. Adults who are more afraid of death are also likely to be higher in neuroticism and to have lower opinions of their own competence or worth. Higher fear is also associated with uncertain positions on religious questions, whereas those with very high or no religious commitment are typically lower in fear of death.
4. Preparations for death include wills and insurance (more common among older adults) and may include a process of reminiscence or life review.

5. Immediately prior to death, there are also signs of "terminal" changes in intellectual performance and emotional response. Adults within a year of death show declining intellectual performance, declining memory, reduced emotional complexity and introspectiveness, and a more passive, accepting self-concept.
6. Kübler-Ross proposes five stages in the actual dying process: denial, anger, bargaining, depression, and acceptance. However, research does not support the contention that all dying individuals show all these emotions, in this or any other order. The process of dying is more individual, more varied, less sequential than Kübler-Ross proposed.
7. Many individuals, when they know they are dying, specifically plan for farewells to those they love, often through gifts or personal conversations.
8. Individual variations in adaptation to dying are parallel, to at least some degree, to individual variations in handling other life dilemmas or changes. Limited research evidence suggests that adults who are least depressed or anxious and appear to cope best with their own deaths are likely to have strong and supportive relationships, to have had contact with someone else who was dying, to have a history of coping well with earlier crises, and to report an intrinsic (versus an extrinsic) religious orientation.
9. Where a death occurs may also have an impact on the degree of acceptance and comfort the individual experiences. Hospice care is a relatively new form of care in which the dying individual is largely cared for by family members (often at home) and controls major decisions about care.
10. Research comparing hospice with normal hospital care shows few differences except that hospice patients and their family care givers are slightly more satisfied with the quality of care.
11. Those left to mourn after a death are helped by clear rituals associated with death, which provide roles for the bereaved and for friends, and may give a sense of transcendant meaning to the death.
12. Once past the rituals, the grieving person is thought to move through a complex grief process which may be accomplished in four stages: shock or numbness, awareness of loss or yearning, conservation-withdrawal or despair, and finally healing or reorganization.
13. There is disagreement among researchers and theorists about whether these aspects of grieving are stage-like, or even if they are universal or necessary. Some adults appear to adjust rapidly to bereavement, with little evident despair; others show high levels of disorganization and despair for many years, with little evidence of healing. A response to another's grief requires sensitivity to such variations.

Suggested Readings

ALSOP, S. (1973). *Stay of execution. A sort of memoir.* New York: Lippincott. A very personal, moving, and informative description of one man's journey from the beginning of his illness with leukemia until his death.

FEIFEL, H. (1990). Psychology and death. Meaningful rediscovery. *American Psychologist, 45,* 537–543. A good, brief, review of many current themes in psychologists' current research on death and dying, along with an exploration of why it has taken so long for psychologists to begin to study this important subject.

KÜBLER-ROSS, E. (1969). *On death and dying.* New York: Macmillan. This was the original major book by Kübler-Ross that significantly changed the way many physicians and other health professionals viewed the dying process. It is full of case material and reflects very well Kübler-Ross's great skill as a listener and clinician.

LYELL, R. (1980). *Middle age, old age: Short stories, poems, plays, and essays on aging.* New York: Harcourt Brace Jovanovich. I've recommended this anthology before (see the suggested readings in Chapter 7). Since it includes several stories about death and dying, from many perspectives, it is a good source here as well. Bunin's "The Gentleman from San Francisco," Tolstoy's "The Death of Ivan Ilych," and Dylan Thomas's "Do Not Go Gentle into That Good Night" all touch on attitudes toward death.

SANDERS, C. M. (1989). *Grief. The mourning after.* New York: Wiley-Interscience. This book will give you a good, non-technical look at the "traditional" view of the grieving process, with lots of examples from the reactions of real-life people and some practical advice about intervention strategies.

SCHREIBER, L. (1990). *Midstream.* New York: Viking. Stewart Alsop's book gives a first-hand account of the time leading up to death; Le Anne Schreiber—a sportswriter of some renown—gives an equally moving second-hand account, in this instance the death of her mother from cancer, detailing both her own feelings and reactions and those of other family members.

SHNEIDMAN, E. S. (1983). *Deaths of man.* New York: Jason Aronson. This is a less clinical book than Kübler-Ross's but much broader and equally sensitive. Shneidman deals with some of the medical and legal aspects of death as well as the personal process.

CHAPTER 15

Pathways Through Adulthood

In Chapter 2, I introduced you to five young people, all in their early 20s, all just beginning the journey of adult life: Tom Kleck, the extroverted working class man with dreams of success beyond his father's; Cathy Stevens, the All-American Girl, with all the advantages of education and temperament; Laura Rogers, married and a mother by 16, divorced by 21, facing welfare or underemployment as she struggles to rear her two children; Walter Washington, the bright, introverted black man with dreams of improving himself through education; Christopher Linton, also bright, with the advantages of education already completed and more to come, and the disadvantages of a pessimistic attitude and difficulty making friends.

What I have been talking about in the last two chapters are the ways in which the lives of these five might move in similar ways through the next six or seven decades—the common changes of body, mind, and personality, and the likely-to-be-shared challenges of marriage, childrearing, work demands, and relationships. Such a normative approach to understanding the adult years has its uses. It tells us something about the average or expectable pathway. It also underlines the fact that the very perception that there *is* a common or modal pattern affects our expectations, goals, and aspirations: For there to be "off-time" events, there has to be some shared concept of "on-time."

But the normative approach, however helpful, cannot give us a full description or explanation of adult life. True, Tom, Cathy, Laura, Walter, and Chris will share certain experiences as they age, but to understand the process of adult development and change we also have to understand the ways in which their lives are likely to differ, the variations in their reactions to the stresses and challenges they will encounter and in the eventual satisfaction or inner growth they may achieve. To put it another way, if we are to comprehend adult lives, we not only need to understand the lawfulness and order that makes us the same, we also have to understand the rules or laws that underlie the immense diversity.

Reaching such understanding is as immense a task as the diversity is great. But let me offer two approaches, beginning with an exploration of the growing literature touching on variations in what has come to be called "successful aging" (Palmore, 1979; Baltes & Baltes, 1990), and concluding with my own attempt at a model of both normative and individual aging.

Successful Aging

How might we define "successful aging?" We might say someone is a successful adult if he or she has fully traversed the sequence of stages or levels I described in Chapters 10 and 11. Or we might use more objective or external criteria, such as whether the individual has achieved occupational success, or a lasting marriage, or avoided substance addiction, or has created positive relationships with his children, or remained healthy. Alternatively, we might use an entirely subjective criteria, by simply asking adults whether they are satisfied with their lives or happy, and then judge as "successful" any life pathway that leads an individual to happiness or high satisfaction with himself and his life.

All of these approaches have been used, but the subjective approach has been by far the most common, so let me start there.

A First Look at Individual Differences in Successful Aging: Life Satisfaction as a Measure of Success

In their long-standing effort to understand why some adults are happier or more satisfied with themselves than are others, psychologists and sociologists have devised dozens of measures of happiness, well-being, or life satisfaction (Diener, 1984). Some have used only a single question, such as "taking all things together, how would you say things are these days—would you say you are very happy, pretty happy, or not too happy?" (Campbell, 1981). Others, such as Cantril (1965), give subjects a nine-rung ladder marked at the top with "best life for you" and at the bottom with "worst life for you." Each subject is asked to mark the rung that best represents her current life. Among researchers who use more than one question to tap life satisfaction, Bradburn's (1969) "affect balance" approach is one of the most widely used. Bradburn argued that overall life satisfaction reflects the combination of positive and negative feelings. His scale includes a set of items about negative emotions (loneliness, depression, boredom, restlessness, or being upset with criticism) and a set about positive emotions (feeling on top of the world, excited or interested in something, pleased with an accomplishment, pride). The resultant sum of the positive and negative feelings Bradburn calls "affect balance."

Each of these measures captures a somewhat different facet of life satisfaction or happiness, but all these measures normally correlate quite highly with one another, suggesting that there is a single dimension being tapped by all, a conclusion further bolstered by the fact that studies of happiness using these many measures also have yielded quite consistent results.

Age and Life Satisfaction

Interestingly, age seems to have very little systematic relationship to the level of reported well-being (Palmore, 1981; Stock, Okun, Haring, & Witter, 1983). Happily, we have longitudinal as well as cross-sectional data to draw on here. In the Duke longitudinal studies, for example, Palmore found no change in overall life satisfaction over a six-year period among adults originally aged 47 to 68. Paul Costa and his colleagues (Costa, Zonderman, McCrae, Cornoni-Huntley, Locke, & Barbano, 1987) have found the same thing in a much larger, nine-year longitudinal study of a nationally representative sample of adults originally aged 25 to 65. The major longitudinal findings from this study are shown in Figure 15–1. You can see that there is some minor fluctuation over the nine-year period, but age accounts for less than one percent of the variation in life satis-

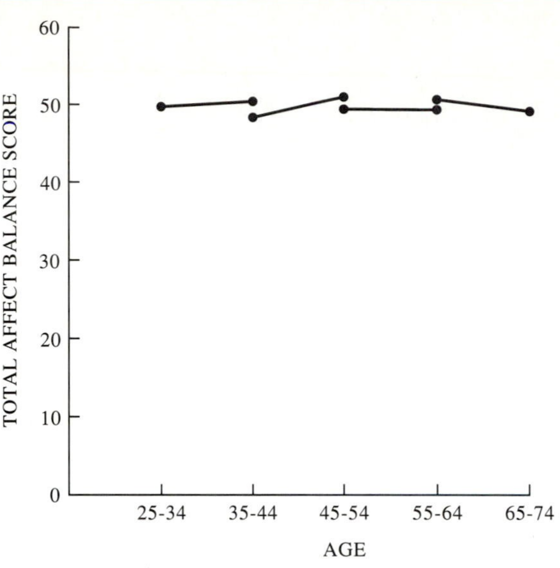

Figure 15–1 Nearly 5,000 subjects in this nationally representative sample were interviewed twice, 9 years apart. Subjects were grouped into 10-year age groups, so each line in this figure represents the average life satisfaction score, measured by affect balance, for one age group at the initial interview and then again 9 years later. There is no sign here of either cross-sectional or longitudinal difference in life satisfaction over the years of adulthood. (Source: Costa, Zonderman, McCrae, Cornoni-Huntley, Locke, & Barbano, 1987, data from Table 1, p. 52).

faction as measured in this study. Yet age is not irrelevant in our understanding of life satisfaction. Costa's study, along with other evidence, suggests that while the overall score is about the same across age, younger adults may experience both positive and negative feelings more strongly (higher highs and lower lows) than do older adults. Furthermore, the ingredients that make up life satisfaction change somewhat with age, a pattern that makes perfectly good sense given the descriptions of the various age periods I have already given in Chapter 13. Health, for example, is a more significant predictor of life satisfaction or happiness among older adults than it is among the young or the middle-aged (Bearon, 1989), and income is a less significant predictor among young adults than among either middle-aged or older adults (George, Okun, & Landerman, 1985). Still, these age variations seem insignificant beside the overall consistency in life satisfaction with age. On average, older adults are as satisfied with themselves and their lives as are younger or middle-aged adults. To understand happiness or well-being, then, we will have to go beyond age as a benchmark and look at both demographic and personal differences.

Demographic and Personal Differences And Life Satisfaction

A number of demographic and personal variations are linked to life satisfaction or happiness. I've summarized the major findings in Table 15.1, but let me comment on a few of the especially interesting or significant patterns.

TABLE 15.1. Factors Associated with Life Satisfaction Among Adults.

Demographic Variables	
Income satisfaction	Higher income is associated with higher life satisfaction, but the effect appears to be relative rather than absolute.
Education	A very weak relationship: Higher educated adults are only slightly more satisfied.
Gender	Essentially no difference, although women may have slightly higher highs and lower lows than men.
Employment	Employed adults (including those employed as homemakers) are more satisfied than unemployed adults, even when income is matched.
Marital status	Married adults are more satisfied than unmarried.
Parenthood	Adults with children still at home are slightly less satisfied but have higher levels of life-meaning.
Personal Qualities	
Personality:	
Extroversion	Extroverted adults are higher in life satisfaction than are introverts.
Neuroticism	Adults high in neuroticism are less satisfied than those low on this dimension, although the difference is not as large as that for extraversion/introversion.
Sense of control	Adults who feel they can and do control their own choices and opportunities are more satisfied than are those who think they are mostly controlled by outside forces.
Social Interaction:	
Amount	Those adults who are satisfied with their level of social interaction have higher life satisfaction.
Quality	Adults whose social interactions are more intimate and more supportive have higher satisfaction. This is especially true for marital interaction; if marital relationship is poor, life satisfaction is adversely affected.
Health	Those adults with better self-perceived health are more satisfied than those who perceive themselves ill or disabled, especially in later years of adulthood.
Religion	Adults who describe themselves as religious, or who say that religion is important in their lives, are more satisfied.
Life Events	The more "negative" life changes an adult has recently experienced, the lower the life satisfaction.
Goals	Adults who are committed to very long-term goals, with little short-term reward, are less satisfied than are adults whose goals are shorter-term or less difficult to achieve.

SOURCES: The most comprehensive source is Diener, 1984. More current sources for specific items included are: Gibson, 1986; Gove, Style, & Hughes, 1990; Koenig, Kvale, & Ferrell, 1988; Lee, 1988; Umberson & Gove, 1989; Willits, & Crider, 1988).

PERCEIVED DIFFERENCES AND PERCEIVED ADEQUACY One of the recurrent themes evident in the table is that in many areas it is not absolute differences that matter but the adult's *perception* of some quality or characteristic—yet another illustration of the point I made in Chapter 11 when talking about meaning systems. So, for example, an adult's perception of his own health is a better predictor of life satisfaction than is a doctor's objective health rating (Diener, 1984; Palmore, 1981), and it is the perceived adequacy of social interactions and not absolute quantity that is most strongly related to happiness (Gibson, 1986).

Something similar seems to operate in the relationship between income and life satisfaction: The relationship is relative rather than absolute. (Money really can't buy happiness after all!) If you have more money than others with whom you compare yourself, you are likely to be slightly happier than are those who are lower on the comparative totem pole. But if everyone in your comparison group experiences a rise in income, your level of life satisfaction or happiness doesn't go up, even though you can now afford things you couldn't afford before (Campbell, 1981; Diener, 1984). The general lack of age differences in happiness is further evidence for the same point. Middle-aged adults generally have higher incomes than younger adults or than they themselves had when they were younger, yet-middle-aged adults are not on average more satisfied with their lives than are young adults. This makes sense if we assume that an adult's primary comparison group is his own cohort. Since the whole cohort has risen in income between the age of 20 and 45, there is no overall increase in happiness. Only those adults who gained comparatively more than their cohort are likely to be more satisfied with their lives. Conversely, those who gained less than the typical amount are likely to be less satisfied.

Combining income and education into a single analysis, Campbell (1981) reports the interesting finding from several large national surveys that income or standard of living is *least* predictive of well-being among the college-educated. Such a finding fits roughly with what Maslow might predict on the basis of his hierarchy of needs. College-educated adults are likely to earn enough money to take care of their basic physiological and safety needs. Once these more fundamental needs are met, higher-order needs emerge, such as the need for love, for self-esteem, and for self-actualization. And these higher needs are not readily met by more money.

PERSONALITY AND TEMPERAMENT Among the most interesting effects listed in Table 15.1 are those connecting personality or temperament with life satisfaction. I have mentioned this connection in earlier chapters, but let me provide some specific numbers.

Costa and McCrae have found such relationships both concurrently and predictively in longitudinal studies of men (Costa & McCrae, 1980b; Costa, McCrae, & Norris, 1981). Those men who score higher on measures of extroversion and lower on measures of neuroticism described themselves as happier at first testing and still described themselves as happier 10 to 17 years later when happiness was again measured. Some sample findings from these studies are given in Table

15.2, a pattern of findings replicated in a six-year longitudinal study in Australia (Heady & Wearing, 1989).

Recent research by Stephen Hotard and his colleagues (Hotard, McFatter, McWhirter, & Stegall, 1989) takes us a step further by exploring the links between neuroticism, extroversion, and life satisfaction. Studying a group of undergraduates, they found that happiness or "subjective well-being" was low only among introverts who were either also high in neuroticism or who were dissatisfied with their social relationships. Introverts low in neuroticism or those who had established at least some satisfying social relationships reported just as much well-being as did extroverts. Whether this same pattern would hold for older adults we don't know, but the findings are helpful and suggestive.

The third personality dimension listed in Table 15.2, a sense of personal control, has a similarly small but consistent relationship with life satisfaction. Those adults who feel they are in charge of their own lives and responsible for their own decisions are generally happier than those who feel that their lives are controlled by others or by fate or chance. Furthermore, adults who feel that they *have* some choices and options are generally happier than those who perceive themselves as being trapped in circumstances they cannot control (Diener, 1984). You may recall that the sense of personal control is also part of the dimension of "hardiness" I

TABLE 15.2. The Relationship Between Extroversion, Neuroticism, and Life Satisfaction.

Concurrent Relationships		
	Correlation with Neuroticism	*Correlation with Extroversion*
Scores on the Bradburn Affect Balance Scale:		
Positive Affect	−.10*	.25*
Negative Affect	.34*	−.12*
Affect Balance	−.27*	.25*
Predictive (Longitudinal) Relationships		
Scores on the Affect Balance Scale 10 years after Neuroticism and Extroversion were measured:		
Positive Affect	−.08	.23*
Negative Affect	.39*	.03
Affect Balance	−.30*	.14*
Scores on a single measure of life satisfaction 10–17 years after Neuroticism and Extroversion were measured:		
Life Satisfaction Score	−.08	.35

NOTE: Those correlations marked with an asterisk are statistically significant at the .05 level or better.

SOURCES: Costa & McCrae, 1980b, data from Table 4, p. 674 and from text; Costa, McCrae, & Norris, 1981, data from Table 3, p. 81.

talked about in Chapter 12. Thus, adults high in "internal" rather than "external" control may be more satisfied with their lives in part because they are better able to deal with the major problems and life strains that come along.

None of the correlations in these studies is particularly large; clearly, many other factors affect life satisfaction. But these studies do suggest that it may be possible to make some prediction of happiness in middle or old age from knowing something of the personality or temperament of young adults. In particular, any temperamental or personality qualities that allow an individual to form satisfying and supportive relationships appear to be especially good predictors of long-term life satisfaction. This conclusion is further supported by the repeated finding that the life satisfaction of socially isolated adults can be increased by providing them with training that increases their social skills (e.g., Fordyce, 1977). We cannot rule out the possibility that the causal chain runs the other way as well: Being happy with yourself and your life may help you to relate more positively to the people around you. But the preponderance of evidence points to the opposite effect—that positive social interactions, perhaps especially close relationships, contribute strongly to happiness and life satisfaction.

Relative Importance of Predictors of Happiness

The list in Table 15.2 is informative, but it doesn't tell you how these different variables might be weighted. Which factors are the most important? Do they simply add up, or do they interact?

The one thing that is clear is that there is no one element in adult life that guarantees high life satisfaction for everyone who possesses it, nor any one experience or quality that leads automatically to unhappiness. Happiness seems to be made up of a great many small things which are probably weighted differently by each person. Even combining the four key demographic variables (income, gender, education, marital status), we can account for no more than about ten percent of the variation in happiness (Diener, 1984). Health and personality each account for no more than a similar 5 to 10 percent.

Of all the variables I have listed, the single most potent in predicting overall happiness has been the person's reported happiness in marriage or family relationships. In several national surveys, the correlations between satisfaction with marriage or family life and overall life satisfaction are in the range of .40 to .45, which means that perhaps as much as 15 to 20 percent of the variation in happiness is attributable to this feature of adult life (Campbell, 1981; Glenn & Weaver, 1981). It is not a magic happiness pill; the correlation is far from perfect. But satisfaction with one's relationships is a better predictor of overall life satisfaction than either demographic factors or satisfaction with such other key aspects of adult life as one's work. This is even true among highly educated men, among whom work commitment is typically very high.

In his autobiography, Chrysler chairman Lee Iacocca makes this point clearly: "Yes, I've had a wonderful and successful career. But next to my family, it really hasn't mattered at all" (1984, p. 289). Robert Sears (1977) often heard similar comments from 60 to 70-year-old men he interviewed as part of Terman's 50-year longitudinal study of a group of gifted subjects. Sears reports that of six areas studied (family, occupation, friends, culture, service, and joy), "family experience was reported retrospectively to have been the one most important for securing satisfaction" (pp. 125–126).

Since the amount of social contact is also related to happiness, it appears likely that the size and variety of your social network, as well as the quality of social support available in your key intimate relationships, not only affects your ability to handle stress or life change, but also strongly affects your ongoing level of life satisfaction or happiness.

Going Beyond Life Satisfaction: Other Measures of Success

The degree of happiness an adult experiences may be one measure of "success" in the adult years. But there are other ways of defining successful adulthood that rely more on professional assessments of an individual's "psychological health" or on objective measures of life success. Two approaches, both involving analyses of rich longitudinal data, are particularly interesting.

Researchers working with the Berkeley longitudinal data have developed a measure of ideal adult adjustment or "psychological health" based on the Q-sort of personality I described in Chapter 9. In this research, psychotherapists and theorists agreed on the pattern of qualities of an optimally healthy person, which included the "capacity for work and for satisfying interpersonal relationships, a sense of moral purpose, and a realistic perception of self and society" (Peskin & Livson, 1981, pp. 156). According to this view, ideally healthy adults are high in warmth, compassion, dependability and responsibility, insight, productivity, candor, and calmness. They value their own independence and autonomy as well as intellectual skill and behave in a sympathetic and considerate manner, consistent with their own personal standards and ethics.

The Q-sort for each subject in the study was then compared to this "ideal" profile, and each adult was given a score on psychological health. When this measure was correlated with the subjects' reported satisfaction with work, with family life, and with the closeness or affection in marriage, they found that adults who are rated by observers as having more "healthy" qualities also describe themselves as more satisfied with their lives.

George Vaillant has approached the definition of successful aging somewhat differently in his studies of the Harvard men included in the Grant study. He has searched for a set of reasonably objective criteria reflecting what he calls *psychosocial adjustment* and then has asked what factors in the men's childhood or in their adult lives are predictive of good or poor psychosocial adjustment (Vaillant, 1974, 1975; Vaillant & Vaillant, 1990).

You'll remember from earlier chapters that the Grant study men were evaluated and assessed in college and then regularly thereafter, with in-depth assessments at age 45 to 50 and again most recently at roughly age 63. Unfortunately, Vaillant has *not* used the same criteria to judge psychosocial adjustment in the men at each age, although the basic strategy has been the same. When the men were 45 to 50, their interview and questionnaire information was evaluated against a 32-point Adult Adjustment Scale; at age 63, only nine items were used to measure adjustment, all of which are listed in Table 15.3, along with a selection of the items from the longer midlife scale. You'll see from the table that the midlife scale is phrased in terms of *maladjustment* while the 63-year-old scale is turned around and phrased positively, but the intent is clearly the same. In each case, following Freud's lead, Vaillant has included items that touch on successful or unsuccessful "working and loving," as well as items that describe medical or psychiatric problems. Like the Berkeley researchers, he has found that this relatively objective assessment is correlated with other measures of adult success, including both a measure of maturity of defense mechanisms and life satisfaction (Vaillant & Vaillant, 1990).

Despite their quite different strategies for measuring successful aging, the findings from the two studies are reasonably consistent and lead to some intriguing suggestions about the ingredients of a healthy or successful adult life.

Both studies show that the most successful and well-adjusted middle-aged adults were those that grew up in warm, supportive, intellectually stimulating

TABLE 15.3. Vaillant's Psychosocial Adjustment Scales.

Selected Items from the Midlife Psychosocial Adjustment Scale (all scored yes or no)	Full Set of Items in Age–63 Psychosocial Adjustment Scale
No steady advance in career	Continued employment (1 = full, 3 = retired)
Earned income < $20,000 (in 1970)	Sustained job success (1 = yes, 2 = no)
No public service beside job	Job or retirement satisfaction (1 = clear satisfaction, 3 = clear dissatisfaction)
Lacks 10-year stable marriage	3+ weeks of vacation (1 = yes, 2 = no)
No pleasant contact with parents/siblings	Few psychiatric visits (1 = 0, 3 => 10)
No objective evidence of friends	Little tranquilizer use (1 ≤ 5 days use per year; 3 ≥ 30 days use per year)
No pastimes with nonfamily members	<5 sick days per year (1 = yes, 2 = no)
Stints vacation	Marital satisfaction (1 = clear satisfaction, 3 = clear dissatisfaction)
No clear enjoyment of job	Recreation with others (1 = yes, 2 = no)
Heavy use of drugs or alcohol	
Psychiatric diagnosis	
> 10 psychiatric visits	
2 or more sick leave days/year	
Often seeks medical attention	

SOURCES: Vaillant, 1975, Table 1, p. 422; Vaillant & Vaillant, 1990, Table 1, p. 32.

families. In the Berkeley study, Livson and Peskin (1981, Peskin & Livson, 1981) found that those who were higher in psychological health at age 30 or 40 grew up with parents who were rated as more open-minded, more intellectually competent, with good marital relationships. Their mothers were warmer, more giving and nondefensive, more pleasant and poised. Similarly, Vaillant found that the men who were rated as having the best adjustment at midlife had come from warmer families and had better relationships with both their fathers and mothers in childhood than had the least well-adjusted men (Vaillant, 1974).

Both studies also show that well-adjusted or successful middle-aged adults began adulthood with more personal resources, including better rated psychological and physical health at college age, a practical, well-organized approach in college (Vaillant, 1974) and greater intellectual competence (Livson & Peskin, 1981).

Both of these sets of findings are pretty much what we might expect. To put it most baldly and simply: Those who age well are those who start out well. To be sure, none of the correlations is terribly large, so even among the midlife subjects, there were some who began with two strikes against them who nonetheless looked healthy and successful at 45 or 50, and some who started out with advantages who did not turn out well. But in general, these findings point to a kind of consistency.

Yet when Vaillant looked at his subjects again when they were at retirement age, a very different picture appeared (Vaillant & Vaillant, 1990). Among these 173 men, *no* measure of early family environment remained a significant predictor of psychosocial adjustment at 63, nor did any measure of early adult intellectual competence. Those who turned out to be "successful" 63-year-olds had been rated as slightly more personally "integrated" when they were in college, and they had had slightly better relationships with their siblings. But other than that, there were simply no childhood or early adulthood characteristics that distinguished between those who had turned out well and those who had turned out less well.

What does predict health and adjustment at age 63 among these men is health and adjustment at midlife. The least successful 63-year olds were those who had used mood-altering drugs at midlife (primarily prescribed drugs intended to deal with depression or anxiety), abused alcohol or smoked heavily, and who used mostly immature defense mechanisms in their 30s and 40s.

Obviously, these findings come from only a single study, including only men, and only very well-educated professional men at that. So we shouldn't make too many huge theoretical leaps from this empirical platform. Still, the pattern of results suggests one (or both) of two possibilities:

1. It may be that each era in adult life simply calls for different skills and qualities, so that what predicts success or healthy adjustment at one age is simply not the same as what predicts it at another age. As one example, college-age intellectual competence may be a better predictor of psychosocial health at midlife simply because at midlife an adult is still in the midst of his most productive working years, when intellectual skill is more central. By retirement age, this may not be so critical an ingredient.

2. Alternatively, we might think of a successful adult life not as something foreordained from one's childhood or one's early adult qualities, but rather as something created out of the resources and opportunities available over the course of the decades. Those who start out with certain familial and personal advantages have a greater chance of encountering still further advantages, but it is what one does with the experiences—stressful as well as constructive—that determines the long-term success or psychosocial health one achieves. The choices we make in early adulthood help to shape the people we become at midlife; those midlife qualities in turn help to shape the kind of older people we become—a process I might describe as *cumulative continuity*. Early childhood environment or personal qualities such as personality or intellectual competence are not unimportant, but by age 65 their influence is indirect rather than direct.

It seems likely to me that both of these options are at least partially true, but it is the second possibility that I find especially compelling. It helps to make sense out of a series of other facts and findings.

One relevant fragment comes from yet another longitudinal study in which George Vaillant has been involved. In this case, he studied a group of 343 Boston men, all white, and nearly all from lower class or working class families. As teenagers, these men had all been part of a non-delinquent comparison group in a major study of delinquency originated by Sheldon and Eleanor Glueck (1950, 1968). They had been interviewed at length when they were junior high school age and were then reinterviewed by the Gluecks when they were 25 and 31, and by Vaillant and his colleagues when they were in their late 40s. In one particular analysis, John Snarey (Snarey, Son, Kuehne, Hauser, & Vaillant, 1987) looked at the outcomes for those men who had not had children at the normative time to see how the men had handled this childlessness. Of this group of childless men, those independently rated at age 47 as clearly "generative" in Erikson's sense were those who were likely to have responded by finding someone else's child to parent, such as by adopting a child or joining an organization like Big Brothers or becoming an active uncle. Those childless men who were rated as clearly not generative at 47 were much less likely to have adopted a child; if they had chosen a substitute it was more likely a pet. Among the childless men, the generative and the nongenerative had not differed at the beginning of adult life in either social class or level of industry, so the eventual differences in psychosocial maturity do not seem to be the result of differences that already existed at age 20. Rather, they seem to be a result of the way the man responded to or coped with an unexpected or nonnormative event in early adult life.

Another type of finding that fits into the same overall picture is one I talked about in Chapter 10 in discussing the consistency of personality over the adult years. You may remember that when researchers have measured personality characteristics several times in the same individuals, they find that the correlations between such measurements at adjacent ages, even ages a decade or two apart, are reasonably robust. But when continuity is examined over longer periods, such as 40 or 50 years, the correlations drop to a much more modest level.

The whole process reminds me a bit of predicting the weather. To predict tomorrow's weather, your best bet is to predict that it will be just like today. You will be right more than half the time. But predicting next week's weather is more difficult, and next month's is virtually unknown. Each day is linked to the day before and the day after, and all are part of a long causal chain of influences; but the weather today is only very indirectly related to the weather six months ago or to what will happen six months from now.

The central point for me is that there are many pathways through adulthood. The pathway each of us follows is affected by the departure point, but it is the choices we make as we go along and our ability to learn from the experiences that confront us that shapes the people we become 50 or 60 years later. If we are going to understand the journey of adulthood, we need a model that will allow us to make some order out of the diversity of lifetimes that results from such choices and such learning or lack of it. So as a final step in the synthesis I have been attempting in this last chapter, let me try my hand at just such a model.

A Model of Adult Growth and Development: Trajectories and Pathways

On the several occasions when I have tried to depict the pathways of adult development with some kind of visual picture, it has become clear very quickly that no two-dimensional drawing, however skillful (and my drawings are never skillful!) can successfully depict the process. At least three dimensions are required, and even that does not quite capture the complexities. Since three- and four-dimensional models are difficult or impossible to depict on these two-dimensional pages, I will content myself with a set of four propositions, several of which can at least be converted into schematic drawings.

The first proposition takes us back to many of the points I made in Chapter 13, as I summarized the information we have on normative or common pathways:

PROPOSITION 1: THERE ARE SHARED, BASIC, SEQUENTIAL PHYSICAL AND PSYCHOLOGICAL DEVELOPMENTS OCCURRING DURING ADULTHOOD, ROUGHLY (BUT NOT PRECISELY) AGE-LINKED.

Whatever other processes may influence adult life, it is clear that the entire journey is occurring along a road that has certain common features. The body and the mind change in predictable ways with age. These changes, in turn, affect the way adults define themselves and the way they experience the world around them. As I said in Chapter 13, I also place the sequence of changes in self-definitions or meaning systems outlined by Loevinger, Fowler, and others in this same category. The difference is that unlike physical and mental changes, the process of ego development or spiritual change is not an inevitable accompaniment of aging but a *possibility* or potentiality.

Within the general confines of these basic processes and sequences of development, however, there are many individual pathways—many possible sequences of roles and relationships, many different levels of growth or life satisfaction or "success"—which brings me to the second major proposition:

PROPOSITION 2: EACH ADULT'S DEVELOPMENT OCCURS PRIMARILY WITHIN A SPECIFIC PATHWAY OR TRAJECTORY, STRONGLY INFLUENCED BY THE STARTING CONDITIONS OF EDUCATION, FAMILY BACKGROUND, ETHNICITY, INTELLIGENCE, AND PERSONALITY.

I can best depict this individuality by borrowing Waddington's (1957) image of the **epigenetic landscape**, a variation of which is shown in Figure 15–2. Waddington introduced this idea in a discussion of the strongly "canalized" development of the infant years, but the same general concept can serve for a discussion of adulthood.

The original Waddington image, like Figure 15–2, was of a mountain, down which ran a series of gullies. In my version of this metaphor, the bottom of the mountain represents old-age while the top of the mountain represents early

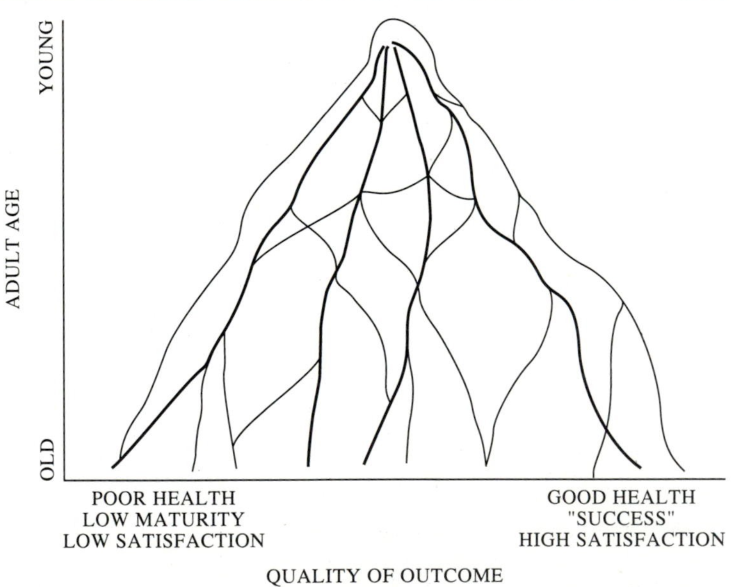

Figure 15–2 The image of a mountain with gullies running down it is one way to depict the alternative pathways through adulthood. The journey down the mountain (from youth to old-age) can begin in any one of many tracks. As the adult moves down the track, there are periods of stability as well as transitions or disequilibria during which the individual may shift from one track to another.

adulthood. In our adult years, each of us must somehow make our way down this mountain. Since we are all going down the same mountain (following the same basic "rules" of physical, mental, and spiritual development), all journeys will have some features in common. But this metaphor also allows for wide variations in the specific events and outcomes of the journey.

Imagine a marble placed at the top of the mountain. The particular pathway it follows to the bottom of the mountain will be heavily influenced by the gully in which it starts. If I also assume that the main pathways are deeper than the side tracks, then shifting from the track in which one starts is less probable than continuing along the same track. Nonetheless, the presence of choice points or junctions makes it possible for marbles starting in the same gully to end up in widely varying places at the bottom of the mountain. From any given starting point, some pathways and some outcomes are much more likely than others. But many possible pathways diverge from any one gully.

I am aware that the mountain metaphor has at least one major drawback; it risks the implication that our progress through adulthood is nothing but a downhill slide involving only decline or loss. The mountain metaphor fails to convey the possibility of growth or development that I have been emphasizing throughout these last few chapters. I have nonetheless chosen to use this image because it is the only metaphor I can think of that conveys the *momentum* that is created by the sequence of choices we make in early adulthood and as we move through our adult years. So bear with me.

This model or metaphor certainly fits with the general findings from Vaillant's long-term study of the Grant study men. The gully one starts in certainly does have an effect on where you are likely to be on the mountain at midlife. But the eventual ending point is much more strongly linked to where you were at midlife than where you started out.

The model also fits with another finding I mentioned in Chapter 13, that there is an increase in variability of scores on various measures of health, mental skill, personality, and attitudes with increasing age. In early adulthood, the various alternative gullies are more like each other (closer together) than is true 40 or 60 years later.

Still another feature implicit in Figure 15–2 as I have drawn it is significant enough to state as a separate proposition:

PROPOSITION 3: EACH PATHWAY IS MADE UP OF A SERIES OF ALTERNATING EPISODES OF STABLE LIFE STRUCTURE AND DISEQUILIBRIUM.

In the mountain-and-gully metaphor, the stable life structures are reflected in the long straight stretches between junction points, while the junctions represent the disequilibria. This aspect of the model is obviously borrowed from Levinson's theory of adult personality development (1978, 1980, 1986). Like Levinson, I conceive of each stable life structure as a balance achieved by an individual among the collection of role demands she is then facing, given the skills and temperamental qualities at her command. This balance is normally reflected in a stable externally observable life pattern—getting up at a particular time every day to get the kids off to school, going off to your job, doing the grocery shopping on Saturday, having dinner with your mother every Sunday, going out to dinner with your spouse every Valentine's day, or whatever. It is also reflected in the quality and specific features of relationships and in the meaning system through which we filter all these experiences. These patterns are not totally fixed, of course. We all make small adjustments regularly, as demands or opportunities change. But there do appear to be times in each adult's life when a temporary balance is achieved.

The Relationship of Stable Periods and Age These alternating periods of stability and disequilibrium or transition appear to be *related* to age. I've suggested such a rough age-linkage in Figure 15–2 by showing more choice points at some levels of the mountain than at others. But I think this age-linkage is much more approximate, much less stage-like, than Levinson originally proposed. The evidence I have described throughout the book simply does not conform well to the strict age-grading of stability and transition that Levinson suggests. Johannes Schroots (1988), who has also used Waddington's model as a basis for describing adult development, puts it this way:

> . . . the metaphor of branching . . . development . . . makes abundantly clear that linear models of behavior development with their stages, phases, transitions, seasons, and passages . . . are inadequate descriptions of the human life span. (p. 304)

Nonetheless, the content of the stable structures at each approximate age and the issues dealt with during each transition seem to be somewhat predictable (after all, we are going down the same mountain). There is a set of tasks or issues that confront most adults in a particular sequence as they age, as I outlined in Table 13.1. In early adulthood this includes separating from one's family of origin, creating a stable central partnership, bearing and beginning to rear children, and establishing satisfying work.

In middle adulthood, the tasks include launching one's children into independence, caring for aging parents, redefining parental and spousal roles, exploring one's own inner nature, coming to terms with the body's aging and with the death of one's parents. An adult who follows the modal "social clock" will thus be likely to encounter transitions at particular ages and to deal with shared issues at each transition. But I am not persuaded that there is only one order, or only one set of ages, at which those tasks are or can be confronted. As just one example, it appears that in some cohorts or some cultures, women may deal with the tasks of identity and intimacy in a different order than do men. In this respect, the mountain-and-gully model is misleading since it does not convey the variability in *timing* of major choice points that clearly does exist, such as what happens when an adult does not marry, or does not have children until his or her 30s or 40s, or becomes physically disabled, or widowed, or ill in his early adult years, or the like.

But whatever the variations in timing, it still appears to me to be valid to describe adult life as alternating between periods of stability and transition.

TURNING POINTS The periods of disequilibrium, which we might think of as turning points in individual lives, may be triggered by any one or more of a whole series of events. There is no way to depict these in the mountain-and-gully model, so I have to turn to a more common kind of two-dimensional diagram, the flow chart or path diagram shown in Figure 15–3. The major sources of disequilibrium, listed on the left-hand side of this figure, are the following:

1. *Role changes,* such as marriage, or the birth of a child, or the departure of the last child from home, or retirement, changes in jobs, and so on.
2. *Asynchrony of timing* in the several different dimensions of adult change or growth. This is part of Perun and Bielby's timing model of development, which I talked about in Chapter 3. When physical development, or mental development, or role patterns are "out of synch" there is tension or disequilibrium in the system. Being significantly off-time in any one dimension of adulthood creates such asynchrony automatically and is thus associated with higher rates of stress. Having a first child in your late 30s is not only a role change, it is also an asynchronous role change, which should increase the likelihood of a major disequilibrium, just as will the *failure* to have children at all, such as among the childless men in the Glueck/Vaillant study of working class men I mentioned a few pages ago. The general rule, as I suggested in Chapter 11, is that on-time role changes seldom trigger major crises or self-reexamination precisely because they are shared with one's peers. The individual can easily explain both the change and the strain it may cause as originating "outside" of himself. Nonnormative changes, in contrast, are hard to explain away in any way except with reference to one's self—your own choices or failures or successes. These more individual experiences, then, are far more likely than the normative ones to bring about reassessment or redefinition of the self, of values, of systems of meaning.
3. *Lack of match* between the demands of a particular set of roles and an adult's own temperament or personality. This is, in some sense, another kind of asynchrony. The study by Florine Livson of the several pathways to high level health in middle-age that I described in Chapter 7 is one example of matching or nonmatching patterns. As you'll recall, Livson found that those adults who looked psychologically healthy at 50 but had shown signs of distress or disturbance at 40 were likely to be those whose qualities as teenagers didn't match the then-prevalent sex roles. The less social and more intellectual young women in this group tried to fit into a mold of full-time homemaking and found it distressing; the more creative and emotional men tried to fit into the mold of the gray flannel suit society and were disturbed at 40. Both groups went through a process in their 40s of freeing themselves of the constraints of those early, ill-fitting roles and emerged at 50 looking very much put together.
4. *Major life changes or major chronic stresses,* particularly "exits" such as the death of a close family member or friend, or the loss of a friendship or love relationship. While unanticipated or off-time changes may be the most difficult in most instances, even some anticipated changes, such as the death of your parents

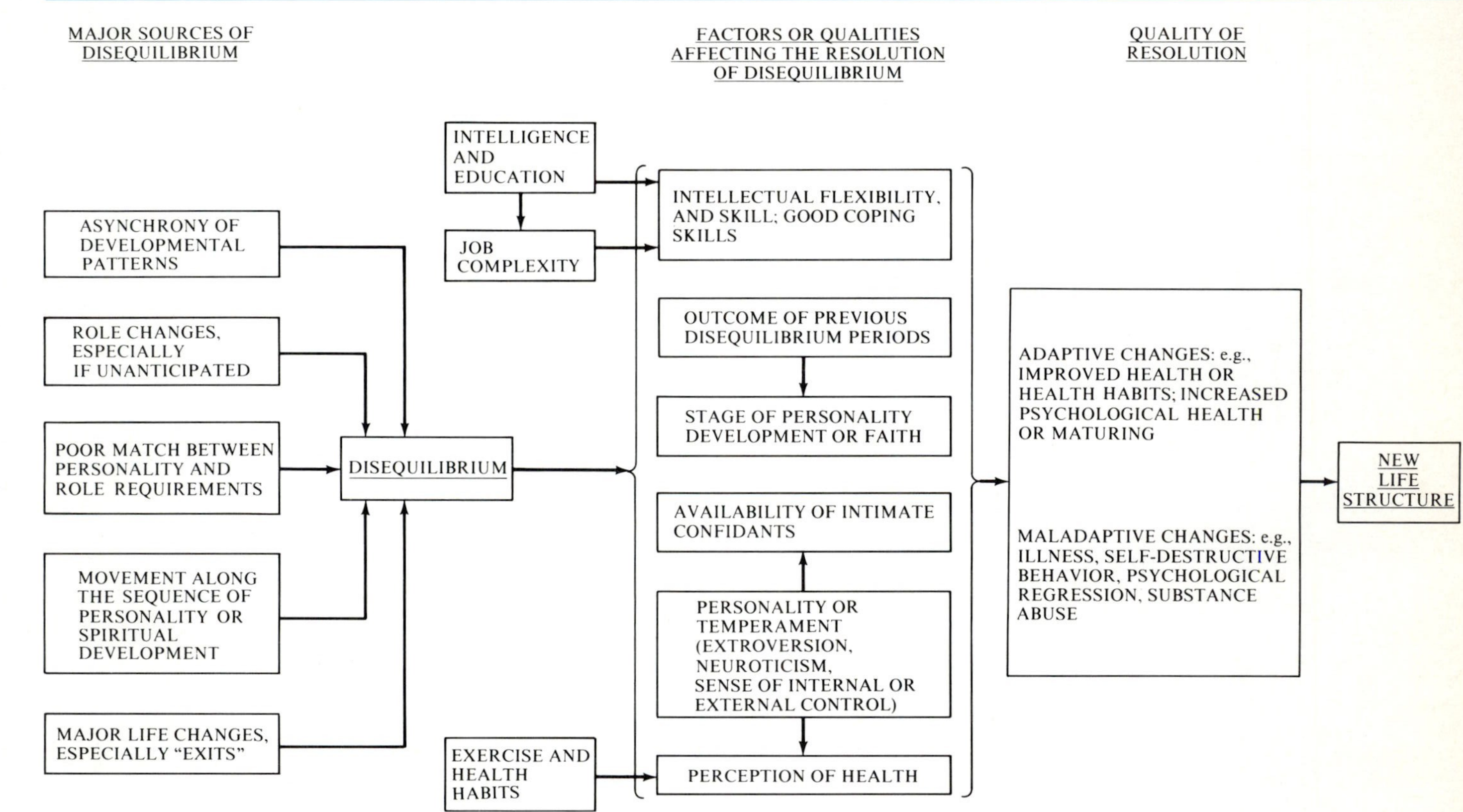

Figure 15–3 *A model of disequilibrium and its resolution. I am suggesting that such a process occurs repeatedly during adulthood, with the effects of these transitions accumulating over time. Each such transition affects the pathway (the gully) along which the adult then moves.*

when you are in your 40s or 50s, still call for significant reassessment and reorganization.

5. Finally, disequilibrium can be triggered by a *change in inner psychological tasks*, such as any movement along the dimension described by Erikson, or Loevinger, or by Fowler's stages of faith. Such inner changes typically occur in *response to* the disequilibrium-causing agents I have just described. But once begun, a transition such as from conformist to conscientious ego structure, or from individuative to conjunctive faith, carries its own disequilibrium. Any new stable life structure that emerges at the end of the disequilibrium period must be built on the new sense of self, or faith, that has evolved.

Whether the individual experiences such a disequilibrium period as a crisis or merely as a rather transitory phase seems to depend on at least two things: the number of different sources of disequilibrium and the individual's own personality and coping skills (as I outlined in Chapter 12). When there is a pile-up of disequilibrium-producing events within a narrow span of years, such as changes in roles, major relationship losses, and asynchronous physical changes, any individual is likely to experience a major transition. But the tendency to respond to this as a crisis may also reflect relatively high levels of neuroticism, low levels of extraversion, or the lack of effective coping skills.

It is in our response to these disequilibrium periods that our particular pathway down the mountain is determined, which leads me to the fourth basic proposition:

PROPOSITION 4. THE OUTCOME OF A PERIOD OF DISEQUILIBRIUM MAY BE EITHER POSITIVE (PSYCHOLOGICAL GROWTH, MATURITY, IMPROVED HEALTH, ETC.), NEUTRAL, OR NEGATIVE (REGRESSION OR IMMATURITY, ILL HEALTH).

Which kind of outcome occurs at any choice point—which channel one follows—is determined or affected by a wide range of variables, which I have sketched in the middle of Figure 15–3.

Intellectual flexibility or skill seems to be a particularly critical ingredient in leading to the later stages of maturity and growth that Vaillant or Loevinger describe. Janet Giele puts it well:

> It is the degree of social complexity on the job or in other aspects of everyday life that appears critical. Those who must learn a great deal and adapt to many different roles seem to be the most concerned with trying to evolve an abstract self, conscience, or life structure that can integrate all these discrete events. By contrast, those with a simple job, limited by meager education and narrow contacts, are less apt to experience aging as a process that enhances autonomy or elaborates one's mental powers. (1982, p. 8)

An adult's intellectual flexibility, in turn, is influenced by the complexity of the environments in which she lives, particularly the complexity of job (either a job outside the home, or even the complexity of housework [Schooler, 1984]). And of course, job complexity is itself partially determined by the level of original education each adult has attained. So well-educated adults are more likely to find complex jobs and are thus more likely to maintain or increase their intellectual flexibility. Linkages like these help to create the pattern of predictability we see between early adulthood and midlife, but since none of these relationships is anywhere near a perfect correlation, there is a good deal of room for shifts from one gully to another. Some blue collar jobs, for example, are quite complex, while some white collar jobs are not, and such variations may tend to push people out of the groove in which they started.

Underlying temperamental tendencies are another key ingredient. Adults who are high in what Costa and McCrae call neuroticism appear to be more likely to respond to disequilibrium by increases in substance abuse, illness, depression, or regressive patterns of defense. Adults with less neurotic or more extraverted temperament, in contrast, respond to disequilibrium by reaching out to others, by searching for constructive solutions.

Figure 15–4 Not all resolutions of transition or disequilibrium periods are adaptive or positive. Some, like increasing alcohol or drug usage, may temporarily deaden the pain or help repress the problem but leave the adult less able to cope with both current and future tasks. (Photo © Jock Pottle, c/o Design Conceptions, 1980. Reprinted with permission.)

The availability of close supportive confidants is also a significant factor, clearly not independent of temperament. Adults who lack close friends or the supportive intimacy of a good marriage are more likely to have serious physical ailments in midlife, or to have significant emotional disturbances, to drink or use drugs and to use more immature forms of defense (Vaillant, 1977a). Such friendless or lonely adults do more often come from unloving and unsupportive families, but even such a poor early environment can be more readily overcome if the adult manages to form at least one close, intimate relationship. Vaillant describes several men in the Grant study who had grown up in unloving or highly stressful families, who were withdrawn or even fairly neurotic as college students, who nonetheless went on to become "successful" and emotionally mature adults. One of the common ingredients in the lives of these men, especially compared to those with similar backgrounds who had poorer outcomes, was the presence of a "healing" relationship with a spouse.

Health may also make some difference in the way an adult responds to a period of disequilibrium. Poor health reduces options; it also reduces your level of energy, which affects the range of coping strategies open to you or the eventual life structures you can create.

Cumulative Effects of Transitions

As a final point, I would argue that the effects of these several disequilibrium periods are cumulative, a process that Gunhild Hagestad and Bernice Neugarten (1985) describe as the "transition domino effect." Such a cumulative effect of earlier stages or transitions is a key element in Erikson's theory of development, as you'll recall from Chapter 3. Unresolved conflicts and dilemmas remain as unfinished business, as excess emotional baggage that makes each succeeding stage more difficult to resolve successfully. Vaillant and others who have studied adults from childhood through midlife have found some support for this notion. Men in the Grant study who could reasonably be described as having failed to develop "trust" in their early childhood did have many more difficulties in the first few decades of adulthood. They were more pessimistic, self-doubting, passive, and dependent as adults and showed many more maladaptive or unsuccessful outcomes compared to those with more "trusting" childhoods.

Other forms of cumulative effect operate as well. One major off-time experience early in life, for example, may trigger a whole series of subsequent off-time or stressful experiences. The most obvious example is the impact of adolescent parenthood, which leads to early marriage and (typically) early school departure, which in turn affects the complexity of the job one is likely to find, which affects intellectual flexibility, and so on through the years.

Another form of cumulative effect occurs when a person's response to an early disequilibrium alters the choices he has available at later forks in the road. For example, in the face of some transition period, perhaps particularly a transition at midlife, an adult might begin a regular exercise program. This decision not only changes her life structure, it is also likely to increase her actual health or perception of health. When she faces the next transition, she does so with the resource of better health, perhaps more vitality. For another adult, one of the

Figure 15–5 Choosing to get more education, as these adults are doing, may often be an adaptive response to a current problem or task. It is also likely to increase the range of resources the individual has available when facing subsequent tasks. Thus, the choices we make at each point along the way have repercussions for later turning points as well. (Photo ©Joel Gordon, 1978. Reprinted with permission.)

resolutions of a prior disequilibrium point might be a change to a more complex job, or a return to school. Such a change not only alters the life structure, it also increases the adult's intellectual flexibility, which in turn affects the range of cognitive coping skills in his repertoire. The next transition might thus be faced more adaptively.

We can see just such cumulative effects in the results of the Grant study. Those men who responded to early adulthood transitions and challenges by drinking more or with prolonged depression reduced their overall coping abilities; they got off track and stayed off track.

ADAPTIVE OR MALADAPTIVE OUTCOMES VERSUS HAPPINESS It is important for me to emphasize that the range of possible outcomes I have labeled "adaptive" and "maladaptive" changes are not identical to happiness and unhappiness. Maladaptive changes such as illness, substance abuse, suicide attempts, or depression obviously are correlated with unhappiness. But such adaptive changes as improved health habits, increased social activity, or movement along the sequence of stages of ego or spiritual development are not uniformly associated with *increases* in happiness. McCrae and Costa, for example (1983), did not find that adults who were at the conscientious or higher levels of ego development reported any higher affect balance than did adults at the conformist stage. Thus, profound changes can result from a disequilibrium period without such changes being reflected in alterations of overall happiness or life satisfaction. Instead, a change in ego development stage may alter the criteria of happiness the person applies to his life. As McCrae and Costa say:

> We suggest that the quality and quantity of happiness do not vary with levels of maturity, but that the circumstances that occasion happiness or unhappiness, the criteria of satisfaction or dissatisfaction with life, may vary with ego level. The needs and concerns, aspirations and irritations of more mature individuals will doubtless be different—more subtle, more individualistic, less egocentric. The less psychologically mature person may evaluate his or her life in terms of money, status, and sex; the more mature, in terms of achievement, altruism, and love. (1983, p. 247)

Maturing clearly does not automatically make an adult happy, as demonstrated by (among other things) the lack of correlation between age and happiness. Maturing and other adaptive changes alter the agenda and thus alter the life structures we create and the way we evaluate those life structures.

Five Young People: Some Forward Predictions

With this model in mind, is it possible to make any predictions about the course of adulthood for Tom Kleck, Cathy Stevens, Laura Rogers, Walter Washington, or Christopher Linton? Unexpected future events will obviously have an impact on their passage through the years, but some reasonable guesses are still possible.

Tom Kleck, the extroverted, bright, working class young man, has more education by age 22 than his father had and has a more complex job. He is also open to new experiences, willing to experiment, low in neuroticism. Certainly, he begins his trip down the mountain in a gully fairly far to the right. The fact that he has already established an apparently satisfying relationship with his girlfriend also bodes well. The most straightforward prediction would be that he will make fairly rapid progress in his career for the next 10 or 15 years, reaching his career peak by about age 40. He is likely to be accompanied on this journey by a reasonably large "convoy" of friends and family, which will make passage through the several transitions somewhat smoother. In general, I would expect Tom both to be fairly happy as an adult and to mature. His openness to new experience, his willingness to buck tradition, are two qualities that especially point in this direction.

Cathy Stevens (the All-American Girl), in contrast, is likely to be happy but is probably less likely to mature. She is following a traditional "social clock," marrying fairly early, having her children at normative times, beginning work only in her 30s or later. For her, some of the issues of identity and independence will be postponed until her 40s or even her 50s. The fact that she is likely to be economically quite well off will buffer her against some of the strains of the roles of wife/mother/worker, thus maintaining the life structure of her 20s or 30s for a longer period. Stability is also indicated by the fact that Cathy's temperament (extroverted, low neuroticism) matches quite well the roles she anticipates filling. For her, the most significant disequilibrium may occur at 40 or 50, when the role demands of motherhood will wane. If her parents should die when she is in that age range, or some other disequilibrium-producing event coincide with the role changes, she is likely to experience a period of depression or distress. Whether she emerges from that time with adaptive growth or not will depend on all the factors I've just listed. Like Tom Kleck, she enters the process with a range of excellent resources, so the likelihood of truly maladaptive responses is not large. But her generally conventional approach may reflect greater resistance to change than is true of Tom.

A quite different prediction can be made for Laura Rogers, who was a mother at 16 and divorced by 22. She has few resources and begins the journey down the mountain in a left-hand track. The sorts of stresses and traumas Laura has already faced *can* have the effect of producing greater maturity. But in Laura's case, given her temperament (high in neuroticism), her lack of education, and the off-timeness of her family life cycle, the greater likelihood is for maladaptive changes. Several events could change that prognosis, however, chief among them the advent of a satisfying and supportive second marriage. She has several close friendships, so she is obviously capable of establishing an intimate relationship. Another "lucky" event would be a job that challenged her or the opportunity to go back to school. It is not so clear, though, that Laura would seek out such opportunities nor seize them if they were offered. She is, in a word, low in "hardiness." She sees the world as largely outside of her own control, and this attitude will make adaptive growth and maturing much less likely.

It is much harder to make a prediction about Walter Washington, the black, inner-city, former basketball player, in part because he has such a mixture of qualities. He shows the kind of intellectual interest and the determination that are often associated with psychological growth and health. In addition, his pursuit of further schooling, and the more complex job he is likely to end up in because of that schooling, predict a high level of cognitive complexity. Also on the positive side of the ledger is his relatively low level of neuroticism. At the same time, Walter is quite introverted and has some trouble establishing really intimate relationships with other people. And, of course, he is black, with all the continuing experience of discrimination that still implies. My prediction is that Walter will be quite successful in his work, achieving satisfaction from that success. But should Walter encounter some really unexpected life change, or when his mother dies, he is likely to have more difficulty dealing with the stress than would someone with stronger social support systems. Walter has the intellectual coping skills that would assist him but not the skill to form the relationships that would be beneficial. This is a man who may very well have a classic midlife crisis, but his inner resources are good enough that he may emerge from such an experience strengthened by it.

Chris Linton, the highly intellectual, introverted law student, also has an interesting mixture of qualities. In some respects, he begins adulthood with a high chance of external success. He is extremely bright, has an excellent education, and the drive to succeed. He will probably become quite wealthy. But he is also likely to be fairly dissatisfied and unhappy most of his life. Like Walter, faced with the inevitable disequilibria in his future, Chris will have the intellectual skill to analyze the alternatives but is likely to lack the friendships and intimate relationships to buffer him from the effects of the stress. But unlike Walter, who is low in neuroticism, Chris's characteristic approach to problems is pessimistic or negative. I will not be surprised if he has a heart attack at 45 or develops some other chronic illness, such as an ulcer. Nor would I be surprised if he becomes an alcoholic. Barring that, he may have serious difficulties at retirement, when his self-definition through work is lost. What could save him from these maladaptive outcomes, among other things, would be a strong, secure, supportive marriage, or even a close relationship with a mentor or friend. Given his personality, the chances of his finding a partner who could provide such unconditional support is not great. But it is possible.

You may have gathered in what I have said about these five young people that I think that *some* stress or disequilibrium is necessary for growth or maturity to occur. Life structures, including stages of ego development or faith, tend to remain stable so long as they work, so long as they provide balance in the system. So without some stresses or strains there would be little change, little growth. Fortunately, the normal course of adult life contains a number of inescapable, built-in stresses or changes, including the fact of physical aging itself. So every adult must cope with some transitions or potential disequilibrating experiences. The ideal arrangement for maximum growth seems to be for those stresses or disequilibria to be substantial enough to stretch the capacity of the individual to cope, but not so major as to overwhelm the adult's resources. An adult who begins life with more intellectual, temperamental, and physical resources can respond with maturing to more complex or pervasive transitions. Other adults, like Laura Rogers, have few resources and are likely to be overwhelmed by the ordinary sequence of life changes, let alone the off-time sequence of experiences she is already coping with.

A research example of this very point comes from the study of the parents of the Berkeley longitudinal subjects (Caspi & Elder, 1986). These parents had been young adults during the Great Depression and many (but not all) of them had to cope with loss of jobs and severe economic hardship. Caspi and Elder have found that of those who faced such hardship, those who had started out in the middle class were actually strengthened by the struggle, while working class adults facing equivalent hardship were adversely affected over the long term. At age 70, the middle class group described themselves as more satisfied with their lives than did equivalently middle-class subjects who had not faced economic reverses in the Depression, while the working class group reported lower life satisfaction than a comparable group of working class adults whose Depression experience had been more benign. Thus, stress can induce growth, may even be necessary for growth to occur, but it can have this effect only when it does not overwhelm the adult's resources.

A Last Look at the Model

I am sure it is clear to you already that the model I have sketched in this chapter, complex as it is, is nonetheless too simplistic. It is doubtless also too culture-specific, although I have tried to state the elements of the model broadly enough to encompass patterns in other cultures. It may also be quite wrong in a number of respects. Among other things, I have assumed throughout this discussion that something like Loevinger's sequence of ego development stages actually exists, and that all adults mature in this pattern if they mature at all. But as you know from Chapters 10 and 11, that assumption is based on slim evidence.

Despite these obvious limitations, however, the model may give you some sense of the rules or laws that seem to govern the richness and variety of adult lives. In the midst of a bewildering array of adult patterns, there does appear to be order, but the order is not so much in fixed, age-related sequences of events as in *process*. To understand adult development, it is useful to uncover the ways in which all pathways, all gullies, are alike. But it is equally important to understand those factors and processes that affect the choices an adult will have and the way she will respond to those choices. Perhaps the most remarkable thing about this journey is that with all its potential pitfalls and dilemmas, most adults pass through it with reasonable happiness and satisfaction, acquiring a modicum of wisdom along the way. May you enjoy your own journey.

Summary

1. To understand the journey of adulthood we need to go beyond the normative approach followed in the last two chapters and look for some kind of orderliness in the enormous variability of individual life patterns.
2. One strategy has been to study "successful aging," with success often defined in terms of life satisfaction. Average levels of life satisfaction do not change significantly with age, although the ingredients may differ from one age period to the next.
3. Life satisfaction is related to several demographic and personal qualities: More highly satisfied adults are likely to have relatively higher income than their peers, to be slightly better educated, to be employed, and married. They are more likely to be extroverted, to be low in neuroticism, and to have a sense of personal control.
4. Perceived adequacy of health and social relationships are also predictors of life satisfaction, again illustrating the central importance of the meaning attached to experiences rather than the experiences themselves.
5. The largest single predictor of life satisfaction appears to be quality (or perceived quality) of social relationships. But no one predictor accounts for a very large percentage of the variation in satisfaction among adults. Individual happiness is composed of many ingredients, many of them highly individual.

6. Other measures of successful aging include subjective ratings of psychological health by experts, or combinations of objective criteria such as success in "work and love."
7. Studies using such measures suggest that family background and early adulthood resources are predictive of midlife psychological health or success, but that such early life experiences are not related to later life health or success. Such late life success is much more strongly related to midlife qualities or skills, suggesting a kind of "cumulative continuity" of life pathways.
8. A preliminary model of adult development includes the metaphor of a mountain with gullies running down it. Each adult, with his own combination of beginning characteristics, moves down the mountain (through adulthood) in a particular gully, somewhat resistant to change.
9. Each pathway can also be thought of as being made up of alternating periods of stable life structures and disequilibrium periods. During the disequilibria, the adult may shift to another 'track' or gully, or continue along the same pathway.
10. In any one culture, the stable periods are age-linked because they are largely defined by the set of family and work roles assumed by adults of particular ages.
11. Disequilibrium may be triggered by role changes, by asynchrony in timing of the several aspects of development, by a lack of match between an individual's characteristics and particular role demands, by unanticipated life changes or stress, and by psychological growth such as movement to a new level in Loevinger's stages of ego development.
12. Whether the outcome of a period of disequilibrium will be positive/adaptive, negative/maladaptive, or neutral will depend on the intellectual flexibility and coping resources of the individual, underlying temperamental qualities, availability of close, supportive confidantes, physical health, and the outcomes of previous disequilibrium periods.

Suggested Readings

ATKINSON, R. (1989). *The long gray line.* Boston: Houghton, Mifflin. The story of 20 years of the lives of the group of young men who formed the class of 1966 at West Point. Only selected young men are highlighted in this story, but you can get some sense of the kinds of pivotal experiences that shaped individual lives, the role of marriage in the lives of the different men, the interplay of personality and life demands. Fascinating reading.

BATESON, M. C. (1989). *Composing a life.* New York: The Atlantic Monthly Press. Mary Catherine Bateson, daughter of Margaret Mead and Gregory Bateson, writes about her own life and that of four other women, exploring many of the very questions of continuity and change that I have examined in this chapter and in this book. Once again, fascinating reading.

BLOCK, J. (1971). *Lives through time.* Berkeley, CA: Bancroft. Like Vaillant's description of the Grant study men, Block's discussion of the early results of the Berkeley/Oakland longitudinal study gives some sense of the elements that affect the pathways of adulthood. At the time this book was written, the subjects were only in their 30s, so this does not describe as long a span of adult years as does Vaillant's discussion, but it is still of great interest.

VAILLANT, G. E. (1977a). *Adaptation to life.* Boston: Little, Brown. I have recommended this book before, so you may already have dipped into it. I recommend it again here because it is one of the really good descriptions of actual lives over time, although it includes information on these men only up to about age 50; the 63-year old interviews Vaillant has recently completed are too recent for the findings to have been part of this book.

GLOSSARY

Achievement motive The disposition to perform activities in competition with a standard of excellence.

Adulthood Arbitrarily defined here as the period from age 18 to death.

Affect General term used by psychologists to mean roughly "emotion," but used more specifically here as a defining attribute of social support.

Affirmation A second defining attribute of social support suggested by Kahn and Antonucci, including expressions of agreement or acknowledgment.

Age norms The set of expectations for the behavior of individuals of any given age group, such as teenagers or the elderly. Such norms are specific to a given culture or subculture, and may change from one cohort to another.

Age strata Layers or groupings by age within any given society. Individuals in each age stratum are expected to occupy certain roles and have certain privileges.

Aging The passage of years in an individual's life—without any connotation of loss or deterioration.

Aid Third defining attribute of social support suggested by Kahn and Antonucci, including direct physical, financial, or informational assistance.

Alzheimer's disease One of several causes of senile dementia, involving loss of brain weight and tangling of neurofibers of the brain resulting in gradual and permanent loss of memory and other cognitive functions.

Androgyny A combination of high levels of both feminine and masculine traits and qualities.

Associative friendship The less intimate form of friendship proposed by Reisman, characterized by some shared activity or interest.

Attachment A positive affective bond between any two individuals, underlying attachment behaviors. A key feature is the enhanced sense of security the individual has when in the presence of the attachment figure.

Attachment behaviors Outward expressions of underlying attachment, such as smiling, trying to be near, writing letters to, hugging, etc. Specific attachment behaviors displayed change over the life cycle.

Autonomous stage The next-to-highest stage proposed by Jane Loevinger, characterized by the capacity to acknowledge and deal with inner conflict.

Being motives Term used by Maslow for a cluster of motives found in humans, to discover and understand, to give love, to find optimum fulfillment of inner potential. Also called "growth motives."

Career consolidation A stage suggested by George Vaillant as an addition to Erikson's stages of adulthood, said to occur in one's early 30s, when attention is focused on work success and achievement.

Climacteric The general term used to describe the period (in both men and women) in which reproductive capacity is gradually lost during adulthood. Menopause is another word to describe the climacteric in women.

Cohort A group of individuals born at approximately the same time who share the same pattern of historical experiences in childhood and adulthood.

Cohort effect An observed difference between the performance of older and younger subjects on any given measure that can be most readily explained as the result of the different historical experiences of the two cohorts.

Cohort-sequential design One of the several sequential research designs, in this case involving two or more consecutive longitudinal studies (e.g. A group born in 1940 is studied from age 20 to age 35, and then another cohort born in 1950 is studied from age 20 to age 35.).

Conformist stage A stage proposed by Loevinger in her theory of adult development, characterized by the identification of one's self with group norms and values.

Confounding The covarying of two measures or properties of individuals or groups such that it is impossible to determine the independent effect of each. In cross-sectional research, age and cohort are confounded.

Conjunctive faith Fifth stage of faith development proposed by Fowler, involving openness to other views, other 'faiths,' and to paradox, myth, and metaphor.

Conscientious stage A stage proposed by Loevinger to follow the conformist and the self-aware level, characterized by the creation of individual rules and ideals.

Conventional level of moral reasoning The middle of the three levels of moral reasoning suggested by Kohlberg, involving reasoning based on the rules or expectations of the family or society.

Coronary Heart Disease (CHD) General term used by physicians to describe a set of disease processes in the heart and circulatory system, including most noticeably a narrowing of the arteries with plaque (atherosclerosis).

Correlation A statistic used to describe the degree to which the scores on two variables covary. A correlation can range from +1.00 to −1.00, with numbers nearer 1.00 reflecting stronger relationships.

Cross-linking An exchange of DNA material between cells of different types, such as skin and connective tissue cells; results in decrease in efficiency of cell protein.

Cross-sectional design Types of research designs in which different age groups are compared on the same measures at a single time point.

Cross-sequential design The most complex of the set of sequential research designs, involving both a series of longitudinal studies and a set of cross-sectional comparisons. (E.g. a group of 25-year-olds, a group of 30-year-olds, and a group of 35-year olds might each be simultaneously studied for 20 years). Schaie's Seattle Study is the best known example.

Crystallized intelligence That aspect of intelligence that is primarily dependent on education and experience: knowledge and judgment acquired through experience.

Decline Term to be used in this book only as a description of some observed lowering or drop in performance over age on some measure.

Defense mechanisms In psychoanalytic theories, these are strategies of the ego for coping with anxiety, including such patterns as denial, repression, projection, and intellectualization. May be organized by levels of maturity.

Deficiency motives Term used by Maslow to describe basic instincts or drives to correct imbalance or to maintain physical or emotional homeostasis.

Dendrites The tree-like branching parts of each nerve cell.

Development Term to be used in this book to refer to any changes with age that appear to involve some systematic improvement, integration, or "growth."

Dialectical thought Proposed form of adult thought that involves recognition and acceptance of contradiction and paradox, and the seeking of synthesis.

Disengagement A proposed process in late life involving a healthy withdrawal from social roles and contacts, and greater freedom from the rules and expectations of earlier adulthood.

Dream A part of Levinson's theory of adult development; in early adulthood each individual is thought to create a mental picture or fantasy of himself or herself creating a particular kind of life or achieving some particular goal.

Ego integrity versus despair The final stage of development proposed by Erikson, confronted in late life, when the adult must come to terms with who she is and has been, or face despair.

Encoding The processes by which information is committed to memory.

Epigenetic landscape A visual metaphor suggested by Wadding that visualizes development as a hill with valleys of various depth and steepness down which individual development moves.

Explanatory style Term used by Seligman to describe either a "helpless" or a non-helpless appraisal of one's environment. Those who explain their experiences by assuming lasting, general, interior causes tend to feel helpless in the face of environmental demands.

Experiment A research design in which the experimenter systematically manipulates one or more variables, assigning subjects randomly to one or more experimental and control groups.

Family life cycle Phrase used by family sociologists to describe the series of steps or stages that occur in the life history of any given family, from marriage, through birth of first child, through various stages in the child's growth, to the children's departure from the family.

Femininity Term used by psychologists to describe a pattern of traits and behavior including high levels of sex-typed female qualities and low levels of sex-typed male qualities.

Fluid intelligence That aspect of intelligence reflecting fundamental, biological processes and less dependent on specific experience.

Gain Term to be used in this book to describe patterns of change with age that involve increases or rises on some measure.

General adaptation syndrome A complex sequence of physiological reactions to stressors proposed by Selye, including initial alarm, intermediate resistance, and finally exhaustion.

Generativity versus stagnation The 7th stage proposed by Erikson, occurring from perhaps age 25 to 50, when the adult must find some way to rear or support the next generation.

Growth motives See *Being motives.*

Hardiness A dimension of personality proposed by Kobasa, including the tendency to respond to situations with commitment, a sense of personal control, and a sense of challenge.

Hospice care Relatively new pattern of care for terminally ill patients in which the majority of care is provided by family members, with control of care and care-setting in the hands of the patient and family. May be at home or in special wards or separate institutions.

Identity The term used in Erikson's theory of development to describe the gradually emerging, and continually changing, sense of self.

Identity versus role confusion The fifth stage in Erikson's theory of development, typifying the teenager and young adult, when the individual must form specific occupational, sexual, and religious identities.

Individualistic level In Loevinger's theory of development, the transitional point between the conscientious and the autonomous stages; central issue is that of dependence and independence.

Individuative-reflective faith Fourth stage proposed by Fowler, in which the source of authority for the adult's model of the world shifts from external to internal.

Integrated stage The final stage of adult development proposed by Loevinger, rarely reached, in which the conflicts of the autonomous stage are transcended.

Intimacy versus isolation The sixth stage proposed by Erikson, typically occurring in the early 20s, when the young adult forms several key, intimate relationships.

Life expectancy The average number of years a person of some designated age (e.g. birth, or age 65) can expect still to live.

Life span The theoretical maximum number of years of life for a given species, which is thought will not be exceeded even with improvements in health care.

Life-span perspective A general perspective shared by a number of theorists that emphasizes that development is a life-long process, that it is multidirectional, involving both gain and loss, and that there is plasticity in human behavior throughout the entire life span.

Life structure Concept suggested by Levinson to describe the pattern of existence, combining roles, relationships, and particular personality adaptations, created by each individual at several points in the adult life.

Locus of control Dimension of individual difference proposed by Rotter. An individual with an inner locus of control sees the source of control within himself; one with an outer locus sees the source of control as in the environment, luck, or the behavior of others.

Longevity A word literally meaning "long life" but used generally in gerontological literature to mean roughly the same as life expectancy.

Longitudinal design Research design in which the same individuals are studied repeatedly over a period of time.

Long-term memory Memory retained over more than a few minutes by means of some encoding process.

Love As defined by Robert Sternberg, includes three elements: intimacy, passion, and commitment.

Marital homogamy The selection of a spouse from among those similar to the self in social class, background, and race.

Masculinity Term used by psychologists to describe a combination of a high level of sex-typed male qualities and traits and a low level of sex-typed female qualities and traits in any one individual.

Maturation Any sequential unfolding of physical changes that is governed by the genetic code, or by other biological processes, and that is shared by all members of the species.

Maximum oxygen uptake (VO_2 max) The amount of oxygen that can be taken into the bloodstream and hence carried to all parts of the body. A major measure of aerobic fitness, VO_2 max decreases with age, but can be increased again with exercise.

Menopause Term used to refer to the female climacteric; that set of physical and hormonal changes associated with the loss of reproductive capacity in women in their 40s and 50s.

Mentor An older adult who may take on the role of guide or supporter for a younger adult in the same profession.

Osteoarthritis Term used generally to describe any significant changes in the bones of the joints of the body associated with the wear and tear of aging.

Osteoporosis The changes in bones, including increased brittleness and porousness, resulting from loss of calcium in the bone.

Panel study A form of cross-sequential research design, common among sociologists, in which a large (usually representative) sample, covering many ages, is studied repeatedly over a period of years.

Parental imperative Phrase used by David Gutmann to describe a possibly "wired in" pattern of intensification of sex-role differentiation after marriage and particularly after the first child is born.

Performance tests Those tests on many IQ tests that rely less on verbal skills and more on basic analytic or memory processes.

Personality An individual's unique, relatively consistent and enduring, patterned methods of behaving in relation to others and the total environment.

Preconventional level of moral reasoning First level of reasoning suggested by Kohlberg, in which the child sees as fair or just that which is rewarded. Self-serving, egocentric view.

Presbycusis A common form of deafness among older adults resulting from basic wear and tear on the auditory system. More common among adults who have worked in noisy environments.

Primary memory See *Short-term memory.*

Principled level of moral reasoning Third major level of moral reasoning proposed by Kohlberg, in which the adult looks behind the rules of society or family for a set of underlying principles on which to base moral judgments.

Q-sort A method of assessing or describing an individual's characteristics involving the sorting of a set of descriptors into a forced normal distribution of "typical" and "atypical" traits.

Recall A type of memory retrieval in which the individual may reproduce the entire stored item without any aids, such as remembering someone's name when you see her again.

Reciprocal friendship The most intimate form of friendship proposed by Reisman, characterized by long-term affectional bonds.

Recognition A type of memory retrieval, easier than recall, in which the individual must simply note that some fact is already known to him (e.g., "Yes, that's the one I saw before").

Resistance resources Collective term for all those personal and social resources that may buffer an individual from the effects of stress; includes social support from others, as well as personality characteristics (such as hardiness) and coping strategies.

Retrieval The process of bringing a particular memory out of short-term or long-term memory.

Role A concept from sociology describing the expected behavioral and attitudinal content of any one social position, such as teacher, or mother, or employer.

Role conflict The experience associated with occupying two or more roles that are wholly or partially logistically or psychologically incompatible.

Role strain The experience associated with occupying a role the demands of which do not match one's own qualities or skills.

Secondary memory See *Long-term memory.*

Self-aware level The step immediately after the conformist level in Jane Loevinger's theory of development; a transitional level in which the individual is beginning to define herself apart from external expectations.

Self efficacy Sense of being able to perform some task or achieve some goal.

Self-protective stage The fourth stage proposed by Loevinger, typically occurring in middle childhood or adolescence, but found occasionally in adults as well. Characterized by attempts to maximize one's own gain in any situation.

Senile dementia Any deterioration of intellectual abilities in old age that is due to some disorder of the nervous system rather than to any normal aging process.

Sensory memory The initial, very brief, sensory impression of some experience that is retained in memory, without encoding, for a very short time.

Sequential designs A family of research designs each of which involves either multiple cross-sectional comparisons, or multiple longitudinal comparisons, or both.

Sex roles Socially-defined collections of traits and behaviors expected to be displayed by male and female persons in any given culture.

Sex role stereotypes Relatively inflexible, widely shared concepts about the personality and behavior expected from men and women in any given culture.

Sex typing The degree of match between an individual's behavior and the prescriptions of the sex role assigned to his or her gender.

Short-term memory That portion of the memory process in which information in the sensory store is attended to, and retained for a slightly longer time. Such memory decays rapidly if there is no further encoding of the item.

Social class A group of people in a given culture who have similar social standing or rank within that culture; typically measured in terms of level of education, occupation, and income.

Social interest Phrase used by Crandall to describe a personality dimension ranging from self-centeredness to interest in and involvement with things beyond the self.

Social mobility The movement of individuals from one social stratum to another within any given society.

Social network Any one individual's collection of relations with family, friends, colleagues, or acquaintances; networks vary in size, rate of contract, interconnectedness, and composition.

Social status Sociologists define a status as a position within a social structure. Many psychologists use the term more loosely as a rough synonym of social class.

Social support The combination of affect, affirmation and aid that an individual receives from those with whom she has relationships.

Speeded tasks Term used for those measures of intellectual ability which have time limits.

Storage The third basic memory process (in addition to encoding and retrieval), involving placing some memory in short-term or long-term memory.

Synthetic-conventional faith Third stage of faith proposed by Fowler, in which the individual selects a model (a faith) from among those available in the social system. Authority is external to the individual.

Temperament A sub class of characteristics included under the general term of "personality"; Normally refers to those aspects of personal style and emotional responsiveness that are detectable early in infancy and appear to have a constitutional basis.

Time-lag design Assessment of a series of groups of subjects, each the same age at the time testing occurs, but representing different cohorts. (E.g., test 20-year-olds in 1970, then another group of 20-year-olds in 1980, then a third group in 1990).

Time sequential design A variety of sequential design in which parallel cross-sectional studies are completed several years apart. (E.g., 20, 40, and 60 year olds might be studied in 1960, and then separate groups of 20, 40, and 60 year olds studied in 1980.)

Type A personality A combination of competitiveness, a sense of time urgency, and hostility or aggressiveness, which has been found to be associated with higher risk of coronary heart disease.

Undifferentiated Term used by psychologists to describe an individual whose self-description includes low levels of both feminine and masculine qualities. Thus the opposite of androgynous.

Universalizing faith The highest (sixth) stage of faith proposed by Fowler, involves some loss of the sense of individuality.

Unspeeded tasks Those measures of intellectual skill that do not have time limits, such as a test of vocabulary or reasoning.

Verbal tests In contrast to "performance tests," those measures of intellectual ability that rely heavily on the ability to manipulate verbal symbols.

REFERENCES

Abbott, D. A., & Brody, G. H. (1985). The relation of child age, gender, and number of children to the marital adjustment of wives. *Journal of Marriage and the Family, 47,* 77–84.

Abrahams, B., Feldman, S. S., & Nash, S. C. (1978). Sex role self-concept and sex role attitudes: Enduring personality characteristics or adaptations to changing life situations? *Developmental Psychology, 14,* 393–400.

Achenbach, T. M. (1978). *Research in developmental psychology: Concepts, strategies, methods.* New York: Free Press.

Ainlay, S. C., & Smith, D. R. (1984). Aging and religious participation. *Journal of Gerontology, 39,* 357–363.

Ainsworth, M. D. S. (1989). Attachments beyond infancy. *American Psychologist, 44,* 709–716.

Ainsworth, M. D. S., Blehar, M. C., Waters, E., & Wall, S. (1978). *Patterns of attachment.* Hillsdale, NJ: Erlbaum.

Aldous, J., Osmond, M. W., & Hicks, M. W. (1979). Men's work and men's families. In W. R. Burr, R. Hill, F. I. Nye & I. L. Reiss, (Eds.), *Contemporary theories about the family* (pp. 226–256). New York: The Free Press.

Aldwin, C. M., Spiro, A. III, Bosse, R., & Levenson, M. R. (1989). Longitudinal findings from the normative aging study: 1. Does mental health change with age? *Psychology and Aging, 4,* 295–306.

Alsop, S. (1973). *Stay of execution.* New York: Lippincott.

Anderson, B. Jr., & Palmore, E. (1974). Longitudinal evaluation of ocular function. In E. Palmore (Ed.), *Normal Aging II* (pp. 24–31). Durham, NC.: Duke University Press.

Anderson, S. A., Russell, C. S., & Schumm, W. R. (1983). Perceived marital quality and family life-cycle categories: A further analysis. *Journal of Marriage and the Family, 45,* 127–139.

Anson, O. (1989). Marital status and women's health revisited: The importance of a proximate adult. *Journal of Marriage and the Family, 51,* 185–194.

Antonucci, T. C. (1985). Personal characteristics, social support, and social behavior. In R. H. Binstock & E. Shanas, (Eds.), *Handbook of aging and the social sciences* (2nd ed. pp. 94–128). New York: Van Nostrand Reinhold.

Antonucci, T. C., & Akiyama, H. (1987). Social networks in adult life and a preliminary examination of the convoy model. *Journal of Gerontology, 42,* 519–527.

Antonucci, T., Tamir, L. M., & Dubnoff, S. (1980). Mental health across the family life cycle. In K. W. Back (Ed.), *Life course: Integrative theories and exemplary populations* (pp. 37–64). American Association for the Advancement of Science Selected Symposium No. 41. Boulder, CO: Westview Press.

Arenberg, D. (1974). A longitudinal study of problem solving in adults. *Journal of Gerontology, 29,* 650–658.

Arenberg, D., & Robertson-Tchabo, E. A. (1977). Learning and aging. In J. E. Birren & K. W. Schaie (Eds.), *Handbook of the psychology of aging* (pp. 421–449). New York: Van Nostrand Reinhold.

Asher, S., Renshaw, P. D., & Hymel, S. (1982). Peer relationships and the development of social skills. In S. G. Moore & C. R. Cooper (Eds.), *The young child: Reviews of research* (Vol. 3, pp. 137–158). Washington, D. C.: National Association for the Education of Young Children.

Assouline, M., & Meir, E. I. (1987). Meta-analysis of the relationship between congruence and well-being measures. *Journal of Vocational Behavior, 31,* 319–332.

Atchley, R. C. (1989). A continuity theory of normal aging. *The Gerontologist, 29,* 183–190.

Atkinson, J. (1987). Gender roles in marriage and the family: A critique and some proposals. *Journal of Family Issues, 8,* 5–41.

Atkinson, R. (1989). *The long gray line.* Boston: Houghton, Mifflin.

Bakan, D. (1966). *The duality of human existence: Isolation and communion in Western man.* Boston: Beacon.

Baker, P. M. (1985). The status of age: Preliminary results. *Journal of Gerontology, 40,* 506–508.

Balkwell, C. (1981). Transition to widowhood: A review of the literature. *Family Relations, 30,* 117–128.

Balkwell, C. (1985). An attitudinal correlate of the timing of a major life event: The case of morale in widowhood. *Family Relations, 34,* 577–581.

Ball, J. F. (1976-77). Widow's grief: The impact of age and mode of death. *Omega, 7,* 307–333.

Baltes, P. B. (1987). Theoretical propositions of life-span developmental psychology: On the dynamics between growth and decline. *Developmental Psychology, 23,* 611–626.

Baltes, P. B., & Baltes, M. M. (1990, in press). Psychological perspectives on successful aging: The model of selective optimization with compensation. In P. B. Baltes & M. M. Baltes (Eds.), *Successful aging: Perspectives from the behavioral sciences.* New York: Cambridge University Press.

Baltes, P. B., Dittmann-Kohli, F., & Dixon, R. A. (1984). New perspectives on the development of intelligence in adulthood: Toward a dual-process conception and a model of selective optimization with compensation. In P. B. Baltes & O. G. Brim, Jr. (Eds.), *Life-span development and behavior* (Vol. 6, pp. 34–77). New York: Academic Press.

Baltes, P. B., Dittmann-Kohli, F., & Dixon, R. A. (1986). Multidisciplinary propositions on the development of intelligence during adulthood and old age. In A. B. Sorensen, F. E. Weinert, & L. R. Sherrod (Eds.), *Human development and the life course: Multidisciplinary perspectives* (pp. 467–508). Hillsdale, NJ: Lawrence Erlbaum Associates.

Baltes, P. B., Dittmann-Kohli, F., & Kliegl, R. (1986). Reserve capacity of the elderly in aging-sensitive tests of fluid intelligence: Replication and extension. *Psychology and Aging, 1,* 172–177.

Baltes, P. B., & Lindenberger, U. (1988). On the range of cognitive plasticity in old age as a function of experience: 15 years of intervention research. *Behavior Therapy, 19,* 283–300.

Baltes, P. B., & Reese, H. W. (1984). The life-span perspective in developmental psychology. In M. H. Bornstein & M. E. Lamb (Eds.), *Developmental psychology: An advanced textbook* (pp. 493–532). Hillsdale, NJ: Lawrence Erlbaum Associates.

Baltes, P. B., Reese, H. W., & Lipsitt, L. P. (1980). In M. R. Rosenzweig & L. W. Porter (Eds.), *Annual review of psychology* (pp. 65–110). Palo Alto, CA: Annual Reviews, Inc.

Baltes, P. B., Reese, H. W., & Nesselroade, J. R. (1977). *Life-span developmental psychology: Introduction to research methods.* Monterey, Ca: Books/Cole.

Bandura, A. (1989). Human agency in social cognitive theory. *American Psychologist, 44,* 1175–1184.

Bankoff, E. A. (1983). Social support and adaptation to widowhood. *Journal of Marriage and the Family, 45,* 827–839.

Baruch, G., & Barnett, R. C. (1983). Adult daughters' relationships with their mothers. *Journal of Marriage and the Family, 45,* 601–606.

Bass, D. M. (1985). The hospice ideology and success of hospice care. *Research on Aging, 7,* 307–328.

Basseches, M. (1984). *Dialectical thinking and adult development.* Norwood, NJ: Ablex.

Basseches, M. (1989). Dialectical thinking as an organized whole: Comments on Irwin and Kramer. In M. L. Commons, J. D. Sinnott, F. A. Richards, & C. Armon (Eds.), *Adult development: Vol. 1. Comparisons and applications of developmental models* (pp. 161–178). New York: Praeger.

Bateson, M. C. (1989). *Composing a life.* New York: Atlantic Monthly Press.

Baugher, R. J., Burger, C., Smith, R., & Wallston, K. (1989-90). A comparison of terminally ill persons at various time periods to death. *Omega, 20,* 103–115.

Baylor, A. M., & Spirduso, W. W. (1988). Systematic aerobic exercise and components of reaction time in older women. *Journal of Gerontology: PSYCHOLOGICAL SCIENCES, 43,* P121–126.

Bearon, L. B. (1989). No great expectations: The underpinnings of life satisfaction for older women. *The Gerontologist, 29,* 772–784.

Beck, R. W., & Beck, S. H. (1989). The incidence of extended households among middle-aged black and white women. Estimates from a 15-year-panel study. *Journal of Family Issues, 19,* 147–168.

Bell, R. R. (1981). *Worlds of friendship.* Beverly Hills, CA: Sage.

Belloc, N. B. (1973). Relationship of health practices and mortality. *Preventive Medicine, 2,* 67–81.

Belloc, N. B., & Breslow, L. (1972). Relationship of physical health status and health practices. *Preventive Medicine, 1,* 409–421.

Belsky, J., Lang, M. E., & Rovine, M. (1985). Stability and change in marriage across the transition to parenthood: A second study. *Journal of Marriage and the Family, 47,* 855–865.

Belsky, J., Perry-Jenkins, M., & Crouter, A. C. (1985). The work-family interface and marital change across the transition to parenthood. *Journal of Family Issues, 6,* 205–220.

Belsky, J., Spanier, G. B., & Rovine, M. (1983). Stability and change in marriage across the transition to parenthood. *Journal of Marriage and the Family, 45,* 567–577.

Bem, S. L. (1974). The measurement of psychological androgyny. *Journal of Consulting and Clinical Psychology, 42,* 155–162.

Bem, S. L. (1977). On the utility of alternative procedures for assessing psychological androgyny. *Journal of Consulting and Clinical Psychology, 45,* 196–205.

Bender, S. (1989). *Plain and simple. A woman's journey to the Amish.* San Francisco: Harper & Row.

Benfante, R., & Reed, D. (1990). Is elevated serum cholesterol level a risk factor for coronary heart disease in the elderly? *Journal of the American Medical Association, 263,* 393–396.

Bengtson. V. L. (1985). Diversity and symbolism in grandparent roles. In V. L. Bengtson & J. F. Robertson (Eds.), *Grandparenthood* (pp. 11–26). Beverly Hills, CA: Sage.

Bengtson, V. L., Cuellar, J. B., & Ragan, P. K. (1977). Stratum contrasts and similarities in attitudes toward death. *Journal of Gerontology, 32,* 76–88.

Benninger, W. B., & Walsh, W. B. (1980). Holland's theory and non-college-degreed working men and women. *Journal of Vocational Behavior, 17,* 81–88.

Berardo, D. H., Shehan, C. L., & Leslie, G. R. (1987). A residue of tradition: Jobs, careers, and spouses' time in housework. *Journal of Marriage and the Family, 49,* 381–390.

Berkman, L. F. (1985). The relationship of social networks and social support to morbidity and mortality. In S. Cohen & S. L. Syme (Eds.), *Social support and health.* Orlando, FL: Academic Press.

Best, D. L., Williams, J. E., Cloud, J. M. Davis, S. W., Robertson, L. S., Edwards, J. R., Giles, H., & Fowles, J. (1977). Development of sex-trait stereotypes among young children in the United States, England, and Ireland. *Child Development, 48,* 1375–1384.

Betz, E. L. (1984). A study of career patterns of women college graduates. *Journal of Vocational Behavior, 24,* 249–263.

Betz, N. E., & Fitzgerald, L. F. (1987). *The career psychology of women.* Orlando, Fl: Academic Press.

Billings, A. G., & Moos, R. H. (1981). The role of coping responses and social resources in attenuating the stress of life events. *Journal of Behavioral Medicine, 4,* 139–157.

Birchler, G. R., Weiss, R. L., & Vincent, J. P. (1975). Multi-dimensional analyses of social reinforcement exchange between maritally distressed and non-distressed spouse and stranger dyads. *Journal of Personality and Social Psychology, 31,* 348–360.

Birren, J. E., & Schaie, K. W. (Eds.) (1990). *Handbook of the psychology of aging* (3rd ed.). San Diego: Academic Press.

Blau, F. D., & Ferber, M. A. (1985). Women in the labor market: The last twenty years. In L. Larwood, A. H. Stromberg, & B. A. Gutek (Eds.), *Women and work. An annual review* (Vol. 1, pp. 19–49). Beverly Hills, CA: Sage.

Blazer, D., & Palmore, E. (1976). Religion and aging in a longitudinal panel. *The Gerontologist, 16,* 82–84.

Block, J. (1971). *Lives through time.* Berkeley, Calif: Bancroft Books.

Block, M. R. (1982). Professional women: Work pattern as a correlate of retirement satisfaction. In M. Szinovacz (Ed.), *Women's retirement* (pp. 183–194). Beverly Hills, CA: Sage.

Block, M. R., Davidson, J. L., & Grambs, J. D. (1981). *Women over forty. Visions and realities.* New York: Springer.

Bloom, B. L., White, S. W., & Asher, S. J. (1979). Marital disruption as a stressful life event. In C. Levinger & O. C. Moles (Eds.), *Divorce and separation. Context, causes, and consequences* (pp. 184–200). New York: Basic Books.

Bloom, B. S. (1964). *Stability and change in human characteristics.* New York: John Wiley & Sons.

Blumenthal, J. A., Emery, C.F., Madden, D. J., George, L. K., Coleman, R. E., Riddle, M. W., McKee, D. C., Reasoner, J., & Williams, R. S. (1989). Cardiovascular and behavioral effects of aerobic exercise training in healthy older men and women. *Journal of Gerontology: MEDICAL SCIENCES, 44,* M147–157.

Blumstein, P., & Schwartz, P. (1983). *American couples.* New York: William Morrow.

Bondareff, W. (1985). The neural basis of aging. In J. E. Birren & K. W. Schaie (Eds.), *Handbook of the psychology of aging* (2nd ed., pp. 95–112). New York: Van Nostrand Reinhold.

Booth, A., & Edwards, J. N. (1985). Age at marriage and marital instability. *Journal of Marriage and the Family, 47,* 67–75.

Booth, A., & Johnson, D. (1988). Premarital cohabitation and marital success. *Journal of Family Issues, 9,* 255–272.

Booth-Kewley, S. & Friedman, H. S. (1987). Psychological predictors of heart disease: A quantitative review. *Psychological Bulletin, 101,* 343–362.

Bornstein, M. H. (1988). Perceptual development across the life cycle. In M. H. Bornstein & M. E. Lamb (Eds.), *Developmental psychology: An advanced textbook* (2nd ed. pp. 151–204). Hillsdale, NJ: Lawrence Erlbaum Associates.

Bortz, W. M., II. (1982). Disuse and aging. *Journal of the American Medical Association, 248* (September), 1203–1208.

Botwinick, J., & Storandt, M. (1974). *Memory, related functions and age.* Springfield, IL: Charles C. Thomas.

Bossé, R., Aldwin, C. M., Levenson, M. R., & Ekerdt, D. (1987). Mental health differences among retirees and workers: Findings from the Normative Aging Study. *Psychology and Aging, 2,* 383–389.

Bowen, G. L., & Orthner, D. K. (1983). Sex-role congruency and marital quality. *Journal of Marriage and the Family, 45,* 223–230.

Bowlby, J. (1969). *Attachment and loss: Vol. 1. Attachment.* New York: Basic Books.

Bowlby, J. (1973). *Attachment and loss: Vol. 2. Separation, anxiety, and anger.* New York: Basic Books.

Bowlby, J. (1980). *Attachment and loss: Vol. 3. Loss, sadness, and depression.* New York: Basic Books.

Bradburn, N. M. (1969). *The structure of psychological well being.* Chicago: Aldine.

Braveman, N. S. (1987). Immunity and aging immunologic and behavioral perspectives. In M. W. Riley, J. D. Matarazzo, & A. Baum (Eds.), *Perspectives in behavioral medicine. The aging dimension* (pp. 94–124). Hillsdale, NJ: Lawrence Erlbaum Associates.

Bray, D. W., & Howard, A. (1983). The AT&T longitudinal studies of managers. In K. W. Schaie (Ed.), *Longitudinal studies of adult psychological development* (pp. 266–312). New York: Guilford Press.

Brecher, E. M. (1984). *Love, sex, and aging.* Boston, MA: Little, Brown.

Bridges, W. (1980). *Transitions.* Reading, MA: Addison-Wesley.

Brigham, M. C., & Pressley, M. (1988). Cognitive monitoring and strategy choice in younger and older adults. *Psychology and Aging, 3,* 249–257.

Brody, E. B., & Brody, N. (1976). *Intelligence: Nature, determinants and consequences.* New York: Academic Press.

Broman, C. L. (1988). Satisfaction among blacks: The significance of marriage and parenthood. *Journal of Marriage and the Family, 50,* 45–51.

Broverman, I. K., Broverman, D. M., Clarkson, F. E., Rosenkrantz, P. S., & Vogel, S. R. (1970). Sex-role stereotypes and clinical judgments of mental health. *Journal of Consulting and Clinical Psychology, 34,* 1–7.

Broverman, I. K., Vogel, S. R., Broverman, D. M., Clarkson, F. E., & Rosenkrantz, P. S. (1972). Sex-role stereotypes: A current appraisal. *Journal of Social Issues, 28,* 59–78.

Brown, G. W., & Harris, T. (1978). *Social origins of depression.* New York: The Free Press.

Brubaker, T. H. (1985). *Later life families.* Beverly Hills, CA: Sage.

Bruch, M. A., Levo, L. C., & Arisohn, B. A. (1984). Conceptual complexity and skill in marital communications. *Journal of Marriage and the Family, 46,* 927–932.

Burkhauser, R. V., Holden, K. C., & Feaster, D. (1988). Incidence, timing, and events associates with poverty: A dynamic view of poverty in retirement. *Journal of Gerontology: SOCIAL SCIENCES, 43,* S46–52.

Burns, J. D. (1958). *The mammalian cerebral cortex* (E. Arnold, Ed.). Monograph of the Physiological Society, No. 5.

Buss, A. H., & Plomin, R. (1986). The EAS approach to temperament. In R. Plomin & J. Dunn (Eds.), *The study of temperament: Changes, continuities and challenges.* Hillsdale, NJ: Lawrence Erlbaum Associates.

Busse, E. W., & Wang, H. S. (1971). The multiple factors contributing to dementia in old age. In *Proceedings of the Fifth World Congress of Psychiatry.* Mexico City. [Reprinted in E. Palmore (Ed.), *Normal aging II* (pp. 151–159). Durham, NC: Duke University Press, 1974.]

Butler, R.N. (1963). The life review: An interpretation of reminiscence in the aged. *Psychiatry, Journal for the Study of Interpersonal Processes, 26.* Reprinted in B. L. Neugarten (Ed.), *Middle age and aging.* Chicago: University of Chicago Press, 1968.

Butler, R. N. (1968). The facade of chronological age: An interpretative summary. In B. L. Neugarten (Ed.), *Middle age and aging* (pp. 235–242). Chicago: University of Chicago Press.

Buunk, B. P., & van Driel, B. (1989). *Variant lifestyles and relationships.* Newbury Park, CA: Sage.

Campbell, A. (1981). *The sense of well-being in America.* New York: McGraw-Hill.

Campbell, J. (1986). *The inner reaches of outer space.* New York: Harper & Row.

Cantril, H. (1965). *The pattern of human concerns.* New Brunswick, NJ: Rutgers University Press.

Carey, R. G. (1974). Living until death: A program of service and research for the terminally ill. *Hospital Progress.* (Reprinted in E. Kübler-Ross (Ed.), *Death. The final stage of growth,* 1975, Englewood Cliffs, NJ: Prentice Hall).

Cargan, L., & Melko, M. (1982). *Singles. Myths and realities.* Beverly Hills, CA: Sage.

Carp, F. M. (1985). Relevance of personality traits to adjustment in group living situations. *Journal of Gerontology, 40,* 544–551.

Carter, H., & Glick, P. C. (1976). *Marriage and divorce: A social and economic study* (Rev. ed.). Cambridge, MA: Harvard University Press.

Caspi, A., Bem, D. J., & Elder, G. H. Jr., (1989). Continuities and consequences of interactional styles across the life course. *Journal of Personality, 57,* 375–406.

Caspi, A., & Elder, G. H. Jr. (1986). Life satisfaction in old age: Linking social psychology and history. *Journal of Psychology and Aging, 1,* 18–26.

Caspi, A., & Elder, G. H. Jr. (1988). Childhood precursors of the life course: Early personality and life disorganization. In E. M. Hetherington, R. M. Lerner & M. Perlmutter (Eds.), *Child development in life-span perspective* (pp. 115–142). Hillsdale, NJ: Lawrence Erlbaum Associates.

Caspi, A., Elder, G. H. Jr., & Bem, D. J. (1987). Moving against the world: Life-course patterns of explosive children. *Developmental Psychology, 23,* 308–313.

Caspi, A., Elder, G. H., Jr., & Bem, D. J. (1988). Moving away from the world: Life-course patterns of shy children. *Developmental Psychology, 24,* 824–831.

Cassileth, B. R., Lusk, E. J., Miller, D. S., Brown, L. L., & Miller, C. (1985). Psychosocial correlates of survival in advanced malignant disease? *New England Journal of Medicine, 312,* 1551–1555.

Cattell, R. B. (1963). Theory of fluid and crystallized intelligence: A critical experiment. *Journal of Educational Psychology, 54,* 1–22.

Cerella, J. (1985). Information processing rates in the elderly. *Psychological Bulletin, 98,* 67–83.

Charness, N. (Ed.) (1985). *Aging and human performance.* Chichester, England: John Wiley & Sons.

Chase-Lansdale, P. L., & Hetherington, E. M. (1990). The impact of divorce on life-span development: Short and long term effects. In P. B. Baltes, D. L. Featherman, & R. M. Lerner (Eds.). *Life-span development and behavior* (Vol. 10, pp. 107–151). Hillsdale, NJ: Lawrence Erlbaum Associates.

Chatters, L. M., & Taylor, R. J. (1989). Age differences in religious participation among black adults. *Journal of Gerontology: SOCIAL SCIENCES, 44,* S183–189.

Childers, P., & Wimmer, M. (1971). The concept of death in early childhood. *Child Development, 42,* 1299–1301.

Chinen, A. B. (1987). Fairy tales and psychological development in late life: A cross-cultural hermeneutic study. *The Gerontologist, 27,* 340–346.

Chiriboga, D. A. (1984). Social stressors as antecedents of change. *Journal of Gerontology, 39,* 468–477.

Chiriboga, D. A. (1989). Mental health at the midpoint: Crisis, challenge, or relief? In S. Hunter & M. Sundel (Eds.), *Midlife myths. Issues, findings, and practice implications* (pp. 116–194). Newbury Park, CA: Sage.

Chiriboga, D. A., & Cutler, L. (1980). Stress and adaptation: life span perspectives. In L. W. Poon (Ed.), *Aging in the 1980s. Psychological issues* (pp. 347–362). Washington, D.C.: American Psychological Association.

Chiriboga, D. A., & Dean, H. (1978). Dimensions of stress: Perspectives from a longitudinal study. *Journal of Psychosomatic Research, 22,* 47–55.

Chirikos, T. N., & Nestel, G. (1985). Longitudinal analysis of functional disabilities in older men. *Journal of Gerontology, 40,* 426–433.

Cicirelli, V. G. (1982). Sibling influence throughout the lifespan. In M. E. Lamb & B. Sutton-Smith (Eds.), *Sibling relationships.* Hillsdale, NJ: Erlbaum.

Cicirelli, V. G. (1983). Adult children and their elderly parents. In Brubaker, T. H. (Ed.), *Family relationships in later life.* Beverly Hills, CA: Sage.

Cicirelli, V. G. (1989). Feelings of attachment to siblings and well-being in later life. *Psychology and Aging, 4,* 211–216.

Clark, R. L. (1988). The future of work and retirement. *Research on aging, 10,* 169–193.

Clark, R. L., & Sumner, D. A. (1985). Inflation and the real income of the elderly: Recent evidence and expectations for the future. *The Gerontologist, 25,* 147–152.

Clarkson-Smith, L., & Hartley, A. A. (1989). Relationships between physical exercise and cognitive abilities in older adults. *Psychology and Aging, 4,* 183–189.

Clausen, J. A. (1981). Men's occupational careers in the middle years. In D. H. Eichorn, J. A. Clausen, N. Haan, M. P. Honzik, & P. H. Mussen (Eds.), *Present and past in middle life* (pp. 321–354). New York: Academic Press.

Clayton, V. P., & Birren, J. E. (1980). The development of wisdom across the life-span: A reexamination of an ancient topic. In P. B. Baltes & O. G. Brim, Jr., (Eds.), *Life-span development and behavior* (Vol. 3, pp. 104–138). New York: Academic Press.

Cohen, G., & Faulkner, D. (1989). Age differences in source forgetting: Effects on reality monitoring and on eyewitness testimony. *Psychology and Aging, 4,* 10–17.

Cohen, L. H. (1988a). *Life events and psychological functioning. Theoretical and methodological issues.* Newbury Park, CA: Sage.

Cohen, L. H. (1988b). Measurement of life events. In Cohen, L. H. (Ed.), *Life events and psychological functioning. Theoretical and methodological issues* (pp. 11–30). Newbury Park, CA: Sage.

Cohen, S., & Wills, T. A. (1985). Stress, social support, and the buffering hypothesis. *Psychological Bulletin, 98,* 310–357.

Colby, A., Kohlberg, L., Gibbs, J., & Lieberman, M. (1983). A longitudinal study of moral judgment. *Monographs of the Society for Research in Child Development, 48,* (Whole # 200).

Cole, S. (1979). Age and scientific performance. *American Journal of Sociology, 84,* 958–977.

Coleman, L. M., & Antonucci, T. C. (1983). Impact of work on women at midlife. *Developmental Psychology, 19,* 290–294.

Commons, M. L., Armon, C., Richards, F. A., Schrader, D. E., Farrell, E. F., Tappan, M. B., & Bauer, N. F. (1989). A multidomain study of adult development. In M. L. Commons, J. D. Sinnott, F. A. Richards, & C. Armon (Eds.) *Adult development* (Vol. 1, pp. 33–56). *Comparisons and applications of developmental models.* New York: Praeger.

Conger, R. D., Elder, G. H. Jr., Lorenz, F. O., Conger, K. J., Simons, R. L., Whitbeck, L. B., Huck, S., & Melby, J. N. (1990). Linking economic hardship to marital quality and instability. *Journal of Marriage and the Family, 52,* 643–656.

Cooney, T. M., Schaie, K. W., & Willis, S. L. (1988). The relationship between prior functioning on cognitive and personality dimensions and subject attrition in longitudinal research. *Journal of Gerontology: PSYCHOLOGICAL SCIENCES, 43,* P12–17.

Corcoran, M. (1978). Work experience, work interruption, and wages. In G. J. Duncan & J. N. Morgan (Eds.), *Five thousand American families—patterns of economic progress.* Ann Arbor, MI: University of Michigan, Institute for Social Research.

Costa, P. T., Jr., Fozard, J. L., & McCrae, R. R. (1977). Personological interpretation of factors from the Strong Vocational Interest Blank scales. *Journal of Vocational Behavior, 10,* 231–242.

Costa, P. T., Jr., & McCrae, R. R. (1980a). Still stable after all these years: Personality as a key to some issues in adulthood and old age. In P. B. Baltes & O. G. Brim, Jr. (Eds.), *Life-span development and behavior* (pp. 64–103). New York: Academic Press.

Costa, P. T., & McCrae, R. R. (1980b). Influence of extraversion and neuroticism on subjective well-being: Happy and unhappy people. *Journal of Personality and Social Psychology, 38,* 668–678.

Costa, P. T., Jr., & McCrae, R. R. (1983). Psychological maturity and subjective well-being: Toward a new synthesis. *Developmental Psychology, 19,* 243–248.

Costa, P. T., Jr., & McCrae, R. R. (1984). Personality as a lifelong determinant of wellbeing. In C. Z. Malatesta & C. E. Izard (Eds.), *Emotion in adult development* (pp. 141–158). Beverly Hills, CA: Sage Publications.

Costa, P. T., Jr., & McCrae, R. R. (1986). Cross-sectional studies of personality in a national sample: 1. Development and validation of survey measures. *Psychology and Aging, 1,* 140–143.

Costa, P. T., Jr., McCrae, R. R., & Arenberg, D. (1983). Recent longitudinal research on personality and aging. In K. W. Schaie (Ed.), *Longitudinal studies of adult psychological development* (pp. 222–265). New York: Guilford Press.

Costa, P. T., Jr., McCrae, R. R., & Norris, A. H. (1981). Personal adjustment to aging: Longitudinal prediction from neuroticism and extraversion. *Journal of Gerontology, 36,* 78–85.

Costa, P. T., Jr., McCrae, R. R., Zonderman, A. B., Barbano, H. E., Lebowitz, B., & Larson, D. M. (1986). Cross-sectional studies of personality in a national sample: 2. Stability in neuroticism, extraversion, and openness.*Psychology and Aging, 1,* 144–149.

Costa, P. T., Jr., Zonderman, A. B., McCrae, R. R., Cornoni-Huntley, J., Locke, B. Z., & Barbano, H. E. (1987). Longitudinal analyses of psychological well-being in a national sample: Stability of mean levels. *Journal of Gerontology, 42,* 50–55.

Cotton, C. C., & McKenna, J. F. (1988). Husbands' job satisfaction and wives' income. In S. Rose & L. Larwood (Eds.), *Women's careers. Pathways and pitfalls* (pp. 83–94). New York: Praeger.

Coverman, S., & Sheley, J. F. (1986). Change in men's housework and child-care time, 1965–1975. *Journal of Marriage and the Family, 48,* 413–422.

Cowan, C. P., & Cowan, P. A. (1987). Men's involvement in parenthood: Identifying the antecedents and understanding the barriers. In P. W. Berman & F. A. Pedersen (Eds.), *Men's transitions to parenthood. Longitudinal studies of early family experience* (pp. 145–174). Hillsdale, NJ: Lawrence Erlbaum Associates.

Coward, R. T., & Dwyer, J. W. (1990). The association of gender, sibling network composition, and patterns of parent care by adult children. *Research on Aging, 12,* 158–181.

Craik, F. I. M. (1977). Age differences in human memory. In J. E. Birren & K. W. Schaie (Eds.), *Handbook of the psychology of aging.* New York: Van Nostrand Reinhold.

Craik, F. I. M., & Rabinowitz, J. C. (1985). The effects of presentation rate and encoding task on age-related memory deficits. *Journal of Gerontology, 40,* 309–315.

Crandall, J. E. (1984). Social interest as a moderator of life stress. *Journal of Personality and Social Psychology, 47,* 164–174.

Crimmins, E. M. (1984). Life expectancy and the older population: Demographic implications of recent and prospective trends in old age mortality. *Research on Aging, 6,* 490–514.

Cristofalo, V. J. (1988). An overview of the theories of biological aging. In J. E. Birren & V. L. Bengtson (Eds.), *Emergent theories of aging* (pp. 118–127). New York: Springer.

Cumming, E. (1975). Engagement with an old theory. *International Journal of Aging and Human Development, 6,* 187–191.

Cumming, E., & Henry, W. E. (1961). *Growing old.* New York: Basic Books.

Cunningham, J. D., & Antill, J. K. (1984). Changes in masculinity and femininity across the family life cycle: A reexamination. *Developmental Psychology, 20,* 1135–1141.

Cunningham, W. R., & Owens, W. A. Jr. (1983). The Iowa State study of the adult development of intellectual abilities. In K. W. Schaie (Ed.), *Longitudinal studies of adult psychological development* (pp. 20–39). New York: The Guilford Press.

Cutler, S. J., & Grams, A. E. (1988). Correlates of self-reported everyday memory problems. *Journals of Gerontology: SOCIAL SCIENCES, 43,* S82–90.

Cytrynbaum, S., Blum, L., Patrick, R., Stein, J., Wadner, D., & Wilk, C. (1980). Midlife development: A personality and social systems perspective. In L. W. Poon (Ed.), *Aging in the 1980s. Psychological Issues* (pp. 463–474). Washington, D.C.: American Psychological Association.

Daniels, P., & Weingarten, K. (1988). The fatherhood clock. The timing of parenthood in men's lives. In P. Bronstein & C. P. Cowan (Eds.), *Fatherhood today. Men's changing role in the family* (pp. 36–52). New York: Wiley-Interscience.

Dannefer, D. (1984a). Adult development and social theory: A paradigmatic reappraisal. *American Sociological Review, 49,* 100–116.

Dannefer, D. (1984b). The role of the social in life-span developmental psychology, past and future: Rejoinder to Baltes and Nesselroade. *American Sociological Review, 49,* 847–850.

Dannefer, D. (1988). What's in a name? An account of the neglect of variability in the study of aging. In J. E. Birren & V. L. Bengtson (Eds.), *Emergent theories of aging* (pp. 356–384). New York: Springer.

Davidson, B., Balswick, J., & Halverson, C. (1983). Affective self-disclosure and marital adjustment: A test of equity theory. *Journal of Marriage and the Family, 45,* 93–103.

Davis, M. A., Randall, E. Forthofer, R. N., Lee, E. S., & Margen, S. (1985). Living arrangements and dietary patterns of older adults in the United States. *Journal of Gerontology, 40,* 434–442.

Dawber, T. R., Kannel, W. B., & Lyell, L. P. (1963). An approach to longitudinal studies in a community: The Framingham study. *Annals of the New York Academy of Science, 107,* 539–556.

Deaux, K. (1984). From individual differences to social categories: Analysis of a decade's research on gender. *American Psychologist, 39,* 105–116.

Deaux, K., & Lewis, L. L. (1984). The structure of gender stereotypes: Interrelationships among components and gender label. *Journal of Personality and Social Psychology, 46,* 991–1004.

DeLongis, A., Coyne, J. C., Dakof, G., Folkman, S., & Lazarus, R. S. (1982). Relationship of daily hassles, uplifts, and major life events to health status. *Health Psychology, 1,* 119–136.

DeMaris, A., & Leslie, G. R. (1984). Cohabitation with the future spouse: Its influence upon marital satisfaction and communication. *Journal of Marriage and the Family, 46,* 77–84.

Dement, W., Richardson, G., Prinz, P., Carskadon, M., Kripke, D., & Czeisler, C. (1985). Changes of sleep and wakefulness with age. In C. E. Finch & E. L. Schneider (Eds.), *Handbook of the biology of aging* (2nd ed., pp. 692–717). New York: Van Nostrand Reinhold.

Denney, N. W. (1982). Aging and cognitive changes. In B. B. Wolman (Ed.), *Handbook of developmental psychology* (pp. 807–827). Englewood Cliffs, NJ: Prentice Hall.

Denney, N. W. (1984). Model of cognitive development across the life span. *Developmental Review, 4*, 171–191.

Denney N. W., & Heidrich, S. M. (1990). Training effects on Raven's Progressive Matrices in young, middle-aged, and elderly adults. *Psychology and Aging, 5,* 144–145.

Denney, N. W., & Palmer, A. M. (1981). Adult age differences on traditional and practical problem-solving measures. *Journal of Gerontology, 36,* 323–328.

Denney, N. W., & Pearce, K. A. (1989). A developmental study of practical problem solving in adults. *Psychology and Aging, 4,* 438–442.

deTurck, M. A., & Miler, G. R. (1986). The effects of husbands' and wives' social cognition on their marital adjustment, conjugal power, and self-esteem. *Journal of Marriage and the Family, 48,* 715–724.

Dewit, D. J., Wister, A. V., & Burch, T. K. (1988). Physical distance and social contacts between elders and their adult children. *Research on Aging, 10,* 56–80.

Diamond, A. M. Jr. (1986). The life-cycle research productivity of mathematicians and scientists. *Journal of Gerontology, 41,* 520–525.

Dickens, W. J., & Perlman, D. (1981). Friendship over the life-cycle. In S. Duck & R. Gilmour (Eds.), *Personal relationships 2. Developing personal relationships* (pp. 91–122). New York: Academic Press.

Diener, E. (1984). Subjective well-being. *Psychological Bulletin, 95,* 542–575.

Dimond, M., Lund, D. A., & Caserta, M. S. (1987). The role of social support in the first two years of bereavement in an elderly sample. *The Gerontologist, 27,* 599–604.

Dixon, R. A., & Lerner, R. M. (1988). A history of systems in developmental psychology. In M. H. Bornstein & M. E. Lamb (Eds.), *Developmental psychology: An advanced textbook* (2nd ed., pp. 3–50). Hillsdale, NJ: Lawrence Erlbaum Associates.

Dobson, C. (1983). Sex-role and marital-role expectations. In T. H. Brubaker (Ed.), *Family relationships in later life.* Beverly Hills, CA: Sage.

Doherty, W. J., & Jacobson, N. S. (1982). Marriage and the family. In B. B. Wolman (Ed.), *Handbook of developmental psychology* (pp. 667–680). Englewood Cliffs, NJ: Prentice Hall.

Doherty, W. J., Su, S., & Needle, R. (1989). Marital disruption and psychological well-being: A panel study. *Journal of Family Issues, 10,* 72–85.

Dohrenwend, B. S., & Dohrenwend, P. B. (1978). Some issues in research on stressful life events. *The Journal of Nervous and Mental Disease, 166,* 7–15.

Dohrenwend, B. S., & Dohrenwend, B. P. (1980). What is a stressful life event? In H. Selye (Ed.), *Selye's guide to stress research,* Vol. 1 (pp. 1–20). New York: Van Nostrand Reinhold.

Dohrenwend, B. S., & Dohrenwend, B. P. (1981). Life stress and illness: Formulation of the issues. In B. S. Dohrenwend & P. B. Dohrenwend (Eds.), *Stressful life events and their contexts.* New York: Watson.

Dolinsky, A. L., & Rosenwaike, I. (1988). The role of demographic factors in the institutionalization of the elderly. *Research on Aging, 10,* 235–357.

Doty, R. L., Shaman, P., & Dann, M. (1984). Development of the University of Pennsylvania Smell Identification Test: A standardized microencapsulated test of olfactory function. *Physiology and Behavior, 32,* 489–502.

Dressel, P. L. (1988). Gender, race, and class: Beyond the feminization of poverty in later life. *The Gerontologist, 28,* 177–180.

Duara, R., London, E. D., & Rapoport, S. I. (1985). Changes in structure and energy metabolism of the aging brain. In C. E. Finch & E. L. Schneider (Eds.), *Handbook of the biology of aging* (2nd ed., pp. 595–616). New York: Van Nostrand Reinhold.

Duncan, G. J., & Morgan, J. N. (1985). The panel study of income dynamics. In G. H. Elder Jr. (Ed.), *Life course dynamics. Trajectories and transitions, 1968–1980* (pp. 50–74). Ithaca: Cornell University Press.

Dunn, J. (1984). Sibling studies and the developmental impact of critical incidents. In P. B. Baltes & O. G. Brim, Jr. (Eds.), *Life-span development and behavior* (Vol. 6, pp. 335–355). Orlando, FL: Academic Press.

Durlak, J. A. (1972). Relationship between attitudes toward life and death among elderly women. *Developmental Psychology, 8,* 146.

Duvall, E. M. (1962). *Family development* (2nd ed.). New York: Lippincott.

Duvall, E. M. (1971). *Family Development* (5th ed.) Philadelphia: Lippincott.

Duvall, E. M. (1988). Family development's first forty years. *Family Relations, 37,* 127–134.

Eberhardt, B. J., & Muchinsky, P. M. (1984). Structural validation of Holland's hexagonal model: Vocational classification through the use of biodata. *Journal of Applied Psychology, 69,* 174–181.

Eichorn, D. H., Clausen, J. A., Haan, N., Honzik, M. P., & Mussen, P. H. (Eds.) (1981). *Present and past in middle life.* New York: Academic Press.

Eichorn, D. H., Hunt, J. V., & Honzik, M. P. (1981). In D. H. Eichorn, J. A. Clausen, N. Haan, M. P. Honzik, & P. H. Mussen (Eds.), *Present and past in middle life* (pp. 89–116). New York: Academic Press.

Eisdorfer, C., & Raskind, M. (1975). Aging, hormones and human behavior. In B. Eleftheriou & R. Sprott (Eds.), *Hormonal correlates of behavior: Vol. I, A lifespan view* (pp. 369–314). New York: Plenum Press.

Eisdorfer, C., & Wilkie, F. (1972). Auditory changes. *Journal of the American Geriatrics Society, 20,* 377–382.

Ekerdt, D. J. (1987). Why the notion persists that retirement harms health. *The Gerontologist, 27,* 454–457.

Elder, G. H., Jr. (1974). *Children of the great depression.* Chicago: University of Chicago Press.

Elder, G. H., Jr. (1978). Family history and the life course. In T. Hareven (Ed.), *Transitions: The family and the life course in historical perspective* (pp. 17–64). New York: Academic Press.

Elder, G. H., Jr., Caspi, A., & Downey, G. (1986). Problem behavior and family relationships: Life course and intergenerational themes. In A. B. Sorensen, F. E. Weinert, & L. R. Sherrod (Eds.), *Human development and the life course: Multidisciplinary perspectives* (pp. 293–340). Hillsdale, NJ: Lawrence Erlbaum Associates.

Elder, G. H., Jr., Liker, J. K., & Cross, C. E. (1984). Parent-child behavior in the Great Depression: Life course and intergenerational influences. In P. B. Baltes & O. G. Brim, Jr. (Eds.), *Life-span development and behavior* (Vol. 6). New York: Academic Press.

Elman, M. R., & Gilbert, L. A. (1984). Coping strategies for role conflict in married professional women with children. *Family Relations, 33,* 37–327.

Elsayed, M., Ismail, A. H., & Young, R. S. (1980). Intellectual differences of adult men related to age and physical fitness before and after an exercise program. *Journal of Gerontology, 35,* 383–387.

Emery, C. F., & Gatz, M. (1990). Psychological and cognitive effects of an exercise program for community-residing older adults. *The Gerontologist, 30,* 184–192.

Erbes, J. T., & Hedderson, J. J. C. (1984). A longitudinal examination of the separation/divorce process. *Journal of Marriage and the Family, 46,* 937–941.

Erdwins, C. J., & Mellinger, J. C. (1984). Mid-life women: Relation of age and role to personality. *Journal of Personality and Social Psychology, 47,* 390–395.

Erdwins, C. J., Tyler, Z. E., & Mellinger, J. C. (1983). A comparison of sex role and related personality traits in young, middle-aged, and older women. *International Journal of Aging and Human Development, 17,* 141–152.

Erikson, E. H. (1950). *Childhood and society.* New York: Norton. (Reissued 1963).

Erikson, E. H. (1959). *Identity and the life cycle.* New York: International Universities Press. (Reissued by Norton, 1980).

Erikson, E. H. (1968). *Identity: youth and crisis.* New York: W. W. Norton.

Erikson, E. H. (1980). Themes of adulthood in the Freud-Jung correspondence. In N. J. Smelser & E. H. Erikson (Eds.), *Themes of work and love in adulthood* (pp. 43–76). Cambridge, MA: Harvard University Press.

Erikson, E. H., Erikson, J. M., & Kivnick, H. Q. (1986). *Vital involvement in old age.* New York: W. W. Norton.

Eron, L. D. (1987). The development of aggressive behavior from the perspective of a developing behaviorism. *American Psychologist, 42,* 435–442.

Eron, L. D., Huesmann, L. R., Dubow, E., Romanoff, R., & Yarmel, P. (1987). Aggression and its correlates over 22 years. In D. Crowell, I. Evans, & C. O'Donnell (Eds.), *Childhood aggression and violence: Sources of influence, prevention and control* (pp. 249–262). New York: Plenum Press.

Estes, R. J., & Wilensky, H. L. (1978). Life cycle squeeze and the morale curve. *Social Problems, 25* (No. 3)., 277–292.

Evans, D. A., Funkenstein, H. H., Albert, M. S., Scherr, P. A., Cook, N. R., Chown, M. J., Hebert, L. E., Hennekens, C. H., & Taylor, J. O. (1989). Prevalence of Alzheimer's disease in a community population of older persons. *Journal of the American Medical Association, 262,* 2551–2556.

Evans, G. W., Brennan, P. L., Skorpanich, M. A., & Held, D. (1984). Cognitive mapping and elderly adults: Verbal and location memory for urban landmarks. *Journal of Gerontology, 39,* 452–457.

Evans, L. (1988). Older driver involvement in fatal and severe traffic crashes. *Journal of Gerontology: SOCIAL SCIENCES, 43,* S186–193.

Evans, L., Ekerdt, D. J., & Bossé, R. (1985). Proximity to retirement and anticipatory involvement: Findings from the Normative Aging Study. *Journal of Gerontology, 40,* 368–374.

Evans, R. I. (1969). *Dialogue with Erik Erikson.* New York: Dutton.

Farmer, Y. M., Reis, L. M., Nickinovich, D. G., Kamo, Y., & Borgatta, E. F. (1990). The status attainment model and income. *Research on aging, 12,* 113–132.

Farrell, M. P., & Rosenberg, S. D. (1981). *Men at midlife.* Boston: Auburn House.

Featherman, D. L. (1980). Schooling and occupational careers: Constancy and change in worldly success. In O. G. Brim, Jr. & J. Kagan (Eds.), *Constancy and change in human development* (pp. 675–738). Cambridge, MA: Harvard University Press.

Featherman, D. L. (1983). Life-span perspectives in social science research. In P. B. Baltes & O. G. Brim, Jr., (Eds.), *Life-span development and behavior* (Vol. 5, pp. 1–59) New York: Academic Press.

Featherman, D. L., & Hauser, R. M. (1975). Design for a replicate study of social mobility in the United States. In K. Land & S. Spilerman (Eds.), *Social indicator models.* New York: Russell Sage Foundation.

Feifel, H. (1990). Psychology and death. Meaningful rediscovery. *American Psychologist, 45,* 537–543.

Feifel, H., & Branscomb, A. B. (1973). Who's afraid of death? *Journal of Abnormal Psychology, 81,* 282–288.

Feifel, H., & Strack, S. (1989). Coping with conflict situations: Middle-aged and elderly men. *Psychology and Aging, 4,* 26–33.

Feldman, S. S., & Aschenbrenner, B. (1983). Impact of parenthood on various aspects of masculinity and femininity: A short-term longitudinal study. *Developmental Psychology, 19,* 278–289.

Fendrich, M. (1984). Wives' employment and husbands' distress: A meta-analysis and a replication. *Journal of Marriage and the Family, 46,* 871–879.

Ferraro, K. R. (1984). Widowhood and social participation in later life: isolation or compensation? *Research on Aging, 6,* 451–468.

Field, D., Schaie, K. W., & Leino, E. V. (1988). Continuity in intellectual functioning: The role of self-reported health. *Psychology and Aging, 3,* 385–392.

Filsinger, E. E., & Thoma, S. J. (1988). Behavioral antecedents of relationship stability and adjustment: A five-year longitudinal study. *Journal of Marriage and the Family, 50,* 785–795.

Finch, C. E. (1986). Issues in the analysis of interrelationships between the individual and the environment during aging. In A. B. Sorensen, F. E. Weinert, & L. R. Sherrod (Eds.), *Human development and the life course: Multidisciplinary perspectives* (pp. 17–30). Hillsdale, NJ: Lawrence Erlbaum Associates.

Finch, C. E. (1988). Aging in the female reproductive system: A model system for analysis of complex interactions during aging. In J. E. Birren & V. L. Bengtson (Eds.), *Emergent theories of aging* (pp. 128–152). New York: Springer.

Finley, N. J. (1989). Theories of family labor as applied to gender differences in caregiving for elderly parents. *Journal of Marriage and the Family, 51,* 79–86.

Fischer, C. S., & Phillips, S. L. (1982). Who is alone? Social characteristics of people with small networks. In L. A. Peplau & D. Perlman (Eds.), *Loneliness* (pp. 21–39). New York: Wiley.

Fischman, J. (1987, February). Type A on trial. *Psychology Today, 21,* 42–50.

Fiske, M. (1980). Changing hierarchies of commitment in adulthood. In N. J. Smelser & E. H. Erikson (Eds.), *Themes of work and love in adulthood* (pp. 238–264). Cambridge, MA: Harvard University Press.

Fitzpatrick, J. L., & Silverman, T. (1989). Women's selection of careers in engineering: Do traditional-nontraditional differences still exist? *Journal of Vocational Behavior, 34,* 266–278.

Flavell, J. H. (1970). Developmental studies of mediated memory. In H. W. Reese & L. P. Lipsitt (Eds.), *Advances in child development and behavior* (pp. 181–211). New York: Academic Press.

Folkman, S., Lazarus, R. S., Pimley, S., & Novacek, J. (1987). Age differences in stress and coping processes. *Psychology and Aging, 2,* 171–184.

Fordyce, M. W. (1977). Development of a program to increase personal happiness. *Journal of Counseling Psychology, 24,* 511–521.

Fowler, J. W. (1981). *Stages of faith.* New York: Harper & Row.

Fowler, J. W. (1983, November). Stages of faith. PT conversation with James Fowler. *Psychology Today, 17,* 56–62.

Fozard, J. L., Metter, E. J., & Brant, L. J. (1990). Next steps in describing aging and disease in longitudinal studies. *Journal of Gerontology: PSYCHOLOGICAL SCIENCES, 45,* P116–127.

Frank, S. J., Avery, C. B., & Laman, M. S. (1988). Young adults' perceptions of their relationships with their parents: Individual differences in connectedness, competence, and emotional autonomy. *Developmental Psychology, 24,* 729–737.

Frankl, V. E. (1984). *Man's search for meaning* (3rd ed.). New York: Simon & Schuster.

Frazier, P. H., & Foss-Goodman, D. (1988–89). Death anxiety and personality: Are they truly related? *Omega, 19,* 265–274.

Friedman, M., & Rosenman, R. H. (1974). *Type A behavior and your heart.* New York: Knopf.

Furstenberg, F. F. Jr., Brooks-Gunn, J., & Morgan, S. P. (1987). *Adolescent mothers in later life.* Cambridge: Cambridge University Press.

Ganellen, R. J., & Blaney, P. H. (1984). Hardiness and social support as moderators of the effects of life stress. *Journal of Personality and Social Psychology, 47* 156–163.

Geerken, M., & Gove, W. R. (1983). *At home and at work. The family's allocation of labor.* Beverly Hills, CA: Sage.

George, L. K., Okun, M. A., & Landerman, R. (1985). Age as a moderator of the determinants of life satisfaction. *Research on Aging, 7,* 209–234.

Gesser, G., Wong, P. T. P., & Reker, G. T. (1987–88). Death attitudes across the life-span: The development and validation of the death attitude profile (DAP). *Omega, 18,* 113–128.

Gibson, D. M. (1986). Interaction and well-being in old age: is it quantity or quality that counts? *International Journal of Aging and Human Development, 24,* 29–40.

Giele, J. Z. (1982a). Women in adulthood: Unanswered questions. In J. Z. Giele (Ed.), *Women in the middle years* (pp. 1–36). New York: Wiley.

Giele, J. Z. (1982b). Women's work and family roles. In J. Z. Giele (Ed.), *Women in the middle years* (pp. 115–150). New York: Wiley.

Gilligan, C. (1977). In a different voice: women's conceptions of the self and of morality. *Harvard Educational Review, 47,* 481–517.

Gilligan, C. (1982). *In a different voice: Psychological theory and women's development.* Cambridge, MA: Harvard University Press.

Gilmour, R., & Duck, S. (1986). *The emerging field of personal relationships.* Hillsdale, NJ: Lawrence Erlbaum Associates.

Ginsberg, D., & Gottman, J. (1986). Conversations of college roommates: similarities and differences in male and female friendships. In J. M. Gottman & J. G. Parker (Eds.), *Conversations of friends. Speculations on affective development* (pp. 241–291). Cambridge, England: Cambridge University Press.

Glenn, N. D., & McLanahan, S. (1981). The effects of offspring on the psychological well-being of older adults. *Journal of Marriage and the Family, 43,* 409–421.

Glenn, N. D., & Weaver, C. N. (1981). The contribution of marital happiness to global happiness. *Journal of Marriage and the Family, 43,* 161–168.

Glenn, N. D., & Weaver, C. N. (1985). Age, cohort, and reported job satisfaction in the United States. In A. S. Blau (Ed.), *Current perspectives on aging and the life cycle. A research annual.* Vol 1, (pp. 89–110). *Work, retirement and social policy.* Greenwich, CT: Jai Press.

Glick, P. C. (1977). Updating the life cycle of the family. *Journal of Marriage and the Family, 39,* 5–13.

Glick, P. C. (1979). The future of the American family. *Current Population Reports* (Special Studies Series P-23, No. 78). Washington, D. C.: U.S. Government Printing Office.

Glick, P. C. (1984). Marriage, divorce, and living arrangements. Prospective changes. *Journal of Family Issues, 5,* 7–26.

Glick, P. C. (1989). The family life cycle and social change. *Family Relations, 38,* 123–129.

Glick, P. C., & Lin, S. (1986). Recent changes in divorce and remarriage. *Journal of Marriage and the Family, 48,* 737–747.

Glueck, S., & Glueck, E. (1950). *Unraveling juvenile delinquency.* New York: The Commonwealth Fund.

Glueck, S., & Glueck, E. (1968). *Delinquents and nondelinquents in perspective.* Cambridge, MA: Harvard University Press.

Goetting, A. (1986). The developmental tasks of siblingship over the life cycle. *Journal of Marriage and the Family, 48,* 703–714.

Golant, S. M. (1987). Residential moves by elderly persons to U.S. central cities, suburbs, and rural areas. *Journal of Gerontology, 42,* 534–539.

Goldberg, E. L., & Comstock, G. W. (1980). Epidemiology of life events: Frequency in general populations. *American Journal of Epidemiology, 111,* 736–752.

Goldberg, E. L., Comstock, G. W., & Harlow, S. D. (1988). Emotional problems and widowhood. *Journal of Gerontology: SOCIAL SCIENCES, 43,* S206–208.

Goldberger, L., & Breznitz, S. (Eds.). (1982). *Handbook of stress. Theoretical and clinical aspects.* New York: The Free Press.

Goodwin, D. W. (1984). Studies of familial alcoholism: A growth industry. In D. W. Goodwin, K. T. Van Dusen, & S. A. Mednick (Eds.), *Longitudinal research in alcoholism* (pp. 97–106). Boston: Kluwer-Nijhoff Publishing.

Gottman, J. M., & Levenson, R. W. (1984). Why marriages fail: affective and physiological patterns in marital interaction. In J. C. Masters & K. Yarkin-Levin (Eds.), *Boundary areas in social and developmental psychology.* New York: Academic Press.

Gottman, J. M., & Porterfield, A. L. (1981). Communicative competence in the nonverbal behavior of married couples. *Journal of Marriage and the Family, 43,* 817–824.

Gould, R. (1978). *Transformations: Growth and change in adult life.* New York: Simon & Schuster.

Gould, R. (1980). Transformations during early and middle adult years. In N. J. Smelser & E. H. Erikson (Eds.), *Themes of work and love in adulthood* (pp. 213–237). Cambridge, MA: Harvard University Press.

Gove, W. R. (1972). Sex roles, marital roles, and mental illness. *Social Forces, 51,* 34–44.

Gove, W. R. (1979). Sex, marital status, and psychiatric treatment: A research note. *Social Forces, 58,* 89–93.

Gove, W. R., & Geerken, M. R. (1977). The effect of children and employment on the mental health of married men and women. *Social Forces, 56,* 66–76.

Gove, W. R., Style, C. B., & Hughes, M. (1990). The effect of marriage on the well-being of adults: A theoretical analysis. *Journal of Family Issues, 11,* 4–35.

Greene, A. L., & Boxer, A. M. (1986). Daughters and sons as young adults: Restructuring the ties that bind. In N. Datan, A. L. Greene, & H. W. Reese (Eds.), *Life-span developmental psychology. Intergenerational relations* (pp. 125–150). Hillsdale, NJ: Lawrence Erlbaum Associates.

Greenstein, T. N. (1986). Social-psychological factors in perinatal labor-force participation. *Journal of Marriage and the Family, 48,* 565–571.

Greenstein, T. N. (1990). Marital disruption and the employment of married women. *Journal of Marriage and the Family, 52,* 657–676.

Greer, D. S., Mor, V., Morris, J. N., Sherwood, S., Kidder, D., & Birnbaum, H. (1986). An alternative in terminal care: Results of the National Hospice Study. *Journal of Chronic Diseases, 39,* 9–26.

Greer, S., Morris, T., & Pettingale, K. W. (1979). Psychological response to breast cancer: Effect on outcome. *Lancet, 2,* 785–787.

Guillen, M. A. (1984, October). The face of change. *Psychology Today, 18 (10),* 76–77.

Guralnick, J. M., LaCroix, A. Z., Everett, D. F., & Kovar, M. G. (1989). Aging in the eighties: The prevalence of comorbidity and its association with disability. *National Center for Health Statistics, Advance Data,* # 170, May 26, 1989.

Gurin, P., & Brim, O. G., Jr. (1984). Change in self in adulthood: The example of a sense of control. In P. B. Baltes & O. G. Brim, Jr. (Eds.), *Life-span development and behavior* (Vol. 6, pp. 282–334). Orlando, FL: Academic Press.

Gutmann, D. (1975). Parenthood: A key to the comparative study of the life cycle. In N. Datan & L. H. Ginsberg (Eds.), *Life-span developmental psychology. Normative life crises* (pp. 167–184). New York: Academic Press.

Gutmann, D. (1977). The cross-cultural perspective: Notes toward a comparative psychology of aging. In J. E. Birren & K. W. Schaie (Eds.), *Handbook of the psychology of aging* (pp. 302–326). New York: Van Nostrand Reinhold.

Gutmann, D. (1987). *Reclaimed powers. Toward a new psychology of men and women in later life.* New York: Basic Books.

Gwartney-Gibbs, P. A. (1988). Women's work experience and the "rusty skills" hypothesis: A reconceptualization and reevaluation of the evidence. In B. A. Gutek, A. H. Stromberg, & L. Larwood (Eds.), *Women and work. An annual review* (Vol. 3, pp. 169–188). Newbury Park, CA: Sage.

Haan, N. (1976). ". . . change and sameness . . ." reconsidered. *International Journal of Aging and Human Development, 7,* 59–65.

Haan, N. (1981). Common dimensions of personality development: Early adolescence to middle life. In D. H. Eichorn, J. A. Clausen, N. Haan, M. P. Honzik, & P. H. Mussen (Eds), *Present and past in middle life* (pp. 117–153). New York: Academic Press.

Haan, N. (1982). The assessment of coping, defense, and stress. In L. Goldberger & S. Breznitz (Eds.), *Handbook of stress. Theoretical and clinical aspects.* New York: The Free Press.

Haan, N., Millsap, R., & Hartka, E. (1986). As time goes by: Change and stability in personality over fifty years. *Psychology and Aging, 1,* 220–232.

Hagestad, G. O. (1979). *Patterns of communication and influence between grandparents and grandchildren in a changing society.* Paper presented at the World Congress of Sociology, Uppsala, Sweden.

Hagestad, G. O. (1984). The continuous bond: A dynamic, multigenerational perspective on parent-child relations between adults. In M. Perlmutter (Ed.), *Minnesota symposia on child psychology* (Vol. 17, pp. 129–158). Hillsdale, NJ: Erlbaum.

Hagestad, G. O. (1985). Continuity and connectedness. In V. L. Bengtson (Ed.), *Grandparenthood* (pp. 31–48). Beverly Hills, CA: Sage.

Hagestad, G. O. (1988). Demographic change and the life course: Some emerging trends in the family realm. *Family Relations, 37,* 405–410.

Hagestad, G. O., & Neugarten, B. L. (1985). Age and the life course. In R. H. Binstock & E. Shanas (Eds.), *Handbook of aging and the social sciences* (2nd ed., pp. 35–61). New York: Van Nostrand Reinhold.

Haight, B. K. (1988). The therapeutic role of a structured life review process in homebound elderly subjects. *Journal of gerontology: PSYCHOLOGICAL SCIENCES, 43,* P40–44.

Halford, W. K., Hahlweg, K., & Dunne, M. (1990). The cross-cultural consistency of marital communication associated with marital distress. *Journal of Marriage and the Family, 52,* 487–500.

Hall, D. T. (1972). A model of coping with role conflict: The role behavior of college educated women. *Administrative Science Quarterly, 17,* 471–486.

Hall, D. T. (1975). Pressures from work, self, and home in the life stages of married women. *Journal of Vocational Behavior, 6,* 121–132.

Hansen, J. E., & Schuldt, W. J. (1984). Marital self-disclosure and marital satisfaction. *Journal of Marriage and the Family, 46* 923–926.

Haring, M. J., Okun, M. A., & Stock, W. A. (1984). A quantitative synthesis of literature on work status and subjective well being. *Journal of Vocational Behavior, 25,* 316–324.

Haring-Hidore, M., Stock, W. A., Okun, M. A., & Witter, R. A. (1985). Marital status and subjective well-being: A research synthesis. *Journal of Marriage and the Family, 47,* 947–953.

Harkins, S. W., & Warner, M. H. (1980). Age and pain. In C. Eisdorfer (Ed.), *Annual review of gerontology & geriatrics* (Vol. 1). New York: Springer.

Harman, S. M., & Talbert, G. B. (1985). Reproductive aging. In C. E. Finch & E. L. Schneider (Eds.), *Handbook of the biology of aging* (2nd ed., pp. 457–510). New York: Van Nostrand Reinhold.

Harney, M. K., & Brigham, T. A. (1985). Tolerance of aversive stimuli in relation to life change. *Journal of Behavioral Medicine, 8,* 21–35.

Harriman, L. C. (1983). Personal and marital changes accompanying parenthood. *Family Relations, 32,* 387–394.

Harris, L. (1981). *Aging in the eighties: America in transition.* Washington, D. C.: National Council on the Aging.

Harris, R. L., Ellicott, A. M., & Holmes, D. S. (1986). The timing of psychosocial transitions and changes in women's lives: An examination of women aged 45 to 60. *Journal of Personality and Social Psychology, 51,* 409–416.

Hartley, A. A., & Anderson, J. W. (1986). Instruction, induction, generation, and evaluation of strategies for solving search problems. *Journal of Gerontology, 41,* 650–658.

Hartnell, J. M., Morley, J. E., & Mooradian, A. D. (1989). Reduction of alkali-induced white blood cell DNA unwinding rate: A potential biomarker of aging. *Journal of Gerontology: BIOLOGICAL SCIENCES, 44,* B125–B130.

Hartup, W. W. (1975). The origins of friendships. In M. Lewis & L. A. Rosenblum (Eds.), *Friendship and peer relations.* New York: John Wiley & Sons.

Hauser, R. M., & Dickinson, P. J. (1974). Inequality on occupational status and income. *American Educational Research Journal, 11,* 161–168.

Hausman, P. B., & Weksler, M. E. (1985). Changes in the immune response with age. In C. E. Finch & E. L. Schneider (Eds.), *Handbook of the biology of aging* (2nd ed., pp. 414–432). New York: Van Nostrand Reinhold.

Havighurst, R. J. (1982). The world of work. In B. B. Wolman (Ed.), *Handbook of developmental psychology* (pp. 771–787). Englewood Cliffs, NJ: Prentice Hall.

Hayflick, L. (1965). The limited *in vitro* lifetime of human diploid cell strains. *Experimental Cell Research, 37,* 614–636.

Hayflick, L. (1975). Why grow old? *The Stanford Magazine, 3* (1), 36–43.

Hayflick, L. (1977). The cellular basis for biological aging. In C. E. Finch & L. Hayflick (Eds.), *Handbook of the biology of aging* (pp. 159–186). New York: Van Nostrand Reinhold.

Hayflick, L. (1987). Origins of longevity. In H. R. Warner, R. N. Butler, R. L. Sprott, & E. L. Schneider (Eds.), *Aging: Vol 31. Modern biological theories of aging.* New York: Raven Press.

Hayward, M. D., Grady, W. R., & McLaughlin, S. D. (1988). The retirement process among older women in the United States. Changes in the 1970s. *Research on Aging, 10,* 358–382.

Hayward, M. D., & Hardy, M. A. (1985). Early retirement processes among older men: Occupational differences. *Research on Aging, 7,* 491–518.

Headey, B., & Wearing, A. (1989). Personality, life events, and subjective well-being: Toward a dynamic equilibrium model. *Journal of Personality and Social Psychology, 47,* 731–739.

Heaton, T. B., & Pratt, E. L. (1990). The effects of religious homogamy on marital satisfaction and stability. *Journal of Family Issues, 11,* 191–207.

Helson, R., Mitchell, V., & Moane, G. (1984). Personality and patterns of adherence and nonadherence to the social clock. *Journal of Personality and Social Psychology, 46,* 1079–1096.

Helson, R., & Moane, G. (1987). Personality change in women from college to midlife. *Journal of Personality and Social Psychology, 53.*

Hennig, M., & Jardim, A. (1976). *The Managerial Woman.* Garden City, N.Y.: Doubleday (Anchor Books).

Herzog, A. R., & Rogers, W. L. (1989). Age differences in memory performance and memory ratings as measured in a sample survey. *Psychology and Aging, 4,* 173–182.

Herzog, A. R., & Schaie, K. W. (1986). Stability and change in adult intelligence: 1. Analysis of longitudinal covariance structures. *Psychology and Aging, 1,* 159–171.

Herzog, A. R., & Schaie, K. W. (1988). Stability and change in adult intelligence: 2. Simultaneous analysis of longitudinal means and covariance structures. *Psychology and Aging, 3,* 122–130.

Hetherington, E. M., & Camara, K. A. (1984). Families in transition: The processes of dissolution and reconstitution. In R. D. Parke, R. N. Emde, H. P. McAdoo, & G. P. Sackett (Eds.), *Review of child development research: Vol. 7. The family* (pp. 398–440). Chicago: University of Chicago Press.

Hetherington, E. M., Cox, M., & Cox, R. (1978). The aftermath of divorce. In J. H. Stevens, Jr., & M. Matthews (Eds.), *Mother-child, father-child relations* (pp. 149–176). Washington, D.C.: National Association for the Education of Young Children.

Hill, M. S. (1988). Marital stability and spouses' shared time: A multidisciplinary hypothesis. *Journal of Family Relations, 9,* 427–451.

Hill, R. (1965). Decision making and the family life cycle. In E. Shanas & G. F. Streib (Eds.), *Social structure and the family: Generational relations* (pp. 114–126). Englewood Cliffs, NJ: Prentice Hall.

Hill, R. (1986). Life cycle stages for types of single parent families: Of family development theory. *Family Relations, 35,* 19–30.

Hinton, J. (1975). The influence of previous personality on reactions to having terminal cancer. *Omega, 6,* 95–111.

Hodgkinson, V., Weitzman, M., & the Gallup Organization Inc. (1988). *Giving and volunteering in the United States: 1988 edition.* Washington, D. C.: Independent Sector.

Hofferth, S. L. (1987). Social and economic consequences of teenage childbearing. In S. L. Hofferth & C. D. Hayes (Eds.), *Risking the future. Adolescent sexuality, pregnancy, and childbearing. Working papers* (pp. 123–146). Washington, D.C.: National Academy Press.

Hoffman, L. W., & Manis, J. D. (1978). Influences of children on marital interaction and parental satisfactions and dissatisfactions. In R. M. Lerner & G. B. Spanier (Eds.), *Child influences on marital and family interaction* (pp. 165–214). New York: Academic Press.

Hogan, D. P. (1978). The variable order of events in the life course. *American Sociological Review, 43,* 573–586.

Holahan, C. J., & Moos, R. H. (1990). Life stressors, resistance factors, and improved psychological functioning: An extension of the stress resistance paradigm. *Journal of Personality and Social Psychology, 58,* 909–917.

Holahan, C. K. (1988). Relation of life goals at age 70 to activity participation and health and psychological well-being among Terman's gifted men and women. *Psychology and Aging, 3,* 286–291.

Holahan, C. K., Holahan, C. J., & Belk, S. S. (1984). Adjustment in aging: The roles of life stress, hassles, and self-efficacy. *Health Psychology, 3,* 315–328.

Holland, J. L. (1973). *Making vocational choices: A theory of careers.* Englewood Cliffs, NJ: Prentice Hall.

Holland, J. L. (1985). *Making vocational choices* (2nd ed.). Englewood Cliffs, NJ: Prentice Hall.

Holloszy, J. O. (1988). Minireview: Exercise and longevity: Studies on rats. *Journal of Gerontology: BIOLOGICAL SCIENCES, 43,* B149–151.

Holmes, T. H., & Rahe, R. H. (1967). The Social Readjustment Rating Scale. *Journal of Psychosomatic Research, 11,* 213–218.

Horn, J. C. (1988, December). The peak years. *Psychology Today, 22,* 62–63.

Horn, J. L. (1982). The aging of human abilities. In B. B. Wolman (Ed.), *Handbook of developmental psychology* (pp. 847–870). Englewood Cliffs, NJ: Prentice Hall.

Horn, J. L., & Donaldson, G. (1980). Cognitive development in adulthood. In O. G. Brim, Jr., & J. Kagan (Eds.), *Constancy and change in human development* (pp. 415–529). Cambridge, MA: Harvard University Press.

Horner, K. W., Rushton, J. P., & Vernon, P. A. (1986). Relation between aging and research productivity of academic psychologists. *Psychology and Aging, 1,* 319–324.

Hotard, S. R., McFatter, R. M., McWhirter, R. M., & Stegall, M. E. (1989). Interactive effects of extraversion, neuroticism, and social relationships on subjective well-being. *Journal of Personality and Social Psychology, 57,* 321–331.

Houseknecht, S. K. (1979). Childlessness and marital adjustment. *Journal of Marriage and the Family, 41,* 259–265.

Houseknecht, S. K. (1987). Voluntary childlessness. In M. B. Sussman & S. K. Steinmetz (Eds.), *Handbook of marriage and the family.* New York: Plenum.

Houseknecht, S. K., & Macke, A. S. (1981). Combining marriage and career: The marital adjustment of professional women. *Journal of Marriage and the Family, 43,* 651–661.

Houston, J. P., Bee, H. L., & Rimm, D. C. (1983). *Invitation to psychology* (2nd ed.). New York: Academic Press.

Hughes, D. C., Blazer, D. G., & George, L. K. (1988). Age differences in life events: A multivariate controlled analysis. *International Journal of Aging and Human Development, 27,* 207–220.

Hunsberger, B. (1985). Religion, age, life satisfaction, and perceived sources of religiousness: A study of older persons. *Journal of Gerontology, 40,* 615–620.

Hunt, M. (1974). *Sexual behavior in the 1970s.* New York: Playboy Press.

Hunter, J. E. (1986). Cognitive ability, cognitive aptitudes, job knowledge, and job performance. *Journal of Vocational Behavior, 29,* 340–362.

Hunter, S., & Sundel, M. (1989). *Midlife myths. Issues, findings, and practice implications.* Newbury Park, CA: Sage.

Huston, T. L., McHale, S. M., & Crouter, A. C. (1986). When the honeymoon's over: Changes in the marriage relationship over the first year. In R. Gilmour & S. Duck (Eds.), *The emerging field of personal relationships* (pp. 109–132). Hillsdale, NJ: Lawrence Erlbaum Associates.

Huston, T. L., Surra, C. A., Fitzgerald, N. M., & Cate, R. M. (1981). From courtship to marriage: Mate selection as an interpersonal process. In S. Duck & R. Gilmour (Eds.), *Personal relationships 2. Developing personal relationships* (pp. 53–90). New York: Academic Press.

Huston-Stein, A., & Higgens-Trenk, A. (1978). Development of females from childhood through adulthood: Career and feminine role orientations. In P. B. Baltes (Ed.), *Life-span development and behavior* (Vol. 1, pp. 258–297). New York: Academic Press.

Iacocca, L. (1984). *Iacocca. An autobiography.* Toronto: Bantam Books.

Irion, J. C., & Blanchard-Fields, F. (1987). A cross-sectional comparison of adaptive coping in adulthood. *Journal of Gerontology, 42,* 502–504.

Ishii-Luntz, M. & Seccombe, K. (1989). The impact of children upon social support networks throughout the life course. *Journal of Marriage and the Family, 51,* 777–790.

Jackson, J. J., & Perry, C. (1989). Physical health conditions of middle-aged and aged blacks. In K. S. Markides (Ed.), *Aging and health* (pp. 111–176). Newbury Park, CA: Sage.

Jacobs, S. C., Kosten, T. R., Kasl, S. V., Ostfeld, A. M., Berkman, L., & Charpentier, P. (1987–88). Attachment theory and multiple dimensions of grief. *Omega, 18,* 41–52.

Jacobson, P. H. (1964). Cohort survival for generations since 1940. *Milbank Memorial Fund Quarterly, 42*(3), 36–53.

James, W. (1902). *The varieties of religious experience.* New York: Mentor edition, 1958.

Jaques, E. (1965). Death and the mid-life crisis. *International Journal of Psychoanalysis, 46,* 502–514.

Jarvik, L. F., & Bank, L. (1983). Aging twins: Longitudinal psychometric data. In W. K. Schaie (Ed.), *Longitudinal studies of adult psychological development* (pp. 40–63). New York: Guilford Press.

Jeffrey, R. W. (1989). Risk behaviors and health. Contrasting individual and population perspectives. *American Psychologist, 44,* 1194–1202.

Johansson, B., & Berg, S. (1989). The robustness of the terminal decline phenomenon: Longitudinal data from the digit-span memory test. *Journal of Gerontology: PSYCHOLOGICAL SCIENCES, 44,* P184–186.

Johnson, D. (1983). *Spirals of growth.* Wheaton, IL: Theosophical Publishing House.

Kagan, J. (1980). Perspectives on continuity. In O. G. Brim, Jr. & J. Kagan (Eds.), *Constancy and change in human development* (pp. 26–74). Cambridge, MA: Harvard University Press.

Kahn, R. L., & Antonucci, T. C. (1980). Convoys over the life course: Attachment, roles, and social support. In P. B. Baltes & O. G. Brim, Jr. (Eds.), *Life-span development and behavior* (Vol. 3, pp. 254–286). New York: Academic Press.

Kahn, S. B., Alvi, S., Shaukat, N., Hussain, M. A., & Baig, T. (1990). A study of the validity of Holland's theory in a non-western culture. *Journal of Vocational Behavior, 36,* 132–146.

Kallman, D. A., Plato, C. C., & Tobin, J. D. (1990). The role of muscle loss in the age-related decline of grip strength: Cross sectional and longitudinal perspectives. *Journal of Gerontology: MEDICAL SCIENCES, 45,* M82–88.

Kalish, R. A. (1985). The social context of death and dying. In R. H. Binstock & E. Shanas (Eds.), *Handbook of aging and the social sciences* (2nd ed., pp. 149–170). New York: Van Nostrand Reinhold.

Kalish, R. A., & Reynolds, D. K. (1976). *Death and ethnicity: A psychocultural study.* Los Angeles: University of Southern California Press. Reprinted 1981, Farmingdale, NJ: Baywood Publishing Co.

Kane, R. L., Klein, S. J., Bernstein, L., Rothenberg, R., & Wales, J. (1985). Hospice role in alleviating the emotional stress of terminal patients and their families. *Medical Care, 23,* 189–197.

Kane, R. L., Wales, J., Bernstein, L., Leibowitz, A., & Kaplan, S. (1984). A randomized controlled trial of hospice care. *Lancet,* 890–894.

Kannel, W. B., & Gordon, T. (1980). Cardiovascular risk factors in the the aged: The Framingham study. In S. G. Haynes & M. Feinleib (Eds.), *Second conference on the epidemiology of aging* (pp. 65–89). U.S. Department of Health and Human Services, NIH Publication No. 80–969. Washington, D. C.: U.S. Government Printing Office.

Karp, D. A. (1988). A decade of reminders: Changing age consciousness between fifty and sixty years old. *The Gerontologist, 28,* 727–738.

Kasl, S. V., & Cobb, S. (1982). Variability of stress effects among men experiencing job loss. In L. Goldberger & S. Breznitz (Eds.), *Handbook of stress. Theoretical and clinical aspects* (pp. 445–465). New York: The Free Press.

Kastenbaum, R., & Aisenberg, R. (1976). *The psychology of death.* New York: Springer.

Katz, P. A. (1979). The development of female identity. *Sex Roles, 5,* 155–178.

Kausler, D. H., Lichty, W., & Freund, J. S. (1985). Adult age differences in recognition memory and frequency judgments for planned versus performed activities. *Developmental Psychology, 21,* 647–654.

Keen, S. (1983). *The passionate life: Stages of loving.* New York: Harper & Row.

Kegan, R. (1980). There the dance is: Religious dimensions of developmental theory. In J. W. Fowler & A. Vergote (Eds.), *Toward moral and religious maturity* (pp. 403–440). Morristown, NJ: Silver Burdette.

Kegan, R. (1982). *The evolving self.* Cambridge, MA: Harvard University Press.

Keith, P. M. (1981–82). Perceptions of time remaining and distance from death. *Omega, 12,* 307–318.

Keith, P. M. (1985). Work, retirement and well-being among unmarried men and women. *The Gerontologist, 25,* 410–416.

Keith, V. M., & Finlay, B. (1988). The impact of parental divorce on children's educational attainment, marital timing, and likelihood of divorce. *Journal of Marriage and the Family, 50,* 797–809.

Kellam, S. G., Ensminger, M. E., & Turner, R. J. (1977). Family structure and the mental health of children: Concurrent and longitudinal community-wide studies. *Archives of General Psychiatry, 34,* 77–86.

Kellehear, A., & Lewin, T. (1988–89). Farewells by the dying: A sociological study. *Omega, 19,* 275–292.

Kenshalo, D. R. (1977). Age changes in touch, vibration, temperature, kinesthesis, and pain sensitivity. In J. E. Birren & K. W. Schaie, (Eds.), *Handbook of the psychology of aging* (pp. 562–579). New York: Van Nostrand Reinhold.

Kenshalo, D. R. (1986). Somesthetic sensitivity in young and elderly humans. *Journal of Gerontology, 41,* 732–742.

Kiecolt-Glaser, J. K., & Glaser, R. (1988). Behavioral influences on immune function: Evidence for the interplay between stress and health. In T. M. Field, P. M. McCabe, & N. Schneiderman (Eds.), *Stress and coping across development* (pp. 189–206). Hillsdale, NJ: Lawrence Erlbaum Associates.

King, P. M., Kitchener, K. S., Wood, P. K., & Davison, M. L. (1989). Relationships across developmental domains: A longitudinal study of intellectual, moral, and ego development. In M. L. Commons, J. D. Sinott, F. A. Richards & C. Armon (Eds.). *Adult development, Vol. 1. Comparisons and applications of developmental models* (pp. 57–72). New York: Praeger

Kinsey, A. C., Pomeroy, W. B., & Martin, C. E. (1948). *Sexual behavior in the human male.* Philadelphia: Saunders.

Kinsey, A. C., Pomeroy, W. B., & Martin, C. E. (1953). *Sexual behavior of the human female.* Philadelphia: Saunders.

Kitson, G. C. (1982). Attachment to the spouse in divorce: A scale and its application. *Journal of Marriage and the Family, 44,* 379–393.

Kitson, G. C., Babri, K. B., & Roach, M. J. (1985). Who divorces and why. A review. *Journal of Family Issues, 6,* 255–293.

Kleemeier, R. W. (1962). Intellectual changes in the senium. *Proceedings of the Social Statistics Section of the American Statistics Association, 1,* 290–295.

Klein, E. (March 5, 1989). 'You can't love without the fear of losing.' *Parade Magazine,* p. 4–6.

Klenow, D. J., & Bolin, R. C. (1989–90). Belief in an afterlife: A national survey. *Omega, 20,* 63–74.

Kliegl, R., Smith, J., & Baltes, P. B. (1989). Testing-the-limits and the study of adult age differences in cognitive plasticity of a mnemonic skill. *Developmental Psychology, 25,* 247–256.

Kluwe, R. H. (1986). Psychological research on problem-solving and aging. In A. B. Sørensen, F. E. Weinert, & L. R. Sherrod (Eds.), *Human development and the life course: Multidisciplinary perspectives* (pp. 509–534). Hillsdale, NJ: Lawrence Erlbaum Associates.

Kobak, R. R., & Sceery, A. (1988). Attachment in late adolescence: Working models, affect regulation, and representations of self and others. *Child Development, 50,* 135–146.

Kobasa, S. C. (1979). Stressful life events, personality, and health: An inquiry into hardiness. *Journal of Personality and Social Psychology, 37,* 1–11.

Kobasa, S. C. (1982). Commitment and coping in stress resistance among lawyers. *Journal of Personality and Social Psychology, 42,* 707–717.

Kobasa, S. C., Maddi, S. R., & Kahn, S. (1982). Hardiness and health: A prospective study. *Journal of Personality and Social Psychology, 42,* 168–177.

Koenig, H. G., Kvale, J. N., & Ferrell, C. (1988). Religion and well-being in later life. *The Gerontologist, 28,* 18–28.

Kogan, N. (1990). Personality and aging. In J. E. Birren & K. W. Schaie (Eds.), *Handbook of the psychology of aging* (3rd ed., pp. 330–346). San Diego: Academic Press.

Kohlberg, L. (1958). *The development of modes of thinking and choices in the years 10 to 16.* Ph.D. dissertation, University of Chicago.

Kohlberg, L. (1964). The development of moral character and ideology. In M. L. Hoffman and L. W. Hoffman (Eds.), *Review of child development research* (Vol. 1, pp. 383–432). New York: Russell Sage.

Kohlberg, L. (1973). Continuities in childhood and adult moral development revisited. In P. B. Baltes & K. W. Schaie, (Eds.), *Life-span developmental psychology: Personality and socialization* (pp. 180–207). New York: Academic Press.

Kohlberg, L. (1976). Moral stages and moralization: The cognitive-developmental approach. In T. Lickona (Ed.), *Moral development and behavior: Theory, research and social issues.* New York: Holt, Rinehart and Winston.

Kohlberg, L. (1981). *Essays on moral development:* Vol. I. *The philosophy of moral development.* San Francisco: Harper & Row.

Kohlberg, L. (1984) *Essays on moral development:* Vol. II. *The psychology of moral development.* San Francisco: Harper & Row.

Kohlberg, L., & Kramer, R. (1969). Continuities and discontinuities in children and adult moral development. *Human Development, 12,* 225–252.

Kohlberg, L., Levine, C., & Hewer, A. (1983). Moral stages: a current formulation and a response to critics. *Contributions to human development 10.* Basel: S. Karger.

Kohn, M. L. (1980). Job complexity and adult personality. In N. J. Smelser & E. H. Erikson (Eds.), *Themes of work and love in adulthood* (pp. 193–212). Cambridge, MA: Harvard University Press.

Kohn, M. L., & Schooler, C. (1978). The reciprocal effects of the substantive complexity of work and intellectual flexibility: A longitudinal assessment. *American Journal of Sociology, 84,* 24–52.

Kohn, M. L., & Schooler, C. (1983). *Work and personality: An inquiry into the impact of social stratification.* Norwood, NJ: Ablex Press.

Konner, M. (1988, December 4). Mortality. *New York Times Magazine,* pp. 100–102.

Korman, A. K., Mahler, S. R., & Omran, K. A. (1983). Work ethics and satisfaction, alienation, and other reactions. In W. B. Walsh & S. H. Osipow (Eds.), *Handbook of vocational psychology* (Vol. 2, pp. 181–206). *Applications.* Hillsdale, NJ: Erlbaum.

Koplowitz, H. (1990). Unitary consciousness and the highest development of mind: The relation between spiritual development and cognitive development. In M. L. Commons, C. Armon, L. Kohlberg, F. Richards, T. A. Grotzer, & J. D. Sinott (Eds.), *Adult development: Vol. 2. Models and methods in the study of adolescent and adult thought* (pp. 105–112). New York: Praeger.

Krause, N. (1986). Social support, stress, and well-being among older adults. *Journal of Gerontology, 41,* 512–519.

Krause, N. (1987a). Chronic financial strain, social support, and depressive symptoms among older adults. *Psychology and Aging, 2,* 185–192.

Krause, N. (1987b). Life stress, social support, and self-esteem in an elderly population. *Psychology and Aging, 2,* 349–356.

Krause, N. (1987c). Satisfaction with social support and self-rated health in older adults. *The Gerontologist, 27,* 301–308.

Krause, N. (1987d). Understanding the stress process: Linking social support with locus of control beliefs. *Journal of Gerontology, 42,* 589–593.

Krause, N., Liang, J., & Yatomi, N. (1989). Satisfaction with social support and depressive symptoms: A panel analysis. *Psychology and Aging, 4,* 88–97.

Kübler-Ross, E. (1969). *On death and dying.* New York: Macmillan.

Kübler-Ross, E. (1974). *Questions and answers on death and dying.* New York: Macmillan.

Kübler-Ross, E. (1975). *Death. The final stage of growth.* Englewood Cliffs, NJ: Prentice Hall.

Kunitz, S. J., & Levy, J. E. (1989). Aging and health among Navajo Indians. In K. S. Markides (Ed.) *Aging and health* (pp. 211–246). Newbury Park, CA: Sage.

Kunze, K. R. (1974). Age and occupations at Lockheed-California: Versatility of older workers. *Industrial Gerontology, 1,* 57–64.

Kurdek, L. A., & Schmitt, J. P. (1986). Early development of relationship quality in heterosexual married, heterosexual cohabiting, gay, and lesbian couples. *Developmental Psychology, 22,* 305–309.

Labouvie-Vief, G. (1980). Beyond formal operations: Uses and limits of pure logic in life-span development. *Human Development, 23,* 141–161.

Labouvie-Vief, G. (1990). Modes of knowledge and the organization of development. In M. L. Commons, C. Armon, L. Kohlberg, F. A. Richards, T. A. Grotzer, & J. D. Sinnott (Eds.), *Adult development: Vol. 2. Models and methods in the study of adolescent and adult thought* (pp. 43–62). New York: Praeger.

Labouvie-Vief, G., & Schell, D. A. (1982). Learning and memory in later life. In B. B. Wolman (Ed.), *Handbook of developmental psychology* (pp. 828–896). Englewood Cliffs, NJ: Prentice Hall.

Lakatta, E. G. (1985). Heart and circulation. In C. E. Finch & E. L. Schneider (Eds.), *Handbook of the biology of aging* (2nd ed., pp. 337–413). New York: Van Nostrand Reinhold.

Lakatta, E. G., Goldberg, A. P., Fleg, J. L., Fortney, S. M., & Drinkwater, D. T. (1988). Reduced cardiovascular and metabolic research in older persons: Disuse, disease, or aging? In R. Chernoff & D. A. Lipschitz (Eds.), *Aging: Vol. 35. Health promotion and disease prevention in the elderly.* New York: Raven Press.

Langer, E. J. (1989a). *Mindfulness.* New York: Merloyd Lawrence.

Langer, E. J. (1989b, April). The mindset of health. *Psychology Today, 23,* 49–51.

Larsen, P. C. (1982). Gay male relationships. In W. Paul, J. D. Weinrich, J. C. Gonsiorek, & M. E. Hotvedt (Eds.), *Homosexuality. Social, psychological, and biological issues.* Beverly Hills, CA: Sage.

Lauer, J., & Lauer, R. (1985, June). Marriages made to last. *Psychology Today, 19,* (6), 22–26.

Lawton, M. P. (1985). Housing and living environments of older people. In R. H. Binstock & E.Shanas (Eds.), *Aging and the social sciences* (2nd ed., pp. 450–478). New York: Van Nostrand Reinhold.

Lawton, M. P. (1990). Residential environment and self-directedness among older people. *American Psychologist, 45,* 638–640.

Lazarus, R. S., & DeLongis, A. (1983). Psychological stress and coping in aging. *American Psychologist, 38,* 245–254.

Lazarus, R. S., & Folkman, S. (1984). *Stress, appraisal, and coping.* New York: Springer.

Lee, G. R. (1988). Marital intimacy among older persons. *Journal of Family Issues, 9,* 273–284.

Lee, G. R., & Ellithorpe, E. (1982). Intergenerational exchange and subjective well-being among the elderly. *Journal of Marriage and the Family, 44,* 217–224.

Lee, G. R., & Ihinger-Tallman, M. (1980). Sibling interaction and morale: The effects of family relations on older people. *Research on Aging, 2,* 367–391.

Leean, C. (1985). *Faith development in the adult life cycle, Module 2.* Working paper of the Faith Development in the Adult Life Cycle Project, The Religious Education Association of the United States and Canada, 1985.

Lehman, H. C. (1953). *Age and achievement.* Princeton, NJ: Princeton University Press.

Leigh, G. K. (1982). Kinship interaction over the family life span. *Journal of Marriage and the Family, 44,* 197–208.

Leon, G. R., Gillum, B., Gillum, R., & Gouze, M. (1979). Personality stability and change over a 30-year period—middle age to old age. *Journal of Consulting and Clinical Psychology, 47,* 517–524.

Lerner, R. M. (1986). *Concepts and theories of human development* (2nd ed.). New York: Random House.

LeShan, L. (1966). *The medium, the mystic, and the physicist.* New York: Ballantine.

Levinson, D. J. (1978). *The seasons of a man's life.* New York: Knopf.

Levinson, D. J. (1980). Toward a conception of the adult life course. In N. J. Smelser & E. H. Erikson (Eds.), *Themes of work and love in adulthood* (pp. 265–290). Cambridge, MA: Harvard University Press.

Levinson, D. J. (1986). A conception of adult development. *American Psychologist, 41,* 3–13.

Lewis, R. A., & Spanier, G. B. (1979). Theorizing about the quality and stability of marriage. In W. R. Burr, R. Hill, F. I. Nye & I. L. Reiss (Eds.), *Contemporary theories about the family* (Vol. 1, pp. 268–294). New York: Free Press.

Lieberman, M. A. (1965). Psychological correlates of impending death: Some preliminary observations. *Journal of Gerontology, 20,* 182–190.

Lieberman, M. A. (1982). The effects of social supports on responses to stress. In L. Goldberger & S. Breznitz (Eds.), *Handbook of stress. Theoretical and clinical aspects* (pp. 764–784). New York: The Free Press.

Lieberman, M. A., & Coplan, A. S. (1970). Distance from death as a variable in the study of aging. *Developmental Psychology, 2,* 71–84.

Lieblich, A. (1986). Successful career women at midlife: Crises and transitions. *International Journal of Aging and Human Development, 23,* 301–312.

Lindsay, R. (1985). The aging skeleton. In M. R. Haug, A. B. Ford, & M. Sheafor (Eds.), *The physical and mental health of aged women* (pp. 65–82). New York: Springer.

List, N. D. (1988). Cancer screening in the elderly. In R. Chernoff & D. A. Lipschitz (Eds.), *Aging. Vol. 35. Health promotion and disease prevention in the elderly*. New York: Raven Press.

Livson, F. B. (1976). Patterns of personality development in middle-aged women: A longitudinal study. *International Journal of Aging and Human Development, 7,* 107–115.

Livson, F. B. (1981). Paths to psychological health in the middle years: Sex differences. In D. H. Eichorn, J. A. Clausen, N. Haan, M. P. Honzik, & P. H. Mussen (Eds.), *Present and past in middle life* (pp. 195–222) New York: Academic Press.

Livson, N., & Peskin, H. (1981). Psychological health at 40: Prediction from adolescent personality. In D. H. Eichorn, J. A. Clausen, N. Haan, M. P. Honzik, & P. H. Mussen (Eds.), *Present and past in middle life* (pp. 184–194). New York: Academic Press.

Locksley, A. (1982). Social class and marital attitudes and behavior. *Journal of Marriage and the Family, 44,* 427–440.

Loehlin, J. C. (1989). Partitioning environmental and genetic contributions to behavioral development. *American Psychologist, 44,* 1285–1292.

Loevinger, J. (1976). *Ego development.* San Francisco: Jossey-Bass.

Loevinger, J. (1984). On the self and predicting behavior. In R. A. Zucker, J. Aronoff, & A. I. Rabin (Eds.), *Personality and the prediction of behavior* (pp. 43–68). New York: Academic Press.

Lohr, M. J., Essex, M. J., & Klein, M. H. (1988). The relationships of coping responses to physical health status and life satisfaction among older women. *Journal of Gerontology: PSYCHOLOGICAL SCIENCES, 43, P54–60.*

Longino, C. F. Jr. (1988). Who are the oldest Americans? *The Gerontologist, 28,* 515–523.

Longino, C. F. Jr., Warheit, G. J., & Green, J. A. (1988). Class, aging, and health. In K. S. Markides (Ed.) *Aging and health. Perspectives on gender, race, ethnicity, and class* (pp. 79–110). Newbury Park, CA: Sage.

Lonky, E., Kaus, C. R., & Roodin, P. A. (1984). Life experience and mode of coping: Relation to moral judgment in adulthood. *Developmental Psychology, 20,* 1159–1167.

Lopata, H.Z. (1969). Loneliness: forms and components. *Social Problems, 17,* 248–262.

Lopata, H. Z. (1973). *Widowhood in an American city.* Cambridge, MA: Schenkman Publishing Co.

Lopata, H. Z. (1979). *Women as widows: Support systems.* New York: Elsevier.

Lopata, H. Z., Heinemann, G.D., & Baum, J. (1982). Loneliness: Antecedents and coping strategies in the lives of widows. In L. A. Peplau & D. Perlman (Eds.), *Loneliness* (pp. 310–326). New York: Wiley.

Lowenthal, M. F., Thurnher, M., & Chiriboga, D. (1975). *Four stages of life.* San Francisco, CA: Jossey-Bass.

Lyell, R. (1980). *Middle age, old age: Short stories, poems, plays, and essays on aging.* New York: Harcourt Brace Jovanovich.

Maas, H. S., & Kuypers, J. A. (1974). *From thirty to seventy.* San Francisco: Jossey-Bass.

Maccoby, E. E. (1990). Gender and relationships. A developmental account. *American Psychologist, 45,* 513–520.

Maccoby, N. (1980). Promoting positive health behaviors in adults. In L. A. Bond & J. C. Rosen (Eds.), *Competence and coping during adulthood* (pp. 195–218). Hanover, NH: University Press of New England.

Maccoby, N., Farquhar, J. W., Wood, P., & Alexander, J. K. (1977). Reducing the risk of cardiovascular disease. *Journal of Community Health, 3,* 100–114.

Madden, D. J. (1989). Visual word identification and age-related slowing. *Cognitive Development, 4,* 1–29.

Madden, D. J., Blumenthal, J. A., Allen, P. A., & Emery, C. F. (1989). Improving aerobic capacity in healthy older adults does not necessarily lead to improved cognitive performance. *Psychology and Aging, 4,* 307–320.

Main, M., Kaplan, N., & Cassidy, J. (1985). Security in infancy, childhood, and adulthood: A move to the level of representation. In I. Bretherton & E. Waters (Eds.), Growing points of attachment theory and research. *Monographs of the Society for Research in Child Development, 50* (Whole No. 209), pp. 66–104.

Manton, K. G. (1988). A longitudinal study of functional change and mortality in the United States. *Journals of Gerontology: SOCIAL SCIENCES, 43,* S153–161.

Marcia, J. E. (1980). Identity in adolescence. In J. Adelson (Ed.), *Handbook of adolescent psychology* (pp. 159–187). New York: Wiley.

Maret, E., & Finlay, B. (1984). The distribution of household labor among women in dual-earner families. *Journal of Marriage and the Family, 46,* 357–364.

Markides, K. S., & Krause, N. (1985). Intergenerational solidarity and psychological well-being among older Mexican Americans: A three-generations study. *Journal of Gerontology, 40,* 390–392.

Martocchio, J. J. (1989). Age-related differences in employee absenteeism: A meta-analysis. *Psychology and Aging, 4,* 409–414.

Maslow, A. H. (1968). *Toward a psychology of being* (2nd ed.). New York: Van Nostrand Reinhold.

Maslow, A. H. (1970a). *Religions, values, and peak-experiences.* New York: Viking. (Original work published 1964)

Maslow, A. H. (1970b). *Motivation and personality* (2nd ed.). New York: Harper & Row.

Maslow, A. H. (1971). *The farther reaches of human nature.* New York: Viking.

Masuda, M., & Holmes, T. H. (1978). Life events: Perceptions and frequencies. *Psychosomatic Medicine, 40,* 236–261.

Matarazzo, J.D. (1972). *Wechsler's measurement and appraisal of adult intelligence* (5th ed.). Baltimore: Williams & Wilkins.

Matthews, K. A. (1988). Coronary heart disease and Type A behaviors: Update on and alternative to the Booth-Kewley and Friedman (1987) quantitative review. *Psychological Bulletin, 104,* 373–380.

McAdams, D. P. (1985). Motivation and friendship. In S. Duck & D. Perlman (Eds.), *Understanding personal relationships. An interdisciplinary approach* (pp. 85–106). London: Sage.

McClearn, G., & Foch, T. T. (1985). Behavioral genetics. In J. E. Birren & K. W. Schaie (Eds.), *Handbook of the psychology of aging* (2nd ed., pp. 113–143). New York: Van Nostrand Reinhold.

McClelland, D. C. (1981). Is personality consistent? In A. I. Rabin, J. Aronoff, A. M. Barclay, & R. A. Zucker (Eds.), *Further explorations in personality* (pp. 87–113). New York: Wiley-Interscience.

McClelland, D. C. (1989). Motivational factors in health and disease. *American Psychologist, 44,* 675–683.

McCrae, R. R. (1989). Age differences and changes in the use of coping mechanisms. *Journal of Gerontology: PSYCHOLOGICAL SCIENCES, 44,* P161–169.

McCrae, R. R., & Costa, P. T., Jr. (1983). Psychological maturity and subjective well-being: Toward a new synthesis. *Developmental Psychology, 19,* 243–248.

McCrae, R. R., & Costa, P. T., Jr. (1984). *Emerging lives, enduring dispositions: Personality in adulthood.* Boston: Little, Brown.

McCrae, R. R., & Costa,. T., Jr. (1988). Psychological resilience among widowed men and women: A 10-year follow-up of a national sample. *Journal of Social Issues, 44,* No. 3, 129–142.

McCready, W. C. (1985). Styles of grandparenting among white ethnics. In V. L. Bengtson & J. F. Robertson (Eds.), *Grandparenthood* (pp. 49–60). Beverly Hills, CA: Sage.

McEvoy, G. M., & Cascio, W. F. (1989). Cumulative evidence of the relationship between employee age and job performance. *Journal of Applied Psychology, 74,* 11–17.

McGandy, R. B. (1988). Atherogenesis and aging. In R. Chernoff & D. A. Lipschitz (Eds.), *Aging: Vol. 35. Health promotion and disease prevention in the elderly.* New York: Raven Press.

McGrath, J. E. (1970). A conceptual formulation for research on stress. In J. E. McGrath (Ed.), *Social and psychological factors in stress.* New York: Holt.

McIntosh, J. L. (1985). Suicide among the elderly: Levels and trends. *American Journal of Orthopsychiatry, 52,* 288–293.

McLanahan, S., & Booth, K. (1989). Mother-only families: Problems, prospects, and politics. *Journal of Marriage and the Family, 51,* 557–580.

Meer, J. (1986, June). The reason of age. *Psychology Today, 20,* 60–64.

Menaghan, E. G., & Lieberman, M. A. (1986). Changes in depression following divorce: A panel study. *Journal of Marriage and the Family, 48,* 319–328.

Midlarsky, E., & Hannah, M. E. (1989). The generous elderly: Naturalistic studies of donations across the life span. *Psychology and Aging, 4,* 346–351.

Mindel, C. H., & Vaughan, C. E. (1978). A multidimensional approach to religiosity and disengagement. *Journal of Gerontology, 33,* 103–108.

Minkler, M., & Stone, R. (1985). The feminization of poverty and older women. *The Gerontologist, 25,* 351–357.

Model, S. (1981). Housework by husbands. Determinants and implications. *Journal of Family Issues, 2,* 225–237.

Moen, P. (1985). Continuities and discontinuities in women's labor force activity. In G. H. Elder, Jr., (Ed.), *Life course dynamics* (pp. 113–155). Ithaca: Cornell University Press.

Monroe, S. M., & Peterman, A. M. (1988). Life stress and psychopathology. In L. H. Cohen (Ed.), *Life events and psychological functioning. Theoretical and methodological issues.* Newbury Park, CA: Sage.

Moore, K. A., Hofferth, S. L., Wertheimer, R. F., Waite, L. J., & Caldwell, S. B. (1981). Teenage childbearing: Consequences for women, families, and government welfare expenditures. In K. G. Scott, T. Field, & E. G. Robertson (Eds.), *Teenage parents and their offspring* (pp. 35–54). New York: Grune & Stratton.

Moos, R. H., & Billings, A. G. (1982). Conceptualizing and measuring coping resources and processes. In L. Goldberger & S. Breznitz (Eds.), *Handbook of stress. Theoretical and clinical aspects* (pp. 212–230). New York: The Free Press.

Morgan, D. L. (1988). Age differences in social network participation. *Journal of Gerontology: SOCIAL SCIENCES, 4,* S129–137.

Morris, J. N., Mor, V., Goldberg, R. J., Sherwood, S., Greer, D. S., & Hiris, J. (1986). The effect of treatment setting and patient characteristics on pain in terminal cancer patients: A report from the National Hospice Study. *Journal of Chronic Diseases, 39,* 27–35.

Mortimer, J. T. (1974). Patterns of intergenerational occupational movements: a smallest-space analysis. *American Journal of Sociology, 5,* 1278–1295.

Mortimer, J. T. (1976). Social class, work and family: some implications of the father's occupation for family relationships and son's career decisions. *Journal of Marriage and the Family, 38,* 241–256.

Mosher, F. A., & Hornsby, J. R. (1966). On asking questions. In J. S. Bruner, R. R. Olver, & P. M. Greenfield (Eds.), *Studies in cognitive growth* (pp. 86–102). New York: Wiley.

Moss, M. S., Moss, S. Z., & Moles, E. L. (1985). The quality of relationships between elderly parents and their out-of-town children. *The Gerontologist, 25,* 134–140.

Mueller, D. P., & Cooper, P. W. (1986). Children of single parent families: How they fare as young adults. *Family Relations, 35,* 169–176.

Murrell, S. A., & Himmelfarb, S. (1989). Effects of attachment bereavement and pre-event conditions on subsequent depressive symptoms in older adults. *Psychology and Aging, 4,* 166–172.

Murrell, S. A., Norris, F. H., & Grote, C. (1988). Life events in older adults. In L. H. Cohen (Ed.), *Life events and psychological functioning. Theoretical and methodological issues* (pp. 96–122). Newbury Park, CA: Sage.

Murstein, B. I. (1970). Stimulus-Value-Role: A theory of marital choice. *Journal of Marriage and the Family, 32,* 465–481.

Murstein, B. I. (1976). *Who will marry whom? Theories and research in marital choice.* New York: Springer.

Murstein, B. I. (1986). *Paths to marriage.* Beverly Hills, CA: Sage.

Mussen, P. (1987). Longitudinal study of the lifespan. In N. Eisenberg (Ed.) *Contemporary topics in developmental psychology* (pp. 375–393). New York: Wiley-Interscience.

Myers-Walls, J. A. (1984). Balancing multiple role responsibilities during the transition to parenthood. *Family Relations, 33,* 267–271.

Nagy, M. (1948). The child's view of death. *Journal of Genetic Psychology, 73,* 3–27.

Nash, S. C., & Feldman, S. S. (1981). Sex role and sex-related attributions: Constancy and change across the family life cycle. In M. E. Lamb & A. L. Brown (Eds.), *Advances in developmental psychology* (Vol. 1, pp. 1–36). Hillsdale, NJ: Erlbaum.

Nathanson, C. A., & Lorenz, G. (1982). Women and health: The social dimensions of biomedical data. In J. Z. Giele (Ed.), *Women in the middle years* (pp. 37–88). New York: Wiley.

Neimeyer, R. A., & Chapman, K. M. (1980-81). Self/ideal discrepancy and fear of death: the test of an existential hypothesis. *Omega, 11,* 233–239.

Neugarten, B. L. (1968). The awareness of middle age. In B. L. Neugarten (Ed.), *Middle age and aging* (pp. 93–98). Chicago, IL: University of Chicago Press.

Neugarten, B. L. (1974, September). Age groups in American society and the rise of the young-old. *Annals of the American Academy*, 187–198.

Neugarten, B. L. (1975). The future of the young-old. *The Gerontologist, 15,* 4–9.

Neugarten, B. L. (1976). Adaptation and the life cycle. *The Counseling Psychologist, 6,* 16–20.

Neugarten, B. L. (1977). Personality and aging. In J. E. Birren & K. W. Schaie (Eds.), *Handbook of the psychology of aging* (pp. 626–649). New York: Van Nostrand Reinhold.

Neugarten, B. L. (1979). Time, age, and the life cycle. *American Journal of Psychiatry, 136,* 887–894.

Neugarten, B. L., & Neugarten, D. A. (1987, May). The changing meanings of age. *Psychology Today, 21* (5), 29–33.

Neugarten, B. L., & Weinstein, K. (1964). The changing American grandparent. *Journal of Marriage and the Family, 26,* 199–204.

Newmann, J. P. (1989). Aging and depression. *Psychology and Aging, 4*, 150–165.

Nieva, V. F. (1985). Work and family linkages. In L. Larwood, A. H. Stromberg, & B. A. Gutek (Eds.), *Women and work. An annual review* (Vol. 1, pp. 162–190). Beverly Hills, CA: Sage.

Nisan, M., & Kohlberg, L. (1982). Universality and variation in moral judgment: A longitudinal and cross-sectional study in Turkey. *Child Development, 53,* 865–876.

Nolen-Hoeksema, S. (1987). Sex differences in unipolar depression: Evidence and theory. *Psychological Bulletin, 101,* 259–282.

Norris, J. E., & Rubin, K. H. (1984). Peer interaction and communication: A life-span perspective. In P. B. Baltes & O. G. Brim, Jr., (Eds.), *Life-span development and behavior* (Vol. 6, pp. 356–383). Orlando, FL: Academic Press.

Norton, A. J. (1983). Family life cycle: 1980. *Journal of Marriage and the Family, 45,* 267–275.

Norton, A. J., & Miller, L. F. (1990). The family life cycle: 1985. *Work and family patterns of American women,* U.S. Bureau of the Census, (Current Population Reports, Series P-23, No. 165). Washington, D. C.: U.S. Government Printing Office.

Nuckolls, K. B., Cassel, J., & Kaplan, B. H. (1972). Psychosocial assets, life crises, and the prognosis of pregnancy. *American Journal of Epidemiology, 95,* 431–441.

Olsho, L. W., Harkins, S. W., & Lenhardt, M. L. (1985). Aging and the auditory system. In J. E. Birren & K. W. Schaie (Eds.), *Handbook of the psychology of aging* (2nd ed., pp. 332–377). New York: Van Nostrand Reinhold.

Ornstein, S., & Isabella, L. (1990). Age vs stage models of career attitudes of women: A partial replication and extension. *Journal of Vocational Behavior, 36,* 1–19.

Ostrow, A. C. (1984). *Physical activity and the older adult. Psychological perspectives.* Princeton, NJ: Princeton Book Co.

Over, R. (1989). Age and scholarly impact. *Psychology and Aging, 4,* 222–225.

Paffenbarger, R. S., Jr., & Hyde, R. T. (1984). Exercise in the prevention of coronary heart disease. *Preventive Medicine, 13,* 3–22.

Palmore, E. (1970). Health practices and illness. *The Gerontologist, 10,* 313–316.

Palmore, E. (1979). Predictors of successful aging. *The Gerontologist, 19,* 427–431.

Palmore, E. (1981). *Social patterns in normal aging: Findings from the Duke Longitudinal Study.* Durham, NC: Duke University Press.

Palmore, E. B., Burchett, B. M., Fillenbaum, G. G., George, L. K., & Wallman, L. M. (1985). *Retirement. Causes and consequences.* New York: Springer.

Palmore, E. B., & Cleveland, W. (1976). Aging, terminal decline, and terminal drop. *Journal of Gerontology, 31,* 76–81.

Palmore, E., & Stone, V. (1973). Predictors of longevity. *Gerontologist, 13,* 88–90.

Parlee, M. B. (1979, October). The friendship bond. *Psychology Today,* pp. 43–54, 113.

Parnes, H. S., Crowley, J. E., Haurin, R. J., Less, L. J., Morgan, W. R., Mott, F. L., & Nestel, G. (1985). *Retirement among American men.* Lexington, MA: Lexington Books.

Paul, W., & Weinrich, J. D. (1982). Whom and what do we study: Definition and scope of sexual orientation. In W. Paul, J. D. Weinrich, J. C. Gonsiorek, & M. E. Hotvedt (Eds.), *Homosexuality. Social, psychological, and biological issues* (pp. 23–28). Beverly Hills, CA: Sage.

Paykel, E. S. (1974). Life stress and psychiatric disorder: Applications of the clinical approach. In B. S. Dohrenwend & B. P. Dohrenwend (Eds.), *Stressful life events. Their nature and effects* (pp. 135–150). New York: Wiley.

Pearce, K. A., & Denney, N. W. (1984). A lifespan study of classification preference. *Journal of Gerontology, 39,* 458–464.

Pearlin, L. (1975). Sex roles and depression. In N. Datan & L. H. Ginsberg (Eds.), *Life-span developmental psychology: Normative life crises* (pp. 191–208). New York: Academic Press.

Pearlin, L. I. (1980). Life strains and psychological distress among adults. In N. J. Smelser & E. H. Erikson (Eds), *Themes of work and love in adulthood* (pp. 174–192). Cambridge, MA: Harvard University Press.

Pearlin, L. I. (1982a). Discontinuities in the study of aging. In T. K. Hareven & K. J. Adams (Eds.), *Aging and life course transitions: An interdisciplinary perspective.* New York: Guilford Press.

Pearlin, L. I. (1982b). The social contexts of stress. In L. Goldberger & S. Breznitz (Eds.), *Handbook of stress: Theoretical and clinical aspects* (pp. 367–379). New York: The Free Press.

Pearlin, L. I., & Lieberman, M. A. (1979). Social sources of emotional distress. In R. Simons (Ed.), *Research in community and mental health.* Greenwich, Conn.: JAI Press.

Pearlin, L. I., & Schooler, C. (1978). The structure of coping. *Journal of Health and Social Behavior, 19,* 2–21.

Peck, M. S. (1978). *The road less traveled.* New York: Simon and Schuster.

Peplau, L. A., & Amaro, H. (1982). Understanding lesbian relationships. In W. Paul, J. D. Weinrich, J. C. Gonsiorek, & M. E. Hotvedt (Eds.), *Homosexuality: Social, psychological, and biological issues* (pp. 233–248). Beverly Hills, CA: Sage.

Peplau, L. A., Bikson, T. K., Rook, K. S., & Goodchilds, J. D. (1982). Being old and living alone. In L. A. Peplau & D. Perlman (Eds.), *Loneliness* (pp. 327–350). New York: Wiley.

Perkins, D. V. (1982). The assessment of stress using life events scales. In L. Goldberger & S. Breznitz (Eds.), *Handbook of stress: Theoretical and clinical aspects* (pp. 320–331). New York: The Free Press.

Perlman, D., & Fehr, B. (1987). The development of intimate relationships. In D. Perlman & S. Duck (Eds.), *Intimate relationships. Development, dynamics, and deterioration* (pp. 13–42). Newbury Park, CA: Sage.

Perlmutter, M. (1986). A life-span view of memory. In P. B. Baltes, D. L. Featherman, & R. M. Lerner (Eds.), *Life-span development and behavior* (Vol. 7, pp. 271–313). Hillsdale, NJ: Lawrence Erlbaum Associates.

Perlmutter, M., Adams, C., Berry, J., Kaplan, M., Person, D., & Verdonik, F. (1987). Aging and memory. In K. W. Schaie & C. Eisdorfer (Eds.), *Annual review of gerontology and geriatrics* (pp. 57–92). New York: Springer.

Perry-Jenkins, M., & Crouter, A. C. (1990). Men's provider-role attitudes. Implications for household work and marital satisfaction. *Journal of Family Issues, 11,* 136–156.

Perun, P. J., & Bielby, D. D. (1980). Structure and dynamics of the individual life course. In K. W. Back (Ed.), *Life course: Integrative theories and exemplary populations.* AAAS Selected Symposium 41 (pp. 97–120). Boulder, CO: Westview Press.

Peskin, H., & Livson, N. (1981). Uses of the past in adult psychological health. In D. H. Eichorn, J. A. Clausen, N. Haan, M. P. Honzik, & P. H. Mussen (Eds.), *Present and past in middle life* (pp. 158–194). New York: Academic Press.

Philliber, W. W., & Hiller, D. V. (1983). Relative occupational attainments of spouses and later changes in marriage and wife's work experience. *Journal of Marriage and the Family, 46,* 161–170.

Piaget, J. (1952). *The origins of intelligence in children.* New York: International Universities Press.

Piaget, J. (1964). Development and learning. In R. Ripple & V. Rockcastle (Eds.), *Piaget rediscovered.* Ithaca, NY: Cornell University Press.

Piaget, J., & Inhelder, B. (1969). *The psychology of the child.* New York: Basic Books.

Pitcher, B. L., Spykerman, B. R., & Gazi-Tabatabaie, M. (1987). Stability of perceived personal control for older black and white men. *Research on Aging, 9,* 200–225.

Pitts, D. G. (1982). The effects of aging on selected visual functions: Dark adaptation, visual acuity, stereopsis and brightness contrast. In R. Sekuler, D. W. Kline, & K. Dismukes (Eds.) *Aging and human visual function.* New York: Alan R. Liss.

Pleck, J. (1977). The work-family role system. *Social Problems, 24,* 417–427.

Plomin, R., Pedersen, N. L., McClearn, G. E., Nesselroade, J. R., & Bergeman, C. S. (1988). EAS temperaments during the last half of the life span: Twins reared apart and twins reared together. *Psychology and Aging, 3,* 43–50.

Plowman, S. A., Drinkwater, B. L., & Horvath, S. M. (1979). Age and aerobic power in women: A longitudinal study. *Journal of Gerontology, 34,* 512–520.

Pollack, J. M. (1979-80). Correlates of death anxiety: a review of empirical studies. *Omega, 10,* 97–121.

Poon, L. W. (1985). Differences in human memory with aging: Nature, causes, and clinical implications. In J. E. Birren & K. W. Schaie (Eds.), *Handbook of the psychology of aging* (2nd ed., pp. 427–462). New York: Van Nostrand Reinhold.

Poon, L. W., & Schaffer, G. (1982). Prospective memory in young and elderly adults. Presented at the Annual Meetings of the American Psychological Association, Washington, D. C.

Powell, B. (1977). The empty nest, employment, and psychiatric symptoms in college-educated women. *Psychology of Women Quarterly, 2,* 35–43.

Pratt, M. W., Golding, G., & Hunter, W. J. (1983). Aging as ripening: Character and consistency of moral judgment in young, mature, and older adults. *Human Development, 26,* 277–288.

Pratt, M. W., Golding, G., & Hunter, W. J. (1984). Does morality have a gender? Sex, sex role, and moral judgment relationships across the adult lifespan. *Merrill-Palmer Quarterly, 30,* 321–340.

President's Commission on Mental Health (1979). *Mental health and the elderly: Recommendations for action.* Reports of the task panel on the elderly and the secretary's committee on mental health and illness of the elderly. (OHDS 80–20960). Washington, D. C.: Government Printing Office.

Rabinowitz, J. C. (1989). Age deficits in recall under optimal study conditions. *Psychology and Aging, 4,* 378–380.

Rakowski, W. (1988). Age cohorts and personal health behavior in adulthood. *Research on Aging, 10,* 3–35.

Rawlings, S. W. (1989). Single parents and their children. In *Studies in Marriage and the Family,* U.S. Bureau of the Census, Current Population Reports, (Series P-23, No. 162). Washington, D.C.: U.S. Government Printing Office.

Regier, D. A., Boyd, J. H., Burke, J. D., Rae, D. S., Myers, J. K., Kramer, M., Robins, L. N., George, L. K., Karno, M., & Locke, B. Z. (1988). One-month prevalence of mental disorders in the United States. *Archives of General Psychiatry, 45,* 977–986.

Reich, J. W., Zautra, A. J., & Guarnaccia, C. A. (1989). Effects of disability and bereavement on the mental health and recovery of older adults. *Psychology and Aging, 4,* 57–65.

Reinke, B. J., Holmes, D. S., & Harris, R. L. (1985). The timing of psychosocial changes in women's lives: The years 25–45. *Journal of Personality and Social Psychology, 48,* 1353–1364.

Reis, H. T. (1986). Gender effects in social participation: Intimacy, loneliness, and the conduct of social interaction. In R. Gilmour & S. Duck (Eds.), *The emerging field of personal relationships* (pp. 91–108). Hillsdale, NJ: Lawrence Erlbaum Associates.

Reisman, J. M. (1981). Adult friendships. In S. Duck & R. Gilmour (Eds.), *Personal relationships 2. Developing personal relationships* (pp. 205–230). New York: Academic Press.

Reker, G. T., & Wong, P. T. P. (1988). Aging as an individual process: Toward a theory of personal meaning. In J. E. Birren & V. L. Bengtson (Eds.), *Emergent theories of aging* (pp. 214–246). New York: Springer.

Rest, J. R., Davison, M. L., & Robbins, S. (1978). Age trends in judging moral issues: A review of cross-sectional, longitudinal, and sequential studies of the Defining Issues Test. *Child Development, 49,* 263–279.

Rest, J. R., & Thoma, S. J. (1985). Relation of moral judgement to formal education. *Developmental Psychology, 21,* 709–714.

Rexroat, C. (1985). Women's work expectations and labor-market experience in early and middle family life-cycle stages. *Journal of Marriage and the Family, 47,* 131–142.

Rexroat, C., & Shehan, C. (1987). The family life cycle and spouses' time in housework. *Journal of Marriage and the Family, 49,* 737–750.

Rhodes, S. R. (1983). Age-related differences in work attitudes and behavior: A review and conceptual analysis. *Psychological Bulletin, 93,* 329–367.

Rice, G. E., & Meyer, B. J. F. (1986). Prose recall: Effects of aging, verbal ability, and reading behavior. *Journal of Gerontology, 41,* 469–480.

Rikli, R., & Busch, S. (1986). Motor performance of women as a function of age and physical activity level. *Journal of Gerontology, 41*, 645–649.

Riley, M. W. (1976). Age strata in social systems. In R. H. Binstock & E. Shanas (Eds.), *Handbook of aging and the social sciences* (pp. 189–243). New York: Van Nostrand Reinhold.

Riley, M. W. (1983). The family in an aging society. A matrix of latent relationships. *Journal of Family Issues, 4,* 439–454.

Riley, M. W. (1986). Overview and highlights of a sociological perspective. In A. B. Sorensen, F. E. Weinert, & L. R. Sherrod (Eds.), *Human development and the life course: Multidisciplinary perspectives* (pp. 153–176). Hillsdale, NJ: Lawrence Erlbaum.

Riley, M. W., Foner, A. and associates. (1968). *Aging and society.* Vol. 1. *An inventory of research findings.* New York: Russell Sage Foundation.

Riley, M. W., Johnson, M., & Foner, A. (1972). *Aging and society: A sociology of age stratification* (Vol. 3). New York: Russell Sage Foundation.

Ritchie, R. J., & Moses, J. L. (1983). Assessment center correlates of women's advancement into middle management: A 7-year longitudinal analysis. *Journal of Applied Psychology, 68,* 227–231.

Roberts, P., & Newton, P. M. (1987). Levinsonian studies of women's adult development. *Psychology and Aging, 2,* 154–163.

Rocca, W. A., Amaducci, L. A., & Schoenberg, B. S. (1986). Epidemiology of clinically diagnosed Alzheimer's disease. *Annals of Neurology, 19,* 415–424.

Roche, G. R. (1979). Much ado about mentors. *Harvard Business Review, 10,* 14–28.

Rollins, B. C., & Feldman, H. (1970) Marital satisfaction over the family life cycle. *Journal of Marriage and the Family, 32,* 20–27.

Rollins, B. C., & Galligan, R. (1978). The developing child and marital satisfaction of parents. In R. M. Lerner & G. B. Spanier (Eds.), *Child influences on marital and family interaction. A life-span perspective* (pp. 71–106). New York: Academic Press.

Rook, K. S. (1984). The negative side of social interaction: Impact on psychological well-being. *Journal of Personality and Social Psychology, 46,* 1097–1108.

Roosa, M. W. (1988). The effect of age in the transition to parenthood: Are delayed childbearers a unique group? *Family Relations, 37,* 322–327.

Rose, R. J., Koskenvuo, M., Kaprio, J., Sarna, S., & Langinvainio, H. (1988). Shared genes, shared experiences, and similarity of personality: Data from 14,288 adult Finnish co-twins. *Journal of Personality and Social Psychology, 54,* 161–171.

Rosenbaum, J. E. (1984). *Career mobility in a corporate hierarchy.* New York: Academic Press.

Rosenfeld, A., & Stark, E. (1987, May). The prime of our lives. *Psychology Today, 21* (5), 62–72.

Rosenfield, S. (1980). Sex differences in depression: Do women always have higher rates? *Journal of Health and Social Behavior, 21,* 33–42.

Rosenkrantz, P., Vogel, S., Bee, H., Broverman, I., & Broverman, D. M. (1968). Sex-role stereotypes and self-conceptions of college students. *Journal of Consulting and Clinical Psychology, 32,* 287–295.

Rosenman, R. H., & Friedman, M. (1983). Relationship of Type A behavior pattern to coronary heart disease. In H. Selye (Ed.), *Selye's guide to stress research* (Vol 2, pp. 47–106). New York: Scientific and Academic Editions.

Rosenthal, C. J., (1985). Kinkeeping in the familial division of labor. *Journal of Marriage and the Family, 49,* 965–974.

Rosow, I. (1985). Status and role change through the life cycle. In R. H. Binstock & E. Shanas (Eds.), *Handbook of aging and the social sciences* (2nd ed., pp. 62–93). New York: Van Nostrand Reinhold.

Ross, H. G., & Milgram, J. I. (1982). Important variables in adult sibling relationships: A qualitative study. In M. E. Lamb & B. Sutton-Smith (Eds.), *Sibling relationships* (pp. 225–250). Hillsdale, NJ: Erlbaum.

Rossi, A. S. (1980). Life-span theories and women's lives. *Signs: Journal of Women in Culture and Society, 6,* 4–32.

Rossi, A. S., (1989). A life-course approach to gender, aging, and intergenerational relations. In K. W. Schaie & C. Schooler (Eds.), *Social structure and aging: Psychological processes* (pp. 207–236). Hillsdale, NJ: Lawrence Erlbaum Associates.

Rossman, I. (1980). Bodily changes with aging. In E. W. Busse & D. G. Blazer (Eds.), *Handbook of geriatric psychiatry*. New York: Van Nostrand Reinhold.

Rothbart, M. K., & Derryberry, D. (1981). Development of individual differences in temperament. In M. E. Lamb & A. L. Brown (Eds.), *Advances in developmental psychology* (Vol. 1, pp. 37–86). Hillsdale, NJ: Lawrence Erlbaum.

Rotter, J. B. (1966). Generalized expectancies for internal versus external control of reinforcement. *Psychological Monographs: General and Applied, 80,* (Whole No. 609).

Rotter, J. B. (1975). Some problems and misconceptions related to the construct of internal versus external control of reinforcement. *Journal of Consulting and Clinical Psychology, 43,* 56–67.

Rowe, I., & Marcia, J. E. (1980). Ego identity status, formal operations, and moral development. *Journal of Youth and Adolescence, 9,* 87–99.

Rubin, L. B. (1985). *Just friends. The role of friendship in our lives.* New York: Harper & Row.

Rubin, Z. (1973). *Liking and loving. An invitation to social psychology.* New York: Holt, Rinehart, & Winston.

Rychlak, J. F. (1982). *Personality and life-style of young male managers.* New York: Academic Press.

Ryder, R. G. (1973). Longitudinal data relating marriage satisfaction and having a child. *Journal of Marriage and the Family, 35,* 604–606.

Ryff, C. (1982). Self-perceived personality change in adulthood and aging. *Journal of Personality and Social Psychology, 42,* 108–115.

Ryff, C. (1984). Personality development from the inside: The subjective experience of change in adulthood and aging. In P. B. Baltes & O. G. Brim, Jr., (Eds), *Life-span development and behavior* (Vol. 6, pp. 244–281). Orlando, FL: Academic Press.

Ryff, C. D. (1989). In the eye of the beholder: Views of psychological well-being among middle-aged and older adults. *Psychology and Aging, 4,* 195–210.

Ryff, C., & Baltes, P. B. (1976). Value transition and adult development in women: The instrumentality-terminality sequence hypothesis. *Developmental Psychology, 12,* 567–568.

Ryff, C., & Heincke, S. G. (1983). The subjective organization of personality in adulthood and aging. *Journal of Personality and Social Psychology, 44,* 807–816.

Salthouse, T. A. (1990). Working memory as a processing resource in cognitive aging. *Developmental Review, 10,* 101–124.

Salthouse, T. A., Kausler, D., & Saults, J. S. (1988). Investigation of student status, background variables, and feasibility of standard tasks in cognitive aging research. *Psychology and Aging, 3,* 29–37.

Sanders, C. M. (1989). *Grief. The mourning after.* New York: Wiley Interscience.

Sands, L. P., Terry, H., & Meredith, W. (1989). Change and stability in adult intellectual functioning assessed by Wechsler item responses. *Psychology and Aging, 4,* 79–87.

Sangiuliano, I. (1978). *In her time.* New York: Morrow.

Sattler, J. M. (1974). *Assessment of children's intelligence.* Philadelphia: W. B. Saunders.

Saunders, C. (1977). Dying they live: St. Christopher's Hospice. In H. Feifel (Ed.), *New meanings of death.* New York: McGraw-Hill.

Savage, R. D., Gaber, L. B., Britton, P. G., Bolton, N., & Cooper, A. (1977). *Personality and adjustment in the aged.* London: Academic Press.

Sayetta, R. B. (1986). Rates of senile dementia—Alzheimer's type in the Baltimore longitudinal study. *Journal of Chronic Disease, 39,* 271–286.

Scarr, S. (1981). *Race, social class, and individual differences in I.Q.* Hillsdale, NJ: Lawrence Erlbaum.

Schaefer, C., Coyne, J. C., & Lazarus, R. S. (1982). The health-related functions of social support. *Journal of Behavioral Medicine, 4,* 381–406.

Schafer, R. B., & Keith, P. M. (1984). A causal analysis of the relationship between the self-concept and marital quality. *Journal of Marriage and the Family, 46,* 909–914.

Schaie, K. W. (1983a). What can we learn from the longitudinal study of adult psychological development? In K. W. Schaie (Ed.), *Longitudinal studies of adult psychological development* (pp. 1–19). New York: Guilford Press.

Schaie, K. W. (1983b). The Seattle longitudinal study: A 21-year exploration of psychometric intelligence in adulthood. In K. W. Schaie (Ed.), *Longitudinal studies of adult psychological development* (pp. 64–135). New York: Guilford Press.

Schaie, K. W. (Ed.) (1983c). *Longitudinal studies of adult psychological development.* New York: Guilford Press.

Schaie, K. W. (1986). Beyond calendar definitions of age, time, and cohort: The general developmental model revisited. *Developmental Review, 6,* 252–277.

Schaie, K. W. (Ed.) (1987). *Annual review of gerontology and geriatrics.* (Vol. 7). New York: Springer.

Schaie, K. W. (1989a). The hazards of cognitive aging. *The Gerontologist, 29,* 484–493.

Schaie, K. W. (1989b). Individual differences in rate of cognitive change in adulthood. In V. L. Bengtson & K. W. Schaie (Eds.), *The course of later life. Research and reflections* (pp 65–86). New York: Springer.

Schaie, K. W. (1990). Intellectual development in adulthood. In J. E. Birren & K. W. Schaie (Eds.), *Handbook of the psychology of aging* (3rd ed., pp. 291–309). San Diego, CA: Academic Press.

Schaie, K. W., & Hertzog, C. (1983). Fourteen-year cohort-sequential analyses of adult intellectual development. *Developmental Psychology, 19,* 531–543.

Schaie, K. W., Orchowsky, S., & Parham, I. A. (1982). Measuring age and sociocultural change: The case of race and life satisfaction. In R. C. Manuel (Ed.), *Minority aging* (pp. 223–230). Westport, CT: Greenwood.

Schaie, K. W., & Parham, I. A. (1976). Stability of adult personality traits: Fact or fable? *Journal of Personality and Social Psychology, 34,* 146–158.

Schaie, K. W., & Willis, S. L. (1986). Can decline in adult intellectual functioning be reversed? *Developmental Psychology, 22,* 223–232.

Schiamberg, L. B., & Chin, C. (1987). *The influence of family on educational and occupational achievement of adolescents in rural low-income areas: An ecological perspective.* Paper presented at the biennial meetings of the Society for Research in Child Development, Baltimore, Md.

Schooler, C. (1984). Psychological effects of complex environments during the life span: A review and theory. *Intelligence, 8,* 259–281.

Schooler, C. (1990). Psychosocial factors and effective cognitive functioning in adulthood. In J. E. Birren & K. W. Schaie (Eds.), *Handbook of the psychology of aging,* (3rd ed., pp. 347–358). San Diego, CA: Academic Press.

Schreiber, L. (1990). *Midstream.* New York: Viking.

Schroots, J. J. F. (1988). On growing, formative change, and aging. In J. E. Birren & V. L. Bengtson (Eds.), *Emergent theories of aging* (pp. 299–332). New York: Springer.

Schuckit, M. A. (1984). Prospective markers for alcoholism. In D. W. Goodwin, K. T. Van Dusen, & S. A. Mednick (Eds.), *Longitudinal research in alcoholism* (pp. 147–164). Boston: Kluwer-Nijhoff.

Schultz, N. R. Jr., Elias, M. F., Robbins, M. A., Streeten, D. H. P., & Blakeman, N. (1986). A longitudinal comparison of hypertensives and normotensives on the Wechsler Adult Intelligence Scale: Initial findings. *Journal of Gerontology, 41,* 169–175.

Schulz, J. H. (1988). *The economics of aging.* (4th ed.). Dover, MA: Auburn House.

Schulz, R., & Aderman, D. (1974). Clinical research and the stages of dying. *Omega, 5,* 137–143.

Schulz, R., & Curnow, C. (1988). Peak performance and age among superathletes: Track and field, swimming, baseball, tennis, and golf. *Journal of Gerontology: PSYCHOLOGICAL SCIENCES, 43,* P113–120.

Scott, J., & Alwin, D. F. (1989). Gender differences in parental strain. Parental role or gender role? *Journal of Family Issues, 10,* 482–503.

Scott, J. P. (1983). Siblings and other kin. In T. Brubaker (Ed.), *Family relationships in later life* (pp. 47–62). Beverly Hills, CA: Sage.

Sears, R. R. (1977). Sources of life satisfactions of the Terman gifted men. *American Psychologist, 32,* 119–128.

Seccombe, K. (1986b). The effects of occupational conditions upon the division of household labor: An application of Kohn's theory. *Journal of Marriage and the Family, 48,* 839–848.

Seccombe, K. (1987). Children. Their impact on the elderly in declining health. *Research on Aging, 9,* 312–326.

Seccombe, K. (1988). Financial assistance from elderly retirement-age sons to their aging parents. *Research on Aging, 10,* 102–118.

Secord, P. F. (1982). The origin and maintenance of social roles: The case of sex roles. In W. Ickes & E. S. Knowles (Eds.), *Personality, roles, and social behavior* (pp. 33–54). New York: Springer-Verlag.

Seiden, A. M. (1980). Time management and the dual-career couple. In F. Pepitone-Rockwell (Ed.), *Dual-career couples.* Beverly Hills, CA: Sage.

Sekuler, R., & Blake, R. (1987, December). Sensory underload. *Psychology Today, 21,* 48–51.

Seligman, M. E. P. (1988, October). Boomer blues. *Psychology Today, 22,* 50–55.

Seligman, M. E. P., Kamen, L. P., & Nolen-Hoeksema, S. (1988). Explanatory style across the life span: Achievement and health. In E. M. Hetherington, R. M. Lerner & M. Perlmutter (Eds.), *Child development in life-span perspective* (pp. 91–114). Hillsdale, NJ: Lawrence Erlbaum Associates.

Selmanowitz, V. J., Rizer, R. L., & Orentreich, N. (1977). Aging of the skin and its appendages. In C. E. Finch & L. Hayflick (Eds.), *Handbook of the biology of aging* (pp. 496–509). New York: Van Nostrand Reinhold.

Selye, H. (1936). A syndrome produced by diverse nocuous agents. *Nature, 138,* 32.

Selye, H. (1976). *The stress of life* (rev. ed.). New York: McGraw-Hill.

Selye, H. (1982). History and present status of the stress concept. In L. Goldberger & S. Breznitz (Eds.), *Handbook of stress. Theoretical and clinical aspects* (pp. 7–20). New York: The Free Press.

Serfass, R. C., & Gerberich, S. G. (1984). Exercise for optimal health: Strategies and motivational considerations. *Preventive Medicine, 13,* 79–99.

Serow, W. J. (1987). Why the elderly move. Cross-national comparisons. *Research on Aging, 9,* 582–597.

Shapiro, G. L., & Farrow, D. L. (1988). Mentors and others in career development. In S. Rose & L. Larwood (Eds.), *Women's careers. Pathways and pitfalls* (pp. 25–40). New York: Praeger.

Sheehy, G. (1974). *Passages*. New York: E. P. Dutton.

Shelton, B. A. (1990). The distribution of household tasks. Does wife's employment status make a difference? *Journal of Family Issues, 11,* 115–135.

Shimokata, H., Tobin, J. D., Muller, D. C., Elahi, D., Coon, P. J., & Andres, R. (1989). Studies in the distribution of body fat: I. Effects of age, sex, and obesity. *Journal of Gerontology: MEDICAL SCIENCES, 44,* M66–73

Shneidman, E. S. (1980). *Voices of death*. New York: Harper & Row.

Shneidman, E. S. (1983). *Deaths of man*. New York: Jason Aronson.

Shneidman, E. (1989). The Indian summer of life. A preliminary study of septuagenarians. *American Psychologist, 44,* 684–694.

Shock, N. W. (1977). System integration. In C. E. Finch & L. Hayflick (Eds.), *Handbook of the biology of aging*. New York: Van Nostrand Reinhold.

Shock, N. W. (1984). *Normal human aging: The Baltimore Longitudinal Study of Aging*. (NIH Publication No. 84–2450). U. S. Department of Health and Human Services, National Institute on Aging. Washington, D. C.: U.S. Government Printing Office.

Shock, N. W. (1985). Longitudinal studies of aging in humans. In C. E. Finch & E. L. Schneider (Eds.), *Handbook of the biology of aging* (2nd ed., pp. 721–743). New York: Van Nostrand Reinhold.

Siegler, I. C. (1983). Psychological aspects of the Duke Longitudinal Studies. In K. W. Schaie (Ed.), *Longitudinal studies of adult psychological development* (pp. 136–190). New York: Guilford Press.

Siegler, I. C., & Botwinick, J. (1979). A long-term longitudinal study of intellectual ability of older adults: The matter of selective attrition. *Journal of Gerontology, 34,* 242–245.

Siegler, I. C., George, L. K., & Okun, M. A. (1979). Cross-sequential analysis of adult personality. *Developmental Psychology, 15,* 350–351.

Siegler, I. C., McCarty, S. M., & Logue, P. E. (1982). Wechsler memory scale scores, selective attrition, and distance from death. *Journal of Gerontology, 37,* 176–181.

Siegler, I. C., Nowlin, J. B., & Blumenthal, J. A. (1980). Health and behavior: Methodological considerations for adult development and aging. In L. W. Poon (Ed.), *Aging in the 1980s* (pp. 499–612). Washington, D. C.: American Psychological Association.

Silver, R. L., & Wortman, C. B. (1980). Coping with undesirable life events. In J. Garber & M. E. P. Seligman (Eds.), *Human helplessness: Theory and applications*. New York: Academic Press.

Simonton, D. K. (1989). The swan-song phenomenon: Last-works effects for 172 classical composers. *Psychology and Aging, 4,* 42–47.

Sinnott, J. D. (1986). Prospective/intentional and incidental every day memory: Effects of age and passage of time. *Psychology and Aging, 1,* 110–116.

Sirignano, S. W., & Lachman, M. E. (1985). Personality change during the transition to parenthood: The role of perceived infant temperament. *Developmental Psychology, 21,* 558–567.

Skolnick, A. (1981). Married lives: Longitudinal perspectives on marriage. In D. H. Eichorn, J. A. Clausen, N. Haan, M. P. Honzik, & P. H. Mussen (Eds.), *Present and past in middle life* (pp. 270–300). New York: Academic Press.

Smelser, N. J., & Erikson, E. J. (1980). *Themes of work and love in adulthood*. Cambridge, MA: Harvard University Press.

Smith, B. D., Thompson, L. W., & Michalewski, H. J. (1980). Averaged evoked potential research in adult aging: Status and prospects. In L. W. Poon (Ed.), *Aging in the 1980s* (pp. 135–154). Washington, D.C.: American Psychological Association.

Smith, D. W., Bierman, E. L., & Robinson, N. M. (1978). *The biologic ages of man*. Philadelphia: W. B. Saunders.

Smith, M. B. (1968). Competence and socialization. In J. A. Clausen (Ed.), *Socialization and society* (pp. 270–320). Boston, MA: Little, Brown.

Snarey, J. R., Reimer, J., & Kohlberg, L. (1985). Development of social-moral reasoning among kibbutz adolescents: A longitudinal cross-cultural study. *Developmental Psychology, 21,* 3–17.

Snarey, J., Son, L., Kuehne, V. S., Hauser, S., & Vaillant, G. (1987). The role of parenting in men's psychosocial development: A longitudinal study of early adulthood infertility and midlife generativity. *Developmental Psychology, 23,* 593–603.

Sørensen, A. (1983). Women's employment patterns after marriage. *Journal of Marriage and the Family, 45,* 311–321.

Sorock, G. S., Bush, T. L., Golden, A. L., Fried, L. P., Breuer, B., & Hale, W. E. (1988). Physical activity and fracture risk in a free-living elderly cohort. *Journal of Gerontology: MEDICAL SCIENCES,43,* M134–139.

Spanier, G. B. (1983). Married and unmarried cohabitation in the United States: 1980. *Journal of Marriage and the Family, 45,* 277–288.

Sparrow, P. R., & Davies, D. R. (1988). Effects of age, tenure, training, and job complexity on technical performance. *Psychology and Aging, 3,* 307–314.

Spence, J. T., & Helmreich, R. L. (1978). *Masculinity and femininity.* Austin, Texas: University of Texas Press.

Spenner, K. I. (1988). Occupations, work settings and the course of adult development: Tracing the implications of select historical changes. In P. B. Baltes, D. L. Featherman, & R. M. Lerner (Eds.), *Life-span development and behavior* (Vol. 9, pp. 244–288). Hillsdale, NJ: Lawrence Erlbaum Associates.

Spitze, G. (1988). Women's employment and family relations: A review. *Journal of Marriage and the Family, 50,* 595–618.

Spitze, G., & Logan, J. (1990). More evidence on women (and men) in the middle. *Research on Aging, 12,* 182–198.

Spreitzer, E., & Riley, L. E. (1974). Factors associated with singlehood. *Journal of Marriage and the Family, 36,* 533–542.

Srole, L., & Fischer, A. K. (1986). Gender, generations, and well-being: The Midtown Manhattan longitudinal study. In L. Erlenmeyer-Kimling & N. E. Miller (Eds.), *Life-span research on the prediction of psychopathology* (pp. 223–238). Hillsdale, NJ: Lawrence Erlbaum Associates.

Stack, S. (1989). The impact of divorce on suicide in Norway, 1951–1980. *Journal of Marriage and the Family, 51,* 229–238.

Stadel, B. V., & Weiss, N. S. (1975). Characteristics of menopausal women: A survey of King and Pierce Counties in Washington, 1973–74. *American Journal of Epidemiology, 102* (Sept), 209–216.

Stanley, S. C., Hunt, J. G., & Hunt, L. L. (1986). The relative deprivation of husbands in dual-earner households. *Journal of Family Issues, 7,* 3–20.

Steindl-Rast, Brother David. (1977). Learning to die. *Parabola, 2,* 22–31.

Sternberg, R. J. (1987). Liking versus loving: A comparative evaluation of theories *Psychological Bulletin, 102,* 331–345.

Stevens, D. P., & Truss, C. V. (1985). Stability and change in adult personality over 12 and 20 years. *Developmental Psychology, 21,* 568–584.

Stevens, G. (1986). Sex-differentiated patterns of intergenerational occupational mobility. *Journal of Marriage and the Family, 48,* 153–163.

Stewart, A. J., & Healy, J. M. Jr. (1989). Linking individual development and social change. *American Psychologist, 44,* 30–44.

Stock, W. A., Okun, M. A., Haring, M. J., & Witter, R. A. (1983). Age and subjective well-being: A meta-analysis. In R. J. Light (Ed.), *Evaluation studies: Review annual* (Vol. 8). Beverly Hills, CA: Sage.

Streib, G. F., & Schneider, C. J. (1971). *Retirement in American society.* Ithaca, NY: Cornell University Press.

Stroebe, M. S., & Stroebe, W. (1983). Who suffers more? Sex differences in health risks of the widowed. *Psychological Bulletin, 93,* 279–301.

Stroebe, W., & Stroebe, M. S. (1986). Beyond marriage: The impact of partner loss on health. In R. Gilmour & S. Duck (Eds.), *The emerging field of personal relations* (pp. 203–224). Hillsdale, NJ: Lawrence Erlbaum Associates.

Stroebe, W., Stroebe, M. S., & Domittner, G. (1988). Individual and situational differences in recovery from bereavement: A risk group identified. *Journal of Social Issues, 44,* No. 3, 143–158.

Stroud, J. G. (1981). Women's careers: Work, family, and personality. In D. H. Eichorn, J. A. Clausen, N. Haan, M. P. Honzik, & P. H. Mussen (Eds.), *Present and past in middle life* (pp. 356–392). New York: Academic Press.

St. Teresa of Avila. (1960). *The life of Teresa of Jesus.* (E. Allison Peers, Trans.). Garden City, NY: Image Books. (Original work written in 1562)

St. Teresa of Avila. (1960) *Interior castle.* (E. Allison Peers, Trans.). New York: Image Books. (Original work written in 1577)

Stull, D. E., & Hatch, L. R. (1984). Unravelling the effects of multiple life changes. *Research on Aging, 6,* 560–571.

Sullivan, E. V., McCullough, G., & Stager, M. (1970). A developmental study of the relationship between conceptual, ego, and moral development. *Child Development, 41,* 39–411.

Super, D. E. (1985). Coming of age in Middletown. Careers in the making. *American Psychologist, 40,* 405–414.

Swensen, C. H., Eskew, R. W., & Kohlhepp, K. A. (1981). Stage of family life cycle, ego development, and the marriage relationship. *Journal of Marriage and the Family, 43,* 841–853.

Szinovacz, M. (1982). Personal problems and adjustment to retirement. In M. Szinovacz (Ed.), *Women's retirement* (pp. 195–204), Beverly Hills, CA: Sage.

Tait, M., Padgett, M. Y., & Baldwin, T. T. (1989). Job and life satisfaction: A reevaluation of the strength of the relationship and gender effects as a function of the date of the study. *Journal of Applied Psychology, 74,* 502–507.

Tamir, L. M. (1982). *Men in their forties. The transition to middle age.* New York: Springer.

Tamir, L. M. (1989). Modern myths about men at midlife: An assessment. In S. Hunter & M. Sundel (Eds.), *Midlife myths. Issues, findings, and practice implications* (pp. 157–180). Newbury Park, CA: Sage.

Terkel, S. (1972). *Working.* New York: Avon.

Terkelsen, K. G. (1980). Toward a theory of the family life cycle. In E. A. Carger & M. McGoldrick (Eds.), *The family life cycle.* New York: Gardner Press.

Teti, D. M., Lamb, M. E., & Elster, A. B. (1987). Long-range socioeconomic and marital consequences of adolescent marriage in three cohorts of adult males. *Journal of Marriage and the Family, 49,* 499–506.

Thomas, A., & Chess, S. (1977). *Temperament and development.* New York: Brunner/Mazel.

Thomas, A., & Chess, S. (1986). The New York Longitudinal Study: From infancy to early adult life. In R. Plomin & J. Dunn (Eds.), *The study of temperament: Changes, continuities and challenges* (pp.39–52). Hillsdale, NJ: Lawrence Erlbaum Associates.

Thompson, L., & Walker, A. J. (1984). Mothers and daughters: Aid patterns and attachment. *Journal of Marriage and the Family, 46,* 313–322.

Thompson, L., & Walker, A. J. (1989). Gender in families: Women and men in marriage, work, and parenthood. *Journal of Marriage and the Family, 51,* 845–871.

Tice, R. R., & Setlow, R. B. (1985). DNA repair and replication in aging organisms and cells. In C. E. Finch & E. L. Schneider (Eds.), *Handbook of the biology of aging* (2nd ed., pp. 173–224). New York: Van Nostrand Reinhold.

Trussell, J., & Rao, K. V. (1989). Premarital cohabitation and marital stability: A reassessment of the Canadian evidence. *Journal of Marriage and the Family, 51,* 535–539.

Tschann, J. M., Johnston, J. R., & Wallerstein, J. S. (1989). Resources, stressors, and attachment as predictors of adult adjustment after divorce: A longitudinal study. *Journal of Marriage and the Family, 51,* 1033–1046.

Tun, P. A. (1989). Age differences in processing expository and narrative text. *Journals of Gerontology: PSYCHOLOGICAL SCIENCES, 44,* P9–15.

Uhlenberg, P., Cooney, T., & Boyd, R. (1990). Divorce for women after midlife. *Journal of Gerontology: SOCIAL SCIENCES, 45,* S3–11.

Ullian, D. Z. (1981). The child's construction of gender: Anatomy as destiny. In E. K. Shapiro & E. Weber (Eds.), *Cognitive and affective growth* (pp. 171–186). Hillsdale, NJ: Erlbaum.

Umberson, D., & Gove, W. R. (1989). Parenthood and psychological well-being. Theory, measurement, and stage in the family life course. *Journal of Family Issues, 10,* 440–462.

Underhill, E. (1961). *Mysticism.* New York: E. P. Dutton. (original work published 1911)

U.S. Bureau of the Census (1989a). *Statistical Abstract of the United States: 1989* (109th ed.). Washington, D. C.: U.S. Government Printing Office.

U.S. Bureau of the Census, (1989b). *Population Profile of the United States: 1989.* (Current Population Reports, Series P–23, No. 159). Washington, D.C.: U.S. Government Printing Office.

U.S. Bureau of the Census (1989c). Current Population Reports, Series P–23, No. 162). *Studies in Marriage and the Family.* Washington, D. C.: U.S. Government Printing Office.

Upton, A. C. (1977). Pathobiology. In C. E. Finch & L. Hayflick (Eds.), *Handbook of the biology of aging* (pp. 513–535). New York: Van Nostrand Reinhold.

Vaillant, G. E. (1974). Natural history of male psychological health. II. Some antecedents of health adult adjustment. *Archives of General Psychiatry, 31,* 15–22.

Vaillant, G. E. (1975). Natural history of male psychological health. III. Empirical dimensions of mental health. *Archives of General Psychiatry, 32,* 420–426.

Vaillant, G. E. (1977a). *Adaptation to life: How the best and brightest came of age.* Boston: Little, Brown.

Vaillant, G. E. (1977b). The climb to maturity: How the best and the brightest came of age. *Psychology Today, 11,* (No. 4), 34–42, 48–49.

Vaillant, G. E., & Vaillant, C. O. (1990). Natural history of male psychological health, XII: A 45-year study of predictors of successful aging at age 65. *American Journal of Psychiatry, 147,* 31–37.

Van Velsor, E., & O'Rand, A. M. (1984). Family life cycle, work career patterns, and women's wages at midlife. *Journal of Marriage and the Family, 46,* 365–373.

Vaughn, D. W. (1977). Age-related deteriorations of pyramidal cell basal dendrites in rat auditory cortex. *Journal of Comparative Neurology, 171,* 501–516.

Verbrugge, L. M. (1984). A health profile of older women with comparisons to older men. *Research on Aging, 6,* 291–322.

Verbrugge, L. M. (1985). An epidemiological profile of older women. In M. R. Haug, A. B. Ford, & M. Sheafor, (Eds.), *The physical and mental health of aged women* (pp. 41–64). New York: Springer.

Verbrugge, L. M. (1989). Gender, aging, and health. In K. S. Markides (Ed.), *Aging and health* (pp. 23–78). Newbury Park, CA: Sage.

Veroff, J., Douvan, E., & Kulka, R. A. (1981). *The inner American. A self-portrait from 1957 to 1976.* New York: Basic Books.

Veroff, J., Reuman, D., & Feld, S. (1984). Motives in American men and women across the adult life span. *Developmental Psychology, 20,* 1142–1158.

Vitaliano, P. P., Breen, A. R., Albert, M. S., Russo, J., & Prinz, P. N. (1984). Memory, attention, and functional status in community-residing Alzheimer Type dementia patients and optimally healthy aged individuals. *Journal of Gerontology, 39,* 58–64.

Waddington, C. H. (1957). *The strategy of the genes.* London: Allen & Unwin.

Walker, A. J., & Thompson, L. (1983). Intimacy and intergenerational aid and contact among mothers and daughters. *Journal of Marriage and the Family, 45,* 841–849.

Walker, H. A. (1988). Black-white differences in marriage and family patterns. In S. M. Dornbusch & M. H. Strober (Eds.), *Feminism. Children and the new families* (pp. 87–112). New York: Guilford.

Walker, L. (1984). Sex differences in the development of moral reasoning: A critical review. *Child Development, 55,* 677–691.

Wallerstein, J. S. (1986). Women after divorce: Preliminary report from a ten-year-follow-up. *American Journal of Orthopsychiatry, 56,* 65–77.

Walsh, W. B., Horton, J. A., & Gaffey, R. L. (1977). Holland's theory and college degreed working men and women. *Journal of Vocational Behavior, 10,* 180–186.

Walster, E., & Berscheid, E. (1974). A little bit about love: A minor essay on a major topic. In T. L. Huston (Ed.), *Foundations of interpersonal attraction* (pp. 355–381). New York: Academic Press.

Waring, J. (1981). The middle years: A multidisciplinary view. In A. C. Eurich (Ed.), *Major transitions in the human life cycle.* Lexington, MA: D. C. Heath.

Waterman, A. S., & Archer, S. L. (1990). A life-span perspective on identity formation: Developments in form, function, and process. In P. B. Baltes, D. L. Featherman, & R. M. Lerner (Eds.). *Life-span development and behavior* (Vol 10, pp. 30–59). Hillsdale, N.J.: Lawrence Erlbaum Associates.

Watson, R. E. L. (1983). Premarital cohabitation vs. traditional courtship: Their effects on subsequent marital adjustment. *Family Relations, 32,* 139–147.

Weaver, C. N. (1978). Sex differences in the determinants of job satisfaction. *Academy of Management Journal, 21,* 265–274.

Wechsler, D. (1939). *The measurement of adult intelligence.* Baltimore: Williams & Wilkins.

Wechsler, D. (1955). *Manual for the Wechsler Adult Intelligence Scale.* New York: Psychological Corporation.

Weg, R. B. (1983). The physiological perspective. In R. B. Weg (Ed.), *Sexuality in the later years. Roles and behavior* (pp. 40–81). New York: Academic Press.

Weiffenbach, J. M., Cowart, B. J., & Baum, B. J. (1986). Taste intensity perception in aging. *Journal of Gerontology, 41,* 460–468.

Weingarten, H. R. (1985). Marital status and well-being: A national study comparing first-married, currently divorced, and remarried adults. *Journal of Marriage and the Family, 47,* 653–662.

Weishaus, S., & Field, D. (1988). A half century of marriage: Continuity or change? *Journal of Marriage and the Family, 50,* 763–774.

Weisman, A. D., & Worden, J. W. (1975). Psychosocial analysis of cancer deaths. *Omega, 6,* 61–75.

Weiss, R. S. (1982). Attachment in adult life. In C. M. Parkes & J. Stevenson-Hinde (Eds.), *The place of attachment in human behavior* (pp. 171–184). New York: Basic Books.

Weiss, R. S. (1984). The impact of marital dissolution on income and consumption in single-parent households. *Journal of Marriage and the Family, 46,* 115–127.

Weiss, R. S. (1986). Continuities and transformations in social relationships from childhood to adulthood. In W. W. Hartup & Z. Rubin (Eds.), *On relationships and development* (pp. 95–110). Hillsdale, NJ: Lawrence Erlbaum Associates.

Weiss, R. S. (1988). Loss and recovery. *Journal of Social Issues, 44,* 37–52.

Weitzman, L. J. (1985). *The divorce revolution: The unexpected social and economic consequences for women and children in America.* New York: The Free Press.

Weitzman, L. J. (1988). Women and children last: The social and economic consequences of divorce law reforms. In S. M. Dornbusch & M. H. Strober (Eds.), *Feminism. Children and the new families* (pp. 212–248). New York: The Guilford Press.

Werner, H., & Kaplan, B. (1956). The developmental approach to cognition: Its relevance to the psychological interpretation of anthropological and ethnolinguistic data. *American Anthropologist, 58,* 866–880.

Whelihan, W. M., Lesher, E. L., Kleban, M. H., & Granick, S. (1984). Mental status and memory assessment as predictors of dementia. *Journal of Gerontology, 39,* 572–576.

White, A. T., & Spector, P. E. (1987). An investigation of age-related factors in the age-job-satisfaction relationship. *Psychology and Aging, 2,* 261–265.

White, L. R., Cartwright, W. S., Cornoni-Huntley, J., & Brock, D. B. (1986). Geriatric epidemiology. In C. Eisdorfer (Ed.), *Annual review of gerontology and geriatrics* (Vol. 6, pp. 215–311). New York: Springer.

White, N., & Cunningham, W. R. (1988). Is terminal drop pervasive or specific? *Journals of Gerontology: PSYCHOLOGICAL SCIENCES, 43,* P141–144.

Wilkinson, R. T., & Allison, S. (1989). Age and simple reaction time: decade differences for 5,325 subjects. *Journal of Gerontology: PSYCHOLOGICAL SCIENCES, 44,* P29–35.

Willemsen, E. W. (1980). Terman's gifted women: Work and the way they see their lives. In K. W. Back (Ed.), *Life Course: Integrative theories and exemplary populations.* AAAS Selected Symposium, #41 (pp. 121–132). Boulder, CO: Westview Press.

Williams, D. G. (1988). Gender, marriage, and psychosocial well-being. *Journal of Family Issues, 9,* 452–468.

Williams, J. E., & Best, D. L. (1982). *Measuring sex stereotypes: A thirty-nation study.* Beverly Hills, CA: Sage.

Willis, L., Thomas, P., Garry, P. J., & Goodwin, J. S. (1987). A prospective study of response to stressful life events in initially healthy elders. *Journal of Gerontology, 42,* 627–630.

Willis, S. L. (1989). Cohort differences in cognitive aging: A sample case. In K. W. Schaie & C. Schooler (Eds.), *Social structure and aging: Psychological processes,* (pp. 95–112). Hillsdale, NJ: Lawrence Erlbaum Associates.

Willis, S. L., & Schaie, K. W. (1986). Training the elderly on the ability factors of spatial orientation and inductive reasoning. *Psychology and Aging, 1,* 239–247.

Willits, F. K., & Crider, D. M. (1988). Health rating and life satisfaction in the later middle years. *Journal of Gerontology: SOCIAL SCIENCES, 43,* S172–176.

Wilson, M. R., & Filsinger, E. E. (1986). Religiosity and marital adjustment: Multidimensional interrelationships. *Journal of Marriage and the Family, 48,* 147–151.

Wohlwill, J. F. (1970). Methodology and research strategy in the study of developmental change. In L. R. Goulet & P. B. Baltes (Eds.), *Life-span developmental psychology. Research and theory* (pp. 150–193). New York: Academic Press.

Woodruff-Pak, D. S. (1988). *Psychology and aging*. Englewood Cliffs, NJ: Prentice Hall.

Wortman, C. B., & Silver, R. C. (1987). Coping with irrevocable loss. In G. R. VandenBos & B. K. Bryant (Eds.), *Cataclysms, crises, and catastrophes: Psychology in action* (pp. 189–235). Washington, D.C.: American Psychological Association.

Wortman, C. B., & Silver, R. C. (1989). The myths of coping with loss. *Journal of Consulting and Clinical Psychology, 57,* 349–357.

Wright, L. (1988). The type A behavior pattern and coronary artery disease: Quest for the active ingredients and the elusive mechanism. *American Psychologist, 43,* 2–14.

Yin, P., & Shine, M. (1985). Misinterpretations of increases in life expectancy in gerontology textbooks. *The Gerontologist, 25,* 78–82.

Yinger, J. M. (1977). A comparative study of the substructures of religion. *Journal for the Scientific Study of Religion, 16,* 67–86.

AUTHOR INDEX

SUBJECT INDEX

ART CREDITS

Chapter-opening art for the following chapters is reproduced by permission of the Metropolitan Museum of Art:

Chapter 1: *Terrace at Sainte-Adresse.* Monet, Claude Oscar (1840–1926). Purchased with special contributions and purchase funds given or bequeathed by friends of the Museum, 1967.

Chapter 2: *The Mountain.* Balthus. Purchase, Gift of Mr. and Mrs. Nate B. Spingold and Nathan Cummings, Rogers Fund and The Alfred N. Punnett Endowment Fund, by exchange, and Harris Brisbane Dick Fund, 1982.

Chapter 3: *Sean O'Casey.* John, Augustus Edwin (1878–1961). Bequest of Stephen C. Clark, 1960.

Chapter 4: *The Coiffurs.* Picasso, Pablo Ruiz (1881–1973). Wolfe Fund, 1951; Acquired from the Museum of Modern Art, Anonymous Gift.

Chapter 5: *Aux Fortifications.* Hopper, Edward. Harris Brisbane Dick Fund, 1925.

Chapter 6: *L'Arlesienne: Madame Joseph-Michel Ginoux (Marie Julien, 1848–1911).* van Gogh, Vincent (1853–1890). Bequest of Sam A. Lewisohn, 1951.

Chapter 7: *The Monet Family in Their Garden.* Manet, Edouard (1832–1883). Bequest of Joan Whitney Payson, 1975.

Chapter 8: *The Card Players.* Cezanne, Paul (1839–1906). Bequest of Stephen C. Clark, 1960.

Chapter 9: *Cherry Orchard.* Vallotton, Felix (1865–1925). Bequest of Miss Adelaide Milton de Groot (1876–1967), 1967.

Chapter 10:: *Head of a Woman.* Picasso, Pablo Ruiz (1881–1973). Bequest of Miss Adelaide Milton de Groot (1876–1967), 1967.

Chapter 11: *A Woman with Chrysanthemums.* Degas, Hilaire Germain Edgar (1834–1917). Bequest of Mrs. H. O. Havemeyer, 1929. The H. O. Havemeyer Collection.

Chapter 12: *The Furnished Room.* Soyer, R. Harris Brisbane Dick Fund, 1940.

Chapter 13: ***The Old Italian Woman.*** Degas, Hilaire Germain Edgar (1834–1917). Bequest of Charles Goldman, 1966, subject to life estate.

Chapter 14: ***Autumn Landscape with a Flock of Turkeys.*** Millet, Jean François (1814–1875). Bequest of Isaac D. Fletcher, 1917. Mr. and Mrs. Isaac D. Fletcher Collection.

Chapter-opening art for Chapter 15, ***Le Tre Finestre*** (1924) by Jessie Boswell, is reproduced by permission of the Galleria d'Art Moderna, Torino.